utsa
memorial
fund
in memory
of

Gloria Dykes

from a gift
to utsa
by

*Pauline Cochran
and
Samuel Cochran*

NONVERBAL BEHAVIOR
AND COMMUNICATION
2nd Edition

NONVERBAL BEHAVIOR AND COMMUNICATION

2nd Edition

Edited by

ARON W. SIEGMAN
STANLEY FELDSTEIN
UNIVERSITY OF MARYLAND BALTIMORE COUNTY

LEA LAWRENCE ERLBAUM ASSOCIATES, PUBLISHERS
1987   Hillsdale, New Jersey   London

Lawrence Erlbaum Associates, Inc., Publishers
365 Broadway
Hillsdale, New Jersey 07642

Library of Congress Cataloging-in-Publication Data
Main entry under title:

Nonverbal behavior and communication.

  Includes bibliographies and indexes.
  1. Nonverbal communication (Psychology)   I. Siegman,
Aron Wolfe. II. Feldstein, Stanley, 1930–   .
BF637.C4N62   1986   153.6   85-20651
ISBN 0-89859-646-7
ISBN 0-8058-0018-2 (pbk.)

Printed in the United States of America
10 9 8 7 6 5 4 3 2 1

Contents

PART III: FACIAL AND VISUAL BEHAVIOR

List of Contributors

Robert Crawford, *University of Duisburg*

James M. Dabbs, Jr., *Georgia State University*

Allen T. Dittmann, *United States Office of Education*

Joyce Edinger, *University of Missouri*

Paul Ekman, *University of California, San Francisco Medical Center*

Mark S. Evans, *Georgia State University*

Ralph V. Exline, *University of Delaware*

Stanley Feldstein, *University of Maryland Baltimore County*

B.J. Fehr, *University of Delaware*

Siegfried Frey, *University of Duisburg*

Alan J. Fridlund, *University of Pennsylvania*

Eckhard H. Hess, *University of Chicago*

Hans-Peter Hirsbrunner, *University of Duisburg*

Joseph Jaffe, *Columbia University*

Adam Kendon, *Connecticut College*

Harriet S. Oster, *University of Pennsylvania*

Miles L. Patterson, *University of Missouri*

Slobodan B. Petrovich, *University of Maryland Baltimore County*

Howard M. Rosenfeld, *University of Kansas*

Barry Ruback, *George State University*

Aron W. Siegman, *University of Maryland Baltimore County*

Joan Welkowitz, *New York University*

Introduction

An attractive feature of nonverbal communication as a research area is that it has captured the interest of scholars of different disciplinary backgrounds — psychologists, linguists, anthropologists, psychiatrists, and sociologists — with each discipline bringing to the area its peculiar theoretical and methodological perspectives and biases. Each of these disciplines also tend to have a favorite topic or problem area within the general domain of nonverbal communication. For example, for fairly obvious reasons, psychiatrists primarily have been interested in the expressive correlates of affective experiences, especially anxiety, whereas anthropologists have done most of the early work on proxemics. Along with the varying yet overlapping topical concerns that the different disciplines bring to the area of nonverbal communication are major differences in methodology.

METHODOLOGICAL ISSUES

Psychologists who are very much concerned with objectivity, measurement, and quantification have brought nonverbal communication into the laboratory. The advantages of this approach are obvious, but there are disadvantages as well. Typical of the experimental method is the manipulation of one variable, and the monitoring of the effects of this manipulation on the dependent variable. It is, of course, possible to manipulate more than one independent variable at a time, but even in such increasingly popular multivariate designs, the experimenter tends to look at the effects of the manipulations, individually and in combination, upon a single dependent variable. The reason for this is that although researchers are becoming familiar with statistical procedures that assess the interaction of several independent variables, few of them are familiar with procedures that assess the interaction of several dependent variables. This methodological constraint may account for the fact that psychological research concerned with nonverbal communication tends to focus on a single channel, be it eye contact, body movements, or some vocal characteristic of speech. This approach is reflected in the very organization of this book, which is primarily, although not exclusively, in terms of identifiable single channels of communication. One problem with the single-channel approach is that different people may use different channels for the same message. Thus, some individuals may express their liking for other persons via the vocal channel, whereas some may do so via the visual channel. To the extent that there is such functional equivalence between channels, the single-channel paradigm is clearly an inappropriate one. By way of contrast, social scientists less concerned with quantification and tests of significance tend to look at functionally organized behavioral domains, such as courtship behavior or greeting behavior, and to monitor an individual's nonverbal communications in a variety of channels. The latter approach, however, tends to be descriptive and, therefore, does not allow for causal statements about the observed relationships.

It should be stressed that although the examination of single channels versus multiple channels of communication may be related to methodologial preferences, it is not an inevitable consequence of such preferences. It is possible to manipulate experimentally behavior that is functionally meaningful, such as approval seeking, and to monitor the effects of the manipulation on a variety of channels, as has in fact been done by Rosenfeld (1966a, b). The important point is that the particular organization of this book notwithstanding, there is a clear recognition, even on the part of psychologists who use the experimental method, that communication is multichanneled and that different channels may be used by different people for the same message; it is a recognition that any general model of interpersonal communication must take into account.

Another problem with the usual experimental paradigm is that it fails to consider the interactional, reciprocal nature of interpersonal communication. Typically, in experimental studies of nonverbal communication, the behavior of one of the participants, usually a confederate of the experimenter, is controlled. For example, if the experimentally manipulated variable is eye contact, one of the participants in an interaction is trained to behave in a uniform and consistent manner with all his or her partners, except in relation to eye contact, which is controlled according to a predetermined schedule (e.g., it may be withheld all of the time from some subjects in a between-subjects design, or some of the time from all subjects in a within-subjects design). Thus, the continuous feedback and readjustment that characterizes dyadic communication is not taken into consideration. By way of contrast, naturalistic studies of conversation can capture the cybernetic nature of interpersonal communication. Clearly, then, the use of the experimental rather than the naturalisitc paradigm involves a trade-off between level of control and appropriateness of the model.

DEFINITIONAL ISSUES

A major concern in the area of nonverbal communication is that of definition. For the author in this field, as well as the teacher, the problem — which may appear to be a fairly abstract one — has a very practical implication: what to include and what to exclude from his or her book or course. Some topics, such as proxemics or the facial, vocal, and bodily expressions of emotion, are included in most textbooks on nonverbal communication. Then there are topics, such as dress codes, which are included by some authors and excluded by most others. Some implicitly held definitions of nonverbal communication are broad enough so that any behavior would qualify. Of course, definitions that are broad enough to include almost any behavior, as long as it is not verbal, are not very useful. Wiener, Devoe, Rubinow, and Geller (1972) have suggested a definition that takes as its starting point the term *communication*. For them, communication implies that one person (an encoder) is actively making his or her experience known to some other person (a decoder) by means of a shared code. The difficulty with this definition is that it may be too restrictive. The difficulty is caused by the term *code*, which implies an arbitrary relationship between the elements that make up the code and their referents. This definition excludes from the domain of nonverbal communication any behavior that bears a direct, nonarbitrary relationship to that which it signifies. Potential candidates for exclusion are the facial, vocal, and bodily correlates of affective experiences, the various hesitation phenomena that appear to signify cognitive processing and at least certain aspects of proxemics. Indeed, the definition excludes much of what is included in this book!

Wiener et al. (1972) are quite explicit about the assumption that nonverbal communication must be in the form of a code that bears an arbitrary relationship to its referents. "To find invariance of behavioral form and referent across cultures would to us be prima facie evidence that the behavior is not part of a coding system. We could agree that some forms of behavior (e.g., facial variations) might be more likely than others to be used in making public some sets of experience (e.g., mood state). However, a behavior whose significance is found to be invariant across cultues (i.e., observers attribute the same significance to the behavior in all cultures) would be difficult to include as a code component, which for us involves an assumption of an arbitrary relationship between symbol and referent" (p. 203). In effect, then, these authors argue that communication can take place only via symbols (which have an arbitrary relationship to their referents) and not via signs (which have a nonarbitrary relationship to their referents).

The distinction between signs and symbols is an old one, but the argument that communication should be limited to symbols seems unnecessarily restrictive. In making their argument, Wiener and his associates explicitly state that language, which is a system of mostly arbitrary symbols, provided them with their criteria for their definition of nonverbal communication. In other words, their limited definition of communication is clearly a consequence of viewing language as the prototype of all communication. But the concern with nonverbal communication is precisely a result of the increasing realization that there is more to communication than language. Infants communicate before they have even the rudimentary form of language, and it is not unreasonable to assume that nonverbal communication predated communication in the history of mankind as well. It simply will not do, therefore, to formulate a model of nonverbal communication based on verbal communication. What we need, instead, is a model of communication that includes the essential features of both verbal and nonverbal communication.

Some of the difficulties associated with the definition offered by Wiener and his associates can be avoided by simply defining communication as the act of making one's experiences known to another person, whether it is via symbols or via signs. The emphasis here is on the act rather than on the medium. Nonverbal communication, then, could include all nonverbal behaviors that are involved in the transmission of experiences or information from one person to another (or others). This definition includes all behaviors that are part of an individual's communicative act and excludes those that are not. The definition, however, has its own difficulties, not the least of which is that it involves us in the issue of intent. Nevertheless, it should be pointed out that even the adoption of a more restrictive definition does not necessarily exclude topics such as the facial expressions of emotion from consideration, as long as they are considered under the rubric of nonverbal behavior rather than communication.

SUBSTANTIVE ISSUES

The sections into which the book is divided roughly organize the chapters in terms of their concerns with the bodily structures and zones that are involved in nonverbal behavior. The chapters subsumed by Part V, however, take a functional approach to nonverbal behavior that is amenable to a cross-channel perspective.

It is clearly traditional to begin the examination of almost any sort of behavior by paying attention to relevant biological considerations. Jaffe

(Chapter 1) does so with regard to the study of conversation, although his concern is at the level of neurobiology. He speculates that the neurophysiology of the brain, particularly the asymmetrical specialization of its hemispheres, can account for much of the structure and efficiency of face-to-face conversation. His primary interest is in the alternation of speakers in a conversation and he argues that "cerebral hemispheric specialization in man has evolved under the selective pressure of efficient face-to-face conservations" (p. 27). In amassing evidence for his position, he provocatively probes such issues as the differential lateralization of linguistic and nonlinguistic behavior, the role of interjections, and the implications of delayed auditory feedback and speech-linked gestures. Moreover, he suggests, and explores in some detail, the possibility that the "mutual illumination of physiology and ordinary conversation" provides a clearer interpretation and understanding of aphasic disorders. The chapter is richly suggestive of a neurophysiological perspective from which to view many of the behaviors discussed in subsequent chapters.

There is little doubt that face-to-face human communication involves more than the exchange of verbal messages. It includes patterns of visual interactions, facial expressions, gestures, body postures and movements, and tone of voice. The chapters in the second section are devoted to the role of body movement and gestures.

Dittmann's chapter (2) is used as the introductory chapter for this section, because it addresses itself to some fundamental issues of definition and classification. The term *body language,* a term frequently used in the early popular literature on nonverbal communication, leads Dittmann to raise the question: What are the criteria of a language? Dittmann concludes "that language is a code . . . . [an] agreed upon system in which: (1) The thoughts and ideas we wish to convey are simplified and grouped into categories. (2) These categories are organized so that the relationships among the categories can be clear. (3) The results of these processes are restructured into symbols of a form that can be communicated from one person to another. To the extent that any communication system is a code in this sense, a great deal of information can be transmitted from sender to receiver in a short period of time with great dependability" (p. 41). According to Dittmann, then, efficiency and reliability are the two hallmarks of language as a code. The author then examines in detail two nonverbal codes, American Sign Language and Indian Sign Language, and concludes that they are codes in the same sense that spoken languages are codes.

With American Sign Language as the prototype of a true body language, Dittmann examines the body movements that accompany speech. According to Dittmann, there are only few discrete body movements that behave like coded material in that they are easily understood by most members of the community. These include the hitchhiker's movement for thumbing a ride, whirling the ear with the index finger to say, "He's crazy," the index finger to the lips for "shhh," and the airman sign for "A-OK." These discrete and categorical emblems have meanings that everyone in the language community can agree upon. "Most movements are not of that type, however, and they take as their organizing principles either the rhythmical structure of the concurrent speech, or their association with the state of being of the person, either long-term or situationally influenced. We use these less specific behaviors as cues to make inferences about those states in the person and the success of those inferences varies with a number of factors. Extended discourse in body language, parallel to that possible in spoken language or ASL (American Sign Language) does not seem to occur" (p. 62).

Adam Kendon in his chapter, "On Gesture: Its Complementary Relationship with Speech," which is one of three new chapters that have been added to this second edition, takes the position that gestures are an integral part of verbal communication. The earlier edition of this book was criticized by some reviewers for giving short shrift to the "movement movement" (Davis, 1972, p. vii), which to some is synonymous with nonverbal behavior. The reason for this lacuna in our first edition is not that we failed to recognize the role of gestures in communication, or that we were unaware of the pioneering work done in this area by Birdwhistell (1970), Scheflen (1965), Kendon (1972), and others. We did feel, however, that the impressionistic nature of much of this work — which at least in part is a result of not having had until recently an efficient coding system for body movements — makes it unlikely that it would generate a reliable and reproducible data base. If one compares the explosion of findings in the areas of facial expression, vocal behavior, and proxemics — all of which are behaviors that can be readily measured and quantified — with the progress that has occurred in the area of body movement since the publication of our first edition, it would seem that our prognostication was not too far off the mark. Nevertheless, we concede to our critics that a book on nonverbal behavior and communication should include a discussion of at least those body movements that so clearly are an integral part of interpersonal communication, even though they seem hopelessly refractory to codification and quantification (or so it seemed until recently). The result is Kendon's chapter. Kendon distinguishes movements that people make when they are nervous (such as self-groomings, clothing adjustments, and repetitive manipulations of rings or other personal accoutrements) from movements that are involved in the regulatory aspects of interactions, and from movements that are intended to be communicative (i.e., to convey meaning). He suggests that the term *gestures*, and especially the term *gesticulations,* should be reserved for these latter type of body movements. Kendon buttresses the aforementioned distinctions with findings from brain-damaged individuals. These findings strongly suggest that communicative gestures, but not the expressive or regulatory movements, are goverened by the same part of the brain that governs speech production. Kendon suggests that speech and gesture are separate representational modalities, under the control of a single "central organizer."

As have others before him, Kendon distinguishes between communicative gestures that are standardized in form and function, and are utterances in themselves, independent of speech, and gestures that occur in association with speech and seem to be integrated with it as part of the total utterance. Kendon further identifies several types of speech-related gestures, based on the nature of their relationship to speech. In the tradition of the structuralist school, these distinctions are based on the form and especially on the function of these speech-related gestures, but unlike some other structuralists, Kendon is concerned with the objectivity and reliability of his coding system.

In reviewing the studies on speech-related gestures, Kendon concludes that gestures are organized separately from speech. However ideas are stored in our heads, they must be stored in a way that allows them to be as readily encoded in gestural form as in verbal form. This, of course, is not to deny the exquisite rhythmic coordination of gesticulation with speech, both are employed in the service of the same overall aim. This view of gesture should, as Kendon points out, lead to some dethronement of language. It leads to a view in which spoken language is regarded as no "deeper" than the gestural representation of meaning.

The chapter (4) by Hirsbrunner, Frey, and Crawford, which is also new to this edition, completes the series of chapters dealing with the role of body movements and dyadic communication. As pointed out earlier, the lack of progress in this area of research is in no small part a result of the lack of an objective, reliable notation system that captures the complexity of human movements. Previous existing notational systems tended to assign verbal labels to a limited number of complex movement patterns. The problem with such systems is that they refer to only a limited number of movements and that their verbal labels fail to capture potentially sgnificant variations (i.e., they have low resolution power). Taking their cue from the use of the alphabet for speech notation, Frey and his colleagues developed a system, which has come to be known as the Bernese system, that is based on time-series notations. What the Chinese script achieves with some 50,000 symbols is done by our alphabet with only 26 symbols. The impressive efficiency of the alphabet results from breaking down complex speech utterances into their phonetic and temporal components. The phonetic component of speech is coded by the letters of the alphabet. The temporal dimension (i.e., the convention of writing the alphabetic symbols in lines from left to right or vice versa) permits the notation of verbal utterances of unlimited complexity with a limited set of symbols. Frey and his colleagues argue that just as complex speech can be resolved into a phonetic and temporal component, complex movements too can be resolved into their spatial and temporal constituents. In the Bernese system, movements are described as a series of positions over time. In this way, they have been able to overcome the low resolution that is characteristic of the labeling systems. The time-series notation approach is especially well suited to the analysis of videotaped records, which themselves resolve complex movements into a position time-series. Thus, the same principle that is used for the visual recording of complex movement behavior is now used to transcribe the visual record into a data protocol.

The system described in this chapter allows the coder to record the changes in the positional state of a speaker's head, trunk, shoulders, upper arms, hands, legs, and feet over time. The position of each of these parts of the body is assessed by reference to two or more dimensions. For example, the position of the head is coded in terms of sagital, rotational, and lateral dimensions that correspond to up–down movements of the head, left–right rotation of the head, and left–right tilting of the head. An interesting recent addition is the synchronization of these rotations with the subject's speech.

The Bernese system yields a huge data matrix that can, however, be reduced in a variety of ways. For example, a recent study (Fisch, Frey, & Hirsbrunner, 1983) using the Bernese system compared the body movements of depressed patients when first hospitalized and on recovery on three movement dimensions: complexity, mobility, and dynamic activation. The system is very popular in Europe where it has been used to describe mother–infant interactions, student–teacher interactions, and the movement behavior of type-A individuals under stress. In our own laboratory, we are now using this system for the development of objective behavioral indices of coronary-prone behavior. It is hoped that the inclusion of this methodological, or measurement-oriented, chapter in this book will make the system more accessible to researchers in this country.

The chapters of Part III are concerned primarily with the roles of facial and visual behavior in emotion and interpersonal interactions. The first of these (Chapter 5) is by Fridlund, Ekman, and Oster, and presents an exhaustive review of facial expressions of emotions. Cross-cultural evidence for the universality of emotional expression in the face, which was the focus of Ekman's chapter, "Facial Expression," in the first edition of this book, takes up only about 15% of this new chapter. Other facets of emotional expression in the face reviewed in the current chapter are: the neuromuscular substrates of facial behavior, phylogenetic bases of human facial action (central to this topic is the concern with the homology of emotional expressions among humans and other species — homologies that may indicated evolutionary bases for these behaviors), the ontogenetic aspects of facial expression, the measurement of facial actions (including a review of facial electromyography), the autonomic nervous system correlates of emotional expression, individual differences in the encoding and decoding of emotional expressions in the face, and facial expressions associated with psychopathology. The focus of this survey is on research published since the Ekman (1978) and Ekman and Oster (1980) reviews. Nearly 200 of the 430 inferences in the current chapter have appeared in print since 1978.

Intense research activity on a particular issue does not always result in fewer unanswered questions. The opposite may very well be the case. For example, early studies on hemispheric specialization for the facial expression of emotion suggested right hemisphere specialization (Galin, 1974), with later studies suggesting right hemisphere specialization for negative emotions and left hemisphere specialization for positive emotions (e.g., Sackheim et al., 1982). Moreover, more recent analysis of these studies have revealed a number of methodological problems and have led the authors of this chapter to conclude that "the explosion of studies concerning asymmetry and laterality in the generation of facial expressions has generated more heat than light" (p. 150). The one conclusion that does seem to emerge from these studies is that asymmetries are apparent most often when the facial expression is deliberate rather than spontaneous. These and many other differences that exist between spontaneous and deliberate facial expressions (and which are reviewed in this chapter) raise serious questions about the use of feigned emotions or command performances of emotions for studying the facial expression of emotions. Yet, many classical studies, including most of the cross-cultural studies by Ekman and his associates, are based on such feigned or acted-out emotions. The question, "How often do people in *natural situations* [italics added] actually show the distinctive, universal patterns of facial expression?", is in fact listed by the authors among the as yet unanswered questions. The problem with naturally occurring emotional responses is that they do not come neatly packaged according to the needs of the experimenter. Depending on the circumstances and the individual, a fear-arousing situation may at the same time produce frustration and anger. Similarly, a frustrating experience may produce not only anger but also shame or depression, and so on. Of course, the experimental manipulation of emotional responses does not necessarily guarantee that there would be no such confoundings.

The developmental aspects of the expression of emotion in the face, which as recently as 1980 was described by Ekman and Oster, as cited by Fridlund et al., (Chapter 5), as a "terra incognito," has become yet another burgeoning research area. The findings are reviewed by the authors, although the findings are not much help in settling the controversy about the role of innateness versus learning in facial emotional expressions. It is surprising that with all the research on the facial expression of emotion in the face, we still lack a detailed study on the congenitally blind, which could go a long way in furthering our understanding of the role of imitation in facial expressions of emotion.

In their review, the authors occasionally venture beyond the confines of facial expressions of emotions and address borader issues such as the relationship of encoding and decoding skills, gender differences, the role of the different nonverbal channels in the expression of emotion and the role of peripheral feedback in the experience of emotion. Clearly, it is an extremely comprehensive review.

In the first edition of this volume, Exline and Fehr reviewed the research concerned with gaze behavior that had been conducted in Exline's laboratory and integrated it with related research by other investigators. In this edition, Chapter 6 by Fehr and Exline is a complete revision of the earlier one and may be said to be the most complete review of the relevant literature now available. Moreover, instead of the earlier emphasis on the theory of Charles Morris as a vehicle for structuring the review, the current chapter emphasizes the semiotic theory of Umberto Eco, who is considerably more explicit than Morris about the role of nonverbal behavior in signification. As in the case of the earlier chapter, however, the findings of the studies reviewed in this one stand on their own. Although Eco's theory may lend a broader context in which to place the studies, their findings are not at variance with the frameworks provided by other theories.

The chapter's first concern is with a conceptual orientation and it takes the view that human interaction is based "on an underlying shared code, the signs, symbols, or expressions of which have similar referents or meaning for code users" (p. 228). The authors are aware of the problems attending the view of nonverbal behavior as embodying a set, or sets, of shared codes and they propose Eco's position that the meaning of a nonverbal behavior derives, at least in part, from its use in one or more social contexts, its relation to those contexts and the cultures of which they are part, and its selection as communicative by the participants in such contexts.

After presenting a brief synopsis of Eco's theory, the authors proceed to discuss visual interaction, particularly in terms of research concerned with the activity of the eyes, the orienting movements of the head and body, and their implications for the perceptions and behaviors of the interactants. The discussion is relatively brief, but it sets the stage for the remainder of the chapter.

Beginning with nonhuman primates and moving to infants, children, and adults, Fehr and Exline carefully review studies that have to do with the occurrences of mutual gaze behavior and the functions it serves. Developmental differences in the use of, and response to, mutual gaze have been reported in the literature, as well as cross-cultural differences. Especially interesting are the findings that gender differences appear very early in life, and that the visual attention of children appears to reflect the social organization of which they are a part.

Most of the chapter, however, is concerned with studies of adult visual interaction. The review of these studies is divided into three major sections.

The first has to do with the role of visual behavior in ongoing interactions, the second relates gaze behavior to enduring characteristics of individuals, and the third is concerned with the relations of transient psychological states and cultural differences to gaze behavior. The impact of the review is considerable. It is clear that visual attention plays an important and, at times, critical communicative role in interpersonal encounters. It is also clear that the information communicated frequently can be "understood" only in terms of the context within which it occurs and the expectations of the recipient. That it is so constrained, however, does not make it less potent in its influence upon the course of an interaction and its participants' interpretations of each other's contributions. Direct and indirect gazes help to structure and regulate an interaction both to the extent that they operate to organize the alternation of the speakers and to the degree to which they offer and/or permit approaches and withdrawals on the parts of the interactants. Visual attention serves not only to impart information, it serves also as an information-gathering strategy and, as such, apears to be particularly crucial during infancy. Gaze behavior also appears to reflect, somewhat differently for males and females, the affective tone of an interaction. Finally, such behavior also appears to communicate certain personality characteristics of the participants in an interaction.

In short, the chapter integrates an extensive empirical and theoretical literature about visual attention with a conceptualization of how the "sign-function" relationships of such attention operates in interpersonal contexts.

In addition to the communication afforded by eye-to-eye contact, Hess and Petrovich (Chapter 7) make a case for "pupil-to-pupil communication." They present a broad survey of the studies concerned with the role of pupillary behavior in interpersonal communication. Such behavior is limited; the pupil can expand, contract, or remain the same. The majority of studies suggest that pupillary dilation conveys interest, presumably positive interest. Negative stimuli appear to elicit pupillary constriction. The authors review in detail the studies Hess and others have conducted that related changes in pupil size to heterosexual and homosexual interest (Don Juans display the same pupillary response to women as do homosexual men) and preferences of children for peers and parents. They also point out that pupil size is inversely related to age and suggest that the relationship is a result of evolutionary selection because of the greater appeal that children with larger pupils appear to have for adults. Other research has demonstrated that even schematically drawn eyes (*eyespots*) can elicit pupillary responses in viewers. Paired eyespots elicited pupillary dilation, whereas sets of single and triple eyespots elicited constriction. Such findings, the authors propose, suggest an "innate schema for two eyespots." It also seems to be the case that the lack of a change in pupil size is perceived as an indication of disinterest. It is the evidence that individuals appear to respond to changes in pupil size on the parts of those with whom they interact that entitles pupillary behavior to be considered a nonverbal channel of communication.

Although they do so briefly, the authors carefully review the methodological problems that have attended the investigations of pupillary behavior. Moreover, they suggest areas that still need to be explored and issues that need to be faced.

The fourth section of this book is devoted to the vocal channel. Unlike many authors who write about nonverbal communication as if it were a field *sui generis,* independent of verbal communication, we view nonverbal communication as very much related to the verbal message, not subordinate to it but rather as an integral part of the total communicative act.

Siegman's contribution (Chapter 8), "The Telltale Voice: Nonverbal Messages of Verbal Communication," is divided into five parts. In the introduction, which is devoted to a definition of terms, he proposes a typology of vocal cues in terms of their functions. He distinguishes between vocal cues that impart meaning to the verbal message, those that regulate the flow of verbal interaction between the participants, and those that are expressive of the speaker's background, his or her affective states, his or her attitudes and feelings toward the person being addressed, and of speech production and information processing. It is this third category of vocal cues with which the chapter is most concerned.

The second part is an historical and critical review of "personality and speech" research, an area that generated much research during an earlier period, subsequently went out of fashion, and is now showing signs of new life. Until recently, common wisdom had it that although people attribute specific personality traits to certain vocal qualities, these attributions, although quite reliable, lack validity. Siegman suggests that a variety of methodological problems may account for the lack of validity. Furthermore, he argues that at least as far as extraversion, the type-A behavior pattern and, to a lesser degree, dominant and assertive behaviors, are concerned, there is objective evidence for specific vocal correlates. Finally, he argues that personality attributions, whether valid or not, are an important basis for person perception, and that they influence our reactions to other people.

The third part of the chapter deals extensively with the effects of anxiety, and more briefly, with the effects of depression, anger, and hostility, on some vocal parameters of speech: tempo, speech disruptions, indices of hesitation, and verbal productivity. Although much of this research was prompted by clinical concerns, Siegman argues for the value of conceptualizing these issues in terms of general psychological principles.

The fourth part summarizes studies about how the relationship between two or more communicants is expressed in the vocal channel, an area about which there are many speculations, but precious little solid empirical data.

In the fifth and last part, Siegman cites numerous studies that demonstrate that most, if not all, of the vocal indices (pauses, filled and unfilled, and speech disturbances) that have been identified as vocal correlates of affective experiences, are also affected by speech production and other cognitive processes. These findings cast considerable doubt on the frequently cited proposition that the nonverbal channels of communication are primarily devoted to the encoding of affect. Siegman argues that a given hesitation phenomenon, such as silent pauses, can serve different functions (cognitive or affective) and, conversely, that different hesitations, such as pauses and speech disruptions, can serve the same function, depending on the context in which they occur. This, of course, enormously complicates the decoding task, a point that was made earlier in relation to visual contact cues, and it buttresses the proposition that the nonverbal channels of communcation are inherently ambiguous.

Feldstein and Welkowitz (Chapter 9) are also concerned with vocal behaviors. Unlike Siegman, however, their interest is in the temporal organization of vocal behaviors within the context of conversation. The model they use to analyze the temporal organization considers the speaking turn a temporal unit. It is also the unit that most adequately characterizes conversational interaction in that it implies the participation of more than one person. Their definition of the turn is empirical and objective and wholly dependent on the sound–silence sequence of a conversation. Thus, it is in keeping with their contention that the temporal parameters of a conversation ought not to be defined in terms of any other verbal or nonverbal channel of communication. The chapter briefly reviews the research that initiated the area of conversation chronography and presents the classification of conversational time patterns preferred by the authors. However, a major portion of the chapter describes the frequency and durational characteristics of speaking turns and simultaneous speech (that is, when both participants in a conversation talk at the same time). It also discusses the differences between the authors' definition of turns and simultaneous speech and those of other investigators. Another major part of the chapter begins with a discussion of what Feldstein and Welkowitz call conversational "congruence," or "interpersonal accommodation," which refers to "the occurrence, within the span of one or more conversations, of similar intensity, frequency, or durational values for the participants on one or more of the parameters that characterize temporal patterning" (p. 468). The authors then review in detail the studies that relate the occurrence of interpersonal accommodation to such psychological constructs and issues as interpersonal perception, psychological differentiation, social contact, social desirability, interpersonal warmth, and level of socialization. Finally, the authors review and discuss the three major theories that have been proposed to account for interpersonal accommodation.

A point made by the chapter, one important enough to be implied by its title, is that prior to investigating the interaction of several channels, or dimensions, of nonverbal communication, each dimension ought be delineated and examined separately as objectively and thoroughly as possible.

In the final chapter (10) of Part IV, Dabbs, Ruback, and Evans describe their very recent investigations of the temporal patterning of group interactions. They propose a model, called *grouptalk,* that represents an extension of the original work of Jaffe and Feldstein (1970) and of the subsequent studies of dialogic interactions reviewed by Feldstein and Welkowitz (Chapter 9). The model posits two modes of interactive behavior in a group. The first mode is identical to the two-person model of Jaffe and Feldstein and applies to interactions that occur between pairs of group members. The other mode occurs when two or more members of the group talk at the same time. In that mode, the parameters that describe the interactions are similar to those that describe dyadic interactions, but they characterize the group.

The critical distinction between the two modes appears to be the definition of the speaking turn. In dyadic interaction, only one person can have the turn (i.e., hold the floor) at any one time. In the grouptalk model, it is the group that has the turn, on the assumption that when two or more of the group members begin talking simultaneously, it is not possible to identify a single turnholder in a way that has intuitively sensible consequences.

After presenting the basic model, the chapter describes various methods for examining the predictability of the temporal patterns within groups and offers speculations about some of the implications of greater and lesser degrees of predictability. It then describes the hardware and software that make the temporal analyses of groups feasible. As one example of potential studies, the chapter reports the results of investigating 20, mixed-gender, five-person groups who were asked to engage in problem-solving interactions. Finally, the chapter closes with a discussion of other possible applications of the model.

Although there are other models that are capable of providing a description of the time patterns of multilogues (e.g., see Lustig, 1980, for an alternative model), it is clearly the model proposed by Dabbs and his colleagues that has received the most careful development with the most sophisticated hardware and software support. It is also the only such model that is undergoing extensive empirical testing. Thus, it represents the most important extension of the two-person model of Jaffe and Feldstein that is now available.

Unlike previous chapters in the book, the two chapters of Part V take the broader approach of examining the functions of nonverbal behavior in interpersonal exchanges. In the first edition of this volume, Patterson reviewed in detail studies of the role of space in social interaction and delineated those issues with which the literature seemed to be principally concerned (i.e., territoriality and personal space, reliability and validity of the construct of personal space, and a variety of epidemiological, situational, and dispositional characteristics). It was only at the end of that review that he tentatively implied that the use of space might most profitably be understood in terms of the functions that such use serves. It is in this edition that Patterson and Edinger (Chapter 11) describe the functional analysis that attempts to integrate the findings of the many diverse investigations of spatial behavior.

In fact, the model proposed by Patterson and Edinger to account for spatial behavior is the same sequential functional model proposed by Patterson (1982) to account for the role of all nonverbal behavior within the context of interpersonal interactions. The feature of the model that distinguishes it from related models (e.g., Cappella & Greene, 1982; Thakerar, Giles, & Cheshire, 1982) is its primary concern with the functions served by nonverbal behavior or, in terms of the model, nonverbal involvement. Patterson and Edinger delineate five functions of nonverbal involvement and assume that the same nonverbal behaviors may, at different times and in different contexts, serve different functions. They also assume that all nonverbal behaviors are "potentially informative," but propose a distinction between those informative behaviors that are communicative and those that are indicative. The former is apparently behavior that is goal-directed, initiated to achieve a particular purpose. Indicative behavior, on the other hand, is "relatively spontaneous, not goal-directed, and less likely to be prominent in cognitive awareness" (p. 524).

In addition to the functions served by nonverbal involvement, the model specifies antecedent factors that mediate the initiation and development of the functions. Culture, gender, and personality are antecedent variables that are relatively constant over time and apparently constant in their influence upon the nonverbal involvement of a particular individual. The other antecedent factors specified by the model are behavioral predispositions, arousal change, and cognitive expectancies, and these "pre-interaction mediators" are said to "determine the functional perspectives of interactants and their initial levels of nonverbal involvement" (p. 526).

The authors review many of the studies of spatial behavior that were reviewed in the first edition of this volume, but here they do so in terms of the functions served by the spatial behaviors and as illustrative of the antecedent factors that help determine the functions. One of the virtues of thus organizing the review is that it makes clear what further studies are needed to test the usefulness of the model, at least with regard to spatial behavior. There are very few studies, for example, that concerned themselves with the influences of experience on the use of interpersonal space. Not much more research has examined the influences of relationship by situational effects upon spatial behavior.

In keeping with the implied position of the model vis-á-vis nonverbal behavior, the chapter closes with a call for coordinated, multichannel analyses of a variety of social psychological processes. It is a call that cannot yet be effectively answered.

The principal concern of Rosenfeld's chapter (12) is with the "problem of how conversants use nonverbal behavior to regulate the flow of information throughout the main body of their interaction" (p. 000). It is the regulatory aspect of nonverbal behavior that he calls its "conversational control function" and his general goal in the chapter is to provide a unified conceptualization of the process and to evaluate the research that relates to it.

Rosenfeld's basic assumption is that conversation is an information exchange process. The assumption raises a number of issues that Rosenfeld attempts to clarify. He recognizes at the start that the analysis of conversational control functions demands that a conversational sequence be segmented into units. The segmentation is initially obvious; each participant in a conversation takes turns speaking and the turns of the two participants alternate. Thus, the first segmentation of the conversation is into complementary speaker–listener roles. The second level of segmentation occurs within the role periods and consists of "informational units." Further segmentation becomes more complex. The informational units are separable into two classes: those that anticipate a shift of the speaker–listener roles, and those that indicate a continuation of the roles as they are. The listener signals that accompany the speaker's informational untis are also differentially classifiable.

If role alternation is the behavior that grossly structures the exchange of information, there must be regulatory signals — conversational control mechanisms — that render the alternation relatively smooth and predictable. How do we identify the signals? But first, how do we decide whether a role shift has occurred, that is, whether a remark made by the person who was presumably listening represents his or her acquisition of the speaker role or a "listener response"? And how do we define *information*? Rosenfeld is aware that these are urgent questions in need of careful answers. He thoughtfully reviews the range of criteria that might be helpful in formulating the answers. He also examines at length the potential answers offered by research concerned with the various dimensions of nonverbal and vocal behavior and concludes that progress has been made in identifying some of the nonverbal control mechanisms and in determining where they occur in the conversational stream. Rosenfeld anticipates, however, that further progress will depend on the correction of certain methodological problems that limit much of the existing research.

CLOSING COMMENTS

The contributors to this edition bring different theoretical and methodological perspectives to their respective chapters. On the other hand, they also hold certain important views in common. They regard nonverbal behavior as an integral part of the total communication act. They are aware of the close relationship between verbal and nonverbal communication and, as a consequence, there is a greater recognition among the contributors to this volume of the cognitive factors in nonverbal communication than is usually the case. Many contributors resort to general psychological models and principles, in order to obtain a handle on the phenomena they deal with. More importantly, perhaps, they are all psychologists who are committed to the proposition that empirical verification is the ultimate test of any hypothesis or theory about nonverbal behavior.

Many contributors bemoan the lack of reliability of many of the indices used in nonverbal communication research and the lack of comparability between indices even when they are reliable. Clearly, much remains to be done in developing reliable and valid measuring instruments.

Several authors argue that nonverbal behavior is inherently ambiguous in the sense that any one cue could communicate a variety of specific messages, depending on the context and so on. It is generally agreed that this ambiguity can be reduced by looking at a multiplicity of cues, which we may very well do when we decipher nonverbal cues in everday communication. Our research paradigms, however, have yet to take this into consideration. In this context, it should be pointed out that in real life both the encoding and decoding of nonverbal communication are dynamic processes with continuous feedback and readjustments between the communicants. It is only very recently that our experimental paradigms have begun to take this cybernetic dimension of nonverbal communication into consideration.

REFERENCES

Birdwhistell, R. L. (1970). *Kinesics and context: Essays on body motion communication.* Philadelphia: University of Pennsylvania Press.

Cappella, J. N., & Greene, J. O. (1982). A discrepancy-arousal explanation of mutual influence in expressive behavior for adult and infant–adult interaction. *Communication Monographs, 49,* 89–114.

Davis, M. (1972). *Understanding body movement. An annotated bibliography.* New York: Arno Press.

Ekman, P. (1978). Facial expression. In A. W. Siegman & S. Feldstein (Eds.), *Nonverbal behavior and communication* (pp. 97–116). Hillsdale, NJ: Lawrence Erlbaum Associates.

Fisch, H. V., Frey, S., & Hirsbrunner, H. P. (1983). Analyzing nonverbal behavior in depression. *Journal of Abnormal Psychology, 92,* 307–318.

Galin, D. (1974). Implications for psychiatry of left and right cerebral specialization. *Archives of General Psychiatry, 31,* 572–583.

Jaffe, J., & Feldstein, S. (1970). *Rhythms of dialogue.* New York: Academic Press.

Kendon, A. (1972). Some relationships between body motion and speech: An analysis of an example. In A. W. Siegman & B. Pope (Eds.), *Studies in dyadic communication* (pp. 177–210). New York: Pergamon Press.

Lustig, M. W. (1980). Computer analysis of talk-silence patterns in triads. *Communication Quarterly, 28,* 3-12.

Patterson, M. L. (1982). A sequential functional model of nonverbal exchange. *Psychological Review, 89,* 231-249.

Rosenfeld, H. M. (1966a). Instrumental affiliative functions of facial and gestural expressions. *Journal of Personality and Social Psychology, 4,* 65-71.

Rosenfeld, H. M. (1966b). Approval-seeking and approval-inducing functions of verbal and nonverbal responses in the dyad. *Journal of Personality and Social Psychology, 4,* 597-605.

Sackheim, H. A., Greenberg, M. S., Weiman, A. L., Yur, R. C., Hungerbuhler, J. P., & Geschwind, N. (1982). Hemispheric asymmetry in the expression of positive and negative emotions: Neurological evidence. *Archives of Neurology, 39,* 210-218.

Scheflen, A. E. (1965). Stream and structure of communicational behavior: Context analysis of a psychotherapy session. Commonwealth of Pennsylvania: E.P.P.I., *Behavioral Studies Monograph,* No. 1.

Thakerar, J. N., Giles, H., & Cheshire, J. (1982). Psychological and linguistic parameters of speech accommodation theory. In C. Fraser & K. R. Scherer (Eds.), *Advances in the social psychology of language* (pp. 205-255). Cambridge: Cambridge University Press.

Wiener, M., Devoe, S., Rubinow, S., & Geller, Y. (1972). Nonverbal behavior and nonverbal communication. *Psychological Review, 79,* 185-214.

A NEUROPSYCHOLOGICAL PERSPECTIVE

1 Parliamentary Procedure and the Brain

Joseph Jaffe
*College of Physicians and Surgeons of Columbia University
and
New York State Psychiatric Institute*

Parliamentary procedure, codified in *Robert's Rules of Order,* assures the efficient and equitable conduct of business by an assembly. It requires that only one person hold the floor at a time. Yet people who have something to tell one another could conceivably do so simultaneously. The fact that they don't suggested the following experiment.

While listening to a news broadcast on the radio, I began to tell an interesting story aloud. This "split attention" task yielded an eerie experience. When I tried to speak fluently, the broadcast was reduced to gibberish, like the babble of peripheral conversation at a large cocktail party. It was unquestionably speech but was as meaningless as a poorly understood foreign language. Conversely, if I made a concerted effort to follow the gist of the newscast, my own speech became halting and repetitious and I lost the thread of my story. Performance on this task did not improve with practice. Apparently, a listener cannot simultaneously be a speaker and vice versa; the brain cannot generate and decipher novel sentences concurrently.

"Novel" is a key word here, for there was indeed one way out of the bind. The newscast remained comprehensible provided my own speech was highly automatic and overlearned. Examples of such speech are simple counting and familiar nursery rhymes, both of which can be produced at a low level of attention. Receptive capacity is not "jammed" by these automatic sequences.

Another apparent counterexample to speaking-listening incompatability is the phenomenon of simultaneous translation, in which the two activities indeed appear to proceed concurrently. Yet even this unusual skill is partly illusory. Henri Barik (1970) showed that the simultaneous translator attempts to make good use of the speaker's pause to deliver his own version, so as to have more time to listen without having to speak concurrently. These findings were similar for all translators studied regardless of their proficiency level or of our nature of the translation task. Such contrived experiments illuminate one of our most commonplace experiences; speaking–listening incompatibility is the biological foundation of politeness, which apportions the speaking time in conversations.

Two people in informal conversation share the available speaking time; when one takes a turn as the speaker the other synchronously becomes the listener. The sending and receiving roles remain neatly reciprocal, as if an invisible parliamentarian were presiding over the interchange, signalling switches of "possession of the floor." This interaction pattern is established early in childhood and is maintained by a complex and as yet poorly understood set of coupling rules. Like most dependable prescriptions for human conduct, they are noticed more in the breach than in the observance. The participants in verbal exchange dovetail their sending–receiving states so automatically that the switching mechanism is largely unconscious until the rules are inadvertently or experimentally violated.

One breach of the reciprocity rule occurs when both partners listen simultaneously, each waiting for the other to speak. If the ensuing silence is not broken within a reasonable length of time, the verbal conversation dies. Another breach occurs when both partners speak simultaneously. If the resultant interruption was inadvertent, one of the concurrent speakers falls silent within about .5 sec, leaving the other in possession of the floor. On the other hand, a purposeful interruption by an erstwhile listener may lead to a prolonged contest for the floor with a determined speaker. These common sense illustrations suggest the following principle. There are four possible configurations of a linguistic system composed of two persons (A and B): B listens while A speaks; A listens while B speaks; both listen; both speak. *Only the first two of these configurations are compatible with stable verbal conversation.*

The case of mutual listening is trivial, but why is joint speaking so intolerable? The simplest explanation of the speaking–listening incompatibility is that a common neural substrate is employed for both the production and comprehension of speech. Linguistic machinery functions as a unit. It can be biased toward speaking or listening, but it can't do both at once.

I became intrigued by the force of conversational expectancies 30 years ago, as a young psychitarist trying his wings in Freudian psychoanalysis (Fig. 1). The technique of this therapy required the patient to recline on a couch and to verbalize, continuously and without censorship, all thoughts "that came to mind." To facilitate this state of "free association" the doctor sat behind the patient and adopted an attitude of passive listening, that is, refraining from all vocal response for periods of up to 50 minutes. The violation of social expectancies in the name of this technique included (1) the

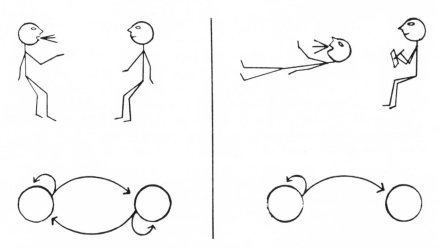

FIG. 1. On the left, a social conversation (above) and a flow diagram (below) showing the source and destination of *overt* vocal and gestural messages. Each participant can monitor himself and can send and receive messages. The system is "closed loop" in both senses. On the right, a psychoanalytic "conversation" (above) and its flow diagram (below). The patient can send and monitor himself but cannot receive; the doctor can receive but not send. The system is "open loop" (Jaffe, 1958).

requirement for continuous monologue by the patient who was unable to see the doctor's facial expression or gestures and (2) an enforced inhibition of the doctor's customary verbal responsiveness. Thus, awkward silences in the patient's monologue were allowed to continue to the point of discomfort and questions were not answered. One purpose of these arbitrary maneuvers was to discourage conventional social discourse. This abrogation of the ordinary rules of conversational interchange made me poignantly aware of the precise social expectancies that were being frustrated. For example, the participants are not face-to-face, a situation we accept in telephone conversations but rarely in the physical presence of the other person. Another violation occurs when the patient demands a response, for example, by asking a question. While waiting for the answer, which may not be forthcoming, a mutual listening state may persist for many minutes before the patient's monologue resumes or the doctor encouragingly asks what thoughts "come to mind." Perhaps of greatest present interest is the speaker's depriviation of "listener feedback," both gestural and vocal.

Gestural feedback must be seen and includes all the body language now treated by the discipline known as kinesis. Such visual signals are highly redundant, as attested to by ordinary telephone communication and by the conversations of blind persons. In both, the information burden of the visual channel is completely assumed by the acoustic channel. Yet though redundant, some type of feedback is necessary. Purposeful omission of all vocal interjections by the listener in a telephone call is profoundly upsetting to the speaker, as anyone can verify in a few minutes.

The gestural and vocal components of interjections are synchronized. For example, when the speaker pauses at the end of a phrase, the listener may nod and say, "I see." Vocal feedback includes all the snorts, chuckles, grunts, murmurs, and brief remarks that let us know that somebody exists at the other end of a telephone call while we are speaking. These interjections account for about one-third of the speaker switches in informal social conversation (Fig. 2).

Monosyllabic interjections by the listener are variously transcribed as "Hmmm.," "Hmmm!," "Hmmm?," "Yes.," "Yes!," "Yes?" and so forth. They possess a melodic, emotional quality, an average duration longer than that of syllables in polysyllabic speech and a time course matching the nonverbal gestures such as head nods with which they are synchronized. It is not generally realized that monosyllabic utterances are always stressed and that stressed syllables are always longer than unstressed syllables, even in polysyllabic speech (for example, MAry HAD a LITtle LAMB). Even when interjections take the form of stereotyped, polysyllabic, semisentences such as "I see," "Go on," "Too bad," "Indeed," "Really," "How's ABOUT that?" and so forth, the melodic contour alone virtually conveys the complete message in the absence of the articulated words (Fig. 3). Such mavericks of spoken messages, midway between speech and music, are generally banished by linguists to a wastebasket named *paralanguage, that is, nonlinguistic noises made with the vocal tract, which occur in a code situation between speaker and listener.* Research on paralanguage, as on kinesics, is in a rudimentary stage. Most attention to date has been directed to the utterances of the speaker rather than of the listener, for example, to the intonation contours of whole sentences, rendered orthographically as comma, period, and question mark at phrase endings. These features modify, quantify, or qualify the meaning of the sentence and partake more of the steady-state, melodic quality of vowels than of the transient, articulated quality of consonants. We now examine the nature of the information conveyed by this qualitative dichotomy between "language" and "paralanguage."

For many years, degradation of speech signals by means of bandpass filtering has been a standard research technique. The effective range of the speech signal from about 30 to 12,000 Hz has been electronically dissected. When the *low* frequency range of the voice spectrum is rejected, intelligibility of speech is preserved, but *biological* parameters such as the sex, age, and emotional state of the speaker are indeterminate. On hearing such filtered speech one is struck by the preservation of the crisp, high-frequency consonant information and the relative loss of low frequency vowel information. The impression gained is that of a sort of acoustic speedwriting, as would be produced if one could pronounce a text from which all vowel sounds were

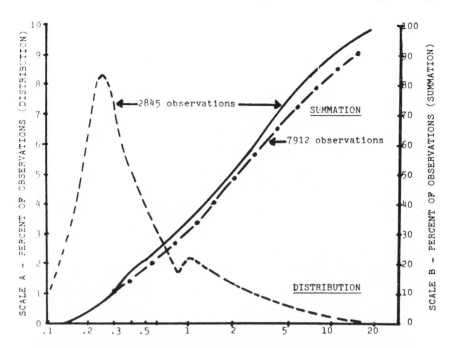

FIG. 2. Frequency distribution of the length of time between speaker switches (dashed line) and its summation (solid line). Redrawn from a pioneering study conducted almost 40 years ago at the Bell Telephone Laboratories by Norwine and Murphy (1938), who tabulated the durations of holding the floor. They defined the event as "speech by one party, including his pauses, which is preceded and followed, with or without intervening pauses, by speech from the other party." On the basis of 2845 such events they concluded, "Since most telephonic speech syllables are shorter than 0.3 second the modal value of .25-sec makes it clear that monosyllabic replies are by far the most numerous." It may be seen that these, in conjunction with terse replies or questions under one second duration, constitute about one-third of the events. More extensive data from our own laboratory on face-to-face conversations confirm this (7912 observations, shown as summation only, in a dot-dash line). The telephonic data from Bell Labs suggest that speakers who can't see their listeners should expect to hear a brief vocal interjection every 14 seconds on the average. In the face-to-face situation in our laboratory the rate drops to one every 18 sec since silent gestures probably substitute for some of the vocal ones. (Adapted with permission from *The Bell System Technical Journal.* Copyright 1938, The American Telephone and Telegraph Company.)

deleted. In contrast, when the signal is filtered to reject the *higher* frequency range of the voice spectrum, speech becomes unintelligible. Yet the emotional state of the speaker and the distinction of male from female and child from adult speakers is retained. Now the effect is that of hearing a murmured conversation, as through a thick door, perhaps the way a text from which all consonants had been deleted might sound if read aloud. Thus the latter technique of low bandpass filtering has become an established method for study-

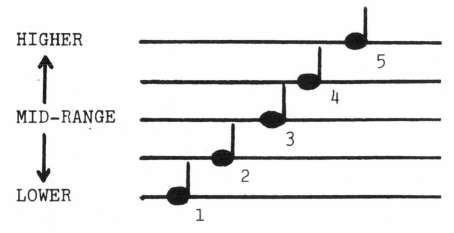

HIGHER

↑

MID-RANGE

↓

LOWER

FIG. 3. These are significant noises, occurring independently of language, that differ from one another only by the parameter of tone. In relative musical notation, they are labeled by numbers 1–5 as shown. Level 3 is variously written as ah, er, uh, hm, and is called a "hesitation vowel," signalling *Wait, I'm not finished* if produced by the speaker, or *Go on!* if interjected by the listener. A 3–4 sequence indicates assent and contrasts with a 3–5 sequence (*I thought so! I told you so.*). The 3–2 pattern signifies negation and contrasts with the 3–5 pattern *Too bad! Sorry you hurt yourself.*). Adapted from an original analysis of the interjections called "vocal segregates" (Austin, 1972).

ing the biological parameters of speakers such as maturity, sex, mood, state of alertness, and so forth, irrespective of *what* is being said but preserving information as to *who* is speaking and *how* they feel. Recalling our previous characterization of paralanguage in general, and listener's interactions in particular, as biased toward a vowel-like, steady-state, musical, emotional quality, one can characterize the results of these filtering experiments as a rough separation between the linguistic and paralinguistic aspects of spoken messages. The plight of a speaker who cannot see or hear his listener now becomes clearer. He is deprived of both paralinguistic and gestural feedback regarding the impact of his message. Is the listener drowsy, excited, bored, delighted, angry, confused, incredulous, depressed? Feedback of such information from receiver to sender "closes the loop" and permits ongoing modification of transmitted messages. Deprived of all feedback, a speaker is in an "open-loop" situation and can only guess at the quality of the human relationship in which he is engaged.

The placement of vocal interjections is never random. A fluent speaker has the option to pause briefly at phrase endings without sounding hesitant. Such "juncture pauses" mark syntactic boundaries in the speech stream and aid the listener in the decoding task. Investigators agree that listeners' interjections occur preferentially during such permissible pauses, hence the literal meaning of "interject" or the paralinguist's term "vocal segregate." Several years ago, Louis Gerstman, Stanley Feldstein, and I showed that a syntactic boundary with its characteristic intonation, especially in conjunction with a somewhat longer than average pause, is a powerful signal of a switching opportunity that virtually triggers the listener's response (Jaffe & Feldstein, 1970). About one-third of the latter are simple interjections of less than one second which "throw the conversational ball" right back to the previous speaker. To pursue the metaphor of parliamentary procedure, the listener has been briefly recognized by the chariman but the lower term sending–receiving configuration is preserved. An apt analogy might be a procedural "point of order" which when recognized by the chairman takes momentary precedence over the motion on the floor. The quality of an interjection signals the cognitive-emotional state of the interjector and also conveys the message that, having briefly said his piece, he relinquishes the floor. In the interchange some metacommunicative bookkeeping has been transacted, that is, an embedded message wich calibrates the existential and/or biological state of the conversational system. This is familiar to users of one-way communication channels such as walkie-talkies. When a message ends with the question, "Do you read me? Over!", the listener replies, "Loud and clear, over!," whereupon the sender continues his substantive message.

What is the special quality of such procedural speaker switches? They have been characterized as primarily paralinguistic but their real explication requires us to delve more deeply into the neurophysiology of conversation. I shall argue that *cerebral hemispheric specialization in man has evolved under the selective pressure of efficient face-to-face conversation*. The proposed mechanism is a compulsory linguistic coupling of the left and somewhat more optional paralinguistic–kinesic coupling of the right "brains" (hemispheres) of speaker and listener, respectively. The net effects is the preservation of sending–receiving roles in the face of brief metacommunicative speaker switches.

Consider two brains confronting each other as in Fig. 4, and assume that both reside in right-handed persons, who comprise roughly 90% of the population. In general, the brain relates to the environment in bisymmetric crossed fashion. Each half of the brain can see, listen to, feel and act upon, primarily, the contralateral half of the environment. But when "the environment" consists of another person in face-to-face conversation a set of abilities come into play that are asymmetrically organized. Thus, when brain A is speaking and brain B is listening the *left half* of each is preoccupied with the same message. Brain A is encoding and transmitting; brain B is receiving and decoding.

Recent investigation has shown the two halves of the brain to be differentially specialized for the biologically significant sounds produced by the human voice. The left-brain, right-ear system is maximally sensitive to the rapid rhythm of spoken syllables, particularly those composed of the stop conso-

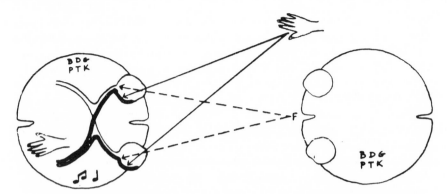

FIG. 4.   Confrontation between speaker (right) and listener (left) in aerial perspective. The listener's fixation on the speaker's face (point F and dotted lines), established a stable optical geometry such that the images of the speaker's gesturing right hand and right half-face both project to the listener's right cerebral hemisphere. This results from the fact that the right half of each retina connects to the right half-brain (heavy lines). It is of interest that a stroke that interferes specifically with the "speaking role" also paralyzes the right hand and right half of the face in 80% of the cases. In contrast, this paralysis pattern occurs in only 20% of the strokes that specifically interfere with the "listening role."

nants b, d, g, p, t, and k. The right-brain, left-ear system is maximally sensitive to the slower rhythms of melodies and nonlinguistic vocal sounds such as coughing, laughing, and crying. Spoken vowels, intermediate between consonants and melody, are not preferentially lateralized. In addition, the system composed of the right-brain and left half of visual space (see Fig. 4) seems to be specially sensitive to movement, depth perception, facial recognition and emotional qualities. Most of these asymmetrical discriminations are present at birth or soon thereafter.

The realization by nineteenth century neurologists that the brain was asymmetrically specialized for speech was at first a static concept, that is, speech capacity was simply "located" in the left cerebral hemisphere. The crowning achievement of that fertile period was the dynamic approach of John Hughlings Jackson (1932). He proposed that speech is a continuum of activity ranging from stereotyped "automatic" forms at one end, carrying primarily emotional information, to more creative sentences that are original in their juxtaposition of ideas. The latter were characterized as "propositional" speech. His facetious illustration, "Thank God, I am an atheist!" was an attempt to illustrate both extremes of the continuum, the emotionally expressive expletive and the propositional assertion, which are not logically contradictory in this example in that they are not commensurate levels of discourse. He suggested different neural levels of speech organization, some under continuous cognitive control and others that are fired off "balistically," that is, without detailed monitoring (closed-loop control) of their time course. The latter comprise stereotyped expressions, clichés, curses, expletives, swearing, and exclamations, all of which have the emotional quality of nonverbal, paralinguistic interjections. Such "automatic" speech was often preserved following left-sided brain lesions which interfered with more purposeful sentence production. These patients might say things spontaneously, in an emotional state of mind, that they could not repeat voluntarily out of the original context. Jackson's clinical insights have been amply vindicated by contemporary research.

Evidence for the continuum from emotional to propositional speech derives from studies of the control mechanisms of speech production. Continuous, or "closed-loop" control requires that the output be monitored and fed back to the generating mechanism. The extent to which this feedback is actually utilized for ongoing control varies. An alternative mode of control might be ballistic, or "open-loop," in which a complete sequence of instructions is issued to the speech musculature and runs its course without correction. One way to assess the degree of closed-loop control is to tamper with the feedback signal. A speaker literally listens to himself via air- and bone-conducted feedback, and it is technically simple to introduce a vocal–aural time lag. To the extent that control is closed-loop, the artificial delay will interfere with articulation. James Abbs and Karl Smith (1970) have shown that the right-ear, left-brain system is more affected by delayed auditory feedback then is the left-ear, right-brain system, an effect which they attribute to the susceptibility of consonants rather than vowels. Thus the right ear is engaged in monitoring the left hemisphere speech output, at least during the propositional speech which was tested. Richard Chase and his co-workers (1967) have shown that delayed auditory feedback has less of an effect upon the automatic speech that occurs, without awareness, during epileptic attacks than upon consciously produced speech. Still another index of the degree of self-monitoring is pausing during speech. Using this index, Donald Boomer and Alan Dittmann (1964) have shown that filled pauses decrease when speech is produced spontaneously without excessive deliberation whereas they increase when the speech task is rendered highly self-conscious and therefor less automatic. It is additionally significant that about 60% of all possessions of the floor in social conversation contain no pauses whatsoever. These include all the replies under one second in duration, which we have characterized as metacommunicative or procedural speaker switches, attesting to their automatic, stereotyped quality.

If the left brains of both speaker and listener are saturated by the linguistic processing of the conversation, do their right brains remain available for the kinesic and paralinguistic phenomena that calibrate the emotional quality of the conversation? Intriguing support for such speculation has recently been provided by Doreen Kimura (1973). She found that right-handers actually use their right hands more *during speaking*, but not during listening. These gestures are listener-directed and tend to synchronize with the primary stress of phrases, which occur about one per second. In effect, the right hand acts as a conductor, beating the phrase rhythm on which the 3 per second syllable rhythm is superimposed. Such gestures are often seen by the listener and it is instructive to ask, "Where are they seen?

The gaze fixations of listeners are fortunately more constrained than the roving gaze of speakers. Most investigators agree that a listener's eyes are usually fixated on the speaker's face (Fig. 4). This finding establishes the listener's fixation point and permits the conclusion that the speaker's right-hand gestures are confined to the listener's left-visual-field, right-brain system. The same system is known to be specialized for facial recognition, and Brenda Milner (1962) has implicated the right hemisphere in a perceptual discrimination of tonal patterns.

What biologically significant purpose could be served by such arrangements? The *speaker's* right ear is primarily engaged in monitoring his own ongoing speech; it would seem an efficient scheme to have his left ear turned to the procedural, paralinguistic interjections of the listener. The *listener's* right ear is engaged in selecting the properly linguistic syllables of the speaker for decoding; it would seem an efficient scheme to have *his* left ear turned to the intonational aspects of the message (Blumstein & Cooper, 1974). The time course of intonation contour is that of the phrase structure, which is also the rhythm of the speaker's right-hand gestures in the listener's left-visual field. That these paralinguistic and kinesic patterns should both arrive in the listener's right brain seems only fitting. The net effect of such hypothetical mechanisms would be the linkage of right brains for kinesic and paralinguistic rhythms just as the left brains are coupled for linguistic temporal sequences. The hypothesis has testable consequences.

This mutual illumination of physiology and ordinary conversation is curiously applicable to the communication disturbances resulting from brain disease. Here we focus upon the left hemisphere exclusively. Discrete brain damage is produced when a clot forms in an artery, cutting off the blood supply to part of a hemisphere ("stroke"). The resultant communication disturbance, known as *aphasia,* occurs in two extreme forms depending on the location of the damage in the left brain (Geschwind, 1972). They can be characterized as *disorders of the speaking role and of the listening role,* respectively. Documented cases in the neurological literature reveal the coexistence of both disorders in the same individual (Brain, 1965; Lhermitte *et al.,* 1973).

We have seen that the speaker's role in a conversation imposes an output bias on the linguistic system such that speech input is jammed. Phrases are fluently generated by the motor apparatus of the left brain under continuous control of the receptive apparatus of the same hemisphere. Occasional pauses between phrases anticipate paralinguistic interjections by the listener, the quality of which may be processed by the speaker's idling right brain. Finally, the left hemisphere activation during speaking entails a rhythmic gesture of the right hand which is synchronized with the phrase rhythm. When left-brain damage produces a disorder of the speaking role, the patient seems to be *locked in the listening role of conversation.* He comprehends rather well. Although there is minimal paralysis of the muscles of articulation, speech is slow, labored, and is produced in short phrases. In the severest forms, the phrase may consist of a stressed monosyllable with prolonged vowel, such as "Yes" or "Damn," formally reminiscent of a listener's paralinguistic interjections. In less severe forms, initial unstressed syllables of words such as "untie" or "define" may be dropped. When normally unstressed grammatical parts of speech, such as articles and prepositions, are omitted the output may read like a telegram. That these patients monitor themselves accurately is attested to by their overt frustration and suffering with their dysfluent articulation and by their emotional depression. Finally, the frequent paralysis of the right hand and right half of the face in these patients renders the normal gestural accompaniment of the speaking role, beamed to the listener's right hemisphere, inoperative.

In contrast, the normal listener's role biases the linguistic system toward reception, with output confined to brief vocal interjections accompanied by head nods. The motor apparatus is subordinate to the perceptual process and its output is suppressed. When left-brain damage produces a disorder of the listening role, the patient seems to be *locked in the speaking role of conversation.* That is, he has difficulty comprehending speech although there is no deafness in the acoustic sense. He seems to have lost the ability ot monitor his own speech as well, since word and/or syllable sequences exhibit destructive permutations which render them incomprehensible. We infer defective self-monitoring from the fact that these patients may be charming conversationalists, cheerfully unaware that their spoken messages don't make complete sense. They make little attempt to correct their obvious errors and, if frustrated by the communication breakdwon, the frustration is not with themselves but with the listener for not comprehending. The rhythm, melody, and grammatical phrasing of speech is preserved, as is the fluency of articulation in spite of the disorganized sequencing. Inasmuch as paralysis of the opposite half of the body is infrequent in these cases, right hand and facial gestures are normally synchronized with the primary stress of the spoken phrases.

The analogy should not be pushed too far; these polar forms of aphasia are admittedly caricatures of normal speaking and listening roles. However, they do underscore the necessary interplay of these states which temporarily lock two brains into complementary configurations during normal conversation.

There has been much speculation as to why man is left-brained for handedness and speech, a specialization which must have evolved, at least within the primates, because of some selective advantage. The thrust of current theory is to invoke social and emotional determination as preferable to geographic and technological explanations. From this viewpoint, it is apparent that the sensorimotor systems that maximally dispense with symmetry in the available neural layout are precisely those that subserve face-to-face conversations. Most serious speculation postulates some sort of protoconversation which long preceded the presently evolved form. If not completely gestural, such predecessors were conceivably highly ritual, co-actional, paralinguistic, and musical; perhaps involving cheers, prayer, work songs, incantations and the like. Such displays are usually highly redundant and the matching of rhythms therein is often functionally more important than the content of speech. If only information processing efficiency were at issue as the biological utility behind speech lateralization, that asymmetry would be equiprobable, half left and half right. The same argument applies to right hemispheric specialization for slower rhythmic and spatial processing, etc. However, a congruence of left speech dominance and right spatial dominance would confer an additional advantage upon certain matched individuals as a consequence of the interpersonal geometry presented in Figure 4.

In summary, the sheer fact of hemispheric specialization is explained by division of labor in the service of efficient processing of information, linguistic by the left; paralinguistic and kinesic by the right. Interpersonal geometry further suggests why such specialization should optimally be the same for conversing individuals. Perhaps the evolutionary question is better rephrased, "Why is the pattern of specialization the same for most people?" One might imagine that some random "initial kick" toward our own asymmetric pattern conferred a selective advantage upon such individuals when engaged in face-to-face conversation.

ACKNOWLEDGMENTS

Supported in part by a general research support grant from Research Foundation for Mental Hygiene, Inc.

REFERENCES

Abbs, J. H., & Smith, K. U. Laterality differences in the auditory feedback control of speech. *Journal of Speech and Hearing Research,* 1970, *13,* 298–303.

Austin, W. M. Nonverbal communication. In A. L. Davis (Ed.), *Culture, class and language variety.* Urbana, Illinois: National Council of Teachers of English, 1972, 140–169.

Barik, H. C. Some findings on simultaneous interpretation. *Proceedings of 78th Annual Convention of American Psychological Association,* Miami Beach, Fla., 1970.

Blumstein, S. & Cooper, W. E. Hemispheric processing of intonation contours. *Cortex,* 1974, *10,* 146–158.

Boomer, D. S. & Dittmann, A. T. Speech rate, filled pause and body movements in interviews. *Journal of Nervous and Mental Disease,* 1964, *139,* 324–327.

Brain, W. R. *Speech disorders.* Washington, D.C.: Butterworths, 1965.

Chase, R. A., Cullen, J. K., Jr., Niedermeyer, E. F. L., Stark, R. E., & Blumer, D. P. Ictal speech automatisms and swearing: Studies on the auditory feedback control of speech. *Journal of Nervous and Mental Disease,* 1967, *144,* 406–420.

Geschwind, N. Language and the Brain. *Scientific American,* 1972, *226,* 76–83.

Jackson, J. H. *Selected writings.* London: Hodder and Stoughton, 1932.

Jaffe, J. Communication networks in Freud's interview technique. *Psychiatric Quarterly.* 1958, *32,* 456–473.

Jaffe, J., & Feldstein, S. *Rhythms of dialogue.* New York: Academic Press, 1970.

Kimura, D. The asymmetry of the human brain. *Scientific American,* 1973, *228,* 70–78.

Lhermitte, F., Lecours, A. R., Ducarne, B., & Escourolle, R. Unexpected anatomical findings in a case of fluent jargon aphasia. *Cortex,* 1973, *9,* 436–449.

Milner, B. Laterality effects in audition. In: V. B. Mountcastle (Ed.), *Interhemispheric relations and cerebral dominance.* Baltimore: Johns Hopkins University Press, 1962.

Norwine, A. C. & Murphy, O. J. Characteristic time intervals in telephonic conversation. *Bell System Technical Journal,* 1938, *17,* 281–291.

11 BODY MOVEMENT

2 The Role of Body Movement in Communication

Allen T. Dittmann
National Institute of Mental Health[1]

When we think of body movements as communicative events, most of us are likely to get rather dramatic in our fantasies. A phrase that comes readily to mind is "body language," and there has even been a book from the popular press with that phrase as its title (Fast, 1970). The topic has everything: the hope of reading the romantic intentions of one's girl- or boyfriend, the adventure of outsmarting a shrewd salesman, the sure thing of predicting the next move of a poker-faced gambler, the suprise of "reading through" the white lies of one's friends, the advantage of knowing what a prospective employer wants to hear.

Everybody knows, of course, that these fantasies are fantasies, that nobody can make himself invisible and listen in on forbidden conversations. And yet there is a lot of truth in the notion that people communicate in many different ways, by words, by tone of voice, by facial expressions, by body movements, by the use of the physical space between one person and another, even by certain psychophysiological responses like blushing and speed or depth of breathing. We are constantly reading each other, or trying to, using all the information we can get, and we can get it from a lot more sources than just the words that pass between us. The question for this chapter is whether all these sources of information can properly be called language, and what difference it might make if they could or could not be. The particular behaviors the chapter will concentrate on are body movements. There are many other communication media, such as facial expressions, and the principles by

---

[1]Now at United States Office of Education.

which this analysis is organized are general ones and could be applied to those behaviors as well.

The first thing to do in deciding whether any given set of behaviors is a language is to agree on what a language is. That will be the first task of the chapter, spelling out some useful criteria for categorizing body movements as either language or not language. It turns out that there is no handy sharp dividing line for this dichotomy, but there are still some good guidelines, and there won't be much difficulty in applying them.

Next, two genuine languages that use body movements will be described in terms of these guidelines. One is in common use today: the sign language of the deaf. There are many remaining unknowns about this language, but the version of it used in the United States, American Sign Language, is currently under study by a number of linguists, and there are many "native speakers" of it available when examples are needed. The other body language included in this chapter is the sign language used by American Indians to communicate with people from other tribes who had different spoken languages. This language is not common today, and what we know about it comes from historical documents and from the memories of quiet old men.

With the principles and examples of body languages at hand, the chapter can then take up what we ordinarily mean by body language among the hearing, to learn to what extent we use these behaviors as a medium of communication, and to what extent they can serve as dependable sources of information about people.

THE NATURE OF LANGUAGE

Dependability is the hallmark of language. This may seem like a strange statement. When we think of dependability in language the first things that come to mind are the exceptions: words can mean more than one thing; sentences are often unclear as to referent; speech is sometimes so garbled with false starts and "ahs" that it's hard to tell what the person is talking about. But for the most part we get along fine with our languages as a means of communicating. We use the context of the conversation to figure out which meaning of the word is intended and what the sentence is referring to, and we are very forgiving of the difficulties people have casting their thoughts into words—after all, we are all up against the same problems when it is our turn to speak, so we virtually don't hear most of the hesitations and tongue-slips and other fumblings that mess up the King's English (or whatever language we are speaking) as people talk in day-to-day conversations.

Language is as reliable as it is because there is an agreement, for the most part an unwritten one, about what words mean and how they are to be fitted together. In short, language is a code used by speakers and listeners to communicate whatever it is they need to get across to each other: "pure" information, orders and requests, feelings, instructions, and on down the line. The term "code" as it is used here refers to the final result of three parallel processes, simplifying the original material, organizing it so that the relationship among its elements can be clear, and restructuring the whole for easy transmission.

Simplification.   The original material in the case of language consists of thoughts and ideas and all the rest of the things we need to communicate. Just what thoughts and ideas really are is beyond our present knowledge, but we know that they must be some neurophysiological processes or configurations of such processes in the central nervous system. The first step of coding, simplifying, means concentrating on the topic to be conveyed, casting aside irrelevancies, or eliminating noise so as not to confuse the listener. This is done by classifying what one is thinking about into categories so that we will be talking in terms of concepts rather than raw impressions. Our words refer to these general concepts, not to particular experiences the concepts might describe. As a result, words we use lack many of the nuances of our original thought and impressions. The great linguist, Edward Sapir (1921), wrote eloquently of this process, using the category "house" as his example:

> The elements of language, the symbols that ticket off experience, [are] associated with whole groups, delimited classes of experience rather than with the single experiences themselves. Only so is communication possible, for the single experience lodges in an individual consciousness and is, strictly speaking, incommunicable. To be communicated, it needs to be referred to a class which is tacitly accepted by the community as an identity. Thus, the single impression which I have had of a particular house must be identified with all my other impressions of it. Further, my generalization memory or my "notion" of this house must be merged with the notions that all other individuals who have seen the house have formed of it. The particular experience that we started with has now been widened so as to embrace all possible impressions or images that sentient beings have formed of the house in question. This first simplification of experience is at the bottom of a large number of elements of speech [pp. 12–13].

So collapsing all those individual experiences of "house" into one category is the essence of simplifying our thoughts.

The idea of categorzing in language is applied not only to words but to the sounds that make up words, and here the procedure is even more clear because the number of categories is so small. The words and sentences of all languages are made up of sequences of a few sounds, or phonemes (see Brown, 1958, pp. 27–50). Needless to say, there are exceptions and complications to this rule, but speakers and listeners believe that it is true, and act on it all the time. To analogize from written language, we can spell any word in our language with the few letters in our alphabet. English speech uses about 35 phoneme categories, plus or minus a few depending on dialect, and we can say anything in English using only the sounds that fall into those categories. and the categories are not only finite in number, but also sharply delineated so that there is no overlap between them in our "mind's ear," even though the differences between some of the pairs may be quite small from the standpoint of the physics of sound.

Simplifying and categorizing is one characteristic of all codes. In the case of language, very complicated material is handled by the system, and often we must be able to express the nuances and the individualized impressions that the simplification has eliminated. How do we manage to do that? We do it by adding as modifiers other categories that refer to those nuances, like "Victorian" or "white-chimneyed" to "house." Using another concept or two helps recover some of what was lost, and has an added advantage: since the modifying categories have also been tacitly agreed upon and are used commonly by all speakers and listeners, we end up being able to express ourselves very precisely. It is thus a characteristic of coded material that the information density in the final results is very high. True, each category is a simplification of many impressions, but a number of categories can be used in a short time period, and a speaker can depend heavily on his listener's sharing the meaning of what he wants to communicate.

Organization. If a number of categories are to be used to explain and modify and include all the nuances, however, there must be some way of keeping track of everything, of making clear what the relationships are among all of the categories. Every language has a set of rules and regulations for this purpose, namely the syntax or grammar of that language. The information about organization is conveyed in many ways in each language, and in an even wider variety of ways from one language to another—special words, suffixes and prefixes, word order, pitch changes, and so on. No language could possibly do without this sort of information. It tells us which are the main categories and which the modifiers, how smaller elements are combined into larger units, and those in turn into still larger ones, how these units are to be related to each other, when one sequence ends and the next one begins, and a host of other things.

Restructuring. The final characteristic of a code to be considered here is that of restructuring, and that consists of assigning some communicable labels to the categories and structural elements. The original categories and the ways they are related to each other, remember, are patterns of neurophysiological events in the speaker's central nervous system, and those are invisible and inaudible to others. They must be recast into some form or symbol that can be communicated, one symbol per configuration so as to avoid confusion. In language as we ordinarily think of it, the symbols are groupings of sounds, and the restructuring is carried out by unbelievably complex instructions to the vocal articulators to produce those sounds.

Throughout this description of what a language code is, there has been repeated reference to agreement among the members of the language community about the various aspects of the process. A bit more explanation of that agreement is due now that the elements of the process have been outlined. It would make no sense for a person to develop a coding system all for himself except for personal record-keeping. The result would certainly serve no function in communicating anything to anyone else. Every step of a coding system must be shared, be agreed upon by at least two people, and language systems are used in common by many more people than that. Where language communities number into the millions, some aspects of the agreement become fuzzy, so that there may be pockets of misunderstandings based on regional differences, social class differences, occupational differences, differences in degree of formality, and the like. Within each of these subcommunities, however, agreement will be high. Even across the subcommunities, there will be enough agreement for useful communication — especially if there is a sort of additional agreement to avoid the areas of disagreement, to stick to basics. No communication is possible without community.

Summary: Some aspects of the nature of language as a code.   Codes, in the sense that language is a code, are agreed-upon systems in which:

1. The thoughts and ideas we wish to convey are simplified and grouped into categories.
2. These categories are organized so that the relationships among the categories can be clear.
3. The results of the processes are restructured into symbols of a form that can be communicated from one person to another.

To the extent that any communication system is a code in this sense, a great deal of information can be transmitted from sender to receiver in a short period of time with great dependability. In short, codes make for very efficient communication.

TWO BODY LANGUAGES

So far in this chapter, spoken language has been the prime example of a coded communication system. It is certainly the most common one, since most people have all the apparatus to produce and receive it, as well as the social surroundings to learn it. There are a few, however, who lack either the apparatus or a common speech community, and cannot use speech as their medium of exchange. This does not mean that they are without any means of communicating or that the means they use is not language. This section of the chapter will use two such languages as examples, one the sign language of the deaf, and the other the system by American Indians to communicate across tribal (and therefore language community) barriers. The former is a more complete linguistic system than the latter, for reasons that should become clear as the two are described.

American sign language.   The fact that deaf people do not use speech to communicate with each other is not news. The obvious reason is that the receiver cannot hear what is spoken to him, but the more subtle reason is that hearing people learn to adjust their vocal apparatus to produce the sounds and combinations of sounds they hear other people producing, and lacking the sense of hearing, deaf people do not know either what sounds to imitate or how successful they are in their imitations. Many deaf people have been taught to speak and to read lips, but the process is laborious, and the resulting speech usually doesn't sound quite right, even though in many cases it is very usable in communicating with hearing people.

But the need to communicate is as great among the deaf as among the hearing, and many systems have been devised for this purpose over many centuries in all parts of the world, using the hands as the source mechanisms and the eyes as the receiving apparatus. Since there are comparatively few people who use these methods of communicating (profound deafness is relatively rare), few hearing people have learned them, the chief exceptions being those who have deaf family members and professionals who work with the deaf. So deaf people and their communication system are set apart and have often been viewed with suspicion, even persecuted. And those prejudices do not simply belong to the unenlightened past, but persist today: since they have difficulty speaking and reading (because writing is based on speech), deaf people do not do well on academic and ability tests designed for the hearing, and are often labeled as intellectually retarded. In addition, the dominant language community, English speakers in this country, assumes that its language is the only true one, and that different ones are not simply different, but inferior. Thus, American Sign Language (ASL) is looked down upon by those who do not understand its structure, and some version of English using a few signs and fingerspelling (a one-to-one hand configuration-to-alphabet letter set) is ordinarily insisted upon in schools, both for the deaf and for hearing people who wish to learn to communicate with the deaf. The result is that most deaf people are taught to deprecate ASL, to deny that it is a "true language," to claim that it "has no grammar," and to say that it is "incorrect." Those same people, however, use the true ASL in casual conversation with each other, and to communicate with their children.

There is a frightening parallel between this situation and that of Black English: the same attitudes prevail toward both and are held both by the dominant language community and also by the users of the special language themselves. In actual fact, both ASL and Black English have different origins than standard English: ASL is more closely related to French because it was imported from France, but it developed in this country quite rapidly so that it is now quite different structurally from both French and English; Black English came from Africa through European traders of slaves and other "merchandise," and has features of both African and European languages in addition to English. Thus the deaf comprise a true minority group so far as their language is concerned and everything that follows from it. As a group they are unfairly discriminated against. It is not an accident that many deaf people are able to understand the problems that Blacks have in the United States from having lived through very similar experiences.

Of all the manual communication systems throughout the world today, we know most about the one used by the deaf in the United States, ASL.[2] The reasons for this greater knowledge are many: the rapid growth of interest in linguistics in this country over the past 15 years, in which a wide range of language and other cognitive processes have been examined; the increased breadth of educational efforts geared for people with all sorts of handicaps; the fortunate positions of certain specialized institutions such as Gallaudet College, a Federally sponsored college for the deaf. Consequently, ASL is coming to be regarded by more and more people as a language in its own right, not as an imcomplete communication system that limits the intellectual accomplishments of its users.

American Sign Language starts where every language starts: its users simplify their thoughts and ideas, boiling them down to a set of commonly used categories to be communicated from person to person. The form of the communication is peculiar to ASL: it consists of hand positions, configurations, and movements, each a set of agreed-upon categories in the same sense that the phonemes that make up the syllables of speech are for any given language; these are put together into symbolic representations of concepts parallel to words, and arranged in sequences according to syntactic rules. The result is that ASL, like all languages, can serve to express anything that a user of the language wishes to express or that any user of any other language can express.

The easiest part of the language for a nonuser to understand is the way signs are made and what they "mean" in another language. There have been identified 12 hand positions (such as at the forehead, mid-face, or some posi-

---

[2]Stokoe's work, applying the methods of structural linguistics to ASL, has formed the basis for this section (see Stokoe, Caterline, and Croneberg [1965] and Stokoe [1972]). Harry W. Hoemann read this section very carefully and kindly sent thoughtful notes which have helped make a more realistic description of ASL.

tion related to the other hand), 19 configurations (mostly identified by their similarities to letters of the alphabet or to numbers in fingerspelling), and 24 movements (such as vertical, sideways, interactional), and one of each of these is used in combination to form any given sign. The numbers of positions, configurations, and movements should not be considered precise at this stage in our knowledge, because detailed study of ASL is not yet complete. Furthermore, the very list is itself more complicated than mere numbers might lead one to expect, because of the possibility of combining elements of the three factors. For example, the left hand in one configuration may serve as the position for the right hand in another configuration to relate to. In short, the number of concepts that ASL may refer to is very large, many times that of the vocabulary in common use today. In addition, facial expressions, gaze direction, and other elements of "body English" can specify, add nuances, and even contribute to the content of being signed. The face can be more a part of sign language than of spoken language for an obvious and important reason: in speech many facial muscles are in movement simply in the course of articulating the speech sounds, so that many expressive facial movements are interrupted by the very act of speaking. In signing, on the other hand, all of the facial muscles are continuously available to he signer in contributing to his communication. Many people claim, in fact, that they "watch the face" of the signer and see the manual elements out of the corner of their eyes.

A given sign, then, is a combination of position, configuration, and movement. A hand is formed into one of the configurations at a particular location with respect to the signer's body (or other hand), and moved in a certain way. In the sign for *good, the right hand is flat with fingers together, palm in; this hand first touches the fingertips to the lips, and then moves forward and down ending with its back placed in the palm of the left hand. In college* the two hands are flat and in front of the body, right hand palm to palm over left. The sign begins with a hand clap, then the right hand circles counterclockwise just above the left.

Many signs have histories that make them seem like pantomines, such as the sign for *girl*: the right hand is folded except for the thumb, which is left extended; the thumb is brushed across the right cheek, beginning almost at the ear and moving toward the chin. This originally referred to the ribbon under the chin for an old-fashioned girl's bonnet, so in this sense it is pantomimic, but by now that movement is so abbreviated that all pictorial representation has been lost — and anyway, why should one indicate a chin ribbon with one's thumb? A number of other signs originated with the fingerspelled initial letter of the English word as the sign was invented, rather like abbreviations, for example the "V" hand used to sign "vinegar." But V also begins the English words "vacation," "valuable," and so on, so initial letters cannot be distinguishing marks for many signs. In short, signs in ASL, whatever their origins, become arbitrary inventions to refer concepts, just like words in speech. It may be that there are more pantomimic signs in ASL than there are onomotopeic words in spoken English, because many signs were invented quite recently and the picturelike quality of some of them has not yet disappeared in the regularization process, but those would probably amount to only a small proportion of the total vocabulary. Only a handful of ASL signs could be guessed correctly by a nonsigner.

The structure of ASL is difficult to understand, because the terms of grammar we are accustomed to using in analyzing spoken languages often do not apply in the same way to ASL. One fundamental reason for this situation lies in the basic difference in dimensionality of the two types of language: in speech the smallest elements of the code are strung together one after the other, whereas in signs they are superimposed upon each other simultaneously. It is as though speech had one dimension, that of the line, whereas signs had four, those of the three dimensions of space plus time. In addition, the signer can add to the elements of his code a good deal of other information: he can indicate comparatives and superlatives by emphasis either of the speed or amount of space devoted to the movement elements; he can add personal pronouns and demonstratives by head and eye movements (so can the speaker, as discussed further, below, but these elements are more regular parts of signing), and so on. Thus what is called a single sign, with all this additional material, is often more than the equivalent for a word in English speech, and may be more comparable to the stem plus endings that make up the words of a language like Latin. In some cases a sign is even equivalent to an English phrase or brief sentence.

Thus, ASL operates differently from spoken language, and specifically from English, the dominant language of the country where it is used. The nature of those differences makes it appear to English speakers that ASL is deficient, since it lacks a number of features that are regularly used in English: it has no endings to indicate tense, number, or grammatical class — indeed the same sign can be used for the "noun" form and the "verb" form of the same concept, like "a dance" and "he danced;" ASL has no articles, nor does it have a copula (*is, are,* and other forms of *be*); it does not use the auxilliary verb *do* to form negatives and past constructions or to emphasize, and so on. The functions contributed by these various forms are not absent, but the forms themselves are not needed in ASL for a sentence to be a proper sentence in that language. If we look at spoken languages from a larger perspective than English, we find that ASL is not so unusual in any of these respects. Many languages do not use endings to words for grammatical structure. Many others have no articles or copula. Those that lack one or another of these features are not deficient as compared with those that have them; they are only different.

In spite of the very different structure of ASL, there are broad similarities to English in the way its larger units are arranged. Where subjects and predicates call for separate signs, they generally follow the same order in ASL and

English. Indirect and direct objects also follow English order, and so on. There are also similarities to the original French: adjectives often follow the nouns they modify. So structure is expressed in different ways than it is in English, but it is still true structure. It provides the organization for individual signs in the same way that all coding systems take care of organizing their elements. Thus, the first two processes in coding are present in ASL: the original thoughts and ideas are simplified by classifying them into agreed-upon categories, and a system of organization helps keep track of the relationships among the categories. The third process, restructuring the resulting categories into communicable form, is achieved by ASL by casting them into combinations of specified visible forms of body movements rather than the audible forms used in speech. The specified forms comprise in their turn a set of agreed-upon categories of hand positions, configurations, and movements similar to the set of phonemes that each spoken language specifies for its community of users. In short, ASL is a body language that really is a language.

Indian sign language. [3]   The American Indians had a very different motivation for developing a sign language than deaf people have: they needed to communicate with people who did not share their spoken language, so as to be able to trade with them and carry on other intertribal business, and later on to deal as a large group with the encroaching white man. As individuals growing up in families they were not dependent on some visible method of communication, for they could hear and therefore speak — or like us, the vast majority of them could. So these were people with fully developed spoken languages who set about inventing an auxilliary language to be used across the language barriers that existed between tribes.

We know very little about the origins of Indian Sign Language (ISL) for the same reasons we know so little about the distant background of any language. By the time missionaries and soldiers began making notes about it, the language had already been in use for some time. The claim that ISL's history is not very long, that it came into being only when the whites began invading Indian lands, seems on the face of it unlikely, since the language would have had to develop too rapidly to be believed. In addition, the development of sign languages for communication among neighboring tribes is not unknown

---

[3]Mallery's monograph (1881) is perhaps the most important historical document on ISL, and it has recently been reprinted. Tomkins (1926) made up a manual of ISL for Boy Scouts that is very valuable. West's dissertation (1960), available in photocopy from University Microfilms of Ann Arbor, Michigan, analyzed ISL using structural linguistics and drawing data from living informants. ISL is used in specialized circumstances today, since English serves as the *lingua franca* in intertribal business. Certain ceremonies and demonstrations are about all that remain as occasions for using ISL, and in most of them the signers give running translations in English.

elsewhere in the world. One such language on which research is now beginning is the system used among the widely diverse peoples of Australia.

We might expect that ISL, being used as an auxilliary means of communicating for rather limited purposes, would be quite primitive and capable of expressing only a few ideas. To some extent that expectation is indeed borne out: its vocabulary is not very large, and some aspects of its structure are quite simple. The surprising thing about ISL, however, is that it appears to be a complete language in the same sense that spoken language and ASL are: one can express virtually anything in it, although one would have to take some roundabout means in some cases.

The signs that make up ISL are combinations of 40 referents (these include positions plus pointing to people and directions), 18 hand configurations, and 24 movements. Not all of these elements are used very often, especially not all the referents, but they are all possible. So the total of the frequently used elements of signing in ISL is not much different from that of ASL. Some of the referents, configurations, and types of movement are the same as those of ASL, or at least very similar, and some are quite different. This should not be surprising for the same situation obtains in the case of any two spoken languages. In English and French, for example, the "n" sounds are for all practical purposes identical, but English has no sound similar to the French "u," nor French to the English "r." The point is that both languages, English and French in the case of spoken languages, and ASL and ISL in signed languages, have their own set of agreed-upon categories of elements with which their users make up the larger units of the languages.

The ideas that are expressed in ISL are the same as those expressed in any other language: thoughts, feelings, or whatever, that are basically neurophysiological processes in the central nervous system. These are simplified and regularized, as they must be with any language, into an agreed-upon set of categories to be expressed. The number of categories appears to be somewhat smaller in ISL than ASL, although no complete inventory of them has yet been developed. And the simplification does not seem to have gone as far for most concepts in ISL as it has for those in ASL, for the signs that express them are a good deal closer to pantomine, as if the users still had some doubts about whether their intentions might be mistaken. Some 98% of ISL signs are of this form, according to one estimate (West, 1960, Vol. I, p. 29). Such elaborate pantomiming means that each concept needs more time to be cast into ISL, with the result that it is more cumbersome and slow than ASL for the same material. Finally ISL wastes time by failing to utilize one whole communication channel: the ideal signer is quite stolid as to facial expression while signing. Although signers are probably not as poker-faced as this ideal would dictate, many nuances that ASL routinely conveys in facial behavior are either lost to ISL or must be expressed in some other way.

Being pantomimic might lead to the expectation that almost anyone could understand the signs. But the regularization has gone too far for that. "Nonspeakers" of the language can guess correctly only somewhat fewer than half of the signs when they are given out of context with plenty of time for guessing, and fewer than that when a conversation is under way and the next signs keep coming along. The fact is that there was a good deal of boiling down of concepts and agreement on how the signs for them were to be formed, agreement on what were the "essential" aspects of each idea that should be made the basis for its sign. Since the language was used with neighboring tribes only, some slight differences developed as to what those essential features were when communicating with different neighbors. Under these conditions, dialects had a good chance to develop. Indeed, there was one area where differences were slight, namely that of the Great Plains, and a dropping off of mutual intelligibility to the East, West, and South.

So the concepts themselves were agreed upon along with their signs, at least within a broad geographical area, but how about the way they were organized? Was that also subject to agreement so that anyone wuld know how a signer was relating one concept to another in connected discourse?

The structure of grammar of ISL, like that of ASL, is difficult to study in the same terms that apply to spoken language, so we do not know as much about it. Apparently the internal structure of the signs was a lot more tightly knit than the external: the way each sign was to be formed was strictly dictated, while the order in which any sequence of signs was to be presented was not. Within broad limits and with only four exceptions, the order of signs within an utterance was determined more by the style of the signer, by convenience, and by the broader line of the narrative than by anything we might consider grammatical or syntactical relationships. ISL, like ASL, is a multidimensional language, so that each sign may contain structural information, unlike individual "words" in English speech. It is in the formation of each individual sign that the grammatical rules lie, and these were apparently very strict. Thus the order of signs in an extended string was not a necessary contributor to information about how the concepts were organized. The four excpetions were the signs for beginning and ending a long utterance or narrative, the sign for questions, and the sign for negation. The first two are self-explanatory. The question sign came before the group of signs, indicating that a question was to follow. The negative, on the other hand, came at the end of the group that was to be negated.

The two processes of regularizing ideas and organizing them, the first two necessities of a coding system, are thus present in ISL, although to a lesser extent than we are used to in other languages, including ASL. It is lesser in the regularizing in that the process does not go so far as it does in other languages, most of the signs being pantomimic in character. And it is lesser in organizing in that the rules of relating one sign to another, by order or any other method, appear looser in ISL than in other languages. The third process, that of presenting the categories in some form communicable to others who are in the language community, has been worked out quite precisely in ISL, partly by the strict internal rules of organizing the elements of form and movement within the signs as they are portrayed, and partly by the pantomimic character of the signs themselves.

Summary: Coding as applied to bodily expression.   The two languages, ASL and ISL, are really codes in the same sense that spoken languages are codes. They are different in the extent to which the information they convey has been subjected to the total process of coding, but they are still codes. In both cases, ideas have been boiled down, organized, and presented in ways that both the signer and the viewer have come to a tacit agreement about, so that when a string of signs comes along the two people can both know what the original idea was. The viewer does not have to guess, and the signer can be confident that he has really communicated. This description is an ideal, of course, for we all know that there are slips — the boiling-down leaves out nuances, the organization does not eliminate all ambiguities, and the means of presentation is not absolutely exact — but the system still admits of considerable precision. The users of both languages can depend on that precision quite securely as they do their daily business communicating with each other.

BODY LANGUAGE: IS IT A CODE?

From languages using body movements as their medium to "body language" as that term is used so often today, is a long step. When we talk about body language, we do not mean that we really carry on conversations through our bodies about any and all topics, but rather than there is more to conversation than an audio tape or a typescript of the words could tell us. We mean that people express themselves in all sorts of ways, sometimes adding to, sometimes — and this is the interesting part — altering or negating what they are saying in words. When we say we are "really reading" someone, we mean that we are tuned in on all of these wavelengths. Sometimes that is good, when we are feeling really at home with a friend, and sometimes it makes us uncomfortable, when the messages we feel we are getting do not add up to a very friendly total atmosphere.

But how dependable are these messages, in the sense that language is a dependable method of communicating? That is the question for this section of this chapter. To answer it, the best set of concepts is that of coding: to the extent that the source information for any system of communication is coded and the elements that make up the messages are also coded, the result is precise communication. Conversely, to the extent that the material has not been subjected to the coding processes, we are left guessing about what the messages really are. To anticipate briefly, there are a few body movements that behave like coded material in that they are easily understood by all or most members of the community. By far the greater majority of movements, however, serve more as cues from which we make inferences. If all the cues add up right, our guesses from these messages can be very good ones, but usually we don't have time for much inferring if we are to keep up with the conversation, and besides, because of the way our perceptual apparatus works, our attention in conversations is drawn to decoding the speech.

First a word about a couple of other interlocking issues. Usually when we talk about "communication" we are referring to situations where one person is deliberately sending messages to one another. He *intends* to do so, and his intentions are fully conscious. Those two characteristics, in fact, are part and parcel of many writers' definitions of communication. But the very idea of body language as it is usually thought of, especially when it refers to cues from which we infer something about a person, precludes both awareness and intention as necessary features of the process. Indeed, some of the stuff that these messages are made of, such as fidgetiness or generalized muscular tension, could not be controlled even if we intended to do so. Others, like posture and how often we look at our conversational partner, are so automatic as to be out of our usual range of consciously thought-out activities. Therefore, the term "communication" will have to take on a more general sort of meaning for the rest of this chapter. It should not be dropped as a term, however, because the messages in question are still messages whether they are deliberate ones ore not: they still consist of information of some sort that is transmitted from one person to another. Both the deliberate messages and not-so-deliberate ones should obey the same laws and be accounted for by the same concepts and theories. So communication is still a good word to cover *all* messages that pass between us.

In order to examine the various movements that comprise body language from the standpoint of coding, one of the basic concepts introduced earlier needs to be spelled out more precisely: the one of categorical information. It came up first in connection with the simplifying and regularizing process we use in boiling our thought down into concepts. Information that has been treated this way is called discrete information. It comes in separate, distinct packages that do not overlap each other, and these are usually of a finite, countable number. This sort of information has another characteristic, too: the packages recur again and again, and are made up of roughly the same elements in the same configuration each time they reappear. In short, they become categories to which some community of people may assign labels or meanings. In the case of simplifying thought processes for use in language, we form our thoughts, ideas, and impressions into categories to be used over and over again, and the language community agrees to stick to those categories or concepts as their medium of exchange, and name them with words or signs.

The opposite of discrete information is the continuous, in which there may be an infinite number of values distributed along a continuum, each one shading into the next one imperceptably. One of the features of continuous information is that it can be made artificially discrete by dividing the continuum into step intervals as we do every day in stating our age. No adult ever gives his age in steps any finer than the year unless he is specially asked to, and we have much broader age categories where we do not require the precision that years can give: baby, child, teenager, young adult, and so on. Everyone knows, of course, that these categories are artificially imposed on what is really a continuum, that not all eight-year-olds are more different in age than some pairs made up of an eight-year-old and a nine-year-old. But for most practical purposes a finer distinction is not needed: we know roughly what is meant by "an eight-year-old child."

In dealing with body movements there is another use of the two terms, discrete and continuous, and that is how movements appear in time. Some are performed discretely — the head nod is a good example — that is, they are brief movements that begin and end suddenly and are sharply separated from the movements that precede them and also from those that follow. Other movements are continuous over time — like one hand stroking the other — and are not seen as different events in time but rather as an activity that spans some period of time.

This difference between discretely performed and continuous movements has two features that are important to understand in the discussion that follows: First, continuous movements cannot sensibly be made into discrete categories simply by dividing them into step intervals. We might divide them, all right, at the changes in direction of continuous stroking, for example, but there would be no meaningful way of naming the resulting categories. On the contrary, we may more easily transform discretely performed movements into continuous information, both as we notice them in social situations and also as we study them in the laboratory, by counting their frequency of occurrence over some period of time. We may then use the results of our counting to make such statements as, "John nods more frequently when talking to Mary than he does when talking to Tom."

The second thing to note about the use of continuous and discrete in talking about movements is that not all discrete movements are necessarily categories of movement. The head nod is both: it is performed discretely, and it is recognized as a category of movement whose meaning is agreed upon by members of the language community. In answer to a question that calls for a "Yes" or a "No," a nod means "Yes." In conversations, listeners insert nods from time to time, and while their meaning is not quite so specific, they are still very wordlike, interchangeable with "Mm-hm," "I see," and so on. Thus the head nod is both discrete and categorical. Many other discretely performed movements, however, do not make up categories that any group might agree has any meaning. Some of the gesticulations that accompany talking, such as those that seem to punctuate the rhythm of speech, are a good case in point. They are usually performed discretely in time, have distinct beginnings and endings, but most of them do not fall into nameable categories. They can be counted, as nods can, and their frequency used as continuous information, and this is the most common way these movements have been dealt with in research studies.

With all the necessary concepts finally at hand, the discussion may now proceed with an examination of body language as a code.[4] It follows the same general outline as the last section, but differs from it in one major respect. The two sign languages, ASL and ISL, are true language systems, both coded, although one is somewhat more completely coded than the other. The task for this chapter was simply to describe them as examples of coded systems. In the case of body language, on the other hand, it is not so clear that there is a code, or if so, what aspects of it the code applies to, and to what extent. We must therefore be more cautious in our approach to describing body language, examining each feature carefully to see if it could be a part of a coded system.

The elements of body language.   In describing ASL and ISL, it was possible to enumerate all the elemental movements, positions, and configurations of the hands that make up the larger groupings called signs. The elements, and the larger groupings as well, are discrete and categorical in nature, agreed upon by the language community. In body language it is not clear that there exists any set number of elements of this sort: perhaps some movements or postures could be thought of as proper elements, while others could not. This discussion will leave the question open at the outset by listing those behaviors that have been studied by various researchers, and treating them as candidates for elemental categories. No claim for completeness is made, because of the practical considerations researchers must weigh in deciding what to study: they want to study what they think is important according to the theoretical ideas they hold, but they also want some assurance of success, and they may be tempted to stick to things that will be easier to handle with the techniques they already have available. Most investigators also include items others have studied, partly because there may be alternative theories that may thus be put to the test, and partly as a check on their methods. The most likely candidates for elements in a body language system

---

[4]The consistency and accuracy of many points in this section have benefited greatly from discussions with Daphne Bugental, Paul Ekman, Wallace Friesen, Karl Heider, Maureen O'Sullivan, and others during a workshop held at Ekman's laboratory in June, 1973.

will be listed here first, the discrete, categorical behaviors, then some that are less likely, and so on down the line.

Discrete Behaviors

Categorical Behaviors

Emblems[5] are the most eligible of the discrete, categorical behaviors. They are *the* movements that have meaning and may be translated directly into words. In some parts of the world, such as Mediterranean countries, a quite complete system of emblems has been worked out and has been used for centuries by people who can hear perfectly well. Some of the stories of these gesture languages may have been exaggerated by the astonished (and artistically gifted) visitors who have described them, but clearly those people's gesture vocabulary enables them to carry on conversations far beyond the bounds that American speakers of English can do with anything but words. Mallery (1881, pp. 295–296) quotes Alexandre Dumas recounting two narratives he observed in Sicily and southern Italy, where he had an opportunity to check independently on what the Italian translation was. Efron (1941) describes emblems used by southern Italian immigrants to New York City, and the republication of his work includes a short dictionary of these gestures.

We are not entirely lacking in emblems but their number is probably not large. Many are highly pantomimic so that it would be difficult to decide if they are truly symbolic emblems—if indeed anyone had already decided that only the symbolic could qualify as emblems. The hitch-hiker's movement for thumbing a ride, for example, when it is used in its context, does not require an interpreter of some strange language to translate. Circling the ear with the index finger to say, "He's crazy!" on the other hand, has no obvious movement-to-words connection. Just how many emblems we have is not known precisely, although a survey is currently being made,[6] nor is there any information on how frequently they are used in comparison to other movements day by day. A number of facial expressions other than those of emotion are emblems, and the emotional expressions themselves, may be used as emblems—the surprise expression, for example, to refer to an experience of surprise. Whether the actual facial expressions of emotion are emblems is a

---

[5]The term "emblem" was used by Ekman and Friesen (1969), who used it to refer to "those nonverbal acts which have a direct verbal translation, or dictionary definition, usually consisting of a word or two, or perhaps a phrase. This verbal definition or translation of the emblem is well known by all members of a group, class, or culture [p. 63]." Ekman and Friesen credit Efron (1941) with proposing the term, although he used it in a more restrictive sense as those symbolic acts that had no relationship between their form and meaning, that is, that were not at all pantomimic.

[6]John Johnson, working with Ekman and Friesen (personal communication, 1973).

moot point since they seem to be biologically determined (Ekman, Friesen, & Ellsworth, 1972). Certainly they function as emblems in daily life.

A related sort of movement, probably used more commonly, is referred to by Birdwhistell (1967) as the *kinesic marker*. These movements mark some aspect of the speech that is going on at the same time, such as head movements to indicate the person in a group to whom the speaker is referring in some part of his utterance (similar to ASL but not so precisely defined). Other such markers may serve as place holders in presenting contrasting ideas, to accompany "On the one hand . . . while on the other . . . ," and the like.

Eye contact (for an extensive review, see Ellsworth & Ludwig, 1972) may seem an odd behavior to include in a chapter on body movement, but one of the best ways of identifying it in a research situation is by observing the accompanying head movements: one usually turns his head to look at another person (if the two are not squared off to begin with, and people in our culture seldom place themselves that way), and if one is looking at another, he is usually looking in his eyes. Since people do not maintain eye contact for long periods at a time, the beginning and end of each contact can easily be told, and the behavior qualifies as discrete. Since it is repeated the same way each time, it is a categorical behavior.

The *smile* is an unmistakable facial behavior that has a sudden onset and usually a slow fade, and is usually of short enough duration to be called a discrete event. Smiles are not all the same, and there may be some subcategories that could be identified, although this work has only begun. One possible subtype is the listener smile (Dittmann & Llewellyn, 1968, p. 83), which has both sudden onset and sudden fade and appears to be another equivalent to the head nod and brief vocalization ("m-hm" etc.)

The *nod* is a discrete, categorical behavior whose dual meanings ("yes" and "m-hm") were mentioned earlier in this section. There may be other categories of nod, based perhaps on number of movements, but these, along with other smiles, have not been studied sufficiently for any definite statements at this time.

These three discrete, categorical behaviors, eye contact, smiles, and nods, lend themselves to forming continuous variables by counting their frequencies over longer periods of time. Most research studies concentrate on these frequencies, and people in social situations probably do, too: one notices that a friend is smiling a lot more today than last week, or a lot less, and so on. In addition, eye contact can be treated as a continuous variable by measuring the duration of each contact, or by totalling the duration of contact in a larger time period.

The *head shake,* meaning "no," usually occurs only in answer to questions that demand either a "yes" or a "no," and since those questions are rather rare, so is the head shake. The movement may also be seen in an almost continuous form in some people under some circumstances, such as during the expression (in words) of a strongly positive attitude: a person may say, "There was really beautiful photography in that movie," while shaking his head continuously.

Two postures that are discrete and categorical round out this part of the list: *arms akimbo* (or hands on hips) and the *open–closed positions of arms or legs* (hands and arms apart and knees separated for open, and arms crossed or folded and legs crossed for closed). There is some question about whether these should be called elements in the same sense as those listed above, since there are many ways of striking these poses, but the variations are not great, and they do fall into definite categories. The akimbo posture is probably rare except in the standing position.

Noncategorical Behaviors

The *gesticulations accompanying speech* are perhaps the best examples of this kind of movement, as mentioned earlier. They are hand movements, usually of small extent (although in some cultures they are quite extensive), brief, and appear to follow the rhythmic structure of the speech they accompany. They are thus discretely performed, with definite beginnings and endings. Whether they are categorical is another matter. The pattern of the movements may be quite repetitive for a given individual, or there may be a limited number of patterns a person uses, but no research results show that these patterns fall into categories that any community of people agree upon as elements for assignment of meanings. Rather, most of them appear to be formed almost randomly.

The location of these movements in the stream of speech has been the subject of two research efforts. The results show that many of the speech-accompanying gesticulations are tied to the location of hesitation forms in speech described by Boomer (1978) (Dittman, 1972a). And many of them begin and end with the onset and completion of units of utterance (Kendon, 1967). Kendon (1972) has discussed many more details of these issues.

In social situations we probably notice gesticulations mostly by their frequency, and researchers have followed that lead. Number of movements per minute, per experimental condition or whatever, can be determined many ways such as by counting them in actual experimental sessions or from movies or video tapes of those sessions, by measuring muscle potentials, by attaching miniature accelerometers, and so on. The resulting numbers are distributed continuously, even though they are made up of discrete events.

Posture shifts, such as changing posture in the chair, crossing and recrossing the legs, and the like are discrete movements, again made up of many possible elements and notable chiefly by their frequency over some longer period of time.

Possibly Discrete and Categorical Behaviors

These are all variations of posture and position, and the variables on which they are measured are certainly continuous. Yet it appears that the continua are divided into step intervals just as age was seen to be, in the explanation of discrete and continuous information at the beginning of this section. The result is a set of categories within each of the behaviors.

Forward and backward lean may be measured in degrees of the trunk from the vertical, a measurement that is obviously on a continuum. But as we interact with people, we cannot discriminate between slight differences in number of degrees, and we do not need to for the most practical purposes. We need only to be able to say that a person is sitting upright, is leaning forward or leaning backward. We may go further than that in some cases, saying that he is leaning slightly forward, way forward, and so on, but these are still discrete steps made of an underlying continuum. The fact that they are so easy to name indicates that they are treated as categories.

Distance between persons is also clearly a continuum, but it, too, is commonly divided into discrete step intervals, again perhaps only three: too close, comfortable distance, and too far. Just where the dividing lines are between these intervals depends on the sex and age composition of the group of people involved, and on the culture they come from (see Watson, 1970).

Body orientation means the angle formed by imaginary lines drawn through the shoulders of two people interacting. If they are facing each other squarely the angle is 0°. The usual conversational angle is a little less than 90°. It is not so clear for this variable, as for the two listed above, that discrete steps are made by people in ordinary, day-to-day situations, but it may work something like distance in that very low angles are too close and at some point beyond the right angle it becomes too distant.

Continuous Behaviors

These are intrinsically continuous over time, not discrete movements made into continuous variables by counting how often they occur. *Adaptors*[7] are often intrinsically continuous movements, such as stroking an arm or a leg, playing with a pencil, rubbing one hand with the other, squeezing the fingers of one hand in the other, moving the hands back and forth over the arm of a chair. While these movements, like all others, have beginnings and endings, we tend not to notice those features, and in research many such movements seem most meaningfully measured in terms of their duration. Some take on

---

[7]These movements have been studied by several investigators who began their work on them independently and called them by different names: body-focused movements (Freedman & Hoffman, 1967); self-manipulations (Rosenfeld, 1966); and adaptors (Ekman & Friesen, 1969).

the appearance of fidgetiness, but just how people in social situations notice them — or if they do at all — is not known.

Rhythmical movements of various parts of the body are also performed continuously. They include foot swinging (usually with legs crossed), foot tapping, finger drumming, and a number of others.

There are a number of other continuous movements that have not been studied specifically, but which may be noticeable in social situations. Certain movements of the feet comprise one group, flexing, turning, and the like; sometimes these movements are almost invisible because the person is moving his toes inside his shoes. Turning back and forth in a swivel chair or rocking in a rocker, when those chairs are present, make up another group.

The organization of body language. In the description of languages so far in this chapter, organization has been an easy topic, because the elements of those languages are arranged very systematically into the groupings that make up their words and signs, with relatively little variation permitted in the total configuration for each. Emblems probably behave in about the same way, although they have not been studied enough for anyone to say for sure. Neither do we know whether they occur frequently enough to be considered an important part of body language in the usual sense of that term. Other than emblems, there appear to be only a few groupings to talk about. Chief among these are postures: in the arms akimbo and the open–closed positions, a total of elements adds up to what the viewer interprets as one of those positions. But the way the elements are arranged is quite variable. In arms akimbo position, the hands may be open or made into a fist, the hands may be rotated forward or backward, and they may be placed toward the front or the back just so long as they are vaguely on the hips, and so on. For any of these variations, a number of viewers would agree that the person is standing "with arms akimbo." The open–closed positions can be made up of even more variable elements.

Some of the acts listed above under discrete, categorical behaviors might be considered groupings, since they contain more than one movement — the head nod, for example — but those constituents are so few that to talk about organization into a larger grouping seems like over-formalizing things. This is not to say that there may not be more than one kind of nod, depending on the details of the constituent movements, but we need a good deal more research on these details before we can differentiate among such acts in a useful way.

Most of the organization of body movements we ordinarily think of as making up body language is determined by the organization of the concurrent speech. As we talk, we divide up our stream of talk into packages of a few words, and these are marked by rhythmical features like recurring stresses toward the end of each unit and a characteristic slowing down as the unit is finished. The organization of these units is made up of the syntactic rules, or grammar, of the language (e.g., see Boomer, 1978). Many body movements follow this unit formation, as if the fact of speaking were a powerful determiner of much of what the speaker does at the same time. When the speaker looks at his listener, and how he changes his line of regard (and also the direction his head is facing); when he inserts the kinesic markers to indicate who is being referred to, to emphasize one topic or another, or whatever, when he initiates the more random-appearing gesticulations — all these are tied to the rhythm structure of the speech that the movements are accompanying. Even larger movements such as posture shifts appear to be related to larger speech units like change of topic, beginning or ending of longer utterances, and so forth. These units of speech in turn are related to the way the speaker sorts out his thoughts, organizes them, and forms them into words. Thinking on one's feet while talking in conversational situations lays the groundwork for all sorts of "nonverbal behavior." It is nonverbal in that it does not consist of words, but it is directly influenced by the very act of talking (see Kendon, 1972)

A different organization related to speech concerns the mechanics of changing speaker turns from one person to another (see Duncan, 1972). A large number of behaviors is involved in this system, from the rhythmical packaging of the speech itself and the concomitant grammatical structure to changes in eye contact (or head orientation), to certain gesticulatory behaviors and a number of others.

In the descriptions of other languages in this chapter, one of the easily recognizable features of words and signs was that they referred to concepts that members of the language community had agreed were to be used to represent their various thoughts, ideas, feelings, and impressions. In the case of body language, some of the acts and postures have similar referents, and it will be instructive to go over the list again to see what the nature of those referents may be. Again, research findings will be the basis for the interpretations.

Among the discrete, categorical behaviors, emblems clearly have the most specific referents. Some of them are truly arbitrary, just as words are, and their referents may vary from culture to culture. The airman's sign for "A-OK," for example, used by United States astronauts and seen worldwide on television, is interpreted in some quarters as an obscene gesture. There are probably not more than a dozen or two of these arbitrary emblems in common use in the United States today. Many more of obvious pantomimic origin, the hitchiker's thumb, for example, or the index finger to the lips for "shhh!" have referents that are just as specific as the arbitrary emblems. The movements that Birdwhistell (1967) has termed "kinesic markers," referred to above, should probably also be included among the emblems as having quite specific reference. Whether all of these should be considered parts of body language as that term is popularly intended is an open question.

The two main functions of nodding, the signal that the listener is keeping up and the specific "Yes" substitute, have already been mentioned. Frequent nodding, when this movement is thus made into a continuous variable, would seem to be a sign of friendliness (Fretz, 1966), but it has not always turned out that simply in research studies: it seems also to be the *result* of a friendly atmosphere (Rosenfeld, 1967). Frequent smiling definitely indicates a wish to be friendly and to be accepted by the other person (Fretz, 1966; Rosenfeld, 1966), a finding quite in line with anyone's expectations. Eye contacts are timed in conversation to help regulate whose turn it is to talk: a person who is about to begin talking will look away from his conversational partner, and he looks back toward the end of rhythmical units of speech as if to seek the feedback that an "m-hm" or a nod would provide (Kendon, 1967). The total length of time that a person looks at another during a conversation is associated with several variables: women look more than men, people attracted to each other look longer, extraverts look more than introverts, and so on (see Ellsworth & Ludwig, 1972, for these and related findings). Staring at another is an upsetting stimulus, possibly an aggressive one (it is definitely aggressive in other mammals), from which the recipient will usually wish to escape (Ellsworth, Carlsmith, & Henson, 1972).

The two postures, arms akimbo and the open position of arms and legs, are used by people interacting with others of lower status. In addition, the akimbo position is more likely when one is with someone whom one dislikes.[8] Forward lean, as might be expected, occurs more among people who like each other. A more complicated pattern has been found with both distance and body orientation in ordinary conversational situations: one feels more comfortable at a greater distance and greater angle of orientation when dealing with a disliked person; he can be closest and oriented at the most direct angle with a neutral person, and somewhere in between with someone he likes.

Discretely performed hand movements (the gesticulations accompanying speech) are organized according to their relationships to speech rhythms. As mentioned above, they occur more frequently at times when the flow of speech is interrupted by hesitations, "ahs," retraces, and other fumblings (Dittmann, 1972a; Dittmann & Llewellyn, 1969). These nonfluencies are far more frequent than we realize, since the listener very kindly edits them out as he tries to follow what the speaker is saying. So nonfluent passages have more gesticulating associated with them than the fluent. When these movements are treated as continuous information by counting them over longer periods of time, they take on another, less specific meaning. A person who gesticu-

---

[8]These interpretations are based on an experiment (Mehrabian, 1968) where subjects were asked to imagine how they would act under different circumstances and may thus have encouraged responses that subjects felt were expected of them in addition to natural behaviors.

lates a great deal may be seen as having Mediterranean background, where people are known to gesticulate a lot, for example, or if his family is obviously not from one of those countries, as being nervous and high strung. He may also be under some strain at this time of his life or in this particular social situation or at this specific moment (Dittmann, 1962; Sainsbury, 1955).

Among the behaviors called possibly discrete, organization does not play much of a role since the behaviors are not made up of constituent pairs in the same way as arms akimbo. The meaning is fairly clear and similar for all of these behaviors: people who lean forward toward their conversational partners, who stand close (but not too close for comfort), and who face squarely (but not completely so) are seen as friendly and warm.

The truly continuous behaviors are even less specific as to meaning. One does not know for sure, for example, if a person engaged in adaptor movements, such as stroking one hand with the other, is upset right now in this immediate situation or if he is inclined to move this way all the time. The same applies to rhythmical movements like swinging the feet and drumming the fingers. They provide information that must be interpreted in some way, not information that carries its own interpretation as discrete categories of behaviors like words and signs do.

As a matter of fact, this differentiation of the sort of information given by continuous and discrete behaviors may be applied to the whole list of movements given in this exposition of body language. The discrete, categorical movements, those that were listed as the most likely candidates for elements in a body language system, were also the most specific as to "meaning," in that the members of the community agree on what they refer to. They are thus the items with the highest information density. As the list progressed toward continuous behaviors, or as discrete behaviors were treated as continua by counting their frequencies over longer periods of time, more broadly probablistic statements had to be made and phrases like "is associated with" began to crop up. The information density of these types of movement is lower. And these behaviors turn out to constitute most of the movements we see in social situations such as conversations.

With a few exceptions, then, we cannot look at a person's movements and know definitely what they mean in body language, the way we can see a series of signs in ASL and know the concepts they refer to. We must rather make probablistic statements about them. If there are enough movements to yield enough problbisitic statements, we can feel more satisfied with our accuracy. In short, we can observe movement cues and make inferences from them about what is going on in the person we are observing, about what he is feeling, what his intentions are, and so on. These inferences cannot be couched in very specific terms, the way one might paraphrase what someone has said—that is, the precision of the conclusions we can draw from our inferences is not very high — but they can still serve us quite well in dealing with others day by day.

The conclusion in the last paragraph implies that the probablistic statements were made up from individual, isolated events, like unconnected lists of words rather than sentences. But the topic for this section of the chapter is organization in body language — is there no organization into larger chunks of meaning here, comparable to the sentences of spoken language or ASL? From what is available in current thinking and research, the answer to that question would have to be "No." People "say" things about themselves in body language, but not in the form of statements that could be part of any discourse. What they say, or what is available to others to "read," has a certain unity to it, to be sure, in that it does not consist of isolated events, but the interrelationships come from the basic state a person finds himself in at any given time, from which all his behaviors derive, not from the connectedness of any syntax such as that which relates words together in sentences.

By stretching a point one could find a few systematic relationships: for example, eye contact and distance are inversely related, probably because of the implications both have for intimacy (for a review of several experiments, see Argyle & Ingham, 197.). A sort of balance is struck, aparently such that if two people are standing or sitting very close to each other, they look at each other less than they would from greater distance. In the case of emblems, usually more than one is needed to get a point across: letting someone know of a mock astonishment at hearing a piece of gossip might entail producing the "surprise" facial expression followed by a wry smile. But longer discourse could take place only under the most artificial circumstances even with emblems and probably not at all with other sorts of movement. Finally, the relationships among all of the behaviors that are involved in changing speaker turns (Duncan, 1972) include messages in body language. These messages do not make up any discourse in and of themselves, but rather contribute to a larger system of social interaction.

Summary: Body language as a limited system of communication.   In this section I have examined body language from the standpoint of its membership in the family of coded communication systems, and found it to qualify in only a few of its features. Discrete behaviors, performed in much the same way each time they appear, like emblems and a few postures, have meanings that everyone in the language community can agree upon. Most movements are not of that type, however, and they take as their organizing principles either the rhythmical structure of the concurrent speech, or their association with the state of being of the person, either long-term or situationally influenced. We use these less specific behaviors as cues to make inferences about those states in the person, and the success of those inferences varies with a number of factors. Extended discourse in body language, parallel to that possible spoken language or ASL, does not seem to occur.

THE PAYOFF: HOW MUCH DO WE USE MOVEMENTS TO "READ" PEOPLE?

The conclusion that body language is only a limited method of communicating may be a disappointment, but it should not come as news, to return to the first paragraphs of this chapter. It should also not be construed as a death-knell for body language, for we do take in movements as we interact with other people, and we do make inferences from them. The question of how much we use them cannot be answered fully at this stage in the development of the field of social interaction because virtually no research has been done on that aspect of the problem. Still, some quite well-informed speculations can be made even now, and as long as they are recognized for what they are, as speculations, they can serve very well until more facts come in — even guide research efforts to find those facts.

The speculations derive from another field of psychology, that of perception, and more specifically from the thinking and work of D. E. Broadbent.[9] He found that what gets through our perceptual apparatus, or what we attend to, depends on a number of features of the stimuli before us, as these relate to a specific characteristic of the perceptual apparatus itself. This characteristic is its limited capacity to handle information. It can deal with so much and no more. When we say that we cannot attend to two things at once, that is only partly true: what we cannot do is exceed the capacity of the system. Given two stimuli, the apparatus gives preference to (1) the one whose information density is the higher, and (2) the one with the greater intensity.

The application to conversations is clear: the speech we hear, being of high information density, plus any of the more highly coded body language events, are likely to get through at the expense of any other less completely coded activities that may be going on at the same time. The intensity feature becomes a leavener that allows body language material to pass the perceptual apparatus. Noncoded body language events that are intense enough will override the attention demandingness of the coded. Or a long succession of them can add up suddenly and make an impression, when for some reason attention becomes available.

The reasons attention might become available are many. There are fairly frequent lulls in conversations during which we do not need to concentrate on

---

[9]Broadbent's original research had as its focus the problem of the inference of signals coming in from various planes in an aircraft control tower. For an explanation of the application of his thinking to human communication, see Dittmann (1972b, pp. 156–161).

decoding the speech of the other person or on encoding into speech what we are trying to say. In addition, the conversation is not always about something we are eager to hear about, so we find our minds wandering. Likely, the wanderings take us to preoccupations from earlier times or to plans for what we are going to do next, but attention could turn at those times to the less densely packed information in body movements. And we need not simply become bored to have attention available for lower information messages: some topics of conversation are inherently more difficult to grasp, and demand a good deal of brain power of all sorts, while others are much simpler, and some parts of most people's talk about them are highly predictable. The amount of attention paid to body language, then, varies from moment to moment, and we get intermittent chances to glimpse at the lower information movements from which we might make inferences about the people with whom we are dealing.

These are fairly solid lines of speculation about how body language can serve as communication, even those aspects of it that have relatively low information density. Very little of it can be read as specifically as the words and signs of the more completey coded languages, but often we do not need that degree of specificity: if we keep observing, hard as that may be when we are trying to keep up with a conversation, we will find more such messages and be able to get more out of the total communication situation. We may even be able to train ourselves to be increasingly alert to body language, though there are no research results yet available that would tell us how successfully we could do so. Perhaps that should be the next step for researchers to take.

ACKNOWLEDGMENTS

Derek C. Hybels gave considerable assistance during the preparation of this chapter, both in searching the literature and in finding meaningful trends in the many results.

REFERENCES

Argyle, M., & Ingham, R. Gaze, mutual gaze, and proximity. *Semiotica,* 1972, *6,* 32–49.

Birdwhistell, R. L. Some body motion elements accompanying spoken American English. In L. O. Thayer (Ed.), *Communication: concepts and perspectives.* Washington, D.C.: Spartan, 1967.

Boomer, D. S. The phonemic clause: Speech unit in human communication. In A. W. Siegman & S. Feldstein (Eds.), *Nonverbal behavior and communication.* Hillsdale, NJ: Lawrence Erlbaum Associates, 1978.

Brown, R. *Words and things.* Glencoe, Illinois: Free Press, 1958.

Dittmann, A. T. The relationship between body movements and moods in interviews. *Journal of Consulting Psychology,* 1962, *26,* 480.

Dittmann, A. T. The body movement–speech rhythm relationship as a cue to speech encoding.

In A. W. Siegman & B. Pope (Eds.), *Studies in dyadic communication*. New York: Pergamon Press, 1972. (a)

Dittmann, A. T. *Interpersonal messages of emotion*. New York: Springer, 1972. (b)

Dittmann, A. T., & Llewellyn, L. G. Relationship between vocalizations and head nods as listener responses. *Journal of Personality and Social Psychology*, 1968, *9*, 79–84.

Dittmann, A. T., & Llewellyn, L. G. Body movement and speech rhythm in social conversation. *Journal of Personality and Social Psychology*, 1969, *11*, 98–106.

Duncan, S., Jr. Some signals and rules for taking speaking turns in conversations. *Journal of Personality and Social Psychology*, 1972, *23*, 283–292.

Efron, D. *Gesture and environment*. New York: King's Crown, 1941.

Ekman, P., & Friesen, W. V. The repertoire of nonverbal behavior: categories, origins, usage, and coding. *Semiotica*, 1969, *1*, 49–98.

Ekman, P., Friesen, W. V., & Ellsworth, P. C. *Emotion in the human face: Guidelines for research and an integration of findings*. New York: Pergamon Press, 1972.

Ellsworth, P. C., Carlsmith, J. M., & Henson, A. The stare as a stimulus to flight in human subjects: a series of field experiments. *Journal of Personality and Social Psychology*, 1972, *21*, 302–311.

Ellsworth, P.C., & Ludwig, L. M. Visual behavior in social interaction. *Journal of Communication*, 1972, *22*, 375–403.

Fast, J. *Body language*, New York: Evans, 1970.

Freedman, N., & Hoffman, S. P. Kinetic behavior in altered clinical states: approach to objective analysis of motor behavior during clinical interviews. *Perceptual and Motor Skills*, 1967, *24*, 527–539.

Fretz, B. R. Postural movements in a counseling dyad. *Journal of Counseling Psychology*, 1966, *13*, 335–343.

Kendon, A. Some functions of gaze direction in social interaction. *Acta Psychologica*, 1967, *26*, 22–63.

Kendon, A. Some relationships between body motion and speech, an analysis of an example. In A. W. Siegman & B. Pope (Eds.), *Studies in dyadic communication*, New York: Pergamon Press, 1972.

Mallery, G. Sign language among North American Indians. *First Annual Report of the Bureau of American Ethnology*, pp. 263–552. Washington, D.C.: U.S. Government Printing Office, 1881. Republished, The Hague: Mouton, 1972.

Mehrabian, A. Inference of attitudes from the posture, orientation, and distance of a communicator. *Journal of Consulting and Clinical Psychology*, 1968, *32*, 296–308.

Rosenfeld, H. M. Approval-seeking and approval-reducing functions of verbal and nonverbal responses in the dyad. *Journal of Personality and Social Psychology*, 1966, *4*, 597–605.

Rosenfeld, H. M. Nonverbal reciprocation of approval: an experimental analysis. *Journal of Experimental Social Psychology*, 1967, *3*, 102–111.

Sainsbury, P. Gestural movement during psychiatric interview. *Psychosomatic Medicine*, 1955, *17*, 458–469.

Sapir, E. *Language: An introduction to the study of speech*. New York: Harcourt, Brace, 1921.

Stokoe, W. C., Ur. *Semiotics and human sign languages*. The Hague: Mouton, 1972.

Stokoe, W. C., Casterline, D. C., & Croneberg, C. G. *A dictionary of American sign language on linguistic principles*, Washington, D.C.: Gallaudet College Press, 1965.

Tomkins, W. *Universal American Indian sign language*. San Diego, California: Tomkins, 1926.

Watson, M. O. *Proxemic behavior, a cross-cultural study*. The Hague: Mouton, 1970.

West, L., Jr. The sign language, an analysis. Vols. I and II. Unpublished doctoral dissertation, Indiana University, 1960. (*Dissertation Abstracts*, No. 60-2854).

3 On Gesture: Its Complementary Relationship with Speech

Adam Kendon
Department of Anthropology
Australia National University

The study of gesture has a long history (Kendon, 1982). The earliest books devoted exclusively to it appeared in the 17th century (e.g., Bulwer 1644). In the 18th century, especially in France, gesture was looked upon as having great relevance for the understanding of the natural origin of language and the nature of thought. Condillac (1754/1971) and Diderot (1751/1916), in particular, wrote about it quite extensively. In the 19th century gesture continued to command serious attention. Edward Tylor (1878) and Wilhelm Wundt (1900) both dealt with it at length. They believed that its study would throw light upon the transition from spontaneous, individual expression to the development of codified language systems. For much of this century, however, the study of gesture appears to have languished. The question of language origins, which has always provided an important justification for its study, fell into disrepute (Stam, 1976). Psychology neglected gesture because it seemed too much connected with deliberate action and social convention to be of use for the understanding of the irrational or to be easily accommodated in terms of behavioristic doctrine. It has been neglected by linguists because it has seemed too much a matter of individual expression. In any case it could not be accommodated into the rigorous systems of phonology and grammar with which linguists were preoccupied (Bolinger, 1946). Even the growth of interest in what came to be known as *nonverbal communication* did not stimulate the study of gesture as one might have expected. This was because the preoccupation here has been with how behavior functions communicatively in the regulation of interaction and in the management of interpersonal relations (Kendon, 1982). Gesture is too much a part of conscious expression and too closely connected with the verbal for it to be of central relevance here.

Recent developments suggest that gesture may soon again receive serious attention. A revival of interest in speculation about the origin of language (Hockett, 1978), and in particular Gordon Hewes' (1973, 1976) argument in favor of the gestural origin of language, the discovery that chimpanzees can be taught at least some aspects of sign language, and the development of the linguistic study of sign language itself (Stokoe, 1980), have all created a climate in which the study of gesture once again seems to be important. The interest that linguists have been showing in how language is used in interaction has led to a realization that, from a functional point of view, spoken utterances often only work because they are embedded in contexts of other forms of behavior, including gesture. Psychology has lately restored higher mental processes to center stage in the array of topics it considers important, and so gesture, as a form of symbolic expression, is suddenly seen to be of interest.

Here I discuss some of the questions the study of gesture appears to raise, in particular in respect to the relationship between gesture and spoken language. I argue that gesture stems from processes of representation of meaning that are as basic as those from which spoken language springs. It is a separate mode of representation and its study provides us with an understanding of symbolic processes that cannot be achieved by the study of spoken language alone.

DEFINITION OF GESTURE

A modern definition of *gesture* (as given in the Oxford English Dictionary, for instance) is that it is a movement of the body, or any part of it, that is considered expressive of thought or feeling. At first sight this appears to include practically everything that a person might do. However, a brief consideration of how the word is commonly used shows that it usually refers to only certain kinds of bodily movements that are considered expressive of thought or feeling.

As commonly understood, gesture refers to such actions as waving goodbye, or giving the thumbs up signal, or thumbing the nose at someone. It includes pointings and pantomimes that people sometimes engage in when they are too far away from one another to talk (or where talk would interfere). It includes the head waggings and arm wavings of vigorous talk, as well as the movements a person may improvise to convey something for which his words seem inadequate. However, there are other kinds of action that, though expressive, seem less appropriately called "gesture". For example, we would not refer to weeping as a gesture or, if we did, we would imply, I think, that the weeping was "put on," that it was a show or a performance, and not wholly genuine as an expression of emotion. I also suggest that the term *gesture* is not usually applied to the movements that people make when they are nervous, such as hair pattings, self-groomings, clothing adjustments, and the repetitive manipulations of rings or necklaces or other personal accoutrements. In ordinary interaction such movements are normally disregarded, or they are treated as habitual or involuntary, and although they are often revealing and may sometimes be read by others as symptoms of the individual's moods or feelings, they are not, as a rule, considered as gestures.

Further, there are many actions that a person must engage in if he is to participate in interaction with others, which, again, though they may be quite revealing of the person's attitudes and feelings, are not regarded as gestures because they are regarded as being done for the practical necessities of interaction, and not for the sake of conveying meaning. Consider the movements that a person in interaction must engage in to establish, to maintain, or to change his distance and orientation in respect to the other participants. The distance a person may establish between himself and his partner in interaction may often be taken as an indication of his attitude toward the other or of his understanding of the nature of the interaction that is taking place. Such spatial and orientational movements are not considered gestures, however, for they are treated as being done, not for their own sake, but for the sake of creating a convenient and appropriate setting for the interaction. Even when someone seems to edge closer to another than the other expects, or when they sit far off and do not move up, despite the far-reaching consequences that may sometimes follow, such actions are yet not considered "gestures" if, as is usually the case, they are done in a way that subordinates them to actions that must be done merely to maintain such spatial and orientational arrangement as is essential for the carrying out of a conversation (Kendon, 1973, 1977, 1985).

We may also note that practical actions are not normally considered gestures even when such actions play a part in social interaction. For example, when people have conversations they may also engage in such activities as smoking, drinking, or eating. The actions required for such activities may sometimes be used as devices to regulate the social interaction. People who meet for talk over coffee and a cigarette may vary the rate at which they drink up their coffee or smoke their cigarette and, as a result, vary the amount of time to be spent in conversation. Lighting a cigarette or relighting a pipe can often be elaborated as a way of "buying time," as when a person needs to think a little before he replies. Yet, despite the communicative significance such activity undoubtedly may have, it is not typically treated as intended to communicate anything. To spend time getting one's pipe ready to light up is to take "time out" of a conversation; it is not to engage in a conversational move or turn, even though it may play a part in structuring the moves or turns of which the conversation is composed.

The actions of smoking, or of any practical action, may be performed in ways that can be highly expressive, however. There are many different ways in which smoke may be exhaled, for example, in a thin and elegant jet, in untidy clouds. It may be directed at people or away from them. One may wave one's cigarette about in elaborate balletic movements; one may stub it out with force or with delicacy. Practical actions, thus, may become embellished with flourishes to the point that their expressive dimension may be openly recognized. As this happens they come to take on the qualities of gesture.

If practical actions can be given some of the qualities of gesture, it is also possible to observe that gestures may sometimes be disguised so that they no longer appear as such. It has been reported that in Germany there is a gesture in which the forefinger touches the side of the head and is rotated back and forth. It is used to mean "he's crazy" and it is regarded as a grave insult. Its use has been the cause of fights and one may be prosecuted for performing it in public. A surreptitious version of it has appeared, however, in which the forefinger is rotated in contact with the cheek. In this version the gesture is performed in such a way that it could be mistaken for scratching the cheek or for pressing a tooth that was giving discomfort. Likewise, in Malta, the gesture known as the Italian Salute or the *bras d'honneur* is regarded as so offensive that one can be prosecuted for performing it in public. Apparently the Maltese have evolved a way of performing this gesture in such a way that it could be mistaken for a mere rubbing of the arm, and not a gesture at all. In this version the left arm is held straight with the hand clenched in a fist, while the right hand gently rubs the inside of the left elbow (Morris, Collett, Marsh, & O'Shaughnessy, 1979).

Such examples are of interest because they make it clear that participants are able to recognize, simply from the way in which the action is performed, whether it is intended as a communicative action or not. Apparently, for an action to be treated as a "gesture" it must have features that make it stand out as such. Such features may be grafted on to other actions, turning practical actions or emotional displays into gestures. Such features may also be suppressed, turning movements from gestures into incidental mannerisms or passing comfort movements.

What are the features an action must have for it to be treated as a gesture? In a study designed to pursue this question (partially reported in Kendon, 1978) 20 people were each shown, individually, a film of a man giving a speech to a fairly large group of people. The film had been made among the Enga, who live in the Western Highlands of Papua New Guinea. The people who watched the film were all Caucasian, English-speaking Australians, and none of them were students of psychology or of any other behavioral science. The film was about 4 minutes in length and it was shown without sound. Each person was asked to tell, in his own words, what movements he had seen the man make. Each subject was allowed to see the film as many times as he liked, and, in discussing his observations, care was taken to use only the vocabulary that he himself proposed. The aim was to find out what movements the subjects picked out in their descriptions and to find out what different sorts of movements they identified.

In the course of the film the man who was speaking engaged in elaborate movements of his arms and head, he walked forward, he manipulated the handle of an axe he was holding, he tugged at his jacket, he touched his face and nose. All subjects, without exception, first said that they saw movements that, they said, were deliberate, conscious, and part of what the man was trying to say. All subjects also said that they saw some other movements that, they said, were just natural, ordinary, or movements of no significance. Thus not only was a sharp distinction drawn by all 20 people between "significant" movements and other movements; all 20 mentioned these "significant" movements first and only later, and sometimes only after some probing did they mention that they had seen some other movements.

A stop-action projector was used so it was possible for the subject to point out precisely where the different movements identified as significant occurred. All subjects were able to do this without any hesitation, and there was very considerable agreement as to which movements were considered a "significant" part of what the man was trying to say and which were "natural" or "ordinary" or of no significance. Thus 37 movement segments were commented on. In all cases a majority of subjects assigned them to either the gestural or the natural category, and there were only 4 segments in respect to which more than 5 out of the 20 subjects differed from the majority in how these movements were to be assigned.

A consideration of the characteristics of the movement segments selected as part of the orator's deliberate expression as compared to those selected as "natural" or "ordinary" or of "no significance" allows us to arrive at some understanding of the features of deliberately expressive movement, as compared to other kinds of movement.

Deliberately expressive movement was movement that had a sharp boundary of onset and that was seen as an *excursion,* rather than as resulting in any sustained change of position. Thus for limb movements deliberately expressive movements were those in which the limb was lifted sharply away from the body and subsequently returned to the same position from which it started. In the head, rotations or up–down movements were seen as deliberately expressive if the movements were rapid or repeated, or if they did not lead to the head being held in a new position, and if the movements were not done in coordination with eye movements. If they were, then the observers would say that the man was engaged in changing where he was looking and this was considered different from movements that were part of what he was saying. Movements of the whole body would be regarded as part of the man's deliberate expression if it was seen as *returning* to the position from which it began, and not resulting in a sustained change in spatial location or bodily posture.

Movements that involved manipulations of an object, such as changing the position of an object, were never seen as part of the man's expression. They were usually referred to, if noticed at all, as "practical." Movements in which the man touched himself or his clothing were also never regarded as parts of deliberate expression. These movements were, by almost all subjects, completely overlooked at the outset. They were dismissed as "natural" or "nervous" or "of no importance" when the subject's attention was drawn to them.

I suggest that these 20 observers were doing what all of us normally do in our dealings with others. Like all of us, they were attending to the behavior of another in a highly differentiated way, and what stood out for them, what was most salient and worth reporting, were those movements that shared certain features that identify them, for the observer, as deliberate and, in this case, intended as communicative. Just as a hearer perceives speech whether comprehended or not as "figure" no matter what the "ground" may be, and just as speech is always regarded as fully intentional and intentionally communicative, so I suggest that if movements are made so that they have certain dynamic charcterics they will be perceived as "figure" against the "ground" of other movement, and such movements will be regarded as fully intentional and intentionally communicative. I suggest that we may recognize a number of features that a movement may have — features that, for the sake of a name, I refer to as the features or manifest deliberate expressiveness. Any movement a person produces may share these features to a lesser or greater degree. The more a movement does so, the more likely is it to be given privileged status in the attention of another and the more likely is it to be seen as part of the individual's effort to convey meaning. What we normally call "gesture" are those movements that partake of these features of manifest deliberate expressiveness to the fullest extent. They are movements at the extreme end of the scale, so to speak. The word gesture serves as a label for that domain of visible action that participants routinely separate out and treat as governed by an openly acknowledged communicative intent.

I say "openly acknowledged communicative intent" because, as my discussion of smoking or of the illegal German and Maltese gestures suggests, it is possible to engage in movements deliberately for the interactional effects they may have, but to do so in such a way that they will *not* be treated as deliberately communicative. Indeed, we do this all the time, and I believe that our ability to do this and our willingness to treat the behavior of others as if it may be differentiated in this way is an important component of our abilities to engage in daily interaction adequately (Kendon, 1985).

It is worth noting, in this connection, that whereas it is possible for me to produce a movement that is ambiguous in its deliberate expressiveness it is not possible for me to do this with speech. I either say something or I do not. If I say something that you can't quite make out, it yet remains that I undoubtedly said *something*, and if you are my partner in an interaction it is your right to challenge me and to ask "what did you say?" Gestures are rarely challenged. I can make movements that might or might not be gestures, but very rarely am I allowed to make noises that might or might not be speakings. It would be most interesting to know whether this also is true in sign language interactions. Is it possible to produce, in a sign language interaction, movements that might or might not be signings, or is there a way in which certain movements are always assigned to intentional discourse, whereas other movements are permitted the sort of ambiguity that we find is permitted for the movements made by speakers? It seems possible that when, for sign language users, all expression must be in one modality, it is more difficult to engage in the kind of "unofficial" communication that is routine for hearing interactors. It is often said that deaf signers are more "open" to one another in their conversation and give expression to their feelings so readily (compare discussion in Washabaugh, 1981). It is suggested here that users of sign language are more open because they have no choice. They cannot, as speakers can, draw the kind of sharp distinction between definite, deliberate utterance, and something that can vary in its definite deliberateness that the availability of both speech and gesture permits.

Now although, as already suggested, it is possible for people to modify their performance of gestural acts so that they do not look like gestures and although features can be added to nongestural actions to give them some of the character of gestures, this remains a capacity of performance that interactants make use of in their management of behavior or in interaction. It does not alter the proposal that participants effectively operate with one another in terms of a notion of bodily movements that are clearly part and parcel of the individual's openly acknowledged intention to convey meaning. It is to this that I apply the term *gesture*. I have proposed an approach to an understanding of how that term may be defined from the point of view of the participant in interaction. I have suggested that gesture is behavior that is *treated* as intentionally communicative by coparticipants and that such behavior has certain features that are immediately recognizable. I have suggested that there are other aspects of behavior that have other characteristics that, as a result, are seen as "incidental" or "practical" and that are treated as quite distinct from "gesture," notwithstanding the role they can be shown to play, and are often deliberately employed to play, in the organization of interaction.

It would appear, then, that participants perceive each other's behavior in terms of a number of different systems of action — the deliberately communicative or gestural, the postural, the practical, the incidental, and, perhaps although I have not explored this here, the emotional. We have also reason to suppose that these different streams of action are produced under the guidance of different systems of control. Actions that are treated as "gestural," it appears, are intimately associated, in their production, with the action of spoken utterance whereas actions that are treated as belonging to other functional systems appear to be under different systems of control.

NEUROLOGICAL CONSIDERATIONS

Neurologists have long recognized a distinction between "voluntary" and "emotional" systems of expression (Myers, 1976). Recent neurologically oriented investigations of gesture suggest that gesture is governed by the same part of the brain that governs speech production, where other aspects of action such as those that are involved in the regulation of interaction are differently controlled.

Thus, Kimura (1976) and Feyereisen (1977) have reported that in right-handed individuals there is a marked tendency for gesticulations to be performed with the right hand, whereas no such hand preference is found for nongesticulatory movements or movements of the hand made during activities other than speech. In left-handed individuals, who are known to be not as fully lateralized for speech control as right-handed individuals, it is found that gesticulations tend to be produced with both hands. These findings have been interpreted to mean that gesticulation and speech are under the governance of the same part of the brain. However, more recent work has suggested that lateralization may be found only for gestures that represent the content of what is being said. Souza-Poza, Rohrberg, and Mercure (1979) and McNeill and Levy (1982) have both reported that gestures that are merely rhythmic and that do not appear to represent content are not lateralized, although representational ones are.

Further light is shed on the neurological control of gesture and its relationship to speech by studies of people with brain damage. Clinical neurologists have long recognized that patients suffering from brain damage that impairs speech (left-hemisphere damage in most cases) also show impairment in their ability to use gesture. This has usually been attributed to apraxia and considered somewhat separate from aphasia, although there is a minority tradition of long standing that has maintained that gestural impairment in aphasia has the same fundamental origin as the aphasia itself: that it stems from an impairment in the capacity to make use of symbols (Duffy & Liles, 1979). Recently, systematic studies of the gestural capacities of aphasics have been reported.

Cicone, Wapner, Foldi, Zurif, and Gardner (1979) report a study of four aphasic patients, with two normals for comparison, in which the character of their gesticulation and its relationship to speech was studied as it could be observed in informal interviews. So far, this is the only study of its kind. Of the four patients observed, two had been diagnosed as having lesions in the anterior (pre-Rolandic) region of the brain. They exhibited the sparse, agrammatic but intelligible speech of the Broca's aphasic. The other two exhibited fluent but gramatically and semantically incoherent speech. They were diagnosed as Wernicke's aphasics, probably suffering from posterior temporal lobe lesions. Cicone et al. report that the character of the gesticulations of these patients closely matched the character of their speech. Thus, according to Cicone et al. (1979), for the Broca's aphasics "output in both modalities is relatively complex, often elaborated" but generally unclear and confusing, like their speech (p. 332). It should be mentioned that Alajouanine and Lhermitte (1964) report summaries of clinical experience that are fully in accord with Cicone et al.'s findings.

Cicone et al. discuss several possible explanations of their findings and they conclude that the best explanation is that gesture and speech are separate, but both under the control of a single "central organizer" – a conclusion exactly in accord with the view being put forward here.

All the other studies of gesture in aphasia have examined patients in formal test situations for their abilities to recognize or to employ pantomimes and, in some studies, standardized symbolic gestures as well. All the studies reported so far show a good correlation between degree of aphasia and degree of impairment in gestural abilities. Goodglass and Kaplan (1963), whose investigation was the first of these systematic studies, concluded that the gestural impairment they found could best be understood as a consequence of apraxia. Their interpretation has been criticized on various grounds by Duffy, Duffy, and Pearson (1975) and by Pickett (1974). These authors offer further data and they conclude that gestural impairment in aphasia is best accounted for by an impairment of symbolic capacities rather than in terms of apraxia. Duffy and Duffy (1981) provide three additional studies that strengthen this conclusion. Other support is provided by Gainotti and Lemmo (1976), who show how gestural impairment in aphasia is strongly correlated with impairment in ability to recognize word meanings.

Several other studies have reported, however, that such a capacity to perceive symbolic meaning may sometimes be impaired only for the aural modality. In these cases patients have been able to benefit from training in the use of gesture systems derived from American Indian sign language (Amerind, devised by Skelly, 1979) or from American Sign Language. Several investigators have reported that patients who can benefit in this way can also read. Peterson and Kirshner (1981), who review these studies, suggest, accordingly, as does Varney (1978), that symbolic abilities may to some extent be modality specific. Although it is clear that they are closely related, neurologically, visual symbolic abilities do show some degree of separateness from aural symbolic abilities. This is just what we would expect to find if gesture and speech are separate representational modalities, yet both recruited to the service of the same aim. Such studies show, thus, the intimate nature of the relationship between the parts of the brain that control "gesture," in the sense that we are using here, and speech.

It is also beginning to be seen that other aspects of behavior that are relevant to communication may have a different neurological mediation. Thus a few authors have pointed out that aphasics are often capable of dealing quite well with all the regulatory aspects of interaction — they can maintain an appropriate spacing and orientation, they recognize when it is their turn to make a conversational move. Their impairment lies in their ability to mobilize speech and gesture to produce coherently meaningful units of utterance. Duffy and Buck (1979) at the University of Connecticut have shown, for instance, that left-hemisphere-damaged aphasics, although impaired in their abilities to produce and to recognize pantomimes in proportion to the degree of their impairment in verbal language, are not significantly different from normals, or, indeed, from right-hemisphere-damaged patients, in their production of appropriate and coherent facial expressions of affect. Markel and his colleagues in Florida (Katz, LaPointe, & Markel, 1978) have reported a study in wich they have shown that aphasics show little impairment in those aspects of behavior that communicate emotional states, attitudes, relative status in the interaction, and the regulation of turn taking. Gardner (Foldi, Cicone, & Gardner, 1982) and his colleagues in Boston after a review of relevant studies have reached a somewhat similar conclusion.

All this supports the view that gesture is indeed to be distinguished from emotional expression, and from those aspects of behavior that serve in the structuring and regulation of face-to-face interaction.

TYPES OF GESTURE

"Gesture," as defined so far, remains a very broad notion. Most who have written on the subject have offered classifications, however, suggesting various types of gesture.

A classification that arranges gestures according to how they achieve their meanings has been offered by Wundt (1900). More recently, Mandel (1977) and Kendon (1980b, c, d) have offered somewhat similar classifications in discussions of sign language. These classifications, which may be called *semiotic*, recognize distinctions between gestures that realize their meaning through *pointing*, gestures that *characterize* or *depict* their meaning in some way, and gestures that have purely conventional connections with their referents.

Classifications of a more functional sort have been offered by Barakat (1969), Efron (1941), Ekman (1977), Freedman (1972), Kaulfers (1931), McNeill and Levy (1982, and Wiener, Devoe, Rubinow, and Geller (1972). Kaulfers (1931) distinguishes from other gestures those that serve in interactional management such as gestures of greeting, request, demand, or refusal, setting them apart from gestures that play a role in discourse. This distinction is useful, and probably sound. There is reason to think that gestures of this sort have a different developmental history from those that are concerned with discourse (Bates, 1979; Bruner, 1978).

Of the other authors listed we find that Efron (1941/1972), Barakat (1969), Ekman (1977), and Wiener et al. (1972) all recognize a class of gestures that function as complete utterances in themselves, independently of speech, and which show a high degree of formalization. Various terms have been proposed: *semiotic gestures* (Barakat), *symbolic or emblematic gestures* (Efron), *emblems* (Ekman), *formal pantomimic gestures* (Wiener).

In regard to speech-related gestures Efron (and Ekman, following Efron, see especially, Ekman, 1977), Freedman, Wiener et al., and McNeill and Levy all recognize a distinction between those that appear to represent some aspect of the content of what is being said, and those that have a more abstract relationship. Various terms have been employed. McNeill and Levy distinguish "iconic" gestures from "beats." Freedman refers to "motor primacy" movements and "speech primacy" movements. "Speech primacy" movements are not representational, but "motor primacy" movements include a group that are. Efron distinguishes pictorial gestures from those that seem to relate to the logical structure of the discourse. He speaks of "physiographic" and "ideographic" gesture, respectively.

In the present chapter I refer to all gesturing that occurs in association with speech and that seems to be bound up with it as part of the total utterance as *gesticulation*. The particular kinds of relationship between gesticulation and the speech with which it is associated is discussed on their merits, and I do not adhere to any of the classification schemes referred to previously. Gestures that are standardized in form and that function as complete utterances in themselves, independently of speech, I refer to as *autonomous gestures* (this includes those that are quite often referred to today as *emblems*).

It must also be recognized that under certain circumstances gesturing can come to take on all the functions of spoken utterance. When it does so it comes to be organized into what is referred to as a *gesture system* and, in circumstances where complete generality of communicative function is required, we observe the emergence of *sign languages*. In the present chapter the phenomena of autonomous gestures and sign languages are not discussed. Let me note my view, however, that such phenomena are to be considered as continuous with gesticulation. In the case of sign languages we may observe how when gesture becomes completely autonomous as an instrument of communication it must depend on itself for its own discourse contexts. When this happens it undergoes changes that lead to gestures coming to have functions much closer to those of words in a spoken language. Further discussion of the phenomena of autonomous gesture may be found in Kendon (1981a).

GESTICULATION

When a person speaks, muscular systems besides those of the lips, tongue, and jaws often become active. There are movements of the face and eyes, of the head, arms and hands, and sometimes of the torso and legs that even to a casual observer, are seen as integrated with the flow of speech. Detailed analyses of films of speakers by Condon (summarized in Condon, 1976) have shown that there is a rhythmic coordination or synchrony between the smallest discriminable phrases of movement and those of speech, even below the level of the syllable. This is not surprising, for the individual speaker is a single organism. Where lack of coordination has been observed, as Condon has proposed, marked pathology is indicated. Condon's findings imply that a similar integration of action would be found if we were to analyze in a similar way the flow of movement in someone engaged in other activities than speaking, although to my knowledge this has not been done.

For Condon, the flow of movement is organized into a succession of phrases that are themselves incorporated into phrases of movement at higher and higher levels of integration (Condon, 1976). At these higher levels of integration, however, there is much differentiation in the way in which the various parts of the body are involved. For example, one may observe the sweep of an arm or the turn of a head occurring over an entire phrase of several words, while movements in the face or the fingers are coordinated with smaller units of speech.

Just which patterns of movement are regarded by others as gesticulations has never been systematically examined. It would appear, however, that some degree of body–part differentiation is required and that the phrases of movement must have a level of integration at least equivalent to that of a phrase of several words, before being picked out in this manner. Movements that are regarded as gesticular phrases occur most frequently in the hands and arms and in the head and face. Hand and arm gesticulation has been most fully investigated and the studies discussed in most detail later are all concerned with this. However, much more attention should be paid to the participation of the head and face. The very few studies that have dealt with them are mentioned first.

Ekman (1979) has described some examples of facial gesturing during talk and he has proposed some criteria by which such actions be distinguished from facial affect displays. Birdwhistell (1970) describes face and head action as serving as kinesic markers of linguistic stress and pronominal and diectic words. The involvement of the head in gesticulation has also been noted by Efron (1941/1972), and the patterning of head and eye movements with speech has been described by Scheflen (1964) and Kendon (1972).

If one observes manual gesticulation in a speaker, it is possible to show how such movements are organized as *excursions,* in which the gesticulating limb moves away from a rest position, engages in one or more of a series of movement patterns, and is then *returned* to its rest position. Ordinary observers identify the movement patterns that are performed during such excursions as "gestures." They see the movement that precedes and succeeds them as serving merely to move the limb into a space in which the gesture is to be performed. A *Gesture Phrase* may be distinguished, thus, as a *nucleus* of movement having some definite form and enhanced dynamic qualities, which is preceded by a preparatory movement and succeeded by a movement that either moves the limb back to its rest position or repositions it for the beginning of a new Gesture Phrase (Kendon 1972, 1980a).

If the flow of gesticulatory activity is thus analyzed into its component Phrases and these phrases are plotted out on a time-based chart against a time-based transcript of the concurrent speech, it is found that there is a close fit between the phrasal organization of gesticulation and the phrasal organization of the speech. For example, if the flow of speech is segmented into Tone Units (which are phonologically defined syllabic groupings united by a single intonation tune — the term used here follows Crystal and Davy, 1969), it is usually found that there is a Gesture Phrase to correspond to each Tone Unit.

A Tone Unit, as just mentioned, is a phonologically defined unit of speech production; however it quite closely matches units of speech that may be defined in terms of units of content or "idea units." The association between Gesture Phrases and Tone Units arises because Gesture Phrases, like Tone Units mark successive units of meaning. Gesture Phrases are not, thus, by-products of the speech production process. They are directly produced, as are Tone Units, from the same underlying unit of meaning. There are several observations that can be adduced to support this. Thus it is found that Gesture Phrases are often begun in advance of the Tone Unit to which they are related and they are often completed before the Tone Unit's completion. The "stroke" of the Gesture Phrase never follows the nucleus of the Tone Unit. Thus Gesture Phrases must be organized at the same time as Tone Units, if not a little in advance of them. Further, when there is a disruption in the flow of speech within a Tone Unit, this typically occurs before the production of the nucleus, that is, before the production of the high-information word. Such disruptions are often attributed to some failure in the process of word retrieval. If a Gesture Phrase is in progress at the moment of such a disruption, one finds that the Gesture Phrase is not interfered with, but it continues to completion with perfect coherence. In such cases it is possible to see how the "idea" is fully available and is serving to govern the production of gesture, although there has been an interruption in speech production. Sometimes both speech and gesture are interrupted, of course, and one may observe an individual producing a succession of incomplete gesture phrases at the same time as he produces a successsion of incomplete phrases of speech. In these cases, however, disruption is at a deeper level, for here the ideas to be expressed have not yet been organized (Kendon, 1980e).

McNeill (1979) and Schegloff (1984) have reported observations of gesture that are very similar to the ones just summarized. McNeill (1979) reports a study of gesticulation observed in a conversation of two mathematicians engaged in a technical discussion. In this analysis he examined what he called gestures (defined in a way that is quite similar to my notion of the Gesture Phrase) in terms of the relationship they exhibited with the conceptual structure of the concurrent speech. He found a close fit between the occurrence of a gesture and the occurrence of a speech unit expressing whole concepts or relationships between concepts. In further analyses McNeill reports that the "peak" of the gesture (that is to say, the most accented part of the movement that I call the "stroke") coincides with what was identified as the conceptual focal point of the speech unit. McNeill has suggested that each new unit of gesture, at least if it is of the sort that can be considered representational of content, appears with each new unit of meaning. Each such gesture manifests, he suggests, a representation of each new unit of meaning the utterer wishes to present.

We may conclude that these studies of how gesticulation is related to the speech it accompanies indicate that it is organized separately but brought into coordination with speech because it is being employed in the service of the same overall aim. The detailed rhythmic coordination of gesticulation with speech arises at the level of the organization of the execution of motor acts. The forms that gestures assume are organized directly from original conceptual representations in parallel with linguistic forms, but independently of them.

Studies in the development of gesture in children appear to support the view that gesture is separately organized. Rather few studies have been conducted but the child's capacity to make use of gesture expands in close association with growth in his capacity for spoken language. However, the way in which children use gesture appears to be different from the way it is used by adults. It seems that in adults gesture is used in relation to speech in a much more precise and specialized way. It appears that, with age, there is an increase in the degree to which the two modalities are coordinated.

Recent longitudinal studies of social interaction of the very young with their mothers show that the gestured actions that provide the first evidence of the ability of the child to engage in language-like communication, far from being replaced as the capacity for speech emerges, expands, and elaborates. Elizabeth Bates (1979) is quite explicit on this point. In summarizing her longitudinal study of 24 children between the ages of 9 and 14 months she writes: "Our findings do not support a model of communicative development in which preverbal communication is replaced by language" (p. 112). Language and gesture, she says, "are related via some common base involving both communication and reference" (p. 112). As this common base develops, the capacity for using both gesture and speech develops. A similar conclusion has been reached in other longitudinal studies. Wilkinson and Rembold (1981) write for instance that "as children become more aware of grammar and more facile at expressing it verbally, they also become more skilled in expressing grammar gesturally" (p. 184).

Studies of gesture in older children have, for the most part, concentrated on the evidence this can provide about changes in the child's capacities for symbolization and they do not address the question of the spontaneous employment of gesture in relation to speech. There are four recent studies that do, however. Each has been conducted independently of the other and they all appear to suggest a very similar picture. I refer here to a study by Norbert Freedman (1977) of changes in gesturing with age as children provide definitions of common words; to studies by David McNeill (in press) and by Morton Wiener and his students (Jancovic, Devoe, & Wiener, 1975) of gesturing in children of different ages as they retell the story of an animated cartoon they have watched; and to a study by Evans and Rubin (1979) of children between the ages of 5 and 10 years as they explain to an adult the rules of a simple game they had just been taught. Evans and Rubin looked at the nature of the gestures the children employed and the role these gestures played in making the explanations intelligible. Taken together, these four studies are consistent with one another in a number of respects. All agree in noting an increase in gesticulation with age. All of them indicate, however, that there are important changes in the kinds of gesticulation that occur and in the way these gesticulations are related to speech. There appears to be a shift away from elaborate enactments or pantomimes that serve instead of speech, towards a use of gesture that is more selective and that is much more closely coordinated with what is being said in words. Thus Freedman described how the 4-year-old, as he attempts to offer a definition of a word such as "hammer," may first pantomime the use of the hammer before attempting a verbal definition. A 10-year-old gestures elaborately while he is talking as if, as Freedman puts it, he "surrounds himself with a visual, perceptual and imagistic aspect of his message." The 14-year-old, on the other hand, uses gesture selectively, usually only in relation to specific words, with which the gesture is highly coordinated. Likewise McNeill describes how children under the age of 8 enact whole scenes and do not relate their words and gestures. In adults, by contrast, "iconic" gestures tend to be precisely coordinated with spoken units of meaning. Furthermore, these gestures become more symbolic in the adult, serving as signs of actions or events. There is no attempt, as there is in the child, to engage in total reenactments.

These studies suggest, thus, that the employment of gesture for the representation of meaning increases in its elaborateness as the child gets older, but that at first it is used separately from speech. Later, as the child's command of speech develops, gesture comes to be used in conjunction with it. It is as if there is an increasing convergence and coordination between the two originally separate froms of expression.

Analyses of how gesticulation is organized in relation to speech and analyses of changes in how gesture is used by children both are compatible with the view that gesture and speech must be considered separate representational modes that may nevertheless be coordinated and closely associated in utterance because they may be employed together in the service of the same enterprise.

USES OF GESTICULATION IN INTERACTION

I turn now to a consideration of what gesticulation may be used for. If, as I suggest, gesture is employed for the same purposes for which speech is employed, I mean this in a very broad sense. I mean by this that gesture and speech are both employed in the task of the production of patterns of action that may serve for others as representations of meaning. I do not mean that they serve this task in the same way. When speech cannot be used, circumstances may make it possible for it to come about that gesture can be organized to do all the things that speech can do. Where speech is available, then we find that gesture and speech are employed differentially, in complementary roles, speech serving one set of communicative functions, gesture another.

Gesture and speech are very different from one another. In particular, because gesture employs space as well as time in the creation of expressive forms, where speech can only use time, the way in which information may be preserved in the two media is very different. Furthermore, it seems likely that important differences may arise from the fact that gesture is a visual medium, where speech uses sound. This may mean that the impact of gesture on a recipient may sometimes be very different from the impact of speech (Kendon, 1981a).

It is remarkable how little work there is that has explored these issues. One or two studies have compared the rate with which people gesticulate when talking to someone they cannot see and when talking to someone they can see. Cohen (1977; Cohen & Harrison, 1973) has investigated this by observing people giving routine directions to another, either face-to-face or over a telephone line. He found that people produced more directional gestures in the presence of another person than they did when they could not see them. However, he also found that when subjects were alone, giving directions into a tape recorder, as practice for a later session with a recipient, they used no gestures at all, although, in spite of this practice, they used them again extensively in a face-to-face situation that followed the practice sessions. In these studies it was clear that speakers were producing gesticulations only when they thought they would be available for a recipient.

Graham and Heywood (1976) compared the speech of subjects who were engaged in a task of describing geometrical shapes to recipients under conditions in which they were allowed to use gesture and under conditions where they were not. They showed that in a condition in which gestures were not permitted there was no disruption of speech (as some would have expected), but there was a change in the way in which the descriptions were accomplished. In the situation where gesturing was not permitted there was a significant increase in the use of phrases or words describing spatial relations, and a decrease in the number of demonstratives used. Speakers paused more when they did not use gestures, but otherwise they were fluent.

This study shows that, for the task of describing geometrical shapes, gesticulation is part of the communicative effort. But what communicative value do gestures have for recipients? This question has been examined experimentally by Berger and Popelka (1971), Graham and Argyle (1975), and Riseborough (1981). Observational studies of value include Sherzer (1972), Birdwhistell (1970), and Slama-Cazacu (1976).

Berger and Popelka (1971) presented 20 sentences to subjects whose instructions were to write what they heard. In one condition the sentences were uttered with an accompanying gesture that fitted the meaning of the sentence, in the other condition no gesture was employed. The sentences were short and the gestures chosen to accompany them were autonomous gestures selected from a list that, in a separate study, had been found to be similarly understood in a sample of 20 students drawn from the same population as the subjects. Berger and Popelka found that accuracy in writing the spoken sentences was greater when they were uttered with an accompanying gesture than when they were not. It is clear that here the gesture assisted in accurate reception of the sentence, although the experiment leaves it open as to how it did so. It might have been interesting to see if it would have made a difference if the accompanying gesture *did not* fit the meaning of the sentence.

Graham and Argyle (1975) established a situation in which subjects were required to make drawings of complex geometrical shapes that were described to them by senders who either were or were not allowed to use gestures as they did so. The likeness to the originals of the recipients' drawings, as judged by a panel of independent judges, was a measure of the effectiveness of the communication. It was found that recipients made more accurate drawings when the senders used gestures, and that this effect was most marked when the figures being described were complex and could not be described with a simple label.

Riseborough (1981) has reported three studies. She showed that subjects were better able to identify objects from descriptions if these descriptions were accompanied by "physiographic gestures." She further showed that subjects, in two recall tasks, could recall word lists more accurately, and could recall a story more accurately if appropriate "physiographic" gestures were employed. She also showed that where the sound channel was obstructed by white noise physiographic gestures made an increased contribution to comprehension.

Other studies that bear on the communicative functions of gesticulation are observational or anecdotal. Birdwhistell (1970) has presented several detailed studies of how movement concurrent with speech is patterned in relation to it and he describes how contrastive movement patterns differentially mark stress in speech and also how they mark pronominals and deictic particles. He provides a highly interesting summary of these observations that suggest that the *direction* of movement of a moving body part marking a pronominal or deictic particle is systematically related to the meaning of the particle. Thus in association with "this," "here," "now," "I," and "we," the body part moves toward the speaker. In association with "that," "there," "then," "you," "they," the body part moves away from the speaker. He also says that the form of the movement differs according to whether the word being marked kinesically is plural or singular. Some of these regularities were observed in analyses of my own of British speakers (Kendon, 1972).

As to the communicative role of such patterned movements, Birdwhistell makes two suggestions. He suggests, in one place, that such movements are of communicative value because, in paralleling speech in this way, they contribute to the redundancy of the uttered message. The availability of the same message in more than one channel allows for communication to take place in a wider range of circumstances and among people more variously equipped with capacities to send and receive than would otherwise be the case (Birdwhistell 1970, pp. 107–108). He also suggests, however, that certain kinesic actions may be functionally *equivalent* to linguistic items. Thus he says "both the kinesic and the linguistic markers may be alloforms, that is, structural variants of each other" (Ibid, p. 127).

Sherzer (1972) has illustrated this last point in some detail in his study of lip pointing among the Cuna Indians of Panama. In this study he shows how lip pointing can be used in conjunction with spoken utterance in a wide variety of ways. He argues, however, that the analysis of the functions of lip pointing must be done in conjunction with an analyss of the discourse structure of Cuna speech events. Thus he shows how a gestural element must be considered as fully integrated with spoken linguistic elements in the Cuna linguistic system.

The view that gestural elements may serve at the same level of functioning as spoken elements within a discourse has also been urged by Slama-Cazacu (1976). She has pointed out how kinesic elements, whether of the face or of the hands, can be inserted into utterances in such a way that they can replace elements that might otherwise have been spoken. She refers to this phenomenon as "mixed syntax" and gives a series of examples. She (Slama-Cazacu, 1976) argues that kinesic elements can achieve, with words, a synthesis into a single code: "structured *sui generis* and comprising verbal and [kinesic] elements mutually modified and fused in *linguistically* analyzeable units" (p. 225, original emphasis).

The observations of Sherzer and Slama-Cazacu are of particular interest because they show how gestures may function on the same level as speech. That is to say they are not serving as alternative representations of concepts; they are being inserted in *speech* sequences as functionally equivalent with the verbal components of such sequences.

OBSERVATIONS ON GESTURAL USAGE

It is clear from the foregoing that gesticulation does indeed play a part in the utterance from a communicational point of view. These observations of the use of gesture in everyday life, however, make it clear that the complexities of gestural use have only just begun to be appreciated. To reinforce this point I conclude with some examples taken from a collection of utterances of gestural usage that I have been maintaining for some time now for the purposes of developing a more systematic understanding of how speakers employ gesture.

First of all, we may note that gesture is often made use of when the communication circumstances make it difficult or impossible for speech to be received. Distance is one such circumstance and too high a level of ambient noise is another.

Within occasions of conversation it sometimes happens that a momentary increase in ambient noise makes hearing impossible. It seems that interactants may be quite sensitive to this and that they may, in conjunction with such noise increases, bring in the use of gesture to overcome the momentary blocking of the speech channel. Thus, a boy was explaining to his father something about fencing. He said "you know, how they do in fencing." Just as he said the word "fencing" a large truck went by, making the word inaudible. He immediately continued "you know/GESTURE/fencing." For the gesture he used a movement of the hand then enacted a bit of the hand movement one might employ if one were using a sword in a duel. Here he brought in a gestural representation of part of the action of fencing just as he began his restatement. What is notable here is that the recourse to gesture was directly in response to the increased ambient noise. He appreciated exactly what it was that had not been heard in the sentence he had just uttered, and, without hesitation, he was able to deploy an alternate mode of expressing it that overcame the transmission difficulties that the sudden increase in ambient noise had created. In other words, he had a clear appreciation of the communication conditions prevailing and he brought in gesture, as appropriate, to meet them.

The speech channel may be momentarily blocked by noise, but it may also be blocked because it is already occupied. In multiparty conversations one may occasionally observe the employment of gesture by participants who are not, for the moment, engaged directly in a current spoken utterance exchange, so that some additional exchange may be accomplished. Thus, seven people were at dinner in a country cottage in the mountains. One person, a guest and also a notorious monologuist, is holding forth at length. A strange noise is heard outside in the valley. One member looks across the table to another with raised eyebrows. The other replies by raising two fisted hands, palms facing downwards, and then lowering them sharply, as if pushing down a blaster's plunger, thereby suggesting that the strange noise was due to blasting. Later, when the hostess must tell her husband to go and make the coffee, she can do so without interrupting the monologuist, again by means of gesture. Gesture, evidently, need not intrude upon the sustained focus of talk. It can be both enacted, at least briefly, and received concurrently, with the sustainment of the main focus of involvement, when this is being sustained in talk.

Such exchanges may, of course, involve the talker himself. A professor giving a talk to a seminar of about 30 people found himself at a loss for a particular expression. A member of the audience held up her hands in an arrangement that suggested to the speaker the word "brackets," which exactly fitted the sense of what it was that he was trying to say. In this case the listener, by employing gesture, made her suggestion to the speaker without interrupting his flow of speech and without altering the attention structure of the seminar situation. By making this suggestion gesturally the listener did not establish a turn for herself in the audience–speaker system, and, thereby, she did not force the speaker to specifically acknowledge her suggestion as she would have done if she had made her suggestion verbally. Her gesture, thus, served to make her suggestion merely available to the speaker that he was free to take up or to ignore as he chose.

This example draws our attention to a feature of gesture which is that, for its employment, people do not seem to have to enter into the same kind of relationship of mutual obligation with regard to one another that they do when they engage in a spoken utterance exchange. It would appear that gestural exchanges can take place between people who have not otherwise established themselves in a "state of talk" together and who have not, thus, entered into the complex of ritual obligations that are thereby implied, such as the turn-taking system. Clearly, it takes time for people to negotiate such a state of talk and accordingly, if in the employment of gesture such negotiations may be bypassed, gestural exchanges may, under some circumstances, be much faster than speech exchanges. Furthermore, because gestural exchanges do not require the ritual arrangements of talk, to address someone in gesture may sometimes be undertaken as a way of addressing them without demanding that they relinquish their current involvement, whatever that may be, and without implying that one is oneself expecting to establish a sustained encounter with them.

For example, a travel agent is talking on the phone, sitting behind a desk that faces toward the glass door of the agency that opens onto the street. A man opens the door, leans in toward the travel agent while still holding the door with his left hand. He extends his right hand toward the agent, jerks his extended thumb upwards, and then rotates his forearm to point his thumb downwards. The travel agent responds with an upwardly jerked thumb, cups his hand over the phone, and calls out a date to him. In this instance the customer, by addressing the travel agent in gesture, not only employed a mode of address to which the recipient could have replied without relinquishing his current involvement, but by employing that mode of address he at the same time indicated that he intended to ask his question in passing, and that he did not intend to enter with the travel agent into any sort of sustained focused interaction.

That gestural exchanges can be undertaken without the full establishment of the ritual obligations of focused interaction that spoken utterance exchanges seem to require derives, we suggest, from its character as a silent, visual medium of expression. In consequence, we find not only that gestural exchanges can be employed in such "in passing" interactions as we have just described. We find also that gesture is often adopted as a medium of utterance where the utterer seeks to be less fully bound or officially committed to what he has to say. Thus it is that we find gesture being adopted as a substitute for speech, where speech might be regarded as too explicit or indelicate.

For example K, a dinner guest of D, was sitting with D in D's living room after dinner, drinking coffee. D himself had not taken a cup of coffee and this fact became a topic of conversation when D offered K a second cup. D, in fact, wanted K to go home, although it was still early and not long since D and K had finished eating. D explained why he was not having any coffee. He said: "Last night I had more coffee than usual at the restaurant and I didn't sleep well, so maybe we oughta/GESTURE/." In this gesture he placed his two extended index fingers side by side and then extended both arms away from himself and upwards in the direction of the door. He thereby clearly indicated that he and K should leave (D had to drive K home). In this example, thus, for just that part of the utterance that was socially awkward for D, a gestural expression was chosen.

It is also seen, in this example, how D's gesture was fully integrated with the *spoken* part of the utterance. A complete analysis of his utterance would not be possible except by considering his gestural expression, fully on a par with what he had said in words. This is an excellent example of the phenomenon of "mixed syntax" described by Slama-Cazacu to which we have already referred.

So far, all the examples I have given are examples in which the gestural element alternates with a spoken element, either serving as a complete utterance in itself or, as in the last example, as an element in an utterance in which spoken elements and gestured elements are mixed. However, gestured elements may cooccur with spoken utterances where the spoken utterance, taken by itself, is grammatically complete. In many of these cases, however, we find that if the gestural element is ignored the utterance remains informationally incomplete and its function within the discourse in which it occurs cannot be accounted for.

A common form of such concurrent use of gesture can be observed in the employment of directional or pointing movements by speakers. These directional or pointing movements often serve to point to referents that are referred to, in speech, only by determiners of pronominals and the pointing movements may, thus, disambiguate the referents of such particles.

Sherzer (1972), as I have already mentioned, has provided quite a detailed study of the different ways in which the Cuna Indians may use lip pointing. He fails to mention, however, whether the Cuna use other methods of pointing as well. American and British English speakers do not use lip pointing, as far as I know, but they readily employ any other body part that happens to be available for a directional movement, as well as pointing with the index finger. The head, the eyes, the elbows, even the whole body, may be employed in producing a directional movement with a deictic function. Birdwhistell (1970), as I have also mentioned, drew our attention to this some years ago in his analysis of what he called kinesic pronominal markers. Such directional movements in association with pronominals and other deictic words are often important, for they provide a necessary disambiguation. Thus, at a recent meeting of anthropologists a colleague, on seeing the chairman of a symposium in which he was to participate, approaching him said: "Where are we gonna be?" The chairman replied, as he hurried forward with his arms fully loaded with books and slide boxes, "Oh/GESTURE/in here." Between "oh" and "in here" he jerked his head backwards in a rapid movement, directing the back of it toward the door of the room from which he had just emerged. The deictic word "here," without the clarification the head jerk provided, would not have sufficed.

Such pointing movements do not only occur in association with pronominals and determiners, however. A husband, at the end of the day, was sitting in the living room talking in a casual way with his wife about what the children had done during the day. At one point he said: "They made a cake, didn't they?" The word "cake" in this phrase received primary stress. It was also marked by a movement of the head. In this case, the head moved in a rightward tilt over "cake" in the direction of the window that overlooked the garden. Here the speaker was pointing with his head to the garden in which, so he had been told by the children, a mud cake had been made. By pointing to the garden as he said "cake" he referred the cake to its location, thereby specifying that it was indeed the mud cake to which he was referring and not some other cake (this example was reported earlier in Kendon, 1972).

The uses of pointing are many, and the two examples I have given here serve only as reminders of some of them. In the last example note how what was referred to in the head point could have been accommodated in a phrase, such as "in the garden." Had the speaker said this, however, it would have taken him more time, and it is possible that on occasion concurrent gesture is employed as a means of "telescoping" what one wants to say where the turn-space that one has available is smaller than one would really like it to be. The following example, involving this time a characterizing gesture rather than a pointing gesture, may be an instance of this. It also shows how a characterizing gesture may be used for disambiguation.

I have a Minolta SLR camera, and whenever I refer to this in my family I always refer to it as "my Minolta." Recently, I acquired a Minolta super-8 movie camera. In consequence the word "Minolta" became ambiguous, for it could refer either to my SLR camera or to the super-8 movie camera. In the course of some conversation with my son, soon after this new camera had been acquired, he said to me: "you could do it with yours, your Minolta." As he said "Minolta" he lifted his hands up, thumb and forefinger of each hand extended at right angles to one another and held on either side of his face, thereby modeling the action of holding a camera in front of his eyes, as one would when snapping a photograph with it. By doing this he disambiguated "Minolta," clearly indicating that it was the SLR he was referring to and not the movie camera. In this instance it would appear that the speaker had anticipated his recipient's possible misunderstanding and he added a gestural characterization as he said "Minolta" as a way of making sure that it was clear what it was he meant. One can also see that he succeeded in specifying the particular camera he meant within the time it takes to utter the word "Minolta." Had he been less urgent about his talk or had the turn slot he had available to him at that time been longer, he might have employed a verbal expression instead. It would seem that gesture can be employed in this way as a way of telescoping into a currently available time segment, more than could otherwise be provided if only words were being used.

Gesture, of course, does not only serve as an alternative or substitute for what otherwise might be said in words. It is also useful because, being the kind of expressive medium that it is, it allows for the possibility of representing aspects of experience that can be represented in words at best only indirectly and in some respects not at all. It is impossible to display the *appearance* of action except by some form of action, for example. The representation of spatial arrangements cannot be accomplished directly in words, but by moving the hands or the body about in space it is possible to demonstrate them.

Accordingly, it is not uncommon to observe speakers incorporating gesture into their utterance where the gesture is employed, not as a substitute or alternative to speech, but as an additional component of the utterance in which aspects of what they are referring to are represented, which are not represented in the words that are being used.

Three examples are given here. When an Englishman first arrives in the Eastern United States and encounters the Sunday edition of the *New York Times,* he is always amazed at its enormous bulk. It is almost always a matter for remark. An Englishman who has lived for many years in the United States encountered one Monday morning a compatriot who had only arrived the week before and he fell into conversation with him at a railroad station, while waiting for the arrival of a train. In the course of exploring his reactions to things American, the resident Englishman said: "Have you made your acquaintance with the/GESTURE/ *New York Times.*" The gesture he here employed was one in which he first placed his two hands forward, palms facing each other, and he then placed them one above the other, palms facing downwards, thereby depicting a thick oblong object. The newly arrived Englishman laughed in response and comments on the enormity of the Sunday *New York Times* were duly exchanged. This gesture, in this example, it is noted, provided a visual representation of just that feature of the Sunday *New York Times* that always surprises an Englishman. What the speaker was attempting to do here was to recreate the surprising appearance of the Sunday *New York Times* for his recipient, for in doing so he thereby can make a direct reference to that moment when the Sunday *New York Times* is first encountered and he thereby can recreate that first encounter in something like the form in which it actually occurs. A verbal description of the size and weight of the Sunday *New York Times* could not achieve this. In his effort to get his compatriot to relive that surprising moment, he provides him, in his gesture, with a depiction that will call up again the reaction that he had upon first seeing and handling the Sunday *New York Times.*

It is noted, of course, that although "Have you made your acquaintance with the *New York Times*" is a perfectly good sentence in itself, unless we had the gestural component, we could not give a proper account of how it functioned within the particular context in which it occurred. Although, in this example, the gesture does not substitute for any element within the spoken part of the utterance, as we have seen it can do in other instances, it is, nevertheless, an integral part of what the utterer had said. We cannot here say, any more than we can in our previous examples, that the gestural component can be left out of any analysis of the utterance as a linguistic unit. The gesture, it is further noted, occurred precisely as the speaker said "with the," the first part of it over "with," the second part over "the." This makes it clear that the gesture was not added in as an afterthought but was incorporated from the very first as an integral part of the entire utterance plan. The utterance, in its construction, thus, had both verbal and gestural components. The gestural component was designed to take care of an aspect of the utterance that the verbal component was not appropriate for. There was, thus, differentiation of function incorporated into the utterance plan.

The second example further exemplifies this point. A lecturer was discussing the behavioral forms of baboons. He was describing how a certain behavioral form was to be seen as having an evolutionary history and how a current behavioral form was to be seen as being the outcome of a long process of natural selection. He said: "under the influence of/GESTURE/ in the end natural selection." The gesture here was inserted in a pause between "of" and "in" and the gesture consisted in moving the hand, with index finger extended, from a position where the hand was extended well above the lecturer's head, to close to the lecturer, in a series of arc-like movements. In this gesture the lecturer appeared to be diagramming a series of steps or stages, thereby indicating that the influence of natural selection he was referring to was an indirect one, working through a long and complex chain of influences. The gesture, thus, augmented the verbal form at just the point where the verbal formulation did not incorporate the notion the lecturer clearly had of an extended succession of stages of influence. However, what we may further note is that the lecturer's pause here was just long enough for him to accomplish the gesture. The *preparation* for the gesture (cf. Kendon 1980a), which involved lifting the hand on an extended arm to the raised position from which the series of downward arc-like movements could be performed, was accomplished during the portion of the utterance in which he said "under the influence of." This means that the gestural form, here dealing with an aspect of what was to be expressed that was not included in the verbal formulation, was conceived of as an integral part of the whole utterance, well in advance of the point at which it would be needed. The program for carrying out the utterance was thus both verbal and gestural when it was initiated, yet the gestural form served to take care of an aspect of what was to be expressed that was not included in the verbal formulation adopted.

A third example. A 14-year-old boy had just returned from an excursion, and he was recounting his experience to his father, who had remained at home. The excursion had been to an open-air museum located close to a large interstate highway. The boy described the very large queue of cars off the highway into the museum, how he had visited a blacksmith's shop there, and how they had had lunch at the cafeteria. He then described how he had seen a lady taking photographs of her children, but there were features of the woman's actions, her expression, and the behavior of the children that he found very amusing. When he reached this part of his narration he suddenly moved away from his father to the center of the room and acted out the actions of someone standing back, holding a camera to their eye as if they were preparing to take a photograph. He then took up another position and acted out the actions of the children whom the woman was trying to pose for the photograph. Throughout he was talking, explaining what the woman and then the children did. It appeared that, in this instance, those parts of the boy's narrative that referred to events, such as the queue of cars, or settings such as cafeterias and blacksmith's shops that were familiar to both father and son, the son could narrate without using gesture. However, the incident involving the woman taking photographs was a unique event, an event that had, for the son, specific features unlike others he might have witnessed. In his recounting he wanted to represent those unique features, those features that had struck him as interesting or amusing. Thus he sought to represent the event more completely, to represent it in a form that came closer to the form in which he had actually witnessed it. A spoken account, no matter how well wrought, would not approach a re-presentation of the event in a form that was similar to the event as it had been witnessed.

What the boy wished to reproduce was the event in the form in which he had witnessed it so that the event could become for his father, as it was for him, an event to be remarked upon and laughed at. A verbal recounting could not achieve this. In his effort to get the father to appreciate the event in the way he had when he had witnessed it, the boy had no other means but to act parts of it out. His endeavor, in this instance, was to recreate the event just as it had been witnessed with as little as possible of the transformation and reorganization that a verbal recounting would have required.

In these examples, it is seen, it is the character of gesture as a form of graphic representation that is being exploited. This character is, in these examples, being exploited to meet not transmission conditions of the interactional event, but the requirements of representational adequacy. In the last two of these examples, especially, the utterer decides where gestural action is required in the light of his understanding of the relationship between the verbal formulation he has available and the image that he wishes to convey.

In this discussion I have given emphasis to the way in which an utterer will select a model of formulation, not only in the light of a comparison between its adequacy of representation and the image that it is intended to convey, but also in the light of what the current communication conditions are. These include transmission conditions, as we have seen, but they also include an appreciation of the kind of impact a gestural formulation may have on a recipient as compared to a verbal formulation. I take it that gestural forms are often resorted to for insults and for urgent commands because a gestural action can be reminiscent of actual physical action, and it may derive some of its added forcefulness from this. Here, however, I wish to point out how gesture may also be selected because it is able to remind the recipient of the visual features of what is being referred to. As we saw, in the *New York Times* example, this may be done to induce a particular mood or reaction in the recipient. By employing gesture, the visual experience itself may be more directly recalled for the recipient and his response to this experience may thus also be recalled.

The use of gesture to recall the visual appearance of something may also be done, as the last example I now offer suggests, as a way of showing that one particularly appreciates the visual appearance of something.

In this example a *recipient* of a spoken utterance engages in a gestural utterance, simultaneously with the spoken utterance, and in doing so displays his understanding and appreciation of the event the speaker is describing. As Gail Jefferson (1973) had described, in her study of precision timing of spoken utterances, recipients in conversation will sometimes make a remark that overlaps precisely with a stretch of speech of a current speaker and that has the same form as the speech that it overlaps, and in doing this the recipient displays how exact is his understanding of what the current speaker is saying. In the example about to be givn this overlap was accomplished gesturally. Here the choice of gesture was especially apt because it was an impressive visual event that the speaker was describing.

In this example, A was in conversation with T and he was listening as T described how he had watched a kestrel hover and then fold its wings and plunge to earth. T said: "I saw a kestrel — ooh he must have been 500 feet up. He hovered there and then he suddenly folded his wings and plummeted to earth."

Precisely over "folded his wings," A lifted his extended arm to shoulder height, folded the fingers of his hand together, and then dropped his hand rapidly. A was here in anticipation of T's description and, by producing this gesture, which depicts the sight that T was describing, he shares this description, displaying his appreciation of what it was that T was saying he had seen. Notice how appropriate a *gestural* utterance was here. T was describing something that it is very impressive to see. What A did, in this gesture, was to depict the event in *visual* terms. Thus it is not only current speakers that will bring in gesture where their current verbal formulations are not adequate to the image they wish to convey. Recipients also may display their grasp of what another is saying by gestural utterance, which is chosen because it is a medium of graphic representation, capable of showing that it is the visual aspect of the event being described that is understood and appreciated.

CONCLUSIONS

The view of gesture I have been putting forward in this chapter has a number of implications. First, it seems to me, it should lead to some dethronement of spoken language. That is to say, it should lead to a view in which spoken language forms are regarded as no "deeper" than other forms by which meaning may be represented. As Teodorrson (1980) has suggested in a recent discussion, spoken language is but one kind of manifestation or *delological form* of the representational process. There is no doubt that spoken language has been elaborated into a communicative code of extraordinary flexibility and generality. However, this is an elaboration that has come about because spoken language has been chosen as the instrument for main use, so to speak. As the phenomena of primary (i.e., deaf) sign languages make clear, gesture can also be elaborated into a flexible and functionally general communicative code to a degree that is quite comparable to spoken language, if circumstances are appropriate. Among the circumstances required, it should be noted, is the existence of a communication *community* in which gesture, rather than speech, is the main modality, and it is further important that such a community be fairly large and that it persist through time. In the past there has been much discussion about the limitations of sign languages. The work on primary sign languages of the last decade leads me to believe that these languages are, in principle, no more limited than spoken languages. Hitherto communities of sign language users that are large enough and that have persisted for long enough have not been available for study. As the brief history of American Sign Language makes clear, such languages can be elaborated, given enough time, and given a large enough community of users.

Secondly, I believe that the view of gesture I have here been advocating will have important implications for theories of mental representation. It is seen that since gestural expressions are fully integrated with spoken aspects, they must be planned for together at the outset. This means that, however ideas are stored in our heads, they must be stored in a way that allows them to be at least as readily encoded in gestural form as in verbal form. The issue of the mental representation of ideas has been the subject of some debate recently. There are those who maintain that ideas are represented in an abstract proposition format that is the same as the format used to encode verbal information (e.g., Pylyshyn, 1973). On the other hand there are those who believe that the representation of ideas is modality specific and that visual ideas are encoded in terms of structures that are spatial and that are analogous transforms of the things they represent (e.g., Metzler & Shepard, 1974; Shepard, 1978). In a review of these positions Anderson (1978) concluded that at the present time it will not be possible, using the techniques available in experimental psychology, to decide whether all ideas are encoded propositionally or whether they may be encoded somehow "pictorially" as well. Either hypothesis, he argues, accounts equally well for current experimental findings. Here it is suggested that the observation that gesture is deployed as an integral part of utterance shows that any theory of representation that gives primacy to a representational format modeled on spoken language structures will not do. A close examination of how gesture and speech are deployed in an utterance makes it clear, as I have tried to show, that meanings are not transformed into gestural form by way of spoken language formats. They are transformed directly and independently. Thus such meanings, however they are stored, are stored in a way that is separate from the formats of spoken language, however abstractly these may be conceived.

As I said at the outset, I believe that we are on the threshold of a new era in the study of gesture. I believe that the study of it will have important consequences for our understanding of representational processes, of the nature of language, and for the ways in which different expressive modalities are exploited in the organization of communication in interaction. It has been my purpose in this chapter to review some of the recent work that bears on these issues.

Gesture, it seems, is of great interest precisely because we can see, on the one hand, how it is a manifestation of a spontaneous mode of representation of meaning but how, on the other, such manifestations can become standardized and transformed into arbitrary symbolic forms. The study of gesture allows us to look both ways, so to speak. It allows us to look inward toward the processes of mental representation, on the one hand, and outward to the social processes by which communication codes become established on the other. Gesture stands at the point at which individual efforts at meaning representation fuse with the processes of codification. As such it is invaluable for the study of the central communicative processes of the human species.

ACKNOWLEDGMENTS

This chapter incorporates material from a lecture entitled "Current Issues in the Study of Gesture" delivered to the Seminar on Biological Foundations of Gesture: Motor and Semiotic Aspects, sponsored by the Toronto Semiotic Circle and the Canadian Hearing Society, May 27–29, 1982. Portions of this chapter have also been taken from a chapter entitled Some Uses of Gesture that has now appeared in its complete form in D. Tannen and M. Saville-Troike (Eds.), *Perspectives on Silence*. Ablex Publishing Corp., Norwood, New Jersey, 1985. I would like to acknowledge a grant from the Henry R. Luce Foundation to Connecticut College that made possible my presence at that institution when much of the work on this chapter was done. During the period of work on this chapter I was also in receipt of a National Science Foundation Grant, BNS 8024173.

REFERENCES

Alajouanine, T., & Lhermitte, F. Nonverbal communication in aphasia. In A. DeReuck & M. O'Connor (Eds.), *Disorders of language* (pp. 168–182). London: Churchill, 1964.

Anderson, J. R. Arguments concerning representations for mental imagery. *Psychological Review*, 1978, *85*, 249–277.

Barakat, R. A. Gesture systems. *Keystone Folklore Quarterly*, 1969, *14*, 105–121.

Barten, S. S. Development of gesture. In N. R. Smith & M. Franklin (Eds.), *Symbolic functioning in childhood* (pp. 139–151). Hillsdale, NJ: Lawrence Erlbaum Associates, 1979.

Bates, E. *The emergence of symbols*. New York: Academic, 1979.

Berger, K. W., & Popelka, G. R. Extra-facial gestures in relation to speech reading. *Journal of Communication Disorders*, 1971, *3*, 302–308.

Birdwhistell, R. L. *Kinesics and context*. Philadelphia: University of Pennsylvania Press, 1970.

Bolinger, D. Some thoughts on "Yep" and "Nope." *American Speech*, 1946, *21*, 90–95.

Bruner, J. S. Learning how to do things with words. In J. S. Bruner & A. Garton (Eds.), *Human growth and development* (pp. 62–84). Oxford: Clarendon Press, 1978.

Bulwer, J. *Chirologia: Or the natural language of the hand . . . whereunto is added chironomia: Or the art of manual rhetoric*. J. W. Cleary (Ed.). Carbondale and Edwardsville: Southern Illinois University Press, 1974 (Originally published 1644).

Cicone, M., Wapner, W., Foldi, N., Zurif, E., & Gardner, H. The relation between gesture and language in aphasic communication. *Brain and Language*, 1979, *8*, 324–349.

Cohen, A. A. The communicative functions of hand illustrators. *Journal of Communication*, 1977, *27*, 54–63.

Cohen, A. A., & Harrison, R. P. Intentionality in the use of hand illustrators in face-to-face communication situations. *Journal of Personality and Social Psychology*, 1973, *28*, 266–270.

Condillac, Etienne Bonnet de. *An essay on the origin of human knowledge: Being a supplement to Mr. Locke's essay on the human understanding* (Thomas Nugent, Trans. London: J. Nourse, 1756). Gainesville, Florida: Scholars' Facsimiles and Reprint, 1971 Facimile Reprint. (Originally published, 1754).

Condon, W. S. An analysis of behavioral organization. *Sign Language Studies*, 1976, *13*, 285–318.

Crystal, D., & Davy, D. *Investigating English style*. Bloomington: Indiana University Press, 1969.

Diderot, D. Lettre sur les Sourds et Muets. See M. Jourdain (Ed.), *Diderot's early philosophical works*. Chicago: Open Court, 1916.

Duffy, R. J., & Buck, R. A. A study of the relationship between propositional (pantomime) and subpropositional (facial expression) extra verbal behaviors in aphasics. *Folia Phoniatrica*, 1979, *31*, 129–136.

Duffy, R. J., & Duffy, J. R. Three studies of deficits in pantomimic expression and pantomimic recognition in aphasia. *Journal of Speech and Hearing Research*, 1981, *46*, 70–84.

Duffy, R. J., Duffy, J. R., & Pearson, K. Pantomimic recognition in aphasics. *Journal of Speech and Hearing Research*, 1975, *18*, 115–132.

Duffy, R. J., & Liles, B. Z. A translation of Finkelnburg's (1870) lecture on aphasia as 'asymbolia' with commentary. *Journal of Speech and Hearing Disorders*, 1979, *44*, 156–168.

Efron, D. *Gesture and environment, etc.* New York: Kings Crown Press, 1941. Republished as *Gesture, race and culture*. The Hague: Mouton, 1972.

Ekman, P. Biological and cultural contributions to bodily and facial movement. In J. Blacking (Ed.), *The anthropology of the body* (pp. 39–84). London: Academic, 1977.

Ekman, P. About brows. In M. Von Cranach, K. Foppa, W. Lepenier, & D. Ploog, (Eds.), *Human ethology: Claims and limits of a new discipline* (pp. 169–202). Cambridge: Cambridge University Press, 1979.

Evans, M. A., & Rubin, K. H. Hand gestures as a communicative mode in school-aged children. *Journal of Genetic Psychology*, 1979, *135*, 189–196.

Feyereisen, P. Hand preference for the different types of movement accompanying speech. *Journal de Psychologie Normale et Pathologique*, 1977, *74*, 451–470. (Original in French)

Foldi, N. S., Cicone, M., & Gardner, H. *Pragmatic aspects of communication in brain-damaged patients.* Unpublished manuscript, 1982.

Freedman, N. The analysis of movement behavior during clinical interviews. In A. Siegman & B. Pope (Eds.), *Studies in dyadic communication* (pp. 152–172). Elmsford, NY: Pergamon, 1972.

Freedman, N. Hands, words and mind: On the structuralization of body movements during discourse and the capacity for verbal representation. In N. Freedman & S. Grand (Eds.), *Communicative structures and psychic structures: A psychoanalytic approach* (pp. 109–132). New York and London: Plenum, 1977.

Gainotti, G., & Lemmo, M. Comprehension of symbolic gestures in aphasia. *Brain and Language,* 1976, *3,* 451–460.

Goodglass, H., & Kaplan, E. Disturbance of gesture and pantomime in aphasia. *Brain,* 1963, *86,* 702–703.

Graham, J. A., & Argyle, M. A cross-cultural study of the communication of extra verbal meaning by gestures. *International Journal of Psychology,* 1975, *10,* 56–67.

Graham, J. A., & Heywood, S. The effects of elimination of hand gestures and of verbal codability on speech performance. *European Journal of Social Psychology,* 1976, *5,* 189–195.

Hewes, G. W. Primate communication and the gestural origins of language. *Current Anthropology,* 1973, *14,* 5–24.

Hewes, G. W. The current status of the gestural theory of language origin. *Annals of the New York Academy of Sciences,* 1976, *280,* 482–504.

Hockett, C. F. In search of Jove's brow. *American Speech,* 1978, *53,* 243–313.

Jefferson, G. A case of precision timing in ordinary conversation: Overlapped tag-positioned address terms in closing sequences. *Semiotica,* 1973, *9,* 47–96.

Jancovic, M. A., Devoe, S., & Wiener, M. Age related changes in hand and arm movements as non-verbal communication: Some conceptualizations and an empirical exploration. *Child Development,* 1975, *46,* 922–928.

Katz, R., LaPointe, L., & Markel, N. Coverbal behavior and aphasic speakers. In R. H. Brookshire (Ed.), *Clinical aphasiology: collected proceedings 1972–1976.* Minneapolis: BRK Publisher.

Kaulfers, W. V. Curiosities of colloquial gesture. *Hispanica,* 1931, *14,* 249–264.

Kendon, A. Some relationships between body motion and speech: An analysis of an example. In A. Seigman (Ed.), *Studies in dyadic communication* (pp. 177–210). New York: Pergamon, 1972.

Kendon, A. The role of visible behaviour in the organization of face-to-face interaction. In M. von Cranach & I. Vine (Eds.), *Movement and social communication in man and chimpanzee.* London: Academic, 1973.

Kendon, A. Gesticulation, speech, and the gesture theory of language origins. *Sign Language Studies,* 1975, *9,* 349–373.

Kendon, A. *Studies in the behavior of face-to-face interaction.* Lisse: Peter de Ridder Press, 1977.

Kendon, A. Differential perception and attentional frame: Two problems for investigation. *Semiotica,* 1978, *24,* 305–315.

Kendon, A. Gesticulation and speech: Two aspects of the process of utterance. In M. R. Key (Ed.), *Nonverbal communication and language* (pp. 207–227). The Hague: Mouton, 1980, (a).

Kendon, A. A description of a deaf–mute sign language from the Enga Province of Papua New Guinea with some comparative discussion. Part 1: The formational properties of Enga signs. *Semiotica,* 1980, *31,* 1–34. (b)

Kendon, A. A description of a deaf–mute sign language from the Enga Province of Papua New Guinea with some comparative discussion. Part II: The semiotic functioning of Enga signs.

Semiotica, 1980, *32,* 81–117.

Kendon, A. A description of a deaf–mute sign language from the Enga Province of Papua New Guinea with some comparative discussion. Part III: Aspects of utterance construction. *Semiotica,* 1980, *32,* 245–313. (d)

Kendon, A. Gesticulation and speech: two aspects of the process of utterance. In M. R. Key (Ed.), *The relationship between verbal and nonverbal behavior.* The Hague: Mouton, 1980. (e)

Kendon, A. Current issues in "nonverbal communication." In A. Kendon (Ed.), *Nonverbal communication, interaction and gesture: Selections from 'Semiotica.'* The Hague: Mouton, 1981. (a)

Kendon, A. Geography of gesture. *Semiotica,* 1981, *37,* 129–163. (b)

Kendon, A. The study of gesture: Some observations on its history. *Recherches Semiotiques/ Semiotic Inquiry,* 1982, *2,* 45–62.

Kendon, A. Behavioral foundations for the process of frame attunement in face-to-face interaction. In G. P. Ginsburg, M. Brenner & M. von Cranach (Eds.), *Discovery strategies in the psychology of action.* London: Academic (1985).

Kimura, D. The neural basis of language via gesture. In H. Whitaker & H. A. Whitaker (Eds.), *Studies in neurolinguistics* (Vol. 2) pp. 145–156). New York: Academic, 1976.

Mandel, M. Iconic devices in American Sign Language. In L. A. Friedman (Ed.), *On the other hand: New perspectives in American Sign Language* (pp. 57–107). New York and London: Academic, 1977.

McNeill, D. *The conceptual basis of language.* Hillsdale, NJ: Lawrence Erlbaum Associates, 1979.

McNeill, D. Iconic gestures of children and adults. In A. Kendon & T. Blakely (Eds.), *Approaches to gesture.* Special issue of *Semiotica,* (in press).

McNeill, D., & Levy, E. Conceptual representations in language activity and gesture. In R. J. Jarvella & W. Klein (Eds.), *Speech, place and action: Studies in deixis and related topics.* Chichester: Wiley, 1982.

Metzler, S., & Shepard, R. Transformatonal studies of the internal representation of three dimensional objects. In R. Solso (Ed.), *Theories in cognitive psychology.* Hillsdale, NJ: Lawrence Erlbaum Associates, 1974.

Morris, D., Collett, P., Marsh, P., & O'Shaughnessy, M. *Gestures: Their origins and distribution.* London: Jonathan Cape, New York: Stein Day, 1979.

Myers, R. E. Comparative neurology of vocalization and speech: Proof of a dichotomy. *Annals of the New York Academy of Sciences,* 1976, *280,* 745–757.

Peterson, L. N., & Kirshner, H. S. Gestural impairment and gestural ability in aphasia: A review. *Brain and Language,* 1981, *14,* 333–348.

Pickett, L. An assessment of gestural and patomimic deficit in aphasic patients. *Acta Symbolica,* 1974, *5,* 69–86.

Pylyshyn, Z. W. What the mind's eye tells the mind's brain: A critique of mental imagery. *Psychological Bulletin,* 1973, *80,* 1–24.

Riseborough, M. G. Physiographic gestures as decoding facilitators: Three experiments exploring a neglected facet of communication. *Journal of Nonverbal Behavior,* 1985, *5,* 172–183.

Scheflen, A. E. The significance of posture in communication systems. *Psychiatry,* 1964, *27,* 316–331.

Schegloff, E. A. On some gestures' relation to talk. In J. M. Anderson & J. Heritage, (Eds.), *Structures of social action: Studies in conversational analyses.* Cambridge: Cambridge University Press 1984, pp. 266–296.

Shepard, R. N. Externalization of mental images and the art of creation. In B. S. Randharva & W. E. Coffman (Eds.), *Visual learning, thinking and communication.* New York: Academic, 1978.

Sherzer, J. Verbal and nonverbal deixis: The pointed lip gesture among the San Blas Cuna. *Language and Society,* 1972, *2,* 117-131.

Skelly, M. *Amerind gestural code based on universal American Indian hand talk.* New York: Elsevier, 1979.

Slama-Cazacu, T. Nonverbal components in message sequence: "Mixed syntax." In W. C. McCormack & S. A. Wurm (Eds.), *Language and man: Anthropological issues* (pp. 217-227). The Hague: Mouton, 1976.

Sousa-Poza, J. F., Rohrberg, R., & Mercure, A. Effects of type of information (abstract-concrete) and field dependence on asymmetry of hand movements during speech. *Perceptual and Motor Skills,* 1979, *48,* 1323-1330.

Stam, J. H. *Inquiries into the origin of language: The fate of a question.* New York: Harper & Row, 1976.

Stokoe, W. C. Sign language and sign languages. *Annual Review of Anthropology,* 1980, *9,* 365-390.

Teodorrson, S. T., Autonomy and linguistic status of non-speech language forms. *Journal of Psycholinguistic Research,* 1980, *9,* 121-145.

Tylor, E. B. *Researchers into the early history of mankind* (3rd ed.). London: John Murray, 1878.

Varney, N. R. Linguistic correlates of pantomime recognition in aphasic patients. *Journal of Neurology, Neurosurgery and Psychiatry,* 1978, *41,* 546-568.

Washabaugh, W. Sign language in its social context. *Annual Review of Anthropology,* 1981,*10,* 237-252.

Wiener, M., Devoe, S., Rubinow, S., & Geller, J. Nonverbal behavior and nonverbal communication. *Psychological Review,* 1972, *79,* 185-214.

Wilkinson, L. C., & Rembold, K. L. The form and function of children gestures accompanying verbal directives. In P. S. Dale & D. Ingram (Eds.), *Child language: An international perspective* (pp. 175-190). Baltimore: University Park Press, 1981.

Wundt, W. *The language of gestures.* The Hague: Mouton, 1900/1973. (Translation of Volkerpsychologie: Eine Untersuchung der Entricklungsgesetze von Sprache, Mythus und Sitte Vol.I, 4th Ed., Part I, Chap. 2. Stuttgart: Alfred Kroner Verlag, 1921)

4 Movement in Human Interaction: Description, Parameter Formation, and Analysis

Hans-Peter Hirsbrunner
Siegfried Frey
Robert Crawford
Department of Psychology of the University of Duisburg

Although speech has been the primary focus in communication research for many years, interest in the nonverbal aspects of communication has increased dramatically during the last decade. The surge of the "movement movement" (Davis, 1972, p. VII) in communication has attracted so much attention that today, according to Galloway (1979), "An awareness of the value of nonverbal communication appears everywhere: businessmen and salesmen, administrators and managers, actors and dancers, as well as teachers and parents have voiced an interest" (p. 197). With this new awareness of the importance of the nonverbal in communication, it has become standard research practice to start an investigation with the production of a video record. Agreement among investigators usually ends, however, right at the moment the recording machinery is turned off, when it comes to the question of how to transcribe visible movement from the video tape into a data protocol. As Badler and Smoliar (1979) have noted, the most pertinent feature of current research on movement behavior "is an almost total lack of agreement on how movement should be described. It is almost as if each research project started from scratch with an arbitrary set of movement characteristics to be observed" (p. 19).

The origins of this "rather disorganized state of the movement research art" (Davis, 1979, p. 55) can be attributed to the fact that the science of nonverbal communication is still in its preliterate phase. In contrast to verbal behavior that can be easily transcribed in great detail into a written protocol by means of the alphabet, the transcription of movement remains a major problem. Coding schemes currently employed for movement notation offer so little resolution that an investigator who enters this field of research finds himself in a dilemma very similar to that of an analphabetic who sets out to investigate verbal behavior: Just as an analphabetic can hear perfectly well what the subjects say, the nonverbal researcher can see perfectly well how subjects move. The problem, however, is how to notate what is heard and seen.

The joint research efforts of "scholars of different disciplinary back-grounds — psychologists, linguists, anthropologists, psychiatrists, sociolo-gists" (Siegman & Feldstein, 1978) have, so far, done little to improve this awkward state of affairs. As Davis (1979) has observed, the most obvious re-sult of the present research endeavor is a:

> chaotic welter of terms scattered throughout the literature. Every researcher seems to adopt his own terms, often without clearly defining what exactly he is referring to. Sometimes the terms are simple everyday action words such as "crossed her legs" or "smiled". Sometimes the terminology is adapted from an-other discipline such as linguistics [e.g., "kinemorphic construction"] or com-puter technology [e.g., "monitors" or "regulatory behaviors"]. In other cases the terms are interpretive ones [e.g., "sad face" or "receptive postures"]. (p. 55)

Up to now, most researchers have not even attempted to develop a coding strategy that can portray the complex movement behavior we encounter in social interactions. Some investigators have even felt that "The task of devising notation systems for these human behaviors defies even the most ingenious person and group of persons" (Key, 1977, p. 55). Despite such pes-simism one need not, however, conclude that a major discovery is necessary to dislodge the science of nonverbal communication from its present prelit-erate state. As Frey and Pool (1976) have shown, current difficulties in move-ment description do not originate from the complexity of the phenomena to be described, but from the investigators' failure to base their coding systems on the principle of time-series notation. The efficacy of the time-series nota-tion in the assessment of the rapidly changing audible and visible phenomena has been long known. From the writing of a musical score to the technical registration of the audible and the visible on devices such as disc, film, or videotape, to the alphabetic transcription of speech, the time-series notation forms the methodological basis for literally every efficient approach to the registration and storage of audiovisual information.

Here we describe the possibilities time-series notation offers for research in nonverbal communication. To do this, we first analyze current coding strate-gies with regard to the possibilities they provide and the limitations they impose upon the investigation of nonverbal interaction. We then explain how time-series notation opens up the way to a unified approach to the coding of speech and movement. Then, the main features of a coding system developed specifically for the time-series notation of nonverbal interaction are described. We also explain how the time-series protocols of speech and movement can be integrated into a common data matrix. Finally, with an example from current research, we show in great detail how the information contained in these data matrices can be used to quantify multiple behavioral parameters, to visualize the interactive organization of movement in a dyad, and to uncover hidden behavioral relationships.

CURRENT CODING STRATEGIES

The fact that the video record itself does provide a highly detailed and accurate account of movement behavior provides no solution to the notation problem. As Ekman, Friesen, and Taussig (1969) remind us, filmed or video taped "records are not data. While records may be the raw input for intriguing ideas and discovery, they must be converted into some digital form in order to be analyzed" (p. 298).

Because of the lack of an efficient coding language, investigators have always been compelled to carry out the main data reduction at a very early stage of their investigation — at the moment of raw data collection. As a consequence, nonverbal behavior research has regularly begun with the production of a coding scheme designed to suit the particular questions pursued in a particular study. Over the past 50 years, this strategy has triggered the production of an awesome array of notational schemes. Most of them have been employed only by their developer and often in only one single study. Frey and Pool (1976) have demonstrated that, according to the principles employed for item definition, most researchers have adopted one of three basic strategies for immediate data reduction:

1. Classification of the vast number of visually different movement patterns into a few global categories whose definitions correspond to what the investigator believes to be "relevant" (Generic Coding).
2. Restriction of behavioral assessment to a small number of movements that are well defined, easily observed, and difficult to mistake (Restrictive Coding).
3. Avoidance of behavioral notation by directly transforming observations into psychological dimensions, or by ascribing a functional "meaning" to the behavior under observation (Direct Evaluation).

Each of these coding strategies impose serious limitations upon the investigators' ability to detect and prove existing relationships between nonverbal behavior and other variables. It is worthwhile, therefore, to examine each in some detail before suggesting an alternative approach.

Generic Coding

Frey and Pool speak of "Generic coding" if data reduction is achieved by constructing code catalogues with generic terms, each covering a wide spectrum of visually different behaviors. Observers using such coding schemes are required to lump a variety of visually different movement patterns into the same generic category that might be labeled as *walk, point, sit, illustrate, hit, automanipulate, forearm sweep, touch, gesture,* etc. So, although coders are visually sensitive to apparently limitless variations in movements, once they begin to label, they are forced to ignore all the variations except those that relate to the differences between code categories. If the data protocol then reports various behaviors to fall in one particular category, say "walk," this does, of course, not at all mean that the coders saw no differences in the way subjects walked. The coders might have been aware of major differences in the way the subjects were walking, but the coding scheme forced them to ignore these differences, simply because it did not provide the codes necessary to describe the observed differences.

Several problems arise from a generic coding of visually discriminable behaviors. First, there is the problem of item selection. Categories contained in current generic codes are, in most cases, simply compiled from common language. This alone drastically limits the possible scope of movement investigation simply because everyday language provides ready labels for only a very limited set of movements. Additionally the labels offered by common language are biased in a way that renders these terms of doubtful value for most studies of face-to-face interactions. Our language offers a wide variety of labels for the very conspicuous, high-impact behaviors, which (probably for that very reason) rarely occur in normal adult interaction. On the other hand, there is only a very limited set of words for the notation of the complex movement accompanying speech in the ordinary face-to-face interaction.

An impressive demonstration of this problem is given by the numerous ethological coding schemes produced in the early 1970s (e.g., Blurton Jones, 1972b; Brannigan & Humphries, 1972; Leach, 1972; McGrew, 1972; Smith & Conolly, 1972). They are meant to contribute to the development of a comprehensive code for the assessment of human nonverbal behavior, but they actually reflect only the biased labeling of our language. These codes offer numerous labels for a registration of rare events such as *hit, beat, punch, pound, clap, push, grab, tug, wrestle, embrace, kick, stamp, slide, jump, somersault.* If we look at the possibilities such schemes offer for the assessment of the less conspicuous behaviors that actually account for the biggest part of the movement displayed in interaction, the resolution is close to zero. Even such an elaborate system as the one compiled by Brannigan and Humphries (1972) includes, within a total of 136 categories, some items that are so globally defined that they can readily accommodate most of the behavioral variation observed in an interaction. The two categories "Demonstrate" and "Gesture," for instance, can probably encompass almost all hand activity that might be displayed during any conversation.[1]

The problems associated with the low resolution of common language can, of course, not be solved by finding a few more labels in the dictionary. Even the less globally defined codes such as "hit," "push," "beat," "punch" present basically the same problem: If such behaviors should occur in a communicative situation, it would be highly important indeed to know exactly how these behaviors were performed, because psychological implications might well be different for different ways of hitting, different ways of pushing, etc.

A second problem is that the generic codes always imply a high risk of damaging research efficacy, because they deliberately permit heterogeneous behaviors to be attributed to the same category. Cronbach (1958), called this a "research strategy which stirs all data into a single pot" (p. 360) and warned that the more globally the categories are defined the more likely it is that significant relations are overlooked, because "different aspects of the global composite, may be related to the criterion in opposite ways. If so, these effects tend to cancel each other and the global index shows little difference between the criterion groups" (p. 362). In addition, existing relations between nonverbal behavior and other variables can already be obscured simply by lumping the critical behavior with behaviors unrelated to the independent variable. As Blurton Jones (1972a) reminds us, if the nonverbal behaviors attributed to the same category:

> do not in fact co-vary and measure the same 'thing' then there is no future in looking for causes . . . . Relationships between cause A and behaviour A will be obscured by lumping that behaviour with behaviour patterns B and C which vary independently of A. (p. 18)

In this case, the relation to the independent variable would hold only for a fraction of the behaviors lumped together. A statistical test administered to such data would, therefore, most likely result in a confirmation of the null hypothesis.

Then, there is the problem of research economy. If the investigator does not find a systematic relation between the independent variables and the behavior measures, it is always possible to define a new generic coding scheme that then lumps behaviors according to the new definitions. However, any subsequent decision to categorize the behavior by redefined generic codes necessitates a return to the original video record and a tedious and expensive

---

[1]Brannigan and Humphries (1972) offer the following definitions: *"Demonstrate* — A movement of arm, hand or fingers used to describe the direction, shape, size or other qualities of that which is being talked about . . . *Gesture* — Variable movements of arm, hand or fingers, usually during conversation, not covered by other gestural unit definitions" (p. 61).

recoding procedure. As there are virtually as many possibilities for lumping visually discriminable behaviors as there are labels for generic categories, it may take an extended search to arrive at an optimal coding scheme; one that is capable of uncovering the relationship between the independent variables and the movement behavior displayed by the subjects. Clearly, the problem of finding the best generic coding scheme arises anew in each study, since the generic coding scheme that is optimal for one study may well turn out to be useless for the next.

Restrictive Coding

Frey and Pool speak of "Restrictive coding" when behavioral description is confined to the assessment of a small subset of specific movements that are well defined, easily observed, and difficult to mistake. This strategy offers the advantage of generating homogeneous data, because coders are not allowed to subsume visually different behaviors into the same category. The investigator thus avoids problems originating from the heterogeneity of the behaviors lumped into generic categories. Homogeneity is, however, typically achieved by greatly reducing the scope of behavioral description. Application of this approach can be adequate if an hypothesis about the occurrence of a very specific movement is to be tested, or even in cases when highly ritualized, emblematic types of movement are to be assessed, such as shrugs, eyebrow flash, obscene gestures, etc. But it does not solve the problem of assessing the fine web of complex movement interlocutors display in a face-to-face interaction. On the contrary, the more rigidly movement patterns are defined, the less behaviors will suit the item definitions, and the more behaviors will fall outside the scope of the investigation. Thus, the kind of data reduction achieved through restrictive coding presents not fewer but only different problems: Whereas generic coding resorts to a "data reduction by lumping," the principle employed in restrictive coding can be best described as "data reduction by ignoring."

Direct Evaluation

In view of the difficulties inherent in movement notation, investigators have often tried to circumvent the whole problem by asking raters to directly transform their observations into psychological dimensions. Coders using this principle of data reduction do not have to bother at all with a notation of the behavior a subject displays during the observation period. Instead the coder is asked to directly evaluate, in his/her own subjective way, what the subject's movements mean in terms of the psychological dimensions of interest to the investigator. Thus, depending on the questions being asked in a particular study, the coders might be required to decide, at their own discretion, to what degree the observed subject is "extroverted," "defensive," "cold," "anxious," "friendly," "nervous," "dominant," etc.

This strategy of research is, of course, an all too simple and naïve way of finding out the hidden meaning of nonverbal behavior. For most rating dimensions there is, up to now, neither agreement about their definitions, nor agreement about what their nonverbal referents are. To ask a rater to establish such a connection means, therefore, to demand of the rater an achievement the investigator himself is not able to produce.

Clearly, a rater's impression can be an interesting datum in its own right. Yet the problem remains that we have no way of knowing how this impression relates to nonverbal behavior as long as we cannot describe the behavior observed. The major failing of the rating techniques in this area of research, therefore, is that they completely bypass the visible behavior itself. They presumably establish a link between a condition (the independent variable) and a psychological state (the rating), the link being observed in the visible behavior. Yet there is absolutely no characteristic of the observable behavior that is itself defined or described, so we end up knowing nothing more about the features and meanings of nonverbal behavior. A reliable connection may be found between, for instance, a stress-inducing experimental condition and the observers' rating of "anxiety," but we will never know what behaviors established this connection: hyperactivity, hypoactivity, specific kinds of movement, or different behaviors in different subjects?

TIME-SERIES NOTATION: A CODING PRINCIPLE FOR A UNIFIED ASSESSMENT OF SPEECH AND MOVEMENT

At the core of the problem of movement description has always been the attempt to resolve the continuous stream of behavior into a nominal scale of discrete spatiotemporal patterns. The inefficiency of this approach to movement notation has already been shown by Frey and Pool (1976):

> It is fairly easy to demonstrate, why movement labelling systems must necessarily be low-resolution instruments. 'Movement' implies change of position over time. If one were to abstract from a continuous stream of human behavior by defining each movement as a sequence of four different positions, each position being selected from a set of only ten defined positions, then the number of distinguishable movements is over 5,000. Increase the sequence to five successive positions and the number of different possible movements becomes more than 30,000. No useful system for labelling movements could be constructed with 30,000 different category labels. Yet even for one component of body movement (e.g. movements of the left hand) it is clear that with our eyes we can discriminate many more than ten possible locations and we see movements as virtually continuous, not restricted to a sequence of five points in time. (p. 4)

The inefficiency of a coding procedure that assigns a label to an entire sequence of spatiotemporal units can probably be best illustrated by considering its use for a transcription of speech behavior. If speech notation were based on labels referring to entire sound sequences, one would, depending on the level of complexity chosen, need a specific symbol for each syllable, for each word, or even for each sentence. The implications this would have are perfectly clear if we consider the coding scheme used to transcribe Chinese. As Martin (1972) notes: "The K'anghsi' [Kangxi] dictionary of 1716 lists 40,545 different characters; Morohashi's recent dictionary carries nearly fifty thousand . . . . If we were to take all the characters that have ever existed it is said, the total number would reach eighty thousand" (p. 83).

The methodological basis on which alphabetic notation achieves a highly sophisticated protocol from just a few symbols is the principle of time-series notation. Instead of assigning a label to a complex vocal-temporal pattern, alphabetic writing systems resolve the stream of verbal behavior into two dimensions, a temporal dimension and a phonetic dimension. Speech behavior is, in effect, coded into two separate components, the phonetic and temporal component. The phonetic component of speech is coded by a small number of symbols, e.g., the 26 letters of the Latin alphabet.[2] The coding of the temporal component of speech results directly from the convention of writing the symbols in lines, e.g., from top left to bottom right. In this way a temporal vector is assigned to each sound symbol, which differentiates the temporal aspects of speech on an ordinal scale level.

The bivariate coding of speech can be easily visualized by simply deleting one of the two constituents from a written transcript. If the temporal component is eliminated, the phonetic information in the transcript collapses into an undefineable aggregate of sound symbols. If the phonetic component is eliminated, the "temporal vectors" are still preserved, but the speech product is, of course, also underdetermined. An illustration of this principle with the example "HI THERE" is given in Fig. 4.1.

It is now apparent that the principle of the bivariate coding of speech into a temporal and a phonetic dimension is the basis for the ingenious way the alphabet achieves a highly sophisticated protocol of speech with just a few symbols. This principle can, as Frey and Pool (1976) have shown, also be successfully applied to the transcription of complex movement behavior. Instead of being labeled as a complex spatiotemporal pattern, "movement" is then "spelled out" as a series of positions over time. Thus, besides presenting a clear solution to the notation problems inherent in current coding strategies,

---

[2]In a survey of current writing systems, Gair (1971) points out that there are currently about 50 individual alphabets in use. Most alphabets contain between 20 to 30 symbols, the lower limit being 12 symbols (Hawaiian Alphabet), the upper limit about 100 symbols (International Phonetic Alphabet, IPA).

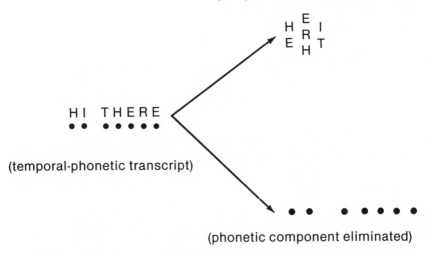

FIG. 4.1   Bivariate coding of a speech product as a time-series of sound symbols.

time-series notation also opens up the way for a unified approach to the notation of speech and movement in the face-to-face interaction. Just as the stream of verbal behavior can be resolved into a phonetic and a temporal component, complex movement can be resolved into its spatial and temporal constituents. And just as the problem of protocolling complex speech can be reduced to the comparatively simple task of ascribing letters to a small number of sounds, the problem of coding "movement" can be reduced to the problem of coding static positions — a much more manageable task. The use of time-series notation is particularily useful in the analysis of filmed or videotaped records, because the records themselves resolve the complex movement into a position-time-series. Thus, the same principle utilized in the registration of movement on film or videotape can again be used to transcribe visible movement into a data protocol.

The Bernese Coding System for Time-Series Notation of Body Movement

The coding system described here was designed by Frey and Pool (1976) for the transcription of the spontaneous movement activity of interlocutors who communicate with each other while in a seated position. The temporal component of body movement is determined from the serial number assigned to each video frame by a standard video timer. The spatial component is assessed by determining the positional states of the following parts of the body: head, trunk, shoulders, upper arms, hands, upper legs, and feet. Table 4.1

TABLE 4.1

Summary of Coding Scheme for the Time-Series Description of Nonverbal Behavior in Face-to-Face Interaction (from Time-Series-Notation: A Coding Principle for a Unified Assessment of Speech and Movement in Communication Research by S. Frey, H. P. Hirsbrunner, and U. Jorns. In E. W. B. Hess-Lüttich (Ed.) *Multimedial Communication: Semiotic problems of its notations.* Tübingen, West-Germany: Narr, 1982. Reprinted by Permission).

Body Part	# of Coded Dimensions	Dimension	Type of Scale # of Units	Type of Movement Defined by Dimension
(1) Head	3	Sagittal	Ordinal/ 5	Up/down tilt of head
		Rotational	Ordinal/ 5	Left/right rotation of head
		Lateral	Ordinal/ 5	Left/right tilt of head
(2) Trunk	3	Sagittal	Ordinal/ 5	Forward/backward tilt of trunk
		Rotational	Ordinal/ 5	Left/right rotation of trunk
		Lateral	Ordinal/ 5	Left/right tilt of trunk
(3) Shoulders[a]	2	Vertical	Ordinal/ 3	Up/down shift of shoulder
		Depth	Ordinal/ 3	Forward/backward shift of shoulder
(4) Upper arms[a]	3	Vertical	Ordinal/ 8	Up/down lift of upper arm
		Depth	Ordinal/ 8	Forward/backward shift of upper arm
		Touch	Nominal/ 7	Upper arm contact with chair/body areas

108

(5) Hands[a]	9	Vertical	Ordinal/14	Up/down shift of hand
		Horizontal	Ordinal/ 9	Left/right shift of hand
		Depth	Ordinal/ 8	Forward/backward shift of hand
		x/y orientation	Ordinal/ 9	Angle of hand in vertical plane
		z orientation	Ordinal/ 5	Outward/inward sway of hand
		Turn	Ordinal/ 5	Up/down turn of palm
		Closure	Ordinal/ 4	Opening/closing of fist
		Folding	Nominal/ 2	Folding together of hands
		Touch	Nominal/52	Hand contact with chair/body areas
(6) Upper legs[a]	3	Vertical	Ordinal/ 5	Up/down shift of upper leg
		Horizontal	Ordinal/ 5	Left/right shift of upper leg
		Touch	Ordinal/ 3	Contact between knees
(7) Feet[a]	7	Vertical	Ordinal/ 9	Up/down shift of foot
		Horizontal	Ordinal/ 7	Left/right shift of foot
		Depth	Ordinal/ 7	Forward/backward shift of foot
		Sagittal	Ordinal/ 5	Up/down tilt from ankle
		Rotational	Ordinal/ 5	Left/right rotation from ankle
		Lateral	Ordinal/ 5	Left/right tilt from ankle
		Touch	Nominal/10	Foot contact with chair/floor/body areas
(8) Position on chair	2	Horizontal	Ordinal/ 3	Left/right position on chair
		Depth	Ordinal/ 3	Front/back position on chair

[a]Left and right coded separately.

summarizes the coding system, showing for each part of the body the dimensions that can be coded, the type of scale used, and the number of positional states that can reliably be distinguished in the different dimensions. The table shows that the number of dimensions into which positions can be coded varies for different parts of the body. This reflects their differential potential to engage in complex movement variation. The shoulders, for instance, can only move forward/backward and upward/downward and, thus, need to be coded in only two dimensions. The hands, in contrast, can move in a much more complex manner and thus need to be coded in more dimensions in order to register their complex variation over time.

The positions that can be distinguished within a particular dimension have been defined, in most cases, as displacements or "flexions" from a standard "upright" sitting position. For example, the five positions distinguished for the lateral dimension of the head, the trunk, and the feet are defined as "strongly tilted to the left," "slightly tilted to the left," "straight," "slightly tilted to the right," "strongly tilted to the right." When positions are assessed in cartesian coordinates, the different positions are referenced to anatomical features of the subject to permit easy and reliable positional classification. For example, the code for the assessment of hand position in the vertical dimensions runs as follows: The middle of the hand is located "above the head" (Code 1), "on the same level as the head" (Code 2), "in the area of the neck" (Code 3), "in the upper part of the trunk" (Code 4),. . . "on the same level as the knee" (Code 10),. . . "on the floor" (Code 14). The full details of the code and a manual for its application is given in Frey (1986).

Coding Accuracy

The coding of the temporal component of movement does not present any serious problems when a video timer is available to assign a serial number to each frame of the video record. The accuracy of the movement description is, therefore, dependent only on the resolution the code offers for the discrimination of the spatial component. The higher a code's resolution in differentiating among positional states, the more accurate is the description of the interlocutors' complex movement behavior.

A special advantage of the coding strategy employed by Frey and Pool is that it provides a highly detailed and accurate description of complex movement behavior, even if coders can differentiate only between a small number of positions in each dimension. The reason for this is that the code's resolution is defined by the product of the number of positions distinguished in each dimension. Thus, for head position alone, the code can differentiate between 125 different head positions if only five positions in each, sagittal, rotational, and lateral dimension are discriminated. The seven ordinal dimensions used to describe hand movement provide, on the basis of the positional states listed in Table 4.1, a descriptive potential for almost a million different hand positions.

It is no surprise then that with this coding strategy the spatial component of movement behavior can be assessed with high precision, without requiring coders to pass a lengthy training period. Frey and Pool have shown that their scheme can be applied after a very short training period, usually not more than a day. Reliability figures obtained after a day's training were over 90% for both retest and intercoder reliability. To assess the validity of positional codings, Frey and Pool performed an additional study in which they tried to reconstruct 40 randomly selected positions on the basis of the coded data. For this purpose, the head, trunk, hands, thighs, and feet of a human model were placed in specific positions, read back from the codings obtained from the original subjects. Pictures taken of this model were then coded and compared with the codings obtained for the original positions. Over 98% of 2,400 data items obtained from each set of photos were in agreement. Figure 4.2 illustrates the resolution and accuracy with which the subjects' original positioning can be documented with this system.

Coding Procedure

Video systems portray a subject's nonverbal behavior at 50 or 60 frames per second. But it is not necessary to make a frame-by-frame transcription of positional states even if one decides to exhaust fully the temporal resolution provided in the video recording. After the subject's position at the first time mark has been assessed, the next measurement has to be made only when a movement occurs. As long as the subject does not move, the previous position code applies to all subsequent points in time. Because a rest period can easily be distinguished from a movement period if the video tape is viewed at normal speed, it would be a waste of time to ascertain the existence of a rest period via frame-by-frame analysis. Thus, in order to obtain a time-series protocol that corresponds to the information on visible movement present in the video record, only movement phases need to be transcribed frame-by-frame. As various studies have shown, even movement phases can be coded in less frequent intervals than frame by frame; half-second or even one-second intervals usually suffice. This degrades the resolution of the protocol to a certain extent, but it does not change the research strategy in any other way. For most applications, a half-second interval appears to provide a more than adequate data base.

Because the different parts of the body vary widely in the degree to which they participate in the total movement activity, it is simpler and easier to code each part of the body in a separate run of the video record. Most of the studies done with this system have employed the following coding procedure: The video tape is set at the first time mark and put into "Stop Motion" mode to al-

Positions of original subjects

Positions of model, read back from the codings

FIG. 4.2 Comparison of positions of original subjects with positions reconstructed from the coded data. The upper half of the picture shows positions of the original subjects, the lower half the positions of the human model, as read back from the codings. From "The Assessment of Similarity" by S. Frey. In M. von Cranach (Ed.), *Methods of Inference from Animal to Human Behavior.* The Hague: Mouton, 1976. Reprinted by permission.

low the coder to assess the position of a single part of the body in all its different coding dimensions. The video recorder is then set in "Normal Play" mode until a movement appears in this part of the body. As long as there is no movement, the previous position code is simply continued. If there is motion in this part of the body, the tape is rewound a short distance and played back to find the exact time of the positional change. The new positions are then coded for each half-second for the duration of the movement period. Then the video recorder is put back into "Normal Play" mode for the duration of the new rest period.

With this procedure, coding costs are tied directly to the amount of information gathered about movement variation. If there is little change in the behavior displayed during the observation period, measurements are infrequent and coding costs are low. If behavior varies in a complex fashion over time and space, measurements must be more frequent and coding costs increase, as does the amount of information gathered about complex movement variation.

Upgrading the Temporal Resolution of Speech Transcriptions

Although time-series notation can be used to transcribe both, speech and movement, the transcripts resulting from the alphabetic notation of verbal behavior cannot be readily integrated with a position-time-series transcript of movement. The reason is that the alphabetic speech transcription degrades the temporal resolution available in the audio track from an interval scale to an ordinal scale level. This means that in the process of speech transcription, the information about the duration of the different sounds is lost. Time-series protocols of movement, in contrast, preserve the interval-level scaling of the time dimension. The movement transcript, therefore, contains information about the relative, and (within the limits of the sampling interval) even the absolute duration for each position and movement. If transcripts of speech and movement are to be integrated into a common data matrix, it is necessary, therefore, to first upgrade the time reference inherent in alphabetic speech transcriptions from their ordinal scale level to the higher order scale employed for movement transcription.

One possibility is acoustical cuing. Condon (1970), for example, suggested manually transporting a sound film:

> forward (with a back-and-forth motion) until the next sound change is detected. There is some sound distortion because of the manual operation that varies with speed. With some practice, however, one learns to transport the film at approximately normal speed and can detect points of sound change and the frame number at which they occur. (p. 51)

Another technique is to insert an oscilloscopic display of the sound wave directly into the video picture and to attempt a visual segmentation of speech. Due to the high ambiguity of the speech signal, use of this technique has long been limited to a recognition of the on–off pattern of speech and silence. The ambiguity of the speech signal can, however, be greatly reduced by suppressing the redundancy inherent in the various phonemes (Hirsbrunner, 1980). For the insertion of a redundancy-suppressed speech signal into the video picture, the "Sequel-Analysis-Module (SAM)" has been developed (Hirsbrunner, 1986). This device takes the audio signals from the sound track of the video recorder, translates the complex speech signal into a series of discrete patterns, or "sequels," visualizes these patterns on an oscilloscope, and inserts them back into a part of the video picture. As has been described elsewhere (Frey, 1984), insertion of a redundancy-suppressed speech signal facilitates visual segmentation and time-marking of continuous speech to such a high degree, that protocols of speech and movement can be time-matched with an accuracy of plus/minus 20 milliseconds.

Integrating Multiple Time Series of Speech and Movement into a Common Data Matrix

The time-series approach described here resolves the complex stream of behavior into multiple data strings. Each data string contains the behavioral variation in one particular aspect of the interlocutor's movement and/or speech activity. Since all data strings refer to a common time code it is possible to integrate, in a second step, the multiple data strings obtained from the two interlocutors into a common data matrix. This data matrix provides the empirical basis for the assessment of the behavioral characteristics which constitute the dependent variables in a particular study. It is worthwhile, therefore, to note in detail how such data matrices are organized and what information they contain.

Contents of the Data Matrix

In Fig. 4.3 we have an example of a data matrix obtained from a time-series notation of 1 minute of a conversation between a male and female student. The left half of the data matrix shows the behavior of the female subject (INTERLOCUTOR A), the right half that of her partner (INTERLOCUTOR B). The numbers and letters at the top of this matrix correspond to the different parts of the body and their respective coding dimensions as enumerated in Table 4.1. The time code, in the middle of the matrix, refers to both subjects. The alphabetic transcript of the interlocutors' verbal behavior is placed next to the time code. Adjacent rows in this matrix describe the nonverbal and verbal behavior of the two interlocutors at intervals of one-half second.

The first row of this matrix, indexed by the time-mark 0005 (= one-half second), shows the positional state for each of the two subjects at the beginning of their conversation. The numbers in each column represent the specific position value within the dimension coded. An entry is made only if there is a change in position. Blanks signify that the position coded at the previous time mark remained unchanged. Thus, the particular way in which the interlocutors moved and rested over the course of the conversation is shown in detail by the vertical succession of entries and blanks.

How to Read a Data Matrix

The data matrix shows the enormous complexity of the behavioral information preserved in the video taped record. For the nonverbal behavior alone, this complexity is resolved into 12,480 data points (6240 for each subject), this covering a time period of only 1 minute. This large amount of information can be directly accessed by computer programs, allowing its efficient use in the definition and quantification of behavioral parameters. Yet before specific parameters are defined, the investigator may often find it worthwhile to look at the matrix at its full level of resolution. In most cases it is surprisingly easy to directly glean from this abundance of information a number of interesting relationships simply by visual inspection of the data matrix. Here are a few possibilities:

–By comparing the white areas with areas blackend by the entries, one can obtain, at a glance, an estimate of the relative amount of movement activity displayed by each of the interlocutors.

–Instances of high movement-complexity can be determined by examining the data matrix for densely clustered entries.

–The suddenness with which movement activity is initiated and terminated can be assessed by determining how many dimensions are simultaneously activated at the onset and offset of movement clusters.

–By comparing the activity of different parts of the body (given in data fields 1 to 8), one immediately gets an idea of the degree of their involvement in the total movement activity.

–By inspecting the movement activity of symmetrical parts of the body, such as right and left hand, one can estimate lateral dominance in movement activity.

–By comparing the vertical succession of entries and blanks, one can easily determine how movement duration and rest periods are temporally structured.

Inspection of the data given in Fig. 4.3 shows that there are marked differences in the way entries are clustered over time, suggesting that there are two

INTERLOCUTOR a | INTERLOCUTOR b

#O	#PITIME	#P	#C	SPEECH
				WARUM DU DICH
				HAST
				HIEFFUR
				GEMELDET
				WAS HAT DICH
				SO DARAN INT
				ERESSIERT
				JA
				HAST GAR KEI
				NE BEDENKEN
				GEHABT
				SO
				MHM
				WAS MUSSTEST
				DA
				MHM

SPEECH (interlocutor a):

- MM
- ACH SO
- NA JA
- HM
- DAS WAR GANZ SPONTAN
- VON EZ
- VON EM TOBIA
- G SHOERT
- DASS
- BEZIEHUNGSWE
- ISE VON DER
- KENIA ICH
- SOLL DAS MAC
- HEN WEIL SIE
- KEINE ZEIT
- HAT NIMAB IC
- H GESAGT JA
- JA MACH ICH
- SCHON /125
- MM
- ACH NE
- MIR WAR
- DAS IM
- PRINZIP
- EGAL ICH HAB
- MIR HALT GED
- ACHT NAJA
- WARUM NICHT
- ICH HAB IRGE
- NDWANN MAL
- SCHON MAL SO
- N KOMISCHEN
- VERSUCH MITG
- EMACHT
- DA MUSST ICH
- IMMER SAGEN
- OB TR
- RICHTIG RUM
- ODER VERKEHR
- T RUM STEHT
- ODER SO
- HA DA HAM SE
- MIR LAUTER
- ERS
- GEZEIGT
- UND MAL MARS
- RECHTS RUM

116

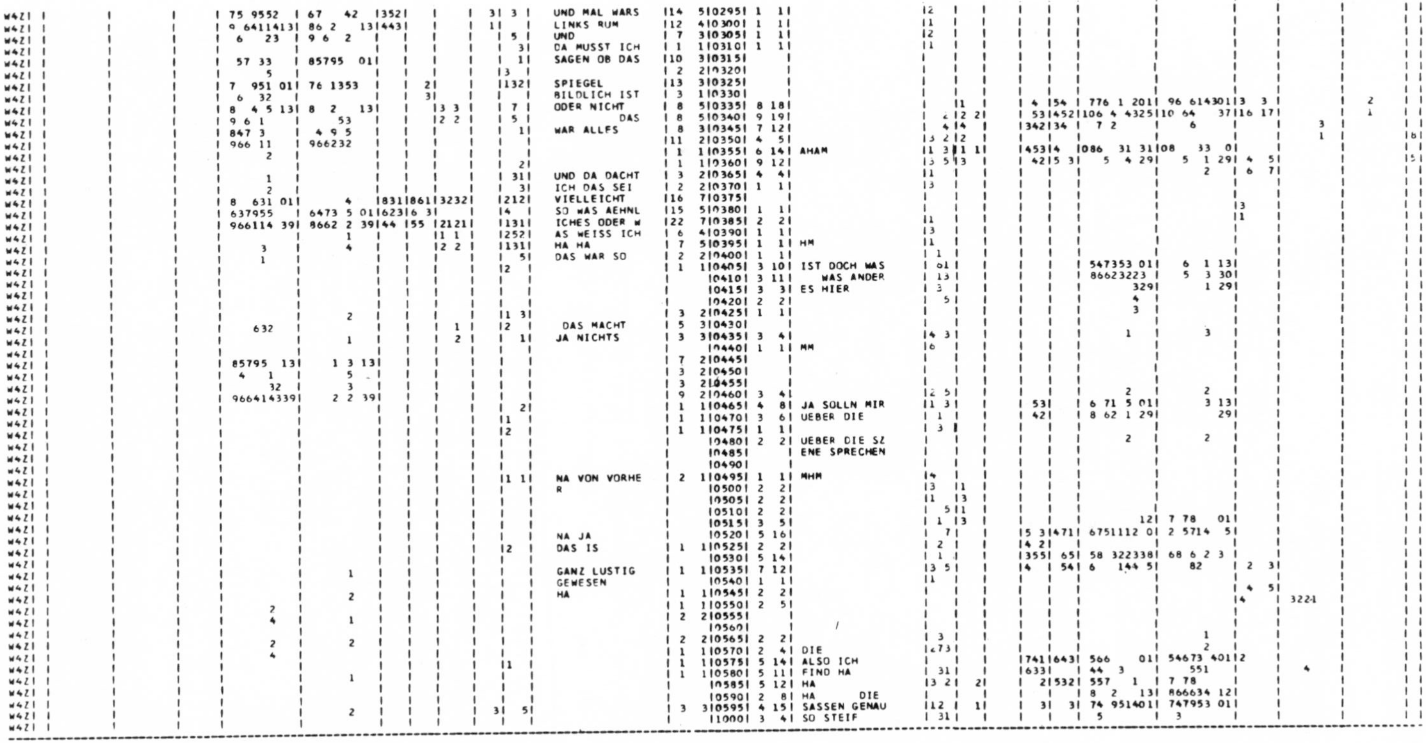

FIG. 4.3   Data matrix resulting from a time-series-notation of nonverbal and verbal behavior of two interlocutors for a time period of 1 minute. From "A Unified Approach to the Investigation of Nonverbal and Verbal Behavior in Communication Research" by S. Frey, H. P. Hirsbrunner, A. Florin, W. Daw, and R. Crawford. In W. Doise and S. Moscovici (Eds.), *Current Issues in European Social Psychology*. Cambridge, England: Cambridge University Press, 1983. Reprinted by permission.

different modes of movement. We see that the male subject (B) initiates and terminates his movement sequences quite abruptly, while the movement behavior of the woman (A) shows high fluidity. This can be seen by the serial arrangement of the cluster of entries. The movement activity of the male is structured into about nine abrupt bursts of complex movement, each lasting for only 2 to 3 seconds. In contrast, the female subject's data entries are far less distinctly structured. Although she has instances of high movement-complexity, too, (e.g., at the time-marks "0240" or "0380"), the clusters extend over larger areas of time and are more blurred in their outlines, indicating that movement activity flows more smoothly.

The differences in the rhythmical structure of movement are mirrored in the speech activity. As can be seen from the matrix, B's verbal utterances are quite short in duration with relatively long time intervals between successive utterances, whereas each of subjects A's verbal utterances covers a comparatively long time span and — at least during the first 40 seconds of the conversation — follows each other in rapid succession. This strongly suggests that speech and movement are closely interrelated, and, in fact, as is obvious from the matrix, phases of movement tend to coincide with phases of verbal utterances. Yet there are also some exceptions. Each subject shows movement when there is no speech and speech when there is no movement. To examine these exceptions in detail, it would be necessary to look up the exact code designations represented by the entries. Then we could determine the particular paths of movement and find out what they have in common in order to get an initial impression as to their function, e.g., "back-channel responses," "interruptions," "attempts to take the floor," etc. This, however, cannot be achieved simply by a visual inspection of the data matrix.

Yet there remain a number of other questions that can be answered by direct inspection of the data matrix. Thus, a comparison of the entries for the right and left hand shows that in this behavioral sample there was no lateral dominance of hand activity for either of the two subjects: In most cases, if one hand moves, the other moves, too. The differential degree to which the different parts of the body engage in the total movement activity is also evident. In this dyad, the rank order seems to be very similar for both subjects: The head is by far the most active part of the body, followed by the hands, with legs and feet showing the least amount of movement activity.

PARAMETER FORMATION FROM MULTIPLE TIME SERIES

Relationships that emerge from a visual inspection of the data matrix must, of course, be further investigated and substantiated by systematic quantitative analysis. To do this, it is necessary to define, on the basis of the coded data, the parameters that are to function as the dependent variables in a particular study. These parameters may be defined with reference to a single data string representing the behavioral variation in one particular coding dimension. But, it is also possible for a parameter to incorporate a great variety of behavioral features represented in different coding dimensions. This is possible because the various data strings representing the interlocutors' complex behavioral pattern are all connected by a common time code. Thus, by integrating the information available from different data strings into a common data matrix, the time-series approach opens the way for a large-scale quantitative analysis of the dyadic interaction with virtually unlimited possibilities for the definition and quantification of behavioral parameters.

Each parameter derived from the data matrix captures a particular aspect or describes a certain characteristic of the complex behavioral stream. Due to the richness of the information available from the data matrices, the definition of these parameters can vary widely in complexity. Thus, depending on the questions being asked in a particular study, the investigator might want to measure a set of parameters as global as, for instance, the amount of verbal and nonverbal activity in an entire dyad during a given observation period, the complexity of the interlocutors' hand movement, the lateral dominance of right-hand activity over left-hand activity, the symmetry in the interlocutors' positional alignment, the disparity between verbal and nonverbal activity, the immediacy of the interactive response, the degree of simultaneous activity or inactivity, the degree to which speech or movement activity predominantes or underscores the partner's activity, the rapidity with which an initial predominance disappears or further increases as time passes, etc. Besides such complex parameters, very specific behavioral aspects might be of interest, e.g., the size of the vertical hand movement, closure of the arms at a given moment, the degree to which an interlocutor turns his head away from the partner, the frequency of trunk movements, the percentage of time an interlocutor holds his head higher than his partner, etc. Or the investigator might want to monitor the occurrence of a wide variety of very specific events whose definition can assume any complexity, from a simple head nod or shoulder shrug, to a more complicated hand movement consisting, for example, of a simultaneous lifting, opening, and upward turning of both hands, or to highly complex verbal/nonverbal patterns, involving a specific sequence of changes in all coding dimensions.

The data needed for the quantification of such parameters can be generated directly from the data matrix. For an easy and efficient data management a comprehensive software system has been developed, designed for use with a Tektronix 4050-Series GCS or 6130 Graphic Work Station. It permits parameter formation in direct interaction with the computer and offers a multitude of options for subsequent graphic and quantitative analysis of the information provided in the data matrix. Figure 4.4 gives an example of how

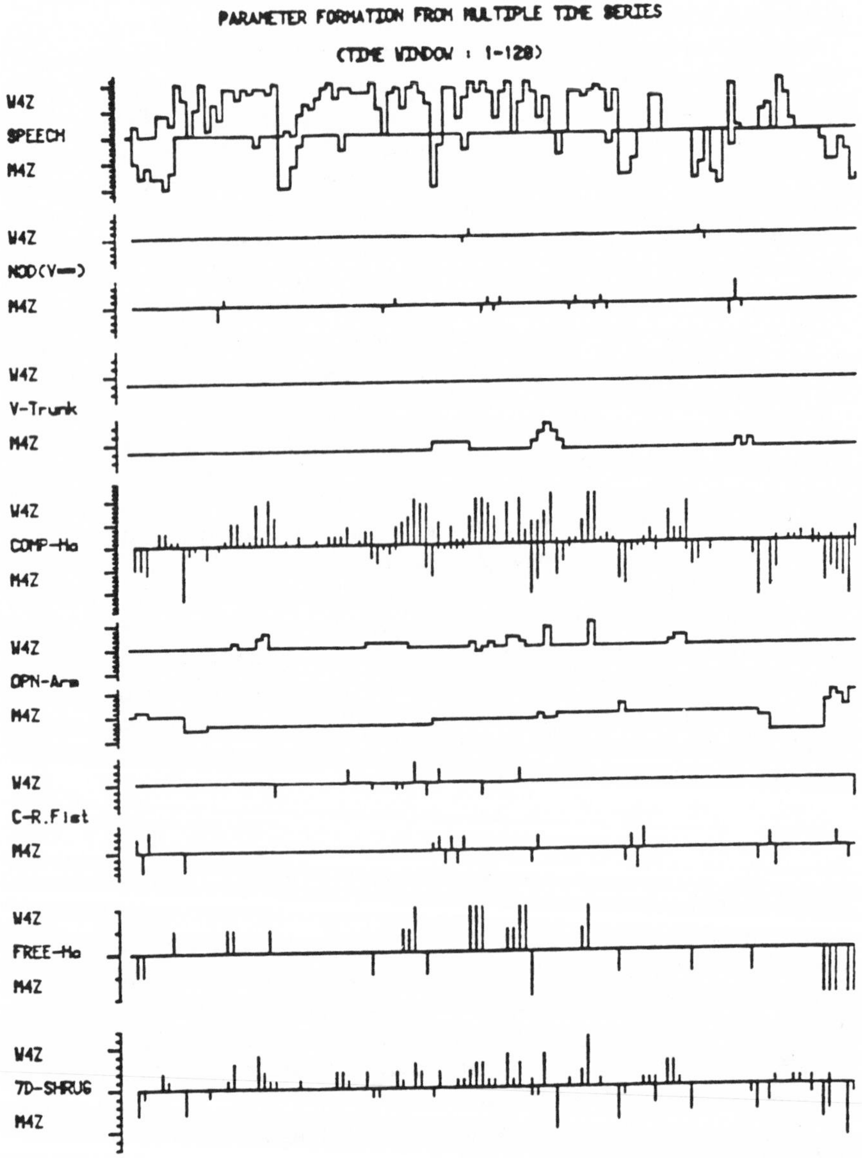

FIG. 4.4 Example of raw data strings generated from the data matrix for the purpose of subsequent graphic and quantitative analysis. The data strings represent, for each of the two interlocutors, the time-series of momentary values for eight behavioral aspects, of varying complexity. From "*Die nonverbale Kommunikation*" by S. Frey. Stuttgart, West Germany: Standard Elektrik Lorenz-Foundation, 1984. Reprinted by permission.

the system can be used to create, at the investigator's discretion, raw data strings that provide information about the temporal organization of any specific or global behavioral characteristic the investigator wishes to analyze. The data were compiled from the matrix and describe, for a time period of 1 minute, the intra and interindividual organization of the interlocutors' activity for eight behavioral characteristics. Time is displayed horizontally, from left to right, all 16 curves refer to the same time scale. The eight behavioral aspects extracted from the data matrix are stacked one above the other, with the data of the female interlocutor (ID: W4Z) being displayed always in the upper part and the data of the male interlocutor (M4Z) in the lower part of each graph. Each curve portrays the actual data strings as they were extracted from the data matrix for subsequent quantitative analysis.

The curve at the top of the graph [SPEECH] visualizes the temporal organization of the subjects' vocal activity, the vertical axis representing the number of phonemes uttered in a half-second interval. The curves are inverted against each other, so that values near the center line indicate low speech activity for both subjects. The second set of two curves NOD (V = =) shows, for each interlocutor, at what times head nods were displayed. Head nods were defined not simply as vertical movements of the head, but more specifically as a head movement involving displacement in only the vertical dimension. This definition accounts for the fact that as soon as there is a simultaneous displacement in the horizontal and/or lateral dimension, we no longer conceive a vertical head movement as a "head nod." The program, therefore, commands a check of all three dimensions into which head position is coded and lists only those types of head movement that suit this specific definition. The direction in which the head nod started is reflected in the vertical line going either up or down; the length of the vertical lines represents the size of the displacement. As long as the lines go in the horizontal direction, no head nod occurred. The third set of two lines [V-Trunk] describes, for each interlocutor, the postural pattern of the trunk in the forward/backward dimension. The vertical axes represent, from bottom to top, the seven positions discriminated in this dimension, from leaning way back (bottom) to tilting way forward (top), with the middle of the axes representing the upright position. The fourth curves [COMP-Ha] refer to the complexity of the subjects' hand movements, describing, for each interlocutor and for each point in time, how many of 14 coding dimensions (seven for each hand) were simultaneously active. The next two lines [OPN-Arm] give the horizontal distance between the hands, indicating when and to what degree the arms of each interlocutor were crossed or opened. The middle of the vertical axes represents a configuration in which the hands are horizontally located at the same place, if the arms cross the curve is below, and if they open the curve is above. The sixth curve-set [C-R.Fist] checks the movements of the right hand for instances of opening and closing. The vertical axes represent the size of the movement by which the hand is opened or closed, with the middle representing "no change." If the hand was opened the line goes up and if closed the line goes down. The seventh curve [FREE-Ha] shows the instances when both hands touch some part of the body or the surroundings (curve at the center), when just one hand is touching (W4Z: one unit above center; M4Z one unit below center), or when both hands are free (two units above or below center). The eighth curve [7D-Shrug] monitors the interlocutors' behavior for the occurrence of a specific movement pattern, a "head–arms–hands–shrug," consisting of a sideways tilt of the head with a simultaneous lifting and opening of both arms and an upside turn of the palms. This curve shows, for each subject, the number of dimensions that are moved according to the directional characteristics defining this movement pattern. It thus indicates, at each point in time, the degree to which the actual movement behavior displayed by each subject approximates the specific movement pattern of interest. If the curve is at the bottom, none of the seven dimensions defining that movement meet the conditions. The vertical lines are of maximum length (W4Z: upward; M4Z: downward) when all conditions are met.

QUANTITATIVE ANALYSIS OF RAW DATA STRINGS: AN EXAMPLE FROM DOCTOR–PATIENT INTERACTION

The data strings compiled from a matrix provide the raw material for the subsequent quantitative analysis into the effects independent variables exert upon the interlocutors' behavior and upon the interactive organization. In order to illustrate how this procedure works we here analyze the interactive organization of four data strings that represent the time pattern of vertical head posture displayed in two dyadic interactions. The example was taken from Frey, Jorns, and Daw (1980), who studied doctor–patient interaction in an attempt to identify nonverbal indicators of recovery from depression. To this end, the nonverbal behavior of 15 depressed patients and their therapists was analyzed in two interview conditions. The first interview took place when the patient was in a severely depressed state, the second shortly before discharge. One particularily interesting finding emerging from their analysis of 30 doctor–patient interactions was that the doctors' perception of the patient as being depressed appeared to be mirrored in the doctors' own vertical head positioning. In the first interview, when the patients were considered severely depressed, the doctors systematically held their heads in an even lower position than did the patients. In the second interview, when doctors were conversing with a patient considered to be recovered, they positioned their heads at a significantly higher level.

The Structure of the Raw Data

Fig. 4.5 gives a graphic illustration of this phenomenon for the case of a patient who had been classified by the therapist as "highly depressed" in the first interview, and as "completely recovered" in the second. The graphs contain the time series of vertical head postures generated from the data matrix for both patient and therapist for the first 3 minutes of each interview. The horizontal axis represents time, each picture covers the first 3 minutes of the interview. The vertical axis represents the interlocutors' head postures, the upper half refers to those of the patient, the lower half to those of the doctor. The curves are inverted against each other, so that values near the center indicate, for both interlocutors, a strong upward tilt of the head.

A comparison of the postural patterns depicted in Fig. 4.5 shows that there were postures that were relatively stable over time and other postures that tended to be assumed only in transition, in the form of short-lasting deflexions from a preferred, basic posture. Although the posture preferred by the patient is, in the first and in the second interview, the upright "level" head posture, the doctor showed a clear preference for this posture only in the second interview. In the first interview, when the patient was classified as being in a highly depressed state, the doctor assumed two stable postures, the upright "level" and the "slightly lowered" head posture. The curves also show an important difference with respect to the short-lasting postures: In the first interview there were nine incidents in which the doctor held his head in a strongly lowered position, whereas the patient did not show this position at

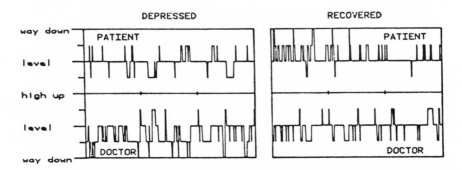

FIG. 4.5   Time-series of vertical head posture of doctor and patient in an interview when the patient was in a highly depressed state, and in an interview when the patient was fully recovered. Time is shown on the horizontal axis. Each graph covers the first 3 minutes of the interview. The postural values for the patient are represented in the upper half of each display; those of the interviewing therapist are shown in the lower half of each display. The curves are inverted against each other; values near the horizontal axis indicate, for both subjects, a strong upward tilt of the head.

TABLE 4.2
Pattern of Vertical Head Posture Displayed by Each Interlocutor.

	Depressed		Recovered	
Parameters	Patient	Doctor	Patient	Doctor
Usage of repertoire	24.3 %ot	39.6 %ot	26.4 %ot	28.1 %ot
Postural stability	5.4 sec	3.6 sec	2.5 sec	3.7 sec
Basic posture	0	− 1	0	0
Inclination	0.05 s.u.	− 0.55 s.u.	− 0.21 s.u.	− 0.09 s.u.
Postural drift	0.00 u/m	0.13 u/m	0.15 u/m	0.13 u/m
Usage of posture				
Head Raised	12.2 %ot	4.2 %ot	1.4 %ot	6.7 %ot
High up	0.0 %ot	0.0 %ot	0.0 %ot	0.0 %ot
Slightly up	12.2 %ot	4.2 %ot	1.4 %ot	6.7 %ot
Level	80.6 %ot	43.9 %ot	78.9 %ot	77.5 %ot
Slightly down	7.2 %ot	44.4 %ot	17.2 %ot	15.8 %ot
Way down	0.0 %ot	7.5 %ot	2.5 %ot	0.0 %ot
Head lowered	7.2 %ot	51.9 %ot	19.7 %ot	15.8 %ot
Rhythm of recurrence				
Head raised	20.0 sec	30.0 sec	60.0 sec	20.0 sec
High up	—	—	—	—
Slightly up	20.0 sec	30.0 sec	60.0 sec	20.0 sec
Level	7.5 sec	6.2 sec	5.1 sec	6.2 sec
Slightly down	12.9 sec	5.3 sec	6.0 sec	8.2 sec
Way down	—	15.0 sec	30.0 sec	—
Head lowered	12.9 sec	6.4 sec	5.6 sec	8.2 sec
Postural persistence				
Head raised	2.4 sec	1.3 sec	0.8 sec	1.3 sec
High up	0.0 sec	0.0 sec	0.0 sec	0.0 sec
Slightly up	2.4 sec	1.3 sec	0.8 sec	1.3 sec
Level	6.0 sec	2.7 sec	4.1 sec	4.8 sec
Slightly down	0.9 sec	2.4 sec	1.0 sec	1.3 sec
Way down	0.0 sec	1.1 sec	0.8 sec	0.0 sec
Head lowered	0.9 sec	3.3 sec	1.1 sec	1.3 sec
Postural mobility	12.1 %ot	22.3 %ot	20.3 %ot	16.4 %ot
Rhythm of recurrence	6.2 sec	3.3 sec	4.5 sec	4.4 sec
Movement duration	0.8 sec	0.7 sec	0.9 sec	0.7 sec
Size of upward shift	1.0 s.u.	1.2 s.u.	1.1 s.u.	1.0 s.u.
Size of downward shift	1.0 s.u.	1.0 s.u.	1.2 s.u.	1.0 s.u.
Size of displacement	1.0 s.u.	1.1 s.u.	1.1 s.u.	1.0 s.u.

%ot stands for *percentage of observation time*
sec stands for *seconds*
s.u. stands for *spatial units of displacement*
u/m stands for *spatial units per minute*
Basic posture: 0 represents the *level* head posture
         − 1 represents the *slightly lowered* posture

all. In the second interview, when the patient was considered "completely recovered," these positions also disappeared from the doctor's postural repertoire.

The Quantification of Individual Differences

Table 4.2 shows how the individual differences in the behaviors depicted in Figure 4.5 can be expressed in quantitative terms. The list of parameters presents a detailed account of each subject's postural repertoire, the dynamics involved in its usage, and the behavioral changes observed in the two interview conditions. The parameter USAGE OF REPERTOIRE gives an overall measure of the degree to which the postural repertoire is used. It reaches a maximum of 100% if the subject spends an equal amount of time in each of the 5 possible positions distinguished in the vertical dimension. The minimum is zero, it indicates that the same posture is assumed all the time. POSTURAL STABILITY measures the average period of time the head is held in a certain position, BASIC POSTURE is defined as the position occurring most of the time. INCLINATION refers to the average degree to which a head is tilted downward (negative values) or upward (positive values) from the level head position. POSTURAL DRIFT is the slope of the regression line of the time graph, indicating the degree to which a subject's average vertical head posture tended to drift upward (pos. values) or downward (neg. values) as a function of time. USAGE OF POSTURE refers to the percentage of time the head was placed in each of the positions distinguished in the vertical dimension. RHYTHM OF RECURRENCE indicates, for each posture, the average length of the time interval between two successive occurrences of the same posture. POSTURAL PERSISTENCE gives the average durations of each posture. The six parameters following refer to dynamic characteristics of vertical head movement, providing quantitative information about the percentage of time spent in motion (POSTURAL MOBILITY), the temporal organization of movement activity (RHYTHM OF RECURRENCE, MOVEMENT DURATION), and the size and direction of posture shifts (SIZE OF UPWARD SHIFT, SIZE OF DOWNWARD SHIFTS, SIZE OF DISPLACEMENT).

The Postural Pattern Displayed by the Patient

The preceding parameters express, in quantitative terms, the behavioral characteristics visualized in the four curves given in Fig. 4.5. A comparison of the data describing the patient's postural activity when depressed and when recovered shows that the positional repertoire was used only to a very limited extent (USAGE OF REPERTOIRE 24.3 vs. 26.4%), with the BASIC POSTURE being assumed during 80.6% of the observation time in the first interview and during 78.9% in the second. In contrast to commonly held beliefs that would suggest that a depressed patient typically displays a strongly lowered head position, the basic posture this patient assumed was the "Level" head position in both interview conditions. There was even a tendency for the head to be oriented more upward than downward when the patient was depressed (Head Raised: 12.2% time; Head Lowered: 7.2% time) and more downward than upward when the patient was recovered (Head Raised: 1.4% time, Head Lowered 19.7% time). This patient's tendency to position the head upward rather than downward with depression is additionally stressed by the lack of any POSTURAL DRIFT in the first interview, as well as by the fact that the increased USAGE of the high posture in depression is not due to a more frequent occurrence of a raised head, but to its higher persistence (RECURRENCE: Head Raised every 20.0 sec; Head Lowered every 12.9 sec; PERSISTENCE: Head Raised for 2.4 sec; Head Lowered for 0.9 sec).

The tendency to position the head more downward than upward with recovery is more equivocal: On the one hand, there is a positive POSTURAL DRIFT indicating that the patient's lowered head position drifted upward as a function of time (0.15 spatial units per minute). On the other hand, the predominance of the downward posture in recovery is additionally emphasized by the occurrence of a number of "way-downward-postures," a posture in which the head is bent downward to a degree that the chin almost touches the chest. As Fig. 4.5 shows at a glance, this posture did not occur at all during depression but was displayed during recovery to such an extent that it alone accounted for a larger proportion of time than did all instances of a raised head posture (Way down: 2.5% of the time; Head Raised: 1.4% of the time).

The Postural Pattern Displayed by the Therapist

The type of vertical head behaviors one would expect the depressed patient to display are more readily identifiable in the postural pattern displayed by the therapist. In contrast to the patient, the therapist assumed a lower head posture when the patient was depressed and distinctly raised his head when the patient was recovered (BASIC POSTURE: -1 versus 0; INCLINATION: -0.55 versus -0.09). This difference extends also to the occurrence of the "way-downward-postures" commonly held to be highly characteristic of depressed patients: When the patient was in a depressed state, the doctor displayed these postures about four times per minute (RECURRENCE: 15.0 sec; PERSISTENCE: 1.1 sec; USAGE: 7.5% time). When the patient was considered recovered these postures completely disappeared from the doctor's repertoire as did the previously strong preference for the "Slightly Lowered" head position, whose USAGE was reduced from 44.4% of the time to 15.8% of the time in favor of the "Level" head posture whose USAGE increased from 43.9% of the time to 77.5% of the time. The POSTURAL

DRIFT measured during the first interview remained at the same level in the second (.13 spatial units per minute). This indicates that the doctor's whole posture pattern shifted to a higher level of vertical head positioning, without affecting his tendency to hold the head in a lower position at the beginning of the interview and to slowly shift his head upward during the course of the interview.

Interactive Organization of Postural Dynamics in the Dyad

Because the behavioral data obtained from the two interlocutors are connected by a common time code, it is possible to relate each subject's head posture to the posture displayed by the partner. One way to study this relation is to add up the interlocutor's momentary postural values to produce a summation curve that represents the interactive postural configuration (IPC) for the dyad as a whole. This new data string can then be analyzed to give a refined picture of the interactive organization of the dyad's postural pattern and of the dynamics involved in its change. Figures 4.6a and 4.6b illustrate this procedure for the data given in Fig. 4.5. The diagrams in each figure contain graphic/quantitative information about: (a) the temporal pattern of activity phases and rest periods (Upper Part), (b) the organization of the interactive postural configuration (Center), (c) the dynamics inherent in turn-taking (Lower Part). Figure 4.6a gives the data for the first interview, Fig. 4.6b gives those for the second. Time is displayed horizontally, from left to right. All three graphs on each diagram refer to the same time scale. The time window chosen in this example is "1–360" (marked below graph title), indicating that the first 360 half seconds (3 min) of the conversation were analyzed. The time scale has marks at 1-minute intervals (beneath upper graph). At the right side of each diagram one finds a listing of behavioral measures describing some characteristics of the interactive organization of vertical head posture in the dyad. To avoid a visual overload of the graph, the listing contains information for only 22 of the 44 parameters that are routinely calculated for each postural dimension extracted from the data matrix. The complete listing of the behavioral aspects that were measured in connection with the analysis given in Figures 4.6a and 4.6b can be found in Table 4.3.

The Temporal Pattern of Activity Phases and Rest Periods

Legend. The upper graph represents the on–off pattern of activity phases and rest periods in the dyad as whole. Vertical bars indicate, in half-second intervals, that either one or both subjects displayed vertical head

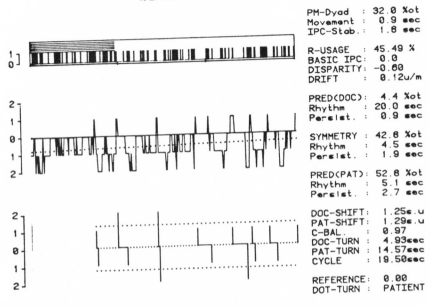

INTERACTIVE ORGANIZATION OF POSTURAL DYNAMICS IN A DYAD
(DEPRESSED COND., 1-360)

PM-Dyad	: 32.0 %ot
Movement	: 0.9 sec
IPC-Stab.	: 1.8 sec
R-USAGE	: 45.49 %
BASIC IPC	: 0.0
DISPARITY	: -0.60
DRIFT	: 0.12u/m
PRED(DOC)	: 4.4 %ot
Rhythm	: 20.0 sec
Persist.	: 0.9 sec
SYMMETRY	: 42.8 %ot
Rhythm	: 4.5 sec
Persist.	: 1.9 sec
PRED(PAT)	: 52.8 %ot
Rhythm	: 5.1 sec
Persist.	: 2.7 sec
DOC-SHIFT	: 1.25s.u
PAT-SHIFT	: 1.29s.u
C-BAL.	: 0.97
DOC-TURN	: 4.93sec
PAT-TURN	: 14.57sec
CYCLE	: 19.50sec
REFERENCE	: 0.00
DOT-TURN	: PATIENT

FIG. 4.6a   Interactive organization of vertical head posture of doctor and patient in the depressed condition. The upper diagram shows the on-off pattern of vertical head movement in the dyad as a whole, the middle diagram gives the time-series of the interactive postural configuration (IPC), and the lower diagram shows the dynamics inherent in turn-taking. To the right, one finds a partial listing of the parameters calculated for the quantification of the behavioral characteristics depicted in the three graphs (for a complete listing of the parameters, see Table 4.3).

movement. As long as no movement occurs, no vertical line is drawn. The section marked by horizontal lines portrays the degree of overall postural mobility, the remaining "white" section is the percentage of time when no vertical head movements were displayed.

Quantitative information about the dyad's postural mobility, the average duration of a movement phase, and the average time period a given interactive postural configuration lasted is provided by the top three parameters on the right side of the graph. "PM-Dyad" is the amount of time the dyad spent in motion expressed as percentage of the total observation time, "Movement" gives the average duration of a movement phase, "IPC-Stab," the average duration of an interactive postural configuration before it was changed. Additional information about the interactive organization of the dyads' activity phases and rest periods is given in Table 4.3 where the overall postural activity is broken down into four types of dyadic configuration: SIMULTANE-

INTERACTIVE ORGANIZATION OF POSTURAL DYNAMICS IN A DYAD

(RECOVERED COND., 1-360)

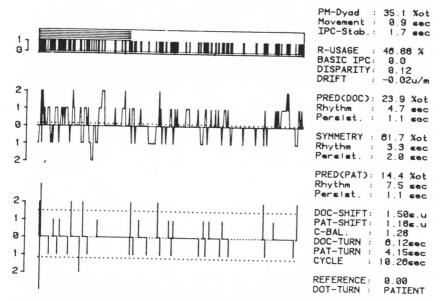

```
PM-Dyad   : 35.1 %ot
Movement  :  0.9 sec
IPC-Stab. :  1.7 sec

R-USAGE   : 46.88 %
BASIC IPC:  0.0
DISPARITY:  0.12
DRIFT     : -0.02u/m

PRED(DOC): 23.9 %ot
Rhythm    :  4.7 sec
Persist.  :  1.1 sec

SYMMETRY  : 61.7 %ot
Rhythm    :  3.3 sec
Persist.  :  2.0 sec

PRED(PAT): 14.4 %ot
Rhythm    :  7.5 sec
Persist.  :  1.1 sec

DOC-SHIFT:  1.50s.u
PAT-SHIFT:  1.18s.u
C-BAL.    :  1.28
DOC-TURN  :  6.12sec
PAT-TURN  :  4.15sec
CYCLE     : 10.26sec

REFERENCE:  0.00
DOT-TURN  :  PATIENT
```

FIG. 4.6b   Interactive organization of vertical head posture of doctor and patient in the recovered condition. The upper diagram shows the on–off pattern of vertical head movement in the dyad as a whole, the middle diagram gives the time-series of the interactive postural configuration (IPC), and the lower diagram shows the dynamics inherent in turn-taking. To the right, one finds a partial listing of the parameters calculated for the quantification of the behavioral characteristics depicted in the three graphs (for a complete listing of the parameters, see Table 4.3).

OUS ACTIVITY (Type 1), SIMULTANEOUS INACTIVITY (Type 2), LONE ACTIVITY OF DOCTOR (Type 3), and LONE ACTIVITY OF PATIENT (Type 4). For each type of activity, calculations were made indicating the percentage of total observation time (Portion of Time Spent in Type of Activity), the length of the time period between two successive occurrences (Rhythm of Recurrence), and their average duration (Persistence).

Content of graph.   A comparison of the information given in Fig. 4.6a and 4.6b shows that the dyad's overall activity was of remarkable constancy both in depression and recovery. When the patient was recovered, there was only a small increase in the overall postural mobility (32.0% time vs. 35.1% time), and almost no difference in the temporal structuring of activity phases and rest periods. On the average, IPC's were held for 1.8 sec when the patient was in a depressed state and for 1.7 sec when the patient was recovered.

TABLE 4.3
Interactive Organization of Vertical Head Posture in Two Dyads

Parameters	Depressed	Recovered
Repertoire usage	45.5 %	46.88 %
Stability of IPC	1.8 sec	1.7 sec
Basic IPC	0	0
Degree of Disparity in IPC	− 0.60 s.u.	0.12 s.u.
Postural drift in IPC	0.12 s.u.	− 0.02 s.u.
Interactive alignment		
Symmetry in IPC	42.8 %ot	61.7 %ot
Disparity in IPC	57.2 %ot	38.3 %ot
Percentage time doctor holds head higher	4.4 %ot	23.9 %ot
Percentage time patient holds head higher	52.8 %ot	14.4 %ot
Rhythm of realignment		
Symmetrical IPC assumed every	4.5 sec	3.3 sec
Doctor assumes higher position every	20.0 sec	4.7 sec
Patient assumes higher position every	5.1 sec	7.5 sec
Persistance of IPC		
Symmetrical IPC lasts for a period of	1.9 sec	2.0 sec
Doctor holds head higher for a period of	0.9 sec	1.1 sec
Patient holds head higher for a period of	2.7 sec	1.1 sec
Turn-taking		
Floor possession doctor	25.3 %ot	59.6 %ot
Floor possession patient	74.7 %ot	40.4 %ot
Turn acquisition (full cycle)	19.5 sec	10.3 sec
Turn-tenure of doctor	4.9 sec	6.1 sec
Turn-tenure of patient	14.6 sec	4.2 sec
Shift, initiating turn-acqu. by doctor	1.3 s.u.	1.5 s.u.
Shift, initiating turn-acqu. by patient	1.3 s.u.	1.2 s.u.
Postural distance during doctor's turn	− 0.2 s.u.	− 0.5 s.u.
Postural distance during patient's turn	− 0.8 s.u.	− 0.4 s.u.
R-latency before doctor takes turn	0.7 sec	0.9 sec
R-latency before patient takes turn	1.7 sec	0.7 sec
Doctor's immobility during own turn	0.3 sec	0.1 sec
Patient's immobility during own turn	5.5 sec	1.4 sec
Postural mobility of the dyad	32.0 %ot	35.1 %ot
Rhythm of recurrence	2.7 sec	2.6 sec
Movement period	0.9 sec	0.9 sec
Interactive organization of movement activity		
Portion of Time Spent in Type of Activity		
Type 1: Simultaneous activity	3.1 %ot	1.7 %ot
Type 2: Simultaneous inactivity	68.0 %ot	64.9 %ot
Type 3: Lone activity of doctor	19.2 %ot	14.8 %ot
Type 4: Lone activity of patient	9.8 %ot	18.7 %ot
Rhythm of recurrence of type of activity		
Type 1 occurring every	22.4 sec	35.9 sec
Type 2 occurring every	2.7 sec	2.6 sec

TABLE 4.3 *(Continued)*

Parameters	Depressed	Recovered
Type 3 occurring every	3.6 sec	4.7 sec
Type 4 occurring every	7.5 sec	4.6 sec
Persistance of type of activity		
Type 1 lasted for	0.7 sec	0.6 sec
Type 2 lasted for	1.8 sec	1.7 sec
Type 3 lasted for	0.7 sec	0.7 sec
Type 4 lasted for	0.7 sec	0.9 sec

Movements lasted for the same period of time (0.9 sec) and occurred at nearly the same rate in both interview conditions (every 2.7 sec vs. every 2.6 sec). A look at the additional information given in Table 4.3 reveals, however, that behind this seemingly stable performance of the dyad as a whole, there were major changes in the way the interlocutors' movement was interactively organized. In the first interview, the lone activity of the doctor accounted for 19.2% of the total observation time, whereas that of the patient lasted for only 9.8%. In the second interview, the doctor's lone activity was reduced to 14.8% of the time, whereas the patient's lone activity almost doubled to 18.7% which suggests that the doctor took the more active part in the interaction when the patient was depressed, and that the patient assumed this role with recovery.

The Dyad's Interactive Postural Configuration (IPC)

Legend.   The diagram in the center of Fig. 4.6a and 4.6b shows how the two interlocutors' vertical head postures were organized with regard to each other. The vertical dimension represents the differences between the momentary head postures assumed by the two subjects. The upper half of the scale indicates, in spatial units, the degree to which the doctor held his head higher than the patient, the lower half the degree to which the patient held his head higher than the doctor. The zero level represents postures in which there is symmetry in vertical head alignment. The dotted line is the regression line of the time graph. Its average distance from the zero level indicates which interlocutor's head was held higher and to what degree. The slope of the regression line indicates the postural drift in IPC, that is, the degree to which postural predominance in vertical head position shifts from one interlocutor to the other as a function of time. If the line is oriented upward, postural disparity gradually shifted toward a predominance of the doctor; if the line is oriented downward, predominance drifted toward the patient. The size of the initial bias in vertical predominance is indicated by the value at which the regression line crosses the vertical axis. Equivalently, the degree of symmetry or disparity toward which the overall IPC is heading can be seen from the vertical value the regression line assumes at the end of the observation period.

Quantitative information about the interactive organization of the interlocutors vertical head postures is given at the right side of the graph. "R-USAGE" represents the degree to which the different IPC's were used. It reaches a maximum of 100% when the interlocutors spent an equal amount of time in each of the IPC's given on the vertical axis, and a minimum of zero if the same IPC was used all the time. "BASIC IPC" is the postural configuration occurring most of the time, with zero representing a symmetrical configuration, positive values a configuration with the doctor holding the head higher, negative values a configuration in which the patient's head is higher. "DISPARITY" measures, in spatial units, the average degree to which interlocutors position their heads at a different height. Positive values indicate the margin by which the doctor held his head higher than the patient, negative values the margin by which the patient's head was higher. The next nine parameters provide information about the temporal organization of predominance and symmetry in the interlocutors' vertical head posture. "PRED(DOC)" shows the percentage of time the doctor held his head higher than the patient, "Rhythm" indicates the average time interval between two successive occurrences of postural predominance, and "Persist." measures their average duration. The six parameters following give the equivalent data for symmetry in vertical head alignment, and for the predominance in the patient's vertical head posture.

Content of graph.   A gross comparison of the dyad's overall IPC-pattern would again suggest that there was little difference in the interactive postural configuration in depression and recovery. REPETOIRE-USAGE increased only slightly from 45.5 to 46.9% with the symmetrical head posture being chosen as the dyad's BASIC IPC in both interviews. A closer look at the details of the interactive organization of the behaviors depicted in Fig. 4.6a and 4.6b reveals, however, that behind this seemingly stable behavioral frame, there was a near complete reversal in the interactive organization of the interlocutors' vertical head postures. When the patient was in a depressed state, there was a pronounced postural disparity in favor of the patient, whose vertical head posture was higher than the doctor's by an average of 0.60 spatial units at every point in time. With recovery, postural disparity was taken over by the doctor who now held his head higher than the patient by a margin of 0.12. The rate of recurrence of predominating head postures showed the same trend. In the first interview, it took 20 seconds, on the average, until the doctor assumed a higher head posture than the patient, and only 4.7 sec in the second interview. For the patient, this tendency was reversed, with a predominant head posture occurring every 5.1 sec in depression and every 7.5 sec with recovery. The persistence of predominating head postures considerably changed with the interview conditions, too. In the first interview, the patient's predominating head postures lasted three times as long as did those of the doctor (2.7 sec vs. 0.9 sec), a difference that completely disappeared with the patient's recovery (1.1 sec both). The most obvious changes concerned, however, the overall predominance of the interlocutors' IPC: When the patient was depressed, the doctor displayed a predominating head posture during less than 10% of the time the patient did (4.4% time vs. 52.8% time). With recovery, the doctor's postural predominance increased from 4.4% of the time to 23.9% of the time, whereas the patient's predominance decreased from 52.8% of the time to 14.4% of the time.

Interestingly, the difference described here did not develop during the course of the interview but existed right from the start of the interaction. As the positive postural drift in the first interview indicates, the disparity in favor of the patient was particularily pronounced at the beginning of the interaction, diminishing rather than increasing as time went on (by a ratio of .12 spatial units per minute). The reversed disparity found in the second interview was also there right from the start, and again there was a tendency toward decreases rather than increases as a function of time (by a ratio of .02 spatial units per minute). It is worthwhile, however, to note that the behavioral changes taking place with the patient's recovery ultimately resulted in a more balanced interactive postural configuration. This is indicated by the lower absolute value of the disparity measure (.60 vs. .12), and by the better counterbalance between the proportions of total postural predominance, as well as in the reduction of the differences between the interlocutors in both frequency and persistence of postural predominance. It is also directly expressed in the changes found with regard to symmetrical postures. As a comparison of Fig. 4.6a and 4.6b shows, symmetrical IPCs were assumed more often in the second interview (every 3.3 sec vs. every 4.5 sec), and with higher persistence (2.0 sec vs. 1.9 sec). The percentage of the time in which symmetrical head postures were displayed thus increased from 42.8% of the time in the first interview to 61.7% of the time in the second, with the occurrence of disparate postures being reduced from 57.2 to 38.3% of the time.

The Dynamics Inherent in Postural Turn-Taking

Legend. The lower diagram in Fig. 4.6a and 4.6b provides, together with the data given under the heading TURN-TAKING in Table 4.3, a detailed and multifaceted picture about the temporal organization of postural turn-taking. Within the context of the behavior investigated here, a turn begins the moment an interlocutor raises his head to a higher position than his partner's and ends when the other interlocutor assumes the higher position. The moments of turn-taking are visualized by the vertical lines, with the beginning of the doctor's turn being indicated by an upward line, the beginning of the patient's turn by a downward line. The size of the displacement initiating an exchange of the turn is indicated by the length of the vertical lines, with the average size of the displacements at the moment of turn-acquisition being represented by dotted lines. The duration of each turn is visualized at the zero level, with the solid parts of the line representing the duration of the doctors' turns, the dotted parts the duration of the patient's turns. The completion of an entire TURN-CYCLE, that is, the time period between two successive turn acquisitions by the same interlocutor, is given by the distance between two vertical lines oriented in the same direction (either upward or downward).

Part of the quantitative information about the organization of postural turn-taking is given at the right-hand side of the diagram. The complete set of parameters calculated for each dyad is given under the heading TURN-TAKING in Table 4.3. FLOOR POSSESSION is the percentage of the total observation time an interlocutor possesses the turn. TURN-TENURE is the average duration of an interlocutor's turn. TURN-CYCLE is the average time period between the beginnings of two successive turns of the same interlocutor. The average size of the displacement initiating an exchange of turn is represented by the parameter SHIFT. The average size of the difference between the vertical head position subjects display during a turn is given by the parameter POSTURAL DISTANCE DURING TURN. RESPONSE-LATENCY refers to the period of time both subjects are at rest before turns are exchanged. IMMOBILITY measures the average period of time an interlocutor remains immobile during his own turn.

Content of graph.   The information given in Fig. 4.6a and 4.6b shows that with recovery, turn-taking became more lively and turn-tenure more balanced. When the patient was in a depressed state, it took the dyad 19.50 seconds, in the average, to pass a turn-cycle, with the patient holding on to the floor for about 75%, the doctor for about 25% of each cycle (14.57 sec vs. 4.93 sec). When the patient was recovered, a TURN-CYCLE was completed every 10.26 seconds, with a ratio of FLOOR POSSESSION of about 40 to 60% in favor of the doctor (4.15 sec vs. 6.12 sec). A closer look at the size of the displacement initiating each interlocutor's turn suggests that there was a tendency for the doctor to be less assertive with regard to floor acquisition when the patient was in a depressed state than when the patient was recovered. In the first interview the average size of the displacement initiating a turn-acquisition by the doctor was lower than the displacement initiating the patient's turn (C-Bal: 0.97). In the second interview this tendency was reversed (C-Bal: 1.28), with the size of the displacement increasing when the doctor acquired the turn and decreasing when the patient did. The assumption that there was a tendency of the doctor to yield FLOOR POSSESSION when the patient was in a depressed state, and to claim FLOOR POSSES-

SION when the patient was recovered, is additionally supported by the fact that the average postural distance during the doctor's turn was more pronounced when the patient was recovered than when depressed (0.5 spatial units vs. 0.2 spatial units), with the opposite taking place when the patient had the turn (0.4 s.u. vs. 0.8 s.u.).

Further Steps in the Analysis

The parameters discussed here illustrate the vast possibilities time-series matrices offer in the sophisticated analysis of complex behavior patterns. The graphic and quantitative procedures applied here to the analysis of the interactive organization of vertical head posture can, of course, be equally applied to the multitude of other behavioral aspects that can be generated from the data matrix (cf. page 118ff). If such analyses are done within the framework of any conventional experimental design (cf. Campbell, 1957; Campbell & Stanley, 1963; Cook & Campbell, 1979), the parameters can be further treated by the usual inference-statistical procedures, which permit a large-scale screening of the systematic effects the independent variables exert upon the interlocutors' behavior. The present example has, in fact, been taken from a study investigating the behavioral interaction in a total of 30 dyads, involving 15 depressed patients and 10 therapists. Within the context of this research, vertical head posture was just one (and not even the most salient) aspect of the behaviors monitored in connection with the attempt to identify nonverbal indicators of recovery from depression. The application of standard inference-statistical procedures was found to be highly instrumental in the quick identification of the strongest contingencies existing between the multiple dependent variables representing the interlocutors' complex nonverbal behavior and the clinical data describing the patients' psychiatric status. In this way, it was possible not only to unravel the intricacies of the behavioral organization in specific doctor–patient interactions, but also to identify those aspects of behavior which, on a more general level, indicate recovery from depression. The details of this work were reported separately (Fisch, Frey & Hirsbrunner, 1983).

CONCLUDING REMARKS

During the recent rush to study the nonverbal element in communication, it has become almost an obsession among behavioral scientists to proclaim body movement preeminently important in the understanding of the human social interaction. And, in fact, research in this area has never suffered from a lack of awareness of the importance of the nonverbal. As Davis (1972) has noted:

> The list of those who have written about expressive movement and nonverbal communication since 1872 reads like a Who's Who in the behavioral sciences; yet writers still defend the relevance of such study or introduce the subject as if it were esoteric and unheard of. It is as if a great many serious behavioral scientists have shown a fleeting interest in body movement and then gone on. (p. 2)

In view of the formidable problems inherent in this field of research, this hegira of serious behavioral scientists is very understandable. The movement behavior we encounter in social interaction is very difficult to study because it is an extremely variable and complex phenomenon, probably no less complex than the internal states and subtle communicative processes it is believed to mirror.

With the advent of film and video, it has become possible to provide a highly detailed permanent record of a subject's complex movement behavior. Until now, however, there has been little success in solving the problem of how to transcribe the information on visible movement from film or video tape into a data protocol. Researchers have usually shied away from detailed behavior description by devising coding schemes that confined the universe of visually discriminable movement patterns into a few global categories. But, in doing this, they have forced the coder to produce a very distorted and blurred picture of spontaneous movement activity. Clearly, progress in nonverbal communication cannot be expected from a research strategy that ignores most of the behavioral differences it sets out to explain. In order to be able to advance our knowledge in this field, the problems inherent in raw data collection must first be solved.

We have shown here that the same principle of time-series notation already used in speech transcription for thousands of years can also be used in the transcription of movement behavior. Data protocols based on this coding principle provide a highly detailed and accurate account of complex spontaneous movement activity and they can be directly related to speech. The data matrices so obtained open up so many possibilities for quantification of behavioral features of widely varying complexity that the limits of behavioral quantification and analysis are more likely to be found in the limits of the equipment used for data processing than in the available information.

Until recently, data processing has had to be done on large computers whose limitations necessitated a lengthy training period for learning how to manage the data. This constituted a considerable hinderance to rapid analysis and even limited the efficient usage of the vast amount of behavioral information available from data matrices. With the recent rapid developments in computer technology, this picture has changed dramatically. The data can now be managed completely on desk-top computers and data handling is now not much more difficult than playing a record or a video tape. More importantly, this new technology gives the investigator direct access to the data matrices so that behavioral patterns can be examined in direct dialogue with the computer. This allows the investigator great freedom in following a trail of behavioral clues in order to uncover previously unnoticed relationships.

In turn, this opens the way to the development of more efficient research strategies when dealing with complex behavioral patterns. With all the behavioral information available at his fingertips, the investigator can create, at his own discretion, data strings representing the behavioral characteristics momentarily of interest. These data can then be processed, visualized, and interrelated in a multitude of graphic and quantitative ways in order to study in detail the flow of movement and to make transparent the intra and interindividual organization of the complex behavior displayed in face-to-face interaction.

Our initial explorations into these procedures (Hirsbrunner, Florin, & Frey, 1981) immediately showed that the new technology offers unique possibilities for the investigator to make full use of his inquisitive, imaginative, and investigative potential. The payoff has been so impressive that we have decided to create a comprehensive software system for a BASIC-programmable desk-top computer. This system permits the investigator to do the complete data management in direct dialogue with the computer, including: (a) the compilation and editing of the raw data matrix, (b) the formation and extraction of multiple data strings representing behavioral parameters of widely varying complexity, (c) the graphic analysis of these data strings, (d) the formation of parameters for their quantitative analysis, (e) the inference-statistical evaluation of multiple dependent variables in studies involving a large number of subjects.

The system has been designed for use with a Tektronix 4050-Series GCS or with a 6130 Graphic Work Station. The size of the data matrices the system can handle is virtually unlimited in the temporal dimension. In the behavioral dimensions it can, in its present form, handle up to 216 coding dimensions describing the complex communicative behavior of two interlocutors in four channels:

1. The motor behavior of two interlocutors, coded with the Bernese System for the time-series notation of nonverbal interaction: 55×2 coding dimensions, describing the movement activity of the different parts of the body for two interlocutors.

2. The facial activity coded with the Facial Action Coding System (Ekman & Friesen, 1978): 49×2 coding dimensions that describe the temporal pattern of the activation of the various facial muscles for two interlocutors.

3. The verbal behavior of two interlocutors as given in an alphabetic transcript of the dialogue: 1×2 coding dimensions.

4. The paraverbal behavior of two interlocutors, coded with regard to voice amplitude, intonation contour, and speech rate (sequel-density): 3×2 coding dimensions.

These possibilities open the way for a sophisticated analysis of complex behavior patterns and permit, together with the high descriptive potential of the time-series notation, a large-scale investigation into the communicative process. The number of investigative possibilities being so large, no single investigator will ever be able to use the system's full potential. But he will be able to define on the basis of the vast amount of information available in the data matrices, those behavioral parameters that are of special interest to him. And, whatever parameters the investigator decides to study in his own data, these same parameters can also be assesed in the data matrices of other studies focusing on different aspects of behavior. Thus, it will be possible to pool the information obtained from different studies in order to explore how human communicative behavior varies with independently controlled conditions. In this way, it should be possible to rapidly advance our knowledge of the intricacies of human communication, and, ultimately, to arrive at a better understanding of the human interaction.

ACKNOWLEDGMENTS

Development of the methodology of time-series notation of nonverbal interaction described in this chapter would not have been possible without the extensive support we have received from the Swiss National Science Foundation (Grant Nos. 1.913-0. 73; 1.467-0.76; 1.070-0.79). We gratefully acknowledge their support over the years.

The present chapter has been prepared following an international workshop on the "Times-Series Notation of Nonverbal Interaction" held at the Laboratoire Européen de Psychologie Sociale (LEPS) of the Maison des Sciences de l'Homme in Paris, from Sept. 21 to 24, 1982. The authors would like to thank the Maison des Sciences de l'Homme for their generous financial support and Madame Adriana Touraine for her superb organization of the conference. We would also like to thank the participants in the workshop for their intensive discussions which have been most helpful in clearing up some of the methodological issues addressed in this chapter.

We are very much indebted to Catherine Darnaud, a close collaborator in the past few years, whose critical contribution has done much to shape our work.

REFERENCES

Badler, N. I., & Smoliar, S. W. Digital representations of human movement. *Computing Surveys*, 1979, II, 19–38.

Blurton Jones, N. Characteristics of ethological studies of human behaviour. In N. Blurton Jones (Ed.), *Ethological studies of child behaviour* (pp. 3–33) Cambridge: Cambridge University Press, 1972.

Blurton Jones, N. Categories of child–child interaction. In N. Blurton Jones (Ed.), *Ethological studies of child behaviour* (pp. 97–127). Cambridge: Cambridge University Press, 1972. (b)

Brannigan, C. R., & Humphries, D. A. Human non-verbal behaviour, a means of communication. In N. Blurton Jones (Ed.), *Ethological studies of child behaviour* (pp. 37–64). Cambridge: Cambridge University Press, 1972.

Campbell, D. T. Factors relevant to the validity of experiments in social settings. *Psychological Bulletin, 54,* 1957, 297–312.

Campbell, D. T., & Stanley, J. C. Experimental and quasi-experimental designs for research on teaching. In N. L. Gage (Ed.), *Handbook of research on teaching* (pp. 171–246). Chicago: Rand McNally, 1963.

Condon, W. S. Method of micro-analysis of sound films of behavior. *Behavior Research Methods and Instrumentation,* 1970, 51–54.

Cook, T. D., & Campbell, D. T. *Causation and quasi-experimental design.* Chicago: Rand McNally, 1979.

Cronbach, L. J. Proposals leading to analytic treatment of social perception scores. In R. Tagiuri & L. Petrullo (Eds.), *Person perception and interpersonal behavior* (pp. 353–379). Stanford: University Press, 1958.

Davis, M. *Understanding body movement: An annotated bibliography.* New York: Arno, 1972.

Davis, M. The state of the art: Past and present trends in body movement research. In A. Wolfgang (Ed.), *Nonverbal behavior: Applications and cultural implications.* New York: Academic, 1979.

Ekman, P., & Friesen, W. V. *Facial Action Coding System.* Palo Alto, CA: Consulting Psychologists Press, 1978.

Ekman, P., Friesen, W., & Taussig, T. Vid-R and SCAN: Tools and methods for the automated analysis of visual records. In G. Gerbner, O. Holsti, K. Krippendorf, W. Paisley, & P. Stone (Eds.), *Content analysis.* New York: Wiley, 1969.

Fisch, H. U., Frey, S., & Hirsbrunner, H. P. Nonverbal indicators of recovery from depression. *Journal of Abnormal Psychology,* 1983, 307–318.

Frey, S. The assessment of similarity. In M. von Cranach (Ed.), *Methods of inference from animal to human behavior.* The Hague: Mouton, 1976.

Frey, S. *Die nonverbale Kommunikation.* Stuttgart, West Germany: Standard Elektrik Lorenz-Foundation, 1984.

Frey, S. *Analyzing patterns of behavior in dyadic interaction. A system for the integrated analysis of multiple time series of nonverbal and verbal behavior.* Toronto: Huber, 1986 (in press).

Frey, S., Hirsbrunner, H. P., Florin, A., Daw, W., & Crawford, R. A unified approach to the investigation of nonverbal and verbal behavior in communication research. In S. Moscovici & W. Doise (Eds.), *Current issues in European social psychology* (pp. 143–199). Cambridge: Cambridge University Press, 1983.

Frey, S., Hirsbrunner, H. P., & Jorns, U. Time-Series-Notation: A coding principle for the unified assessment of speech and movement in communication research. In E. W. B. Hess-Lüttich (Ed.), *Multimedial communication: Semiotic problems of its notation* (pp. 30–58). Tübingen: Narr, 1982.

Frey, S., Hirsbrunner, H. P., Pool, J., & Daw, W. Das Berner System zur Untersuchung nonverbaler Interaktion: I. Die Erhebung des Rohdaten-Protokolls. In P. Winkler (Ed.), *Methoden der Analyse von Face-to-Face Situationen* (pp. 203–236). Stuttgart: Metzler, 1981.

Frey, S., Jorns, U., & Daw, W. A systematic description and analysis of nonverbal interaction between doctors and patients in a psychiatric interview. In S. A. Corson (Ed.), *Ethology and nonverbal communication in mental health* (pp. 231–258). New York: Pergamon, 1980.

Frey, S., & Pool, J. *A new approach to the analysis of visible behavior.* Research Reports from the Department of Psychology of the University of Berne, 1976.

Gair, J. W. Alphabet. In *Collier's Encyclopedia* (Vol I, 588–606). New York: Crowell-Collier, 1971.

Galloway, C. M. Teaching and nonverbal behavior. In A. Wolfgang (Ed.), *Nonverbal behavior: Applications and cultural implication* (pp. 197–207). New York: Academic, 1979.

Hirsbrunner, H. P. *Sequel-analysis. Ein zeitgenaues Verfahren zur visuellen Verlaufsanalyse des Sprachsignals.* Doctoral Dissertation, University of Berne, 1980.

Hirsbrunner, H. P. *Reference manual for the sequel analysis module SAM 259.* Research Reports from the Department of Psychology of the University of Berne, 1986.

Hirsbrunner, H. P., Florin, A., & Frey, S. Das Berner System zur Untersuchung nonverbaler Interaktion: II. Die Auswertung von Zeitreihen visuell-auditiver Information. In P. Winkler (Hrsg), *Methoden der Analyse von Face-to-Face Situationen* (pp. 237–268). Stuttgart: Metzler, 1981.

Key, M. R. *Nonverbal communication.* Metuchen, NJ: The Scarecrow Press, 1977.

Leach, G. M. A comparison of the social behaviour of some normal and problem children. In N. Blurton Jones (Ed.), *Ethological studies of child behaviour* (pp. 249–281). London: Cambridge University Press, 1972.

Martin, S. E. Nonalphabetic writing systems: Some observations. In J. M. Kavanaugh & I. G. Mattingly (Eds.), *The relationship between speech and reading.* Cambridge, MIT Press, 1972.

McGrew, W. C. *An ethological study of children's behavior.* London: Academic, 1972.

Siegman, A., & Feldstein, S. *Nonverbal behavior and communication* (Vol. 1). Hillsdale, NJ: Lawrence Erlbaum Associates, 1978.

Smith, P. K., & Connolly, K. Patterns of play and social interaction in pre-school children. In N. Blurton Jones (Ed.), *Ethological studies of child behaviour.* Cambridge: Cambridge University Press, 1972.

III FACIAL AND VISUAL BEHAVIOR

5 Facial Expressions of Emotion: Review of Literature, 1970–1983

Alan J. Fridlund
The University of Pennsylvania

Paul Ekman
University of California, San Francisco

Harriet Oster
The University of Pennsylvania `

Research on facial expressions of emotion has been episodic. The topic flourished from 1920 to 1940, drawing the attention of well-known psychologists, e.g., Allport, Boring, Goodenough, Guilford, Hunt, Klineberg, Landis, Munn, Titchener, and Woodworth. However, the cumulative knowledge was unimpressive. In the opinion of influential reviewers (Bruner & Tagiuri, 1954; Hunt, 1941; Tagiuri, 1968), there were no consistent answers to the most fundamental questions about the accuracy of information provided by facial expressions, their universality and possible innateness, etc. During the next 20 years there were comparatively few studies of facial expression, with the exception of Schlosberg's reports (Schlosberg, 1941, 1952, 1954) that categorical judgments of emotion could be ordered in terms of underlying dimensions.

A number of recent trends have contributed to the resurgence of interest in facial expression. Tomkins (1962, 1963) provided a theoretical rationale for studying the face as a means for learning about personality and emotion. He also showed that observers can obtain very high agreement in judging emotion if the facial expressions are carefully selected to show what he believes are the innate facial affects (Tomkins & McCarter, 1964). Tomkins greatly influenced both Ekman and Izard, helping each of them to plan their initial cross-cultural studies of facial expression. The resulting evidence that there is universality in facial expression rekindled interest in this topic in psychology and anthropology.

The evidence for universals in facial expression not only fits with Tomkins' theory, but also with the newly emerging interest in applying ethological methods and concepts to human behavior. Interested in the biological bases of behavior, human ethologists welcomed evidence of commonalities in social behavior across cultures. Human ethologists provided the first detailed "catalogs" describing naturally occurring facial behavior (Blurton Jones, 1972; Brannigan & Humphries, 1972; Grant, 1969; McGrew, 1972). In recent years, developmental psychologists investigating attachment, mother–infant interaction, and the development of emotion have also begun to study facial expression.

Interest in facial expression also reflects the current popularity of nonverbal communication. Whereas most of the research done under this rubric has focused on hand and body movement, gaze direction, or posture, some studies have included facial measures or have used observer judgment approaches to assess the face.

Within psychophysiology, there is renewed interest in the functioning of physiological systems in emotion, and its relation to facial expressions of emotion. This interest is shown in recent studies that attempt to correlate facial behavior with neural and visceroautonomic responses. Additionally, findings relating to cerebral hemisheric specialization (see Bradshaw & Nettleton, 1981) have triggered a flurry of research concerning hemispheric participation in facial-expression generation, perception, and interpretation.

A number of reviews covered the literature on facial expression up to 1970. Ekman, Friesen, and Ellsworth (1982) reanalyzed many of the experiments conducted from 1914 to 1970. They found, contrary to Bruner and Tagiuri's (1954) assessment, that the data yielded consistent, positive answers to fundamental questions about the language used to describe facial expression, the influence of context on judgments of facial expression, the accuracy of judgments, and similarities across cultures. For other reviews of facial expression see: Charlesworth and Kreutzer (1973) on infants and children; Chevalier-Skolnikoff (1973) and Redican (1975, 1982) on nonhuman primates; Ekman (1973) on cross-cultural comparisons; Izard (1977) on theories of emotion.

We focus primarily on studies since these reviews, substantially updating and expanding the review by Ekman and Oster (1978). We first consider the neuromuscular substrates of facial behavior. We then discuss five topics we deem of major importance, either because of their longstanding theoretical significance (ethological, cross-cultural, developmental, and accuracy studies) or because of recent methodological advances (facial measurement systems). We subsequently consider the influence of facial feedback on emotion and explore the relationships between facial expression and visceroautonomic systems, in the context of theories of emotion. Finally, studies of facial action in psychopathology are reviewed. Rather than providing exhaustive coverage of each area, we summarize exemplary findings, point out gaps in empirical knowledge, and delineate questions for future study.

MECHANISMS FOR THE GENERATION OF FACIAL EXPRESSIONS

Facial expressions are generated by a sublimely complex neuromuscular network that shows close connections with other functions of the central nervous system. It is tempting to regard the facial-expressive apparatus as simply a "dedicated system" specialized for facial displays of emotion. However, it is just as much a "paralinguistic" display system (Fridlund & Gilbert, 1985). The role of the face is underestimated in its involvement not only with (a) production of speech but also (b) eating and drinking (c) regulation of oral and nasal respiration, gustation, and olfaction and (d) protection and lubrication (through lacri- mation) of the eyes. Neuroanatomical and physiological studies point to its critical articulation with many other organismic functions. Thus any complete account of facial action in emotion must include a consideration of other functional properties of facial action. The parsing of emotional from nonemotional facial actions is a thread woven throughout this chapter. Prerequisite is a brief summary of the mechanisms underlying facial action.

What Has Been Found

Both neuromuscular and nonneuromuscular factors contribute to facial expressions.   It is often assumed that facial expressions of emotion result only from neuromuscular activity. In fact, many other factors contribute to facial expression and to the perception of emotion from faces.

Ekman (1978) has distinguished four separate sources of information ("sign vehicles") in the face that are utilized in judgments of facial expressions: (a) "static" sign vehicles, which remain relatively (though not completely) constant; e.g., bony structure, sizes and shapes of features, skin pigmentation; (b) "slow" sign vehicles, which reliably change with age; e.g., bags, sags, pouches, hair distribution, skin blotching, fatty deposits; (c) "rapid" sign vehicles, consisting of muscular movements, changes in facial coloration (blanching or blushing), temperature, sweat production, pupillary reponses, and alteration of gaze or head position; and (d) "artificial" sign vehicles, reflecting cosmesis or facial defects, e.g., eyeglasses, cosmetics, hair removal or supplementation with hairpieces, plastic-surgical repairs, appliances, or scars.

The nonneuromuscular signs are frequently (and all too often erroneously) associated with judgments of emotion or personality type (see work by

Secord and associates reported by Secord, 1958). As is explained later, these differences in static and slow sign systems can interfere with facial measurement, both visible and electromyographic. They can also contaminate substantive research on facial expressions, particularly research concerned with studies of facial asymmetry (see later).

Within the central nervous system, there are multiple pathways controlling facial expression. The neural systems that mediate facial expression are poorly researched and little understood, but it is clear that the neuromuscular component of facial expression has multiple determinants in the central nervous system, at both cortical and subcortical levels. The most important functional distinction is between "voluntary" and "involuntary" facial expressions.

Voluntary actions are apparently controlled by the corticobulbar pathways (pyramidal tracts) that emanate from precentral "motor" cortex. Extrapyramidal influences are thought to mediate involuntary, emotional facial movements, along pathways probably emanating from the globus pallidus, caudate putamen, red nucleus, and midbrain reticular formation.

This "dual control" of facial movement is shown by the finding that individuals suffering from complete paralysis or hemiparesis of voluntary facial movements (as in cerebral vascular accidents damaging cortex, or pseudobulbar palsy, which affects the corticobulbar tracts) may show spontaneous facial expressions — often grossly exaggerated — when emotion is aroused (Tschiassny, 1953).

Conversely, spontaneous emotional expression but not voluntary movement may be affected by subcortical lesions or by parkinsonism (Ford, 1966; Monrad-Krohn, 1924). Involuntary movements of facial muscles (particularly in the perioral and ocular regions) frequently characterize the tardive dyskinesias that occur as extrapyramidal effects in long-term neuroleptic treatment of schizophrenics (Serra & DiRosa, 1975). There may be some overlap between these dual control systems, because in prefrontal lesions there is also a reduction in spontaneous expressions (Kolb & Milner, 1981). The latter findings may, however, reflect the general affective disengagement seen in frontal patients.

A second functional distinction in the pathways mediating facial expression is their contralateral versus ipsalateral control. Clinical findings (mostly from studies of neurological disorders and brain injury) suggest that, like the limb musculature, the facial motoneuron pathways (i.e., those of CN VII, the facial nerve) are largely crossed (indicating contralateral control) for the muscles in the lower face. However, motoneurons innervating some of the ocular and upper-face muscles (e.g., medial and lateral *frontales, corrugator supercilii, orbicularis oculi*) appear to have more ipsalateral representation (Brodal, 1981; Kuypers, 1958; Mueller, 1983). This differential lateralization of motor control is important when considering (a) accuracy of face perception and facial measurement, (b) deceit and dissimulation, (c) spontaneous versus deliberate facial actions, and (d) asymmetries and lateralization in facial expression (extended discussions of each to follow; also see Ekman, 1982b, for discussion of effects of facial nerve surgery).

Studies of lateralization and asymmetry in the generation of facial expressions have shown inconsistent effects that do not support any of the current conceptualizations of cerebral hemispheric function. Following from recent interest in cerebral hemispheric specialization for emotion (Galin, 1974; Geschwind, 1980; Sackeim, Greenberg, Weiman, Gur, Hungsbuhler, & Geschwind, 1982) have come attempts to measure asymmetry and/or laterality in the production of facial expressions (studies of hemispheric involvement in facial perception are considered in the Accuracy section). Hager (1982) and Hager and Ekman (1983) have provided overviews of this research. Three types of studies are representative.

In the first, researchers have attempted to determine whether static sign vehicles, such as bone structure or skin pigmentation, or slow sign vehicles, such as fatty deposits, skin pouches, and skin texture (see Ekman, 1978, and discussion of sign vehicles aforementioned), show asymmetry or laterality (laterality is specified as asymmetry reliably favoring one side across individuals). The study of static and slow sign vehicles has largely been performed by orthodontists, physical anthropologists, and plastic surgeons. In general, the findings show that some degree of facial asymmetry is typical (Gorney & Harries, 1974; Thompson, 1943). Lateralization also seems evident, especially in maxillary (cheek) bone structure and skin surface area. This lateralization favors the left side of the face in childhood, with a right-side advantage apparent in adults (Burke, 1971; Letzner & Kronman, 1967; Mulik, 1965; Shah & Joshi, 1978; Vig & Hewitt, 1975; Woo, 1931). No evidence is available at present to indicate that this structural laterality is a consistent developmental process.

In the second group of studies, "chimeric" faces are created by photographically aligning two left sides, or two right sides, of one photographed face. This results in two still photos of composite faces, with each composite presenting symmetrical left-face or right-face features. Observer judgments are employed to indicate of differences in left and right facial features, a presumption that began with early research by Wolff (1933, 1943). Hager (1982) has provided a detailed review of this literature. Overall, these studies have tended to show that the right-composite face (at least for unfamiliar faces) is perceived as more similar to the normal face (Lindzey, Prince, & Wright, 1952; McCurdy, 1949; Wolff, 1943). More recent data by Gilbert and Bakan (1973) suggest that this effect may not be due to facial features per se, but instead to a perceptual bias on the part of observers, i.e., the right side of the face appears more like the normal face because it is registered (in normal direct gaze) in the left visual field and projected to the right cerebral hemisphere.

Other investigators using composite faces have requested subjects to make judgments about the emotions expressed in the faces. The general results of these studies are that the expressions are judged to be "more intense" in the left composites (Campbell, 1978, 1979; Knox, 1972; Sackeim, Gur, & Saucy, 1978; the left side of a facial stimulus is typically projected to left occipital cortex), when observers possess an intact right hemisphere (Bruyer, 1981).

Crucial to the use of composite faces in the study of facial asymmetry is the type of facial expression photographed. For example, in the Sackheim and Gur (1978) study, subjects rated most photographs as showing more intense emotion on the left side of the face. However, as Ekman (1980) stated in his critique of the conclusions drawn by these investigators, most of the photographs used in this study were actually poses by trained "facial gymnasts" instructed as to the specific muscles to contract. Ekman further noted that the photographs in which Sackheim and Gur found no asymmetry were the only ones that were generated spontaneously. The sign vehicles presented pictorially were not, therefore, reflective of spontaneous emotion. Thus the authors' interpretation of the findings as reflecting lateralization for facial expressions of *emotion* were of dubious validity. That judgments of facial asymmetry are affected by the "spontaneity" of the composite stimuli was confirmed in research by Cacioppo and Petty (1981).

In the third group of studies, dynamic changes in "rapid" sign vehicles (muscular actions) are evaluated for asymmetry or laterality using direct measures of facial behavior. Typically, expressions are experimentally elicited in subjects, and facial actions on the left and right sides of the face are compared with respect to intensity, timing, and/or duration of contraction. From these studies as well, inferences have been drawn about possible hemispheric contribution to the generation of facial expressions. Hager (1982) has also reviewed these studies. Eliciting stimuli have included "humorous situations" (Lynn & Lynn, 1938), watching humorous movies (Lynn & Lynn, 1943), conversaton with spontaneous smiling (Chaurasia & Goswami, 1975), or instructions to pose facial expressions either according to emotion terms (Borod & Caron, 1980; Campbell, 1978; Rubin & Rubin, 1980) or muscular movement (Alford & Alford, 1981; Chaurasia & Goswami, 1975). These studies have typically found that requested movements are more asymmetrical than "spontaneous" movements, with a small tendency to lateralization favoring the left side of the face in the asymmetrical expressions. A tendency toward greater left-side asymmetry has also been reported for males (Alford & Alford, 1981), and for right-handed individuals in general (Rubin & Rubin, 1980).

Hager's (1982) analysis of these studies suggested that most were critically deficient. Among these studies, shortcomings included: (a) invalid measures of facial asymmetry, often merely involving observer judgments of asymmetry (which risk confounds with perceptual biases); (b) use of only one index of left/right facial action (e.g., intensity, or rapidity of onset) when scoring asymmetry; (c) failure to identify the type of facial expression elicited (e.g., emblematic, emotional, or posed) or to separate types of expressions for analysis. On this latter point, the types of facial expression typically misconstrued as "facial expressions of emotion" have been explicated by Ekman (1978). Among these expression types are (a) "emblems," or symbolic communications, e.g., the wink; (b) "manipulators," or noninstrumental, self-manipulative actions, e.g., lip-biting; (c) "illustrators," or actions accompanying and highlighting speech, e.g., eyebrow and upper-eyelid raising in emphasis; and (d) "regulators," such as nods or smiles, which mediate turn-taking in conversation.

A study by Schwartz, Ahern, and Brown (1979) attempted to discern "lateralization for emotion" using facial EMG techniques (see section on facial measurement, following). Similar data have been reported by Sirota and Schwartz (1982). Subjects were given instructions to ponder affectively toned reflective questions, and left versus right EMG activity was compared for several facial sites, across "positive" and "negative" questions, with a right-sided *zygomatic*-site advantage for "positive" questions (the *zygomatic major* retracts the mouth corners and pulls them slightly upward; it is the principal action in a smile). Ekman, Hager, and Friesen (1981) criticized the use of the reflective questions because of the likelihood that they elicited poses corresponding to the putative affective tone of the question, rather than genuine emotion.

Furthermore, in a recent study, Fridlund (submitted for publication, 1985) duplicated the "lateralization" effect obtained by Schwartz et al. (1979) by simply requesting subjects to make a "neutral face" or pose a smile. Fridlund also formulated criteria for accepting facial EMG lateralization effects as indicating emotion and not motor-control confounds or noncollinearities in bilateral muscular contraction.

Ekman et al. (1981) were the first investigators to compare directly, using anatomically based facial scoring, possible asymmetries in posed versus spontaneous facial expressions. In a sample of children, asymmetrical movements of *zygomatic major* occurred much more frequently in posed than in spontaneous smiles. Asymmetrical deliberate movements showed a general left-side advantage. An extension to a sampling of spontaneous smiles in adult women showed few asymmetrical movements among these spontaneous expressions, and there was no tendency for lateralization. The observed difference in asymmetries between deliberate and spontaneous expressions was regarded by Ekman et al. (1979) as consistent with the dual-control model of facial action, and with the expectation that more cortically mediated (i.e., deliberate) expressions would show increased asymmetry. Convergent validation of this model would also be provided by investigations of laterality and asymmetry in other facial actions with presumed subcortical predominance, i.e., parkinsonoid movements and dyskinesias associated with extrapyramidal cholinergic and dopaminergic pathways.

The most detailed asymmetry/laterality data to date were collected by Hager (1985), who replicated the Ekman et al. (1981) finding that spontaneous actions of *zygomatic major* are more symmetrical than deliberate actions. This pattern was also apparent for the spontaneous actions of *orbicularis oculi* (the eye sphincter, which opens and shuts the eyelids) in smiling and in startle reactions, and of *risorius* (which draws the corners of the mouth laterally) in startle reactions, in contrast to deliberate actions of these muscles. These findings and other evidence indicated that asymmetry in the intensity of bilateral actions was related more to motor control than emotion.

Specialization of a single hemisphere for controlling facial actions could not have accounted for all the observed asymmetry — laterality changed unpredictably, depending on which facial action was being observed. Although the pattern of left–right asymmetry was correlated across four different tasks requiring production of facial actions, striking differences occurred between the performance of requests for bilateral versus unilateral actions. This dependence of asymmetry on type of task suggests a need for more careful validation and selection of asymmetry measures, particularly when the researcher uses only one measure.

In summary, the explosion of studies concerning asymmetry and laterality in the generation of facial expressions has generated more heat than light. The effects are often not obtained. When they are obtained, they tend to be small and are easily washed out by variations in stimulus materials and experimental methods. Which side of the face appears more active seems to vary depending on the muscle, rather than to be general to either the left or the right side. Most importantly, asymmetries are apparent most often when the expression is deliberate and not emotional. Therefore, asymmetry/lateralization may be of most relevance not to the study of emotion, but to issues of instigation of spontaneous versus deliberate expression, and the masking or posing of facial expressions.

As a whole, the findings do not fit models of cerebral hemispheric specialization that posit either (a) right-hemisphere specialization for emotion (see Galin, 1974), (b) right-hemisphere specialization for negative emotions and left-hemisphere specialization for positive emotions (e.g., Dimond, Farrington, & Johnson, 1976; Reuter–Lorenz & Davidson, 1981; Sackeim et al., 1982; Schwartz et al., 1979), or (c) left-hemisphere dominance for motor-control aspects of emotional behavior (Geschwind, 1975). Little knowledge about the functional integration of the cerebral hemispheres has emerged, and no demonstration has been forthcoming that any putative differences in hemispheric control of facial expression have more than incidental significance for theories of emotion.

Unanswered or Unasked Questions

From what level in the nervous system do coordinated facial expressions of emotion arise? Evidence is lacking on this issue. Mueller (1983) has ably noted the circularity inherent in attempting to "locate" emotion (and by implication, the generators for facial expressions of emotion), in the central nervous system. Following from the thinking of the 19th-century neurologist, Hughlings Jackson (Jackson, 1958a, b), it may be that maturely differentiated facial expressions emerge from coordination of reflexive components well manifest during infancy (see Bratzlavsky, 1979; Bruner, 1973). In Jacksonian fashion, the bilateral facial-nerve nuclei located in the pontine area of the brainstem would generate the component facial patterns, the subcortical extrapyramidal structures the full-blown affective displays, and the neocortical pyramidal structures the modulated expressiveness, integrated with cultural display rules of the adult.

There has been surprisingly little work on the neural substrates of *coordinated* facial expression. Generally, motor-cortical stimulation or stimulation of the descending pyramidal tracts elicits discrete, contralateral facial muscle movements in the monkey, although rhythmic mouth and tongue movements suggestive of mastication have been observed (Denny-Brown, 1939). Stimulation of "limbic" and hypothalamic sites (see Mueller, 1982) has produced coordinated emotional responses in the cat, with the appropriate facial concomitants (e.g., exposing of teeth, flattening of ears, hissing; see Ectors, Brookens, & Gerard, 1938; Flynn, 1967; Hess, 1954). Finally, the stimulation of pontine and medullar sites in the brainstem in the monkey has been reported to elicit coordinated facial expressions, including a "tensing grimace," a "faciorespiratory complex simulating laughter," and eyelid closure (Weinstein & Bender, 1943).

These studies are all handicapped because they (a) do not attempt to separate facial-motor elicitation effects of the electrical stimulus from those involving simple induction of pain, hunger, thirst, or other drive states; (b) do not control for density of representation of different facial muscles in the structures stimulated (i.e., electrical stimulation of the facial nucleus results in a much greater "spread of effect" to pathways representing other muscles than would similar stimulation applied to motor cortex; see Potegal, Blau, & Miller, 1980); (c) do not describe the elicited facial actions in terms of anatomically based movements but instead use emotion-related terminology.

Nor can comparative data be taken as a valid indicant of human emotional responding. Profound differences are found between humans and other primate and nonprimate orders. In nonprimates, the facial musculature takes the form of a broad sheet or "platysma." The progression along the phylogenetic tree is accompanied by a specialization of platysma toward expression and display, with humans showing the most differentiated facial expressions. As benefits the finer differentiation of their facial musculature, the facial nucleus in humans is more complex and differentiated than in other species, with separable cell groupings controlling specific subsets of the musculature (Rinn, 1984). Thus, the greater complexity in neuromuscular substrates renders inferences about human emotional behavior from comparative neurophysiological studies (e.g., those employing intracranial stimulation) tenuous at best, because animal studies are most likely to underestimate the subtle differentiations in human emotional expressions.

For ethical reasons, *experimental* human studies (wherein the verbal self-report could act as an indicant of any induced emotion) do not exist, and the anecdotal evidence from clinical neurosurgery is at this point insufficient to clarify this issue. The videotaping of facial behavior of neurosurgery patients undergoing diagnostic stimulation represents an unexploited opportunity to collect the essential human data (see Kolb & Milner, 1981).

What are the Neuroanatomical Substrates for "Facial Feedback"?   As we review later in a separate section, many emotion theorists attempting to explain self-perception of emotion have placed heavy emphasis on the importance of putative feedback pathways indicating momentary patterns of contraction of the facial musculature. Evidence for neuroanatomical substrates is mixed. Although there are reports of proprioceptive spindle organs in facial muscle (Bowden & Mahran, 1956), their existence is still in contention (Moldaver, 1980a, b). Because recent research has verified that spindle outputs from skeletal muscles have direct representation in cortex (e.g., Roland, 1978; Starr, McKeon, Skuse, & Burke, 1981; and see discussion of implications of these findings by Roland, 1978), further anatomical research to ascertain the existence or nonexistence of spindles in facial muscle and their possible cortical representation is essential.

It is possible that feedback of the state of contraction of the facial muscles relies on information from skin exteroceptors through CN V (trigeminal; see Bratzlavsky, 1979), or from facial regional blood flow and temperature changes (see Tomkins, 1979), but evidence is lacking on this point.

How confidently can one infer underlying neural function from analysis of facial behavior?   This question is crucial for investigators who wish to use measures of visible facial action or electrophysiological measures of other facial activity (EMG, bilateral sweat-gland activity, blood flow, etc.) to make statements about pyramidal versus extrapyramidal influences, or hemispheric participation.

Unfortunately, data concerning this issue are scant, and the implicit conceptual issues are thorny. To illustrate this point, let us consider an example involving hemispheric participation in bilateral facial action. In a particular emotion-eliciting situation, one observes that a subject's left *zygomatic major* is slightly more contracted than her right *zygomatic* (i.e., she has an asymmetrical smile). Can one then conclude greater right-hemisphere activity? Not necessarily, because (a) the muscles may be contracting with equal force, yet the skin and fatty deposits are more yielding on the left side and permit greater muscle excursion (see Ekman, 1980); (b) the muscles may be contracting with equal force, yet perhaps because of unequal numbers of muscle fibers, neural activity (at the motoneuron level, from the facial nucleus) may be greater at one muscle than the other; (c) the motor cortical areas for each muscle may show identical activity, yet the corticofugal pyramidal tracts may contain unequal numbers of fibers, accounting for the asymmetrical muscle activity. This analysis is incomplete, but it suffices to illustrate the vexing issues involved in inferring neural function from peripheral action. More confident statements are to be derived by combining multiple indices of facial action, such as onset and offset times, and examining them for convergent and/or divergent information relating to neural substrates.

PHYLETIC BASES OF HUMAN FACIAL ACTION

Ethologists have shown increasing interest in human facial expression as a particularly specialized type of intra- and interspecies signal system. Redican (1982) has capably reviewed the ethological perspective on human facial expressions, one which can be traced to Darwin's perspicacious observations over 100 years ago (Darwin, 1872/1955). Central to this perspective is a concern with the homology of emotional expressions among humans and other species (especially within primates), homologies that may indicate phyletic, evolutionary bases for these expressions.

Most ethological studies of facial expression in nonhuman primates and in nonprimate species have followed the basically empirical approach of identifying species-typical displays and looking for regularities in: (1) the eliciting circumstances; (2) the sender's behavior preceding, accompanying, and following each display; and (3) the responses of recipients. On the basis of such analyses, ethologists draw inferences about the messages conveyed by a particular display, its signal value, and its adaptive functions (cf. Smith, 1977). As Smith indicates, facial, vocal, and postural-gestural displays may convey several different kinds of messages. These range from a general broadcasting of the sender's identity or species, to a specific signaling of the sender's emotional/motivational state and behavioral dispositions. Such signaling may serve crucial adaptive functions in regulating agonistic and sexual encounters, facilitating group cohesion and cooperation, and ensuring parent-infant bonding and parental care.

Extension of the ethological approach to facial expression has resulted in several lines of research: (a) cross-cultural searches for commonalities in human facial expressions (covered separately, later); (b) development of taxa for human facial expressions by inductive, "ethogrammatic" methods (see section on facial measurement); (c) research on facial displays in nonhuman primates; and (d) inductive attempts to pinpoint homologous facial displays and their putative functions (honed by natural selection), across primate and nonprimate orders. We discuss the latter two lines of research in this section.

What Has Been Found

Many nonhuman primates show a variety of highly differentiated facial displays. The development of taxa for facial displays in nonhuman primates is of increasing interest in primatology. Recent studies have shown a variety of distinctive and discriminable facial displays in apes, and in both New World and Old World monkeys (e.g., Marriott & Salzen, 1978; van Hooff, 1969, 1972, 1976; van Lawick-Goodall, 1971; Weigel, 1979; and see Chevalier-Skolnikoff, 1973, and Redican, 1982, for reviews). Nonhuman primates may also have specialized mechanisms for perceiving faces and discriminating among facial expressions (Rosenfeld & Van Hoesen, 1979).

Facial displays in nonhuman primates correspond to reliable and specifiable precursors or releasers. Many primate studies have attempted not only to classify facial displays, but also to specify reliable precursors (and/or consequences) of the displays. Results are encouraging (e.g., Mariott & Salzen, 1978; Martenson, Sackett, & Erwin, 1977; Weigel, 1979; and see Redican, 1983, for review). Regrettably, most researchers have merely used free observation of primate behavior and then inferred the functions of facial displays that were demarcated according to inductively derived taxa. Often the classifications were based on terms related to human emotions (e.g., a "fear grimace"), a type of anthropomorphism that Tinbergen (1959) has warned against. Exceptions include the anatomically based descriptions of displays provided by van Hooff (e.g., van Hooff, 1969), and recent attempts at empirical clustering of behavioral streams (Colgan, 1978).

There are homologous facial displays among humans and nonhuman primates. We suggest that a properly empirical demonstration of facial-display homologues across primates would require (a) anatomically based description of facial actions, (b) validation of homologous *releasers* or precursors to the displays, and (c) validation of homologous *consequences* for the displays. For reasons cited previously, these formal criteria have not been met by most ethological studies of facial displays. Klopfer and Klopfer (1982) have argued against the naive induction of "homology" from comparative ethological studies. However, inductively based studies have largely reached concensus regarding homologies in a few primate displays. Among those in Redican's (1982) summary are the (a) grimace (i.e., the silent bared-teeth face, from van Hooff, 1969; cf. human "fear" or "surprise") (b) tense-mouth display (i.e., lips are compressed and drawn slightly inward; cf. human "anger"); (c) play face (i.e., the mouth is wide-open, with lip corners barely retracted; cf. the human smile and/or laughter). These formulations must be accepted tentatively pending validation using the suggested formal criteria.

Unanswered or Unasked Questions

What Are the Evolutionary and/or Ontogenetic Bases of the Configurations of Facial Action That Constitute Facial Expressions of Emotion? Why are particular facial muscles activated in particular emotional expressions? For example, why are the lip corners raised in happiness and drawn down in sadness, rather than vice versa? Evidence for the universality of certain facial expressions has led some investigators to conclude that these expressions are innate displays whose form and use as specialized communicative signals were shaped by natural selection (Andrew, 1963; Darwin, 1955; Eibl-Eibesfeldt, 1972; Izard, 1977; Redican, 1975, 1982; Tomkins, 1962; but see Ekman, 1972). According to this view, certain distinctive facial expressions may have evolved from highly conspicuous (and hence, informative) behaviors that originally served some direct biological function, e.g., orienting responses or defense reactions (cf. Andrew, 1972; Redican, 1983; Smith, 1977). In some cases, the evolution of such behaviors into specialized displays may have come about through *emanicipations* from their original biological functions and *ritualizations* that enhanced their usefulness as signals. In this way, displays emerge from phyletically more elemental components (e.g., the mammalian sucking reflex was emancipated from its role in infant feeding and then ritualized as primate lipsmacking and human kissing). In attempting to reconstruct the possible phyletic origins of human facial expressions such as smiling and laughter (cf. van Hooff, 1972), ethologists rely primarily on comparative studies of homologous displays in related species (see Redican, 1982, for a critical review of studies from this *phylogenetic* standpoint).

An alternative, *ontogenetic* account of the origins of human facial expressions was proposed by Allport (1924) and Peiper (1963). These writers argued that the principal facial expressions of adults derive, through species-specific learning and individual experience, from the biologically adaptive responses of the newborn: elemental sensory reactions, defensive and orienting responses, crying, sucking, etc. (cf. section on neuromuscular control of facial expressions). According to this view, the facial expressions seen in infants are biologically adaptive behaviors, not yet specialized for communication and not necessarily expressive of emotion.

The crucial data for resolving this question for any particular facial expression exist in only piecemeal fashion. In addition to the comparative data previously mentioned, we would need detailed, longitudinal studies of the facial expressions shown by human infants in several unrelated cultures and in a wide range of situations. Detailed comparisons of blind and sighted infants would reveal the possible importance of imitation and of actions directly involved in vision for the development of facial expressions (cf., Oster & Ekman, 1978). Studies of congenitally blind infants (reviewed by Charlesworth & Kreutzer, 1973) have provided the best evidence that direct imitation is unnecessary for the development of smiling, laughter, and crying. However, descriptions of the actual facial movements corresponding to these and other emotions (e.g., surprise, anger) in blind children have been vague and imprecise. Reports that blind infants and children are less facially expressive than sighted children (Charlesworth & Kreutzer, 1973; Fraiberg, 1974) have also lacked detailed description (see discussion by Oster & Ekman, 1978).

How extensively within the phylogenetic tree can discriminable facial displays be detected? The vast majority of research on nonhuman facial displays has focused on the primates. It is generally held that nonprimates show a much less differentiated facial musculature, approaching the sheet-like quality of *platysma*. This limits the potential of these species for exhibiting discriminable facial displays. Nonprimates appear chiefly to use gross body movement (e.g., tail-wagging, presentation of plumage), posturing (e.g., elevation or lowering of head), autonomic signs (e.g., piloerection, rapid respiration with flared nostrils), in addition to shared channels such as vocalization and gaze, as displays. However, recent studies point to discriminable facial displays in nonprimates. Examples include (a) the open mouth, with or without baring of teeth, seen in reptiles (Andrew, 1964); and (b) flattening of ears in threat or startle, seen in most mammals (Redican, 1982). Miller (1975) has even shown anatomically based evidence of some discriminable facial expressions for greeting, grooming, submission, and threat in fur seals and walruses.

CROSS-CULTURAL STUDIES AND THE ISSUE OF UNIVERSALITY

What Has Been Found

Observers label certain facial expressions of emotion in the same way regardless of culture. A number of studies (reviewed by Ekman, 1973) attempted to show differences across cultures in the way observers judge isolated facial expressions. In fact, their findings were either ambiguous or showed similarity across cultures. More consistent results have been obtained by investigators who used explicit descriptive criteria (based on theory or empirical results) to select photographs of expressions representative of each emotion. These photographs were shown to observers who selected from a list of emotion terms the one that best described each expression. The majority of observers in each culture interpreted the facial expressions as conveying the same emotions (five literate cultures, Ekman, 1972; Ekman, Sorenson, & Friesen, 1969; nine literate cultures, Izard, 1971). Similar experiments have obtained comparable results in Malaysia (Boucher, 1973; Boucher & Carlson, 1980) and in two states of the Soviet Union (Niit & Valsiner, 1977).

Two studies investigated judgments of the intensity of emotional expression. Both found high agreement among members of literate cultures (Ekman, 1972; Saha, 1973).

In spite of this evidence, it could still be argued that facial expressions of emotion are culturally variable social signals, and that the commonality in judgments is attributable solely to common learning experience. By this interpretation, exposure to the same mass media representations of emotional expression might have taught people in each culture how to label facial expressions. This explanation was invalidated by studies of isolated, preliterate cultures not exposed to the mass media: the South Fore in Papua/New Guinea (Ekman & Friesen, 1971) and the Dani in West Iran (Heider & Heider, reported by Ekman, 1973). These observers chose the same facial expressions for particular emotions as members of literate cultures.

A limitation of these cross-cultural experiments is that the facial expressions presented were not genuine but were posed by subjects instructed to show a particular emotion or to move particular facial muscles. One interpreter of this literature (Mead, 1975) suggested that universality in judgments of facial expression might be limited to just such stereotyped, posed expressions. Two experiments argue against this interpretation. Winkelmayer et al. (Winkelmayer, Exline, Gottheil, & Paredes, 1978) chose motion picture samples from interviews with normal and schizophrenic individuals to see if emotion judgments by members of different cultures would differ when spontaneous rather than posed expressions were shown. There was no overall difference among American, British, and Mexican observers. However, the Mexican observers were less accurate than the others in judging the facial expressions of normal but not schizophrenic subjects. This difference had not been predicted, may have been due to language and/or culture, and has not been replicated.

More clear-cut results were obtained in a study by Ekman (1972) in which Japanese and American observers judged whether the facial expressions of Japanese and American subjects were elicited by watching a stressful or neutral film. Observers of both cultures were equally accurate whether they judged members of their own or the other culture. Moreover, persons of either culture who were judged correctly by Americans were also judged correctly by Japanese (correlations above 0.75). This experiment was replicated with different subjects and observers.

Members of different cultures show the same facial expressions when experiencing the same emotion unless culture-specific display rules interfere. Whereas many studies have compared judgments of facial expression by observers from different cultures, few studies have compared the facial expressions actually produced by members of different cultures in comparable situations. Without studies measuring actual facial activity, it is not possible to determine which specific aspects of facial expressions are universal, in what social contexts these configurations are shown, nor how cultural norms for managing emotional expression (display rules) operate. Such questions apply both to intended (posed) and spontaneous facial expressions. There has been but one study of each.

Ekman and Friesen (1971) found that members of a preliterate New Guinea group showed the same facial movements when posing particular emotions as do members of literature cultures. Ekman (1972) and Friesen (1972) also found that when Japanese and American subjects sat alone watching either a stress-inducing or neutral film, they showed the same facial actions. However, as predicted by knowledge of display rules in the two cultures, when a person in authority was present, the Japanese subjects smiled more and showed more control of facial expressions than did the Americans. Similar findings were provided by Kilbride and Yarczower (1980).

Unanswered or Unasked Questions

How many emotions have a universal facial expression?   Research in literate cultures has found distinctive facial expressions for anger, disgust, happiness, sadness (or distress), fear, and surprise (Boucher, 1973; Ekman, 1972, 1973; Ekman et al., 1969; Izard, 1971; Saha, 1973). Izard (1971) also reported evidence for interest and shame, but inspection of his photographs suggests that head position, not facial expression, may have provided the clues for recognizing these emotions. There have been no other cross-cultural studies of these two emotions. In the preliterate cultures studied, fear and surprise expressions were discriminated from anger, sadness, happiness, and disgust but were confused with each other, both in labeling and posing expressions (Ekman, 1973). In summary, there is unambiguous evidence of universality only for the expressions of happiness, anger, disgust, sadness, and combined fear/surprise. Further study might reveal universal facial expressions for other emotions.

A likely candidate is the "startle" reaction. There is considerable disagreement about whether startle should be considered an emotional response related to surprise, or a fundamentally reflexive act (Tomkins, 1962; Vaughan & Sroufe, 1976; Wolff, 1966). Ekman, Friesen, and Simons (1983) extended pioneering efforts of Landis and Hunt (1939) in more closely examining the response topography of the startle. Classifying the startle reaction as "on the boundary between emotion and reflex," Ekman et al. found marked, reliable stereotypy within 20 msec of the startle stimulus. This stereotypy was unaffected in topography or timing by attempts to inhibit the reaction. These findings await cross validation in several other cultures.

How many universal expressions are distinguishable for any emotion? Tomkins (1962, 1963) hypothesized that each emotion would have both universal and culture-specific expressions, but he did not describe the appearance of the latter in any detail. The cross-cultural studies used only a few examples of each emotional expression and did not analyze observers' judgments to see whether different versions of each expression were judged differently.

Even within a single culture, it is not known how many expressions there are for any single emotion. Perhaps another way cultures might differ is in the number of facial expressions associated with a particular emotion; e.g., there might be four or five expressions for anger in one culture, and eight or nine in another.

How great are the cultural differences in facial expression? Most accounts of extreme cultural variability in the expression of emotion come from qualitative observations made by single observers who did not control for observer or sampling bias or take display rules into account (Birdwhistell, LaBarre, Leach, Mead, & Montague, reviewed by Ekman, 1972, 1977). One quantitative study of cultural differences is the previously cited finding by Ekman (1972) and Friesen (1972) that facial expressions in Japanese and American subjects differed in a social situation but not when the same subjects were alone. This fit the authors' hypothesis that socially learned *display rules* for managing facial expressons in various context are a major source of cultural variation in facial expression. In another discussion of display rules,

Heider (1974) confirmed his prediction that one West Irian culture, but not another, would substitute disgust expressions for anger when asked to portray angry themes. There has been no further cross-cultural study of display rules. A study of yearbook photographs and conversations (Seaford, 1976) found evidence for a facial expression "dialect" in patterns of smiling among Southeastern Americans. The origin and interpretation of this dialect remain unclear.

Many questions could be asked about display rules within a single culture, as well as in cross-cultural comparisons. What are these rules? How are they acquired—with what levels of specificity in terms of the characteristics of the social situation and persons to which they apply? When facial behavior is managed or attenuated in two cultures, is the resultant facial behavior similar? For example, if in two cultures the display rule for adult females is to deintensify sadness when hearing about the husband's prolonged departure, is the facial appearance of the deintensified sadness the same in both cultures? Or does one culture deintensify sadness by restricting the expression to just the brow (producing a *partial* expression), and the other culture deintensify by reducing the duration of the expression (producing a *micromomentary* expression)? Ekman (1972) postulated that learned triggers for each emotion were another source of cultural variation, but he hypothesized that the elicitors may share some underlying characteristics. Boucher (1973) and Cunningham (1977) found evidence for similarities—but not for the hypothesized differences—in the specific elicitors of certain emotions in quite divergent cultures. In summation, there probably are important cultural differences in facial expression that are attributable to learning, but precisely what these are, and how they come to be, are unknown.

How often do people in natural situations actually show the distinctive, universal patterns of facial expression? Are these expressions (see Ekman & Friesen, 1975) common or relatively rare? Does their occurrence vary with culture, sex, age, or the particular social context? There have been notable initiatives toward measuring expressions under naturalistic conditions (Lockard, Fahrenbruch, Smith, & Morgan, 1977), but overall there is little evidence indeed.

The most fine-grained measurement of facial expressions under naturalistic conditions was performed by Ekman and Friesen (unpublished data), who viewed videotapes of psychiatric interviews of patients who were largely diagnosed as having affective disorders. In this population, wherein more emotional expressions might have been expected, less than one third of the corpus of facial actions—nearly 6000 facial expressions, scored for 30 ten-minute interviews—were classifiable as emotional expressions. To restate, Ekman and Friesen regarded this proportion as perhaps an overestimate of what may occur in nonpatients, because the patients interviewed were mostly "discussing their feelings"!

Obviously, more data are needed. However, detailed measurement of the facial expressions occurring in more than one circumstance in different cultures, as well as knowledge of each culture's display rules, are not available for even one culture.

DEVELOPMENTAL ASPECTS OF FACIAL ACTION

Most research on facial expression in infants has been concerned with the timetable of emotional development. At what age and in what order do particular emotions emerge? Unfortunately, the behavioral criteria by which various emotional responses have been "recognized" and labeled are often subjective and imprecise, with little attention paid to detailed description of the facial movements themselves. Most early studies also lacked independent, convergent measures for assessing the infant's presumed emotional state. Several recent studies have attempted to deal with these methodological problems (Campos, Emde, Gaensbauer, & Henderson, 1975; Hiatt, Campos, & Emde, 1979; Lewis, Brookes, & Haviland, 1978; Waters, Matas, & Sroufe, 1975; Young & Decarie, 1977). Nevertheless, it is still not known precisely when the distinctive, universal facial expressions corresponding to certain emotions appear, nor how they develop. Part of the problem is that the questions left unanswered by research on infants have not been pursued in studies of toddlers and young children.

What Has Been Found

The facial musculature is fully formed and functional at birth. Many observers have been struck by the newborn's considerable facial mobility (Gesell, 1945; Haviland, 1975). Using a fine-grained measurement system (description later), Oster has confirmed that all but one of the discrete facial muscle actions visible in the adult can be identified and finely discriminated in full-term and premature newborns (Oster & Ekman, 1978; Oster & Rosenstein, in press). Evidence for organization and temporal patterning in expressive movements such as smiling, brow-knitting, and pouting in young infants has also been found by fine-grained analysis (Josse, Leonard, Lezine, Robinot, & Rouchouse, 1973; Oster, 1978, 1982; Oster & Ekman, 1978).

Distinctive facial expressions resembling certain adult expressions are present in early infancy. Crying, the universal expression of *distress,* is of course present at birth, but there has been little careful description since

Darwin's of the facial signs of distress and no study of developmental changes, if any, in cry faces. It is not known whether different facial movements correspond to acoustically different cry types or different sources of distress. Newborn infants show expressions resembling adult *disgust* in response to unpleasant tastes (Peiper, 1963; Rosenstein & Oster, 1981; Steiner, 1973). These facial responses have been found in anencephalic and hydrocephalic infants, suggesting a brainstem origin (Steiner, 1973). The processes by which these facial reactions become associated with a wide range of psychological elicitors are not known. The *startle* reaction can be triggered in the newborn by sudden, intense stimulation and often occurs as a spontaneous discharge in non-REM sleep. The facial response is quite different from surprise and is said not to change throughout life.

Contrary to previous belief, neonatal smiles are neither random nor produced by flatulence. They occur primarily during REM sleep and seem to reflect periodic, endogenous fluctuations in CNS activity (Emde, Gaensbauer, & Harmon, 1976; Sroufe & Waters, 1976; Wolff, 1963). Social smiling, i.e., smiling in an alert, bright-eyed infant who is fixating the caregiver, first occurs around 3 to 4 weeks of age (Wolff, 1963). The reliable, full-blown social smile emerges in the third month (Emde et al., 1976; Wolff, 1963). Smiling in 2- to 3-month-olds has been observed in a variety of experimental situations suggesting that it reflects a successful attempt at cognitive assimilation or "mastery" (Papousek & Papousek, 1977; Shultz & Zigler, 1970; Sroufe, 1978; Sroufe & Waters, 1976), or a sense of efficacy and control over the environment (Watson, 1978). Consistent with such interpretations is Oster's (1978) observation that 1- to 3-month-old infants engaged in social interaction frequently break into a smile after several seconds of gazing with intensely knit brows at the caregiver's face. This brow-knitting, according to Oster, reflects the infant's effort to assimilate some puzzling aspect of the mother's behavior.

Beginning around the fourth month, smiling becomes increasingly reserved for the infant's primary caregivers (Ainsworth, 1973; Bowlby, 1969). With the exception of Wolff's classic study, little is known about developmental changes in the morphology of the smile or about differences—if any—in the appearance of "social," "playful," or "cognitive-mastery" smiles (but see Blurton Jones, 1972; Bower, 1982; van Hooff, 1972). Laughter first appears around 4 months. Most studies have focused on changes in the determinants of laughter (Rothrbart, 1973; Sroufe, 1978; Sroufe & Waters, 1976). Insights into the mechanisms underlying smiling and laughter have come from the study of Down's Syndrome infants (Cicchetti & Sroufe, 1978).

To date, there is still no conclusive evidence that infants in the first year of life show discrete, differentiated facial expressions corresponding to the universally recognizable adult expressions of surprise, sadness, anger, and fear. This issue is elaborated later.

Three- to 4-month-olds show differential responses to facial expressions. Early studies (reviewed by Charlesworth & Kreutzer, 1973) indicated that infants do not begin to discriminate among facial expressions until 5 to 6 months. In a more recent study by Caron, Caron, and Myers (1982), infants less than 6 months of age did not show categorical recognition of facial expressions. This finding is in contrast to those of other recent studies that report differential fixation to slides of smiling versus nonsmiling faces by 3-to 4-month-olds (LaBarbera, Izard, Vietze, & Parisi, 1976; Nelson, Morse, & Leavitt, 1979; Young-Browne, Rosenfeld, & Horowitz, 1977). Yet these findings are not definitive. As Oster (1981) suggests in a critical review of this literature, it is unclear which aspects of the faces infants were responding to, because potentially confounding stimulus characteristics were not considered (e.g., the enhanced contrast present in a "toothy" grin). In a recent study that did control for the "toothiness" of facial expressions, Oster and Ewy (1981) found differential smiling but not visual fixation by 4-month-old infants to slides of smiling versus nonsmiling faces independent of toothiness. (Subjects viewed either toothy or nontoothy smiles alternating with toothy fear faces or nontoothy sad faces posed by the same actors.)

There is some evidence that by 2–3 months infants begin to perceive faces configuratively, rather than in terms of isolated features (Maurer & Barrera, 1981). However, the configurative representation of faces may not mature completely until age 10 (Carey & Diamond, 1977). Studies of infants' scan patterns to different facial expressions (cf. Maurer & Salapatek, 1976; and in monkey, Mendelson, Haith, & Goldman-Rakic, 1982) might help to resolve this question.

To answer the more difficult question of when infants begin to perceive the facial expressions of others as meaningful social signals (cf. Oster, 1981), additional studies are needed that examine infants' facial expressions and other behavior in response to the facial expressions of adults in naturalistic social situations. Some relevant findings have come from studies of infant–caregiver social interaction. A number of investigators have found that young infants become "sober" or distressed when the caregiver presents an impassive face, suggesting a sensitivity to the animation and responsiveness of naturally occurring facial behavior (Brazelton, Tronick, Adamson, Als, & Wise, 1975; Stechler & Carpenter, 1967; Trevarthen, 1977, 1979). Detailed study of infants' responses to the dynamic, temporally patterned, often exaggerated facial expressions used by caregivers (cf. Stern, Beebe, Jaffe, & Bennett, 1977) might reveal a greater sensitivity to differences in the expressive movements themselves. In addition, promising work on "social referencing" in 1-year-olds (Klinnert, Campos, Sorce, Emde, & Svejda, 1982) indicates that by the end of the first year infants actively seek and use the information provided by their caregivers' facial expressions in appraising uncertain situations (e.g., novel and potentially frightening toys, or the visual cliff). As Ainsworth, Bell, and Stayton (1974) have pointed out, the tendency of newly mobile infants to heed the urgent nonverbal signals of their parents has obvious adaptive value.

Neonates may have an innate capacity for imitating facial movements. Meltzoff and Moore (1977, 1982) have found differential imitation of specific facial actions such as tongue protrusion and mouth opening in neonates, including (in their recent work) infants only 42 to 72 hours old. Although these findings remain controversial (see critiques by Anisfeld, 1979; Hayes & Watson, 1981; Jacobson & Kagan, 1979; Masters, 1979), Meltzoff and Moore (1979) ably defend their rigorous testing and measurement procedures. After considering a variety of possible mechanisms that might account for neonatal imitation of facial gestures, these authors conclude that the most likely mediator was an innate capacity to apprehend "the equivalences between the act seen and the act done" (p. 295). Further support for these conclusions has come from the findings of Field, Woodson, Greenberg, and Cohen (1982), who reported that 2-day-olds could discriminate and imitate happy, sad, and surprised facial expressions posed by a live model. This study warrants replication using more stringent testing and scoring criteria.

The evidence of neonatal imitation presented in these papers raises the intriguing possibility that direct imitation may indeed play a role in the development of facial expressions. This notion has received little attention in recent years. It has been assumed either that such imitation was impossible in the neonate, or if it was possible, that imitation was unnecessary. Supporting the latter presumption was evidence that the principal human facial expressions are present in all cultures, and even in congenitally blind infants— although, as noted previously, the evidence is far from complete on this score. Neonatal imitation also poses a challenge to the contention of many learning theorists that "imitative behavior" is a set of stimulus and response discriminations shaped by social reinforcement. That imitation may at least play a role in modulating or "fine-tuning" facial expressions is suggested by Kaye and Marcus's (1978) observation that 6-month-olds gradually accommodate their motor performance over a series of trials to match modeled mouth movements.

The abilities to "encode" and "decode" facial expressions, and to deceive and detect deception, improve with age. Earlier experimental studies (reviewed by Charlesworth & Kreutzer, 1973; Oster, 1981) established that by the age of 3 to 5 years, children are familiar with the basic, universally recognized facial expressions of emotion. Using a variety of tasks, investigators have shown that preschool children can (a) match photographs showing the same expression posed by different individuals; (b) identify the expressions that correspond to emotion terms or to pictorial representations of emotion-eliciting situations; and (c) imitate or voluntarily produce recognizable versions of these facial expressions (Borke, 1971; Greenspan, Barenboim, & Chandler, 1976; Hamilton, 1973; Izard, 1971; Odum & Lemond, 1972; Paliwal & Goss, 1981; Zuckerman & Przewuzman, 1979).

One general finding from these studies is that production tasks are more difficult than matching or imitation tasks. The expression of happiness is typically easiest, and fear among the most difficult. By 5 years of age, children can also imitate many of the specific actions found in emotional expressions (Ekman, Roper, & Hager, 1978). Finally, 4- to 6-year-olds associate specific attributes of schematic faces (e.g., brow and mouth curvature) with specific emotions (Paliwal & Goss, 1981). Unfortunately, it is not possible to say how early these skills emerge, because studies of infants between 6 months and 2 years of age are rare. One obvious reason is that the experimental tasks used in most of these studies are beyond the apparent cognitive abilities of preverbal infants and toddlers.

An understanding of facial expressions at an emotional level is shown by reports of preschool-age children's spontaneous responses to the emotional expressions of others (Hamilton, 1973; Leiman, 1978; and review by Hoffman, 1977). According to Hoffman, the capacity for empathic responding may be present very early in life. This view is supported by considerable anectdotal evidence of empathic responding by infants and toddlers in natural social interactions (Darwin, 1877; Hoffman, 1977; Zahn-Waxler, Radke-Yarrow, & Kling, 1979). In one experimental study, Main, Weston, and Wakeling (1979) found expressions of "concerned attention" in 1-year-olds when a stranger with whom they had been interacting became distressed. Empathic responding was more likely in subjects who had secure attachment relationships with their caregivers than in those without secure attachment. This suggests that early experience can influence the tendency to show expressions of empathy.

Studies using the slide-viewing paradigm developed by Buck (1975) have shown that the spontaneous nonverbal expressions of preschool children watching sides can be "decoded" by adults and by other preschool children, at least in terms of the pleasantness or unpleasantness of the sender's reaction. Buck (1975, 1977) and more recently Field and Walden (in press) have presented evidence that the "internalizer/externalizer" personality postulated by Jones (1935) is present at an early age. Children who are more "expressive" (i.e., whose expressions can be more accurately decoded by adults) are less physiologically reactive, as measured by electrodermal response or ratings of "internalizer/externalizer" personality traits, than less expressive children, and vice versa.

Field and Walden (in press) have presented data suggestive of individual differences along an "internalizer/externalizer" dimension in neonates — although in the study reported, measures of facial expressiveness and cardiac responsivity were obtained in different testing situations. (The autonomic nervous system correlates of facial expression in adults are discussed later). Unfortunately, most "encoding/decoding" studies in children have not involved any direct measures of the children's facial expressions. Therefore, we cannot be certain what kinds of facial expressions were being shown by children whose expressions were accurately decoded (and who were therefore assumed to be highly expressive). The only direct studies of facial behavior in children have come from an ethological approach (see below).

The general finding from studies of "encoding" and "decoding" abilities in school-age children is that these basic skills improve with age (DePaulo & Rosenthal, 1982). More subtle multichannel aspects of nonverbal communication also begin to emerge during this time; these seem to result in part from the development of increasingly complex cognitive capacities, and from an enhanced ability to manage expressions and thus use them deliberately, even deceptively. In fact, what Ekman and Oster (1978) had described as a "terra incognita" has now become a burgeoning research area (cf. articles in Feldman, 1982). Recent experimental studies have focused on three subtleties of nonverbal communication in children: (a) the ability to perceive discrepancies between different communication channels (e.g., Blanck & Rosenthal, 1982; Volkmar & Siegel, 1982); (b) the capacities to deceive nonverbally and to detect deception in others (DePaulo & Jordan, 1982; Feldman, Devin–Sheehan, & Allen, 1978; Feldman, Jenkins, & Popoola, 1979; Morency & Krauss, 1982; Shennum & Bugental, 1982); and (c) the emergence of display rules for inhibiting expressions of negative feelings and masking these with positive expressions (Saarni, 1982; Shennum & Bugental, 1982).

Saarni (1979) has also found increasing awareness of rules for managing emotional expressions in children from 6 to 10 years of age. In experimental situations (e.g., the slide-viewing paradigm), school-age children have been reported to show a general social inhibition of spontaneous facial expressiveness when experimenters are present (Yarczower & Daruns, 1982; Yarczower, Kilbride, & Hill, 1979). However, a social *facilitation* of facial expressions has also been reported in some natural situations (see following).

Facial expression plays a crucial role in naturally occurring social interactions. The young infant is increasingly being veiwed as an active individual, equipped with basic signaling capacities that serve to ensure certain kinds of attachment-promoting exchanges between infant and caregivers (Ainsworth, 1973; Bowlby, 1969; Brazelton et al., 1975; Lewis & Rosenblum, 1974; Trevarthen, 1977 1979). Facial expression is now recognized as a major component of this signaling system.

Ethological studies of natural social interaction in daycare or nursery-school settings have typically focused on the repertoire of facial and gestural actions associated with agonistic encounters, rough-and-tumble play, and social interaction with adults and peers (Blurton Jones, 1972; and see review by Camras, 1982). Ethologists discuss these actions in terms of their presumed motivation and signal function. However, there has been little quantitative documentation that particular expressive movements actually serve the presumed signaling function. Nor have ethologists systematically related the facial movements shown in such actions to emotional expressions. An exception on both scores is a recent ethologically oriented experimental study showing that certain "aggressive" facial configurations used by children defending a desired object predicted both the children's own and their partners' subsequent behavior (Camras, 1977, 1982). Zivin (1982) has also documented developmental changes in two facial displays ("plus" and "minus" faces), used in social encounters between children. The growing social control over emotional expression is suggested by observations that the presence of others can have a facilitative effect on some emotional expressions such as crying (Blurton Jones, 1972) and humor (Chapman & Wright, 1976), and inhibitory effects under some circumstances (Yarczower & Daruns, 1982).

Unanswered or Unasked Questions

At what age can emotion be inferred from facial expressions seen in early infancy?   Most psychologists have believed that young infants lack the cognitive prerequisites for the experience of emotion. This belief cuts across the nativist/empiricist spectrum (e.g., Allport, 1924; Gesell, 1945; Peiper, 1963), though there have been widely differing views on the presumed cognitive prerequisites for experiencing "true emotion," on the age when these prerequisites are attained, and on the ontogenetic mechanisms presumed to be involved. Recent articles (Emde et al., 1976; Lewis & Brooks, 1978; Saarni, 1978; Sroufe, 1978) have interpreted expressive movements such as crying and smiling in early infancy as purely passive, reflex-like precursors of later expressions of emotion.

There is said to be no "genuine" emotion until the emergence of the first signs of active cognitive processing or "consciousness" around the third month (Emde et al., 1976; Sroufe, 1978), or until the emergence of "self-conscious awareness" around 18 months (Lewis & Brooks, 1978). Electroencephalographic data suggest that there is differential cerebral hemispheric activity in 10-month-old infants exposed to an actor's facial expressions (Davidson & Fox, 1982), but the subjective correlates of these electrophysiological changes, and their relation to the infants' own facial expressions, have not been examined.

Although not denying the importance of these cognitive achievements, several researchers maintain that emotion is present from birth (Izard, 1978;

Tomkins, 1962, 1963). Others suggest a more gradual transition from reflexive instigation to higher order cognitive mediation of emotional expressions (Oster, 1978; Stechler & Carpenter, 1967; Wolff, 1966). This issue cannot be resolved on the basis of available empirical data.

When do adult-like, differentiated facial expressions for the emotions of interest, surprise, sadness, fear, and anger, respectively, first appear? "Brightening" of the eyes and face has been noted in quiet, alert newborns attending to visual or auditory sitmuli. This bright, alert look may be accompanied by widened eyes and raised brows, by knit browns and pursed lips, or by relaxed brows and lower face. Izard's coding systems (Izard, 1979; Izard & Dougherty, 1980) designate all such attentive faces as expressions of "interest." This ignores the possibility that the different facial expressions shown by alert infants may occur in different circumstances and may have different behavioral correlates and meanings. For example, Oster (1978, 1984) has found that brow-knitting in young infants, as in adults, seems to signal an effort to apprehend a "puzzling" object or event. More generally, as we shall see, it is premature to label facial configurations of infants in terms of adult emotion categories until their elicitors, consequences, and behavioral correlates have been determined.

The typical adult suprise face is infrequently observed in infants less than 1 year old (Charlesworth & Kreutzer, 1973; Vaughan & Sroufe, 1976), even though infants in the second half-year may respond to presumably surprising experimental situations in ways suggesting that they were surprised (Dećarie, 1978; Hiattt, Campos, & Emde, 1979; Vaughan & Sroufe, 1976).

We cannot yet specify when discrete negative-affect expressions (as distinct from crying) begin to appear on a regular basis, nor in what natural circumstances they are likely to occur. Sadness and distress faces differ in adults, but this distinction has not been demonstrated in studies of infants and children. The emotions of "wariness" and fear emerge in the second half of life, as inferred from the onset of hesitant, avoidant, or overtly negative reactions to situations that were not previously distressing, such as heights or the approach of a stranger (Campos, Hiatt, Ramsay, Henderson, & Svejda, 1978; Décarie, 1978; Emde et al., 1976; Sroufe, 1977, 1978). The emotion of anger has been inferred from "tantrum" behaviors and from instrumental acts such as hitting, throwing, and biting (Charlesworth & Kreutzer, 1973; Sroufe, 1978). But the facial expressions accompanying these emotional responses have not been described in detail.

To date, there has been no conclusive evidence that infants in the first year of life show discrete, differentiated facial expressions in response to either naturally occurring or experimentally manipulated elicitors of fear, anger, or sadness (Campos et al., 1975; Hiatt et al., 1977; Lewis et al., 1978; Waters et al., 1975; Young & Décarie, 1977). The only study that examined infants' responses in situations designed to elicit several different negative emotions (anger, fear, and distress) found no evidence of specificity in the facial expressions of 9- to 12-month-old infants (Young & Décarie, 1977). More recently, two groups of researchers have reported finding evidence for differentiated facial expressions of discrete negative emotions in infants. Both sets of findings are plagued by severe shortcomings, yet because these studies have been influential, they merit close examination.

Izard, Huebner, Risser, and Dougherty (1980; also see Malatesta & Haviland, 1982) reported that judges could reliably identify in 1- to 9-month-old infants facial expressions that corresponded to adult emotions of joy, interest, surprise, sadness, anger, disgust, contempt, and fear. These findings were obtained in judgment studies using the theoretically based facial coding systems devised by Izard (1979) and Izard and Dougherty (1980; and see criticisms of theory-based facial coding systems following). The findings can be criticized on three grounds: (a) they assert without evidence that "the spontaneous expressions of the fundamental emotions are essentially invariant over the life-span" (Izard & Dougherty, 1980); (b) they do not permit identification of the cues used by judges to discriminate the ostensibly discrete expressions; (c) they provide no evidence that the infants whose facial expressions were correctly "identified" by judges experienced emotional states homologous to those associated with the corresponding adult facial expressions.

In two separate studies, Campos, Emde, and their colleagues examined the facial expressions of 10- to 12-month-olds in happiness-, surprise-, and fear-arousing situations (Hiatt et al., 1979) and of 7-month-olds in an anger-provoking situation (Stenberg, Campos, & Emde, 1983). The coding system in both cases was based on Ekman and Friesen's (1975) descriptors of six universally recognizable adult facial expressions. Like other investigators, Hiatt et al. (1979) found clear differences between the infants' expressions of positive versus negative emotions. However, they did not find any evidence that infants in the fear-arousing situations showed discrete fear expressions, as opposed to distress or other negative affect expressions. Stenberg et al. (1983) maintain that infants showed discrete anger expressions in their anger situation. However, infants were tested in only one emotion-eliciting situation. There was thus no direct test of the claim that the expressions observed were specific to *anger*. In fact, there was considerable overlap in the facial movements observed in the anger situation and those shown by infants in the fear situations of the Hiatt et al. (1979) study. In both studies, the investigators do not report whether any subjects showed full-face expressions of anger or fear. Instead, they simply report the proportion of infants who showed each of the separate "facial expression components" predicted for different discrete emotions. As Ekman and Friesen (1975) have carefully emphasized, the separate components of facial expressions are usually not specific to a single emotion. In fact, the brow/forehead and nose/mouth actions designated by Stenberg et al. (1983) as anger components are also the main components of the distress expression (i.e., the cry face) in infants, which was not included in the coding system used in these studies. Thus, the fact that these components are shown by infants in the anger situation is inconclusive.

As noted previously, 5-year-olds can satisfactorily pose expressions of anger, fear, and sadness. But there has been no systematic study of the actual occurrence of discrete negative-affect expressions in natural or laboratory settings. Crying apparently remains the prepotent expression of virtually all strong negative affect throughout early childhood. However, no studies have investigated Tomkins' proposal (Tomkins, 1963) that different cry faces accompany different negative affects. Nor is it clear whether young children cry because they do not yet "use" more discrete facial expressions (which they can, however, produce voluntarily), or because all negative affect is blended with or produces distress at this age.

We should emphasize that there may well be greater differentiation and specificity in spontaneous facial expressions accompanying negative emotions in infants and young children than has been shown by existing methods. If so, it will require more fine-grained analyses of the facial expressions shown in different circumstances, and more detailed analyses of the patterning of these expressions and their relationship to other behavior (especially crying), to reveal these differences.

When — and how — do facial expressions of emotion come under voluntary control?   Little is known about the first stages of the transition from the automatic, uncontrolled expression of emotion in early infancy to the more modulated, subtle, and voluntary expression of emotion seen in older children and adults. The first step is probably the (not fully conscious) instrumental use of crying and smiling, somewhere in the first 2 to 3 months of life — as suggested by subjective impressions of "fake" crying (Wolff, 1969); by evidence that both crying and smiling can be brought under the control of social reinforcement (Gerwirtz & Boyd, 1976); and by reports suggesting that during the first half year of life, infants begin to acquire a sense of the efficacy of their own signaling behavior (Bell & Ainsworth, 1972). By the end of the first year, one sees what seem to be smiles used as social greetings, deliberate "tantrum" behaviors, and visible efforts to hold back or suppress tears.

As noted previously, one form of voluntary control — deliberately imitating or posing facial expressions when the corresponding emotion is (presumably) not felt — is present to some extent in preschool children. One study investigating children's verbal knowledge of social display rules (Saarni, 1978) found increasing awareness of rules for managing emotional expression from 6 to 10 years. We know of no attempts to study directly children's efforts to control emotional expression or their use of display rules. Despite the general assumption that feedback from others (e.g., "big boys don't cry") plays a crucial role in shaping children's tendencies to manage emotional expression, investigators have only recently explored the kinds of social feedback children actually receive in response to their facial expressions. This question, and the issue of how social feedback might shape children's use of particular expressions and perhaps even their subjective experience of the emotions (cf., discussion of cultural "feeling rules" by Hochschild, 1979), are at the center of the nascent field of "the socialization of emotions" (cf. Lewis & Michalson, 1982). There have been promising first steps toward discovering how parents actually do respond to the emotional expression of their infants (Lewis & Michalson, 1982; Malatesta & Haviland, 1982). However, researchers have not yet attempted to discover whether infants respond differentially to different kinds of caregiver feedback, or whether the age changes observed in infants' use of emotional expressions are dependent on caregiver responses (cf. Malatesta & Haviland, 1982). This is clearly the next step for these important studies.

FACIAL MEASUREMENT

Careful investigations in neurophysiological, ethological, and developmental research require objective methods for observing and quantifying facial action. Two major methods for this purpose have evolved — measurement of visible facial actions using facial coding systems and the measurement of electrical discharges from contracting facial muscle tissue (facial electromyography).

Measurement of Visible Facial Action

Since Landis' report almost 60 years ago (Landis, 1924), there has been a plethora of systems developed to structure and analyze the observation of facial action. The measurement systems described share the features of being unobtrusive, requiring a permanent visual record (videotape or cinema) that allows slowed playback and/or multiple viewings rather than realtime observation, and relying on an observer who scores or codes behavior in terms of a set of predetermined categories or items. Many of these systems were not developed as independent contributions, but rather in the course of studying other substantive questions. Typically, the rationale for developing these systems was often ad hoc and not based on either sound theoretical argument or an empirical basis. Ekman (1981) has provided a detailed comparison of 14 major facial coding systems.

A problem encountered by all researchers attempting to understand facial behavior is the selection of appropriate behavioral units for parsing the stream of dynamic, configurative facial activity. This issue is of prime importance, yet many coding systems have been proposed without adequate consideration of it. As Altmann (1968) commented, "What stage in our research could be more crucial than this initial choosing of behavioral units. Upon it rests all of our subsequent records of communication interactions and any conclusions we may draw from them" (p. 501; and see discussions by Buck, Baron, & Barrette, 1982; and Condon & Ogston, 1967a, b).

Two major approaches have been used in the construction of facial coding systems, the *observer judgment* approach, and the *direct measurement* approach. In the judgment approach, observers are asked to make judgments about slides, films, or occasionally, live presentations of facial expressions. For example, slides of psychiatric patients are shown to judges who must then classify each patient as depressed, normal, or schizophrenic. Judgment studies have typically involved either placing expressions along emotion scales (e.g., Schlosberg, 1941, 1962, 1954) or in discrete emotion categories (e.g., Izard, 1971, 1972; and see review of both scaling and categorical approaches by Ekman, Friesen, & Ellsworth, 1982b).

In the direct measurement approach, the slides would be examined for particular differences that would then discriminate the diagnostic categories; e.g., depressive might raise the inner eyebrows more than both other groups, whereas the schizophrenics might show more perioral facial actions.

Both approaches to facial coding have value in selected applications. However, the judgment approach is singularly handicapped; it is impossible within such a system to determine exactly which facial signs result in judgment differences. This liability is particularly pronounced in studying emotional behavior, wherein only an analytic approach to discrete facial actions affords an escape from inappropriate inferences regarding critical facial signs of emotion.

The choice of behavioral units in facial coding systems has been based either on theory (largely ethological formulations), inductive observation, or facial anatomy.

Theory-based selection.   Ekman, Friesen, and Tomkins' (1971) Facial Affect Scoring Technique (FAST) sepcified what they considered, on the basis of previous research, to be the distinctive components of six universal affect expressions (77 descriptors of the hypothesized facial appearance in happiness, sadness, anger, fear, surprise, and disgust). FAST proved useful in studies relating subjects' facial expressions to autonomic responses, experimental conditions, and observers' judgments. FAST could not be used to determine whether actions other than those specified are relevant to emotion, nor to study developmental changes or individual differences in the expression of emotion. No provision was made to code intensity of facial behaviors, and facial descriptors were specified as happening in two states — "on" or "off." Of course, all the liabilities of theoretically based coding systems mentioned earlier apply to FAST as well.

Izard has continued working with theoretically based coding systems, culminating in the Maximally Descriptive Facial Movement Coding System (MAX; Izard, 1979), and the System for Identifying Affect Expression by Holistic Judgment (AFFEX; Izard & Dougherty, 1980). Like FAST, MAX and AFFEX are based on earlier recognition studies which established that certain configurations of facial muscle groups are universally associated with particular emotions. Neither MAX nor AFFEX provides an exhaustive listing of possible facial behaviors; MAX, for example, provides only those 27 descriptors hypothesized by Izard to be necessary to form judgments about seven "primary" emotions. No data are provided establishing that the facial actions *excluded* are not involved in emotional expression, and thus the "exhaustiveness" of the systems cannot be confirmed or disconfirmed using these systems. No provision is made for encoding response intensity, and, like FAST, facial action is seen as "on" or "off."

As just noted, MAX and AFFEX were designed primarily as a tool for coding emotional expressions in infants. Oster and Rosenstein (in press) point out three difficulties inherent in the use of MAX and AFFEX for this purpose. First, there is no attempt in scoring facial behavior to distinguish between organized patterns of facial expression in infants and configurations that match an adult stereotype as a result of an adventitious cooccurrence of facial muscle actions. Second, in these systems infant expressions can be classified as "fitting" a particular adult category on the basis of a small number of facial actions, occurring in only two of the three areas of the face. Because certain facial actions are omitted from MAX and AFFEX, it is impossible to verify whether infant (or even adult) expressions meeting the coding criteria are the same as their standardized adult counterparts. It is also impossible to study other infant expressions that do not resemble adult stereotypes but which might constitute meaningful communicative signals. Third, and perhaps most serious, is the absence of any independent evidence that the configurations specified in MAX and AFFEX indicate the presence of the corresponding discrete emotional states in infants. This last objection likewise applies to the use of MAX and AFFEX for coding adult expressions.

Inductively based selection. Several overlapping listings of facial actions have been derived by observing spontaneous behavior in infants (Nystrom, 1974; Young & Décarie, 1977), children (Blurton Jones, 1971;

Brannigan & Humphries, 1972; Grant, 1969; McGrew, 1972), normal adults, and psychiatric patients (Grant, 1969). These are reviewed in detail by Ekman (1981). The inductively based systems have been useful in generating "ethograms," or catalogs of the salient behaviors in the communications repertoire. Blurton Jones' system has been adopted with some variations by a number of developmental psychologists.

The inductively based facial coding systems cannot be considered general-purpose facial measurement systems. The parsing of facial actions is inconsistent — all include both simple actions and complex movements that are not subdivided into component actions. Behavioral units are occasionally objectively identified but are all too often given names laden with inference (e.g., *angry frown*); these terms make inferences about the facial behavior (e.g., whether the frown signifies anger or not) difficult. Many behavioral units are only vaguely described, so that investigators cannot know if they are coding the same actions. Descriptions of actions are often not in accord with the underlying facial anatomy. For example, Birdwhistell attempted to construct a facial measurement system paralleling linguistic units (see Birdwhistell, 1970), whereas Grant derived measurement units from their ostensible (unvalidated) "function" (Grant, 1969). Static facial signs (e.g., individual, racial, or age-related differences in physiognomy) make it difficult to identify certain actions in systems that describe facial behavior in terms of static configurations (e.g., "oblong mouth").

Anatomically based selection.   Because every facial movement is the result of muscular action, any complex facial movement can be scored analytically in terms of the minimal muscle actions that collectively produced the movement. Seaford (1976) has provided an excellent, detailed critique of the hazards involved in theoretically and inductively derived systems; his description of a regional variation in facial expression showed the parallel advantages that accrue from an anatomical approach.

Several investigators have attempted to derive anatomically based systems (Ermiane & Gregarian, 1978; Frois-Wittman, 1930; Fulcher, 1942; Landis, 1924; and refer to Ekman, 1981, for analyses of these systems). Because only anatomically based coding systems offer the possibility of being comprehensive, the extant systems can be judged against this standard.

Assessment of the comprehensiveness of any facial coding system must proceed with regard to four fundamental criteria. First, all visible facial actions must be included in the system (regardless of theoretical or inductive notions about function or signal value). Second, provision for coding the *intensity* of facial actions must be included; this provision is particularly important in measuring muscular excursions in the left versus the right side of the face, and in studies involving intensity of emotion. Third, *timing* of the facial actions, with regard both to stimulus situations and the patterning of the facial actions themselves, must be included in a comprehensive system. The response dynamics that must be coded include *onset time, apex time* and *offset time*; these fine-grained dynamics have already been implicated in the discrimination of deceptive versus felt expression (Ekman & Friesen, 1982) and deliberate versus spontaneous smiles (Ekman, Hager, & Friesen, 1981). Fourth, the behavioral units must be clearly and operationally defined, with high interrater reliabilities and suitable validity data.

Measured according to these criteria, nearly all the anatomically based systems fall short. Most were devised strictly to measure emotion. The systems devised by Frois-Wittman (1930), Fulcher (1942), and Landis (1924) contained only limited subsets of facial actions, and they made no provision for the timing of actions. Ermiane and Gregarian (1978) offered a system which codes all visible facial actions, including intensity information, but which excludes coding for the timing of facial actions. Ermiane and Gregarian also distinguished the actions of some muscles without data showing that they operated independently in visible behavior.

Ekman and Friesen's Facial Action Coding System (FACS; Ekman & Friesen, 1976, 1978) was developed to fill the need for a comprehensive, general-purpose system applicable in any context, not just in emotion-related situations. As a prerequisite, Ekman and Friesen sought to discover the precise role of each facial muscle on visible facial expression. In order to do so, they resurrected Duchenne's (1862) method of inserting needle electrodes in individual facial muscles. The muscle activity elicited by electrical stimulation at the electrode tip indicated the effect of each muscle on facial appearance. The facial actions that were discerned by Ekman and Friesen were found to be in accord with Hjorstjo's (1970) independent anatomical studies of the appearance of single facial muscle actions.

The descriptions of facial actions comprising FACS resulted not only from the resultant stimulation data, but also from a determination of whether particular muscle combinations resulted in *visibly* discriminable facial actions. On the one hand, distinct muscles that produce morphologically identical facial actions were combined. On the other hand, if a single muscle was found to produce visibly distinct actions, two or more units were designated. Therefore, all facial movements can be given unambiguous codes. From these observations, Ekman and Friesen derived 44 action units (AU's) that can, singly or in combination, account for all visible facial movement. All AU's are scoreable according to 5-point intensity ratings, and full provision is made for coding onset, apex and offset timing for each AU. High interrater reliabilities have been obtained using FACS. Empirical data also guided how precisely the intensity and timing of selected AU's could be rated reliably.

FACS takes considerable time to learn and use, requiring repeated, slow-motion viewing of facial actions. Because slow-motion replay is required, FACS is unsuitable for real-time coding. By its nature, FACS includes more distinctions than may be needed for any particular study, which increases the expense and tedium of measurement. However, once meaningful behavioral units are derived empirically (i.e., not from theoretical or inductive assertions), it is possible within a given study to collapse some of the elementary measurement units, or to disregard subtle distinctions. This point applies especially to studies of emotion—FACS suggests which AU's may, in fact, correlate with specific emotional states. These are presented as hypotheses that require validation.

Although not all the FACS emotion hypotheses have been tested, there is evidence (reviewed by Ekman, 1982a) to support a number of the predictions. From studies of spontaneous emotional expression in which subjective report was used as a validity criterion, predictions about the actions that signal happiness, fear, distress, and disgust have been supported (also see Accuracy section, following). Studies employing observers' attributions of emotion as a validity criterion have supported FACS predictions for these emotions as well as for surprise and anger.

Ekman and Friesen desired to suplement the comprehensive FACS with a standardized alternative that measures broader, emotion-related facial actions. The result, EMFACS, considers only emotional expressions, and among those only the AU's and AU combinations that are best supported by empirical findings or theory as emotion signals. As such, EMFACS is really a theory-based coding system, but with an important difference—its systematic derivation from FACS permits confident statements about what was omitted. The solidity of EMFACS as a system with empirical grounding is suggested by extensive concurrent validation studies with FACS, which indicate high correlations (> .8) of EMFACS with FACS ratings.

Coding time with EMFACS is speeded, albeit at the expense of subtler AU's and AU combinations, including those indicative of conversational signals or self-manipulations. The precise temporal dynamics of the facial actions are ignored in favor of unitary demarcations of peak actions. To maintain an empirical approach to the measurement procedure, the facial actions are, like FACS, described in terms of numerical codes. The coder is also requested not to interpret the actions as emotion signals until they are tabulated post hoc and classified according to EMFACS criteria.

Other measures of visible facial action.   Perhaps the most popular measure of facial activity has been direction of gaze, yet surprisingly this rarely has been studied in relation to emotion or facial expressions (recent exceptions have been provided in research by Graham & Argyle, 1975; Lalljee, 1978; Stechler & Carpenter, 1967; Stern, Beebe, & Jaffe, 1977; Waters, Matas, & Sroufe, 1975). Although pupil dilation has been studied in relation to emotion, we know of no study of associated changes in facial expression. Blood flow, skin temperature, electrodermal responding, and coloration changes in the face are other measures that so far remain unexplored.

Facial Electromyography

Following from earlier work by Malmo, Whatmore, and others (e.g., Malmo & Shagass, 1949; Whatmore & Ellis, 1959, 1962), the use of facial electromyography (EMG) has recently been advanced as a putative measure not only of posed expression, but also of mood and emotional states that are not necessarily accompanied by overt facial action. Because facial EMG attempts to measure activity of specific facial muscles, it can be seen as an exemplar of the direct measurement approach. Fridlund and Izard (1983) detailed the problems and potential of facial EMG and critically reviewed the existing literature.

Principles of electromyography. Electromyographic recording relies on Galvani's discovery that contracting muscle tissue emits electrical discharges. In modern electromyography, sensitive amplifiers detect the secondary spike trains (motor unit action potential trains or MUAPT) generated by the contracting tissue. Contact with the muscle tissue can be made directly by using indwelling fine wires. More frequently, recording proceeds indirectly through skin, using surface electrodes filled with conductive paste and attached to the skin with adhesive collars.

Why use facial EMG? Facial EMG has three advantages over pure facial observation. First, the EMG signal is instantaneously detectable and thereby lends itself to immediate recording. Second, the EMG signal is a precise, nearly linear index of isometric muscle contraction (Moritani & DeVries, 1978), offering a more finely graded measure of muscle activity than can be provided by raters. Third, EMG techniques can allow the detection of muscle contractions that are too small to be observable (see Ekman, 1981).

EMG measurement of facial activity is most applicable when the investigator can specify in advance the emotions and/or facial actions of interest, when unobtrusiveness is not crucial, and when the subject is not called upon to move the face or body excessively. EMG is probably most useful when emotion is elicited by fantasy, recall, listening, viewing a film, etc. EMG is also the only method for studying Birdwhistell's (1970) proposal that there are stable individual differences in the pattern of muscular tension maintained when the subject is "at rest" (see Smith, 1973; but also see Vitti & Basmajian, 1976; and further discussion on this point in the Accuracy section of this chapter).

Liabilities in facial electromyography. Several constraints plague the unencumbered use of facial EMG techniques as measures of facial action. Because the electrodes make direct contact with the face, the subject is usually manifestly aware that he/she is participating in research concerning the face, a condition that can result in distorted or attenuated facial behavior (Kleck, Vaughan, Cartwright-Smith, Vaughan, Colby, & Lanzetta, 1976).

The leads, paste, and tape tend to inhibit movement and may be torn by strong muscle actions. Attachment of recording discs can be problematic on males with heavy beard growth. If fine-wire recording is performed, implantation of the electrodes can be expected to produce some degree of irritation and pain.

Construct validity of facial electromyography as a measure of facial Action. Does facial EMG detect specific facial actions? Facial EMG should allow the detection of the activity of specific facial muscles in a given facial expression, or during an emotional situation. Usually it does not. Identifying the muscle or muscles that act as EMG sources is usually difficult, because the recording selectivity of EMG depends on a number of factors. Chief among these is the type of recording electrode. Pickup-site sensitivity and selectivity are high in the case of indwelling fine wires. These detect even low-amplitude motor units in close proximity, but they may exclude the transduction of distal units that may be part of the same muscle. On the other hand, the more commonly used surface discs are less sensitive and show broad pickup areas not confined to the muscle(s) underlying the electrode site. Selectivity is further lowered by the nonlinear transconductive properties of the intervening skin. Consequently, interpretation of surface EMG sources must be restricted to "muscle regions" or "tensional zones" instead of to specific muscles. The resultant intermuscle crosstalk may be attenuated somewhat through appropriate signal filtering (e.g., a highly restricted passband; see Fridlund & Fowler, 1978; Fridlund, Price, & Fowler, 1982), close spacing of differential paired electrodes over the selected site(s), and electronic "differencing" of signals from nearby sites, but caution is still warranted whenever surface recording is used for multichannel facial electrode montages.

Nor can a facial EMG signal be taken necessarily as an accurate representation of ongoing dynamic muscle activity. The relationship between detected electrical output at an EMG site and the mechanical force exerted by a muscle may change over time as a function of fatigue and learning (Mulder & Hulstijin, 1984). Proper attention is often not given to the influence of EMG signal-processing parameters upon the resultant detected signal. Because of the stochastic, "popcorn"-noise quality of the EMG signal, its transformation to a usable format for recording usually requires integration of the signal over a suitable time period. Unless the integration time constants are appropriately short, the signal dynamics that encode muscle onsets, offsets, and apices may be smoothed so as to be wiped out entirely. The result is that ongoing facial actions may be obscured. Differences in EMG signal-processing modes and parameters also severely limit comparability among facial EMG/ emotion studies.

Additionally, most of the current knowledge regarding how the EMG signal relates to underlying muscle activity was based on research involving the limb musculature, e.g., work performed in kinesiology, rehabilitation, and sports medicine. There is a small body of research concerning biofeedback of EMG activity in *lateral frontalis* as an indicant of "tension," but these findings are severely compromised by misunderstanding of facial EMG techniques and neglect of underlying facial anatomy (see discussions by Basmajian, 1976; Fridlund, Cottam, & Fowler, 1982; Fridlund, Fowler, & Pritchard, 1980).

There is little basic quantitative research concerning measurement parameters in facial EMG, optimal facial electrode placements, etc. Only one study (unpublished) has examined the relationship between the integrated electromyogram and correlated visible facial action. Ekman, Schwartz, and Friesen (reported in Ekman, 1981) found a monotonic yet nonlinear relationship. It is likely that the integrated facial electromyogram may best be modeled as a power function of facial action, using standard magnitude-estimation procedures (see Stevens, 1961, 1975), but this relationship must remain speculative until verified empirically.

The use of facial EMG techniques does not relieve the investigator of the responsibility for defining units of measurement and choosing which facial behaviors to observe. One must decide what features of the EMG signal are salient (i.e., what constitutes the EMG "response"?). Because of the cost in time and effort of using facial EMG techniques (sampling even a small proportion of facial muscles using EMG recording electrodes would require a large number of electrodes and an inordinate amount of subject preparation), the investigator must make a priori judgments about which facial behaviors will be important. Therefore, all facial EMG/emotion research can be seen as necessarily having a theory-based component.

To date, facial EMG techniques have seen use in studies of affective imagery and affective disorder (Brown & Schwartz, 1980; Carney, Hong, O'Connell, & Amado, 1981; Fridlund, Schwartz, & Fowler, 1984; Oliveau & Willmuth, 1979; Schwartz, Brown, & Ahern, 1980; Schwartz, Fair, Mandel, Salt, & Klerman, 1976a, b; Schwartz, Fair, Mandel, Salt, Mieske, & Klerman, 1978; Teasdale & Bancroft, 1977; Teasdale & Rezin, 1978); of posed expressions (Rusalova, Izard, & Simonov, 1975; Sumitsuji, Matsumoto, Tanaka, Kashiwagi, & Kaneko, 1967, 1977); and of social interaction and empathy (Cacioppo & Petty, 1979; Englis, Vaughan, & Lanzetta, 1981; Vaughan & Lanzetta, 1980, 1981). The findings of these studies are incorporated in other sections of this chapter. For a critical review of facial EMG/emotion literature to date, consult the chapter by Fridlund and Izard (1983).

ACCURACY

How can one determine if the information provided by a person's facial expression is an accurate indicant of emotional state? There must exist some criterion—independent of the face itself—for establishing which emotion, if any, was experienced at the moment of facial expression. This is especially problematic considering the fact that most facial behavior is probably not related to emotional display; rather, it appears to be punctuative, gestural, or parapractic (Ekman, 1977, 1978).

The problem of independent validation has been the greatest obstacle to research on accuracy. A common approach has been to ask subjects to report their feelings (usually retrospectively) and to see whether the facial expressions differ when reporting emotion A as compared to emotion B. Such self-reports are error-prone, because subjects may fail to remember, or to distinguish among, the emotions experienced—particularly if several minutes elapse before the report is made. A subject who successively felt anger, disgust, and contempt while watching a film might not recall all reactions, their exact sequence, or their time of occurrence. This problem can be lessened by limiting self-report to grosser distinctions (i.e., between pleasant and unpleasant feelings); however, one then cannot determine with any specificity the correlations between more complex facial behavior and affective states.

A second common approach has involved the use of specific intended elicitors of emotion, e.g., affectively positive versus negative films or slides; anticipation of an electric shock versus a no-shock trial; or hostile versus friendly remarks made by a confederate. The facial expressions of the respondents are then evaluated post hoc for variance attributable to the experimental conditions. Because it is unlikely that all subjects experience the same, discrete, sustained emotion during a particular condition, this approach can usually show only that different facial expressions are used in presumably pleasant and unpleasant conditions, or that there are overriding commonalities in facial behavior engendered by the experimental inductions.

Attempts to pre- or postdict other information about a subject (e.g., whether he/she has many friends) have also been used to assess accuracy. However, this approach implies that facial expressions can provide information about enduring traits in addition to transient states. Difficulties encountered in the operational definition of traits, in addition to the selection of units of facial measurement, encumber this approach.

If particular changes in vocal intensity or prosody, gross body movement, head position, or speech content were infallible indicators of particular emotions, these could then serve as accuracy criteria. Unfortunately, there is no evidence that these channels impart any more accurate information about emotional states than do facial expressions. The same difficulties befall investigators who seek unambiguous benchmarks for emotion in the (peripheral) autonomic nervous system, or in the central nervous system. The few studies that have explored the neural correlates of facial expression were reviewed earlier.

We would suggest that there is, in fact, no single, infallible way to determine an individual's "true" emotional state. We endorse the use of multiple convergent measures: facial, postural, psychophysiological, and others to gain a more reliable indication of the emotions displayed and experienced. The production of such multivariate indices of emotion would then derive from convergent and discriminant validation exercises, these being requisite for definition of the "nomological networks" that define soft constructs like "intelligence," "personality," and "emotion" (see Cronbach & Meehl, 1955).

What Has Been Found

Facial expressions of emotion can provide accurate information about the occurrence of pleasant as compared to unpleasant emotional states.

A reanalysis of studies from 1914 to 1970 concluded that both facial measurement and observers' judgment methods can accurately distinguish pleasant from unpleasant states (see Ekman et al., 1982b). Since then, a number of experiments (cited later) have replicated these findings but have not extended them to possible distinctions among particular positive and negative emotions. There is little information pinpointing the specific facial actions that discriminate pleasant from unpleasant states. In the vast majority of studies, most investigators have used the observer judgment approach, which precludes determining which configurations the observers were responding to. Those who directly measured facial expression have, in large part, failed to report the frequency of specific actions, and/or full-face conformations, that provided information.

Recent experiments using facial electromyography have produced evidence bearing on the discrimination of pleasant versus unpleasant emotional states. Schwartz, Fair, Salt, Mandel, and Klerman (1976a, b) used an affective-imagery task in an attempt to induce emotions. The authors showed that "happy" imagery conditions were separable from negative-affect conditions, largely through the reciprocal activities in EMG sites overlying *corrugator supercilii* (which lowers and draws together the brows) and *zygomatic major* (again, which raises lip corners in a smile). *Corrugator* sites also tend to show EMG activity corresponding with self-reported negative-thought frequency (Teasdale & Rezin, 1978). Fridlund, Schwartz, and Fowler (1984) reported good discrimination of "happy" from negative-affect imagery trials, using four-EMG-site recording montage and multivariate pattern classification. In these EMG studies, the imagery trials are supposed to induce "real" emotions. That they may instead induce a type of posed expression has been suggested by Ekman, Hager, and Friesen (1981), and later by Fridlund and Izard (1983)

A careful analysis of *what* responses are being detected in these EMG experiments has yet to be performed. Are subjects in "negative-affect" conditions just frowning more, and in "positive-affect" conditions smiling more? Or is there more tonic muscular activity signifying an index of mood? No definitive data have been provided. Anecdotal observations by Fridlund et al.

(1984) suggest that the responses to imagery items are often phasic and do not fit the tonic interpretations often provided. A corroborating finding was that the lability of the EMG activity in each recording site was nearly as discriminative of imagery-trial type as overall mean EMG activity (Fridlund et al., 1984). Further developments in temporal analysis of the EMG signal may provide additional clues (Cacioppo, Marshall–Goodell, & Dorfman, 1982). However, videotape recordings of subjects' facial behavior coincident with highly resolved EMG recording would provide a more complete answer.

Facial expressions can provide accurate information about the intensity of emotion and can distinguish among several specific negative and positive emotions.   Surprisingly, there are few "decoding" studies that attempt to categorize putatively spontaneous facial expressions among a range of emotional categories. Most studies have either used posed expressions as stimuli or have instructed subjects merely to classify facial expressions along a pleasant–unpleasant dimension. Yet a few studies offer data that are relevant.

Ekman, Friesen, and Ancoli (1980) used FACS to study the spontaneous facial expressions that occurred while subjects watched motion picture films and then reported on their subjective experience. High correlations were found between specific facial actions hypothesized to be signs of positive and negative emotions and ratings of subjective intensity of those positive and negative emotions, respectively. Facial actions that reliably distinguished reports of disgust were isolated.

Several facial EMG studies have attempted to discriminate among multiple posed emotional states. Highly patterned, multiple-site EMG activity is found with instructions to pose facial expressions of several emotions (Sumitsuji, Matsumoto, Tanaka, Kashiwagi, & Kaneko, 1967). Trained actors generate higher amplitude, more discriminable EMG patterns than untrained controls (Rusalova, Izard, & Simonov, 1975). Factor scores derived from principal-component analyses of facial EMG patterns of posed facial expressions were reported to be congruent with Schlosberg's dimensional emotion typology (Sumitsuji, Matsumoto, Tanaka, Kashiwagi, & Kaneko, 1977).

Other EMG studies have yielded suggestive data for imagery and conditioning-related emotional inductions. In this regard, mere exposure to posed-expression photographs can elicit differential EMG patterns in observers (Dimberg, 1982), although this effect is hard to replicate and may be due to unintended "priming" of subjects to respond emotionally (McHugo & Lanzetta, personal communication, 1983). Lanzetta and colleagues have employed a "vicarious classical conditioning" paradigm, whereby observers are exposed to a model who appears to be experiencing pain. Under these conditions, subjects generate EMG patterns congruent with "anticipaton" and "pain" when models are observed to be (ostensibly) anticipating, then receiving, noxious stimuli (Vaughan & Lanzetta, 1980). Asking observers to either "amplify" or to "inhibit" their facial expressions during conditioning trials does not affect subsequent conditioned facial EMG "empathetic" responding (although, of course, the facial EMG activity during conditioning paralleled the instruction to amplify or inhibit; Englis, Vaughan, & Lanzetta, 1981). Empathic and counterempathic EMG patterns are discriminable when model/observer outcomes are made congruent or incongruent in a gaming situation (Vaughan & Lanzetta, 1981). Finally, Fridlund et al. (1984) showed reliable multivariate classifications of both posed and imagery-related trials across emotional categories of happiness, sadness, anger, and fear.

Facial expressions can be disguised to mislead an observer about the emotion experienced. It is nearly a truism that facial displays manifest by individuals may not only reflect emotional state, but they may also (a) feign emotion when none is present (e.g., the *phony* smile), (b) attenuate or dampen the apparent intensity of any felt positive emotion (e.g., the dampened smile), and/or (c) mask the presence of a typically negative-felt emotion with a simulated alternative emotion (e.g., the *masking* smile). Quite often the literature has obscured these distinctions through the use of the over-inclusive term *deception.* In order to understand by which process subjects are responding, it is therefore necessary in facial deception studies to sample not only facial behavior but also other response systems possibly indicative of emotion. Among the dozens of recent experiments on interpersonal deceit, few (e.g., Ekman & Friesen, 1974a; Harper, Wiens, & Fujita, 1977; Lanzetta, Cartwright-Smith, & Kleck, 1976; Mehrabian, 1971; Zuckerman, DeFrank, Hall, Larrance, & Rosenthal, 1979) explicitly instructed subjects to conceal their emotions and also obtained evidence independent of the face that subjects actually experienced some emotion (also see the developmental section in this chapter for studies on nonverbal deception in children).

These experimental tests of the extent to which the face can be used deceptively have yielded contradictory results. This ambiguity in findings is most likely due to variations in the strength or number of emotions aroused, the subjects' motivation to deceive, and their prior practice in perpetrating such deception. However, these experiments have also differed in other ways: e.g., whether subjects knew they were being videotaped; whether observers knew that deception might be involved; whether the observers were trained; and whether channels other than facial expression were available to observers.

Probably the single most ambiguous piece of facial behavior is the smile (Ekman & Friesen, 1975). When a tachistoscope limits visual exposure to a fraction of a second, smiles are the most easily recognized facial expressions (O'Sullivan, Ekman, & Friesen, unpublished manuscript) and are matched only by surprise expressions in observers' ability to recognize them at a distance. Their decoding by observers as representing either felt or unfelt positive feelings occur at levels no better than chance (O'Sullivan, Ekman, Friesen, & Weiss, unpublished manuscript).

A variety of studies has shown no difference in how often people smile when they are lying or being truthful (Finkelstein, 1978; Helmsley, 1977; Hocking & Leathers, 1980; Knapp, Hart, & Dennis, 1974); Krauss, Geller, & Olson, 1976; Kraut,1978; Kraut & Poe, 1980; McLintock & Hunt, 1975; Mehrabian, 1971; O'Hair, Cody, & McLaughlin, 1981). However, in a detailed analysis of smiles, Ekman and Friesen (1982) surmised that "felt," "false," and "miserable" smiles (miserable smiles are those occurring with negative affect, e.g., in sadness or shame) were discriminable not by frequency of occurrence, but by the topography of the smiles themselves.

In a study of the relationship between the actions of *zygomatic major* and the intensity of reported pleasure at viewing a film (Ekman, Friesen, & Ancoli, 1980), the felt smiles (those that correlated with self-reported emotion ratings) exhibited durations that were typically more than two-thirds of a second, and less than 4 seconds. Within these temporal boundaries, the reported strength of positive emotion correlated with the exact duration of the smile, the intensity of the muscular contractions, and the frequency of smiling.

Ekman and Friesen (1982) have speculated that false (phony or masking) smiles may differ from felt smiles in that they (a) usually do not involve orbicularis oculi activity (the "crinkly-eye" appearance); (b) will tend to be slightly asymmetrical, generally stronger on the left side of the face if the individual is righthanded (also see Borod & Caron, 1980; Ekman, Hager, & Friesen, 1981); (c) may occur with onset times that are socially inappropriate; (d) show excessively long apex durations, short onset times, and irregular offset times. Masking smiles may uniquely cooccur with *leakage cues* to the presence of felt negative emotions.

"Miserable" smiles are usually singularly deliberate, reflecting social acknowledgment of the presence of negative affect. These smiles were thought by Ekman and Friesen (1982) to be (a) asymmetrical, (b) very brief, lasting two thirds of a second or less, (c) cooccur with, or amid, pronounced facial behavior signifying negative emotion.

These proposed differentiations of smile types are presented as assertions, only some of which have been tested to date. Ekman and Friesen (pilot study) found that the smiles shown by depressed patients fit their predictions about unfelt smiles, and this has also since been replicated by Matsumoto (unpublished masters' thesis). Ekman and Friessen also found that the smiles shown by nondepressed individuals when viewing pleasant films fit their predictions about felt smiles, whereas smiles shown in response to unpleasant films fit their predictions about unfelt smiles.

Also consistent with these predictions are data from a recent study by Oster, Rosenstein, and Shapiro (unpublished data), who found significant negative correlations between the Beck Depression Inventory (BDI) scores of undergraduate subjects and the intensity of the smiles these subjects had previously posed when requested to smile for a polaroid snapshot (higher BDI scores indicate greater dysphoria and/or depression). Pronounced contraction of orbicularis oculi accompanied moderate to intense smiles in subjects with the lowest BDI scores. However, in some subjects with high BDI scores, strong orbicularis oculi contraction accompanied very low intensity smiles, in these cases looking more like a "wince." Actions suggesting "leakage" of negative emotions, though rare, were confined to subjects with high BDI scores. Thus, even posed smiles can accurately reflect mood.

To date, there is little research bearing on deceptive facial behaviors other than smiling, and there has been little validation of the kinds of cues that characterize different types of deceptive or otherwise "unfelt" facial behavior. The relationship between facial behavior and nonfacial cues in deception situations is not adequately known, although recent studies suggest that there are individual differences in the ability to deceive that span facial and nonfacial channels (see Zuckerman, DeFrank, Fall, Larrance, & Rosenthal, 1979).

Individuals differ in facial "expressiveness" (encoding ability) and in their ability to judge facial expressions (decoding ability).   In encoding/decoding studies, encoders are videotaped in emotion-arousing situations (while watching slides or undergoing shock). Decoders (often the same subjects) then try to infer, from each encoder's facial expressions, the eliciting condition (category of slides or level of shock) or the encoder's rating of his/her own emotional experience. There are marked individual differences in how accurately an individual's facial expressions are judged, and in how accurately an individual judges the faces of others (Buck, 1977, 1978; Cunningham, 1977; Harper, Wiens, & Fujita, 1977; Lanzetta & Kleck, 1970; Zuckerman, Larrance, Hall, DeFrank, & Rosenthal, 1979). Fridlund et al. (1984) also showed, using facial EMG techniques, a wide range of "discriminability" of facial EMG patterns across subjects in both imagery and posed-expression tasks.

Attempts to study the relationship between encoding and decoding abilities have produced mixed and/or nonsignificant results (see Fujita, 1977, for a careful discussion). Inconsistent but largely negative findings have also been obtained in the search for personality correlates of individual differences in encoding and decoding abilities (O'Sullivan, 1982). An exception is the small but consistent superiority of women in both encoding and decoding (Brunori, Ladavas, & Ricci–Bitti, 1979; Cherulnik, 1979; Friedman, 1979; Gallagher & Shuntich, 1981; Hall, 1977, 1978), although the components of this superiority have not been elaborated. Women have also shown greater sensitivity to facial movements by infants during REM sleep (Briem & Nystrom, 1978). Blacks and whites apparently do significantly better in same-race recognition of photographic poses than they do with photos of individuals of the other race (Brigham & Barkowitz, 1978).

These studies are fraught with methodological problems, which may explain some of the inconsistencies in the findings. In some designs, the subjects must periodically rate their own emotional experience, a task that might affect their facial expression or the emotional experience itself. In many experiments, the actual emotions (if any) experienced by the encoders are not verified. Exceptions are studies that obtained independent ratings of the emotions aroused by their elicitors (Cunningham, 1977; Harper, Wiens, & Fujita, 1977), or that used psychophysiological measures to indicate arousal, though not which emotion was aroused (Lanzetta, Cartwright-Smith, & Kleck, 1976). Most often, the only measure of emotional arousal is the observers' success in inferring the relative pleasantness of the eliciting condition, or the subject's subsequent rating of his/her own feelings (Buck, Miller, & Caul, 1974; Buck, Savin, Miller, & Caul, 1972; Zuckerman, Hall, DeFrank, & Rosenthal, 1976). Such judgment could be made on the basis of cues having nothing to do with facial expression, e.g., posture or gross body movements, or with facial signs of *cognitive* activity.

An additional problem in many decoding tasks is that observers must judge facial expressions that occurred during speech, but with the speech omitted. Only the deaf might have sufficient experience with this condition to develop stable individual differences in decoding such stimuli. Quite a different approach to individual differences is illustrated by findings that the emotional state of the observer can influence the emotion attributed to a facial expression (Rothbart & Birrell, 1977; Schiffenbauer, 1974).

As reviewed extensively by O'Sullivan (1982), many investigators have used standardized materials in studying individual differences in the ability to decode facial expressions of emotion (e.g., Buck, 1976; Buzby, 1924; Langfeld, 1918; O'Sullivan, Guilford, & DeHille, 1965; Tomkins, & McCarter, 1964; Rosenthal, Hall, DiMatteo, Rogers, & Archer, 1979). The resulting measurement scales have varied with regard to both stimulus materials (ranging from sketches of facial expressions, to photographed poses and videotape segments) and response measures (e.g., free verbal labeling, photographic matching, Likert scales of "pleasantness;" structured category-matching). Current examplars of such scales include BART (Brief Affect Recognition Task: Ekman & Friesen, 1974b), CARAT (Communication of Affect Receiving Ability Test: Buck, 1977), and PONS (Profile of Nonverbal Sensitivity; Rosenthal et al., 1979).

There are cerebral-hemispheric differences in the perception of faces. Several converging lines of evidence (clinical observation, research on commissurotomized patients, and recognition, discrimination, and reaction-time ex-

periments with normal and brain-injured subjects) point to a right-hemis-
here (and thus a left visual-field) advantage in recognizing faces (e.g.,
Bruyer, 1981; Cicone, Wapner, & Gardner, 1980; DeKosky, Heilman, Bow-
ers, & Valenstein, 1980; Finlay & French, 1978; Hilliard, 1973; Marzi &
Berlucci, 1977; Safer, 1981; Strauss & Moscovitch, 1981; and see reviews by
Benton, 1980; Bradshaw & Nettleton, 1981; Bruyer, 1980b; and Sergent &
Bindra, 1981).

The right-hemisphere advantage in recognizing faces is especially pronounced (a) when the task requires processing in terms of the higher order,
configurative properties of faces, rather than isolated features (Campbell,
1978; Diamond & Carey, 1977); (b) if the faces to be recognized by subjects
show emotional expressions, rather than when they are affectively neutral
(Suberi & McKeever, 1977; but see Hansch & Pirozzolo, 1980); (c) if the faces
are shown right-side-up (Bruyer, 1980a; Leehey, Carey, Diamond, & Cahn,
1978; however, this effect may hold only for unfamiliar faces — see Phillips &
Rawles, 1979); and (d) if the subject is female (Ladavas, Umilita, & Ricci-
Bitti, 1980). The sex differences may be reflective of sex-related field-
independent versus field-dependent cognitive styles (Pizzamiglio & Zoccolotti, 1981).

It is not clear at what age the right-hemisphere advantage begins to emerge,
but there is concensus that it is seen by the age of 7 or 8 and is reportedly fully
apparent by age 13 (Broman, 1978; Reynolds & Jeeves, 1978; Young & Ellis,
1976).

In their review of this literature, Sergent and Bindra (1981) added that the
right-hemisphere advantage in perception of faces is best observed when (a)
stimulus information is "degraded" by using short tachistoscopic exposure
times, or peripheral-vision presentation; (b) the faces to be compared are
highly discriminable; (c) sets of unfamiliar faces are used; and (d) task requirements allow a lax response criterion (e.g., in recognition or perception
tasks, which require fewer operations than in indentification tasks; Sergent &
Bindra, 1981, p. 541).

The right-hemisphere advantage in facial perception may not reflect specific right-hemispheric specialization for emotion, or for faces in particular.
Rather, the differences may more parsimoniously reflect right-hemisphere
specialization for "holistic," parallel-input perception of gestalten, as opposed to processing according to a seriated, analytic mode. In support of this
conclusion, a reexamination of cases of documented prosopagnosia (inability to recognize faces) reveals that in such cases the patients were not only
"face-blind," but that their deficits also included difficulties in recognizing a
broad range of visually ambiguous, context-dependent stimuli (Damasio,
Damasio, & Van Hoesen, 1982).

There are recent data showing reaction-time differences when subjects
tachistoscopically viewed "happy" or "sad" poses in either the left or right visual field (Reuter–Lorenz & Davidson, 1981). The results were interpreted as

favoring a left-hemisphere advantage for processing positive emotions, and a right-hemisphere advantage in processing negative emotions (see Gur & Gur, 1980). These data must be accepted tentatively, because the results are confounded with relative ease of identification of smiles versus negative-affect expressions (see data by Buchtel, Campari, De Risio, & Rota, 1978). More complex findings were reported by Pizzamiglio, Zoccoltti, Mammucari, and Cesaroni (1983), whose tachistoscopic data showed trends toward left-visual-field superiority for fear, disgust, surprise, sadness, and happiness (significant only in the case of disgust) — and right-visual-field superiority only for anger! These unexpected findings have been replicated in another sample (Pizzamiglio, personal communication, 1983).

The inconsistencies across all the experiments cited in this section on cerebral hemispheric specialization for face perception await clarification. Furthermore, an integration of studies relating putative hemispheric processes in face perception and facial-expression generation has yet to be accomplished.

Unanswered or Unasked Questions

How much information does the face, as compared to voice, speech, and body movement, provide about emotion?   A number of studies have compared observers' judgments about an event perceived via different verbal and nonverbal "channels": audiovisual, aural alone, or visual alone. Others have focused on which of several discrepant cues (delivered across channels) are remembered or acted upon. Since the initial findings by Merabian and Ferris (1967), most experiments have found that the face is more accurately judged, produces higher agreement, or correlates better with judgments based on full audiovisual input than do speech content or tone of voice; this difference has been termed *video primacy* (see Argyle, Alkema, & Gilmour, 1971; Bugental, Kaswan, & Love, 1970; Burns & Beier, 1973; DePaulo, Rosenthal, Eisenstat, Finkelstein, & Rogers, 1978; Zaidel & Mehrabian, 1969). The video primacy is especially apparent when speech content is filtered (Zuckerman, Amidon, Bishop, & Pomerantz, 1982). Results of a few experiments have departed from the Merabian–Ferris (1967) findings and have suggested that the face was less important than another channel (Berman, Shulman, & Marwit, 1976; Shapiro, 1972) or that channel cue varied with the observer (Vande Creek & Watkins, 1972). The factors accounting for these differences in findings are not presently known.

The findings of most "channel" experiments are suspect because the behavior judged was quite contrived. The most extensive series of studies (Cline, Atzet, & Holmes, 1972, on naturally occurring behavior found that what was said mattered more than the visual input, and that knowledge of demographic information produced as much accurate behavioral postdiction as exposure to an audiovisual film. Another problem in this research is that observers judging the "face" channel are usually shown — without sound — facial expressions that occurred embedded in speech. Alternatively, the facial expressions are shown with content-filtered or randomized speech. This could cause misinterpretation of speech-related facial expressions. Moreover, observers who are limited to just the face may obtain more information than they would ordinarily get from the face when it is viewed in context.

A study by Ekman, Friesen, O'Sullivan, and Scherer (1980) found that the relative weight given to facial expression, speech, and body cues depended both on the judgment task (e.g., rating the stimulus object's dominance, sociability, or relaxation) and on the conditions in which the behavior occurred (while subjects frankly described positive reactions to a pleasant film or tried to conceal negative feelings aroused by a stressful film). The correlation between judgments made by observers who saw the face with speech were quite low on some scales (e.g., calm–agitated) and quite high on other scales (outgoing–withdrawn).

Krauss et al. (Krauss, Apple, Morency, Wenzel, & Winton, 1981) also published data bearing on the relative weighting of verbal and nonverbal channels. Krauss et al. (1981) used judgments from observers of a televised political debate and videotaped samples of interviews with college women, alone and in combination with typescripts and content-filtered speech for the debate and interviews, to conclude that there was "no support for the widespread assumption that nonverbal channels . . . form the primary basis for the communication of affect" (p. 312). As such, the Krauss et al. findings have been interpreted as corroborating those of Ekman et al. (1980) in negating video primacy (Zuckerman et al., 1982). However, O'Sullivan, Ekman, Friessen and Scherer (1985) criticized the Krauss et al. findings because (a) no independent evidence was obtained that the videotaped expressors were emotionally aroused; (b) typescripts were selected with bias toward samples rich in verbal content; (c) face and body were not isolated for videotaped presentations; and (d) the rating scales used had low ecological validity. O'Sullivan et al. (1985) reemphasized that the Ekman et al. (1980) data did *not* negate video primacy but rather established the context-dependency of video primacy.

Studies by Bugental et al. have suggested that the influence of facial expression, as compared to other sources, depends on the expressor, the perceiver, the message contained in each channel, and previous experience. Children were less influenced than were adults by a smile shown by an adult female when it was accompanied by negative words and voice tone (Bugetal, Kaswan, Love, & Fox, 1970). Some experimental grounds for distrusting mothers' smiles was found in a study showing that smiling in mothers (but not fathers) was not related to the positive versus negative content of the simultaneous speech (Bugental, Love, & Gianetto, 1971). Also, mothers (but not fathers) of disturbed children produced more discrepant messages (among face, voice, and words) than did parents of nondisturbed children (Bugental, Love, & Kaswan, 1971).

Although Scherer et al. (Scherer, Scherer, Hall, & Rosenthal, 1977) studied judgments of personality rather than emotion, his findings also contradict the simple notion that one channel is better than another. Personality inferences were usually channel specific, some best made from one source, some from another. No one combination of channels (face plus speech, face plus voice, etc.) yielded the most accurate judgments. It varied with the trait judged.

The whole question of how much information is conveyed by separate channels is misleading. There is no evidence that individuals in actual social interaction selectively attend to another person's face, body, voice, or speech, or that the information conveyed by these channels is simply additive. Nor is there evidence that separate channels offer orthogonal contributions to communication. To the contrary, we would speculate that encoding of emotion or other communication among channels is quite configurative. Additionally, the central mechanisms directing behavior cut across channels, so that, for example, certain aspects of face, body, voice, and speech are more spontaneous, whereas others are more closely monitored and controlled.

Evidence on this point is provided by a separate line of studies that focused on the channels that are attended to in detecting deception. Zuckerman, DePaulo, and Rosenthal (1981) summarized several studies comparing face versus body cues in detecting deception and concluded by showing, in accordance with Ekman and Friesen's (1969) concept of the "leakage-cue hierarchy," that body cues were more likely to "leak" deceptive information than facial cues. Zuckerman, Larrance, Spiegel, and Klorman (1981) showed that subjects could achieve more control over facial expressions than tone of voice. Zuckerman, Amidon, Bishop, and Pomerantz (1982) subsequently showed that the tone of voice (the *less* controllable channel) was a more potent source of leakage cues for deception. DePaulo and Rosenthal (in press), using their Nonverbal Discrepancy Test, found that the video primacy effect increases with age (see also the discussion by Blanck & Rosenthal (1982) on the developmental aspects of video primacy in discrepant messages).

It might well be that observers selectively attend not to a particular channel, but to a particular type of information (e.g., cues to emotion, deception, or cognitive activity), which might be available within several channels. No investigator has explored this possibility, or the possibility that different individuals may characterologically attend to different types of information or encoding channels (although clinical supposition indicates they do; see Bandler & Grinder, 1975).

Are encoding and decoding abilities stable?   Although the search for personality correlates of individual differences in encoding and decoding abilities (reviewed earlier) implies that these differences are stable, there has been no study of test–retest reliability in individual encoding ability. One study has explored encoding and decoding abilities in the same subjects (in pre-school-age children) and discovered no relationship (Zuckerman & Przewuzman, 1979).

A persistent notion pertains to whether individuals manifest chronic patterns of tension in their facial musculature that correspond to personality style or character structure. These patterns might conceivably be decoded as personality attributes (Secord, 1958). As mentioned earlier, Birdwhistell (1970) proposed that there might be stable individual differences in facial-muscle patterns that would reflect cultural and characterological influences.

The seeming plausibility of this hypothesis is belied by the neurophysiological data. It is true that the facial muscles manifest a "base-line" tonus. However, this tonus is mechanical, due in great part to the basic turgor of muscle tissue, possibly sustained by low-level tonic humoral stimulation (Bender, 1938) and so-called "nutritive" effects of facial nerve (Drachman, 1974; Gutmann, 1976; and see Ekman, 1982b, for a discussion of the consequences of facial nerve surgery upon facial expressions). The facial muscle tonus is *not* related directly to motoneuron or muscle-tissues electrical activity—most observers agree that relaxed facial muscles demonstrate no base-line electrical activity (Moldaver, 1980b, Vitti & Basmajian, 1976), with the possible exception of nonmimical, antigravity muscles (e.g., the temporalis and masseter, which support the lower jaw). Therefore, no "resting" muscle activity could acount for any encoding of emotional or personality factors.

It is nonetheless possible that individuals may, in social interaction, assume a "social face" that might include stereotyped, characterological patterns of *active* muscular contraction. These patterns could probably be discerned only with ambulatory EMG monitoring performed in social situations, and permitting this, with participants habituated to the presence of the measurement apparatus. No data are yet available on this issue.

What factors account for accurate encoding and decoding of emotion?   It is not clear from the present research which encoder responses in an emotional situation reliably confer affective cues. Correspondingly, the strategies used by decoders in attempt to appraise the emotional state of an encoder, or the affective context of a situation, are not well known. It is probable that *asking* decoders which encoder cues accounted for their responses is not sufficient, as suggested by the finding that there is little relationship between face-recognition ability and ability to verbalize facial descriptors (Goldstein, Johnson, & Chance, 1979). Additionally, the use of static poses (e.g., photographed faces) may not be relevant to how in vivo emotion recognition occurs, because data using black-face makeup and painted white dots on select facial features have shown motion cues to be adequate for decoding some emotions (e.g., Bassili, 1978, 1979). Detailed component analyses of decoding strategies are mandated, with special regard to findings that some facial signs show more discriminative efficiency than others for decoders and for specific emotions (Bassili, 1979; Boucher & Ekman, 1975; and see review by Ekman, Friesen, & Ellsworth, 1982a).

O'Sullivan (1982) has cast the measurement of encoding and decoding abilities in terms of the psychometric procedures of test construction and validation. From this perspective, adherence to psychometric principles can (a) minimize lexical and logical ambiguities in what is being measured (e.g., "nonverbal sensitivity" vs. "receiving ability") and ambiguities as to whether these abilities are to be considered specific or general traits; (b) force experimenters to consider the ramifications of their choices concerning stimulus materials and presentation (schematic or realistic faces, clarity of stimuli, poses versus spontaneous expressions, context in which facial expressions are presented, sampling domain among emotion categories, and possibly confounding speech movements); (c) predict biases that ensue from mode of response (verbal labeling or nonverbal responding such as figure matching); (d) test the robustness of the measured ability through processes of convergent and discriminant validation; and (e) assess the more traditional psychometric properties of internal consistency, test–retest reliability, and difficulty level.

The need for adherence to psychometric procedures in construct definition and validation is revealed in studies that show poor convergent validation among the various scales of "decoding ability" (Fields & O'Sullivan, 1976; Harper, Wiens, & Matarazzo, 1979; Rosenthal et al., 1979). As O'Sullivan (1982) states, "A test that does not correlate highly with itself [or, we would add, with others held to be sampling the same domain] has little chance of correlating with other measures" (p. 311). The elaboration of the constructs of encoding and decoding abilities, and their extension to other research questions, must await the development of more reliable and valid measurement scales.

AUTONOMIC NERVOUS SYSTEM CORRELATES OF FACIAL EXPRESSIONS

There are few studies relating facial behavior to ongoing physiological activity. Such studies are important in that they focus on facial behavior that may signify an internal organismic state (i.e., emotion), and because psychophysiological responses are also used as indicants of emotional responding. Proper investigation of autonomic correlates of facial behavior can lead to construct validation of emotion classifications, to the derivation of typologies of facial expressions (emotional versus others), and to the clarification of the possible role of facial behavior in mediating physiological change and subjective experience.

Historically, investigations of the psychophysiology of emotion have focused on the autonomic nervous system (ANS). A complete discussion of ANS involvement in emotion is beyond the scope of this chapter (see classic paper by Lacey, 1967; and recent reviews by Leshner, 1977 and Tarpy, 1977). However, it is desirable to consider briefly (a) the role of the ANS in emotion, (b) the anatomical articulations of autonomic pathways with those for facial expression, and (c) the extant research exploring facial/autonomic correlates.

What Has Been Found

The ANS is closely related to emotional behavior and experience.   Since James' initial outlining of the importance of autonomic nervous system (ANS) activity in emotional behavior (James, 1884), the ANS has been regarded as "the nervous system for the emotions." Certainly the everyday subjective experience of common ANS-mediated response systems in emotion (facial flushing and blanching, sweat gland activity, altered heart rate and blood pressure, respiratory changes, etc.) lends credence to such a linkage. However, the role of the ANS is instigating and/or mediating emotional behavior and experience still requires clarification.

Research relating to ANS functioning in emotion has been dominated by two traditions. The Jamesian tradition postulates that the peripheral patterning of autonomic and striate-muscle activity determines the specific emotion experienced (anger, fear, happiness, etc.), and within experimental psychophysiology, a number of studies have found such patterns associated with differing emotional states (Arnold, 1945; Averill, 1969; Ax, 1953; Funkenstein, 1957; J. Schachter, 1957). The Jamesian peripheralist position also underlies investigations of the "facial feedback hypothesis" (discussed later).

In contrast, within the "centralist" tradition of W. Cannon (1929), ANS activity (specifically, sympathetic/parasympathetic balance) is regarded as "an undifferentiated physiological soup" (Lang, 1979), which indicates intensity but not valence of emotional *behavior*—the valence is determined by cognitive appraisal (consult the careful review of physiological theories of emotion by Goldstein, 1968, for assumptions of the James and Cannon theories and their derivatives). The supporting evidence for the centralist position has typically been obtained from studies involving social evocation of multiple emotions despite injection of sympathomimetic drugs (Cantril & Hunt, 1932; Maranon, 1924; Schachter & Singer, 1962). The cognitive-appraisal views of emotion have been predominant within social psychology.

Not unexpectedly, both lines of research have yielded results that are inconclusive (see Fridlund, Gibson, & Newman, 1984, for summary of evidence for centralist and peripheralist theories). This is true for several reasons:

1. Hierarchical, servomechanistic views of emotion (Candland, 1977) based on more sophisticated mechanisms of motor organization (Gallistel, 1980) have displaced the relatively simplistic conceptions of both James and Cannon.

2. James' and Cannon's theories focus only on whether visceromotor patterning is necessary or sufficient for emotion. Neither makes strict predictions about the extent of ANS/motor patterning that might accompany, though not necessarily mediate, emotion. Moreover, a careful reading of James (1884, 1890) reveals that he was not a hard-core peripheralist: James believed that "coarse" emotions stemmed largely from perception or visceromotor patterning, whereas the "subtle" emotions were much more psychologically determined.

3. The evidence claimed for each position provides only equivocal support, and often can be reframed as supporting the competing position. For example, studies showing physiological discriminations among emotions are often held to support James' theory. However, in these studies it is never clear that the discriminations mediate the participant's emotional states. The observed patterns may simply be vestigial display components of emotion (i.e., sweating or piloerection) that do not mediate, but merely indicate emotion. Alternatively, the patterns may just reflect compensatory bodily *responses* to differential physiological demands of each emotion. A third possibility is that the obtained patterns may reflect not emotion specificity, but different levels of generalized arousal wherein noncollinear changes in activation of different physiological response systems *look* like "patterning" (see Fridlund, 1985).

Another example of the inconclusiveness of existing research comes from studies that involve injection of diffuse sympathomimetics. The diversity of behaviors observed after injection is taken as support for a centralist theory of emotion (e.g., Schachter & Singer, 1962). However, this finding does not conflict with James' theory: diffuse arousal agents should not be expected to elicit pure or predictable emotion. Only injections that produced a prototypic physiological pattern for an emotion could be expected to elicit that emotion.

4. Physiological theories of emotion have not adequately distinguished between autonomic *neural* mediation, which is highly specific and phasic in action, and endocrine (epinephrine, norepinephrine, corticosteroid, and endorphin) mediation, which is diffuse and tonic. Consideration of the former undercuts Cannon's dictum that ANS processes could not mediate emotion because they were too slow and diffuse.

5. Neither centralist nor peripheralist theorists adequately distinguish between emotional *display* or *behavior,* and emotional *experience* (Cannon spoke mainly about the former, and James about the latter).

In summary, little can be learned about emotion or about the visceromotor responses that accompany it by continuing to pit James' views against Cannon's. What we need to do is to specify the linkages that do exist between facial (and nonfacial) expressions of emotion and the actions of the ANS.

There are close anatomical connections between face and ANS. The precise connections between the facial muscles and the ANS are not well known. Stimulation of motor-cortical tissue (e.g., that mediating facial action) typically evokes concurrent phasic ANS activity (Wall & Pribram, 1950); this phasic activity is generally held to be compensatory to the energetic or circulatory demands of motor activity (Freeman, 1948).

More direct connections may also be involved, and our mention of them serves to underscore the *non*-emotional functions of the face. There is evidence in the cat that the tenth cranial nerve (CN X, vagus), which is the mediator of parasympathetic influences throughout the viscera, contains afferent fibers that impinge directly upon facial motoneurons (also see earlier discussion of neuroanatomical substrates of facial expression). These fibers are suggested to participate in coordination of eating, chewing, and digestion (Tanaka & Asahara, 1981). The facial nuclei are also impinged upon by fibers from other pontine nuclei, such as those mediating ocular and trigeminal (facial-afferent) function. These influences participate in the facial reflexes (e.g., the blink, rooting, and sucking reflexes; Bratzlavsky & vander Eecken, 1977). Other fibers from the auditory systems are hypothesized to mediate facial involvement in orientation and auditory localization (Santibanez, Espinoza, Astorga, & Strozzi, 1974).

Within the biofeedback and stress-management literature, there has been a great deal of research concerning the relationship between "tension" in the lateral frontales and ANS responding. This work has proceeded under the erroneous assumption that *frontalis* activity (typically measured electromyographically) is particularly indicative of "stress" or ANS-mediated "arousal" (see Fridlund, Fowler, & Pritchard, 1980, and Fridlund, Cottam, & Fowler, 1982, for discussion of this issue). Intimate neural connections were posited between the *frontales* and hypothalamic ANS-mediating regions (Gellhorn, 1964; Gellhorn & Kiely, 1972); this association has not been borne out. However, in none of this research were facial *expressions* related to stress or arousal state; this literature is thus excluded from the present review.

Facial behavior is reliably associated with ANS changes. Two different approaches have examined the relationship between facial expression and ANS responding. In one type of study, gross changes in autonomic measures (mostly electrodermal response, EDR) averaged over some period of time are compared with changes in facial expression (as inferred by observers' judgments of emotion). The alternative approach has examined correlated patterning in the moment-to-moment changes in ANS and facial measures. This latter approach has produced more consistent results.

Correlation studies of individual differences in ANS responsivity and facial expressiveness (e.g., in the encoding/decoding studies discussed previously) have typically found negative relationships; i.e., individuals who exhibit greater facial behavior evince lower ANS reactivity (Buck, Miller, & Caul, 1974; Lanzetta & Kleck, 1970; Notarius & Levenson, 1979). For example, subjects whose faces can be accurately judged as anticipating shock (Lanzetta & Kleck, 1970) or as viewing slides arousing positive versus negative affect show lower EDR responsivity than those whose faces are less accurately judged, and vice versa (see review by Buck, 1977). These findings were presaged by Jones (1935), who posited an "internalizer/externalizer" distinction to account for similar findings. "Externalizers" were held to be overtly reactive (and internally quiescent) when exposed to an emotion- or arousal-eliciting stimulus; "internalizers" were held to be outwardly placid yet autonomically hyperreactive. As noted earlier, there is some evidence for such a distinction in infants and young children (Buck, 1975, 1977; Field & Walden, in press).

However, these findings have not been uniformly obtained. In experimental, within-subject studies (e.g., facial feedback and deception studies discussed earlier), increases in facial expressiveness have been shown to be accompanied by increases in ANS responsivity (Kleck et al., 1976; Lanzetta, Cartwright-Smith, & Kleck, 1976; and other studies cited previously). Zuckerman et al., (1981) also found positive correlations for facial expressivity and autonomic reactivity, in both between-subjects and within-subjects analyses.

It is tempting to consider the facial/ANS relationships discovered in these studies as reflecting some "hardwired" mode of emotional processing. They may—but other factors may more parsimoniously account for these data. The positive facial/ANS relationships can be explained in terms of the concomitants of emotional expressivity: When subjects produce more intense facial expressions, there may be more related somatomotor activity. One would expect increased ANS responding on the basis of increased physiolgoical demand. The between-subjects negative correlations are accountable in terms of social learning theory: inhibited facial behavior may have been learned under aversive social conditioning, in which ANS arousal would also be expected (see Lanzetta, Cartwright–Smith, & Kleck, 1976). The type of relationship found would then be highly dependent on the type of eliciting stimulus, social context, and previous conditioning. Further research will clarify the processes involved.

Malmstrom, Ekman, and Friesen (1972), in a pilot study, found that different patterns of tachycardia and bradycardia coincided with facial activity showing elements of disgust versus surprise when subjects viewed a stressful film. Ancoli (1979) found that facial expressions of disgust in subjects viewing a stressful film were related to respiration changes (thoracic as compared to abdominal).

Within a more traditional classical-conditioning model, slides of facial expressions were used as conditional stimuli (CS's) for aversive electrodermal conditioning. The affective valence ("happy" or "neutral" vs. "angry" or "fearful") of the photographed faces modulated conditional response (CR) intensity and rate of acquisition (Orr & Lanzetta, 1980), and persistence of the CR on extinction trials (Ohman & Dimberg, 1978). These differential effects have been observed when the projected faces "shadowed" a neutral tone CS (Lanzetta & Orr, 1980).

Dimberg and Ohman (1983) extended these findings in reporting that an "angry" slide potentiated extinction responding only when the photographed face was "looking at" the subjects. When "angry" slides were used during acquisition trials, showing the same person in the slides from acquisition through extinction enhanced both excitatory (if the extinction face was "angry") and inhibitory (if the extinction face was "happy") influence on CR persistence (Dimberg, 1983). In addition to corroborating a mediational account of classical conditioning (see Bolles, 1979), these findings have been interpreted (Ohman & Dimberg, 1978) as supporting concepts of stimulus preparedness (Seligman, 1971), and phyletically derived "facial affect programs" (predispositions to react sterotypically to specific facial displays; see Tomkins, 1962, 1963).

Using a "vicarious classical conditioning" procedure, Lanzetta and colleagues have measured facial action using integrated surface EMG techniques in addition to electrodermal responding. In the instigation phase of the "vicarious" paradigm, an observer's vicarious (or sympathetic) emotional responses are monitored while a model undergoes conditioning trials involving emotional arousal (typically, conditioning is to an aversive stimulus such as a brief electric shock, and using a tone as the CS). During the conditioning phase, observer responses are monitored after CS offset, before the model has reacted. Vaughan and Lanzetta (1980) found that observer facial EMG and electrodermal responses were congruent with those expected had the observers been *directly* anticipating and receiving shock. When observers were either shocked or rewarded contingent on *opposite* outcomes for the model, differentiable counterempathic responses in facial EMG and electrodermal responding were reported (Englis, Vaughan, & Lanzetta, 1981).

In developmental studies of infants' reactions to an approaching stranger, several investigators (e.g., Campos, Emde, Gaensbauer, & Henderson, 1975; Waters, Matas, & Sroufe, 1975; and see review by Sroufe, 1977) have found greater tachycardia in 6- to 10-month-old infants who showed facial signs of "wariness" or distress than in infants who showed neutral or positive expressions. An "open" or affectively neutral, attentive face was typically accompanied by heart-rate deceleration, thus paralleling the adult "attentional bradycardia" findings (Lacey, 1967). Provost and Gouin-Décarie (1979), who tested 9- and 12-month-old infants in six different emotion-eliciting situations, have also reported that "negative" emotions (anger and distress) evoked significant tachycardic episodes, whereas "positive" emotions (interest and joy) were associated with small, nonsignificant bradycardic episodes. However, specific positive and negative emotions could not be distinguished from each other on the basis of their concurrent cardiac activity. Lewis, Brooks, and Haviland (1978), while finding a relationship between bradycardic periods and attentive faces did not find a significant relationship between tachycardic episodes and negative-affect expressions. (See also discussion of these findings by Field and Walden, in press).

Difficulties common to many studies of facial behavior and ANS correlates are (a) failure to obtain specific measures of facial action and reliance on affect judgments; (b) differential amplitude-time courses of facial behavior (which can change on a millisecond-by-millisecond basis), and ANS measures (whose amplitude-time courses range from tenths of a second to several seconds; and in the case of responses to endogenous epinephrine- or norepinephrine-mediated arousal, up to 20 min); and (c) inadequate consideration of consequences of between-subjects versus within-subjects analyses (see Buck, 1980, for discussion); (d) failure to obtain or verify the induction of pure emotional states rather than confluent emotions; (e) lack of a unifying theory specifying the ANS changes, including magnitude and direction of effects, which are expected to accompany emotional behavior.

Unanswered or Unasked Questions

Are specific ANS changes associated with specific facial expressions? Only one study has examined the ANS correlates of objectively measured facial expressions of multiple emotional states. Ekman, Levenson, and Friesen (1983) employed a group of Stanislavski actors, and another group composed of scientists in the area of facial behavior who were requested to (a) make six different sets of facial actions validated in previous findings (Ekman & Friesen, 1978) as corresponding to emotions of surprise, disgust, happiness, sadness, anger, and fear; and (b) experience each of the six emotions by focusing on a relevant past experience.

FACS was used to verify those facial-action trials on which the requested movements were performed to criterion, and for which ANS data were retained; a self-report inventory established those trials for which subjects reported sufficient reexperiencing of each emotion. Heart rate, skin conductance, bilateral finger temperature, and forearm muscle tension were measured concurrently. Differentiable ANS patterns were obtained that discriminated positive from negative emotions and also discriminated among some negative emotions. Surprisingly, the patterns obtained for the two tasks were congruent. No differences were evident between the actors and scientists, either in type or extent of ANS patterning.

Further experiments incorporating verified emotion, validated facial behavior, and multiple ANS measures will be needed before a model of ANS functioning in discrete emotional states can be constructed. The ANS measures can then be reliably employed as convergent validators of the emotions themselves.

Facial Feedback

How can we account for the subjective experience of emotion? The debate over this issue has been dominated by theorists arguing for the primacy either of "peripheral" visceral and striate-muscle responses (from James, 1884, 1890; Lange, 1885; Tomkins, 1962, 1963, 1982), or for the primacy of "central" cognitive appraisal (e.g., Cannon, 1927, 1931; Lazarus, Averill, & Opton, 1970; Plutchik, 1977; Schachter & Singer, 1962; and see discussion of these theories in preceding section).

Citing Darwin's (1872/1955) classic work on the origins of emotional expressions, Tomkins (1962, 1963, 1982) modified and extended James' theory of emotion, positing that discrete, differentiated emotions derive from feedback from innately patterned facial expressions. Tomkin's assertions set the stage for several experiments designed to test the "facial feedback hypothesis" — that patterned proprioceptive feedback from facial muscle activity (or from integrated facial expressions) is a *necessary* and/or *sufficient* determinant of the experience of emotion (see Buck, 1980, for a detailed account of the facial feedback hypothesis and related research).

A variant of the facial feedback hypothesis, set within the framework of self-attribution theory (e.g., Bem, 1967; Schachter, 1964), postulates that we can use information from our own facial (and other) behavior to *infer* what we feel. Laird's original study (Laird, 1974) provided a model for later facial feedback experiments: subjects were instructed to contract particular facial muscles, producing — presumably without their awareness — a "happy" or "frowning" expression that they maintained on their faces while viewing slides or cartoons. The face manipulation had a significant, though small, effect (compared with the effect of the slides) on their reported feelings. A subsequent series of experiments found that individual differences on the face mainipulation task were related to other indices of an individual's tendency to use "self"- versus "situation"- produced cues (e.g., Duncan & Laird, 1977).

Tourangeau and Ellsworth (1979) failed to confirm the strong version of the facial feedback hypothesis, i.e., that overt facial expression was both necessary and sufficient for the experience of emotion. Facial manipulations had no significant effect on self-reported emotion, and only ambiguous effects on physiological responses. The study was roundly criticized, and the critiques point out the difficulties in testing the facial feedback hypothesis experimentally. Hager and Ekman (1981) cited three main shortcomings: (a) the specific requested movements were not valid analogs of emotional expressions; (b) other expressions besides the requested movements may have occurred; and (c) the procedures were subject to contamination by demand charcteristics. Izard (1981) asserted that any role that facial feedback might play in emotional experience would be reflexive, nearly immediate, and of only a few milliseconds duration. Tomkins (1981) commented on the artificiality of the expression-manipulation procedures, and on the fact that numerous physiological systems normally involved in affect (e.g., respiration and blood flow) were bypassed by the procedure. In response to these criticisms, Ellsworth and Tourangeau (1981) stated that their experiment disconfirmed the "necessity" version of the facial-feedback hypothesis, and not the "sufficiency" variant. The criticisms of the Tourangeau and Ellsworth (1979) experiment, and the authors' rebuttal should be consulted for elaborations of these issues.

Other tests of the facial feedback hypothesis have involved monitoring of facial expressivity and other (usually physiological) indices of emotional behavior (e.g., Zuckerman, Klorman, Larrance, & Spiegel, 1981). A positive correlation between magnitudes of within-trial facial expressions and adjunctive indices of emotion is taken as supporting the hypothesis. These studies were reviewed in the preceding section on ANS correlates of facial expression. Buck (1980) has schematized various interpretations and derivatives of the facial feedback hypothesis and the corresponding methods for testing each.

The strongest evidence for a positive link between voluntary facial expression and emotion comes from a series of experiments by Lanzetta, Kleck, and colleagues (Colby, Lanzetta, & Kleck, 1977; Kleck, Vaughan, Cartwright-Smith, Vaughan, Colby, & Lanzetta, 1976; Lanzetta, Cartwright-Smith, & Kleck, 1976), investigating the effect of overt facial expression on the intensity of emotional arousal produced by shock. Attempts to conceal facial signs of pain consistently led to decreases in both skin conductance and subjective ratings of pain, whereas posing the expression of intense shock significantly increased both measures of arousal. When subjects were told that they were being observed by another person, they showed less intense facial expressions and correspondingly decreased autonomic responses and subjective ratings of pain, even though they received no instructions to inhibit their responses (Kleck et al., 1976).

These findings can be interpreted in various ways (see Lanzetta et al., 1976). Before concluding that facial feedback was directly and causally related to the observed changes in arousal, it would be necessary to rule out the possibility that some other strategy used by subjects might have affected (or comediated) both their facial expressions and emotional experience. It is also not clear that the effect is specific to facial versus bodily signs of emotion. Nevertheless, these findings suggest that overt facial expression is often correlated with intensity of emotional arousal. Evidence that facial feedback can determine which emotion is experienced is far more tenuous.

As reviewed in the section on neuromuscular substrates for facial expression, there are ample pathways by which facial activity could mediate emotional experience, including exteroceptors in the superficial layers of facial skin, distention and thermoreceptors in deeper facial skin, and possible spindle organs in facial muscle tissue sensitive to state of contraction. The studies to date must be seen only as very weak tests of a facial feedback hypothesis. Demand characteristics and possible effects of comediating systems (cognitive or other) for *both* facial action and ANS measures cannot be discounted. One real test of the facial feedback hypothesis — providing subjects with "simulated" multichannel facial feedback to trigeminal afferent fibers — is technologically unfeasible at this time. Clinical evidence is probably not useful, because studies of changed emotionality in facial hemiparetics are confounded with depressive reactions secondary to disability.

Finally, the studies to date have underestimated the impact of external, social feedback, i.e., the micromomentary reactions of conspecifics to an individual's facial displays. From this perspective, the visual, tactile, or auditory feedback from the reactions of others may represent an additional basis for the individual's appraisal of emotion (or even the principal basis, according to those who emphasize the "socialization of emotion"; cf. Lewis & Michalson, 1982).

Although it is intriguing to hypothesize that distorted feedback from others, especially during childhood (e.g., a mother's labeling her child's "angry" expressions as "sad" or vice versa), could produce distortions in the way individuals experience emotions — as suggested by Ekman and Friesen (1975) and Lewis and Michalson (1982) — there is so far little direct evidence for such a process. (Recent work on the socialization of emotions was presented in the section on development of facial expressions.) The possibility that consistent patterns of social feedback may play a role in influencing the experience of emotion highlights the need for more research on facial expressions occurring during social interaction in naturalistic settings. At the same time (and apart from factors in the sender/recipient interaction), independent evidence is still needed to establish which emotion, if any, the sender is experiencing.

FACIAL EXPRESSIONS IN PSYCHOPATHOLOGY

It is widely accepted that facial expressions are an important part of psychodiagnosis (Ekman & Friesen, 1974b). Nearly all clinicians are familiar with the sad or muted "facies" (facial appearance) seen in dysphoria and depression, or with the "worried" face seen in the anxiety disorders. A mask-like face and "reptilian stare" are often reported in patients with parkinsonism or in schizophrenics treated with neuroleptics. Yet there has been little systematic study regarding facial expressions in psychopathology — what is reported is typically anecdotal and consists of emotion-laden terminology instead of specific observations of facial behavior. This lack of research is particularly unfortunate, given the possible role that facial behavior may play in the differential diagnosis of psychological disorder, and given the distortions of social interaction that often occur in individuals with manifest psychopathology.

What Has Been Found

Facial behavior may distinguish dysphoric and/or depressed individuals from those with normal mood. The only systematic research involving visible facial behavior in depression is a pilot study recently completed by Ekman and Friesen (unpublished data). FACS and EMFACS were used to judge two 10-min videotaped interview samples in major depressives, dysthymics, manic, and schizophrenic patients. Composite scores were then generated corresponding to the emotion predictions of FACS and EMFACS. A greater number of composites held to comprise "sadness" discriminated the major depressives from all other diagnostic categories. That depressives may sometimes be *less* facially expressive than normals is corroborated by Ganchrow, Steiner, Kleinger, and Edelstein (1978), who found attenuated facial responses in depressives exposed to a cold-pressor test.

Some facial EMG studies have suggested that depressed individuals may manifest higher EMG activity in certain facial sites than do nondepressed individuals. Schwartz et al. (1976a, b) recorded EMG activity from several facial sites in "depressed" outpatients who were instructed to imagine affectively tainted situations. The depressed patients were observed to show greater *corrugator*-site activity than controls (Schwartz et al., 1976a). This difference was reported to be especially evident with imagery involving "a typical day" (Schwartz et al., 1976b). Problematic in these studies was the diagnosis of depression based solely on self-report scales (which largely measure simple dysphoria, and not the full depressive syndrome). Oliveau and Willmuth (1979) used affective imagery and more stringent diagnostic criteria in a partial replication of the Schwartz et al. (1976b) study and failed to discriminate depressives from nondepressed controls. However, using "resting" EMG of selected facial sites, Carney, Hong, Kulkarni, and Kapila (1982) found higher EMG levels in depressed than in nondepressed individuals. Studies by Teasdale and Bancroft (1977) and Teasdale and Rezin (1978) documented that *within* depressed patients, ratings of mood, or of the "frequency of negative thoughts," were highly correlated with *corrugator*-region EMG activity.

The discrimination of depressives from nondepressives based on facial behavior should be accepted cautiously, because (a) sample size was limited in the Ekman and Friesen pilot study; (b) findings from the facial EMG studies have not been reliable, and (c) the investigators have used inconsistent diagnostic criteria (e.g., they have confused dysphoria with clinical depression).

Corrugator-region EMG activity is correlated with response to antidepressant medication. Schwartz, Fair, Salt, Mandel, Mieske, and Klerman (1978) measured "resting" corrugator-region EMG activity in clinically depressed patients at hospital admission, and after a 2-week trial on tricyclic antidepressants (largely amitriptyline). The authors reported that subjects who evinced higher *corrugator*-region EMG levels showed fewer depressive signs, as measured by clinical ratings. Fridlund and Izard (1983) showed that the statistical analysis of the Schwartz et al. (1978) data were computed erroneously, and that the relationship between *corrugator*-region EMG and lifting of depression did not hold.

More convincing data have been provided by Carney, Hong, O'Connell, and Amado (1981) and Carney (1981). These data have shown that higher initial *corrugator-* and *zygomatic*-region EMG levels correlate well with changes in self-report measures of depression. That both EMG sites correlated with response to medication has been suggested by Fridlund and Izard (1983) as corroborating earlier notions (e.g., Goldstein, 1965; Martin & Davies, 1965; Rimon, Stenback, & Hahmar, 1966; Whatmore & Ellis, 1959, 1962) of a "hyperponesis," or hyperarousal process in certain depressions — paradoxically, the retarded depressions, which are preferentially sensitive to tricyclic effects (Byck, 1975; Kuhn, 1958).

Why might this hyperponetic process be a component of many depressions? Increasingly, evidence points to elevated activity in the hypothalamo-pituitary-adrenocortical (HPA) axis (a response system activated in stressful coping) in many depressives; this finding forms the basis for the attempted diagnostic use of the dexamethosone suppression test (DST) in clinical psychiatry (Nelson, Orr, Stevenson, & Shane, 1982). We would suggest that elevated facial EMG levels in depressives may be reflecting elevated HPA-axis activity. If so, then facial EMG may provide a noninvasive alternative to the DST.

Unanswered or Unasked Questions

Are there facial-behavioral correlates of the schizophrenias? A consistent finding has been a reduced ability among schizophrenics to classify photographed facial expressions (e.g., Harizuka, 1977; Walker, Marwit, & Emory, 1980). The only systematic research on facial expression in the schizophrenias was the previously cited pilot study by Ekman and Friesen (1983). The data for the schizophrenics showed a relative preponderance of composite scores held to be correlated with fear. Research on facial behavior in the schizophrenias is difficult because of the direct anhedonic and pseudoparkinsoid effects of antischizophrenic medication. However, evidence that there are observable extrapyramidal motor deficits (easily measured using ocular tracking tasks) in preschizophrenics and relatives of schizophrenics (Spohn & Patterson, 1979) make differences in fine-grained facial behavior probable, and their potential study intriguing.

What are the facial-behavior correlates of other forms of psychopathology?   Little is known. The manic subjects in the Ekman and Friesen (1983) pilot study showed more facial actions corresponding to happiness than in the other psychiatric groups. Most of these actions were not accompanied by self-reports of happiness. Virtually unknown is how facial behavior might change with response to antimanic medication (typically lithium carbonate, initially in concert with a neuroleptic). More generally, distortions in facial behavior associated with the formal thought disorder seen in the schizophrenias, and often in the major affective disorders, are fertile ground for future research.

FUTURE DIRECTIONS

The study of facial behavior has mushroomed. The findings and their implications have been of interest not only to psychologists—we have reviewed studies indicating the relevance of facial expression to ethology and primatology, physical anthropology, human development and developmental neurobiology, neurology and neurophysiology, psychophysiology and psychiatry. Yet studies to date have hardly broken ground in the attempt to understand the interrelationships among facial expression, visceroautonomic and other somatic processes, enculturation, health and illness. Advances in facial-expression research will proceed both in recognizing the fundamental role of the face in all these areas, and in attempting to grapple with its sophistication as an information encoder.

We close by presenting some exciting research possibilities that would extend our knowledge of facial action considerably; these involve:

1. The relevance of facial expressions to personality disorders and to psychophysiological disorder.

2. Correlations between facial expressivity and intelligence (see Haviland, 1975).

3. Development of an enhanced FACS that uses optical scanning and computer pattern-analysis of split-second facial actons.

4. Neuroanatomical and neurophysiological work, emphasizing the study of individuals with demonstrable neurological involvement, to clarify

(finally) the structural and functional interrelationships among the neural substrates for facial expression and inhibition of facial expression.

5. Detailed studies of facial behavior in schizophrenia, mania, and in various types of organic brain syndromes.

6. Exploration of the relationships between facial display rules and ethnic group, socioeconomic level, and occupation.

7. Detailed studies of congenitally blind individuals in attempt to understand further the role of imitation in the maturation of facial expression.

8. A renascence of cross-cultural investigations of facial expressions focused on explicating the nature of individual differences within cultures.

9. Close investigation of the role of specific facial behaviors in mediating dyadic interaction and group processes.

10. More precise longitudinal study of the ontogeny of differentiated facial expressions and their relationship to early "reflexive" behavior in infants.

REFERENCES

Ainsworth, M. The development of infant–mother attachment. In. B. Caldwell & H. Ricciuti (Eds.), *Review of child development research* (Vol. 3). Chicago: University of Chicago Press, 1973.

Ainsworth, M., Bell, S., & Stayton, D. Infant–mother attachment and social development: Socialisation as a product of reciprocal responsiveness to signals. In M. P. M. Richards (Ed.), *The integration of a child into a social world.* London: Cambridge University Press, 1974.

Alford, R., & Alford, K. F. Sex differences in asymmetry in the facial expression of emotion. *Neuropsychologia,* 1981, *19,* 605–608.

Allport, F. M. *Social psychology.* Boston: Houghton–Mifflin, 1924.

Altmann, S. Primates. In T. Sebeok (Ed.), *Animal communication: Techniques and results of research* (pp. 466–522). Bloomington: Indiana University Press, 1968.

Ancoli, S. *Psychophysiological response patterns to emotions.* Dissertation, University of California, San Francisco, 1979.

Andrew, R. J. Evolution of facial expression. *Science,* 1963, *141,* 1034–1041.

Andrew, R. J. The displays of the primates. In J. Buettner–Janusch (Ed.), *Evolutionary and genetic biology of primates* (Vol. II, pp. 227–309). New York: Academic, 1964.

Andrew, R. J. The information potentially available in displays. In R. A. Hinde (Ed.), *Nonverbal communication.* New York: Cambridge University Press, 1972.

Anisfeld, M. Letter to the Editor. *Science,* 1979, *205,* 214–215.

Argyle, M., Alkema, F., & Gilmour, R. The communication of friendly and hostile attitudes by verbal and nonverbal signals. *European Journal of Social Psychology.* 1971, *1,* 385–402.

Arnold, M. B. Physiological differentiation of emotional states. *Psychological Review,* 1945, *5,* 34–48.

Averill, J. R. Autonomic response patterns during sadness and mirth.*Psychophysiology,* 1969, *5,* 399–414.

Ax, A. F. The physiological differentiation between fear and anger in humans. *Psychosomatic Medicine,* 1953, *5,* 433–442.

Bandler, R., & Grinder, J. *The structure of magic* (Vol. 1). Palo Alto, CA: Science and Behavior Books, 1975.

Bandler, R., & Grinder, J. *Patterns of the hypnotic techniques of Milton H. Erickson, M. D. (Vol. I)*. Cupertino, CA: Meta Publications, 1976.

Basmajian, J. V. Facts vs. myths in EMG biofeedback. *Biofeedback and Self-Regulation*, 1976, *1*, 369–371.

Bassali, J. N. Facial motion in the perception of faces and of emotional expression. *Journal of Experimental Psychology*, 1978, *4*, 373–379.

Bassili, J. N. Emotion recognition: The role of facial movement and the relative importance of upper and lower areas of the face. *Journal of Personality and Social Psychology*, 1979, *37*, 2049–2058.

Bell, S. M., & Ainsworth, M. D. S. Infant crying and maternal responsiveness. *Child Development*, 1972, *43*, 1171–1190.

Bem, D. J. Self-perception: An alternative interpretation of cognitive dissonance phenomena. *Psychological Review*, 1967, *74*, 183–200.

Bender, M. B. Fright and drug contractions in denervated facial and ocular muscles of monkeys. *American Journal of Physiology*, 1938, *121*, 609–619.

Benton, A. L. The neuropsychology of facial recognition. *American Psychologist*, 1980, *35*, 176–186.

Berman, H. J., Shulman, A. D., & Marwit, S. J. Comparison of multidimensional decoding of affect from audio, video and audiovideo recordings *Sociometry*, 1976, *39*, 83–89.

Birdwhistell, R. L. *Kinesics and context*. Philadelphia: University of Pennsylvania Press, 1970.

Blanck, P. D., & Rosenthal, R. Developing strategies for decoding "leaky" messages: On learning how and when to decode discrepant and consistent social communications. In R. S. Feldman (Ed.), *Development of nonverbal behavior in children*. New York: Springer–Verlag, 1982.

Blurton Jones, N. G. Criteria for use in describing facial expression in children. *Human Biology*, 1971, *41*, 365–413.

Blurton Jones, N. G. Non-verbal communication in children. In R. A. Hinde (Ed.), *Nonverbal communication* (pp. 271–296). Cambridge: Cambridge University Press, 1972.

Bolles, R. C. *Learning theory* (2nd ed.). New York: Holt, Rinehart, & Winston, 1979.

Borke, H. Interpersonal perception of young children: Egocentrism or empathy? *Developmental Psychology*, 1971, *5*, 263–269.

Borod, J. C., & Caron, H. S. Facedness and emotion related to lateral dominance, sex, and expression type. *Neuropsychologia*, 1980, *18*, 237–241.

Boucher, J. D. *Facial behavior and the perception of emotion: Studies of Malays and Temuan Orang Asli*. Paper presented at the Conference on Psychology Related Disciplines, Kuala Lumpur, 1973.

Boucher, J. D., & Carlson, G. E. Recognition of facial expression in three cultures. *Journal of Cross-Cultural Psychology*, 1980, *11*, 263–280.

Boucher, J. D., & Ekman, P. Facial areas and emotional information. *Journal of Communication*, 1975, *25*, 21–29.

Bowden, R. E. M., & Mahran, Z. Y. The functional significance of the pattern of innervation of the muscle quadratus labii superioris of the rabbit, cat, and rat. *Journal of Anatomy*, 1956, *90*, 217–227.

Bower, T. G. R. *Development in infancy* (2nd ed.). San Francisco: W. H. Freeman, 1982.

Bowlby, J. *Attachment and loss* (Vol. 1). *Attachment*. New York: Basic Books, 1969.

Bradshaw, J. L., & Nettleton, N. C. The nature of hemispheric specialization in man. *Behavioral and Brain Sciences*, 1981, *4*, 51–91.

Brannigan, C. R., & Humphries, D. A. Human nonverbal behavior, a means of communication. In N. G. Blurton Jones (Ed.), *Ethological studies of child behavior*. Cambridge: Cambridge University Press, 1972.

Bratzlavsky, M. Feedback control of human lip muscle. *Experimental Neurology*, 1979, *65*, 209–217.

Bratzlavsky, M., & vander Eecken, H. Altered synaptic organization in facial nucleus following facial nerve regeneration: An electrophysiological study in man. *Annals of Neurology*, 1977, *2*, 71-73.

Brazelton, T., Tronick, E., Adamson, L., Als, H., & Wise, S. Early mother-infant reciprocity. In *Parent-infant interaction*. Amsterdam: Elsevier Experimental Medicine, 1975.

Briem, V., & Nystrom, M. The detection of infants' facial movements. *Psychological Research Bulletin, Lund. U.*, 1978, *18*, 22.

Brigham, J. C., & Barkowitz, P. Do "They all look alike?" The effect of race, sex, experience, and attitudes on the ability to recognize faces. *Journal of Applied Social Psychology*, 1978, *8*, 306-318.

Brodal, A. *Neurological anatomy*. New York: Oxford University Press, 1981.

Broman, M. Reaction-time differences between the left and right hemispheres for face and letter discrimination in children and adults. *Cortex*, 1978, *14*, 578-591.

Brown, S. L., & Schwartz, G. E. Relationships between facial electromyography and subjective experience during affective imagery. *Biological Psychology*, 1980, *11*, 49-62.

Bruner, J. Organization of early skilled action. *Child Development*, 1973, *44*, 1-11.

Bruner, J. S., & Tagiuri, R. The perception of people. In G. Lindzey (Ed.), *Handbook of social psychology* (Vol. 2). Reading, MA: Addison-Wesley, 1954.

Brunori, P., Ladavas, E., & Ricci-Bitti, P. E. Differential aspects in the recognition of facial expression of emotions. *Italian Journal of Psychology*, 1979, *6*, 265-272.

Bruyer, R. Cerebral lesion and perception of out-of-focus faces. *Année Psychologique*, 1980, *80*, 379-390. (a)

Bruyer, R. Perception of the human face and cerebral hemispheric differences in the normal subject. *Année Psychologique*, 1980, *80*, 631-653. (b)

Bruyer, R. Asymmetry of facial expression in brain damaged subjects. *Neuropsychologia*, 1981, *19*, 615-624.

Buchtel, H., Campari, F., DeRisio, C., & Rota, R. Hemispheric differences in discriminative reaction time to facial expressions. *Italian Journal of Psychology*, 1978, *5*, 159-169.

Buck, R. Nonverbal communication of affect in children. *Journal of Personality and Social Psychology*, 1975, *31*, 644-653.

Buck, R. A test of nonverbal receiving ability: Preliminary studies. *Human Communication Research*, 1976, *2*, 162-171.

Buck, R. Nonverbal communication of affect in preschool children: Relationships with personality and skin conductance. *Journal of Personality and Social Psychology*, 1977, *31*, 644-653.

Buck, R. The slide-viewing technique for measuring nonverbal sending accuracy. JSAS *Catalog of Selected Documents in Psychology*, 1978, *8*, 63.

Buck, R. Nonverbal behavior and the theory of emotion: The facial feedback hypothesis. *Journal of Personality and Social Psychology*, 1980, *38*, 811-824.

Buck, R., Baron, R., & Barrette, D. Temporal organization of spontaneous emotional expressions: A segmentation analysis. *Journal of Personality and Social Psychology*, 1982, *42*, 506-517.

Buck, R., Miller, R. E., & Caul, W. F. Sex, personality, and physiological variables in the communication of affect via facial expression. *Journal of Personality and Social Psychology*, 1974, *30*, 587-596.

Buck, R., Savin, V. J., Miller, R. E., & Caul, W. F. Communication of affect through facial expressions in humans. *Journal of Personality and Social Psychology*, 1972, *23*, 362-371.

Bugental, D. E., Kaswan, J. W., & Love, L. R. Perception of contradictory meanings conveyed by verbal and nonverbal channels. *Journal of Personality and Social Psychology*, 1970, *16*, 647-655.

Bugental, D. E., Kaswan, J., Love, L., & Fox, M. Child versus adult perception of evaluative messages in verbal, vocal, and visual channels. *Developmental Psychology*, 1970, *2*, 367-375.

Bugental, D. E., Love, L., & Gianetto, R. Perfidious feminine faces. *Journal of Personality and*

Social Psychology, 1971, *17*, 314–318.

Bugental, D. E., Love, L., & Kaswan, J. Verbal–nonverbal conflict in parental messages to normal and disturbed children. *Journal of Abnormal Psychology*, 1971, *77*, 6–10.

Burke, P. H. Stereophotogrammetric measurement of normal facial asymmetry in children. *Human Biology*, 1971, *43*, 536–548.

Burns, K. L., & Beier, E. G. Significance of vocal and visual channels in the decoding of emotional meaning. *Journal of Communications*, 1973, *23*, 118–130.

Buzby, D. E. The interpretation of facial expression. *American Journal of Psychology*, 1924, *35*, 602–604.

Byck, R. Drugs and the treatment of psychiatric disorders. In. L. S. Goodman & A. Gilman (Eds.), *The pharmacological basis of therapeutics* (5th Ed.). New York: Macmillan, 1975.

Cacioppo, J. T., Marshall-Goodell, B., & Dorfman, D. D. Topographical analysis of the integrated EMG. *Psychophysiology*, 1982, *19*, 543. (Abstract)

Cacioppo, J. T., & Petty, R. E. (1979). Attitudes and cognitive response: An electrophysiological approach. *Journal of Personality and Social Psychology*, *37*, 2181–2199.

Cacioppo, J. T., & Petty, R. E. Electromyographic specificity during covert information processing. *Psychophysiology*, 1981, *18*, 518–523. (a)

Cacioppo, J. T., & Petty, R.E. Lateral asymmetry in the expression of cognition and emotion. *Journal of Experimental Psychology: Human Perception and Performance*, 1981 *7*, 333–341. (b)

Campbell, R. Asymmetries in interpreting and expressing a posed facial expression. *Cortex*, 1978, *14*, 327–342.

Campbell, R. *Cerebral asymmetries in the interpretation and expression of a posed expression.* Unpublished doctoral dissertation, University of London, 1979.

Campos, J. J., Emde, R. N., Gaensbauer, T., & Henderson, C. Cardiac and behavioral interrelationships in the reactions of infants to strangers. *Developmental Psychology*, 1975, *11*, 589–601.

Campos, J. J., Hiatt, S., Ramsay, D., Henderson, C., & Svejda, M. The emergence of fear on the visual cliff. In M. Lewis & L. Rosenblum (Eds.), *The development of affect* (pp. 149–182). New York: Plenum, 1978.

Camras, L. Facial expressions used by children in a conflict situation. *Child Development*, 1977, *48*, 1431–1435.

Camras, L. A. Ethological approaches to nonverbal communication. In R. S. Feldman (Ed.), *Development of nonverbal behavior in children.* New York: Springer–Verlag, 1982.

Candland, D. K. The persistent problems of emotion. In D. K. Candland, J. P. Fell, E. Keen, A. I. Leshner, R. Plutchik, & R. M. Tarpy (Eds.), *Emotion* (pp. 1–84). Monterey, CA: Brooks/Cole, 1977.

Cannon, W. B. The James–Lange theory of emotions: A critical examination and an alternative theory. *American Journal of Psychology*, 1927, *39*, 106–124.

Cannon, W. B. *Bodily changes in pain, hunger, fear and rage* (2nd Ed.). New York: Appleton, 1929.

Cannon, W. B. Again the James–Lange and the thalamic theory of emotions. *Psychological Review*, 1931, *38*, 281–295.

Cantril, H., & Hunt, W. H. Emotional effects produced by the injection of adrenaline. *American Journal of Psychology*, 1932, *44*, 300–307.

Carey, S., & Diamond, R. From piecemeal to configurational representation of faces. *Science*, 1977, *195*, 312–314.

Carney, R. M., Hong, B. A., O'Connell, M. F., & Amado, H. Facial electromyography as a predictor of treatment outcome in depression. *British Journal of Psychiatry*, 1981, *138*, 454–459.

Carney, R. M., Hong, B. A., Kulkarni, S., & Kapila, A. A comparison of EMG and SCL in normal and depressed subjects. *Pavlovian Journal of Biological Science*, 1982, *16*, 212–216.

Caron, R., Caron, A., & Myers, R. Abstraction of invariant face expressions in infancy. *Child Development,* 1982, *53,* 1008–1015.

Chapman, A. J., & Wright, D. S. Social enhancement of laughter: An experimental analysis of some companion variables. *Journal of Experimental Child Psychology,* 1976, *21,* 201–218.

Charlesworth, W. R., & Kreutzer, M. A. Facial expression of infants and children. In P. Ekman (Ed.), *Darwin and facial expression* (pp. 91–168). New York: Academic Press, 1973.

Chaurasia, B. D., & Goswami, H. K. Functional asymmetry in the face. *Acta Anatomica,* 1975, *91,* 154–160.

Cherulnik, P. D. Sex differences in the expression of emotion in a structured social encounter. *Sex Roles,* 1979, *5,* 413–424.

Chevalier-Skolnikoff, S. Facial expression of emotion in nonhuman primates. In P. Ekman (Ed.), *Darwin and facial expression.* New York: Academic, 1973.

Cicchetti, D., & Sroufe, L. A. An organizational view of affect: Illustration from the study of Down's Syndrome infants. In M. Lewis & L. Rosenblum (Eds.), *The development of affect* (pp. 309–350). New York: Plenum, 1978.

Cicone, M., Wapner, W., & Gardner, H. Sensitivity to emotional expressions and situations in organic patients. *Cortex,* 1980, *16,* 145–158.

Cline, V. B., Atzet, J., & Holmes, E. Assessing the validity of verbal and nonverbal cues in accurately judging others. *Comparative Group Studies,* 1972, *3,* 383–394.

Colby, C. Z., Lanzetta, J. T., & Kleck, R. E. Effects of the expression of pain on autonomic and pain tolerance responses to subject-controlled pain. *Psychophysiology,* 1977, *14,* 537–540.

Colgan, P. W. (Ed.), *Quantitative ethology.* New York: Wiley–Interscience, 1978.

Condon, W. S., & Ogston, W. D. A method of studying animal behavior. *The Journal of Auditory Research,* 1967, *7,* 359–365.

Condon, W. S., & Ogston, W. D. A segmentation of behavior. *Journal of Psychiatric Research,* 1967, *5,* 221–235.

Cronback, L. J., & Meehl, P. E. Construct validity in psychological tests. *Psychological Bulletin,* 1955, *52,* 281–302.

Cunningham, M. R. Personality and the structure of the nonverbal communication of emotion. *Journal of Personality,* 1977, *45,* 564–584.

Damasio, A. R., Damasio, H., & Van Hoesen, G. W. Prosopagnosia: Anatomic basis and behavioral mechanisms. *Neurology,* 1982, *32,* 331–341.

Darwin, C. *The expression of the emotions in man and animals.* New York: Philosophical Library, 1955. (Originally published, 1872).

Darwin, C. A biographical sketch of an infant. *Mind,* 1877, *2,* 285–294.

Davidson, R. J., & Fox, N. A. Asymmetrical brain activity discriminates between positive and negative affective stimuli in human infants. *Science,* 1982, *218,* 1235–1237.

DeKosky, S. T., Heilman, K. M., Bowers, D., & Valenstein, E. Recognition and discrimination of emotional faces and pictures. *Brain & Language,* 1980, *9,* 206–214.

Denny-Brown, D. *Selected writings of Sir Charles Sherrington.* New York: Harper & Brothers, 1939.

DePaulo, B. M., & Jordan, A. Age changes in deceiving and detecting deceit. In R. S. Feldman (Ed.), *Development of nonverbal behavior in children.* New York: Springer–Verlag, 1982.

DePaulo, B. M., & Rosenthal, R. Measuring the sensitivity to nonverbal communcation. In C. E. Izard (Ed.), *Measuring emotions in infants and children.* New York: Cambridge University Press, 1982.

DePaulo, B., Rosenthal, R., Eisenstat, R., Finkelstein, S., & Rogers, P. Decoding discrepant nonverbal cues. *Journal of Personality and Social Psychology,* 1978, *36,* 313–323.

Diamond, R., & Carey, S. Developmental changes in the representation of faces. *Journal of Experimental Child Psychology,* 1977, *23,* 1–22.

Dimberg, U. Facial reactions to facial expressions. *Psychophysiology,* 1982, *19,* 643–647.

Dimberg, U. *Facial expressions as excitatory and inhibitory stimuli for conditioned autonomic responses,* 1983, submitted for publication.

Dimberg, U., & Ohman, A. The effects of directional facial cues on electrodermal conditioning to facial stimuli. *Psychophysiology,* 1983, *20,* 160–167.

Dimond, S. J., Farrington, L., & Johnson, P. Differing emotional response from right and left hemispheres. *Nature,* 1976, *261,* 690–692.

Drachman, D. B. Trophic actions of the neuron: An introduction. *Annals of the New York Academy of Science,* 1974, *228,* 3.

Duchenne, B. *Mechanisme de la physionomie humaine ou analyse electrophysiologique de l'expression des passions.* Paris: Bailliere, 1862.

Duncan, J., & Laird, J. D. Cross-modality consistencies in individual differences in self-attribution. *Journal of Personality,* 1977, *45,* 191–206.

Ectors, L, Brookens, N. L., & Gerard, R. W. Autonomic and motor localization in the hypothalamus. *Archives of Neurology and Psychiatry,* 1938, *39,* 789.

Eibl-Eibesfeldt, I. Similarities and differences between cultures in expressive movements. In R. A. Hinde (Ed.), *Nonverbal communication* (pp. 297–312). Cambridge: Cambridge University Press, 1972.

Ekman, P. Universals and cultural differences in facial expressions of emotion. In J. Cole (Ed.), *Nebraska Symposium on Motivation* (Vol. 19). Lincoln: University of Nebraska Press, 1972.

Ekman, P. Cross-cultural studies of facial expressions. In P. Ekman (Ed.), *Darwin and facial expression* (pp. 169–229). New York: Academic, 1973.

Ekman, P. Biological and cultural contributions to body and facial movement. In J. Blacking (Ed.), *The anthropology of the body.* London: Academic, 1977.

Ekman, P. About brows: Emotional and conversational signals. In M. von Cranach, K. Foppa, W. Lepenies, & D. Ploog, (eds.), *Human enthology.* Cambridge: Cambridge University Press, 1978.

Ekman, P. Asymmetry in facial expression. *Science,* 1980, *209,* 833–834.

Ekman, P. Methods for measuring facial action. In K. Scherer & P. Ekman (Eds.), *Handbook on methods of nonverbal communications research.* New York: Cambridge University Press, 1981.

Ekman, P. *Emotion in the human face* (2nd ed.). Elmsford, NY: Pergamon, 1982. (a)

Ekman, P. Facial expression and facial nerve surgery. In M. D. Graham & W. F. House (Eds.), *Disorders of the facial nerve* (pp. 336–368). New York: Raven Press, 1982. (b)

Ekman, P., & Friesen, W. V. The repertoire of nonverbal behavior: categories, origins, usage, and coding. *Semiotica,* 1969, *1,* 49–98.

Ekman, P., & Friesen, W. V. Constants across cultures in the face and emotion. *Journal of Personality and Social Psychology,* 1971, *17,* 124–129.

Ekman, P., & Friesen, W. V. Detecting deception from the body or face. *Journal of Personality and Social Psychology,* 1974, *29,* 288–298.

Ekman, P., & Friesen, W. V. Nonverbal behavior and psychopathology. In R. J. Friedman & M. M. Katz (Eds.), *The psychology of depression: Contemporary theory and research.* Washington, DC: Winston, 1974. (b)

Ekman, P., & Friesen, W. V. *Unmasking the face.* Englewood Cliffs, NJ: Prentice-Hall, 1975.

Ekman, P., & Freisen, W. V. Measuring facial movement. *Journal of Environmental Psychology and Nonverbal Behavior,* 1976, *1,* 56–75.

Ekman, P., & Friesen, W. V. *The Facial Action Coding System.* Palo Alto, CA: Consulting Psychologists Press, 1978.

Ekman, P., & Friesen, W. V. Felt, false, and miserable smiles. *Journal of Nonverbal Behavior,* 1982, *6,* 238–252.

Ekman, P., Friesen, W. V., & Ancoli, S. Facial signs of emotional experience. *Journal of Personality and Social Psychology,* 1980, *39,* 1125–1134.

Ekman, P., Friesen, W. V., & Ellsworth, P. What components of facial behavior are related to observers' judgments of emotion? In P. Ekman (Ed.), *Emotion in the human face* (2nd Ed., pp. 98–110). Cambridge: Cambridge University Press, 1982. (a)

Ekman, P., Friesen, W. V., & Ellsworth, P. What emotion categories or dimensions can observers judge from facial behavior? In P. Ekman (Ed.), *Emotion in the human face* (2nd Ed., pp. 39–55). Cambridge: Cambridge University Press, 1982. (b)

Ekman, P., Friesen, W. V., & Ellsworth, P. Does the face provide accurate information? In P. Ekman (Ed.), *Emotion in the human face.* (2nd Ed.). Elmsford, New York: Pergamon, 1982. (c)

Ekman, P., Friesen, W. V., O'Sullivan, M., & Scherer, K. Relative importance of face, body and speech in judgments of personality and affect. *Journal of Personality and Social Psychology,* 1980, *38,* 270–277.

Ekman, P., Friesen, W. V., & Simons, R. C. *The boundary between emotion and reflex: An examination of startle.* Manuscript submitted for publication, 1983.

Ekman, P., & Friesen, W. V., & Tomkins, S. S. Facial Affect Scoring Technique (FAST): A first validity study. *Semiotica,* 1971, *3,* 37–38.

Ekman, P., Hager, J. C., & Friesen, W. V. The symmetry of emotional and deliberate facial actions. *Psychophysiology,* 1981, *18,* 101–106.

Ekman, P., Levenson, R. W., & Friesen, W. V. Emotions differ in autonomic nervous system activity. *Science,* 1983, *221,* 1208–1210.

Ekman, P., & Oster, H. Facial expressions of emotion. *Annual Review of Psychology,* 1978, *30,* 527–554.

Ekman, P., Roper, G., & Hager, J. C. Deliberate facial movement. *Child Development,* 1980, *51,* 886–891.

Ekman, P., Sorenson, E. R., & Friesen, W. V. Pan-cultural elements in facial displays of emotions. *Science,* 1969, *164,* 86–88.

Ellsworth, P., & Tourangeau, R. On our failure to disconfirm what nobody ever said. *Journal of Personality and Social Psychology,* 1981, *40,* 363–369.

Emde,R. N., Gaensbauer,T. J., & Harmon, R. J. Emotional expression in infancy: A biobehavioral study. *Psychological Issues Monograph Service Series,* 1976, *10* Monograph 37).

Englis, B. G., Vaughan, K. B., & Lanzetta, J. T. Conditioning counterempathic emotional responses. *Journal of Experimental Social Psychology,* 1981, *38,* 375–391.

Ermiane, R., & Gergarian, E. *Atlas of facial expressions. Album des expressions du visage.* Paris: La Pensee Universelle, 1978.

Feldman, R. S. *Development of nonverbal behavior in children.* New York: Springer–Verlag, 1982.

Feldman, R. S., Devin-Sheehan, L., & Allen, V. L. Nonverbal cues as indicators of verbal dissembling. *American Educational Research Journal,* 1978, *15,* 217–231.

Feldman, R. S., Jenkins, L., & Papoola,O. Detection of deception in adults and children via facial expressions. *Child Development,* 1979, *50,* 350–355.

Field, T., & Walden, T. Perception and production of facial expressions in infancy and early childhood. In H. Reese & L. Lipsitt (Eds.), *Advances in child development and behavior* (Vol. 16). New York: Academic Press, in press.

Field, T. M., Woodson, R., Greenberg, R., & Cohen, D. Discrimination and imitation of facial expressions in neonates. *Science,* 1982, *218,* 179–181.

Fields, B., & O'Sullivan, M. *Convergent validation of five person perception measures.* Paper presented at the meeting of the Western Psychological Association, Los Angeles, 1976.

Finkelstein, S. *The relationship between physical attractiveness and nonverbal behaviors.* Unpublished honors thesis, Hampshire College, 1978.

Finlay, D. C., & French, J. Visual field differences in a facial recognition task using signal detection theory. *Neuropsychologia,* 1978, *16,* 103–107.

Flynn, J. P. The neural basis of aggression in cats. In D. C. Glass (Ed.), *Neurophysiology and emotion.* New York: Rockefeller University Press, 1967.

Ford, F. R. *Diseases of the nervous system in infancy, childhood, and adolescence.* Springfield, IL: Thomas, 1966.

Fraiberg, S. (1974). Blind infants and their mothers: An examination of the sign system. In M. Lewis & L. A. Rosenblum (Eds.), *The effect of the infant on its caregiver*. New York: Wiley, 1974.

Freeman, G. L. *The energetics of human behavior*. Ithaca, NY: Cornell University Press, 1948.

Fridlund, A. J. *Possible motor-control confounds in facial EMG lateralization-for-emotion research*. Manuscript submitted for publication, 1985.

Fridlund, A. J., Cottam, G. L., & Fowler, S. C. In search of the general tension factor: Tensional patterning during auditory stimulation. *Psychophysiology*, 1982, *19*, 136–145.

Fridlund, A. J., & Fowler, S. C. An eight-channel computer-controlled scanning electromyograph. *Behavior Research Methods & Instrumentation*, 1978, *10*, 652–662.

Fridlund, A. J., Fowler, S. C., & Pritchard, D. A. Striate muscle tensional patterning during frontalis EMG biofeedback. *Psychophysiology*, 1980, *17*, 47–55.

Fridlund, A. J., Gibson, E. L., & Newman, J. B. Putting emotion into behavioral medicine: Discrete-emotion psychophysiology and its relevance for research and therapy. In L. Temoshok, C.Van Dyke, & L. S. Zegans (Eds.), *Emotions in health and illness: Applications to clinical practice*. Orlando: Grune & Stratton, 1984.

Fridlund, A. J., & Gilbert, A. N. Emotions and facial expression. *Science*, 1985, *230*, 607–608.

Fridlund, A. J., Hatfield, M. E. Cottam, G. L., & Fowler, S. C. *Anxiety and striate-muscle activation: Evidence from electromyographic pattern analysis*. Manuscript submitted for publication, 1985.

Fridlund, A. J., & Izard, C. E. Electromyographic studies of facial expressions of emotions and patterns of emotions. In J. T. Cacioppo & R. E. Petty (Eds.), *Social psychophysiology: A sourcebook* (pp. 243–286). New York: Guilford Press, 1983.

Fridlund, A. J., Price, A. W., & Fowler, S. C. Low-noise, optically isolated electromyographic preamplifier. *Psychophysiology*, 1982, *19*, 701–705.

Fridlund, A. J., Schwartz, G. E., & Fowler, S. C. (1984). Pattern recognition of self-reported emotional state from multiple-site facial EMG activity during affective imagery. *Psychophysiology, 21*, 622–637.

Friedman, H. S. The interactive effects of facial expressions of emotion and verbal messages on perceptions of affective meaning. *Journal of Experimental Social Psychology*, 1979, *15*, 453–469.

Friesen, W. V. *Cultural differences in facial expressions in a social situation: An experimental test of the concept of display rules*. Unpublished doctoral dissertation, University of California, San Francisco, 1972.

Frois-Wittman, J. The judgment of facial expression. *Journal of Experimental Psychology*, 1930, *13*, 113–151.

Fujita, B. *Encoding and decoding of spontaneous and enacted facial expressions of emotion*. Unpublished doctoral dissertation, University of Oregon, Portland, 1977.

Fulcher, J. S. "Voluntary" facial expression in blind and seeing children. *Archives of Psychology*, 1942, *38*, pp. 1–49.

Funkenstein, D. H. The physiology of fear and anger. *Scientific American* 1955, *192*, 74–80.

Galin, D. Implications for psychiatry of left and right cerebral specialization. *Archives of General Psychiatry*, 1974, *31*, 572–583.

Gallagher, D., & Shuntich, R. J. Encoding and decoding of nonverbal behavior through facial expressions. *Journal of Research in Personality*, 1981, 241–252.

Gallistel, C. R. *The organization of action: A new synthesis*. Hillsdale, NJ: Lawrence Erlbaum Associates, 1980.

Ganchrow, J. R., Steiner, J. E., Kleiner, M., & Edelstein, E. L. A multidisciplinary approach to the expression of pain in psychic depression. *Perceptual & Motor Skills*, 1978, *47*, 379–390.

Gellhorn, E. Motion and emotion: The role of proprioception in the physiology and pathology of the emotions. *Psychological Review*, 1964, *71*, 457–472.

Gellhorn, E., & Kiely, W. F. Mystical states of consciousness: Neurophysiological and clinical aspects. *The Journal of Nervous and Mental Disease,* 1972, *154,* 399–405.

Geschwind, N. The apraxias: Neural mechanisms of disorders of learned movement. *American Scientist,* 1975, *63,* 188–195.

Geschwind, N. Some special functions of the human brain: dominance, language, apraxias, memory, and attention. In V. B. Mountcastle (Ed.), *Medical physiology* (Vol I, 14th ed., pp. 647–665). St. Louis: Mosby, 1980.

Gesell, A. *The embryology of behavior.* New York: Harper, 1945.

Gewirtz, J. L., & Boyd, E. F. Mother–infant interaction and its study. *Advances in Child Development and Behavior,* 1976, *11,* 141–163.

Gilbert, C., & Bakan, P. Visual asymmetry in perception of faces. *Neuropsychologia,* 1973, *11,* 355–362.

Goldstein, A. G., Johnson, K. S., & Chance, J. Does fluency of face description imply superior face recognition? *Bulletin of the Psychonomic Society,* 1979, *13,* 15–18.

Goldstein, I. B. The relationship of muscle tension and autonomic activity to psychiatric disorders. *Psychosomatic Medicine,* 1965, *27,* 39–52.

Goldstein, M. L. Physiological theories of emotion: A critical historical review from the standpoint of behavior theory. *Psychological Bulletin,* 1968, *69,* 23–40.

Gorney, M., & Harries, T. The preoperative and postoperative consideration of natural facial asymmetry. *Plastic and Reconstructive Surgery,* 1974, *54,* 187–191.

Gouin-Décarie, T. Affect development and cognition in a Piagetian context. In M. Lewis & L. Rosenblum (Eds.), *The development of affect* (pp. 183–204). New York: Plenum, 1978.

Graham, J. A., & Argyle, M. The effects of different patterns of gaze combined with different facial expressions. *Journal of Human Movement Studies,* 1975, *1,* 178–182.

Grant, N. G. Human facial expression. *Man,* 1969,*4,* 525–536.

Greenspan, S., Barenboim, C., & Chandler, M. J. Empathy and pseudo-empathy: The affective judgments of first- and third-graders. *Journal of Genetic Psychology,* 1976, *129,* 77–88.

Gur, R. C., & Gur, R. E. Handedness and individual differences in hemispheric activation. In J. Herron (Ed.), *Neuropsychology of left-handedness.* New York: Academic, 1980.

Gutmann, E. Neurotrophic relations. *Annual Review of Physiology,* 1976, *38,* 177.

Hager, J. C. Asymmetries in facial expression. In P. Ekman (Ed.), *Emotion in the human face: Guidelines for research and an integration of findings* (2nd ed., pp. 318–352). New York: Cambridge University Press, 1982.

Hager, J. C. The asymmetry of facial actions is inconsistent with models of hemispheric specialization. *Psychophysiology.* 1985, *22,* 307–318.

Hager, J. C., & Ekman, P. Methodological problems of Tourangeau and Ellsworth's study of facial expression and experience of emotion. *Journal of Personality and Social Psychology,* 1981, *40,* 358–362.

Hager, J. C., & Ekman, P. The inner and outer meanings of facial expressions. In J. T. Cacioppo & R. E. Petty (Eds.), *Social psychophysiology* (pp. 287–306). New York: Guilford, 1983.

Hall, J. *Gender effects in encoding nonverbal cues.* Unpublished manuscript, The Johns Hopkins University, 1977.

Hall, J. Gender effects in decoding nonverbal cues. *Psychological Bulletin,* 1978, *85,* 845–857.

Hamilton, M. L. Imitative behavior and expressive ability in facial expression of emotion. *Developmental Psychology,* 1973, *8,* 138.

Hansch, E. C., & Pirozzolo, F. J. Task relevant effect on the assessment of cerebral specialization for facial emotion. *Brain and Language,* 1980, *10,* 51–59.

Harizuka, S. Perception of schizophrenic patients in classifying pictures of facial expression. *Japanese Journal of Psychology,* 1977, *48,* 231–238.

Harper, R. G., Wiens, A. N., & Fujita, B. *Individual differences in encoding–decoding of emotional expression and emtional dissimulation.* Paper presented at the Annual Meeting of the American Psychological Association, San Francisco, 1977.

Harper, R. G., Wiens, A. N., & Matarazzo, J. D. The relationship between encoding-decoding of visual nonverbal emotional cues. *Semiotica,* 1979, *28,* 171–192.

Haviland, J. Looking smart: The relationship between affect and intelligence in infancy. In M. Lewis (Ed.), *Origins of infant intelligence.* New York: Plenum, 1975.

Hayes, L. A., & Watson, J. S. Neonatal imitation: Fact or artifact? *Developmental Psychology,* 1981, *17,* 655–660.

Heider, K. *Affect display rules in the Dani.* Paper presented at the Annual Meeting of the American Anthropological Association, New Orleans, 1974.

Helmsley, G. D. *Experimental studies in the behavioral indicants of deception.* Unpublished doctoral dissertation, University of Toronto, 1977.

Hess, W. R. *Diencephalon: Autonomic and extrapyramidal functions.* New York: Grune & Stratton, 1954.

Hiatt, S., Campos, J., & Emde, R. Fear, surprise, and happiness: The patterning of facial expression in infants. *Child Development,* 1979, *50,* 1020–1035.

Hilliard, R. D. Hemispheric laterality effects on a facial recognition task in normal subjects. *Cortex,* 1973, *9,* 246–258.

Hjortsjo, C. H. *Mans face and mimic language.* Lund: Student-Literature, 1970.

Hochschild, A. R. Emotion work, feeling rules, and social structure. *American Journal of Sociology,* 1979, *85,* 551–575.

Hocking, J. E., & Leathers, D. G. Nonverbal indicators of deception: A new theoretical perspective. *Communication Monographs,* 1980, *47,* 119–131.

Hoffman, M. L. Empathy, its development and prosocial implications. *Nebraska Symposium on Motivation,* 1977, *25,*

Hunt, W. A. Recent developments in the field of emotion. *Psychological Bulletin,* 1941, *38,* 249–276.

Izard, C. E. *The face of emotion.* New York: Appleton-Century-Crofts, 1971.

Izard, C. E. *Patterns of emotion: A new analysis of anxiety and depression.* New York: Academic, 1972.

Izard, C. E. *Human emotions.* New York: Plenum, 1977.

Izard, C. E. On the ontogenesis of emotions and emotion-cognition relationships in infancy. In M. Lewis & L. Rosenblum (Eds.), *The development of affect* (pp. 389–413). New York: Plenum, 1978.

Izard C. E. *The maximally discriminative facial movement coding system (Max).* Newark: Instructional Resources Center, University of Delaware, 1979.

Izard, C. E. Differential-emotions theory and the facial feedback hypothesis of emotion activation: Comments on Tourangeau's "The role of facial response in the expression of emotion." *Journal of Personality and Social Psychology,* 1981, *40,* 350–354.

Izard, C. E., & Dougherty, L. M. *System for identifying affect expressions by holistic judgment (Affex).* Newark: Instructional Resources Center, University of Delaware, 1980.

Izard, C. E., Huebner, R. R., Risser, D., & Dougherty, L. The young infant's ability to produce discrete emotion expressions. *Development Psychology,* 1980, *16,* 132–140.

Jackson, J. H. Evolution and dissolution of the nervous system. In J. Taylor (Ed.), *Selected writings of John Hughlings Jackson* (Vol. 2). New York: Basic Books, 1958.(a)

Jackson, J. H. On the anatomical and physiological localization of movements in the brain. In J. Taylor (Ed.), *Selected writings of John Hughlings Jackson* (Vol. 2). New York: Basic Books, 1958, 1958. (b)

Jacobson, S., & Kagan, J. Released responses in early infancy: Evidence contradicting selective imitation. Letter to *Science,* 1979, *205,* 215–217.

James, W. What is an emotion? *Mind,* 1884, *9,* 188–204.

James, W. *The principles of psychology.* New York: Holt, 1890.

Jones, H. E. The galvanic skin reflex as related to overt emotional expression. *American Journal of Psychology,* 1935, *47,* 241–251.

Josse, D., Leonard, M., Lezine, I., Robinot, F., & Rouchouse, J. Evolution de la communication entre l'enfant de 4 a 9 mois et un adulte. *Enfance*, 1973, *3*, 175–206.

Kaye, K., & Marcus, J. Imitation over a series of trials without feedback: Age six months. *Infant Behavior & Development*, 1978, *1*, 141–155.

Kilbride, J. E., & Yarczower, M. Recognition and imitation of facial expressions: A cross-cultural comparison between Zambia and the United States. *Journal of Cross-Cultural Psychology*, 1980, *11*, 281–296.

Kleck, R. E., Vaughan, R. C., Cartwright-Smith, J., Vaughan, K. B., Colby, C. Z., & Lanzetta, J. T. Effects of being observed on expressive, subjective, and physiological responses to painful stimuli. *Journal of Personality and Social Psychology*, 1976, *34*, 1211–1218.

Klinnert, M., Campos, J., Sorce, J., Emde, R., & Svejda, M. Emotions as behavior regulators: Social referencing in infancy. In R. Plutchik & H. Kellerman (Eds.), *Emotions in early development* (Vol. 2). *The emotions*. New York: Academic, 1982.

Klopfer, P. H., & Klopfer, L. On 'Human ethology.' *Semiotica*, *1982, 9*, 175–185.

Knapp, M. L., Hart, R. P., & Dennis, H. S. An exploration of deception as a communication construct. *Human Communication Research*, 1974, *1*, 15–29.

Knox, K. A. M. *An investigation of nonverbal behavior in relation to hemispheric dominance.* Unpublished masters thesis, San Francisco State University, 1972.

Kolb, B., & Milner, B. Observations on spontaneous facial expression after focal cerebral excisions and after carotid injection of sodium amytal. *Neuropsychologia*, 1981, *19*, 505–514.

Krauss, R. M., Apple, W., Morency, N., Wenzel, C., & Winton, W. Verbal, vocal, and visible factors in judgments of another's affect. *Journal of Personality and Social Psychology*, 1981, *40*, 4312–320.

Krauss, R. M., Geller, V., & Olson, C. *Modalities and cues in the detection of deception.* Paper presented at the Annual Meeting of the American Psychological Association, Washington, DC, September, 1976.

Kraut, R. E. Verbal and nonverbal cues in the perception of lying. *Journal of Personality and Social Psychology*, 1978, *36*, 380–391.

Kraut, R. E., & Poe, D. On the line: The deception judgments of customs inspectors and laymen. *Journal of Personality and Social Psychology*, 1980, *39*, 784–798.

Kuypers, H. G. J. M. Corticobulbar connexions to the pons and lower brain-stem in man: An anatomical study. *Brain*, 1958, *81*, 364–388.

Kuhn, R. (1958). The treatment of depressive states with G22355 (imipramine hydrochloride). *American Journal of Psychiatry*, 1958, *115*, 459–464.

Lacey, J. T. Somatic response patterning and stress: Some revisions of activation theory. In M. H. Appley & R. Trumbull (Eds.), *Psychological stress: Issues in research* (pp. 14–44). New York: Appleton-Century-Crofts, 1967.

Lalljee, M. The role of gaze in the expression of emotion. *Austrian Journal of Psychology*, 1978, *30*, p. 59–67.

Landis, C. Studies of emotional reactions: II. General behavior and facial expression. *Journal of Comparative Psychology*, 1924, *4*, 447–509.

Landis, C., & Hunt, W. A. *The startle pattern*. New York: Farrar, Straus, & Giroux, 1939.

Lang, P. J. A bio-informational theory of emotional imagery. *Psychophysiology*, 1979, *16*, 495–512.

Lange, C. G. *Om sindsbevaegelser. et psyko. fysiolog. studie.* Copenhagen: Krønar, 1885.

Langfeld, H. E. The judgment of emotions from facial expressions. *Journal of Abnormal and Social Psychology*, 1918, *13*, 172–184.

Lanzetta, J. T., Cartwright-Smith, J., & Kleck, R. E. Effects of nonverbal dissimulation on emotional experience and autonomic arousal. *Journal of Personality and Social Psychology*, 1976, *33*, 354–370.

Lanzetta, J. T., & Kleck, R. E. Encoding and decoding of nonverbal affect in humans. *Journal of Personality and Social Psychology*, 1970, *16*, 12–19.

Lanzetta, J. T., & Orr, S. P. Influence of facial expressions on the classical conditioning of fear. *Journal of Personality & Social Psychology*, 1980, *39*, 1081–1087.

Lazarus, R. S., Averill, J. R., & Opton, E. M. Toward a cognitive theory of emotion. In M. Arnold (Ed.), *Feelings and emotions*. New York: Academic, 1970.

Leehey, S., Carey, S., Diamond, R., & Cahn, A. Upright and inverted faces: The right hemisphere knows the difference. *Cortex*, 1978, *14*, 411–419.

Leiman, B. *Affective empathy and subsequent altruism in kindergarten and first-grade children*. Paper presented at the Annual Meeting of the American Psychological Association, Toronto, August, 1978.

Leshner, A. I. Hormones and emotions. In D. K. Candland, J. P. Fell, E. Keen, A. I. Leshner, R. M. Tarpy, & R. Plutchik (Eds.), *Emotion*. Monterey, CA: Brooks/Cole, 1977.

Letzner, G. M., & Kronman, J. H. A posterioanterior cephalometric evaluation of craniofacial asymmetry. *Angle Orthodontist*, 1967, *37*, 205–211.

Lewis, M., & Brooks, J. Self-knowledge and emotional development. In M. Lewis & L. Rosenblum (Eds.), *The development of affect* (pp. 205–226). New York: Plenum, 1978.

Lewis, M., Brooks, J., & Haviland, J. Hearts and faces: A study in the measurement of emotion. In M. Lewis & L. Rosenblum (Eds.), *The development of affect* (pp. 77–124). New York: Plenum, 1978.

Lewis, M., & Michalson, L. The socialization of emotions. In T. Field & A. Fogel (Eds.), *Emotion and early interaction*. Hillsdale, NJ: Lawrence Erlbaum Associates, 1982.

Lewis, M., & Rosenblum, L. A. (Eds.). *The effect of the infant on its caregiver*. New York: Wiley, 1974.

Lindzey, G., Prince, B., & Wright, H. R. A study of facial asymmetry. *Journal of Personality*, 1952, *21*, 68–84.

Lockard, J. S., Fahrenbruch, C. E., Smith, J. L., & Morgan, C. J. Smiling and laughter: Different phyletic origins? *Bulletin of the Psychonomic Society*, 1977, *10*, 183–186.

Lynn, J. G., & Lynn, D. R. Face-hand laterality in relation to personality. *Journal of Abnormal and Social Psychology*, 1938, *33*, 291–322.

Lynn, J. G., & Lynn, D. R. Smile and hand dominance in relation to basic modes of adaptation. *Journal of Abnormal and Social Psychology*, 1943, *38*, 250–276.

Main, M., Weston, D., & Wakeling, S. *"Concerned attention" to the crying of an adult actor in infancy*. Paper presented at the Annual Meeting of the Society for Research in Child Development, San Francisco, March, 1979.

Malatesta, C., & Haviland, J. Learning display rules: The socialization of emotion expression in infancy. *Child Development*, 1982, *53*, 991–1003.

Malmo, R. B., & Shagass, C. Physiologic studies of reaction to stress in anxiety and early schizophrenia. *Psychosomatic Medicine*, 1949, *11*, 9–24.

Malmstrom, E., Ekman, P., & Friesen, W. V. *Autonomic changes with facial displays of surprise and disgust*. Paper presented at the meeting of the Western Psychological Association, Portland, Oregon, 1972.

Marañon, G. Contribution a l'etude de l'action emotive de 'adrenaline. *Revue Francaise d'Endocrinologie*, 1924, *2*, 301–325.

Marriott, B. M., & Salzen, E. A. Facial expressions in captive squirrel monkeys (Saimiri sciureus). *Folia Primatologica*, 1978, *29*, 1–18.

Martenson, J. A., Sackett, D. P., & Erwin, J. Facial expressions as correlates of overt aggression in pigtail monkeys. *Journal of Behavioral Science*, 1977, *2*, 239–242.

Martin, I., & Davies, B. M. The effect of sodium amytal in autonomic and muscular activity of patients with depressive illness. *British Journal of Psychiatry*, 1965, *111*, 168–175.

Marzi, C. A., & Berlucchi, G. Right visual field superiority for accuracy of recognition of famous faces in normals. *Neuropsychologia*, 1977, *15*, 751–756.

Masters, J. C. Letter to the editor. *Science*, 1979, *205*, 215.

Maurer, D., & Barrera, M. E. Infants' perception of natural and distorted arrangements of a schematic face. *Child Development,* 1981, *52,* 196–202.

Maurer, D., & Salapatek, P. Developmental changes in the scanning of faces by young infants. *Child Development,* 1976, *47,* 523–527.

McCurdy, H. G. Experimental notes on the asymmetry of the human face. *Journal of Abnormal and Social Psychology,* 1949, *44,* 553–555.

McGrew, W. C. *An ethological study of children's behavior.* New York: Academic, 1972.

McLintock, C. C., & Hunt, R. G. Nonverbal indicators of affect and deception in an interview setting. *Journal of Applied Social Psychology,* 1975, *5,* 54–67.

Mead, M. Review of *Darwin and facial expression* (P. Ekman, Ed.). *Journal of Communication,* 1975, *25,* 209–213.

Mehrabian, A. Nonverbal betrayal of feeling. *Journal of Experimental Research in Personality,* 1971, *5,* 64–73.

Mehrabian, A., & Ferris, S. Inference of attitudes from nonverbal communication in two channels. *Journal of Consulting Psychology,* 1967, *31,* 248–252.

Meltzoff, A. N., & Moore, M. K. Imitation of facial and manual gestures by human neonates. *Science,* 1977, *198,* 75–78.

Meltzoff, A. N., & Moore, M. K. Letter to the editor. *Science,* 1979, *205,* 217–219.

Mendelson, M. J., Haith, M. M., & Goldman-Rakic, P. S. Face scanning and responsiveness to social cues in infant rhesus monkeys. *Developmental Psychology,* 1982, *18,* 222–228.

Miller, E. H. A comparative study of facial expressions of two species of pinnepeds. *Behaviour,* 1975, *53,* 268–284.

Moldaver, J. Anatomical and functional characteristics of the muscles supplied by the facial nerve. In J. Moldaver & J. Conley (Eds.), *The facial palsies* (pp. 16–19). Springfield, IL: Thomas, 1980. (a)

Moldaver, J. Muscle tone and the mimetic muscles. In J. Moldaver & J. Conley (Eds.), *The facial palsies* (pp. 26–33) Springfield, IL: Thomas, 1980. (b)

Monrad-Krohn, G. H. On the dissociation of voluntary and emotional innervation in facial paralysis of central origin. *Brain,* 1924, *47,* 22–35.

Morency, N. L., & Krauss, R. M. Children's nonverbal encoding and decoding of affect. In R. S. Feldman (Ed.), *Development of nonverbal behavior in children.* New York: Springer–Verlag, 1982.

Moritani, T., & DeVries, H. A. Reexamination of the relationship between the surface integrated electromyogram (IEMG) and the force of isometric contraction. *American Journal of Physical Medicine,* 1978, *78,* 253–277.

Mueller, J. Neuroanatomical correlates of emotion. In L. Temoshok, C. Van Dyke, & L. S. Zegans (Eds.), *Emotions in health and illness: Theoretical and research foundations.* Orlando: Grune & Stratton, 1982.

Mulder, T., & Hulstijn, W. The effect of fatigue and repetition of the task on the surface electromyographic signal. *Psychophysiology,* 1984, *21,* 528–534.

Mulik, J. F. An investigation of craniofacial asymmetry using the serial twin-study method. *American Journal of Orthodontics,* 1965, *51,* 112–129.

Nelson, C. A., Morse, P. A., & Leavitt, L. A. Recognition of facial expressions by seven-month-old infants. *Child Development,* 1979, *50,* 1239–1241.

Nelson, W. H., Orr, W. W., Stevenson, J. M., & Shane, S. R. Hypothalamic-pituitary-adrenal axis activity and tricyclic response in major depression. *Archives of General Psychiatry,* 1982, *39,* 1033–1036.

Niit, T., & Valsiner, J. Recognition of facial expressions: An experimental investigation of Ekman's model. *Tartu Riikliku Ulikooli Toimetised: Trudy po Psikhologii,* 1977, *429,* 85–107.

Notarius, C. I., & Levenson, R. W. Expressive tendencies and physiological responses to stress. *Journal of Personality and Social Psychology,* 1979, *37,* 1204–1210.

Nystrom, M. Neonatal facial-postural patterning during sleep: I. Description and reliability of observation. *Psychological Research Bulletin*, 1974, *14*, 1-16.

Odum, R., & Lemond, C. Developmental differences in the perception and production of facial expressions. *Child Development*, 1972, *43*, 359-369.

O'Hair, H. D., Cody, M. J., & McLaughlin, M. L. Prepared lies, spontaneous lies, Machiavellianism and nonverbal communication. *Human Communication Research*, 1981, *7*, 325-339.

Ohman, A., & Dimberg, U. (1978). Facial expressions as conditioned stimuli for electrodermal responses: A case of "preparedness"? *Journal of Personality and Social Psychology*, 1978, *36*, 1251-1258.

Oliveau, D., & Willmuth, R. Facial muscle electromyography in depressed and nondepressed hospitalized subjects: A partial replication. *American Journal of Psychiatry*, 1979, *136*, 548-550.

Orr, S. P., & Lanzetta, J. T. Facial expressions of emotion as conditioned stimuli for human autonomic responses. *Journal of Personality and Social Psychology*, 1980, *38*, 278-282.

Oster, H. Facial expression and affect development. In M. Lewis & L. Rosenblum (Eds.), *The development of affect* (pp. 43-76). New York: Plenum, 1978.

Oster, H. *Pouts and horseshoe-mouth faces: Their determinants, affective meaning, and signal value in infants.* Paper presented at the Symposium on the Psychobiology of Affective Development at the biennial meeting of the International Conference on Infant Studies, Austin, Texas, March, 1982.

Oster, H. "Recognition" of emotional expression in infancy? In M. Lamb & L. Sherrod (Eds.), *Infant social cognition: Empirical and theoretical considerations.* Hillsdale, NJ: Lawrence Erlbaum Associates, 1981.

Oster, H. *The determinants and signal value of brow-knitting and smiling in infants.* Paper presented at the Conference on Infant Studies, New York, May, 1984.

Oster, H., & Ekman, P. Facial behavior in child development. *Minnesota Symposium on Child Psychology*, 1978, *11*, 231-276.

Oster, H., & Ewy, R. *Discrimination of sad vs. happy faces by 4-month-olds: When is a smile seen as a smile?* Paper presented at the 6th Biennial Meeting of the International Society for the Study of Behavioral Development, Toronto, August, 1981.

Oster, H., & Rosenstein, D. (in press). Analyzing facial movement in infants. In P. Ekman & W. V. Friesen (Eds.), *Analyzing facial action.* New York: Plenum.

O'Sullivan, M. Measuring the ability to recognize facial expressions of emotion. In P. Ekman (Ed.), *Emotion in the human face* (2nd ed., pp. 281-317). Elmsford, New York: Pergamon, 1982.

O'Sullivan, M., Ekman, P., Friesen, W., & Scherer, K. What you say and how you say it: The contribution of speech content and voice quality to judgments of others. *Journal of Personality and Social Psychology*, 1945, *48*, 54-62.

O'Sullivan, M., Guilford, J. P., & de Mille, R. *The measurement of social intelligence* (Rep. No. 34). Los Angeles: University of Southern California, Psychology Laboratory, 1965.

Paliwal, P., & Goss, A. E. Attributes of schematic faces in preschoolers' use of names of emotions. *Bulletin of the Psychonomic Society*, 1981, *17*, 139-142.

Papousek, H., & Papousek, M. Mothering and the cognitive headstart: Psychobiological considerations. In H. R. Schaffer (Ed.), *Studies in mother-infant interaction* (pp. 63-85). New York: Academic, 1977.

Phillips, R. J., & Rawles, R. E. Recognition of upright and inverted faces. *Perception*, 1979, *8*, 577-583.

Peiper, A. *Cerebral function in infancy and childhood.* New York: Consultants Bureau, 1963.

Pizzamiglio, L., & Zoccolotti, P. Sex and cognitive influence on visual hemifield superiority for face and letter recognition. *Cortex*, 1981, *17*, 215-226.

Pizzamiglio, L., Zoccolotti, P. Mammucari, A., & Cesaroni, R. The independence of face identity and facial expression recognition mechanisms: Relationship to sex and cognitive style. *Brain and Cognition*, 1983, *2*, 176-188.

Plutchik, R. Cognitions in the service of emotions: An evolutionary perspective. In D. K. Candland, J. P. Fell, E. Keen, A. I. Leshner, R. M. Tarpy, & R. Plutchik, (Eds.), *Emotion* (pp. 189–212). Monterey, CA: Brooks/Cole, 1977.

Potegal, M., Blau, A., & Miller, S. Preliminary observations with technique for measuring current spread in the rat brain. *Physiology & Behavior,* 1980, *25,* 769–773.

Provost, M., & Gouin-Décarie, T. Heart rate reactivity of 9- and 12-month-old infants showing specific emotions in natural settings. *International Journal of Behavioral Development,* 1979, *2,* 109–120.

Redican, W. K. Facial expression in nonhuman primates. In L. A. Rosenblum (Ed.), *Primate behavior* (Vol. 4). New York: Academic, 1975.

Redican, W. K. An evolutionary perspective on human facial displays. In P. Ekman (Ed.), *Emotion in the human face* (2nd ed, pp. 212–280). Elmsford, NY: Pergamon, 1982.

Reuter-Lorenz, P., & Davidson, R. J. Differential contributions of the two cerebral hemispheres to the perception of happy and sad faces. *Neuropsychologia,* 1981, *14,* 578–591.

Reynolds, D. M., & Jeeves, M. A. A developmental study of hemispheric specialization for recognition of faces in normal subjects. *Cortex,* 1978, *14,* 578–591.

Rinn, W. E. The neuropsychology of facial expression: A review of the neurological and psychological mechanisms for producing facial expressions. *Psychological Bulletin,* 1984, *95,* 52–77.

Rimon, R., Stenback, A., & Hahmar, E. Electromyographic findings in depressive patients. *Journal of Psychosomatic Research,* 1966, *10,* 159–170.

Roland, P. E. Sensory feedback to the cerebral cortex during voluntary movement in man. *The Behavioral and Brain Sciences,* 1978, *1,* 129–147.

Rosenfeld, S. A., & Van Hoesen, G. W. Face recognition in the rhesus monkey. *Neuropsychologia,* 1979, *17,* 503–509.

Rosenstein, D., & Oster, H. *Facial expression as a means of exploring infants' taste responses.* Paper presented at the Symposium on the Development of Food and Flavor Preferences at the annual meeting of the Society for Research in Child Development, Boston, April, 1981.

Rosenthal, R., Hall, J. A., DiMatteo, M. R., Rogers,P. L., & Archer, D. *Sensitivity to nonverbal communication: The PONS Test.* Baltimore: Johns Hopkins University Press, 1979.

Rothbart, M., & Birrell, P. Attitude and the perception of faces. *Journal of Research in Personality,* 1977, *11,* 209–215.

Rothebart, M. K. Laughter in young children. *Psychological Bulletin,* 1973, *80,* 247–256.

Rubin, D. A., & Rubin, R. T. Differences in asymmetry of facial expression between left- and right-handed children. *Neuropsychologia,* 1980, *18,* 373–377.

Rusalova, M. N., Izard, C. E., & Simonov, P. V. Comparative analysis of mimical and autonomic components of man's emotional state. *Aviation, Space, and Environmental Medicine,* 1975, *46,* 1132–1134.

Saarni, C. Children's understanding of display rules for expressive behavior. *Developmental Psychology,* 1979, *15,* 424–429.

Saarni, C. Cognitive and communicative features of emotional experience, or do you show what you think you feel? In M. Lewis & L. Rosenblum (Eds.), *The development of affect.* New York: Plenum, 1978.

Saarni, C. Social and affective functions of nonverbal behavior. In R. S. Feldman (Ed.), *Development of nonverbal behavior in children.* New York: Springer–Verlag, 1982.

Sackeim, H. A., Greenberg, M. S., Weiman, A. L., Gur, R. C., Hungerbuhler, J. P., & Geschwind, N. Hemispheric asymmetry in the expression of positive and negative emotions: Neurological evidence. *Archives of Neurology,* 1982, *39,* 210–218.

Sackeim, H. A., & Gur, R. C. Lateral asymmetry in intensity of emotional expression. *Neuropsychologia,* 1978, 16, 473–481.

Sackeim, H. A., & Gur, R. C., & Saucy, M. C. Emotions are expressed more intensely on the left side of the face. *Science,* 1978, *202,* 434–436.

Safer, M. A. Sex and hemispheric differences in access to codes for processing emotional expressions of faces. *Journal of Experimental Psychology,* 1981, *110,* 86–100.

Saha, G. B. Judgment of facial expression of emotion—a cross-cultural study. *Journal of Psychological Research,* 1973, *17,* 59–63.

Santibanez, G., Espinoza, B., Astorga, L., & Strozzi, L. Macroelectrodic activity of the facial nucleus of the cat. *Acta Neurobiologiae Experimentalis,* 1974, *34,* 265–276.

Schachter, J. Pain, fear, and anger in hypertensives and normotensives: A psychophysiologic study. *Psychosomatic Medicine,* 1957, *19,* 17–29.

Schachter, S. The interaction of cognitive and physiological determinants of emotional state. In L. Berkowitz (Ed.), *Advances in experimental social psychology* (Vol. 1). New York: Academic, 1964.

Schachter, S., & Singer, J. E. Cognitive, social, and physiological determinants of emotional state. *Psychological Review,* 1962, *69,* 379–399.

Shennum, W. A., & Bugental, D. B. The development of control over affective expressions in nonverbal behavior. In R. S. Feldman (Ed.), *Development of nonverbal behavior in children.* New York: Springer-Verlag, 1982.

Scherer, K. R., Scherer, U., Hall, J. A., & Rosenthal, R. Differential attribution of personality based on multichannel verbal and nonverbal cues. *Psychological Research,* 1977, *39,* 221–247.

Schiffenbauer, A. Effect of observer's emotional state on judgments of the emotional state of others. *Journal of Personality and Social Psychology,* 1974, *30,* 31–35.

Schlosberg, H. A scale for the judgment of facial expression. *Journal of Experimental Psychology,* 1941, *29,* 497–510.

Schlosberg, H. The description of facial expressions in terms of two dimensions. *Journal of Experimental Psychology,* 1952, *44,* 229–237.

Schlosberg, H. Three dimensions of emotion. *Psychological Review,* 1954, *61,* 81–88.

Schwartz, G. E., Ahern, G. L., & Brown, S. L. Lateralized facial muscle response to positive and negative emotional stimuli. *Psychophysiology,* 1979, *16,* 561–571.

Schwartz, G. E., Brown, S. L., & Ahern, G. L. Facial muscle patterning and subjective experience during affective imagery. *Psychophysiology,* 1980, *17,* 75–82.

Schwartz, G. E., Fair, P. L., Mandel, M. R., Salt, P., Mieske, M., & Klerman, G. L. Facial electromyography in the assessment of improvement in depression. *Psychosomatic Medicine,* 1978, *40,* 355–360.

Schwartz, G. E., Fair, P. L., Salt, P. Mandel, M. R., & Klerman, G. L. Facial expression and imagery in depression: An electromyographic study. *Psychosomatic Medicine,* 1976, *38,* 337–347. (a)

Schwartz, G. E., Fair, P. L., Salt, P., Mandel, M. R., & Klerman, G. L. Facial muscle patterning to affective imagery in depressed and nondepressed subjects. *Science,* 1976, *192,* 489–491. (b)

Seaford, H. W. *Maximizing replicability in describing facial behavior.* Paper presented at the Annual Meeting of the American Anthropological Association, Washington, DC, 1976.

Secord, P. F. Facial features and inference processes in interpersonal perception. In R. Tagiuri & L. Petrullo (Eds.), *Person perception and interpersonal behavior.* Stanford: Stanford University Press, 1958.

Seligman, M. E. P. Phobias and preparedness. *Behavior Therapy,* 1971, *2,* 307–320.

Sergent, J., & Bindra, D. Differential hemispheric processing of faces: Methodological considerations and reinterpretation. *Psychological Bulletin,* 1981, *89,* 541–554.

Serra, S., & DiRosa, A. Spontaneous facial-buccal-lingual dyskinesia: Clinical observations and pharmacological experiments. *Acta Neurologica,* 1975, *30,* 576–586.

Shah, S. M., & Joshi, M. R. The assessment of asymmetry in the normal craniofacial complex. *The Angle Orthodontist,* 1978, *48,* 141–148.

Shapiro, J. G. Variability and usefulness of facial and bodily cues. *Comparative Group Studies,* 1972, *3,* 437–442.

Shultz, T. R., & Zigler, E. Emotional concomitants of visual mastery in infants: The effect of stimulus movement on smiling and vocalizing. *Journal of Experimental Child Psychology,* 1970, *10,* 390–402.

Shennum, W. A. & Bugental, D. B. In R. S. Feldman (Ed.), *Development of nonverbal behavior in children.* New York: Springer–Verlag, 1982.

Sirota, A. D., & Schwartz, G. E. Facial muscle patterning and lateralization during elation and depression imagery. *Journal of Abnormal Psychology,* 1982, *91,* 25–34.

Smith, R. P. Frontalis muscle tension and personality. *Psychophysiology,* 1973, *10,* 311–312.

Smith, W. J. *The behavior of communicating.* Cambridge, MA: Harvard University Press, 1977.

Spohn, H. E., & Patterson, T. Recent studies of psychophysiology in schizophrenia. *Schizophrenia Bulletin,* 1979, *5,* 581–611.

Sroufe, L. A. Wariness of strangers and the study of infant development. *Child Development,* 1977, *48,* 731–746.

Sroufe, L. A. The ontogenesis of emotion. In J. Osofosky (Ed.), *Handbook of infancy.* New York: Wiley, 1978.

Sroufe, L. A., & Waters, E. The ontogenesis of smiling and laughter: A perspective on the organization of development in infancy. *Psychological Review,* 1976, *83,* 173–189.

Starr, A., McKeon, B., Skuse, N., & Burke, D. Cerebral potentials evoked by muscle stretch in man. *Brain,* 1981, *104,* 149–166.

Stechler, G., & Carpenter, G. A viewpoint on early affect development. In J. Hellmuth (Ed.), *Exceptional infant* (Vol. I). *The normal infant.* New York: Brunner/Maazel, 1967.

Steiner, J. E. The gustofacial response: Observation on normal and anencephalic newborn infants. In J. F. Bosma (Ed.), *Fourth symposium on oral sensation and perception.* Bethesda, MD: U.S. Department of Health and Human Services, 1973.

Stenberg, C., Campos, J., & Emde, R. The facial expression of anger in seven-month-old infants. *Child Development,* 1983, *54,* 178–184.

Stern, D. N., Beebe, B., Jaffe, J., & Bennett, S. L. (1977). The infant's stimulus world during social interaction: A study of caregiver behaviours with particular reference to repetition and timing. In. H. R. Schaffer (Ed.), *Studies of mother-infant interaction* (pp. 177–202). New York: Academic Press.

Stevens, S. S. The psychophysics of sensory function. In W. A. Rosenblith (Ed.), *Sensory communication* (pp. 1–33). Cambridge, MA: MIT Press, 1961.

Stevens, S. S. *Psychophysics: Introduction to its perceptual, neural, and social prospects.* New York: Wiley, 1975.

Strauss, E., & Moscovitch, M. Perception of facial expressions. *Brain & Language,* 1981, *13,* 308–332.

Suberi, M., & McKeever, W. F. Differential right-hemispheric memory storage of emotional and non-emotional faces. *Neuropsychologia,* 1977, *15,* 757–768.

Sumitsuji, N., Matsumoto, K., Tanaka, M., Kashiwagi, T., & Kaneko, Z. Electromyographic investigation of the facial muscles. *Electromyography,* 1967, *7,* 77–96.

Sumitsuji, N., Matsumoto, K., Tanaka, M., Kashiwagi, T., & Kaneko, Z. An attempt to systematize human emotion from EMG study of the facial expression. *Proceedings of the 4th Congress of the International College of Psychosomatic Medicine,* Kyoto, Japan, 1977.

Tagiuri, R. Person perception. In G. Lindzey & E. Aronson (Eds.), *Handbook of social psychology.* Reading, MA: Addison–Wesley, 1968.

Tanaka, T., & Asahara, T. Synaptic actions of vagal afferents on facial motoneurons in the cat. *Brain Research,* 1981, *212,* 188–193.

Tarpy, R. M. The nervous system and emotion. In D. K. Candland, J. P. Fell, E. Keen, A. I. Leshner, R. M. Tarpy, & R. Plutchik (Eds.), *Emotion* (pp. 149–187). Monterey, CA: Brooks/Cole, 1977.

Teasdale, J. D., & Bancroft, J. Manipulation of thought content as a determinant of mood and corrugator activity in depressed patients. *Journal of Abnormal Psychology,* 1977, *86,* 235–241.

Teasdale, J. D., & Rezin, V. Effect of thought-stopping on thoughts, mood and corrugator EMG in depressed patients. *Behavior Research and Therapy,* 1978, *16,* 97–102.

Thompson, J. R. Asymmetry of the face. *Journal of the American Dental Association,* 1943, *30,* 1859–1871.

Tinbergen, N. Einige Gedanken uber Beschwichtigungs-Gebaerden. *Zeitschrift fur Tierpsychologie,* 1959, *16,* 651–665. (Reprinted as [On appeasement signals]. In N. Tinbergen [Ed.], *The animal in its world* [Vol. 2, pp. 112–129]. Cambridge: Harvard University Press, 1972).

Tomkins, S. S. *Affect, imagery, consciousness* (Vol. 1), *The positive affects.* New York: Springer, 1962.

Tomkins, S. S. *Affect, imagery, consciousness* (Vol. 2), *The negative affects.* New York: Springer, 1963.

Tomkins, S. S. Script theory: Differential magnification of affects. In H. E. Howe, Jr. & R. A. Dienstbier (Eds.), *Nebraska Symposium on Motivation, 1978* (Vol. 26). Lincoln: University of Nebraska Press, 1979.

Tomkins, S. S. The role of facial response in the experience of emotion: A reply to Tourangeau and Ellsworth. *Journal of Personality and Social Psychology,* 1981, *40,* 355–359.

Tomkins, S. S. *Affect, imagery, consciousness* (Vol. 3). New York: Springer, 1982.

Tomkins, S. S., & McCarter, R. What and where are the primary affects? Some evidence for a theory. *Perceptual and Motor Skills,* 1964, *18,* 119–158.

Tourangeau, R., & Ellsworth, P. C. The role of facial response in the experience of emotion. *Journal of Personality and Social Psychology,* 1979, *37,* 1519–1531.

Trevarthen, C. Descriptive analyses of infant communicative behaviors. In H. R. Schaffer (Ed.), Studies of mother-infant interaction (pp. 227–270). New York: Academic, 1977.

Trevarthen, C. Instincts for human understanding and for cultural cooperation: Their development in infancy. In M. von Cranach, K. Foppa, W. Lepenies, & D. Ploog (Eds), *Human ethology: Claims and limits of a new discipline.* New York: Cambridge University Press, 1979.

Tschiassny, K. Eight syndromes of facial paralysis and their significance in locating the lesion. *Annals of Otology, Rhinology, and Laryngology,* 1953, *62,* 677–691.

van Hooff, J. A. R. A. M. The facial displays of the Catarrhine monkeys and apes. In D. Morris (Ed.), *Primate ethology* (pp. 9–88). Garden City, NY: anchor, 1969.

van Hooff, J. A. R. A. M. A comparative approach to the phylogeny of laughter and smiling. In R. A. Hinde (Ed.), *Nonverbal communication* (pp. 209–238). Cambridge: Cambridge University Press, 1972.

van Hooff, J. A. R. A. M. The comparison of facial expression in man and higher primates. In M. von Cranach (Ed.), *Methods of inference from animal to human behavior* (pp. 165–196). Chicago: Aldine, 1976.

van Lawick-Goodall, J. *In the shadow of man.* Boston: Houghton–Mifflin, 1971.

Vande Creek, L., & Watkins, J. T. Responses to incongruent verbal and nonverbal emotional cues. *Journal of Communications,* 1972, *22,* 311–316.

Vaughan, B. E., & Sroufe, L. A. *The face of surprise in infants.* Paper presented at the Annual Meeting of the Animal Behavior Society, Boulder, Colorado, 1976.

Vaughan, K. B., & Lanzetta, J. T. Vicarious instigation and conditioning of facial expressive and autonomic responses to a model's expressive display of pain. *Journal of Personality and Social Psychology,* 1980, *38,* 909–923.

Vaughan, K. B., & Lanzetta, J. T. The effect of modulation of expressive displays on vicarious emotional arousal. *Journal of Experimental Social Psychology,* 1981, *17,* 16–30.

Vig, P. S., & Hewitt, A. B. Asymmetry of the human facial skeleton. *The Angle Orthodontist,* 1975, *45,* 125–129.

Vitti, M., & Basmajian, J. V. Electromyographic investigation of frontalis and procerus muscles. *Electromyography and Clinical Neurophysiology*, 1976, *16*, 227–236.

Volkmar, F. R., & Siegel, A. E. Responses to consistent and discrepant social communications. In R. S. Feldman (Ed.), *Development of nonverbal behavior in children*. New York: Springer-Verlag, 1982.

Walker, E., Marwit, S., & Emory, E. A cross-sectional study of emotion recognition in schizophrenics. *Journal of Abnormal Psychology*, 1980, *89*, 428–436.

Wall, P. D., & Pribram, K. H. Trigeminal neurotomy and blood pressure responses from stimulation of lateral cerebral cortex in *Macaca mulatta*. *Journal of Neurophysiology*, 1950, *13*, 409–412.

Waters, E., Matas, L., & Sroufe, L. Infants' reaction to an approaching stranger: Description, validation, and functional significance of wariness. *Child Development*, 1975, *46*, 348–356.

Watson, J. S. Perception of contingency as a determinant of social responsiveness. In E. P. Thoman (Ed.), *The origin of the infant's social responsiveness*. Hillsdale, NJ: Lawrence Erlbaum Associates, 1978.

Weigel, R. M. The facial expressions of the brown capuchin monkey. *Behavior*, 1979, *68*, 250–276.

Weinstein, E. A., & Bender, M. B. Integrated facial patterns elicited by stimulation of the brainstem. *Archives of Neurology and Psychiatry*, 1943, *50*, 34–42.

Whatmore, G. B., & Ellis, R. M. Some neurophysiological aspects of depressed states. *Archives of General Psychiatry*, 1959, *1*, 70–80.

Whatmore, G. B., & Ellis, R. M. Further neurophysiological aspects of depressed states. *Archives of General Psychiatry*, 1962, *6*, 243–253.

Winkelmayer, R., Exline, R. V., Gottheil, E., & Paredes, A. The relative accuracy of U.S., British, and Mexican raters in judging the emotional displays of schizophrenic and normal U.S. women. *Journal of Clinical Psychology*, 1978, *34*, 600–608.

Wolff, P. H. Observations on the early development of smiling. In B. M. Foss (Ed.), *Determinants of infant behavior II*. New York: Wiley, 1963.

Wolff, P. H. The causes, controls, and organization of behavior in the neonate. *Psychological Issues*, 1966, *5*, (Monograph 17).

Wolff, P. H. The natural history of crying and other vocalizations in early infancy. In B. M. Foss (Ed.), *Determinants of infant behavior* (IV). London: Methuen, 1969.

Wolff, W. The experimental study of forms of expression. *Character and Personality*, 1933, *2*, 168–176.

Wolff, W. *The expression of personality: Experimental depth psychology*. New York: Harper, 1943.

Woo, T. L. On the asymmetry of the human skull. *Biometrica*, 1931, *22*, 324–341.

Yarczower, M., & Daruns, L. Social inhibition of spontaneous facial expressions in children. *Journal of Personality and Social Psychology*, 1982, *43*, 831–837.

Yarczower, M., Kilbride, J. E., & Hill, L. A. Imitation and inhibition of facial expression. *Developmental Psychology*, 1979, *15*, 453–454.

Young, A. W., & Ellis, H. D. An experimental investigation of developmental differences in ability to recognize faces presented to the left and right cerebral hemispheres. *Neuropsychologia*, 1976, *14*, 495–498.

Young-Browne, G., Rosenfeld, H. M., & Horowitz, F. D. Infant discrimination of facial expressions. *Child Development*, 1977, *48*, 555–562.

Young, G., & Décarie, T. G. An ethology-based catalogue of facial/vocal behaviors in infancy. *Animal Behavior*, 1977, *25*, 95–107.

Zahn-Waxler, C., Radke-Yarrow, M., & Kling, R. Child rearing and children's prosocial initiations toward victims of distress. *Child Development*, 1979, *50*, 319–330.

Zaidel, S., & Mehrabian, A. The ability to communicate and infer positive and negative attitudes facially and vocally. *Journal of Experimental Research in Personality*, 1969, *3*, 233–241.

Zivin, G. Watching the sands shift: conceptualizing development of nonverbal mastery. In R. S.

Feldman (Ed.), *Development of nonverbal behavior in children*. New York: Springer–Verlag, 1982.

Zuckerman, M., Amidon, M. D., Bishop, S. E., & Pomerantz, S. D. Face and tone of voice in the communication of deception. *Journal of Personality and Social Psychology,* 1982, *43,* 347–357.

Zuckerman, M., DeFrank, R. S., Hall, J. A., Larrance, D. T., & Rosenthal, R. *Journal of Experimental Social Psychology,* 1979, *15,* 378–396.

Zuckerman, M., DePaulo, B. M., & Rosenthal, R. Verbal and nonverbal communication of deception. In L. Berkowitz (Ed.), *Advances in experimental social psychology* (Vol. 14). New York: Academic, 1981.

Zuckerman, M., Hall, J., DeFrank, R. S., & Rosenthal, R. Encoding and decoding of spontaneous and posed facial expressions. *Journal of Personality and Social Psychology,* 1976, *34,* 966–977.

Zuckerman, M., Klorman, R., Larrance, D. T., & Spiegel, N. H. (1981). Facial, autonomic, and subjective components of emotion: The facial feedback hypothesis versus the externalizer-internalizer distinction. *Journal of Personality and Social Psychology,* 1981, *41,* 919–1944.

Zuckerman, M., Larrance, D. T., Hall, J. A., DeFrank, R. S., & Rosenthal, R. Posed and spontaneous communication of emotion via facial and vocal cues. *Journal of Personality,* 1979, *47,* 712–733.

Zuckerman, M., Larrance, D. T., Spiegel, N. H., & Klorman, R. Controlling nonverbal cues: Facial expressions and tone of voice. *Journal of Experimental Social Psychology,* 1981, *17,* 506–524.

Zuckerman, M., & Przewuzman, S. Decoding and encoding facial expressions in preschool-age children. *Environmental Psychology and Nonverbal Behavior,* 1979, *3,* 147–163.

6

Social Visual Interaction: A Conceptual and Literature Review

B. J. Fehr
Tufts University

Ralph V. Exline
University of Delaware

One of the salient features of other persons in our social world is the action and focus of their eyes. The direction of another's gaze, which seems to indicate something about his or her orientation or focus of attention, may have significance for us and the organization of our own actions, particularly if we happen to be the target of these two distinctive orbs. But others are not invulnerable to the same scrutiny from us and likely will make similar adjustments depending on what they infer about our intentions, based in part on the presence or absence of our apparent attention to them. Whether in a public or private setting, the action of the eyes seems to play an important role in the organization of social behavior. It is with the extensive research literature focused on this apparently simple act that this chapter is concerned. The research is reviewed and a conceptual framework presented, based on a semiotic/structuralist approach to communication, within which the findings are organized. This review draws upon, refers to, and hopefully extends other reviews that have appeared during the last 10 to 15 years (Argyle & Cook, 1976; von Cranach, 1971; Ellsworth, 1975; Ellsworth & Ludwig, 1972; Harper, Wiens, & Matarazzo, 1978; Vine, 1970).

This chapter represents a complete revision of the one we prepared for the first edition of this volume (Exline & Fehr, 1978). In the previous version, the research dealing with social visual interaction was organized within the early semiotic framework of Charles Morris as presented in *Foundations of the Theory of Signs* (1938). Exemplar studies were described as representing syntactic, semantic, and pragmatic aspects of gaze behavior. The present chapter differs from the former by providing a more comprehensive review of the empirical literature, including work published subsequent to the first edition, and a somewhat modified theoretical perspective, which reflects our continuing efforts to understand social visual behavior. Semiotics, the science of signs, continues to play an important role, however, the approach of Umberto Eco (1976) is selected over that of Morris (1938). Further, greater emphasis is given to the developmental and interactive context in which visual behavior occurs, along the lines suggested by von Cranach and Vine (1973) and Goodwin (1981). The discussion of measurement issues is substantially abbreviated as we have in the interim prepared a chapter specifically dealing with this topic (Exline & Fehr, 1982).

Definition and Measurement of Social Visual Behavior

Visual behavior as it is discussed here specifically refers to gazes at and away from the eye–face region of other persons in a social context. Although sophisticated techniques exist for automating the recording of eye fixations, such as eye-marker cameras or infrared video systems, such techniques would be quite obtrusive to ordinary social interaction. Thus, researchers interested in the social aspects of gaze behavior characteristically employ human observers who record the incidence of eye–face fixations either while the interaction is in progress or from video or film records. These observations are recorded using check sheets or notes, frequency counters, event recorders, or computers. The specific gaze variables obtained will obviously depend on the type of equipment that is available; a more detailed record of duration, frequency, and point of occurrence during the interaction is typically only possible if one has access to event recorders or computers. Various indices of gaze have been reported: percent total gaze, or the percentage of the total interaction period spent looking at the eye–face region of the other; mean duration total gaze, or the average duration of glances over the interaction period; and total frequency of gazes for the same period. Researchers interested in the relationship between speech and gaze often record both variables thus producing a number of composite measures: percentage, mean duration, or frequency of looking at the other while speaking, and percentage, mean duration, or frequency of looking while listening to the other speak. If two people are looking at each other in the eye–face region at the same moment, this is referred to as a mutual gaze or eye contact and similarly its percentage, mean duration, and frequency may be noted. Some investigators have employed the assistance of confederates whose gaze is controlled by a prearranged schedule; others observe the behavior of freely interacting participants. In the latter case, the visual behavior of both parties may be recorded. The measures described thus far are all produced by summing or averaging over the total interaction period or some portion of it (e.g., speaking or listening periods). When the interest is the flow or sequencing of gaze, frequency as it relates to speech or other behavioral variables, the records are examined for patterns of initiation, termination, and mutual occurrence of the various behaviors (see Exline & Fehr, 1982 for a fuller description of the preceeding).

The interpretation of visual interaction behaviors depends in part on the validity and reliability of their measurement. Whereas fairly high reliabilities are routinely obtained, questions about the validity of measurement have been raised by a series of experiments conducted by Mario von Cranach and his colleagues (von Cranach, 1971; von Cranach & Ellgring, 1973; see Exline & Fehr, 1982 for a review). These psychophysical experiments have demonstrated that the ability to discriminate (a) gaze at the eyes from gaze at other parts of the face and head and (b) gaze at the face from off-body gazes is adversely affected by a number of factors, e.g. (a) angular, displacement of the head from a straight-on position, (b) increased distance between sender and receiver, (c) decreased duration of gaze, (d) angular displacement of the observer from the line of orientation between sender and receiver, and (e) movements of the eyes or head prior to fixation. Although these results deserve serious consideration and will hopefully promote further analysis of the measurement process, several mitigating factors enable us to retain some confidence in the findings of visual interaction research. Subjects in von Cranach's experiments made judgments about discretely displayed eye fixations from a programmed assistant in a noninteractional context. Vine (1971) found that the reliability of judgment was higher in a naturalistic setting when compared with a format similar to that of the psychophysical experiments. Whereas this does not necessarily demonstrate a concomitant increase in validity, it does suggest that there might be something quite different about the two settings. Argyle (1970) argues that in normal conversation gazes are focused either on the face of a partner or well away, which would simplify the discrimination task. In many situations the perceptions of the receiver regarding the gaze direction of the sender are of more interest than the specification of where the sender is actually looking (Exline, 1972). High reliabilities have been obtained between observers' and receivers' measurement of on-face and off-face gazes suggesting that observers are at least coding receiver perceptions. Finally, Ellgring and von Cranach (1972) have demonstrated that observer validity may be enhanced by feedback provided during the training trials, a procedure that many current researchers employ. Thus, whereas final resolution of the problem will depend on validity studies conducted in naturalistic settings, we can have some confidence in the data produced to date by studies of visual interaction. As von Cranach (1971) argues, however, the validity issues influence what may be considered an appropriate definition of the variable. In the sections to follow, gaze at another person refers to gaze in the eye–face region rather than gaze specifically directed to the eyes alone. "Mutual gaze," rather than "eye contact," will be used to refer to the simultaneous shared baze of two persons.

CONCEPTUAL ORIENTATION

Of particular interest to students of nonverbal communication are those non-word activities of the organism, which, in social contexts, are brought to bear for the purpose of interacting with, influencing, and communicating with others who are minimally copresent.

To be a social animal, as humans are purported to be, is in part to organize one's activities with respect to others of the same species. For this organization to occur there must be some way of connecting with or contacting other conspecifics. Each must be able to obtain information from others and provide information to them; furthermore each must be able to adjust his or her performance in accordance with the information. Part of being social is to be equipped with the capability of doing so. Receptor–effector systems (the sensory systems, neural networks, muscular–skeletal systems) that provide for interaction with the environment in general may be employed to interact with conspecifics who constitute a particularly significant subcomponent of the total environment. With respect to the focus of this chapter, social visual behavior may be used to gather information about others and serve as a signal to others of one's activities. Members may be influenced not only by specific signals, but also by the sheer presence of others, or by information provided by the conduct of daily activities that may enable prediction of what they will do next (Hinde, 1975). But if this process is to constitute more than random impact, some underlying organization must occur such that information from members may be standardly and reliably responded to or interpreted. Any meaning associated with social gaze would be most useful for the organization of social activities if it were standardly thus associated. Some behaviors may have, in fact, evolved for their particular effectiveness in influencing the behavior of others (Hinde, 1975). In organisms with fairly complex repertoires, where a number of choices of next-action are available, signaling is particularly important when the decision about next-action depends on the activities of others. Thus, some sort of signaling or communication system provides for the organization of social activities.

In humans, one such obvious system is language, an underlying system of shared expression-content relationships coupled with the ability for speech production and auditory sensitivity, as well as the necessary neural development upon which the organization of the system rests. Much emphasis and attention has been given to this aspect of our ability to mutually influence each other. The models and methodologies employed have played a role in determining, occasionally detrimentally, approaches to nonverbal activity as it is implicated in human social behavior.

How is the interaction of human social animals organized? The view taken here is that it is based on an underlying shared code, the signs, symbols, or expressions of which have similar referents or meaning for code users. Individuals are capable of encoding, or putting in expression form, contents that are receivable by others. These expressions are then decoded that such some semblance of the original content is retained. The shared code enables predictable, interpretable interaction to be conducted. In the processing of language, encoding and decoding occur virtually simultaneously, albeit in two different individuals. When consideration is also given to the nonverbal behavior of individuals, the distinction between encoder and decoder becomes blurred. For although a person may be silent, he or she still seems to be engaging in activity that is meaningful, as, for example, displays of internal states, or as reactions to the verbal and nonverbal actions of the other. These displays, to be reliably meaningful, must also be systematically organized based on an underlying system of expression-content relationships. The listener encodes nonverbally while decoding the verbal and nonverbal displays of the other. Further, the listener may encode verbal behavior simultaneously with the speech of the other person. The speaker encodes verbal utterances coincident with encoding nonverbal actions and poses. This system does not materialize as a fixed entity in humans but rather develops through phylogenetic, historical, cultural, and ontogenetic processes that continue to operate as the individual progresses through each interaction with others. This chapter reviews what is known about visual behavior in the social lives of both nonhuman primates and humans. Developmental similarities and differences are described for human infants, children, and adults. The majority of the research has been conducted within white western cultural groups, however, when available, cross-cultural work is presented. although not reviewed here, historical similarities and differences would be partially retrievable from etiquette books and novels of earlier historical periods.

Social interaction is said to occur when two or more co-present individuals simultaneously and mutually impact on each other. Communication occurs, as a subcategory of social interaction, when the mutual impact or message exchange is based on a shared code that develops through a shared history, both phylogenetic and ontogenetic. Conscious awareness of the process is not necessary, but neither is it precluded as a possibility. Persons may be aware of what they are doing, even potentially intend to do it, but much of human action occurs out of awareness, without the intervention of conscious attention, and these actions may still be part of a structured or coded system. Further, there will likely be activities that are not conventionally correlated with content as part of a code, activities that other authors have variously referred to as "informative" or "expressive" behavior. Although, it becomes apparent, as the argument progresses, that from the perspective developed here, a good deal less activity is relegated to this category compared with other formulations. It is argued that much nonverbal behavior is patterned through social interactions occurring early in life, leading to actions that are habitually and unreflectively performed, but nonetheless culturally structured. The previous discussion of the interaction system owes much to that presented by von Cranach and Vine (1973).

It is fairly easy and probably not very controversial to say that aspects of nonverbal behavior convey meaning to a receiver. Describing the specific aspects of the behavior (expression), the specific nature of the meaning (content), and the nature of the relationship between the two has been more problematic. Under the influence of the linguistic model in which discrete components (phones/phonemes/morphemes) are arbitrarily related to content, a number of researchers (e.g., Birdwhistell, 1952) have attempted to describe similar minimally discriminable and meaningful components of nonverbal behavior (kines/kinemes/kinemorphs). The goal then is to build from the pieces the overall patterns of nonverbal behavior functional in social interaction. One difference (among many) between verbal and nonverbal behavior suggests that such a strategy is, at least, uneconomical. Language in its various forms appears resolvable to a manageable set of discrete component elements or phonemes capable fo being used to produce a virtually infinite set of strings, with at least a very large set of associated meanings. Nonverbal behavior on the other hand, as Birdwhistell has demonstrated, seems to be composed of an enormous set of discriminable movements, restricted only by the physical limitations of the body. The meaning set associated with these movements however seems much smaller. It may be more profitable to begin with the meaning set, initially as represented in "commonsense" understandings, and expanding from there, to describe the units or clusters of non-word actions associated with the meaning set. For example, the study of social visual behavior may be meaningfully advanced by beginning with the understandings people have of one another and then determining the gaze displays that are called into play in these understandings, rather than cataloging all possible gaze behaviors and measuring their relationship to rating scales structured by the investigator.[1]

Researchers who have been concerned with the issue of coding (Dittman, 1978; Ekman & Friesen, 1969; Scherer & Ekman, 1982) have argued for both similarities and differences between the code structures of verbal and nonverbal behavior. Scherer and Ekman (1982), for example, suggest that a sign-referent relationship may be described on three dimensions: "(1) discrete versus continuous/graded, (2) probabilistic versus invariant, and (3) iconic versus arbitrary" (p. 13). Verbal language signs, they argue, tend to be related to their referents in a discrete (the sign refers to a given thing or not), invariant (the sign-referent relationship is standard across occasions and persons), and arbitrary (the sign bears no relationship to the nature of the referent) manner. On the other hand, relationships between nonverbal signs and their referents may be similar to those proposed for language or,

---

[1]Thanks to David Clarke for stimulating this line of argument.

and perhaps more usually, may refer to some content through a continuous/ graded, probabilistic, iconic relationship. A gesture may vary in intensity of performance related to a graded meaning. This relationship may exist in some contexts and not in others. The gesture may be similar in some respect to the referent, as when one forms one's hands in the shape of a bowl in order to refer to a bowl.

The most general discussion of coding relationships is provided by semiotics, or the science of signs. The semiotitian attempts to understand all instances of sign usage, reasoning that there are probably some general features shared by such activities. A particularly helpful work in this regard is Umberto Eco's *A Theory of Semiotics* (1976). Eco sets himself the task "to explore the theoretical possibility and the social function of a unified approach to every phenomenon of signification and/or communication" (p. 3). Perhaps because of his own interest in aesthetics and architecture, he is particularly sensitive to what he calls the "verbocentric dogmatism" inherent in some treatments of semiotics (e.g., Barthes, 1964, cited in Eco, 1976) and thus deals extensively with nonverbal as well as verbal instances of sign usage.

Eco's general semiotic theory takes account of (a) a theory of codes that deals with all instances of signification, elaborated through the notion of "sign-function," and (b) a theory of sign-production in which "the possibilities provided by a signification system are exploited in order to physically produce expressions for many practical purposes" (p. 4). The theory of codes considers the semiotics of signification including the nature of expressive forms (e.g., various gaze behaviors), the nature of content or meaning (e.g., attention, interest), and their relationship to each other. The theory of sign-production considers the semiotics of communication, dealing with the labor involved in actually producing expressions (in the most general sense, including both verbal and nonverbal), correlating them with a content, and interpreting them. For example, gazes at and away from another are produced in social contexts in which they are interpreted, or associated with meanings. Eco is not proposing an "abstract theory of the pure competence of an ideal sign-producer" (p. 28), but rather "a social phenomenon subject to changes and restructuring, resembling a network of partial and transitory competencies rather than a crystal-like and unchanging model" (p. 28–29). The conventional relationship between social gaze and some meaning is not fixed ("crystal-like") but is subject to temporary and more permanent changes through its use in a social setting over time.

"A sign-function arises when an expression is correlated to a content, both the correlated elements being the functives of such a correlation" (p. 48). This relationship between elements of an expression plane and elements of a content plane is based on cultural convention. Within a culture, social gaze is correlated with some content or meaning. The expression (e.g., gaze) and the content (e.g., interest) are functives or components of the sign-function or correlation. Any expression, even physical events emanating from a natural source (as in the relationship between smoke and fire, or symptoms and disease), may become a functive or a sign-function if the correlation becomes recognized and employed within a culture. A sign-function dos not refer to a physical entity, such as the eyes or a particular gaze direction, but rather it refers to a relationship between an expression and a content. Nor is a sign-function a fixed semiotic entity for the functives may enter into other correlations. The proposed content in any specific instance will be circumscribed by contextual and circumstantial features of the sign-production. For example, the meaning associated with gaze may very with the changing circumstances of its production. The operation of a sign-function is not dependent on the existence of an external referent, for it is possible to refer to things that do not exist (e.g., unicorn) and it is possible to lie (e.g., to refer to events that have not occurred). Eco, in fact, states that "semiotics is in principle the discipline studying everything which can be used in order to lie. If something cannot be used to tell a lie, conversely it cannot be used to tell the truth: It cannot in fact be used 'to tell' at all" (1976, p. 7). If gaze may be understood to "tell" us something about an individual's orientation, interest, or target of attention, it may certainly be used to lie. It is certainly possible to gaze directly at something while attending to something else, even when what is gazed at is another person. This does not mean it is impossible to refer to "reality," but the verification of such statements is outside the domain of semiotics.

The content and expression planes are conceptualized as spaces, structured by mutual opposition between elements based on culturally determined pertinent features, and filled with token expression and content units, shaped from undifferentiated continua of physical and conceptual possibilities. With respect to visual behavior, of all the possible moves and focuses of the eyes (the undifferentiated continua of physical possibilities), some are singled out by a culture in contrast to others (structured by mutual opposition between elements) based on aspects that more or less clearly differentiate them (culturally determined pertinent features). For example, if, as Argyle (1970) suggests, we tend to gaze at or well away from others, this would serve to facilitate contrast between two particular gaze possibilities. Of all the possible meanings that could be correlated with the expressions (the undifferentiated continua of conceptual possibilities), certain ones may be selected by a culture (e.g., interest versus disinterest), which could be contrasted through mutual opposition to each other, based on pertinent features (e.g., the degree of concern of another). A particular gaze at another is a token expression; a particular meaning is a token content. The code, then, is a set of rules coupling items from the expression plane with items from the content plane, a particular instance of which constitutes a sign-function. The code does not refer to a simple point-to-point correlation between expression and content; an expression may refer to a network of contextually and circumstantially constrained denotations and connotations providing for reverberations through the content plane, calling forth various equivalences, emotive associations, and translations. The gaze of another may be correlated with the concept of interest, a favorable emotional feeling, and some notion of the relational implications of the gaze for the recipient. Thus, what is typically referred to as a message may be more like a text (i.e., a set of messages) and, despite the connotations of that term, need not be verbally translatable. As Eco notes, this latter process is similar to Pierce's conception of interpretant. The meaning or content associated with an expression is a "cultural unit" and may be anything that is defined or distinguished as an entity within a culture (p. 67). Something acquires a position in the system by means of opposition to other things based on culturally determined pertinent features. Things or events do not have meaning in and of themselves, based on inherent essences, but rather are meaningful only in terms of their relationship to other things or events. "The laws of signification are the laws of culture. For this reason culture allows a continuous process of communicative exchanges, insofar as it subsists as a system of systems of signification" (p. 28).

Despite the fact that Eco contends it is unnecessary to consider the actual perceptual and interpretive capabilities of any particular addressor/addressee in the definition of the process of signification (although the possibility of such should be foreseen), one cannot but note the similarity of aspects of his formulation to those of structuralist persuasion such as George Kelly (1955) and Jean Piaget (1970). This similarity has not gone unnoticed by others (Culler, 1973; Hawkes, 1977). Hawkes (1977) argues that the perspective of both structuralism and semiotics occurred in part as a result of a shift in the understanding in the nature of perception emanating from changes during the 20th century in the physical sciences. The world was no longer seen to consist of independently existing entities whose features could be both clearly and independently perceived. Rather the active constructive processes of the perceiver became viewed as imposing structure on events by noting a relationship between different events. Events and objects are "defined" not by their inherent essences but by the relationships proposed to exist between them (cf. Eco's definition of meaning aforementioned). As Culler (1973) points out, from this perspective, "if human actions or productions have a meaning there must be an underlying system of conventions which makes this meaning possible" (p. 21-22, cf. discussion on signaling between conspecifics, p. 5). Things are meaningful insofar as they are functional or operative *within* the system, from the "emic" (Pike, 1967) perspective, or the point of view of code users. Whereas things may be described "ethically" (Pike, 1967), from the point of view of an outsider, to understand their content for users, one must attempt to assume the emic perspective. In the present context, the focus of study would be those aspects of social gaze meaningful and relevant to members of a cultural group. This is not meant to imply that the structuring process is totally idealistic or whimsical. If it were we would not be able to successfully interact with our environment, including each other. Further, Lyons (1973) argues that the selection of pertinent features for distinguishing between events may operate on the basis of a "natural hierarchy" such that (in his example) languages may actualize certain features before others because of the perceptual and cognitive predispositions of humans. But the only thing that can be perceived is the relationship between perceivers and the object of perception (Hawkes, 1977; cf. Mead's (1934) definition of the self).

Of particular import to researchers in nonverbal communication is Eco's (1976) discussion of "modes of production." Despite the fact that he has provided a general definition of sign-function proposed to be capable of handling all instances of sign use, Eco notes that there still appears to be different "types" of signs. Some contents, for example, are expressed verbally and some nonverbally. Further, these contents are not always easily translatable with respect to each other. Certain verbal contents can be expressed nonverbally, others cannot. Although perhaps a larger proportion of the nonverbal contents may be expressed verbally, compared with the reverse operation, certain nonverbal contents appear to be inexpressible verbally. Eco critiques a number of sign typologies, focusing particularly on Peirce's trichotomy of: symbol, a sign that bears an arbitrary relation to its referent[2] (as in verbal language); index, a sign that is physically connected to its content (as in symptoms); and icons, a sign that is in some way similar to its referent (as in a drawing of an object). Many nonverbal actions are frequently discussed under the rubric of icons and indices (cf. Scherer & Ekman (1982) discussed earlier). With references to icons, Eco argues that they are able to convey meaning not because of their similarity or analogy to some external referent, but because of the operation of cultural conventions, which specify certain features as pertinent to the expression of a given content. An "iconic" representation of a zebra may include stripes if stripes constitute a culturally relevant feature. However, one can conceive of a culture in which the relevant feature is other than stripes because of the zebra's relationship to other animals within the system. In such a culture, a striped zebra icon may not be immediately effective (example from Eco, 1976, p. 206).

As Culler (1973) points out in his discussion of structuralist approaches to the study of modern culture, it is sometimes difficult to perceive the underlying system organizing and organized by human action because the events of our lives seem "natural." Absent is the initial sensation of strangeness that one encounters in a foreign culture. Researchers are sometimes charged with making elaborate explanations of the obvious, an indictment not unheard of

---

[2]Note that the use of "referent" implies the existence of some external event or object, i.e., something that exists.

with respect to nonverbal communication research. Thus no one is particularly surprised to learn that high-status persons receive a great deal of visual attention until they consider that it could be otherwise, as in Nigeria (Foluki Bank-Auba, personal communication, October, 1982) where it is considered impolite to gaze directly at a superior. Even within American culture, Ashcraft and Scheflen (1976) suggest white children are more likely to hear " 'Look me in the eye, young man!' " (p. 15), whereas black children receive " 'Get your eyes out of my face, boy!' " (p. 16). The job of the researcher then is to bring an element of strangeness into the study of his or her own culture. This amounts to demonstrating that what seems "natural" and the *only* way could be, and often is, otherwise among different groups.

Eco proposes a classification of "modes of sign-production," to replace earlier typologies of signs. Expressions are produced in different ways depending on: (a) the physical labor necessary for the particular production, (b) the type/token ratio, or the relationship between a token expression and its expression type, (c) the type of continuum to be shaped, whether it is similar or different from the material-stuff with which possible referents could be made, and (d) the mode and complexity of articulation (p. 217 ff.).

Elaborating on point (d) above, Eco proposes that it is unreasonable to assume that all sign systems are articulated in a manner similar to that of verbal languages, which are characterized by two levels of articulation. Eco employs the notion of "super-signs," in which the content is an entire proposition, to develop this argument. Super-signs may be analyzed into a first level of articulation that produces signs (sign-functions) that convey content as in the case of morphemes. A second level of articulation that may occur further analyzes the first level into *figurae*, or units that do not represent in themselves any of the content in the first level, as in phonemes. Whereas verbal language is characterized by such double articulation, other sign-systems may not be. It is, for example, possible to consider super-signs that are articulated only to *figurae*. Such may be the case with certain aspects of nonverbal behavior. A particular posture may convey some content about the person assuming it, but the individual positions of body parts that constitute it may be nothing more than *figurae*, without any meaning in and of themselves, but only meaningful as part of the total postural super-sign. In terms of visual behavior, direct gaze at another may mean nothing in and of itself but only because meaningful in the context of an overall orientation.

Visual Behavior and the Eyes

From the point of view of an isolated individual, the eyes are primarily part of the visual system, a portion of our sensory/perceptual apparatus that is designed to interpret certain aspects of the environment. Nielson (1962) suggests that we are often unaware of the *act* of looking; the *object* of perception dominates our attention rather than the *process*. However, a full account of perception is not possible without considering the behavior that produces it.[3]

Once another individual is introduced to the situation, the eyes seem to take on an additional role, that of signal or expression. As Diebold (1968) notes: "If any components of looking behavior have status as communication signs, there is one aspect in which they will be anomalous as visual-gestural signals: the receptors (the eyes) are at one and the same time also the effectors of the signals" (p. 548).[4] It is of use to know to what another is attending. The eyes, unlike some other receptors, must be pointed in the direction of the object of visual attention, despite our considerable capability for peripheral vision. Although we can hear what is going on behind our back, we must turn to see it. Thus the gaze direction of others can be informative of their current orientation, and potentially their next move, providing us with the capability of adjusting to it.

All but the lowest organisms possess receptors for light. With the evolution of higher primates, there was a concomitant increase in visual acuity, but at the expense of the extent of the area of clear focus. It is helpful that so many cues have been localized on the face, and that the face itself became flexible and expressive, perhaps as a result of homeothermal body metabolism and the muscles used for mastication and suckling (Vine, 1970). Thus, not only the eyes, but the ears, nose, mouth, and facial muscles can all provide information about the state and potential next moves of another, certainly all worthy of scrutiny.

Marler (1967) argues that a modality's usefulness in the reception of signals depends on the typical habitat in which it is used. Because vision depends on ambient light it is of restricted use at night and in closed environments, such as bee hives. Also, he suggests that vision is less satisfactory for distance reception of cues from conspecifics (or others) because of the requirement that the eyes be pointed at the source, less satisfactory, that is, unless vision is coupled with other modalities such as audition. The visual modality is advantageous in that, when seen, the source of the cue is immediately apparent. Also, the system can resolve compound signals from others, some elements of which are fairly durable (e.g., general appearance), increasing the likelihood of accurate reception. Marler (1967) concludes that visual signals are ideal for close-range communication in diurnal animals inhabiting a relatively

---

[3]As Argyle and Cook (1976) note, the study of person perception frequently fails to consider this point and instead directs the attention of subjects to experimental stimuli, rather than attempting to evaluate what the individual directs his or her attention to.

[4]A similar point is made by Argyle and Cook (1976): "Gaze is indeed a signal, but it is primarily a channel which can be open or shut, and it must be treated both as a channel and a signal" (p. xi). Also, various functional accounts of visual behavior (e.g., Argyle & Dean, 1965; Kendon, 1967; Vince, 1981) propose both monitoring and expressive components of looking.

open environment as part of a close-knit and complex social organization. Thus, the eyes are part of a perceptual system for gathering information about the environment. The focus or direction of another's eyes may provide us with knowledge of what he or she is oriented toward. The eyes are surrounded by other input/output systems that may also provide useful information regarding another, and the visual modality seems ideally suited for operation within the context of human social organization.

To function as a signal within a communication system, or in Eco's (1976) terms to act as an expression correlated with a content, the actions of the eyes of another must minimally be perceivable. Although the general orientation of another's body can be reliably noted, even at a distance, the detection of the specific focus of another's eyes has narrower limits of accuracy. Particularly as distance increases and head orientation deviates from straight-on to our own, our ability to correctly detect the focus of another's eye diminishes. Whereas some of the factors mitigating problems of validity in experimental work would probably operate for the average person, there certainly are limits to our ability in this respect. Within the distance range of normal conversations (2'-6'), we probably are fairly accurate. Several field experiments (to be discussed later), in which the presence or absence of gaze at a target is manipulated at even greater distances (e.g., Greenbaum & Rosenfeld, 1978), report results dependent on this one shifting cue. This suggests, at least, that people respond to where they think another is looking, particularly when it seems to be at them. Probably within a psychophysical paradigm, these same subjects would not be able to discriminate the specific focus of a gazer from 10 to 12 feet away. However, if we, as Argyle (1970) suggests, tend to look at or well away from another, i.e., producing an easily discriminable cue, it would be of great advantage in detecting another's visual focus.

Occasionally, as part of experimental research in visual interaction, subjects have been asked at the end of the session to estimate the extent to which they were gazed at by a confederate who was instructed to look at them for a particular percentage of time, or at specified moments during the interaction. Results are mixed. Ellsworth and Ross (1975) found subjects able to discriminate gross level differences, whereas Argyle and Williams (1969) found they were not. Ellsworth and Ludwig (1972) suggest that subjective reports may not be a very good measure of the recipients' responsiveness to the cue because many studies report significant effects of gaze for other modes of response. It may be argued, however, that the gaze of another becomes particularly relevant and is therefore monitored at certain points during an interaction (Goodwin, 1981). Global perceptions of a partner's gaze level may depend more on the presence or absence of gaze at these conversational junctures, rather than on the partner's actual level of gazing. Furthermore, Argyle and Williams (1969) found that persons who, in general, felt observed estimated that they had received more direct gaze from an experimental confederate compared to persons who did not tend to feel observed. Further research is needed to clarify these issues.

Von Cranach (1971) suggests that it is important to consider the "phenomenology of the signal" for the receiver (the emic perspective), which is rarely done in research on visual interaction. Most often the aspects of gaze behavior, both measured and manipulated, have been selected a priori by the investigator. The logical possibilities of eye movement and fixation together with the limitations of recording equipment have produced a set of gaze variables that the data indicate are in some way related to subject responses. It may be that intuitions of researchers, as members of the culture they are studying, aided in the selection of variables. The question of the significant features of gaze behavior for receivers, however, has not been fully explored.

Partially as a result of the problems associated with the detection of gaze, von Cranach (1971) views visual behavior as a component of the general "orienting behavior" of the individual: "the orientation of the eyes, head and the whole body towards the partner" (p. 217). This sort of orienting activity is frequently the first response upon reception of signals from another (Marler, 1967). The beginning of a conversation is typically preceded by a shift in head and body orientation toward our proposed interlocutor (von Cranach, 1971; Diebold, 1968; Kendon, 1973). We don't typically converse back to back, unless instructed by an experimenter interested in the extent to which this position disrupts our behavior. Von Cranach (1971) believes this orientation activity to be hierarchically organized, such that the greatest intensity is achieved when the hips and legs, trunk, head, and eyes are all aimed in the same direction. Voluntary gaze almost never occurs alone, rather it is typically coincident with other body adjustments. The general impression created by orienting toward another is a readiness to interact, a readiness to communicate. Conversely, turning away from the partner, bodily and/or visually, may imply the opposite (von Cranach, 1971).

The general orientation of individuals in a social context, of which gaze is an important component, serves to inform others regarding underlying predispositions, transitory states, and probable future actions. Vine (1978) states: "Social communication is thus regarded as a process involving the transmission of interpersonal signals which sets up a relationship between the behaviors of the recipients" (p. 286). From the perspective that suggests that what is perceived is the relationship between perceiver and the object of perception, social communication serves to structure the relationship between the participants themselves. Part of the significance of another's visual behavior, as an aspect of his or her general orientation, is the set of implications these acts have for the recipient, for his or her definition of self, and for the course of the ensuing interaction. The actions are social in that they not only are a "display about the self," but also a "projection about the other" (Goodwin, 1981). The projection about the other suggests a role for the other to play vis-a-vis the actor. A speaker is usually not merely tossing words into the air, but speaking *for* a hearer. A submissive display may propose that another play a dominant role. The participants are both proposing and responding to relationship messages that may result in a stable or precarious definition of the relationship between them. Given the potential complexity of the signals, and the speed with which they must be processed, it would be of biological advantage if at least part of the operation were automated (Vine, 1970). If the expression-content relationships are part and parcel of one's construction of reality, much of the coordination of social interaction may be dealt with without the constant intervention of conscious processing. In instances where the "programming" has gone wrong and the individual has difficulty interpreting and responding appropriately to the social expressions of others, tapping this automatic processing may be difficult.

The remainder of the chapter is devoted to a review and discussion of the visual interaction literature from the perspective of the conceptual orientation described previously. Thus, the focus is the expression-content relationships (sign-functions) for various aspects of visual behavior as it is employed in social settings (sign-productions). As Ellsworth (1975) notes, "meaning," or content, has been inferred from a number of different approaches and operationalizations. Meaning may be inferred from a correlation between an expression (e.g., direct gaze at partner) and an internal state of the expressor. Ellsworth would probably also include in this category correlations between an expression and various measures of individual differences (e.g., personality inventories) and organismic variables (e.g., sex as described in Ellsworth & Ludwig, 1972). Although such investigations do not provide direct evidence of communication, given the model discussed earlier in which an expression may be viewed as projecting a role for another as well as a display, information may be obtained from such research, which, in combination with other studies, may suggest a potential communicative role. It would obviously be necessary to test this supposition more directly than has been done so far. Meaning may further be used to refer to "the sender's intention to communicate a specific meaning, to the receiver's attribution of a meaning to the behavior, or to a generally shared worldlike meaning understood by both the sender and the receiver" (Ellsworth, 1975; p. 54). Sender's intentions have been explored primarily through the use of role-playing designs. From such research, however (e.g., Pellegrini, Hicks, & Gordon, 1970), it is typically unclear to what extent the sender was aware of the particular components of his or her display especially when the instructions were very general (e.g., Subjects are instructed to behave as if they like their interaction partner). Few investigations in nonverbal communication have fully demonstrated the use of a *shared* code (Weiner, Devoe, Rubinow, & Geller, 1972); rather they have chosen some aspect of the total process on which to focus. Many studies, for example, measure a subject's perceptions of another and relate these perceptions to the gaze behavior of the other. Rarely, however, are both encoding and decoding paradigms employed within a single investigation. Finally, meaning is sometimes inferred from the overt behavior or physiological responses of recipients of a particular expression form. This latter procedure becomes necessary when the respondant is not easily interviewed or unable to complete questionnaires, as is the case with human infants and nonhuman primates. However, this strategy has also been used extensively with adult humans. Meaning is further articulated in such cases by observing who introduces a particular expression, who responds to it, and the context or circumstances for both sender and receiver (Marler, 1967). Data from all these types of designs are reviewed in the following four sections. An attempt is made to weave a general pattern in which they each play a part in explicating the role of visual behavior in the social lives of nonhuman primates, and human infants, children, and adults.

NONHUMAN PRIMATES

The work of comparative ethologists and psychologists provides many interesting suggestions regarding the phylogenetic origins and organization of nonverbal behavior in humans. Hinde (1975) argues that so long as we realize the limits of such endeavors, comparative studies may be particularly useful in the investigation of nonverbal behavior because in lower animals it may be observed without the added complication of the interaction between nonverbal behavior and language. Human nonverbal codes might also be more similar in form to the behavior codes of nonhuman mammals than to the coding forms of verbal language (Bateson, 1968), Further, Diebold (1968) suggests that certain endogenous components of human communication appear as "behavioral homologies" in the ethograms of nonhuman primates.

Mutual gaze, particularly in the form of a stare, is a primary component of threatening or aggressive displays of many nonhuman primates: e.g., adult male baboons (Hall & Devore, 1965), gorillas (Schaller, 1963, 1964), rhesus and bonnet macaques (Altmann, 1962; Hinde & Rowell, 1962; Simonds, 1965), and a number of old-world monkeys and apes (van Hooff, 1967). Staring at another male is frequently described as the first component in an increasingly aggressive encounter. A dominance struggle typically ensues until one of the animals averts its gaze away from the face of the other. Chance (1962) describes such aversion as a visual "cut-off", which he proposes reduces the arousal associated with direct gaze. The arousing properties of the stare are not limited to its display by conspecifics. Exline and Yellin (1969; also reported in Exline, 1972) caught the eye of caged rhesus macaques and either continued to hold or immediately broke off the mutual gaze. Significantly more aggressive displays were performed in the presence of the direct versus averted gaze of the two male experimenters, including in the case of one monkey, leaping onto and rattling the front bars of his cage. The brief mutual gaze that was broken by the experimenters would frequently initiate an aggressive display that abruptly ceased at the point of E's gaze aversion. Further, there is some evidence to indicate that the gaze of an experimenter is physiologically arousing to macaques (Wada, 1961).

Dominance hierarchies in primate groups are thought by some ethologists (e.g., Hinde, 1974) to be based on the cumulative outcomes of aggressive and competitive interactions between group members. More dominant animals, from this perspective, are those who "win" in a greater number of such encounters. An individual animal's rank in the hierarchy is secure only so long as he can continue to force submission from animals of lower status. Chance (1967) observes, however, that in some primate groups a stable hierarchy exists despite the absence or relative infrequency of aggressive interactions. As a consequence of these observations, he proposes that the origin of primate dominance hierarchies rests in what he calls their "attention structure." The attention structure of a group may be observed in the differential visual attention given to higher status group members. Lower status members frequently monitor the spatial location and activities of more dominant animals and adjust their own activities and positions in accordance with the cues from above. The attention-attracting qualities of dominance displays are emphasized over what other researchers may regard as their inherent aggressiveness. Chance (1967) suggests that the origins of the attention structure may be found in the dependency experiences of infancy and early childhood, in which individuals are necessarily attentive to adults as their source of care and protection. This suggestion is not unlike Milgram's (1974) discussion of the potential origins of human obedience. In the context of socialization, Milgram describes many circumstances in which humans are trained to be unquestionably obedient (attentive) to the wishes of more dominant individuals. In infancy, certainly, the dependent child's subordination is daily demonstrated; nevertheless, it is possible that some superordinates later in life maintain their position because it is never challenged, rather than for their ability to win in an aggressive struggle.

Keverne, Leonard, Scruton, and Young (1978) compared visual monitoring to the dominance hierarchy produced by assessing the direction of aggressive encounters (who attacks whom) in a group of Talapoin monkeys who had been observed in a laboratory setting for 6 years. The attention structure of the group reflected the aggression hierarchy such that animals that would be classified as more dominant based on the outcome of competitive encounters also received more visual attention. Keverne et al. (1978) believe, however, that the attention structure is a consequence of rather than antecedent to social ranking (see also Hinde, 1974). They observe that following the establishment of a stable hierarchy based on the outcome of aggressive encounters, the overall level of aggressive behavior greatly decreases, thus making it very difficult for the researcher to describe the hierarchy through the observation of such behaviors. Keverne et al. (1978) view the stability of visual monitoring patterns as evidence that group members are still very much aware of the hierarchical structure despite the absence of overt aggression. Hinde (1974) further believes that many opportunities continue to exist for members to learn the aggressive nature of dominance displays. According to Chance (1967), on the other hand, these opportunities are not often taken. Resolution of this controversy may reside in allowing that both aggressive encounters and the socialization of attention may play a role in the creation, maintenance, and evolution of social hierarchies. The attention structure would provide for a measure of intergenerational stability, and the guidance and protection of young group members. Competitive encounters would provide for vitality and adaptive evolution of group structure, as maturing young adults take over the leadership roles of retiring seniors. It is significant that the visual behavior of group members plays a role in both maintenance and evolution of group structure.

Direct gaze is not only a component of aggressive and submissive displays, but also has been described as part of grooming, greeting, and play facial expressions in old-world monkeys and apes (van Hooff, 1967). It thus becomes important to evaluate the total context in which a particular cue is implicated. Signals may be subject to a number of competing interpretations, and Hinde (1975) reports that prediction of next action improves when patterns of behavior as opposed to single-component behaviors are assessed.

Following a survey of the role of eye signals across many species, Argyle and Cook (1976) observe that it is only in primates that gaze functions as an affiliative as well as an aggressive cue, perhaps because of the infant feeding position that enhances eye contact between mother and child.[5] It will be seen that a similar explanation is offered for the affiliative role of gaze in humans. In other lower species, eye spots, eye rings, eye color changes, and direct gaze seem to function as communicative signals primarily in the context of aggressive encounters (Argyle & Cook, 1976). It is interesting that the affiliative aspects of gaze behavior are thought to stem from the same dependency relationship that Chance (1967) argues provides the basis for the attention structure in primate groups. Further, both affiliation and attention structure would function to maintain group stability.

One further study is of interest in this context for its similarity to research conducted with human participants. Thomsen (1974) describes a series of experiments in which he observed the frequency of returned gaze of a number of species of caged monkeys to the steady (2-minute duration) gaze of an ex-

---

[5] Argyle and Cook (1976) thank Dr. Mansur Lalljee for this suggestion, and the same appreciation is extended here.

perimenter. Adult rhesus macaques who had experienced some degree of social deprivation in infancy returned E's gaze less frequently than macaques who were not deprived of early social contact. This pattern remained consistent across four testing sessions. Species differences (5 old world and 1 new world) were also observed in the frequency of returned gaze. Adolescent female rhesus macaques gazed more frequently than males of the same age group, although no sex differences were found for adults. Furthermore, the adolescent monkeys gazed more frequently on the average than the adults. Adult rhesus macaques returned the experimenter's gaze more frequently in their home cage than they did in a new, unfamiliar cage. Finally, across several studies, a greater frequency of returned gaze occurred when the experimenter stood .61 meters from the cage compared to the frequency returned when the experimenter stood 1.8 meters from the cage. Thomsen (1974) reports that all the returned gazes were very brief, precluding the measurement of duration, and he does not provide information on the rest of the display that accompanied the gaze. Nevertheless, the results are intriguingly similar to some of those found with humans, to which we now turn.

HUMAN INFANTS

Visual interaction between caregiver and infant, particularly mutual gaze, is thought to play a significant role in the ontogenesis of normal social behavior (Stern, 1974). The purpose of this section, and the following section dealing with children older than infants, is to illustrate some of the recent work in the development of social, communicative capabilities with emphasis given to the role of interpersonal gaze. The past 15 years have witnessed a significant increase in studies with a truly interactive focus. Schaffer (1977) characterizes the shift in conceptual and methodological issues that has occurred in the investigation of infant–caretaker interactions as follows: The infant is now regarded as an active contributor to early social exchanges rather than a relatively passive responder to the social stimulation with which he[6] is confronted. Activities that were studied predominantly as characteristics of individuals frequently occur in social contexts, and it is now believed that their significance may rest in the social, communicative functions served by their performance in such contexts, rather than merely as descriptors of individual differences. Schaffer (1977) suggests, for example, that language was initially conceived "as a set of behavioral patterns explicable purely in terms of the psychological organization of the individual [but that] it has been increas-

---

[6]The convention employed by Stern (1977) in which the caregiver is referred to with a feminine pronoun and the infant with a masculine pronoun is employed here with the same hope that the disadvantages of such a convention will be outweighed by clarity of reference.

ingly recognized as in fact deriving its significance primarily from its communicative function and is in need consequently of study in dyadic settings." (p. 4) Further, there has been a need to postulate a degree of "preparedness" on the part of the infant for dealing with the social features of the environment in a manner similar to the innate capabilities to cope with other aspects of the physical world, such as breathing and digestion. For example, the infant possesses an oral apparatus to cope with the nipple and food provided by it from the caretaker, visual structures that are particularly sensitive to stimulus configurations associated with the human face, and auditory structures selectively tuned to the human voice (p. 9). Such activities seem to become linked or "entrained" to the behavior of the caretaker in the course of the daily interactions with the child. Emphasis has been given to microanalysis of exchanges along with their temporal patterning. The infant possesses certain social and cognitive capabilities to which the caretaker responds, helping the infant learn how these actions may be used in social exchange.

Vine (1973) provides a comprehensive review of the mother–infant research related to the facial–visual channel of communication, including consideration of the infant's developing sensory capabilities, attentional responses, and smiling behavior, in order to evaluate particularly the role of the eyes and smiling in the development of attachment. Vine concludes that the stimulus configuration of the mother's eyes is not an innate releaser of infant smiling as earlier authors believed. Rather, Vine (1973) argues that the eyes have stimulus qualities to which the infant is particularly sensitive, a view also shared by Stern (1974). Vine (1973) describes the process as follows: The mother gazes at the infant when holding him, which brings her eyes into a distance range in which the infant can focus. The infant's visual attention is directed to the mother's eyes because of their stimulus characteristics of, for example, contrast. The infant begins to develop a schema of this frequently repeated stimulus, the recognition of which produces a smile. The smile seems to occur concomitant with an optimal level of information processing for the infant, such as is the case for a recently acquired schema, or a slight modification of an already established schema. The variety of facial expressions provided by the mother would fill the second requirement. The infant's smile and gaze is reportedly a very pleasurable event for the mother and serves to continue the interaction. It is important for the mother to be sensitive to the infant's capabilities and arousal level to sustain a mutually enjoyable interaction. As the infant develops, the eye schema is expanded to include the entire face, and later the recognition of the mother as a person separate from others, leading to a specific attachment. Similar processes may occur in nonhuman primate mother–infant exchanges, as suggested by Argyle and Cook (1976).

Stern's (1974) microanalysis of mother–infant play further explicates aspects of this process. Thirty-seven play sessions involving eight infants (four sets of twins) were videotaped in the homes of participants. Each of the 37 sessions involves only one infant at a time, and the duration of the period was determined by the mother and her infant rather than the experimenters. The gaze behavior of mother and infant was recorded by observers while the interaction was in progress. Play episodes were of particular interest because they involve mainly social interaction with no other task except interesting and delighting one another. Stern (1974) regards the goal of play as "the mutual regulation of stimulation so as to maintain an optimal level of arousal which is affectively positive" (p. 210).

Stern (1974) argues that the visual system of the infant is the first to mature to the extent that mother and infant have virtually equal internal control over its use. This capacity provides the young infant with at least one system that it can call into operation to control perceptual input and thus regulate his degree of internal physiological arousal. The infant cannot yet leave the field, but he can look away, close his eyes, and turn his head. Similarly, the infant cannot physically approach or reach toward, but he can look. According to Stern (1974), infants will turn away from an over or underarousing stimulus providing early indications of self-regulation and coping.

Along these lines, Waters, Matas, and Sroufe (1975) measured heart rate changes of infants who were approached by unfamiliar females while the infant's mother sat 4 feet away. The infant's heart rate accelerated as the female approached, which may be interpreted as a defensive response, reducing the effects of stimulation (Graham, 1979). Infants who diverted their gaze from the stranger to look at their mothers evidenced a concomitant heart rate deceleration that is thought to be a component of an orienting response, facilitating stimulus intake. Such gaze aversions would typically occur immediately prior to a peak in heart rate acceleration in infants who did not soon cry. The gaze aversion and subsequent heart rate deceleration seemed to function as a coping response, enabling the infant to reestablish visual contact with the stranger without crying, which tended to forestall renewed contact. Such physiological responsivity is not limited to the infant. Leavitt and Donovan (1979) recorded both skin conductance and heart rate of mothers who had 3-month-old infants while they viewed a videotaped presentation of a similar infant who gazed at them (at the lens) or gaze averted. Each mother ($n = 36$) viewed six trials of both gaze and gaze eversion in counterbalanced orders. Gaze aversion produced heart rate deceleration that did not habituate across trials. Direct gaze produced early heart rate deceleration that changed to an acceleratory response by trial 6. The heart rate acceleration was primarily accounted for by mothers who were characterized as externals on Rotter's (1966) internal–external locus of control scale. Leavitt and Donovan (1979) suggest that persons who view the external environment as noncontingent with respect to their own actions (externals) may find aspects of it aversive.

Stern (1974) proposes that mother–infant social interaction is unique in that both parties engage in certain behaviors only in the presence of the other, and consequently they must be studied in this context to fully understand their significance. The mother typically engages in displays that constitute an exaggerated form of those performed with other adults. The use of baby talk, exaggerated facial expressions of, for example, surprise, and very close interpersonal distance are all examples of these simplified "supernormal" forms. Further, the mother engages in very long gazes (30 seconds and longer) at her infant and the presence of the infant's returned gaze (mutual gaze) decreases the likelihood that she will look away from the infant's face. The mother visually takes on the role of an adult listener and treats the infant as if he were communicating with her. Stern (1974) refers to these activities of the mother as "infant elicited behaviors" because of the uniqueness of their production in this context. It is not the *mere* presence of the infant that is important here, as infant gaze, smiles, and coos increase the probability of the production of these exaggerated behaviors on the part of the mother.

The infant frequently engages in facial expressions, vocalizations, and gazes that are emitted in non-social contexts; however these actions tend to take on a form specific to social interaction. Stern (1974) suggests that the infant's visual system is intrinsically or endogenously structured to produce gaze alternation. The eyes move to a focal point and then shift away. While interacting with his mother, this type of eye movement becomes entrained to her own visual behavior, the outcome of which serves to increase the probability of mutual gaze between them. Although the proportion of the interaction time during which the infant looks at his mother varies greatly, across play periods and across infants, the gaze-to-gaze interval (period of time encompassing a gaze at the mother plus the following gaze away) remains fairly stable within a play session. Thus, as Schaffer (1977) proposes, the infant is equipped with behaviors that prepare him for interaction with the environment and further become linked to the actions of others during social exchanges. The mother typically spends a great deal of time looking at her infant. The infant is more likely to return this gaze and not look away if the mother is looking. Given the relatively constant visual attention of the mother, it is the infant who initiates and terminates most (94%) mutual gazes. This enables the infant to regulate the degree of social contact, and the sensitive mother will be able to regulate her play behavior in terms of what the infant signals he can deal with and continue to maintain a positive affect. "In this way the infant's responsivity to maternal stimuli organizes his gaze alternations to serve a social function" (p. 204).

The visual behavior of both infant and mother does not occur alone but is embedded in a more complex social display. Whereas the infant is more likely to look at his mother if she is already looking at him, this probability is increased if the mother is also vocalizing. The action of the eyes may be particularly significant during this early stage of development; however its role may be best understood in relation to the expressive and social context in which it occurs.

The importance of mother–infant gaze may be further demonstrated by considering situations in which it is absent. Fraiberg (1974) has made longitudinal observations in interactions between mothers and their infants who were blind from birth, but otherwise normal. The lack of eye-to-eye contact is particularly disturbing to these mothers who frequently do not feel as if they make meaningful contact with thier child. Fraiberg (1974) notes a similar impact on professionals: "Our consensus, as a team of researchers and clinicians who have worked with blind children for several years, was that we have never overcome this sense of something vital missing in the social exchange" (p. 217). The use of the eyes affords some degree of initiation in the relationship from the infant. Without this capability, the infant has little more than vocalizations of distress with which to elicit an automatic response from the mother. Smiles and vocalizations of blind infants are also reduced in frequency and extent, all of which served to reduce initiations from the parents. Fraiberg (1974) recommends much vocalization and physical contact by the mother to get the relationship going, because those infants who lack such interaction frequently show impairment in object and human relationships as they grow older.

Sex differences in the tendency to make eye contact with an adult have been demonstrated for newborn infants. Hittelman and Dickes (1979) recorded the incidence of returned gaze to a female stranger by male and female neonates between 24 and 60 hours old. Males and females did not differ in the amount of time their eyes were open or in the frequency with which they gazed at the female experimenter. However, female neonates returned E's gaze in significantly greater proportion of the time as compared to males (74 seconds vs. 13 seconds of 297 seconds). Because the frequency of looking was the same for both males and females, this proportion difference is due to the female infants exhibiting a significantly longer duration of glance (3.71 sec. vs 2.53 sec.). This difference in the infant's capacity to maintain eye contact is probably due to the tendency for females to be 1 to 1 weeks more mature than males with respect to skeletal and neurological development. Subtle sex differences such as these could influence the mother's handling of the infant, perhaps resulting in an enhancement of interpersonal relatedness in females. As is seen later, these sex differences in average gaze level are found with older children as well as with adults.

Farren, Hirschbiel, and Jay (1980) examined developmental changes in visual attention between mothers and their children during a 20-minute play period. Eighty-one (43 males, 75 blacks) children were observed from three age groups (6 months, 20 months, 36 months) in interaction with their mothers. The mothers of 6-month-old infants engaged in the greatest amount of visual attention to their child compared to the other two groups. Also, mothers across age groups tended to initiate (look first) more gazes. Although the children did not differ significantly with respect to age in the proportion of looking, the incidence of simultaneous (1-sec. resolution) initiations and terminations of mutual gazing increased with age. Farren et al. (1980) conclude that the 36-month-old child is beginning to show signs of adult synchronous patterns, particularly as the initiation of mutual gaze in this group was frequently preceded by a vocal or verbal signal.

It is not merely the sheer presentation and duration of the mother's expressive displays that seem to be significant. The temporal and sequential patterning of such activity also appears to be important. Stern, Beebe, Jaffe, and Bennett (1977) present a microanalysis of two play sessions in which the vocalizations, facial expressions, and head movements of the adult tend to occur in repetitious, temporally regular patterns. This type of stimulus presentation, they argue, is particularly well suited to the information-processing capabilities of the infant and would likely lead to the formation of social schemata. The stimulus world presented to the infant by its caretaker is composed of human expressive and communicative displays. The rhythmic repetition of such behaviors, with slight modifications on each repetition, enable the infant to develop rich social schemata. "The caregiver thus, in trying to care for and engage the infant, creates themes and variations of sound and movement which the infant's mental processes will gradually re-transpose into classes of human acts of caring and engaging" (p. 193). The temporal patterning may thus be more important than the particular modality employed (Stern et al., 1977), a circumstance that would have positive implications for blind infants.

The mutual coordination of mother–infant exchanges, particularly given the predictable repetitive nature of the adult display, may reach the point of simultaneous action, which occurs so rapidly, it may no longer be considered in stimulus–response terms (Beebe, Stern, & Jaffe, 1979). Further, Beebe et al. (1979) describe instances of behavior-pause sequences that may be the precursors to adult conversation. Jaffe and Anderson (1979) discuss the gestural origins of language and speech, suggesting that conversation may grow ontogenetically from the rhythmic coaction of mother and infant. Condon and Sander (1974) found human neonates to move in synchrony with the sound of human speech (both English and Chinese) more so than to discrete vowel sounds and tapping noises. When the temporal patterning of the four states of dyadic gaze (both look, neither look, and one-way gaze by either) is subjected to Markov analysis, a first-degree Markov model does the best job in describing the transitional probability Matrix (Jaffe, Stern, & Perry, 1973). This result is similar to what is found with the sound–silence patterning of human speech. The foregoing "suggests that the 'bond' between human beings should be studied as the expression of a participation within shared organizational forms rather than as something limited to isolated entities sending discrete messages" (Condon & Sander, 1974, p. 101).

CHILDREN

A growing body of research dealing with the usage and interpretation of and overt response to nonverbal behavior in childhood has produced evidence of significant differences related to sex and age. Before turning to this literature, it should be noted that two investigations have found children (6–7 years of age) to be less accurate in detecting the focus of another's gaze compared to adults. This has been found with respect to the discrimination of gazes to various points within the face (Lord, 1974), and the detecton of on-face versus off-face gazes (Thayer, 1977). Whereas both of these studies employed a psychophysical paradigm and are therefore subject to the reservations associated with similar investigations dealing solely with adults, the relative detection difference should be kept in mind when evaluating the research that follows.

The tendency for females to gaze at another more than do males has also been observed through the years of human childhood (Ashear & Snortum, 1971; Kleinke, Desautels, & Knapp, 1977; Levine & Sutton-Smith, 1973; Russo, 1975; Vlietstra & Manske, 1981). This effect holds both when children (age 3 years to adulthood) interact with a steadily gazing adult female (Ashear & Snortum, 1971; Kleinke et al., 1977) or male (Vlietstra & Manske, 1981), and when they interact with a peer of the same sex without the constraint of either participant's gaze being controlled by the experimenter (Levine & Sutton-Smith, 1973; Russo, 1975). The difference between boys and girls has primarily been confined to percentage and average duration of mutual gaze due to experimental constraints: The use of a steadily gazing confederate limits measurement to mutual gaze, and Russo (1975) only reported data with respect to mutual gaze. Levine and Sutton-Smith (1973) recorded the proportion of total gaze, mutual gaze, looking while listening, and looking while speaking. Girls gazed at their same-sex partners than did boys on measures of mutual gaze and looking while speaking.

Sex differences have also been observed in the interpretation and behavioral response to gaze. Kleinke et al. (1977) found boys (3–5 years of age) to like an adult female less when she gazed steadily than when she rarely gazed at them. Girls, on the other hand, tended to prefer the confederate when she gazed steadily. Four to 5-year-old girls and boys interpreted pictures of children interacting with adults who were portrayed as looking at the child or not (Vlietstra & Manske, 1981). In general the gazing adult was interpreted as more approving. The children viewing pictures of a gazing adult had previously interacted for 10 minutes with a steadily gazing adult male or female. Girls in this latter group gave a more approving interpretation than boys, and boys gave a greater disapproving interpretation than girls. Further, boys' approval ratings were negatively correlated ($-.37$) with their own glances toward the adult in the previous play session, and their disapproval ratings were positively correlated (+ .34) with previous gaze. In both studies, the boys' relatively negative interpretations of the gaze of another were related to research, indicating that boys tend to receive a greater number of reprimands and negative sanctions compared to girls and thus might have come to view the gaze, particularly of an adult, as signaling impending criticism.

An interest in the development of social perception led Post and Hetherington (1974) to investigate suggestions from previous researchers that girls may evidence an earlier and greater sensitivity and responsiveness to cues defining social relationships. Four and 6-year-old boys and girls were presented with stimulus cards depicting a male and female who were either looking or not looking at one another, and who were either close together or far away. The children indicated who liked whom best in a paired-comparisons presentation of the set of cards. Correct responses were scored based on previous literature relating looking and proximity to liking. Four-year-old boys and girls did not differ from one another; however, 6-year-old girls were more accurate than boys in responding to both eye gaze and proximity cues, given the interpretation scheme employed. In a second study dealing only with the proximity cue, boys and girls performed equally in the discrimination of the cue (near vs. far), but girls alone attached reliable meaning to it. Abramovitch and Daly (1978) failed to find sex differences in the interpretation of head orientation and eye gaze, although 6-year-olds more correctly interpreted the gaze cue, which in this case was directed at them, rather than occurring between others who were observed. This difference in cue may explain the diverging results. Post and Hetherington (1974) suggest that girls may be more sensitive to affiliation relationships than boys, but that if aggressive encounter had been employed perhaps the boys would have performed on par with the girls. They also allow that boys may respond to different cues than girls for the interpretation of affiliation.

Intriguing patterns of sex differences are beginning to merge in the work with children that will be reflected in the data from adults; however, a number of complicating factors needs to be considered. Whereas Post and Hetherington (1974) correctly refer to literature relating relatively greater amounts of looking with liking, subsequent research has found this relationship to be modified by other variables, such as, for example, the nature of the verbal exchange (Ellsworth & Carlsmith, 1968). Also, both direct gaze and gaze aversion have been related to the communication of dominance or potency (Ellsworth & Carlsmith, 1973; Exline, Ellyson, & Long, 1975). to the extent that it would be possible to incorporate these variables into work with children, without overly complicating the task, a clearer picture of the relationship between sex and the interpretation of gaze may emerge. This would be useful in studies of the impact of an interaction partner as well as in studies in which standardized pictorial or videotape displays are presented.

Age differences in the extent to which children gaze at an interaction partner have been observed during interactions with peers and adults, although the results indicate differences between these two types of interactions. Ashear and Snortum (1971) recorded the visual behavior of children varying in age from preschool to the eighth grade while they were being interviewed by a steadily gazing adult female. The younger children returned the gaze of the interviewer more than the older children. Within the general decline in gaze across ages, there was a significant peak for the second-grade children and a significant valley for the fifth-grade group. Levine and Sutton-Smith (1973) and Russo (1975) observed the visual behavior of children (ages 4–12 years) during a conversation with a same-sex peer. In both studies gaze at partner increased with age. Status, level of gaze, and sex of partner differences confound comparison of these investigations. A decline in egocentric orientation may facilitate the ability to attend to an interaction partner, but the role of the status and sex of the partner would have to be considered.

The role of visual interaction in the creation of and response to teacher expectancy effects (Rosenthal & Jacoboson, 1968) has been explored by a number of investigators. Most of this work deals with the behavior of adults and thus could be presented in the following section. The implications of the adult's actions, however, are primarily directed at children, thus their discussion in this context. Male and female undergraduate "tutors" gazed more at a 10-year-old male confederate whom they had been led to believe was bright compared with tutors who received no information regarding their pupil's IQ or had been told the student was dull (Chaiken, Sigler, & Derlega, 1974). The higher level of gaze was accompanied with more forward leans, head nods, and smiles, and fewer backward leans. This cluster of behaviors was interpreted as representing a positive attitude toward the student that could influence their performance. A sample of high, compared to low, socioeconomic-status Canadian mothers engaged in greater mutual gaze with their 5-year-old children, which Hore (1970) interpreted as reflecting a similar expectancy for capable performance. The gaze of an adult may reflect other types of expectation as well. Hore (1976) found Australian tutors to engage in more mutual gaze with recently arrived immigrant students compared to native Australians and immigrants who had been in the country for some time, perhaps reflecting an expectation of difficulty in interpreting the speech of the student. Ho and Mitchell (1982) found Australian college-age students to respond differentially to warm (smiling, looking, forward lean, and head nods) versus cold (frowning, little or not evoking, backward lean, and head shakes) tutors. Overall, students looked and smiled at the warm tutor more than the cold tutor. However, a sex of student by warmth of tutor interaction revealed that female students gazed at the warm tutor more than male students, whereas the reverse was true with the cold tutor. Finally, Jones and Cooper (1971) examined the role of interpersonal gaze in the mediation of experimenter effects (Rosenthal, 1963), another application of the general expectancy phenomenon. Male high school students were paired together, one acting as experimenter, the other as subject. Experimenters were instructed to either look quite a bit or hardly at all while giving the instructions on a picture-rating task to their subjects. Subjects receiving the higher level of gaze reported a more favorable mood state and rated the photographs more positively. In summary, a relatively high level of gaze associated with other positive behaviors seems to accompany the expectation of successful performance and influences the subsequent behavior of persons receiving it. As Hore's (1976) study suggests, however, a number of different types of expectation may be accompanied by direct gaze and the positive effects may be limited to particular contexts.

Vaughn and Waters (1981) examined the role of visual behavior as it relates to the social organization of a group of preschool children along the lines suggested by Chance's (1967) concept of attention structure. Vaughn and Waters were primarily concerned with developing a measure of social competence in children free from the problems associated with global ratings, positive and negative sociometric choice, and usual methods of assessing dominance hierarchies. To this end they made daily observations of children in a preschool over the course of a three-term school year. Measures of the three types of behavior described previously were made in addition to attention rank, which was obtained by noting in numerous time samples who a given child looked at. A stable attention structure of hierarchy resulted from the rank measures; children directed more visual attention to high-ranking individuals than would be expected by chance. This structure was based on group consensus rather than the visual activity of one or two individuals. Attention rank was moderately correlated with competition rank (.48), the more usual measure employed to construct dominance hierarchies but was correlated also with a different set of other behavioral measures. In particular attention rank was positively correlated with measures of positive sociometric choice, interactive play, and conversation with peers, whereas competition rank was not so correlated. Further, attention rank proved to be a more stable indicator of group structure than did competition rank. This does not mean that children ranking high in the attention structure were not involved in competitive and aggressive encounters, but they did not necessarily initiate these interactions. Vaughn and Waters (1981) conclude that attention structure reflects social organization, rather than generates it, as Chance (1967) would argue, and further propose that the foundation of social organization in preschool children is social competence. Social competence attracts attention, and much could be learned from observing it.

Lastly, visual behavior has been investigated within the context of psychological problems in childhood. One of the primary overt manifestations of childhood autism is an impairment of social relations, which is in part evidenced by a strong reluctance to make eye-to-eye contact with another person. Hutt and Ounstead (1966) believe gaze aversion in autists may reflect an attempt on their part to reduce external stimulation due to already high levels of internal arousal. They observed eight male autistic children (3–6 years of age) at play and found them to be almost always solitary rather than interacting with others. When approaching adults, to be picked up or for assistance in, for example, opening a door, their overt motor behavior could not be distinguished from other children not so diagnosed. However, the autistic chidren would turn their heads away from the adult, refusing to look at them. Hutt and Ounstead (1966) further observed autistic and non-autistic children's responses to five drawings of faces placed on stands around a familiar room. Autistic children spent less time perusing the faces than non-autistics and spent considerably more time focusing on other inanimate features of the environment. Autists observed by Hutt and Ounstead would only look at others with fleeting glances when not being looked at themselves. Hutt and Vaizey (1966) consider the gaze aversion of autists to represent an appeasement gesture, on the order of Chance's (1962) "cut-off" signals. Compared with other hospitalized but non-autistic children, autists did not become aggressive as room density increased and further were not attacked by other children. The gaze aversion of autists may be part of a more general syndrome rather than specific to the human face. O'Conner and Hermelin (1967) found autistic children to spend less overall time in focused observation compared to other children, but to still look at faces, in a controlled experimental context, more than other visually presented stimuli.

Rutter and O'Brien (1980), concerned with the lack of consideration given to situational variability in most diagnostic designations, compared the visual behavior of withdrawn and aggressive girls during discussions with a male and female adult. Withdrawn girls gazed at their interaction partner less than did aggressive girls while discussing a personal topic, but there was no difference between the groups during an impersonal discussion. Rutter (1976) has reported a similar pattern with adult schizophrenics, who have previously been characterized as gazing less at others in general. Rutter and O'Brien (1980) argue that trait descriptions are unlikely to succeed as they rarely appropriately incorporate consideration of the situational variability of behavior.

ADULTS

A sizeable research literature focused on the social visual behavior of adults has accumulated over the past 20 years. This literature, however, represents a rather heterogeneous mix. Many conceptual and methodological orientations are represented from virtually every subdivision of psychology, with a smattering of papers from sociology and anthropology. The total set constitutes a conglomeration somewhat resistent to meaningful organization. Direct gaze at another versus away gaze is fairly easy to measure reliably, especially compared to other more graded actions such as smiles. Perhaps partially for this reason gaze behavior is selected by so many researchers attempting to study nonverbal aspects of their particular domain of interest. Some papers deal directly with the role of visual behavior in social interaction, whereas others include the variable in projects with some other central focus. Previous reviewers have dealt with this state of affairs by grouping studies based on the variables, other than gaze, which were manipulated or measured. Further, frequent emphasis has been given to the distinction between encoding and decoding activities to clarify those situations in which one may comfortably speak of communication. In this review an attempt is made to integrate the literature within the conceptual organization introduced earlier. Research dealing with the relationship of visual behavior to the flow of interaction, the development of relationships, various individual differences, and more transitory circumstances of the participants are discussed in subsections within the general framework. When available, encoding and decoding studies are discussed together under a shared conceptual unit. The result, it is hoped, is a conceptual mosaic of information, which, when viewed from a distance, as with a pointalist painting, blends to form a meaningful gestalt. Viewed close up, areas for future research should emerge. As with any systematic gestalt, linear linguistic description to some extent distorts the whole. An attempt is made to keep the larger picture in mind while discussing the parts.

Conceptual Orientation: Review and Extension

It has been suggested that humans, as social animals, organize their activities with respect to others based on an underlying system of expression-content relationships, which taken together compose cultural patterns of meaningful interaction. To the extent that gaze behavior plays a significant role in this organization, it seems to do so by providing information regarding the gazer's orientation, attention, interest, and involvement with the object or point of focus. Caregivers and infants initiate, maintain, modulate, terminate, and avoid contact with each other through this early-maturing channel. The repeated, rhythmic, and simplified displays of the caregiver serve to pattern the infant for ongoing and later social exchanges with members of his cultural or subcultural group, without the necessity of constant conscious surveillance of his performance. As the infant matures and develops, these basic patterns of approach, regulation, withdrawal, and avoidance (Stern, 1977) become elaborated and articulated into a number of layers of slowly increasing complexity, enabling a richer array of interaction types. Approach, for example, may become differentiated to include affiliative and dominating styles, adaptively suited to different states of the participant, and different types of interactions. One of these styles may become a relatively stable characteristic pattern approach for a given individual. Gaze directed at a partner, gaze withdrawn from the partner's face, or the apparently active avoidance of gazing at a partner may be viewed as displays of the orientation, attention, interest, and involvement aspects of various states, traits, and interaction sequences. The definition of appropriate behavioral styles of interaction settings within a culture may place constraints on certain types of displays, encouraging or demanding some, and discouraging or refusing to accept others. For example, in white middle-class America, one might hear admonitions to "look at me while I'm speaking to you" or "don't stare at that poor unfortunate person."

Although there appears to be something about gaze at another that represents orientation, attention, interest, and involvement, the relationship is far from simple. Perhaps the attribution of orientation and attention stems from the necessity of directing the eyes, as compared to other sensory receptors, toward an object of perception. The duration and intensity of fixation may provide cues related to interest and involvement. It would further seem to matter whether the gaze was freely given as opposed to being requested or demanded. Given that the eyes function as part of a sensory system, information-processing constraints related to the complexity and ambiguity of the material, as well as to the individuals capabilities for dealing with it, come into play.

Callan, Chance, and Pitcairn (1973) stress the distinction between attention, which they view as a matter of stimulus input only, and "advertence," which they define as the public or official manifestation of attention. Again, as with the gaze shifts of the infant, an inherent process of the individual may become entrained for social purposes. Callan et al. (1973) suggest that the managed display of advertence may be employed to control and manipulate the self vis-a-vis physically present others. Such displays differentiate social presence from mere physical presence. An individual's eyes may be aimed in a particular direction whether or not the actual object of the individual's attention and/or interest is in that direction. In the simplest case, an individual may attend and display this attention through trunk, head, and eye orientation to some aspect of the environment. If the individual is in the presence of others, it would be important to consider whether or not such displayed attention was considered appropriate. Also, an individual may be gazing in one direction but more interested in happenings in another location. Much may be viewed unobtrusively with peripheral vision or perhaps overheard without direct visual orientation. Further, a person may be lost in thought, not really carefully attending to any aspect of the visual field. Thus, the observation of advertence displays by others may, on occasion, be misinterpreted, although there may be cues in the overall display a person presents that routinely enable others to make correct interpretations. Even from disembodied eyes, we may be able to detect the degree of convergence from the angle of the pupils and thus detect a focal point to which the eyes may be attending. In daily social contacts, however, we have available to us a wealth of information, a set of cues that in relation to each other enable us to successfully manage social contacts. Of course we can be fooled, but if we were always fooled it would be difficult to coordinate our activities with others even as well as we do. Bateson (1968) argued that one advantage of the relatively nonconscious production of nonverbal behavior is the consequent reduction in the likelihood of deception. One might argue, though, that as we become patterned in socially acceptable ways, socially skilled false displays may become more easily produced.

The interpretations made by observers may also be influenced by the implications the display has for them. A gaze at or away from another is not only a display about the gazer but has implications for those who receive or fail to receive visual attention. Are they being appropriately or inappropriately attended to, or perhaps ignored? What sort of relationship is proposed? Also, observers may differ with respect to the level of analysis with which they approach the social world (Barker, 1963; Pike, 1967). Are they concerned about the global components or the details of another's display? One may entirely miss or fret about the presence or absence of visual attention.

Finally, the production and interpretations of social visual behavior may partially depend on its placement within a sequence of events. At certain points during a conversation, the presence or absence of partner gaze may be critical to successful continuation, whereas at other junctures it may not matter very much. While describing something of great importance, an individual may be concerned if recipients do not display appropriate advertence, including direct gaze at them. Chitchat, on the other hand, may be comfortably conducted while conversants are performing other activities, and very occasionally glancing at one another. Although, even in the latter example, it may be of importance at what points in the flow of conversation the few glances that are produced actually occur. These issues are developed in the review that follows. The visual behavior of adults is described as it relates to the sequence of interactions, relatively enduring dispositions and characteristics of individuals, temporary states and interaction circumstances, and cultural differences.

Visual Behavior and the Stream of Ongoing Interaction

Initiating versus avoiding interactions.   Individuals daily come together with others to converse and enact the affairs of their lives. Some degree of mutual orientation, even if at times quite minimal, is necessary for these "focused interactions" (Goffman, 1963) to proceed. How is the initiation or avoidance of such encounters negotiated? Goffman (1963) has suggested that the gazes and glances that individuals exchange with each other, or avoid exchanging, play an important role in signaling one's accessibility or inaccessibility to others. Particularly in public settings, people are confronted with numerous others who must be dealt with in some way. Goffman (1963) argues that we frequently signal our lack of interest in, and lack of threat to others, through "civil inattention": "one gives to another enough visual notice to demonstrate that one appreciates that the other is present . . . , while at the next moment withdrawing one's attention from him so as to express that he does not constitute a target of special curiosity or design" (p. 84). This may be accomplished by gazing at the other at a distance, but then dropping the eyes and head as one continues to approach and pass.

Cary (1978a, 1979) made films of persons passing one another on a college campus walkway. Detailed coding of head position and gaze direction failed to confirm Goffman's anecdotal descriptions. Further observations also failed to confirm the presence of tongue shows, compressed lips, and lip-bites which had been described in earlier reports. Cary concluded that the most typical display involved holding the head erect and gazing straight forward, rather than toward others who were present. Looks, if they occurred, were more common among cross-sex than same-sex pairs, although when confronted with a steadily gazing confederate in a latter study, females were more likely to avert their gaze than were males. Although Cary failed to observe the specific features of Goffman's formulation, he did observe a variety of inattention, perhaps without the "civility." It is fairly easy to see peripherally where people are on a sidewalk by simply looking straight ahead, thus enabling one to negotiate past them. One might feel ignored rather than civilly inattended in this case, but certainly the likelihood of any focused interaction, even a brief smile, is minimal. Looking at others in such situation can be a risky business. The consequences of finding that someone is looking back and seeking contact may be unknown and/or unwanted. The desire to make friendly passing contact may result in rejection. Thus, it is safer to avoid any direct contact with other pedestrians.

Givens (1978) observed people negotiating their way through a public market, entering a bar, and passing on campus walkways in order to identify natural behavioral units involved in encounters with strangers. In over 90% of the 150 observations some combination of lip-compression, lip-bite, gaze aversion, and self-touching occurred. Givens characterizes these behaviors as aversive gestures, gestures that signal others who are present that focused contact would not be well received. While these same actions were not replicated by Cary (1979), it would be important to consider the relative density in the different observation settings. Negotiating ones way through a crowd may be more aversive than strolling on a spacious campus walkway.

The probability of making visual contact with others may further depend on the nature of the general community one is in. Newman and McCauley (1977) found that people in a small town (Parkesburg, PA) are more willing to return the gaze of a steadily looking male or female confederate than are those in a suburban (Brynmawr, PA) or an urban (Philadelphia) area.

In the research described, visual contact was avoided and conversation failed to occur. Cary (1978b) suggests that when confronted with a stranger brief glances may be used to evaluate the willingness of the other for further involvement. He videotaped the initial encounters between male and female strangers in same and cross-sex dyads in a laboratory room. One participant was already seated in the room when the second entered. Conversation of any sort (brief, lapsing, continuous) was much more likely if a mutual glance occurred upon entry of the second person. If a mutual glance occurred at the point when the entering person broke contact with the door handle, continuous conversation became very likely. Stable individual differences and transient states would probably influence how one would deal with this subtle maneuvering. A typically outgoing individual or one in a particularly social mood would perhaps be more likely to attempt further interaction despite the lack of gaze on the part of the other.

Krivonos and Knapp (1975) videotaped, in a laboratory setting the greeting activity of college males who were either previously acquainted or not. Mutual gaze was the second most frequent nonverbal display and, along with a head gesture (the most frequent nonverbal action), was again viewed as a way to test the water for possible conversation. Acquainted pairs were more likely to smile and begin to talk to one another. Kendon and Ferber (1973) described a six-step pattern of greeting observed at an outdoor birthday party. Although the filming procedure precluded the recording of gaze direction, apparent sighting and orientation to each other were important components of the typical pattern. Kendon and Ferber (1973) regarded greetings as serving "an important function in the management of relations between people" (p. 592). By way of greeting, individuals are made to feel a part of the party, may confirm or continue their relationships, and signal relative social status, familiarity with others, degree of liking, and the likely nature of subsequent conversation. Parties to a greeting provide information regarding the nature of their orientation to each other, an important element of which is some degree of visual attention.

Gaze in relation to conversational roles.   Once a focused interaction in the form of conversation is properly underway, visual behavior has been found to relate to the interaction roles of speaker and listener. In dyadic interaction, individuals have been repeatedly observed to gaze at their partners a greater proportion of the time when listening to their partners speak, compared to the proportion of looking when they themselves speak (Allen & Guy, 1974; Cherulnik, Neely, Flanagan & Zachau, 1979; Dabbs, Evans, Hopper & Purvis, 1980; Ellyson, Dovidio, Corson & Vinicur, 1980; Ellyson, Dovidio & Fehr, 1981; Exline, Gray & Schuette, 1965; Exline et al., 1975;

Kendon, 1967; Kleinke, Staneski & Berger, 1975; Kleinke, Staneski & Pipp, 1975; Nielson, 1962). In terms of the variables described at the beginning of the chapter, the proportion of looking while listening is greater than the proportion of looking while speaking. Further, Kendon (1967) found the average duration of gaze at one's conversation partner while listening to be greater than the average duration of gazes while speaking.

The term *listener* in this context refers to the individual in a conversation who is not talking while someone else is. Thus, "listening" periods are computed with respect to the speech of another. The proportion of looking while listening = sec. gaze at partner while partner speaks/sec. partner speaks. Such usage is not meant to imply the listener is actively processing the talk of the other, but rather it provides a convenient term to designate the person who is silent while someone else speaks.

The act of speaking, in much of the research described here, is indicated by human coders who depress a switch connected to a pen recorder or computer wherever a particular individual speaks. Systems have been developed to automate this process, providing far more accurate and detailed records of the sound–silence patterning associated with conversation (Jaffe & Feldstein, 1970). When such records are produced coincident with the coding of visual behavior by human coders, similar results are obtained, despite terminological and definitional differences (see Goodwin, 1981, Ch. 1, for discussion of differences). For example, Dabbs, Evans, Hopper, and Purvis (1980) report that the probability of gaze at a partner is greater during the partner's "turn" than during one's own turn.

Exline, Ellyson, and Long (1975) argue that the relative difference between the levels of looking while speaking and looking while listening may be understood in terms of the differential impact of "feedback inhibition" and a "norm of attention" on the conversational roles of speaker and listener. a speaker must not only labor to produce coherent speech, but also, to the extent that he or she monitors a listener, process ongoing feedback provided by the listener's displays. At times this feedback may overload or distract the speaker, necessitating gaze aversion (feedback inhibition) in order to maintain a fluent stream of conversation. These authors further maintain that a norm of attention is operative for both speakers and listeners. Some degree of displayed attention (advertence) would seem to be required through social conventions of courtesy. Whereas the norm of attention would influence the visual behavior of both parties equally, the added factor of feedback inhibition would serve to reduce the speaker's gaze toward a listener, thus producing the observed pattern.

Several studies provide support for the notion that a speaker's gaze level is related to variations in the difficulty of an ongoing speaking task. Exline and Winters (1965b) instructed male participants to make up stories based on categories varying in difficulty (four-legged animals, automobile models, and

European cities). Subjects gazed at a listener significantly less while discussing European cities compared to the other two categories. Kendon (1967) found a lower level of partner-directed looking during hesitant compared to fluent speech. He argues that hesitant speech is associated with utterance planning processes and would be expected to be accompanied by a lower level of gaze. Beattie (1978b, 1979a) also finds gaze aversion associated with certain hesitant compared to fluent aspects of speech. Because, however, he found relatively high levels of partner-directed gaze even during hesitant speech, Beattie (1979a) suggests that the signaling role of visual behavior may, on occasion, be dysfunctional to language production. In two studies (Allen & Guy, 1977; Cegala, Alexander, & Sokuvitz, 1979), the verbal output of freely conversing dyads was transcribed and categorized in terms of the proposed cognitive difficulty or uncertainty associated with its production. Both research groups found a greater proportion of speaker away-gazes associated with more difficult verbal productions. Finally, Ellyson, Dovidio, and Corson (1981) paired together for conversation females with differing levels of self-reported expertise on a series of topics. Participants gazed a significantly greater proportion of the time while speaking about topics on which they were experts compared to their looking while speaking on topics that they knew less about. Expert knowledge may reduce the labor involved in discussing certain topics, enabling a speaker to spend more time monitoring his or her audience without disrupting the flow of discourse.

Intuitively it seems reasonable that a norm of attention exists for listeners. As Goodwin (1981) suggests, speakers talk to and for others upon whom it is incumbent to demonstrate hearership. One way in which appropriate attention may be displayed is to gaze at the speaker. Culturally based prescriptions such as "look at me while I'm speaking to you" further argue for such a norm, at least within white western subcultural groups. Exline (1972) asked a group of Americans to indicate their degree of comfort with several different levels of gaze from another under varying circumstances. Respondents reported expected discomfort in the presence of non-gazing listener, and considerably more comfort if the listener looked at them about 50% of the time. However, it might further be suggested that the cognitive complexity of the conversation material would also influence the gaze of a listener. As the material increases in complexity, the processing task might drive the gaze of a listener away from the distraction of the speaker's face. In the only data available on this issue, however, Ellyson et al.'s (1981) listeners gazed significantly less when discussing a topic on which they were an expert compared to their listening gaze on other topics. The authors argue that the expert need not attend the comments of a person who knows less than they do on a topic. It may be that looking while listening is more directly related to social norms and roles than the difficulty of the conversation topic, although it would be interesting to analyze listening gaze with respect to the cognitive load categories employed by Allen and Guy (1977) and Cegala et al. (1979) for the study of speaking gaze. It may well be that under some circumstances proportion of looking while listening would be lower than the proportion of looking while speaking depending on the relative difficulty of the conversation or material for different participants.

Markov modeling of gaze and speech. The data just described, which relates visual behavior to the conversational roles of speaker and listener, were produced by summing across an entire interaction period. Other authors have considered the nature of the gaze–speech relationship sequentially, as the ongoing interaction proceeds. One approach has been to evaluate the usefulness of Markov models for describing the patterning of gazes at and away from a conversation partner, coincident with whether the partners were speaking or silent. Hedge, Everitt, and Frith (1978) conclude that a first-order Markov model best predicts the occurrence of sound versus silence and gaze at versus gaze away from one's dyadic partner. One should interpret these results with caution, however, because of the fact that the recording of the data was reliably synchronized at .5 sec., but the sampling for the Markov analysis occurred below this level, at .3 sec. It is therefore likely that many of the state changes introduced into the analysis were not reliably coded. Natale (1976) also found a first-degree Markov best predicted the occurrence of gaze for dyad members. In this study, however, the video recording was made from a profile view of the conversants, a measurement technique that von Cranach's research (e.g., 1971) suggests is subject to serious violations of validity. Further analyses of sequential patterning employing Markov as well as more complex models of the temporal organization of social behavior (see Clarke, 1982; von Hoof, 1982) are clearly called for.

Gaze and the construction and exchange of speaking turns. Successfully conducting a conversation requires that the participants not only produce speech but also coordinate their activities meaningfully with respect to each other. In many cases, the evaluation of others is based both on what they have to say and *how* they make their contributions. One of the ubiquitous features of conversation is its tendency to proceed through turns of talk. Although there are obvious exceptions, participants tend to speak one at a time, and in most conversations, a smooth exchange of speaking turns is accomplished without explicit verbal comment governing the process. The gaze behavior of conversants has been suggested as a possible nonverbal cue that, among others, aids in the rapid transfer of the floor from one participant to another.

Nielson (1962) filmed 22 undergraduate males during 12 minutes of a conversation with an experimental assistant. The incidence and coincidence of speech and gaze were recorded from the film, and Nielson reported that participants tended to look away from the conversation partner as they began a speaking turn, and to gaze at the partner as they came to the end of their turn. The gazes away from and at the partner did not necessarily occur precisely at the point of turn initiation or termination but rather became more likely in the period of time surrounding these points, possibly signaling imminent speaker changes. Although this pattern may be seen in the raw data presented, Nielson further elaborates on cases in which it did not hold true. Interviews with participants during and following a viewing of their own film revealed they were frequently able to comment on aspects of their nonverbal display. For cases in which the visual behavior did not correlate highly with speaking versus silence, participants reported feelings of discomfort (gaze-away), or attempts to halt attacks from the assistant or demonstrate aggression (gaze-at).

Kendon (1967) further explored the possibility that speaker gaze may serve as a cue of turn exchange in a descriptive study of seven 30-min. conversations between pairs of strangers who were instructed to get to know one another. Filmed excerpts from these interactions were analyzed in terms of the presence or absence of gaze at the conversation partner surrounding the beginning and ending of "long utterances" (5 sec. or longer). Gaze away from the partner was more likely at utterance beginning, peaking at the actual initiation point. Gaze *at* the partner occurred more frequently at utterance ending, again peaking at the point of termination. In the period of time surrounding utterance beginning, Kendon suggests, participants were planning their remarks. Gaze aversion at this point in the flow could serve to shut off distracting feedback from the interlocutor. As the utterance came to an end, however, a choice point was reached in which the next move of the speaker could depend on information from the listener. Gazing at the partner during this time could provide information regarding the listener's displayed intentions and, further, might signal the partner that comments from them would now be accepted. To further evaluate the potential signaling function, Kendon (1967) further analyzed two conversations in which both gazes at and gazes away from the partner at utterance ending occurred with sufficient frequency that they could be compared. Utterances that terminated with a gaze at the partner were followed more rapidly with an utterance from the partner. Without such gaze, partners either paused before initiating an utterance or failed to respond. It is important to note that Kendon (1967) is interested in the array of actions performed by conversants as they negotiate a change of speaker, with gaze patterning being the most typical, but not only, element in the conversations observed. He provides a detailed account of one turn exchange in which the participants brow, mouth, and head movements are described along with gaze direction, all in conjunction with a transcript of the speech. Whereas summary data are provided only for the coincidence of gaze and utterances, Kendon suggests that speakers and auditors signal, in a number of ways, their intentions regarding their respective conversation roles as well as their desire to change these roles. The extent to which conversants monitor each other and are sensitive to such cues, including gaze direction, may play a role in determining their ability to execute synchronous turn exchanges.

Various attempts to replicate aspects of Kendon's (1967) work have produced mixed results. Beattie (1978a) videotaped four hour-long interactions, three that were tutorials between a student and supervisor and one faculty discussion. Data from five males were evaluated for the presence or absence of partner-directed gaze at the termination point associated with complete utterances leading to a speaker change. Beattie (1978a) was particularly interested in the relationship between gaze direction at utterance termination and the duration of the "switching pause" (silence bounded by the speech of different speakers) that followed. In general, switching pauses were shorter when gaze at the partner was absent. This is the reverse of Kendon's (1967) findings. In a later paper, apparently based on the same interactions, Beattie (1979b) finds the shortest switching pauses to follow hesitant speech accompanied by direct gaze at the conversation partner. He suggests that, although speaker gaze is not an indispensable cue regulating turn exchange, it may be particularly useful in the context of a low overall gaze level. Such a gaze level would possibly be present during hesitant speech, thus rendering the gaze at utterance termination more salient to an auditor and more useful as a cue. Because Kendon (1967) reported overall gaze levels lower than those observed in his own work, Beattie (1979b) employed the same analysis to explain the divergent results in their respective studies. Beattie concluded in a later paper (1981), however, that the most important cue for turn exchange was syntactic clause completion along with the attendant vocal cues.

Mixed results were also reported by Rutter, Stephenson, Ayling, and White (1978) in two studies of conversations. In Study I, same and cross-sex dyads discussed points of disagreement on a previously completed sociopolitical questionnaire in Study II. In both experiments, the first, middle, and final 3 min. of 20-min. interactions were coded for the presence or absence of direct gaze at the partner, by both speakers and listeners, coincident with the termination of utterances (linguistically complete units of 10 or greater words, which ended in a floor change without overlapping speech). In both studies, a majority of utterances leading to turn exchange ended with speaker gaze at the partner. Rutter et al. (1978) argue however that this is not sufficient for speaker gaze to serve as a floor-change cue. Other required conditions are: (a) The gaze at the speaker should be greater at the end compared to the beginning of utterances. This condition was obtained in Study II only; (b) a great deal of mutual gaze by speakers and listeners would be required at turn exchange points because a visual cue must be seen to be useful. Mutual gaze occurred "only" on 48–64% of the potential occasions; (c) there should be less mutual gaze at turn beginning than at turn end, which occurred only in Study II. The authors conclude that insufficient evidence exists to warrant the attribution of floor-exchange cue properties to speaker gaze. Even if mutual gaze were always present at such points in conversation, Rutter et al. (1978) suggest that the speaker may be merely monitoring the listener for cues rather than the converse. Gaze is always accompanied by other visual and vocal cues. They argue that the presence or absence of speaker gaze may be redundant to other cues, which would also explain the ability to successfully converse in no-vision situations (e.g., telephone conversations).

Both Beattie (1978a) and Rutter et al. (1978) speculate that Kendon's findings may have been due to his definiton of an utterance, a definition that is not made explicit in his article. If Kendon included utterances that terminated in the simultaneous speech of the two participants, the consequences may have been to artificially increase the incidence of gaze at turn end. In their respective analyses (Beattie, 1978a; Rutter et al., 1978), such utterances were excluded from consideration.

In response to the papers of Beattie (1978a) and Rutter et al. (1978), Kendon (1978) discusses some of the differences and similarities in their respective results. Kendon (1978) views Rutter et al.'s (1978) Study II as most similar to his own in that both involved a serious (vs. ritualized) discussion among peers (vs. individuals of different status). Study II also produced results that were most similar to Kendon's (1967). Of perhaps greater import, however, Kendon (1978) suggests that actions that serve to cue a next speaker are likely variable, depending on the nature of turn units, current conversational structure, and participant's understandings of each other's conversational intentions. This latter point highlights an essential difference in conceptual orientation. From Kendon's structuralist perspective (see Kendon, 1982), natural units of behavior (turn exchanges) may best be investigated through intensive studies that attempt to describe and explain these behaviors with respect to the contexts in which they are typically produced (conversations of various types). From this perspective, it is not fruitful to test, experimentally, the role of cues isolated from the context in which they occur. This is particularly true if one has not intensively observed and thoroughly described the phenomenon of interest.

A further striking difference between the work of both Nielson (1962) and Kendon (1967) compared to that of Beattie (1978a, 1979b) and Rutter et al. (1978) is the duration of gaze sampling. The latter authors observed the presence or absence of speaker gaze only at utterance termination. Both Kendon (1967) and Nielson (1962) describe changes in the incidence of speaker gaze throughout the interaction, thus enabling them to record changes in the probability of gaze surrounding, rather than only at the point of, turn exchange. Wieman and Knapp (1975) report that the gaze of speakers increases over the period of their turn, and this change in incidence may be one of the criticial cues in smooth floor exchanges.

Charles Goodwin (1981), in a very insightful monograph from within the domain of conversation analysis (see Atkinson & Heritage, in press; West & Zimmerman, 1982), provides the type of intensive investigation that Kendon would favor. Conversation analysis rests on the assumption that human action may best be understood by reference to its placement within sequences of actions, as produced in natural settings. This contextual understanding involves a prospective analysis of what a current acton implicates and projects, which is intimately associated with a corresponding retrospective analysis of its placement relative to prior actions (Atkinson & Heritage , in press). To this end, Goodwin (1981) videotaped approximately 50 hours of conversations as they occurred in 14 different settings (e.g., family dinners, a teenage swim party, butchers in a meat market, etc.). Verbal and vocal aspects of the dialogue of participants was transcribed employing a system developed by Jefferson (see Sacks, Schegloff, & Jefferson, 1974). Constraints imposed by the circumstances of recording necessitated the use of head orientation rather than the details of gaze direction per se to indicate the orientation of speakers and recipients. Throughout the work, Goodwin (1981) uses the term *gaze* to describe these orientations. He justifies this usage by noting that gaze is typically accompanied by a head orientation (see also von Cranach, 1971; Exline, 1972; Stern, 1977).

For Goodwin (1981), conversation is minimally a two-party activity, a mutually constructed and coordinated process requiring more than mere copresence and talk. Conversation, and the construction of turns within conversation, make relevant the two social identities of speaker and hearer. While the actions relevant to each role are performed by individuals and thus display something about the performer, they also project or implicate actions for others who are also present. Incumbency in these identities of speaker and hearer are subject to demonstration. The speaker, the party whose turn is in progress, speaks not just to have the floor but speaks to have the floor while others listen. These actions project an addressee within a particular engagement framework (e.g., focused conversation, talk within disengagement [to be discussed later]). The *social* identity of speaker is ratified not simply by the action of talking, but by the display of hearership on the part of present others, particularly the speaker's addressee(s). Gaze, as well as other actions, may be employed within a sequence of actions to indicate a projected addressee and/or to display hearership. The speaker may project particular addressees by gazing at them; the addressees may display hearership by gazing at the speaker. Ratification of both identities depends on the actions of others. Talk on the part of a speaker is not sufficient to ratify the role of speaker, nor is silence on the part of an addressee sufficient to ratify the role of hearer. Each depends on the other to achieve true social realization. Turns within talk, then, are mutually constructed. A speaker may alter the construction of a turn in progress in response to his or her understanding of the activities of a projected addressee within the ordered sequence of a conversation.

Goodwin (1981) suggests that the gaze of an addressee may be particularly relevant to the construction of a speaker's turn at turn beginning. As the speaker begins to talk, the auditory cue of the voice announces that the services of a hearer are required if the talk is to be regarded as unimpaired. If the gaze of a hearer is directed toward the speaker at turn beginning, hearership *may* be appropriately displayed, and the talk may proceed. If, however, a recipients' gaze is directed elsewhere, it *may* be relevantly absent for the speaker. Because speakers speak *for* hearers and cannot be meaningfully ratified in this social identity without the services of a hearer, it is as if the speaker's turn has not yet really begun. It is in this sense that the speaker's talk may be regarded as impaired. Goodwin (1981) provides numerous examples from his videotaped corpus to demonstrate that speakers may employ both pauses in speech and restarts (sentence reconstruction following a sentence fragment) to request the gaze (appropriate orientation) of a hearer. This may occur at turn beginning and at other points in the conversation when a hearer's gaze is relevantly absent. In the following example (adapted from Goodwin, 1981, p. 56–57), the speaker, Sue, begins a turn by saying "I come in t- . . . ." At this point, the gaze of a recipient, Diedre, arrives, i.e., begins to be directed at Sue (indicated by a solid line). Sue restarts and produces a complete sentence: "I no sooner sit down on the couch in the living room, and the doorbell rings" (p. 56).

Sue (speaker):   I come in t- I no sooner sit down on the couch . . .
Deidre (recipient gaze):   [X_____

A pause may also be used in the same manner to delay the progress of a sentence until appropriate hearership is displayed.

The recipient's gaze need not have actually arrived at the speaker for the speaker to proceed with a complete sentence. Goodwin's (1981) examples suggest it may be sufficient for the hearer's gaze to be in the process of moving toward the speaker. This is an aspect of social visual behavior that has not previously been considered. More usually researchers record only the gazes at and away from others. Goodwin's (1981) work argues, however, that the action of a recipient's eyes moving in the direction of a speaker may display sufficient hearership for talk to proceed and thus prove worthy of further consideration.

The orientation of the recipient of talk becomes relevant to the speaker only when the speaker is monitoring the recipient. This monitoring may be accomplished directly, by looking at the recipient, or peripherally. In the latter case, the speaker may be gazing away from the recipient but be aware peripherally of the general orientation displayed, if not the specific focus of gaze. Goodwin (1981) distinguished between the use of restarts and pauses along these lines. If the speaker monitors a relevantly non-gazing recipient at talk beginning, he may be repeated until the hearer's gaze arrives. The speaker who begins an utterance without monitoring the recipient may pause early in the construction of the utterance to provide time for the recipient to appropriately orient to the talk. The use of a pause in this context enables the progress of the turn to be momentarily halted without regarding previous talk as impaired. Thus, the mutual monitoring (see also M. Goodwin, 1980) engaged in by speakers and hearers enables them to coordinate the construction of a turn.

Goodwin (1981) notes that this description of the role of gaze at turn beginning suggests a preferred ordering of events. The hearer's gaze should move in the direction of the speaker early on in the production of an utterance, whereas the speaker should wait before monitoring the recipient, giving the recipient sufficient time to appropriately orient to the talk in progress. This sort of ordering, if it occurred repeatedly, would produce the pattern of gaze at turn beginning observed by Kendon (1967) and Rutter et al. (1978, Study II).

A quantitative analysis of a 10-minute conversation provides information regarding the statistical probabilities associated with Goodwin's (1981) description of the use of restarts at turn beginning. Cases in which the speaker's gaze arrives at a gazing versus a nongazing hearer are compared for the speaker's subsequent production of a restart. A significant chi-square leads Goodwin (1981) to further examination of the cases contributing to the 2 × 2 matrix (hearer gaze: present vs. absent; speaker: restart, no restart). First, it was found that restarts are much less likely if hearer gaze is present (1 restart in 25 cases). Goodwin does not argue that restarts are *only* used to delay talk in progress but might also be related to other factors such as the complexity of the conversation topic, or planning phases in talk. He is suggesting, however, that restarts, despite the fact that they are typically regarded as instances of the "degenerate quality" (p. 55) of natural speech, may in fact be employed in a socially competent, if not linguistically competent, manner. Secondly, Goodwin carefully analyzes those cases in which hearer gaze was absent but failed to produce a restart (11 of 17 cases). In these 11 instances, hearers were involved in other actions that displayed appropriate orientation for that point in the conversation. Hearers might be performing activities relevant to the talk (e.g., looking away when asked to remember something), or be in the process of moving their gaze toward the speaker. Also, if the speaker's monitoring began coincident with her talk, the hearer's gaze might not yet be relevantly absent. This leeway has limits, however. The longer the delay in realignment, the more likely a restart becomes.

Several points are relevant at this juncture. First, examination of cases that do not fit a proposed pattern (despite overall statistical significance) can lead to an enriched understanding of a phenomena. Second, although the gaze direction of the recipient of talk *may* be *part* of a display of hearership, it need not *always* be present and may at times be *appropriately absent*. Goodwin's (1981) findings argue for further intensive studies of conversational organization in its verbal (including content) and nonverbal aspects. Third, synchronization between the actions of conversational participants need not be perfect for successful interaction to occur. In terms of Goodwin's (1981) example, the speaker who gazes at a recipient coincident with his initiation of talk allows, within limits, time for the recipient to appropriately orient to the talk. This is an interesting phenomenon in and of itself. Differences may be foreseen in the delay afforded by some persons, and in the delay produced by others, given variations in context, sequential position, importance of topic, temperament, etc. Further, this issue of synchronization bears on the definition of units of behavior. The boundary of turn beginning would seem to vary depending on whose point of view is considered, and whether this point of view stems from an emic or etic (Pike, 1967) orientation. Goodwin (1981) also provides examples in which a speaker apparently modifies the vocal aspects of a turn ending to better coordinate with the activities of a recipient. The termination point of a turn may be extended through vocal elongation or the addition of new verbal components in response to a recipients inability to reply because of involvement with accepted competing activities.

Finally, Goodwin (1981) argues that because participants understand the presence or absence of a partner's gaze differently dependent on its placement and participation within the sequence of events, it is inappropriate to sum frequencies or durations over an interaction period, a usual procedure in most experimental work. However, he allows that variations permissible in the use of social visual behavior may mean it can be called to the service of other social processes, such as displays of intimacy or dominance. This issue is returned to in a later section of the chapter.

Interpersonal gaze during interactions involving competing activities. Laboratory investigations of visual behavior are typically structured so that participants have little else to do than converse with each other. Purses, backpacks, cigarettes, and books are left for safekeeping with the experimenter who does not want such articles to be inconsistently employed to justify gaze away from one's interaction partner. In naturalistic conversations, however, participants have freely available the toted paraphernalia of their everyday lives. Moreover, many conversations are directly related to various articles, books, or reports to which the participants legitimately attend. Argyle and Graham (1977) observed the visual behavior of dyads asked to plan a summer holiday. These discussions variously took place in the presence of a complex relevant object (detailed map of Europe), a simple relevant object (outline map of Europe), no object, an irrelevant object (a map when asked to discuss general interests), and finally no object and lowered background stimulation (no map and the blind drawn over the window). Conversational gaze patterns are substantially different under these situations. In the presence of the complex or simple relevant object the gaze of participants is primarily directed toward the items (81.9 and 69.9%) and very little at each other (16.4 and 27.0%). If there is no object or the object is irrelevant, percentage gaze at the partner increases substantially, (58.0 and 64.1%), although there are glances toward background environmental stimuli. When all objects are absent and the window is covered, gaze at the partner reaches its highest level (76.6%).

Elements of the environmental background may draw one's visual attention detrimentally away from a task at hand, either because of the background's interest value or boredom with the task. Breed and Colaiuta (1974) time sampled the visual attentiveness of college students during advanced social psychology lectures. Students who received the highest test scores spent more time looking at the instructor and less time "looking around" than students who performed less well on exams.

The presence of task-relevant material may, further, influence the relationship between gaze and speech. Noller (1980) recorded the presence versus absence of direct gaze in married couples who were discussing their response to a questionnaire they had on the table in front of them. The incidence of looking while speaking was greater than the incidence of looking while listening. This pattern is the reverse of that typically observed in laboratory conversations in which material such as Noller's questionnaire are not present during the discussion.

Because they were videotaped in naturalistic settings, many of Goodwin's (1981) interactions involve multiple participants and a number of potentially competing activities. In a more recent paper, Goodwin (in press) analyzes a segment of a dinner conversation in which one of the participants tells a story. Although a recipient's gaze typically becomes relevant when monitored by the speaker, this rule may be relaxed to enable hearers to deal with other aspects of a multi-activity situation, in this case eating dinner. Although it is still incumbent upon a hearer to display hearership, this may be accomplished by, for example, head nods, if one needs to look at one's plate to accurately scoop up a morsel of food. At points during the talk, however, particularly at the climax of a story, the speaker may prefer the undivided attention of recipients. At such moments, talk may not meaningfully proceed without the gaze of relevant participants, who must pause in their consummatory activities to appropriately orient to the story teller. If such visual attention fails to occur, the speaker has various means available to request it: restarts and pauses; and if these do not achieve the desired orientation, a direct question or command may be employed to solicit the desired attentional display from a recipient.

Such common exigencies and vicissitudes of everyday life frequently entwine conversations. A more complete understanding of the role of visual behavior in social interaction would be enhanced by further exploration of this type of interaction setting.

Alternative orientation frameworks.   The mutual monitoring of focused conversation represents only one of several possible ways to orient to copresent others. Goodwin (1981) discusses other patterns of orientation possible among participants whose state of co-presence has already been established and is being to some degree sustained. During lapses in conversation, for example, interactions seem to "disengage." The participants continue to be physically present but not relevantly present in quite the same sense as when talk flowed easily. Disengagement, as with other forms of orientation, occurs as a result of the coordinated actions of minimally two participants. Goodwin details how, in one example, two women slide into a state of temporary disengagement by signaling through the use of gaze aversion, slowed pace of action, and attention to an alternative activity that continued talk on the previous topic was not regarded as necessarily relevant. As in the case of turn initiation and termination, the boundary between engagement and disengagement is not, in many cases, clear and sharp. Rather each participant allows time for their displayed proposals to be processed and responded to. This transitional display serves as a sort of holding pattern in which the next orientation framework may be negotiated.

In the context of sustained co-presence, participants may continue to monitor the actions of others peripherally, without directly looking at them. This is displayed in Goodwin's (1981) example when one participant looks *with* the other at some aspect of the environment, although neither overtly monitors the other. The orienting head movement may be perceived via peripheral vision and respond to in a manner so as to signal and check upon the possibility of potentially resuming conversation. Thus, to measure only the incidence of direct gaze would overlook indirect visual responsiveness that figures in the coordination of participants' actions.

Changes in gaze level over the course of an interaction.   The majority of researchers interested in the level of gaze directed at a conversation partner report this information only for the total interaction period. Data from four experiments (Allen & Guy, 1974; Coutts & Schneider, 975; Rajecki, Ickes, & Tanford, 1981; Schneider & Hansvick, 1977), however indicate gazel-level changes when the first and second half of brief (3–5 min.) interactions between strangers are compared. In all four cases, gaze level decreased across the interaction period. It may be that aspects of another's behavior become predictable over time, reducing the necessity of a high level of monitoring.

Gaze-level changes over an interaction period are also influenced by manipulated gaze changes produced by experimental confederates. In three investigations (Breed & Porter, 1972; Exline & Eldridge, 1967; Schneider & Hansvick, 1977), confederates were instructed to gaze at participants during the first half of an interaction and gaze away during the second half, or the reverse. Schneider and Hansvick (1977) found male and female subjects to decrease their gaze at a confederate who shifted from gazing at them to gazing away from them. In the away-at condition, however, they maintain the lower level of gaze initiated during the first half of the interaction even though the confederates gaze increased. Breed and Porter (1972) had participants role play a positive or negative attitude toward the confederate whereas a control group received no instructions. While role playing a positive attitude, male participants gazed more frequently at the confederate who first looked toward them and then looked away. The confederate who looked away and then at participants received a higher frequency of gaze from negative role play and control-group males compared to confederates who first gazed at the participants and then gazed away. Exline and Eldridge (1967) found that participants reported greater confidence in their impressions of a confederate when he gazed at them during the second half of an interaction rather than during the first half.

Interaction termination.   Given that initiating and maintaining an interaction involves some degree of partner directed gaze, it is not surprising that the termination (and avoidance) of an encounter is associated with gaze aversion. Knapp, Hart, Friedrich, and Schulman (1973) observe leave-taking behaviors of previously acquainted and unacquainted males, who interviewed a male confederate of similar or different status relative to themselves. Occurrences of verbal and nonverbal behaviors were recorded during the 45 seconds prior to the participant rising from his chair to exit. The act of breaking mutual gaze with the confederate was the most frequently observed nonverbal behavior. The incidence of various nonverbal leave-taking behaviors rose during the final 15 seconds and peaked in the last 5 seconds. Knapp et al. (1973) argue this change in frequency serves to warn another of one's impending departure and consequent inaccessibility. Such foreshadowing of proposed actions enables participants to better coordinate major changes in a sequence of events.

Gaze as it Relates to Relatively Stable Dispositions and Characteristics of Individuals.

In the previous section, discussion centered on aspects of interactions or conversations with which any individual, regardless of his or her relatively stable personal tendencies or transitory states, would have to contend. In this section and the one following, consideration is given to what is known about the relationship between such traits and more temporary circumstances as they relate to the display of visual behavior in social interaction. It may reasonably be hypothesized that what an individual brings to an interaction in the form of socially relevant predispositions and more temporary states would influence gaze patterning associated with the initiation, maintenance, termination, and avoidance of encounters with others. In keeping with the conceptual orientation of this chapter, displays associated with aspects of individual functioning are thought to have social implications for interaction partners. The research described, however, focuses primarily on the displays associated with individual traits and states, without considering the social, communicative projections of such displays.

The majority of the research described in this section evaluates the role of the stable characteristics of individuals as these characteristics relate to the social visual behavior of the same individuals. A few investigators, however, have considered the attention-attracting qualities of relatively stable features of the targets of social gaze. Salient physical qualities of certain individuals are more likely to draw the visual attention of others. These few investigations are described at the end of this section.

Individual differences in gaze levels and their stability. Considerable individual variation has been observed in the gaze one directs at a conversation partner. In Nielson's (1962) study of male undergraduates, the total proportion of the interaction period spent gazing at an experimental assistant varied from 8 to 73%. Looking while speaking and looking while listening varied from 4 to 64% and 11 to 89%, respectively. Kendon (1967) reports similar diversity among both male and female conversants as may be seen in the following ranges: Percentage total gaze, 18–70%; percentage looking while speaking, 20–65%; percentage looking while listening, 30–80%; and percentage mutual gaze, 9.83–30.00%. Kendon (1967) also reports measures of individual variation in the average duration of gazes directed toward a conversation partner: Mean total gaze, 2.10–7.98 sec.; mean looking while speaking, 1.94–7.32 sec.; mean looking while listening, 2.24–7.93 sec.; and mean mutual gaze, 1.44–2.80 sec.

The consistency of such differences has been investigated by several researchers. Daniell and Lewis (1972) report high stability (correlations ranging from .803 to .961) for the gaze of male and female participants toward a steadily gazing assistant, across three weekly interviews. This held true whether the participant was interviewed by the same or three different female interviewers, although there was a slight tendency for somewhat less consistency in the latter case. In two studies, Patterson (1973) obtained similar results for males and females in same or cross-sex interviews. Comparisons were made across a 25-min. ($r = .65$) and a 2-week ($r = .95$) interval. Kendon and Cook (1969) recorded visual behavior and speech for males and females who interacted for 30 min. each with several other individuals. Analyses of variance resulted in significant identity of subject factors for most gaze and speech variables. The relatively high degree of stability for gaze behavior found in these studies, however, must be interpreted with caution. The nature of the different interaction situations was quite similar. Variations in relative status, degree of affiliation, relationship type, complexity of topic, etc. would likely produce somewhat lower levels of consistency.

Sex.   As Ellsworth and Ludwig (1972) state, "in research on visual behavior, sex differences are the rule, rather than the exception" (p. 379). The tendency, observed in infancy and childhood, for females to spend greater time gazing at an interaction partner compared to males has also repeatedly been observed in the context of adult laboratory conversations between strangers (Aiello, 1972; Allen & Guy, 1974; Argyle & Ingham, 1972; Dabbs et al., 1980; Exline, 1963; Exline et al., 1965; Foddy, 1978; La France & Carmen, 1980; Nevill, 1974; Rutter, Morley, & Graham, 1972; Schneider & Hansvick, 1977). The difference in average gaze level between males and females ranged from 10 to 20 percentage points. Confidence in this pattern of sex difference is enhanced by the fact that the investigations vary with respect to the duration of the interaction, topic of conversation, specific gaze variables measured, and whether the conversation partner was an experimental assistant or another participant. Occasionally the gaze-level difference between males and females is restricted to particular gaze variables. For example, Allen and Guy (1974) found females look at their partners more than males only while listening, but not while speaking. Available data does not enable the discriminating factors to be sorted out. When the sex composition of the conversing dyads is taken into account (e.g., Argyle & Ingham, 1972), female–female pairs frequently gaze at each other more than male–male or cross-sex pairs. Further, Coutts and Schneider (1975) found same-sex female dyad members to gaze at each other more than male dyads or cross-sex dyads during an unfocused interaction. In this study, participants were waiting for their experiment to begin in an area where talking was not permitted.

La France and Carmen (1980) examined the import of sex-role identification (masculine, feminine, androgynous) as well as sex in the display of various nonverbal behaviors. A significant main effect revealed females to look while speaking (the only gaze variable measured) more than males. Also, sex-role identification interacted with sex. Masculine males gazed while speaking significantly less than feminine females. Androgynous females gazed more than androgynous males, though not significantly, and their average gaze levels fell between those of the masculine males and feminine females but were not significantly different from them. Thus, the display of visual behavior is related to sex in both its biological and psychological aspects.

When the interaction setting shifts to the public sphere, females, compared to males, avoid visual contact with a steadily gazing stranger (Buchanan, Goldman, & Juhnke, 1977; Cary, 1978a; Greenbaum & Rosenfeld, 1978; and Smith & Stanford, 1977). In such contexts the visual attention of another may appear particularly threatening, connoting a type of interaction in which one might prefer not to be involved.

Explanations of the observed sex differences in visual behavior center on proposed differences in the sex-role socialization experiences of males and females. Exline (1963), for example, suggested that women may be oriented to and affected by social stimuli to a greater extent than men. This argument is continued by Exline et al. (1965), with further reference to the potential origins of women's greater social orientation within the nuclear family. Such proposals are in keeping with the data and interpretation of Hittelman and Dickes (1979). They found female neonates to gaze more at an adult than male neonates, which likely influences the nature of early social encounters. Sex differences in gaze behavior carry into childhood and are accompanied by differential sensitivity to and interpretation of the visual behavior of others. Further, individuals who are less extreme in their sex-role identification and may be characterized as androgynous would be expected to display less difference in visual attention (see La France & Carmen, 1980).

Henley (1977) reminds us, however, that affiliative disposition is not the only quality conveyed by nonverbal behavior. Individuals also differ with respect to the relative power and control they are inclined or permitted to exert over others. The difference in visual attention displayed by men and women may therefore further reflect social-status differentiation in a male-dominated world. In this respect, women may be viewed as submissively attentive to others (cf. Chance (1967) and Vaughn and Waters (1981) on attention structure). In the presence of potentially threatening gaze from another, deference may be displayed by averting the eyes, as observed in public settings (cf. Chance (1962) on "cut-off" actions).

Further discussions of these proposals follows in the section on affiliation and dominance.

Age. Very little is known about possible gaze-level differences associated with advancing age in adults. Two field investigations, however, provide intriguing results that deserve further exploration. Muirhead and Goldman (1979) observed the mutual gaze exchanged by 216 conversing dyads in shopping centers. Dyads were selected on the basis of their apparent previous acquaintance and relatively stationary position on benches or at restaurant tables. Participants were grouped into three age categories (18–30 yrs., 31–55 years, 56 and older) based on estimates made by the observers. The youngest and oldest groups engaged in significantly more mutual gaze than the middle group. Sex composition of the dyads interacted with age such that in the youngest group cross-sex dyads exchanged significantly more mutual gaze than did male–male dyads. The mutual gaze of same-sex female dyads fell between the two extremes but was not reliably different from either. For the middle-aged and older groups the pattern reversed. In both cases, cross-sex pairs shared significantly less mutual gaze than did same-sex male pairs. The gaze of female–female conversants remained in the middle position and was only reliably different from the cross-sex pairs in the oldest group. It is impossible to tell whether the shifts are related to differences in age, degree of acquaintance, duration of relationship, or other unknown factors. The increased mutual gaze level in male dyads, however, is sufficiently different from usually observed patterns to merit further consideration.

Newman and McCauley (1977) observed the responses of pedestrians (who were approaching a post office or large grocery store) to the steady gaze of a male or female confederate. Confederate gaze was returned most often by the youngest and oldest groups. One might wonder if the generally lower visual contact observed for the middle-age group in both of these studies reflects a style of social contact related to this stage of development.

Personality.   Despite the controversy surrounding the relationship between responses on personality inventories and behavior under varying circumstances (Block, 1971; Mischel, 1968), a number of investigators have explored the possibility that individuals with various self-reported stable predispositions may in fact display these tendencies nonverbally while interacting with others. Wiens, Harper, and Matarazzo (1980) further argue that nonverbal behavior, should it relate reliably to responses on personality inventories, may even be used in place of such paper and pencil measures. In many practical settings, they argue, clients may be unable or unwilling to cooperate or read and comprehend the items contained in such questionnaires. A sample of their nonverbal behavior could, in such cases, be employed to aid diagnostic and other types of classification. This optimistic suggestion would require consideration of a wide range of nonverbal actions, across a selection of critical settings, including but not limited to an individual's visual behavior. Social visual interaction has, however, been found to relate significantly, if moderately, to a number of standard personality variables. These investigations have proceeded along two different lines. In one case, participants are pretested on the personality measure in question, and only those who obtain extreme scores are observed during an interaction. In the second case, participants are randomly sampled from some population for observation. Personality scores are then related to coded behaviors.

Extroverts have been observed to spend greater time gazing at an interaction partner than introverts. Mobbs (1968) preselected participants with extreme scores on these two scales and found extroverts to exhibit a longer average duration of mutual gaze compared to introverts. Rutter, Morely, and Graham (1972) found extreme-scoring extroverts to initiate more gazes and display a higher frequency of looking while speaking. The latter authors believe the higher frequency of extrovert gaze to be produced by their tendency to speak more than introverts. When observations were made of nonpreselected participants by Argyle and Ingham (1972) and Kendon and Cook (1969), extroversion was significantly correlated with greater partner-directed gaze. Similarly, Wiens et al. (1980) found shorter gaze duration related to introversion scores. The greater social interest of extroverts, compared to introverts, is typically employed to explain their greater incidence of partner-directed visual attention.

Rajecki, Ickes, and Tanford (1981) paired together for conversation persons with extreme scores on a measure of internal versus external locus of control. Dyads composed of two externals engaged in greater partner-directed gaze than pairs of internals or mixed-disposition pairs. Externals' proposed greater responsiveness to external cues, and internals' tendency to avoid social influence were suggested as explanations for these results. Lefcourt and Wine (1969) found internals to gaze more frequently at an experimental assistant when the assistant was instructed to avoid looking at the participant. Such an observational strategy may allow the internal to obtain information from interaction partners without becoming involved with them. Rajecki et al. (1981) also found the gaze behavior of dyad members to be highly correlated regardless of dispositional classification. Internals and externals in mixed dyads did not differ significantly in their respective tendency to gaze at conversation partners. It would be interesting to know if the externals in these dyads were primarily responsible for the correlation between the gaze behavior of dyad members.

High self-monitors (Snyder, 1974) are characterized as more concerned to adjust their interactional performance to the prevailing social environment compared to low self-monitors. Dabbs et al. (1980) found this proposed tendency of high self-monitors evidenced in their inclination to engage in less frequent but longer gaze at conversation partners compared to lows. This result, however, was only obtained when high self-monitors were paired with others of like disposition. When high and low self-monitors were paired for conversation, lows appeared more responsive to their partners. High self-monitors average duration of gaze remained unchanged, whereas lows increased their gaze duration as if to play the role of listener vis-a-vis the highs.

Socially anxious individuals might be expected to avoid the discomfort associated with social encounters by gazing less at interaction partners. Daly (1978) found less looking while speaking to an interviewer in participants with high as compared to low scores on a test of social anxiety. Daly (1978) cautions, however, that it may be inappropriate to group high and low socially anxious individuals on the basis of their test scores alone. Greater vari-ability in average duration of interviewer-directed gaze was observed for high as compared to low socially anxious participants, suggesting differences in their respective within-group coping styles. The relationship between anxiety and social visual attention may be limited by the specific source of the dis-comfort, as Hobson, Strongman, Bull, and Craig (1973) found gaze level unrelated to a more general measure of trait anxiety.

A number of investigators have developed self-report measures that evalu-ate attentiveness (Nideffer, 1976; Norton & Pettegrew, 1979) and inter-actional involvement (Cegala, Savage, Brunner, & Conrad, 1982) as general social styles. Norton and Pettegrew (1979) found mutual gaze conceptually related to an attentive communication style. In one study, Cegala et al. (1979) reported to an attentive communication style. In one study, Cegala et al. (1979) reported high levels of speaking and listening gaze related to higher levels of self-reported involvement in an interaction. In a second study (Cegala et al., 1982), however, this result was limited to males during periods in which they were speaking. Wiens et al. (1980) correlated subscale scores of Nideffer's (1976) Test of Attentional and Interpersonal Style with the visual behavior of male interviewees. Broad internal and external focus was related to a lower frequency of interviewer-directed gaze. Participants characterized as behaviorally impulsive responded to an increased verbal response latency of the interviewer with an increase in visual attentiveness to the interviewer.

Much attention has been given to the investigation of the relationship be-tween visual behavior and the communciation of dominance and affiliation. This may be seen in studies of individual-difference displays (to be described here), in studies that experimentally manipulate status or power and liking, and in studies that investigate the verbal labels respondents use to describe in-dividuals whose gaze level has been observed (to be discussed later).

Strongman and Champness (1968) were able to construct a stable domin-ance hierarchy for a group of five men and five women based on each individ-ual's tendency to break the initial mutual glance in a brief interaction with other members of the group. These authors originally proposed, in the ab-sence of independent measures of dominance, that the dominant individuals in the hierarchy were the ones who did not glance away from their partners. In a later paper, however, Strongman (1970) reported that mutual glance breaking was positively correlated with a trait measure of dominance, such that the persons at the top of the dominance hierarchy were in fact more likely to break initial mutual glances. Based on Kendon's (1967) work, it was suggested that the dominant participants broke visual contact to begin speak-ing, but they would be expected to maintain steady gaze at partners during mutual silence.

A belief that dominant persons look at others more than submissive per-sons is evident in the assertiveness literature, and assertiveness-skills training usually involves attempting to increase social gazing. Galassi and Galassi

(1976) have, in fact, found more assertive persons to gaze at a confederate interactant more than less assertive persons when role playing assertiveness. Measures of visual behavior contributed most, among a set of measures, to the discrimination of the performances of low-versus medium- and high-assertive persons combined.

More dominant as compared to deferent individuals have been shown to respond differentially to variations in the behavior of an interaction partner. Exline and Messick (1967) categorized males as high- or low-control oriented based on their responses to Schultz's (1960) Firo-B scale. Low controls returned the gaze of a steadily gazing male interviewer more when the interviewer gave few social reinforcers (head nods, smiles, uhuh) than when he gave many. Also, low controls gazed more than high controls in the low-reinforcement condition. These more deferent persons may have been seeking missed feedback on their performance. Low-control males also spend more time visually monitoring a confederate who sweeps the air above their heads while listening to them speak compared to a confederate who gazes steadily at them while listening (Exline, Fairweather, Hine, & Argyle, reported in Exline, 1972). High controls did not visually discriminate between the attentive and inattentive listeners.

When visual behavior is coded with respect to the conversational roles of speaking and listening, high- and low-control (Firo-B) males and females may be further differentiated by their patterns of listener and speaker gaze. Exline, Ellyson, and Long (1975) developed an index of visual dominance behavior that is the ratio of looking while listening divided by looking while speaking. Lower values of the ratio are characterized a representing a more dominant display because, they argue, high-status or controlling individuals would not feel as strongly the force of the norm of attention (discussed earlier) that elevates the level of looking while listening. High-control males produced significantly lower visual dominance ratios than low-control males. This difference was a result of differences in looking while listening, which was lower for high controls. Looking while speaking was not significantly different for the two groups. Ellyson, Dovidio, and Fehr (1982) report similar results for high- and low-control females.

Finally, females who differ with respect to their self-reported degree of expertise on a given topic display, when discussing the topic, look–listen/look–speak patterns similar to those found for high- versus low-control individuals. Women who claimed expertise exhibited relatively equal levels of looking while speaking and listening. If their partner, rather than themselves, knew more about the topic, looking while listening was greater than looking while speaking.

Exline (1963) characterized male and female participants in terms of their level of n affiliation. High-n affiliative females gazed at their like-sex partners significantly more than less affiliative females. High n affiliative males, on the other hand, tended to monitor their male coconversants less than low-affiliative males. Discussions in this study occurred under instructions that emphasized a cooperative or competitive orientation. A post hoc analysis, which more stringently constrained the characterization of high- and low-*n* affiliation, revealed that high-*n* affiliators (regardless of sex) gazed at others more when competition was subdued rather than salient. Low-*n* affiliators gazed at their fellow participants more when competition was salient.

Exline (1963) characterized male and female participants in terms of their level of *n* affiliation. High-*n* affiliative females gazed at their like-sex partners significantly more than less affiliative females. High *n* affiliative males, were more affection and inclusion oriented than males and also tended to return the gaze of a steadily gazing interviewer more than males. A post hoc analysis revealed, however, that both men and women who could be characterized as particularly affection and inclusion oriented gazed at the interviewer more than their less warmly disposed counterparts. Results such as these have been employed to argue that the greater average gaze level of females compared to males reflects females tendency to be relatively more affiliative and socially concerned based on traditional sex-role training. Evidence that less controlling or submissive persons tend to monitor others more than more dominant individuals supports Henley's (1977) counterproposal that sex differences in visual behavior may reflect power differences between the sexes rather than variation in affiliative orientation.

Each of the aforementioned personality dispositions are conceptualized as differing from the others in several respects. Perhaps their common relationship to social gaze behavior reflects what they share in terms of the relative degree of openness to social interaction. Individuals disposed to extroversion, external locus of control, self-monitoring, low social anxiety, attentiveness, deference, affiliation are characterized as open to information from the social world and also tend to gaze at conversation partners more than their respective counterparts.

Psychiatric patients.   Difficulties suggested by Wiens et al. (1980) in the classification of personality types based on self-report questionnaires would be expected to be even greater in the case of psychiatric patients. Harris (1978) further argues that interviews with patients or members of their families may be no more enlightening. Thus, in an attempt to develop behavioral indices of various diagnostic categories, as well as information related to the behavioral concomitants associated with recovery, patients have been observed under a variety of interaction circumstances.

The results of early investigations suggested that both depressives and schizophrenics exhibited a lower level of interviewer-directed gaze than normal controls. For example, Hinchliffe, Lancashire, and Roberts (1970) found depressive patients to return the gaze of a steadily gazing interviewer more than surgical patients matched for age, sex, and socioeconomic status. In a second study (Hinchliffe et al., 1971) recovered depressives gazed more at an interviewer than patients still diagnosed as depressed. Waxer (1974) found judges were able to correctly distinguish depressed from non-depressed hospitalized patients from viewing a videotaped segment of their intake interview. Visual behavior served as an important cue for these judges as depressed patients maintained gaze at the interviewer about 1/4 as much as non-depressed controls. Rutter and Stephenson (1972a, b) found both schizophrenic and depressed hospitalized patients to gaze at an interviewer less than other psychiatric patients and non-psychiatric controls from a chest ward in a general hospital.

Further investigations of Rutter (1976, 1977), however, qualify the conditions under which the lower gaze level of depressives and schizophrenics may be observed. When members of these two diagnostic categories discussed topics unrelated to their patient status, their partner-directed gaze level was similar to that found in various control groups. This result is similar to that reported by Rutter and O'Brien (1980, described earlier) for withdrawn and aggressive girls. Also, Hersen, Miller, and Eisler (1973) found alcoholic males to gaze at their wives less while discussing their drinking problem than while conversing on other topics. Their wives, on the other hand, gazed at their husbands more while talking about alcohol-related issues. Rutter and O'Brien (1980) argue for standard consideration of the situational variability of behavior. In a reanalysis of previously reported data, Rutter (1978) further reports no difference between schizophrenics and other groups with respect to the incidence of partner-directed gaze during exchange.

Further subtleties of the visual behavior of schizophrenics have been investigated. Williams (1974) compared schizophrenics with other psychiatric patients and normal controls in their inclination to gaze at a television compared to a female confederate. Although schizophrenic patients gazed less at the confederate than other groups, they did not avoid looking at the television. Williams (1974) concludes that the interpersonal gaze level of schizophrenics may be associated with an avoidance of persons but not stimulation in general.

Harris (1978) compared the social gaze of male schizophrenics to that of normal controls as they interacted with their mothers, their fathers, an unrelated authority figure, and a peer. Schizophrenics shared a greater number of mutual gazes with their mothers compared to other interaction partners, and schizophrenics exhibited less mutual gaze with all partners compared to the normal controls. Thus, the interactional gaze of schizophrenic patients has been found to be related to the conversation topic, the nature of the target of gaze, and the relationship with the interaction partner.

Finally, Callan, Chance, and Pitcairn (1973) made exploratory observations of advertence displays in two situations involving psychiatric patients.

An informally constituted group of hospitalized schizophrenic patients was observed to develop a set of actions that could be used to manifest, attract, or withdraw advertence. Mutual gaze was one such activity. A further observation is of interest because of its bearing on the research related to turn exchange and the transition between various engagement frameworks. Callan et al. (1973) describe these patients as apparently having difficulty with gradual transitions between interaction segments. They did not seem to be able to hang in limbo as participants negotiated engagement alternatives. Rather they tended to either be in or out of the ongoing interaction focus, switching from one state to another in a very abrupt manner. A second set of observations were made during sessions of a formally structured psychotherapy group. In this setting the authors developed a classification scheme of total advertence performances that they labeled *modes of presentation.* Four such modes were observed in this setting: (a) "Alert," in which patients gazed at others and seemed responsive to the official focus of the group; (b) "huddled," from which patients might enter the discussion voluntarily or be brought in by others; (c) in the "closed" mode, spontaneous contributions failed to occur, although the individual would respond to direct questions; (d) the "away" patient seemed unfocused, gazing into space. As a result of Callan et al.'s (1973) interest in the distinction between attention and advertence, they note that these modes of presentation are to be understood as displays that do not necessarily represent the true attentional state of the individuals performing the display.

Gaze in the presence of salient interpersonal stimuli.   Certain individuals in society, because of their atypical physical appearance, might be expected to simultaneously draw and inhibit visual attention from others. When confronted with a handicapped person, Langer, Fiske, Tayler, and Chanowitz (1976) argue that one may experience conflict between the desire to gather information about a novel stimulus and the force of social sanctions against staring at others. In some settings this would lead to visual avoidance and in others displayed advertence, depending on the relative strength of these opposing forces. Kleck (1968) found male secondary school students to return the gaze of a steadily gazing male confederate when the confederate played the role of a leg-amputee as compared to a physically normal peer. The effect was significant only for listening periods. Langer et al. (1976) suggest that during conversation, monitoring another is acceptable, particularly when listening to the other speak.

Arguing that social norms permit staring at publicly displayed photographs and thus increase the likelihood of novel stimulus perusal, Langer et al. (1976) unobtrusively measured the duration of visual fixation to pictures of handicapped, pregnant, and normal persons. Females stared for longer periods of time at photographs that depicted handicapped as compared to normal members of the same sex. Pregnant women seemed to fall in the "novel" category for female viewers, as they were stared at longer than normal women but less than handicapped. Males were observed to gaze at exhibited photographs less when observed by a female experimental accomplice. While observed, males gazed at photos of normal males more than hunchback males. This pattern was reversed when participants were not obviously observed. In a third study, Langer et al. (1976) reasoned that opportunity for pre-interaction visual access to a novel stimulus (a handicapped or pregnant female) would reduce the proposed conflict as a result of reduction in novelty of the stimulus. Males and females who were able to view the female confederate prior to interaction sat closer to the confederate than participants who were not given such visual access. Lack of prior visual access, and thus lack of reduction in stimulus novelty, led to spatial avoidance of a handicapped or pregnant woman compared to the level of avoidance of the same woman in a normal state.

Thompson (1982) observed the incidence of visual attention directed toward handicapped versus nonhandicapped persons who were either seated in a restaurant or moving through a shopping mall. In the restaurant, handicapped persons, in comparison with nonhandicapped persons, waited longer for the waitress to take their order, had fewer but longer interactions with the waitress, and a lower frequency and percentage of mutual gaze with the waitress. While walking through the mall, the frequency of stares directed toward handicapped and nonhandicapped persons did not differ, but the handicapped persons were stared at significantly longer than the nonhandicapped. Thompson argues that the conflict between novelty and social constraints on staring might exist only when one interacts with the handicapped person. Handicapped persons passed on public walkways, however, may be reduced to a non-person status, which would reduce the social sanction against staring at them.

This line of research points to the importance of considering the attention-attracting salience of a target of interpersonal gaze in addition to the various dispositions, characteristics, and states of the gazer, and the situated social norms for the display of attention. It is likely that other less dramatic aspects of the physical appearance of individuals, such as, for example, attractiveness, would also catch the eye of pedestrians and perhaps be less subject to sanctions against continued visual attention during focused interaction (see Kleinke, Staneski, & Pipp, 1975). Chance's (1967) concept of the attention structure of a group similarly emphasizes the perceptual salience of dominance displays. Further, individuals differ with respect to their tendency to dress and carry themselves in a manner that would attract notice. The study of social gaze in general is based on the premise that other people per se constitute a salient aspect of our social world. The work of Chance (1967),

Langer et al. (1976), and Thompson (1982) leads to the conclusion that some individuals are more salient than others.

Gaze as it is Related to More Temporary States or Circumstances

The research reviewed in this section examines the impact of naturally and experimentally produced circumstances on the production of and response to social visual behavior. Consideration is given to the relationship between social gaze and physiological arousal, emotion, embarrassment, lying and credibility, degree of acquaintance, cooperation and competition, seating position, symmetry of observation, and dominance and affiliation.

Mutual gaze and physiological arousal. Philosophers (e.g., Sartre, 1957) and psychologists (e.g., Argyle & Dean, 1965) have suggested that extended mutual gaze is an extremely arousing interpersonal stimulus. Several investigators have experimentally studied this proposition by evaluating the relationship between mutual versus averted gaze and various measures of physiological arousal. Typically subjects are instructed to gaze steadily in silence at a live or videotaped confederate who returns or averts his or her gaze across trials, in some cases with simultaneous variation in other nonverbal variables. Changes in physiological measures recorded during the session are then related to the presence or absence of confederate gaze.

McBride, King, and James (1965), in a study of the physiological concomitants of interpersonal spacing, reported higher levels of GSR for both male and female participants when they were gazed at by a male or female confederate. Cross-sex dyads evidenced somewhat higher arousal levels than same-sex dyads. Similar results were obtained by Nichols and Champness (1971). Mutual gaze between subject and confederate produced significantly greater frequency and amplitude in GSR compared to that obtained when the confederate's gaze was averted from the subject. In this case however no sex differences were obtained. Leavitt and Donovan (1979) and Donovan and Leavitt (1980) found no skin conductance discrimination between the directed and averted gaze of a videotaped confederate. In the latter study, however, male and female participants produced higher levels of GSR to a male as compared to a female target regardless of gaze condition. The authors suggest that the videotaped display may not be as potent as that provided by a live confederate.

In a series of studies, Gale and his associates have investigated EEG responsiveness to variations in the gaze of a confederate. Both males (Gale, Lucas, Nissim, & Harpham, 1972; Gale, Spratt, Chapman, & Smallbone, 1975) and females (Gale, Kingsley, Brookes, & Smith, 1978) evidenced greater EEG arousal when gazed at than when not. Gale et al. (1978) further demonstrated that this arousal occurred in females (only females participated in this study) both when they were in the role of gazer and the recipient of the gaze. Martin and Gardner (1979), however, failed to replicate EEG responsiveness to gaze variation in male participants when gaze was crossed with smiling. Further, smiling was related to lower amplitude EEG (i.e., greater arousal) only in early trials.

Kleinke and Pohlen (1971) measured the tonic heart rate (HR) of males who played 50 trials of a Prisoner's Dilemma game with a male confederate. Higher HR levels were obtained when the confederate gazed directly at the participant compared to when the confederate averted his eyes from the participant's face. Donovan and Leavitt (1980) presented males and females with videotaped displays of males and females who gazed at (into the lens) or away from recipients. Sex of subject and target interacted with gaze condition. Male subjects confronted with a male target responded with HR deceleration (orienting response) that habituated across trials. All other sex combinations produced HR deceleration that did not habituate over time. Donovan and Leavitt (1980) suggest that these results may reflect a greater tendency for male dyads to engage in power struggles and avoid intimacy in comparison to female and mixed-sex dyads.

Although in these constrained, asocial situations mutual gaze does seem to result in physiological arousal, Martin and Gardner (1979) raise a number of important questions concerning the generalizability of the findings. Nonverbal actions typically occur in combination. When Martin and Gardner (1979) crossed smiling and gaze, the gaze effect did not occur. Gaze may have become a particularly salient, arousing stimulus in these situations in which it was the only thing that varied. Further, in the preceding studies the participants merely gazed at a confederate in the absence of any conversation. As Donovan and Leavitt (1980) point out, steadily unbroken mutual gaze of 10–18 seconds in silence are non-normative. The lab studies relating physiological arousal and gaze may reflect the arousing properties of non-normative situations rather than the arousing properties of mutual gaze per se. An important, if difficult, next step in this line of research would be to distinguish between those contexts in which the direct gaze of another is an arousing cue and those in which it is not.

Gaze and the expression of emotion.   The role of gaze direction in the facial expression of emotion has received relatively limited attention compared to that given the action of the facial muscles. Ekman and Friesen (1975), for example, describe, as part of their six basic facial expressions of emotion, the positions of the brows, and musculature surrounding the eyes, but do not discuss any particular visual focus associated with the expressions. With two exceptions, the photographs in their book show the individual displaying the emotion gazing straight into the lens of the camera, as if gazing at the viewer. The exceptions are two displays of sadness.

Several researchers report less partner-directed gaze concomitant with the display of sorrow, despair, or sadness. Fromme and Schmidt (1972) recorded the gaze behavior of male volunteers as they role played fear, sorrow, and anger as well as a neutral expression. The duration of gaze directed at a male confederate during the expression of sorrow was about half that observed for the expression of the other emotions. Lalljee (reported in Argyle & Cook, 1976, p. 79) had actresses enact emotions to a camera as if the camera was another person. Percentage gaze at the camera was highest for the enactment of surprise, excitement, joy, and scorn, and lowest for despair, rage, annoyance, and anxiety. Female participants induced to feel depressed gazed at a female confederate less frequently and for briefer durations than participants induced to feel elated (Natale, 1977).

Exline, Paredes, Gottheil, and Winkelmayer (1979) filmed schizophrenic and normal-control females while they recounted happy, sad, and angry personal experiences to a male interviewer. For the normal, but not the schizophrenic, women, gaze directed toward the interviewer was greatest during their telling of a happy experience, and downward gaze was greatest for the sad story. This pattern was most clearly displayed for those normal females whose experiences were rated as particularly intense in content. Male and female judges viewed silent recordings of these sessions and rated which of a target person's three film clips they regarded as representing the recounting of a happy, sad, or angry experience. Judges' ratings significantly corresponded to the displayed visual behavior. Stories were rated as happy when the direct gaze minus downward gaze difference was greatest, angry when the difference was intermediate, and sad when the difference score was lowest. This was particularly true for the normal compared to the schizophrenic target females. Direct gaze was, however, not related to judging accuracy (judging a happy story as happy regardless of gaze pattern). Thus, it seems as if the judges had expectations about the gaze pattern associated with the display of these three affects that they employed to make their ratings in the absence of the verbal channel.

Kimble and Olszewski (1980) and Kimble, Forte, and Yoshikawa (1981) recorded gaze directed at a camera and at a male assistant (only Kimble et al., 1981) by female participants who enacted a positive, liking or negative, anger message. Instructions were given to display the message either with great intensity or with ambivalence. In both studies, a greater percentage of gaze was directed at the recipient when the enactment was intense rather than ambivalent. The authors argue that gaze is related more to the intensity of expression than to the specific affective tone.

Gaze has also been found to be related to state anxiety. Wiens et al. (1980) found frequency of interviewer-directed gazes to be positively correlated with a self-report measure of state anxiety. Increased frequency of gaze within a fixed time period is typically negatively related to gaze duration. In this study, however, state anxiety was not significantly related to length of looking. Jurich and Jurich (1974) experimentally induced state anxiety in female participants by having a male assistant interview them on premarital sexual attitudes. Lower levels of returned gaze with the interviewer were significantly associated with subject's increased ratings of their own anxiety ($r = .42$) and observer's ratings of the subject's anxiety ($r = .79$). Lower levels of gaze were further associated with increased physiological arousal as measured by finger sweat prints.

Much work remains to be done to clarify the relationship between gaze direction and the expression of emotion. It may be that the direction of gaze does not play a role in the expression of emotion per se, that, instead, emotion is conveyed through facial patterning. One can imagine the pictured expressions in Ekman and Friesen's (1975) book with the gaze directed at a number of different angles. What seems to change in this exercise is not the emotion expressed, but rather the target or stimulus of the emotion. Lalljee (reported in Argyle & Cook, 1976) suggested that higher levels of camera-directed gaze in his study were associated with emotions that could be characterized as having an external focus. When the target of the affect could be construed as the self, gaze levels were lower. It might also be suggested that the extent of partner-directed gaze in the expression of emotion may reflect the willingness or desire of the individual to involve the other in the emotion. The observed regularities between gaze direction and emotional expression may reflect cultural norms concerning the degree of openness one should feel and display while experiencing particular emotions. The results of Kimble and his associates (Kimble & Olszewski, 1980; Kimble et al., 1981), namely, a positive relationship between gaze level and emotional intensity, may vary depending on the degree of comfort and appropriateness of expressing such intensity toward another particular individual.

Gaze level and embarrassment.   Folk wisdom would have it that the facial blush of embarrassment would be accompanied by the avoidance of (particularly) mutual gaze with other present parties. One does not want to be observed while losing face. Although it is a bit like the ostrich who sticks its head in the sand, avoiding mutual gaze with others enables one to briefly disengage from an uncomfortable interaction.

Modigliani (1971) experimentally created a situation in which male participants succeeded or failed at a task while they were observed by others (publically) or while they were alone (privately). Public failure resulted in decreased mutual gaze with a male confederate compared to public success that was followed by increased confederate-directed gaze. Modigliani (1971) does not regard these gaze changes as reflecting embarrassment, however, because within-group self-reported level of embarrassment was not correlated with gaze level. He suggests that the decreased gaze may have displayed a negative evaluation of a gazing and critical confederate.

Edelmann and Hampson (1979) attempted to embarrass male and female participants by having an interviewer report that he had drawn a picture the participants had chosen as the one they liked least. Self-report measures of embarrassment were obtained. Participants who indicatd embarrassment decreased gaze at the interviewer during the critical phase of the interview, whereas nonembarrassed participants increased their gaze level during this time period. Embarrassed participants also displayed an increase in speech disturbances. Their lower level of gaze may have reflected cognitive planning as well as a desire for momentary reduced involvement with the interviewer.

Gaze level in relation to lying and credibility. Our common social knowledge also proposes that the honest, and therefore, credible, person looks you in the eye when speaking to you. This proposition has been evaluated with both encoding and decoding methodologies.

When instructed to lie or conceal information, experimental participants tend to gaze at an interaction partner more than those not so instructed. For example, Sitton and Griffin (1981) found that both black and white females, told to lie about personal information during an intake interview with a counselor gazed at the counselor more than participants who had not received such instructions.

Lie or conceal instructions have also been found to interact with sex of participant. Burns and Kintz (1976) found females to engage in longer confederate-directed glances compared to males when told to lie. This particularly held true when the confederate was male. Male participants gazed more at a female confederate when instructed to lie as compared to when they told the truth. This difference did not occur with male confederates. Males and females were asked to conceal information or given no instructions during an interview by Exline et al. (1965). Females returned the gaze of a steadily gazing male or female interviewer while listening to the interviewer speak more when concealing versus no instruction. Male participants engage in a greater proportion of looking while listening when not instructed to conceal information rather than when so instructed.

Fugita, Hogrebe, and Wexley (1980) observed males to gaze more when instructed to attempt to deceive an "expert" in deception detection compared with a "non-expert." Other measured facial cues did not vary with the perceived expertise of the recipients in detecting deception.

Lying has also been found to interact with personality. Exline, Thibaut, Hickey, and Gumpert (1970) implicated high and low Machiavellian males and females in cheating during an experimental session. Low Machs decreased their gaze level with an experimenter from a base-line period to a preaccusation interview. Their gaze level dropped even lower when accused of cheating. High Machs, on the other hand, did not decrease their gaze from base line to preaccusation and further increased their gaze when accused. It was suggested that the proposed emotional detachment and social manipulative skills of the high Mach enabled a skilled performance in this setting.

The encoding research just described suggests that folk wisdom educates our attempts to lie and/or conceal, although we may tend to overshoot the mark. The relationship between direct gazing and truthful communication merits further attention. Some truths are more difficult to express than others; some lies are fairly easy to put over. We may be more invested in the communication of certain messages, both true and false. These factors would likely influence our inclination to gaze directly at another while discussing the issues in question.

Within a decoding paradigm, male and female audience members found an informative speech more credible when the speaker gazed at the audience rather than at her notes (Beebe, 1974). Hemsley and Doob (1978) videotaped three male confederates who were portraying an alibi witness in a jury trial. Male and female judges regarded the witness as less credible when he gazed downward while giving testimony than when he gazed at the lens of the camera. Also, the defendant was more likely to be found guilty in the downward compared to direct-gaze condition. Post-experimental interviews suggested that downward but not direct gaze in this situation was a particularly salient cue. The authors argued that the viewers may have expected and therefore not particularly noticed direct gaze, as it did not produce a complementary positive response on the part of the respondants. In line with Goodwin's (1981) work (described earlier), direct gaze was relevantly absent in this context.

Gaze and the degree of quality of relationship. Rutter and Stephenson (1979) observed same-sex dyads of friends or strangers while they discussed items of disagreement from a sociopolitical questionnaire, under competitive or cooperative instructions. The only significant effect revealed that friends gazed less at each other than did strangers. This finding was interpreted to mean that social visual behavior primarily serves an information-gathering rather than an expressive function. Friends would require less information about each other than strangers.

The degree of partner-directed monitoring might be expected to vary with the intensity of a relationship. Rubin (1970) recorded the visual interaction of mixed-sex couples in which both members scored above or below the median on his scale of romantic love. It was hypothesized that the absorption and exclusiveness of romantic love would be displayed through a greater tendency of strong-love couples to visually monitor one another, compared to weak-love couples. During a 3-minute free conversation, there was a tendency for strong-love couples to gaze mutually at one another more than weak-love couples. This occurred only when strong-love couple members were paired with their significant other, but not when they were paired with an opposite-sex stranger who scored similarly on the love scale. Strong-love couples engaged in significantly greater "mutual focus" (the proportion of total looking time which was mutual) than weak-love couples, again, only when together rather than with a stranger. Goldstein, Kilroy, and Van de Voort (1976) demonstrated that this effect was not a result of greater amounts of talking in the strong-love couple conversations. Strong-love couples did spend more time talking than weak-love couples; however they also spent more time gazing at each other during silent periods.

Newlywed couples who differed in their degree of self-reported marital discord were observed by Beier and Sternberg (1977). Couples reporting the least disagreement looked at each other the most, also sat closer to one another, and touched each other more than did high-discord couples.

Sex differences in displayed intimacy were obtained by Smith and Sheahan (1979), who recorded conversations of intimate and non-intimate mixed-sex couples. Males engaged in longer durations of visual monitoring while interacting with a non-intimate. Females, on the other hand, exhibited greater gaze duration in conversation with an intimate.

Variations in visual monitoring between individuals have further been shown to influence the attributions of others regarding the nature of the relationship two people share. Perceived mutual gaze between two males in still photographs was significantly and positively correlated with perceived intimacy by male viewers (Scherer & Schiff, 1973). Thayer and Schiff had judges rate the perceived length of relationship (1974) and the perceived sexual interest (1977) of filmed same- and mixed-sex dyads. One partner gazed at the other briefly or for a more extended duration, and this gaze was either reciprocated or not by the other. Long, reciprocated gazes were associated with attributions of longer relationships than other gaze-pattern combinations. Higher order interactions revealed that long, non-reciprocated gazes in male–male dyads led to the briefest relationship ratings, whereas long, non-reciprocated gaze of a male toward a female led to ratings of the longest term relationships. Sexual interest was perceived to be greater between mixed-sex pairs who reciprocated long gazes.

Kleinke, Meeker, and La Fong (1974) made videotapes of mixed-sex pairs role playing engaged couples. Couples who gazed at each other were perceived as liking each other more and being generally more positive than couples who failed to monitor one another.

Information about the degree of prior acquaintance influenced the perception subjects had of pairs who gazed steadily or did not look at one another

(Abele, 1981). Male judges described steady gazing as more potent and active than no partner gazing if the pair was believed to have been previously acquainted. This difference was not obtained for unacquainted pairs.

Although strangers may monitor each other more than friends, within groups greater amounts of looking seem to be associated with a more positive orientation for both encoders and decoders.

Gaze in cooperative versus competitive interactions. The achievement of both cooperative and competitive interactions would involve an individual's ability to coordinate own actions with others and to this extent likely make use of visual monitoring to accomplish the coordination. However, the differential nature of these interpersonal orientations would suggest different patterns of partner-directed attention.

Foddy (1978) observed males and females in same-sex dyads as they worked on minimum necessary share game under a competitive or cooperative set. Dyads operating within a cooperative set engaged in on the average longer gazes than competitive set dyads. Foddy demonstrates that this effect was not a result of different levels of speaking within the two-set conditions and further argues that the gaze behavior of participants was employed to establish and maintain a type of relationship appropriate to the co-orientation set.

Relatively higher levels of partner-directed gazing in cooperative compared to competitive interactions may not always be perceived favorably. Kleinke and Pohlen (1971) found males to report feeling more friendly toward a confederate cooperator who looked down at the work table rather than gazing at them steadily. In this situation, however, the participants did not converse with each other, and the steady gaze may have become aversive.

In the context of integrative bargaining research, Lewis and Fry (1977) manipulated interaction orientation motives. Participants operating under an individualistic motive were more likely to discover mutually advantageous solutions if visual access during their conversation was blocked by a barrier separating them. When instructed to consider their partner's position, the barrier had no effect on their problem solving. The mutual lack of visual access may have limited personal control tendencies in the individualistic condition.

Orientations that participants bring to an interaction may interact with the structure created by the experimenter. In a post hoc analysis, Exline (1963) reports that high-*n* affiliative men and women gazed less at group (triad) members when competition, rather than cooperation, was made salient through experimental instructions. Low-*n* affiliators, on the other hand, gazed at each other more in competitive versus cooperative interactions.

Jellison and Ickes (1974) considered why an individual would want to see another. With Heider (1958), they suggest that perception gives one some measure of control over the portion of the environment taken in. The power of perception resides in all co-present participants, and further, some interaction formats would potentially minimize or maximize one's desire to see or be seen. Male participants in Jellison and Ickes' (1974) study were led to anticipate a competitive or cooperative interaction with another. Further, they believed they would either interview (see) or be interviewed by (be seen by) this other. Participants were asked to choose whether they would like to have a panel between them during the interview open or closed. Those anticipating a competitive interaction desired the panel closed if they were to be interviewed, and open if they were to be the interviewer. If participants expected a cooperative (vs. competitive) interaction, they were more likely to desire the panel open. This was particularly the case if they were to interview the other. Postexperimental interviews suggested that individuals who selected the atypical panel position when anticipating a competitive encounter did so for their believed ability, or lack of same, to influence the partner.

Gaze and seating position.   Seating position, which refers to the bodily orientation of seated participants (e.g., side-by-side, cornering, directly across), is the variable that has received much attention, particularly following the work of Sommer (1969). Seating positions seem to influence the nature of interactions partially through the ease of visual access afforded by different orientations. The across position is usually accompanied by a greater degree of partner-directed gazing than the side-by-side position (Aiello, 1972, Muirhead & Goldman, 1979). The across position may also stimulate greater levels of participation. Caproni, Levine, O'Neal, McDonald, & Gray, (1977) observed seminar sessions in which the instructor changed his seat across meetings. Students who sat across from the instructor talked more than students in other positions, which the authors believed was because of the easy visual access in this position compared to others. They also noted a tendency for certain individuals to be more likely to take this seat. In a review of the seating literature, Greenberg (1976) reports that leaders tend to sit in positions permitting easy eye contact with the largest number of group members. It would seem, as Jellison and Ickes (1974) suggest, that leaders make use of the perceptual power of, for example, the head of the table position.

Observing and being observed.   Argyle and his associates (Argyle & Ingram, 1972; Argyle, Lalljee, & Cook, 1968; Argyle & Williams, 1969) have investigated conditions that influence one's perception of seeing or observing others, versus being seen or observed by them. In an interview setting (Argyle & Williams, 1969), the person in the interviewee role felt more observed than the interviewer, and females felt more observed than males. Responses to a questionnaire (Argyle & Williams, 1969) revealed that males and females reported feeling more observed when meeting an older as compared to a younger person. These results were somewhat weaker for older respondents. With peers, females reported feeling more observed than males. Argyle and Williams (1969) investigated whether feeling observed could be regarded as a cognitive orientation of the individual or actually related to situational cues of observation. Male and female participants interacted with an opposite sex confederate who gazed at them for a small or large proportion of the interaction period. Feeling observed was unrelated to the confederate's level of gaze. Estimates of confederate gaze level were inaccurate with respect to the extent to which the confederate actually looked at participants but were significantly and positively correlated with the extent to which participants felt observed. Further, those participants who reported feeling observed in general (i.e., in their everyday lives) gazed less at the confederate than those not tending to feel observed.

Argyle, Lalljee, and Cook (1968) questioned participants who interacted in varying conditions of visibility (e.g., wearing sunglasses speaking through a one-way screen, etc.) vis-a-vis another. Greater discomfort was experienced when the conditions of visibility were asymmetrical, although discomfort was somewhat less if the self could see and the other could not. Females reported being more uncomfortable than males by not being able to see their partners, even when they were unseen themselves.

Dominant and affiliative aspects of social gaze.   The implied power associated with the role of observer is reminiscent of the aggressive, threatening stare of nonhuman primates. Ellsworth, Carlsmith, and Henson (1972) investigated the impact of the steady stare on human receivers. In a series of field studies, male and female confederates either gazed steadily (with neutral face) or glanced at and then looked away from motorists and pedestrians waiting at a traffic intersection. When the light changed, those individuals who were stared at crossed the intersection more rapidly than those who were only glanced at. This effect occurred regardless of the same composition of the confederate-motorist/pedestrian dyad. The speedier departures did not seem to be a function of the potentially atypical qualities of the stimulus, as motorist speed was not affected by the presence of an experimenter banging on the sidewalk with a hammer. The authors interpret the steady gaze in this context as threatening. The confederate's display had ambiguous implications for receivers. They fled in response.

Greenbaum and Rosenfeld (1978) varied several aspects of a confederate's nonverbal behavior and measured a wider range of response components in a similar context. Male confederates stared, with a neutral face, or looked away from motorists as they approached a red traffic light. The stare manipulation was produced at eight distances from the curb, and the stare was accompanied or not by lowered brows. Somewhat less than half the motorists avoided the situation by pulling ahead of or staying behind "normal" intersection placement. As this response occurred prior to the stare manipulation, it was likely a response to the confederate's physical distance from the curb. The relative frequency of backward avoidance was greater the closer the confederate was to the curb, and female drivers were more likely to backward avoid than males. About half the motorists pulled to a "normal placement" position but avoided the situation by greater lateral displacement from the curb compared to the forward and backward placement group, especially female drivers. Departure speed was greater in the stare condition, and female motorists gazed at the confederate less when he stared at them than when he gazed away. A very small proportion of motorists behaved as if they regarded the placement and gaze of the confederate as friendly. They pulled to the normal placement position, spoke to the confederate, looked at him, and left the intersection more slowly than the nonverbalizing normal placement participants. This group tended to be composed of males who had their automobile window open. Although most drivers acted as though the stare, especially when performed close to the curb, was aversive, it is significant that a few did not.

Avoidance of a staring confederate has also been reported in library study areas (Smith, Stanford, & Goldman, 1977), elevators (Buchanan, Goldman, & Juhnke, 1977), and church pews (Campbell & Lancioni, 1979). Smith et al. (1977) report sex differences in response to the steady gaze of male and female confederates who sat at a table where a lone student worked in a library. Females left the table sooner than males, particularly when the starer was male. Females also glanced at the confederate less than males. Female confederates on the other hand were glanced at more than male confederates. Smith et al. (1977) describe the male subjects as demonstrating more interest or curiosity and less overt intimidation than females, particularly with a female starer.

In the discussion of their series of studies, Ellsworth, Carlsmith, and Henson (1972) suggested that the flight response they observed might have resulted from the contextual surround of the steady stare rather than the act of staring itself. The stare seemed to demand some sort of interpersonal response, but the ambiguity of the situation made it unclear what specific response would be appropriate. If participants had been able to unambiguously interpret the stare, thus implying a set of potential responses to it, they might have been encouraged to even approach the starer rather than flee. Ellsworth and Langer (1976) provide support for this proposition. Shoppers at a large mall were more likely to approach, without hesitation, a young woman who apparently needed help if her problem was clearly identified (lost contact lens) as compared to the condition in which her situation was more ambiguous (seemed to be unwell). This effect was more likely if the young woman stared at the passerby.

Others have also found the steady gaze versus gaze aversion of a confederate to incrase the likelihood of compliance with both explicit and implicit
unambiguous requests. Further, the sex composition of the confederate-
subject dyad typically influences compliance levels. Male and female hitch-
hikers were more likely to be offered a ride if they stared at approaching drivers than if they looked away from the drivers (Snyder, Grether, & Keller,
1974). A larger proportion of males compared to females stopped, particularly when the hitchhiker was female. Kleinke (1977) found shoppers more
likely to comply with a female confederate's request for a dime if she gazed at
them while making the request. Males were more likely to give her a dime
than were females. Airport patrons were more likely to comply with a legitimate request from a female (asking for a dime to make an important phone
call) if the request was accompanied by gaze versus no gaze (Kleinke, 1980).
Again males were more likely to comply than females. Compliance with an illegitimate request (e.g., asking for a dime for a candy bar) was not effected
by the presence or absence of gaze in one study, but in a second study, gaze
reduced the likelihood of compliance with an illegitimate request. Kleinke
(1980) suggested that gaze aversion in the illegitimate request condition
served to humble the person making the request and therefore make her appear more acceptable to a potential benefactor.

Vallentine and Ehrlichman (1979) observed the effects of gaze or its absence in an implicit request context. Male and female confederates with one
arm in a sling fumbled with and dropped coins at a bus stop in the presence of
an individual who was waiting alone for the bus to arrive. Gaze at the individual (vs. gazing at the dropped coins) was associated with a greater likelihood
of assistance in picking up the money if both confederate and subject were female. Conversely, males were more likely to help another male if gaze was absent rather than present. Employing a similar paradigm, Vallentine (1980)
found the gaze of a female victim (coin dropper) directed toward a potential
helper to reduce the likelihood of the bystander effect. Females waiting at a
bus stop were more likely to assist in picking up the dropped coins when they
were gazed at directly versus not gazed at if another confederate bus patron
was also present. The gaze seemed to target the individual as a helper. When
the second confederate was absent, gazing at the coins was more effective in
soliciting help than gazing at the potential helper.

Lefebvre (1975) instructed half the male participants in his study to attempt to get a female confederate to stay on for a brief discussion after they
completed a task they worked on together. As the pair was not permitted to
speak while they worked on the task, the focus was on nonverbal indicators
of what Lefebvre (1975) called "ingratiation." Participants gazed much more
at the confederate in the ingratiation condition compared to a condition in
which no such instructions were given. Further, the ingratiation males were
rated as much more likeable and attentive by a set of judges who viewed

videotapes of the interactions. The males in this study spontaneously employed partner-directed gaze as a precursor to making a request. It would be interesting to see whether gaze level would be lower under instructions to make an "illegitimate" request, which was found more effective by Kleinke (1980).

The research indicates that the power of the gaze in these contexts is influenced by the ambiguity of the situation, the sex composition of the dyad involved, the legitimacy of the request, and the presence or absence of others. When moving through the public domain, people probably have a set of assumptions about how others will and/or should behave vis-a-vis themselves, and perhaps also stable or transitory inclinations to relate to others in a particular manner.

The pedestrian-passing research, described earlier (see: Initiating Versus Avoiding Interactions), indicates that people frequently display inattention (civil or otherwise) to those around them as they move through public places. The emphasis here is on the word display, for Goodwin's (1981) work would suggest we are peripherally aware of others and from this information can coordinate our activities with theirs. How else would we avoid collision on sidewalks? These displays are further reminiscent of Callan, Chance, and Pitcairn's (1973) "modes of presentation" or advertence among psychiatric patients. They constitute socially appropriate ways of orienting to, or relating to, the many unknown individuals who inhabit and traverse our communities.

To some extent, the field investigations of the impact of steady gaze under varying circumstances presented the participating populace with an atypical social situation. Atypical in the sense that only a small portion of the strangers we encounter in public settings stare steadily at us and/or approach us with requessts. The norm of public inattention is more usually operable. The confederates in these studies were proposing a shift, in Goffman's (1963) terms, from an unfocused to a focused interaction. The displays may be thought of as indicating something about the confederate, whether consistent tendency or temporary condition, which may or may not be correct. Further, the displays have implications for receivers. They suggest a type of focused interaction, a way of relating, in which the receiver may or may not wish to become involved, depending on the interpretation or meaning (both cognitive and affective) they construct about what is going on, and what is required of them. Socially self-confident persons may feel they can handle virtually any situation, and respond on the basis of considerations other than fear. A small proportion of the subjects in Greenbaum and Rosenfeld's (1978) study seemed to accept the invitation to focused interaction and proposed by their own behavior a friendly tone for the interaction. They may not all have necessarily construed the situation as clearly friendly, but rather than have been attempting a relational maneuver of their own, the tendency to do so being likely to depend on stable and/or transitory inclinations for types of involvement. Some individuals might be expected to turn such an encounter into an overt aggressive interaction. Some, perhaps very lonely, persons might be expected to attempt contact with virtually anyone they encounter. This seems to be the case with some senior citizens. These factors might be expected to interact with situational stimulus ambiguity and ambiguity tolerance of the receiver in producing responses to steady gaze in the public domain.

When the nature of the proposed interaction is less ambiguous, as in direct requests for aid, other-directed gaze is associated with generally greater compliance unless the request is regarded as illegitimate, or perhaps socially unacceptable. The individual's ideo-affective (Tomkins, 1965) construction of the situation and their tendency to involve themselves in the understood interaction seems to play a mediating role.

The reported sex effects taken together suggest that females are less willing than males to participate in such encounters, particularly if their proposed co-participant is male. Perhaps females are less certain of their ability to successfully negotiate an acceptable encounter with an unknown male. Female confederates, on the other hand, are approached more often than male confederates by both males and females. Even males may have concern for their ability to impact on other males to produce an acceptable interaction.

The study of minimal social encounters, such as those described previously, provide us with important insights into processes through which we manage our relations in public. Further, they may provide us with clues about the negotiation of interpersonal orientations in conversations, and relationships of longer duration. The incorporation of individual-difference measures may be achieved by having participants complete relevant questionnaires in a laboratory setting and then observing them in a pedestrian-passing context as they leave the laboratory. Another technique would be to send participants to a second location during a study and observe their behavior en route. In this case, it would be easier to request self-report information following an encounter, including their responses to viewing a videotape of an encounter in which they were involved.

Among nonhuman primates, a steady stare directed at conspecifics (as opposed to the more guarded monitoring of low-status members of an attention structure) operates as a threat display. The work of Ellsworth et al. (1972) and other suggests that under certain conditions humans respond as if the steady stare had a similar impact. Primates may avoid or escape an aggressive encounter by averting their gaze from another member of the group. Gaze aversion in such cases seems to function as an appeasement gesture that inhibits aggressive acts that might otherwise be directed at an animal. Ellsworth and Carlsmith (1973) investigated the possibility that gaze aversion might function in a similar manner among humans. Whereas ethologists would argue that averted gaze would inhibit aggression, Ellsworth and Carlsmith (1973) point out that Zimbardo's deindividuation theory would predict the reverse, i.e., that gaze aversion would limit contact between individuals and therefore make it easier to treat others as nonpersons and perhaps behave more aggressively toward them. Male participants who were angered or treated positively by a male confederate were subsequently given the opportunity to deliver shocks to this same confederate. The investigators varied in the visual behavior of the confederate following a warning signal that could be followed by shock. He would: (a) Gaze steadily at the subject following all warning signals, (b) consistently glance at the subject and then gaze avert downward, or (c) vary his behavior by gazing steadily on some trials, and gazing downward following a quick glance on others. The level of shock delivered to nonangered subjects was relatively low and fairly consistent across conditions. Angered subjects, on the other hand, delivered more shock to the confederate who consistently gaze averted compared to the consistently gazing confederate. When the confederate's gaze was variable, he received more shock when he looked at the participant than when he gazed down at the table. This occurred regardless of the affective nature of their prior interaction. Also, regardless of the condition they were in, subjects reported that the confederate's steady gaze was aversive. The aversiveness seemed to inhibit aggression by the angered participants when the gaze was consistent. However, when the confederate's gaze varied, participants acted as though they might be able to gain control of the behavior by punishing (shocking) performances of it. Part of the aversiveness of the steady stare in public settings may relate to its unresponsive nature. People might be more likely to become involved with another on whom they may be able to exert some influence. If their reading of the situation suggests that, not only is the encounter likely to be negative but that it will be one in which they might not be able to negotiate a change in affect, then flight, when possible and available as an alternative, constitutes a very sensible response.

Although consistent gaze aversion failed to thwart aggressive actions in Ellsworth and Carlsmith's (1973) study, it may be sometimes employed in a manner that suggests an appeasement interpretation. The steady stare is sometimes likened to an invasion of another's personal space, albeit accomplished from a distance. When forced into crowded conditions, individuals may signal a lack of interest in relationships of appreciable intensity, whether aggressive or friendly, by gazing away from the faces of others. Hutt and Vaizey (1966) interpret the impact of autists' gaze aversion in crowded conditions along these lines. Efran and Cheyne (1974) arranged for male participants to violate or not to violate the personal space of experimental assistants in a narrow hallway. Being forced to pass between two others (vs. passing by them, or passing by inanimate objects) was associated with downward head and gaze, as well as a number of mouth gestures interpreted as agonistic.

These authors were interested in the effects of crowding that they believe occur as a result of the accumulation of small negative encounters such as the
one they created. When males and females interacted in crowded or uncrowded areas, Ross, Layton, Erickson, and Schopler (1973) found males to
engage in less facial regard in the crowded versus uncrowded condition,
whereas the reverse was true for females. For both sexes, this effect occurred
only if participants were together for 20 compared with 5 minutes.

The deindividuating impact of steady gaze aversion in Ellsworth and
Carlsmith's (1973) study was mediated by the negative affective tone of the
encounter. Interestingly, this is precisely the context of gaze aversion's effectiveness among nonhuman primates. From the work to date it would appear
that a counter threatening signal is more effective in limiting aggressive acts
in humans.

The expectations people have concerning the appropriate orientation of
others to themselves seems to vary with social context. In the course of an ongoing conversation, we might expect greater attention or a more direct orientation from others, particularly when we speak. The tendency to look at a
conversation partner more while listening to them speak, compared to when
we ourselves speak, has been taken as evidence of such a norm of attention
(Exline, Ellyson, & Long, 1975). If steady gaze may be part of a potent
display in public settings, to some extent in violation of a norm of inattention, in conversations the reverse may be the case. It has already been reported (see section on gaze and personality) that more dominant- or control-
oriented persons give less visual attention to another's speech than those less
so inclined. This result has been replicated in contexts in which the relative
power, control, or status of individuals was experimentally manipulated.

Nevill (1974) generated dependency in males and females by withdrawing
assistance on a very difficult anagram task, in comparison to a non-
dependency group for whom help was not withdrawn. During a subsequent
interview, dependent participants gazed at the interviewer significantly more
than nondependents. Exline, Ellyson, and Long (1975) created legitimate
(ROTC officer and cadet) and illegitimate (peers from a physical education
class) power hierarchies by assigning one member (ROTC officer and, randomly, one of the gym class peers) control over the outcomes of a discussion
problem task for both. High-power members were further privately instructed to benefit themselves in the division of rewards. Low-power dyad
members gazed more at their partners than the high-power member gazed at
them while they discussed the tasks. This was more characteristic of legitimate compared to illegitimate power hierarchies.

When visual behavior is coded with respect to conversational role, the
greater attentiveness of subordinate individuals is displayed during listening
rather than speaking periods. In a second study, pairing only ROTC officers
and cadets in identical discussion tasks, Exline et al. (1975) found low-power

members to gaze more at their partners while listening to them speak than when speaking themselves. Proportions of looking while listening and speaking were not different for high-power persons. ROTC officers who received high leadership ratings at a summer camp training program gazed less at their cadet partners than officers who were not rated as favorably.

Similar patterns have been reported for women (Ellyson, Dovidio, & Fehr, 1981). Females were paired for discussion with a female confederate who was presented as being of either higher or lower status than the participant. Participants were also observed in a second conversation with a nonconfederate peer. Peer and lower status social positions were accompanied by greater looking while listening than while speaking. The high-status role produced listening and speaking gaze levels that were not different.

Exline, Ellyson, and Long (1975) argue that individuals with designated power or control in a social context need not attend to subordinates. They are the ones who control outcomes. Lower status persons, however, are to some extent at the mercy of the powers that be. Attention upward in the hierarchy enables them to acquire the information necessary to adjust their performance to those governing costs and rewards. This is precisely the sort of attention structure observed by Chance (1967) among nonhuman primates and Vaughn and Waters (1981) in a preschool setting.

On first pass, it might appear that conflicting interpretations of social visual behavior have been obtained when the results of field and conversational studies are compared. In public settings, steady visual attention is responded to as a potent cue that may produce flight or compliance with a request. In conversational settings, on the other hand, the same attention appears to be a sign of one's subordinate position. Consideration of the specific nature of the visual attention in these two contexts may help resolve the apparent contradiction. Ellsworth and Carlsmith (1973) provide evidence that suggests the importance of the degree of variability in another's gaze behavior. Actions of another that vary are potentially subject to influence. Stable, consistent, and in the extreme, rigid actions may appear uncontrollable, and in this sense unresponsive to counteractions from a receiver. The steady gaze produced by confederates in public settings was unresponsive to displays of the recipients. There is a similar lack of interpersonal responsiveness in the listening gaze of dominant- and high-status conversants who display little visual attention to the speech of others. In both cases, the potency associated with a pattern of social gaze would appear to relate to a seeming lack of concern with the desires and agendas of the recipient. Furthermore, public stares and low levels of listener gaze are produced to some extent in violation of social norms governing displays of attention in the two contexts: a norm of inattention in public settings and a norm of attention in conversations. Thus, although potency in these two contexts is displayed through different patterns of gaze, the patterns share certain unresponsive and non-normative qualities.

Verbal interpretations of gaze behavior have been shown to correspond to the meaning inferred from the behavioral studies. Thayer (1969) found that males rated extended confederate gazes in silence as more dominant than brief gazes. Participants in the extended gaze condition also felt the confederate viewed them as less dominant than those in the brief gaze condition.

Dovidio and Ellyson (1982) produced a series of videotaped interactions in which the looking while listening and looking while speaking of actors and actresses was programmed. Participants viewing the silent tapes were presented with a straight-on picture of one person, shot over the shoulder of the conversation partner. Factor-analyzed semantic-differential ratings revealed that confederates who displayed higher, as compared to lower, visual dominance ratios (looking while speaking/looking while listening) were perceived as more potent by both male and female subjects. Dovidio and Ellyson (1982) reversed the numerator and denominator of the original visual dominance ration generated by Exline et al. (1975). When speaking and listening gaze are analyzed separately, potency ratings increase as looking while speaking increases and decreases as looking while listening increases. The placement of glances in the ongoing stream of events and the facial, postural surround of such glances would probably also influence the degree of perceived submissiveness. Individuals who quickly avert their gaze from another's face whenever the other looks at them would probably be perceived as submissive, regardless of their overall gaze levels. This would especially be the case if the gaze was accompanied by a submissive posture.

At the same time that the act of gazing at and away from another's face has been associated with relations of dominance and potency, it has also been associated with friendly and loving relations. Recall Rubin's (1970) strong-love couples who engaged in greater mutual focus than weak-love couples.

Overall greater levels of partner-directed gazing have been related to positive, friendly encounters. Pellegrini, Hicks, and Gordon (1970) found females who were instructed to role play liking and approval of a female confederate to gaze more at the confederate compared to participants who were given no instruction, or asked to role play dislike. Males' social-emotional evaluation of a male interviewer was positively correlated with their tendency to look at the interviewer (Goldberg, Kiesler, & Collins, 1969). Males and females judged that filmed interviewees liked an interviewer more when they gazed at him for 80 rather than 15% of the interaction period (Kleck & Nuessle, 1968). The higher level of gaze was also associated with a more positive evaluation of the interviewee. Beier and Sternberg (1977) found that couples who reported marital discord were less likely to look at each other while conversing than couples who reported less disagreement. Finally, sexual arousal, which may sometimes be interpreted to involve a positive orientation toward others, has been associated with higher levels of opposite-sex-directed gaze, particularly if the gazer favorably evaluates the arousal

(Griffitt, May, & Veitch, 1974). Artificial manipulation of gaze level, however, does not seem to influence the gazer's evaluation of a conversation partner. Kleinke, Staneski, and Berger (1975) found that experimentally increasing the level of males' visual attention toward a female confederate did not increase their liking for her. They suggested the participants were unaware of the increase in gaze, and it thus was ineffective in changing their attitude. Also, there would seem to be an upper limit to the positive relationship between looking and liking. Argyle, Lefebvre, and Cook (1974) report that participant's evaluations of various patterns of confederate gaze generally increased with gaze level but fell off somewhat when the confederate looked at them continuously.

Clinicians concerned with the nonverbal displays they present in therapeutic sessions have found filmed counselors to be rated as more genuine, competent, self-confident (Tipton & Rymer, 1978), and empathetic (Haase & Tepper, 1972; Tepper & Haase, 1978) the more they look at their clients. A word of caution is in order, however, concerning the generalizability of ratings made while viewing recorded interactions to actual therapy sessions. Fretz, Corn, Tuemmler, and Bellet (1979) found differential ratings of a filmed counselor's behavior not to hold up in actual counseling sessions. They argue that the counselor may have worked to facilitate the interaction in other ways when requested to lower their gaze level for the purposes of experimentation. Although this may be the case, other authors have reported actor–observer differences in ratings of nonverbal displays (e.g., Ellsworth & Ross, 1975; Holstein, Goldstein, & Bem, 1971), the implications of which need to be more fully investigated.

Males and females do not always identically produce, respond to, or interpret visual behavior in affiliative contexts. A number of interesting sex differences have been observed. Exline and Winters (1965a) observed the visual attention of males and females as they performed a creativity task before two steadily gazing confederates of the same sex as themselves. Halfway through the session, participants were asked to state a preference for one of the two confederate evaluators. Following this declaration, females increased their looking while speaking directed toward the preferred evaluator. Males decreased their looking while listening to the nonpreferred evaluator.

Ellsworth and Ross (1975) paired males and females in same-sex dyads ostensibly for a study of encounter-group exercises. One participant, who played the role of a quasiconfederate, was instructed to perform one of four gaze patterns as they listened to their partner speak. These four patterns included: (a) continuous gaze at the partner, (b) visual attention contingent upon an intimate revelation by the partner, (c) gaze aversion contingent on an intimate revelation, and (d) continuous gaze aversion. Females reported liking the participant-confederate more when she was visually attentive versus less so. Males preferred the continuous and contingent gaze avoider. For females, there was a significant positive correlation between the level of gaze they thought they received and (a) their liking for the participant-confederate ($r = .77$), and (b) their perception of the extent to which they were liked by the confederate ($r = .53$). These correlations were nonsignificant for males. The degree of intimate revelation produced by speakers was rated by observers and the speakers themselves. Male and female participants both believed they had been more intimate in the two higher gaze conditions. Observers, however, rated the females as more intimate in the presence of visual attention, and the males as more intimate when partner-directed gaze was lower. Ellsworth and Ross (1975) conclude that females respond to visual attention with intimacy and liking, whereas males respond with less intimacy and some less liking for the gazing partner.

A similar pattern of results was obtained by Kleinke, Bustos, Meeker, and Staneski (1973) employing a different methodology. Instructed to get to know one another, dyads composed of one male and one female talked together for 10 minutes. The experimenter then informed them that the visual attention of one person (SELF) directed toward his or her partner (OTHER) had been recorded during the conversation, and that the SELF (half men and half women) had gazed at the OTHER more than average, average, or less than average. Impression ratings of the dyad members for each other were then obtained. Males in the SELF position evaluated their female OTHER more favorably if they believed they had looked at her at a low rather than high level. Females evaluated their male partner more favorably if they were led to believe they had looked at them a great deal. From the OTHER position males found a female partner less attractive if they were told she had engaged in a low level of gaze at them. Females perceived their male OTHERS as least attractive if they thought the OTHER had given them a high level of visual attention. On the whole, females ratings indicated greater responsiveness to the attributed gaze manipulation compared to males.

The presentation of sex differences in the production and interpretation of visual behavior scattered through primate and human literature is finally complete and warrants comment. Females have been found to visually monitor others more than males across species (Thomsen, 1974) and among humans across the ages from infancy (Hittelman & Dickes, 1979), through childhood (e.g., Ashear & Snortum, 1971; Kleinke et al., 1977; Levine & Sutton-Smith, 1973), into early adulthood (e.g., Argyle & Ingham, 1972; Exline et al., 1965; Schneider & Hansvick, 1977). LaFrance and Carmen (1980) find similar sex differences in visual behavior particularly with sex-typed as compared to androgynous males and females. The maintenance of this pattern into later adulthood remains to be investigated, but preliminary data (Muirhead & Goldman, 1979) forecast potential changes.

Interpretation of this sex difference, as mentioned before, has centered on the impact of differences in sex-role socialization, primarily as such training might influence affiliative tendencies. Thus, females' greater affiliative tendencies (Exline et al., 1965) are thought to be produced by a socialization process that emphasizes interpersonal sensitivity and leads to greater visual monitoring of others compared to males. Whereas females have repeatedly been found to gaze at others more than males, the within-sex relationship between affiliation and social gaze has been found to be consistent for women, and mixed for men. In both encoding and decoding studies, females have routinely been found to associate relatively higher levels of partner-directed gaze with more rather than less affectively positive orientations (e.g., Ellsworth & Ross, 1975; Exline et al., 1965; Rubin, 1970). Males, on the other hand, have sometimes been found to associate higher levels of gaze with more positive orientations (e.g., Goldberg et al., 1975; Kleck & Neussle, 1968; Rubin, 1970) and sometimes with a less positive orientations (e.g., Ellsworth & Ross, 1975; Smith & Sheahan, 1979). The available research does not provide for a clear discrimination between the two cases for males. There is a tendency, however, for a positive relative relationship between affiliation and gaze to be found in the context of cross-sex interactions with previously known partners (e.g., Rubin, 1970), and a negative relationship to be found during interactions with same-sex strangers (e.g., Ellsworth & Ross, 1975; Exline & Winters, 1965a), although exceptions may be found (e.g., Goldberg et al., 1975; Smith & Sheahan).

Male children (Kleinke et al., 1977) and young adults (Ellsworth & Ross, 1975) report preference for a previously unknown other who gazes at them relatively less than the level preferred by females in the same age group. These studies along with Kleinke et al. (1973) lend support to Henley's (1977) suggestion that sex differences in gaze level may also be related to differential orientations with respect to control and power. Males in Kleinke et al.'s (1973) study preferred a female conversation partner they were led to believe they had gazed at relatively little but found a female who had reportedly gazed at them more than average more attractive. The pattern for females was reserved. The differential gaze levels preferred by males are those associated with power differences in conversations. High-status, and more control-oriented men and women gaze at conversation partners, particularly while listening to the partner speak, relatively less than low-status, less controlling persons (Ellyson et al., 1981; Exline et al., 1975). It might be argued that in the context of initial interactions with opposite-sex strangers, males on the average prefer to be in a more dominant position vis-a-vis females, and that females on the average prefer a more deferent or submissive role with respect to males. In the context of ongoing personal relationships, males may feel more comfortable displaying positive feelings through higher levels of visual attention. These suggestions should be regarded as quite tentative, and certainly awaiting clarification and revision.

One source of difficulty in sorting out these issues is that the dominant and affiliative aspects of social visual behavior have primarily been researched separately, so that the interweaving of the two dimensions rarely has been explored. Dominance and affiliation have been regarded as primary themes in the study of social relationships (e.g., Brown, 1965), and also important in humans' interpretation of events (e.g., the potency and evaluation dimensions of Osgood, Suci, and Tannenbaum's, 1957, work on the semantic differential). The relationship between the two dimensions in the context of social relations is unclear. A case can be made for their independence for we know of, for example, dominant persons who are also affiliative, and ones who are nonaffiliative. There is also the question of their relative importance. Haley (1963) would argue that control is primary in all social relations. From this perspective, any social display may be regarded as proposing a relationship along certain lines, the proposal constituting a social-influence attempt. Research that attempts to integrate our understanding of these two dimensions is clearly called for.

The evaluation of relatively high- versus low-gazing partners has also been investigated, whereas the affective tone (positive vs. negative) of explicit or implicit feedback provided by the gazer was concomitantly varied. Ellsworth and Carlsmith (1968) found females to prefer a female interviewer whose conversation had favorable implications for the participant, if the interviewer gazed relatively more during their interaction. When the implications were negative, however, an interviewer who gazed relatively less was preferred. Employing a videotaped confederate as an interaction partner, Scherwitz and Helmreich (1973) extended this line of research. Arguing that Ellsworth and Carlsmith (1968) used feedback that was relatively impersonal, Sherwitz and Helmreich compared responses to feedback identical to that used by Ellsworth and Carlsmith to responses to more personal feedback. The results indicate that males prefer a videotaped same-sex partner providing them with personal feedback if the partner gazes at them (at the lens) when the feedback is negative and gazes away when the feedback is positive. Both males and females preferred a videotaped confederate providing positive feedback who gazed when the feedback was impersonal (replicating Ellsworth & Carlsmith, 1968, and extending to males) and gazed away when the feedback was personal. Four cells of this potentially 16-cell design (2 [Recipient: male, female] × 2 [Confederate gaze: high, low] × 2 [Feedback: positive, negative] × 2 [Feedback: personal, impersonal]) have yet to be investigated: negative, personal feedback with females under high and low gaze; negative, impersonal feedback with males under high and low gaze.

This line of research has potential implication for work in conflict resolution. Feedback provided under certain conditions of visual monitoring may be more likely to result in a favorable disposition toward the other that would likely influence outcomes for both parties. Perhaps a more cooperative approach to negotiations would obtain if feedback, whether positive or negative, was presented in a manner found to favorably impress the recipient.

No discussion of the relationship between affiliation and visual behavior would be complete without mention of the very influential Affiliative Conflict theory introduced by Argyle and Dean (1965) and revised by Argyle and Cook (1976). The theory proposes that opposing forces of approach and avoidance influence the level of intimacy and thus the level of partner-directed gazing, particularly mutual gaze, during social interaction. Affiliative needs, and a need for feedback motivate approach, whereas fears associated with being seen, revealing inner states, and fear of observing rejected responses from another motivate avoidance. Participants enter an interaction with a predisposition toward a certain level of acceptable intimacy to be achieved with others. This leads to the establishment of an equilibrium of intimacy between interactants for the course of their time together. If the intimacy equilibrium is disturbed, compensatory action will be taken to restore it, rather like the operation of a thermostat. A number of behaviors, believed to be linked with an affiliative motivation, function jointly to maintain and restore the equilibrium, e.g., mutual gaze, smiling, physical closeness, and topic intimacy. Relatively greater levels of any of these behaviors would lead to increased intimacy; conversely, lower levels would decrease intimacy. Thus, if participants are seated very close to each other producing an unacceptable level of intimacy, they will, to restore the equilibrium, compensate, for example, by decreasing mutual gaze. It is the equilibrium-maintaining portion of the theory that has received the greatest attention from researchers. In Argyle and Dean's original paper (1965), they report that both males and females decrease mutual gaze with a steadily gazing confederate in same- and mixed-sex dyads as the distance between them reduces 10 to 6, and then 2 feet. The decrease in mutual gaze with increased closeness was greatest to male–female pairs. Cappella (1981) provides a thorough review and critique of the research that followed this original study, the details of which need not be duplicated here. In summary, Cappella (1981) reports that the manipulation of the levels of various verbal and nonverbal variables produced in some cases compensatory actions, and in other cases reciprocation. Cappella (1981) argues that the contradictory results may be integrated by considering the expectations for intimacy that participants brought to the various settings and the expectations for intimacy generated by their initial contact with the behavioral displays of an interaction partner, frequently a trained confederate. An extension and elaboration of Argyle and Dean's (1965) model generated by Patterson (1982) includes consideration of both intimacy and social control processes and allows for both compensatory and reciprocal interaction cycles.

Cultural and subcultural differences in visual attention. Thus far, the discussion has proceeded without regard for the likelihood of cultural differences in the typical display and interpretation of social visual attention. Because cultural comparisons frequently provide a much needed contrast to our own interaction patterns, enabling us to demystify what seems natural, it is unfortunate that so little is known about cultural similarities and differences in the production and understanding of social gaze. A few brief anecdotal accounts are provided by, for example, Hall (1963) and Johnson (1972); but, few detailed descriptions or experimental studies have been conducted. Two lines of work comparing the visual behavior of white Westerners with American Blacks and Arabs are described.

Hall's (1963) anecdotal descriptions of Arab–American differences in typical level of interaction gaze were empirically validated by Watson and Graves (1966). Hall (1963) proposed that Arabs are more visually direct than Americans with respect to his four-point coding system: sharp (focusing directly on the other's eyes), clear (focusing in the region of the other's head and face), peripheral, and no visual contact (as described by Watson & Graves, 1966). Although the distinction between "sharp" and "clear" would be challenged by the psychophysical work of von Cranach (1971), Watson and Graves (1966) report virtually identical interobserver scoring. Arab and American male students, studying at the University Colorado, were paired with male friends of their own culture for a 5-minute conversation in their native tongue. The Arabs were found to gaze more directly at their partners (as well as sit more directly and closer, talk louder, and touch more) than Americans.

Watson (1970) extended this work by observing brief conversations of 106 foreign students from 30 different countries. Interpersonal gaze was less direct for participants from "noncontact" cultures (including the U.S.A.) compared to those from "contact" cultures (including Arab countries). Contact cultures, in comparison with noncontact cultures, are ones characterized by a more direct orientation, smaller interpersonal distance, greater incidence of interpersonal touch, and more direct gaze. In postconversation interviews, the Arabs discussed the importance of direct eye contact in interactions and indicated that less eye contact represents a desire to break off conversation or a lack of interest. Watson (1970) reports that many Arabs indicated annoyance at Americans who gaze less directly in conversations.

Collett (1971) investigated the possibility of improving intercultural contact between Arabs and Englishmen (whose nonverbal displays are more similar to those of Americans rather than Arabs) through training the English in the nonverbal behaviors of the Arabs. Male Arab participants preferred an Englishman who displayed Arab nonverbal behavior (including a high level of direct gaze) to one who did not. English judges did not discriminate in preference for English conversation partners who performed Arab nonverbal displays versus others who were not so trained. Collett (1971) argues that the English may have focused on other aspects of the interaction when evaluating their own countrymen. Nonetheless, the data indicate that Arab males gaze more directly at same-sex conversation partners than do males from Western cultures, and that it is possible to favorably influence the impressions Arab males have of Western interaction partners by training the partners to produce an increased level of direct gaze.

A number of investigations have attempted to test anecdotal descriptions (e.g., Johnson, 1972) that suggest that black Americans engage in less partner-directed gaze than white Americans. In two observational studies LaFrance and Mayo (1976) demonstrated such differences. In Study I, a black male engaged in two 10-minute conversations, one with a black male and one with a white male. Five minutes of each of these conversations were filmed and subjected to a frame-by-frame analysis of partner-directed gaze and speech. The white participant gazed at his partner more when listening to the partner speak than when speaking himself. This replicates the pattern typically observed for whites. The two black participants, however, displayed the reverse pattern, gazing at their respective partners more while speaking than while listening to the partners speak. In the second study, LaFrance and Mayo (1976) observed listening gaze in a number of naturalistic settings as it occurred among Blacks and Whites in same-race dyads of varying sex compositions. A main effect revealed that black participants gazed less at same-race interaction partners while listening to them speak than did white participants. A significant sex composition by race interaction demonstrated that not all race differences were significant across all sex combinations. However, the means do not overlap. Although it is not possible to conclude from the second study that the look–speak/look–listen pattern of Blacks is the reverse of that for Whites, a difference in level of gaze while listening is apparent.

Subsequent research has confirmed a gaze-level difference between Blacks and Whites, such that Blacks gaze less at interaction partners than do Whites. However, the reversed look–speak/look–listen pattern, found in Study I by LaFrance and Mayo (1976), has not been replicated. Exline, Jones, and Maciorowski (1977) found both black and white males to gaze at same-race males more while listening than while speaking. Although the gaze levels of Blacks and Whites could not be directly compared, because they participated in separate studies, the black males gazed less at their partners in general than did the Whites.

Fehr (1977) obtained similar results when comparing the visual behavior of black and white females while they conversed with black and white female interviewers in a laboratory setting. Black females gazed less at interaction partners, regardless of the partners race, than did white females. Both black and white females, however, gazed more while listening than while speaking. In a second study (Fehr, 1981), the visual behavior of pairs of same-race black and white females was compared as they recounted happy and sad personal experiences to each other. Black females tended to gaze less than white females, and both black and white females again gazed more at their partners while listening than while speaking. Also, black and white females gazed more at their partners while recounting a happy as compared to a sad personal experience. This pattern is similar to the one obtained by Exline et al.

(1979) for normal as compared to schizophrenic women. Finally, white females, in a third study (Fehr, 1981), preferred a female confederate, regardless of race (Black or White) who gazed at the average level of white females, as observed in previous research, compared to a confederate who gazed at the average level of black females. This effect is similar to that obtained by Collett (1971) for Arab males. Similarly, Garratt, Baxter, and Rozelle (1981) trained campus police to enact black as compared to white nonverbal behaviors, including gaze, while interviewing black male undergraduates. These students rated the policeman more favorably when they displayed black nonverbal behavior (less direct gaze) compared to white nonverbal behavior (more direct gaze).

DISCUSSION AND CONCLUSIONS

Social visual behavior has been conceptualized in this chapter as an expression component of an underlying, culturally structured code of expression-content relationships, which enables (and probably developed in conjunction with) the organization interactions of humans as social animals. Entrained for social purposes within the social interactions of early infancy, gaze behavior, through the course of development, becomes a component of more elaborated patterns of social exchange in adulthood. Because these visual displays become part of the habitually produced patterns of social interaction, they need not be consciously produced nor consciously interpreted, but neither is conscious attention to the production and interpretation of gazes at and away from others precluded as a possibility.

The literature reviewed indicates that gaze in social settings has been related to numerous characteristics, dispositions, and states of individuals, and also to numerous aspects of naturally occurring and experimentally controlled interaction circumstances. One may very reasonably inquire, in the face of this near plethora of data, whether or not anything general may be said about the meaning of social gaze, whether or not there is any standard content conventionally correlated with this expression form.

Phoebe Ellsworth (1975) proposes that:

> Although glances and gazes do not have specific sign-referent meanings for the observer, they are not completely neutral stimuli which depend entirely on contextual cues for their interpretation . . . a person faced with another's gaze is not free to choose from the whole range of possible interpretations, unconstrained by any intrinsic stimulus properties . . . the behavior itself will narrow the range of variation, resulting in general consistencies of response and interpretation. (p. 55)

Ellsworth (1975) suggests three aspects of visual behavior itself that would limit the range of possible interpretations: "A direct gaze is *salient*; it is *arousing;* and it is *involving*. Gaze aversion is generally none of these things" (p. 56, emphasis in the original). Ellsworth regards these qualities as working limitations on the meaning of gaze, subject to revision as the study of visual behavior continues.

Although the direct gaze of another may be particularly salient under certain circumstances (e.g., steady stares in public settings; Ellsworth et al., (1972), it does not seem as if it would always be so. The eyes do possess attention-attracting qualities, such as contrast between the white of the sclera and the darker regions of the pupil and iris. It is this contrast that promotes visual monitoring in infants (Stern, 1977; Vine, 1973). However, the eyes are always embedded in a physical and social context that would be expected to influence the salience of any particular direct gaze. Facial expressions, body orientation, clothing, etc., and various features of the background environment would play a role in determining the general prominence of the individual, and therefore the prominence of any direct gazes he or she would produce. Regardless of how striking any of these stimulus features might be, for a gaze to be salient to a recipient it must be monitored by the recipient, either directly or peripherally. As Goodwin (1981) proposes, direct gaze or gaze aversion may be relevantly present or absent, the relevance depending on the activities in progress at particular points in the interaction sequence. In conversational settings, the visual behavior of one's partner may become particularly salient when one monitors the partner and finds a visual orientation at variance with one's desires or expectations. This formulation may be applied in public settings, as, for example, in the case of a person who dresses in a particularly flashy manner and then expects and searches for the visual attention of others. Further, the norms of attention or inattention operative in various contexts would interact with the preceeding factors to produce expectations about and therefore the salience of another's gaze. Hemsley and Doob (1978) found the absence of the direct gaze of an alibi witness a salient cue, whereas its presence was not specially noted. The stares in public settings and gaze aversion in conversations associated with dominant or potent displays (e.g., Ellsworth et al., 1972; Exline et al., 1975) may be particularly salient for their lack of responsiveness and violation of normative expectations.

The proposed arousing properties of direct gaze are equally problematic. Although a number of investigators have reported heightened physiological responsiveness in the recipients of direct gaze (e.g., Gale et al., 1972), the social context of the recordings was quite unusual. Prolonged steady mutual gaze in silence is a reasonably infrequent event, perhaps because of its arousing properties. However the disquieting impact of this pattern of visual behavior does not imply that even steady gaze under other circumstances would produce the same effect. In the context of a conversation, the steady visual attention of a listener would likely be less disturbing than gaze aversion, depending on the topic under consideration. This is not meant to deny the arousing properties of gaze in threatening (e.g., Ellsworth et al., 1972) and sexual (Griffit et al., 1974) contexts. However, the arousing properties are strongly influenced by the desires, expectations, and norms for visual attention experienced by participants, rather than primarily residing in the act of gazing itself.

If direct gaze means anything in and of itself, Ellsworth's (1975) third property of involvement may well be the message. Von Cranach (1971) regards visual attention as a component of the general orienting behavior of the individual to his or her social world. As such it is accompanied by other postural/positional behaviors of the upper and lower trunk and limbs providing varying degrees of directness in orientation. The degree of directness would be related to variations in the readiness to connect with another, or readiness for involvement. This conceptualization returns us to the fact that the visual system, is, at base, a sensory/perceptual system that provides the organism with a way to gather information and therefore becomes involved with the environment.

Certain portions of the research literature bear directly on the information gathering and processing aspects of gaze behavior. For example, the tendency for people to look at conversation partners more while listening to the partners speak than while speaking themselves is typically interpreted as reflecting the need of a speaker to occasionally inhibit social feedback (incoming information) from others in order to continue producing fluent speech (e.g., Exline et al., 1975). Several studies have specifically demonstrated that speakers decrease their gaze toward a partner as the complexity and/on difficulty of the speaking task increases (Allen & Guy, 1977; Beattie, 1978b, 1979a; Cegala et al., 1979; Exline & Winters, 1965b; Kendon, 1967). Interpersonal gazing also decreases over the course of an interaction period (Allen & Guy, 1974; Coutts & Schneider, 1975; Rajecki et al., 1981; Schneider & Hansvick, 1977), and as participants have known each other for a longer period of time (Rutter & Stephenson, 1979). These latter two cases, however, are interpreted as reflecting a decrease in the information to be obtained from monitoring an increasingly known entity, rather than reflecting the difficulty of a task at hand. Certain aspects of the social stimulus world have, further, been demonstrated to draw the visual attention of individuals, as, for example, caregiver's eyes for infants (Stern, 1977; Vine, 1973) and handicapped persons for adults (Langer et al., 1976; Thompson, 1982). The caregiver's eyes are thought to be salient for the infant as a result of the nature of the infant's sensory/perceptual system that is sensitive to the contrast between the sclera and darker regions of the eyes. Handicapped persons are thought to be salient for their novelty (information value) in a world in which the proportion of handicapped persons is relatively low, and the fact that they are frequently hidden from public view in institutions. Each of these lines of investigation focuses on particular aspects of the total transaction (Cantril, Ames, Hastdorf, & Ittelson, 1961) between individuals and their social environment, and each sheds light on the information-processing component of person-directed gaze.

The information-processing aspects of visual attention come to have social implications as they become entrained during infancy for social purposes (Stern, 1977). Direct gaze and gaze aversion become important ways of approaching, regulating, withdrawing from, and avoiding others (Stern, 1977). Returning to a theme developed earlier in the chapter, gazing at and away from any entity serves to structure a relationship between the perceiver and the entity (Cantril et al., 1961; Culler, 1973; Eco, 1976). The perceiver and the entity mutually define each other in the context of the act of perception. When the entity is another person, the relationship is social. A bond, however weak or strong, extending through whatever duration and colored by various ideo-affective (Tomkins, 1965) understandings, connects the two individuals. In the context of the bond, each person is constituted as a particular differentiated entity, having mutually defined temporal and spatial boundaries, and is further understood or interpreted as being an entitiy of a particular type (cf. Mead, 1934). Infants make crucial connections with caregivers through the early maturing visual system (Stern, 1977; Vine, 1973). Infants denied this form of social contact as a result of congenital defects in the visual system are in jeopardy of impairment in human relationships (Fraiberg, 1974). Even in adulthood interactions are initiated by looking at another, and other-directed gaze may serve as a way to test the water of a potential interaction by sizing up the other's readiness for social contact (Cary, 1978b). Interactions are avoided (Givens, 1978) and terminated (Knapp et al., 1973) through orienting away from others, of which gaze aversion in an important component. Correlations between gaze level and personality factors such as introversion–extroversion (e.g., Mobbs, 1968), internal and external locus of control (Rajecki et al., 1981), self-monitoring (Dabbs et al., 1980), and social anxiety (Daly, 1978) seem to relate to the basic social approach and withdrawal aspects of these interpersonal tendencies.

It is certainly not our intention to imply, by the singular focus of the discussion on visual attention, that the action of the eyes provides the only means of connecting and disengaging from others in the social world. All our other sensory/perceptual and motor systems are implicated in this process as well, and any understanding of the role of interpersonal gaze in our interactions with others is necessarily incomplete without consideration of the way it relates to these other systems. For example, Fraiberg (1974) proposes that congenitally blind infants may connect with caregivers through touch and audition if the caregivers are educated to pursue these other channels. Also, Goodwin (1981, in press) provides examples of behaviors (e.g., head nods) that may substitute for partner-directed gaze under some circumstances (e.g., interaction involving competing activities).

It is, further, important to note that the information-processing and socially entrained aspects of interpersonal gaze do not always work in harmony. Although relatively lower levels of gaze have been observed during the production as compared to the reception of speech, Beattie (1979a) argues that his observations of partner-directed gaze during hesitant speech suggest that the social signaling function of gaze may be occasionally dysfunctional to language production. A conflict between desires to peruse novel stimuli and social sanctions against staring at others may be seen in Langer et al.'s (1976) work with handicapped persons.

Although the meaning of social gaze in and of itself may be circumscribed to include involvement with, attention to, and orientation toward other persons in the social world, this meaning is further elaborated in the context of culturally and socially situated interactions. People may be involved with and withdraw from others in a variety of ways, and contextual cues can serve to disambiguate the nature of such involvement and withdrawal. It is, however, a matter of degree; perfect clarification is rarely if ever achieved, and as Ellsworth et al. (1972) note, the social implications of visual attention sometimes remain ambiguous. Participants may work to clarify interpersonal ambiguity; they may tolerate it, enjoy it, or, as in Ellsworth et al.'s (1972) study, avoid or escape it.

The research literature provides information regarding two varieties of elaboration on the orienting, attentional, and involving aspects of the meaning of social visual behavior. In situations that may be characterized by a predominance of either affiliative or power themes, the social gaze of participants is displayed and interpreted as representing degrees of interpersonal evaluation and closeness, or degrees of dominance and subordination. A great deal of the visual interaction literature bears directly on these "glances of power and preference" (Exline, 1972, p. 163).

Interactions characterized as involving affectively positive interpersonal orientations have been associated with relatively higher levels of partner-directed gaze in comparison to negatively toned or simply less positive interactions. As stated earlier, this relationship has been consistently observed for females in both encoding (e.g., Pellegrini et al., 1970; Rubin, 1970) and decoding (e.g., Ellsworth & Ross, 1975; Kleinke et al., 1974) research designs but has been found to be less uniform for males, who sometimes associate lower levels of social gaze with more positive orientations (e.g., Ellsworth & Ross, 1975; Rubin, 1970). As might be expected, the relationship between affiliation and social gaze has been found to be influenced by the nature of the conversation topic. Males and females prefer another who gazes at them while providing impersonal positive feedback and gazes away while providing personal positive feedback (Ellsworth & Carlsmith, 1968; Sherwitz & Helmreich, 1973). The complete pattern for negative feedback has yet to be explicated.

With respect to dominance, a consistent pattern of results has emerged for both males and females. Staring at others in public settings has been most frequently responded to as if the stare constituted a threatening cue (Ellsworth et al., 1972; Greenbaum & Rosenfeld, 1978; Smith et al., 1977) except when accompanied by some legitimate, less ambiguous rationale for approach (Ellsworth & Langer, 1976; Kleinke, 1977, 1980). During conversations in laboratory settings, individuals predisposed to dominance displayed less visual attention to a partner's speech than did individuals who describe themselves as typically more deferent. This pattern has also been observed when power differences between participants were experimentally manipulated (Ellyson et al., 1981; Exline et al., 1975). Furthermore, such patterns were perceived as more dominant by observers (Dovidio & Ellyson, 1982).

Potency is further attributed to having asymmetrical control of the visual channel. Jellison and Ickes (1974) found males who anticipated a competitive encounter with another to desire to see, but not be seen by the other, in an anticipated pre-encounter interview. Leaders are most frequently found at head of the table positions, enabling easy view of everyone at the table not afforded to those sitting along the side (Greenberg, 1976). Argyle, Lalljee, and Cook (1968) found participants to report greater discomfort under conditions of asymmetric compared to symmetrical visibility, although discomfort was somewhat less if the participant could see when his or her partner could not. Finally, Argyle and Williams (1969) report that interviewees felt more observed than interviewers.

Once it has been asserted that the meaning of social visual attention may be elaborated by contextual cues of affiliation and dominance, it becomes important to specify how one would know which of these two extensions to apply in any particular situation. Although researchers have tended to focus on one or the other for the purpose of a particular investigation, generally some degree of both affiliation and dominance are present in any interactional setting (e.g., Brown, 1965). It would be important to know how the affiliative and dominating aspects of persons and situations interact to produce the summary perceptions typically provided at the end of interactions, and how they relate to the gaze levels produced by participants.

One point of connection between the dominant and affiliative aspects of social gaze may reside in their relationship to the concept of responsiveness. Earlier, dominant or potent gazes, whether in public or conversational settings, were characterized as relatively unresponsive to the displays of recipients. Deferent or dependent gaze seems to be associated with receptivity toward interaction partners. Conceptually, deference and affiliation may be regarded as sharing a component of responsiveness. Dependence involves a responsiveness to those who control one's outcomes; affiliation implies a sensitivity to the needs and desires of others. A low level of affiliation is associated with a lack of concern for others similar to the orientation of dominant individuals. Investigations that consider the placement of glances and gazes in the ongoing sequence of events would provide information regarding the visual responsiveness of participants. Typically researchers have measured gaze throughout an interaction but not provide summary data on gaze level for the total interaction period, or for listening and speaking subperiods. Both Goodwin (1981) and Stern (1977) provide evidence to indicate that much can be learned by examining the moment-to-moment exchange of gazes by participants. Aspects of Goodwin's (1981) work, for example, could be used to obtain a process view of visual responsiveness. Goodwin finds that speakers may employ pauses and restarts to "request" the gaze of a listener who is not displaying appropriate hearership to the speaker's talk. If it were necessary to use this maneuver repeatedly throughout a conversation, the speaker would be likely to perceive the listener as a recalcitrant participant in conversation. In contexts dominated by power themes, the unresponsive listener may regard as potent; in contexts dominated by affiliation themes, the same person may be perceived as unfriendly. Goodwin's (1981) descriptions of requested gaze forecast other possibilities. Consider, for example, gaze that is freely "given," such that it never needs to be requested. A coconversant who displays this type of orientation to one's talk may be regarded as dependent, or perhaps adoring. Further, gazes given and requested would likely vary in incidence as the topic of conversation changes, or as competing activities are introduced. Giving consideration to the placement of activities within the sequence of events enables one to investigate the transactive construction of an interaction, and therefore the relationship between participants, as it emerges through time.

If social visual behavior may be used to "tell" about involvement with others, however elaborated, it must be able to be used to "lie" or conceal (Eco, 1976). This is precisely the distinction made by Callan et al. (1973) in their conceptualization of attention and advertence. Displays or expressions do not always reflect the underlying orientation of the individual producing them. Experimental participants instructed or induced to lie or conceal information frequently gazed at interaction partners more than did those not so instructed (Fugita et al., 1980; Sitton & Griffin, 1981). Sex (Burns & Kintz, 1976; Exline et al., 1965) and personality (Exline et al., 1970) have, further, been found to interact with these experimental manipulations of concealment. When social norms preclude the observation of handicapped persons, participants display less visual attention toward them. However, when the salience of such norms is relaxed, visual attention increases (Langer et al., 1976; Thompson, 1982). Presumably in these contexts, participants were attempting to display that degree of involvement that they regarded as appropriate for the situation. Subtler forms of this ability may be employed to express and conceal affection for another.

In Eco's (1976) terms, if visual behavior may be used to "lie," and it seems that it can, it may serve as an expressive form, conventionally correlated with various contents of orientation and involvement, contextually elaborated in terms of affiliation and dominance. It is within the context of a culture that sign-functions are formed, that expressions are made meaningful. The study of social visual behavior has not frequently strayed outside of white western cultural groups, and it is to these groups that the participants labor to produce visual behaviors and correlate them with contents for an audience. Such displays, based on an underlying system of signification, serve to structure and are structured by the daily interactions in which we organize our affairs and relationships with each other.

ACKNOWLEDGMENTS

The senior author wishes to thank David Clarke, Bill Husson, and Don Fry for stimulating discussions directly relevant to aspects of the present chapter. Further appreciation goes to Bill Husson, who provided helpful and detailed editorial comments on an earlier version of the chapter.

REFERENCES

Abele, A. Acquaintance and visual behavior between two interactants: Their communicative function for the impression formation. *European Journal of Social Psychology,* 1981, *11*)4), 409–425.

Abramovitch, R., & Daly, E. M. Children's use of head orientation and eye contact in making attributions of affiliation. *Child Development,* 1978, *49*(2), 519–522.

Aiello, J. R. A test of equilibrium theory: Visual interaction in relation to orientation, distance and sex of interactants. *Psychonomic Science,* 1972, *27*(6), 335–6.

Allen, D. E., & Guy, R. F. *Conversational analysis.* The Hague: Mouton, 1974.

Allen, D. E., & Guy, R. E. Ocular breaks and verbal output. *Sociometry,* 1977, *40*(1), 90–96.

Altmann, S. A. A field study of the sociobiology of rhesus monkeys, *macaca mulatta. Annals of the New York Academy of Sciences,* 1962, *102*(2), 338–435.

Argyle, M. Eye-contact and distance: A reply to Stephenson & Rutter. *British Journal of Psychology,* 1970, *61*(3), 395–396.

Argyle, M., & Cook, M. *Gaze and mutual gaze.* Cambridge, UK: Cambridge University Press, 1976.

Argyle, M., & Dean, J. Eye-contact, distance and affiliation. *Sociometry,* 1965, *28,* 289–304.

Argyle, M., & Graham, J. A. The Central Europe Experiment — Looking at persons and looking at things. *Journal of Environmental Psychology and Nonverbal Behavior,* 1977, *1,* 6–16.

Argyle, M., & Ingham, R. Gaze, mutual gaze, and proximity. *Semiotica,* 1972, *6*,(1), 32–49.

Argyle, M., Lalljee, M., & Cook, M. The effects of visibility on interaction in a dyad. *Human Relations,* 1968, *21,* 3–17.

Argyle, M., Lefebvre, L, & Cook, M. The meaning of five patterns of gaze. *European Journal of Social Psychology,* 1974, *4*(2), 125–136.

Argyle, M., & Williams, M., Observer or observed? A reversible perspective in person perception. *Sociometry,* 1969, *32,* 396–412.

Ashcraft, N., & Scheflen, A. E. *People space.* Garden City, NY: Anchor Books, 1976.

Ashear, V., & Snortum, J. R. Eye contact in children as a function of age, sex, social and intellectual variables. *Developmental Psychology,* 1971, *4*(3), 479.

Atkinson, J. M., & Heritage, J. E. Introduction. In J. M. Atkinson & J. E. Heritage (Eds.), *Structures of social action: Studies in conversational analysis.* Cambridge, UK: Cambridge University Press, in press.

Barker, R. G. (Ed.). *The stream of behavior.* New York: Appleton-Century-Crofts, 1963.

Bateson, G. Redundancy and coding. In T. Sebeok (Ed.), *Animal communication.* Bloomington: Indiana University Press, 1968.

Beattie, G. W. Floor apportionment and gaze in conversational dyads. *British Journal of Social and Clinical Psychology,* 1978, *17,* 7–15. (a)

Beattie, G. W. Sequential temporal patterns of speech and gaze in dialogue. *Semiotica,* 1978, *23,* (1/2), 29–52. (b)

Beattie, G. W. Planning units in spontaneous speech: Some evidence from hesitations in speech and speaker gaze direction in conversation. *Linguistics,* 1979, *17,* 61–78. (a)

Beattie, G. W. Contextual constraints on the floor-apportionment function of speaker-gaze in dyadic conversations. *British Journal of Social and Clinical Psychology,* 1979, *18*(4), 391–392. (b)

Beattie, G. W. The regulation of speaker turns in face-to-face conversation: Some implications for conversation in sound-only communication channels. *Semiotica,* 1981, *34*(1/2), 55–70.

Beebe, S. A. Eye contact: A nonverbal determinant of speaker credibility. *The speech teacher,* 1974, *23,* 21–25.

Beebe, B., Stern, D., & Jaffe, J. The kinesic rhythm of mother–infant interactions. In A. W. Siegman & S. Feldstein (Eds.), *Of speech and time: Temporal speech patterns in interpersonal contexts.* Hillsdale, NJ: Lawrence Erlbaum Associates, 1979.

Beir, E. G., & Sternberg, D. P. Marital communication. *Journal of Communication,* 1977, *27,* 92–97.

Birdwhistell, R. L. *Introduction to kinesics.* Louisville, KY: University of Louisville Press, 1952.

Block, J. *Lives through time.* Berkeley, CA: Bancroft, 1971.

Breed, G., & Colaiuta, V. Looking, blinking & sitting: Nonverbal dynamics in the classroom. *Journal of Communication,* 1974, *24*(2), 75–81.

Breed, G., & Porter, M. Eye contact, attitudes, and attitude change among males. *Journal of Genetic Psychology,* 1972, *120,* 211–217.

Brown, R. *Social psychology.* New York: Free Press, 1965.

Buchanan, D. R., Goldman, M., & Juhnke, R. Eye contact, sex, and the violation of personal space. *Journal of Social Psychology,* 1977, *103,*(1), 19–25.

Burns, J. A., & Kintz, B. L. Eye contact while lying during an interview. *Bulletin of the Psychonomic Society,* 1976, *7*(1), 87–89.

Callan, H. M. W., Chance, M. R. A., & Pitcairn, T. K. Attention and advertance in human groups. *Social Science Information,* 1973, *12*(2), 27–41.

Campbell, B. E., & Lancioni, G. E. The effects of staring and pew invasion in church settings. *Journal of Social Psychology,* 1979, *108*(1), 19–24.

Cantril, H., Ames, A. Jr., Hastdorf, A. H., & Ittelson, W. H. Psychology and scientific research. In F. P. Kilpatrick (Ed.), *Explorations in transaction psychology* (pp. 6–35). New York: New York University Press, 1961.

Cappella, J. N. Mutual influence in expressive behavior: Adult–adult and infant–adult dyadic interaction. *Psychological Bulletin,* 1981, *89,* 101–132.

Caproni, V., Levine, D., O'Neal, E., McDonald, P., & Gray, G. Seating position, instructor's eye contact availability, and student participation in a small seminar. *Journal of Social Psychology*, 1977, *103*(2), 315-316.

Cary, M. S. Does civil inattention exist in pedestrian passing? *Journal of Personality and Social Psychology*, 1978, *36*, 1185-1193.

Cary, M. S. The role of gaze in the initiation of conversation. *Social Psychology*, 1978, *41*, 269-271. (b)

Cary, M. S. Gaze and facial display in pedestrian passing. *Semiotica*, 1979, *28*, 323-326.

Cegala, D. J., Alexander, A. F., & Sokuvitz, S. An investigation of eye gaze and its relation to selected verbal behavior. *Human Communication Research*, 1979, *5*(2), 99-108.

Cegala, D. J., Savage, G. T., Brunner, C. C., & Conrad, A. B. An elaboration of the meaning of interaction involvement: Toward the development of a theoretical concept. *Communication Monographs*, 1982, *49*(4), 229-248.

Chaiken, A. I., Sigler, E., & Derlega, V. J. Nonverbal mediators of teacher expectancy effects. *Journal of Personality and Social Psychology*, 1974, *30*(1), 144-149.

Chance, M. R. A. An interpretation of same agonistic postures: The role of "cut-off" acts and postures. *Symposium of the Zoological Society of London*, 1962, *8*, 71-89.

Chance, M. R. A. Attention structures as the basis of primate rank orders. *Man* (new series), 1967, *2*, 503-518.

Cherulnik, P. O., Neely, W. T., Flanagan, M., & Zachau, M. Social skill and visual interaction. *Journal of Social Psychology*, 1979, *104*(2), 263-270.

Clarke, D. The sequential analysis of action structure. In M. von Cranach & R. Harre (Eds.), *The analysis of action* (pp. 191-212). Cambridge, UK: Cambridge University Press, 1982.

Collett, P. On training Englishmen in the non-verbal behavior of Arabs: An experiment in intercultural communication. *International Journal of Psychology*, 1971, *6*, 209-215.

Condon, W. S., & Sander, L. W. Neonate movement is synchronized with adult speech: Interactional participation and language acquisition. *Science*, 1974, *183*, 99-101.

Coutts, L. M., & Schneider, F. W. Visual behavior in an unfocused interaction as a function of sex and distance. *Journal of Experimental Social Psychology*, 1975, *11*, 64-77.

Cranach, M. von. The role of orienting behavior in human interaction. In A. H. Esser (Ed.), *Behavior and environment: The use of space by animals and men* (pp. 217-237). New York: Plenum, 1971.

Cranach, M. von, & Ellgring, J. H. Problems in the recognition of gaze direction. In M. von Cranach & I. Vine (Eds.), *Social communication and movement* (pp. 419-443). New York: Academic, 1973.

Cranach, M. von, & Vine, I. Introduction. In M. von Cranach & I. Vine (Eds.), *Social communication and movement*. London: Academic, 1973.

Culler, J. The linguistic basis of structuralism. In D. Robey (Ed.), *Structuralism: An introduction*. Oxford: Clarendon, 1973.

Dabbs, J. M., Evans, M. S., Hopper, C. H., & Purvis, J. K. Self-monitors in conversation: What do they monitor? *Journal of Personality and Social Psychology*, 1980, *39*(2), 278-284.

Daly, S. Behavioral correlates of social anxiety. *British Journal of Social and Clinical Psychology*, 1978, *17*(2), 117-120.

Daniell, R. J., & Lewis, P. Stability of eye contact and physical distance across a series of structured interviews. *Journal of Consulting and Clinical Psychology*, 1972, *39*(1), 172.

Diebold, A. R. Anthropology and the comparative psychology of communicative behavior. In T. A. Sebeok (Ed.), *Animal communication: Techniques of study and results of research* (pp. 525-571). Bloomington: Indiana University Press, 1968.

Dittman, A. T. The role of body movement in communication. In A. W. Siegman & S. Feldstein (Eds.), *Nonverbal behavior and communication*. Hillsdale, NJ: Lawrence Erlbaum Associates, 1978.

Donovan, W. L., & Leavitt, L. A. Physiological correlates of direct and averted gaze. *Biological Psychology*, 1980, *10*(3), 189–199.

Dovidio, J. F., & Ellyson, S. L. Decoding visual dominance: Attributions of power based on relative percentages of looking while speaking and looking while listening. *Social Psychology Quarterly*, 1982, *45*(2), 106–113.

Eco, U. *A theory of semiotics*. Bloomington: Indiana University Press, 1976.

Edelman, R. J., & Hampson, S. E. Changes in non-verbal behavior during embarrassment. *British Journal of Social and Clinical Psychology*, 1979. *18*(4), 385–390.

Efran, M. G., & Cheyne, J. A. Affective concomitants of the invasion of shared space: Behavioral, physiological, and verbal indicators. *Journal of Personality and Social Psychology*, 1974, *29*, 219–226.

Ekman, P., & Friesen, W. The repertoire of nonverbal behavior: Categories, origins, usage and coding. *Semiotica*, 1969, *1*(1), 49–98.

Ekman, P., & Friesen, W. V. *Unmasking the face*. Englewood Cliffs, NJ: Prentice-Hall, 1975.

Ellgring, J. H., & Cranach, M. von. Process of learning in the recognition of eye-signals. *European Journal of Social Psychology*, 1972, *2*(1), 33–43.

Ellsworth, P. C. Direct gaze as a social stimulus: The example of aggression. In P. Pliner, L. Krames, & T. Alloway (Eds.), *Nonverbal communication of aggression* (pp. 53–76). New York: Plenum, 1975.

Ellsworth, P. C., & Carlsmith, J. M. Effects of eye contact and verbal content on affective response to a dyadic interaction. *Journal of Personality and Social Psychology*, 1968, *10*(1), 15–20.

Ellsworth, P., & Carlsmith, J. M. Eye contact and gaze aversion in an aggressive encounter. *Journal of Personality and Social Psychology*, 1973, *28*(2), 280–292.

Ellsworth, P. C., Carlsmith, J. M., & Henson, A. A stare as a stimulus to flight in human subjects: A series of field experiments. *Journal of Personality and Social Psychology*, 1972, *21*(3), 302–311.

Ellsworth, P. C., & Langer, E. J. Staring and approach: an interpretation of the stare as a nonspecific activator. *Journal of Personality and Social Psychology*, 1976, *33*(1), 117–122.

Ellsworth, P. C., & Ludwig, L. M. Visual behavior in social interaction. *Journal of COmmunication*, 1972, *22*(4), 375–403.

Ellsworth, P., & Ross, L. Intimacy in response to direct gaze. *Journal of Experimental Social Psychology*, 1975, *11*, 592–613.

Ellyson, S. L. Dovidio, J. F., & Corson, R. L. Visual behavior differences in females as a function of self-perceived expertise. *Journal of Nonverbal Behavior*, 1981, *5*(3), 164–171.

Ellyson, S. L., Dovidio, J. F., & Fehr, B. J. Visual behavior and dominance in women and men. In C. Mayo & N. M. Henly (Eds.), *Gender and nonverbal behavior*. New York: Springer-Verlag, 1981.

Ellyson, S. L., Dovidio, J. F., Corson, R. L., & Vinicur, D. L. Visual dominance behavior in female dyads: Situational and personality factors. *Social Psychology Quarterly*, 1980, *43*, 328–336.

Exline, R. V. Explorations in the process of person perception: Visual interaction in relation to competition, sex and need for affiliation. *Journal of Personality*, 1963, *31*(1), 1–20.

Exline, R. V. Visual Interaction: The glances of power and preference. In J. K. Cole (Ed.), *Nebraska Symposium on Motivation*. Lincoln: University of Nebraska Press, 1972.

Exline, R. V., & Eldridge, C. *Effects of two patterns of a speaker's visual behavior upon the perception of the authenticity of his verbal message*. Paper presented at the annual convention of the Eastern Psychological Association, Boston, 1967.

Exline, R. V., Ellyson, S. L., & Long, B. Visual behavior as an aspect of power relationships. In P. Pliner, L. Kramer, & T. Alloway (Eds.), *Nonverbal communication of aggression*, New York: Plenum, 1975.

Exline, R. V., & Fehr, B. J. Applications of semiosis to the study of visual interaction. In A. W. Siegman & S. Feldstein (Eds.), *Nonverbal behavior and communication.* Hillsdale, NJ: Lawrence Erlbaum Associates, 1978.

Exline, R. V., & Fehr, B. J. The assessment of gaze and mutual gaze. In P. Ekman & K. Scherer (Eds.), *Handbook of methods in nonverbal behavior research.* Cambridge, UK: Cambridge University Press, 1982.

Exline, R. V., Gray, D., & Schuette, D. Visual interaction in a dyad as affected by interview content and sex of respondent. *Journal of Personality and Social Psychology,* 1965, *1*(3), 201–209.

Exline, R. V., Jones, P., & Maciorowski, K. *Race, affiliative- conflict theory and mutual visual attention during conversation.* Paper presented at the American Psychological Association Meetings in San Francisco, 1977.

Exline, R. V., & Messick, D. The effects of dependency and social reinforcement upon visual behavior during an interview. *British Journal of Social and Clinical Psychology,* 1967, *6,* 256–266.

Exline, R. V., Paredes, A., Gottheil, E. G., & Winkelmayer, R. Gaze patterns of normals and schizophrenics retelling happy, sad, and angry experiences. In C. E. Izard (Ed.), *Emotions in personality and psychotherapy.* New York: Plenum, 1979.

Exline, R. V., Thibaut, J, Hickey, C. B., & Gumpert, P. Visual interaction in relation to machiavellianism and an unethical act. In R. Christie & F. Geis. *Studies in Machiavellianism* (pp. 53–75). New York: Academic, 1970.

Exline, R. V., & Winters, L. C. Affective relations and mutual glances in dyads. In S. S. Tomkins & C. E. Izard (Eds.), *Affect, cognition, and personality.* New York: Springer, 1965. (a)

Exline, R. V., & Winters, L. C. *The effects of cognitive difficulty and cognitive style upon eye to eye contact in interviews.* Paper presented at the annual convention of the Eastern Psychological Association, Atlantic City, 1965. (b)

Exline, R. V., & Yellin, A. Eye contact as a sign between man and monkey. Proceeding of the XIXth *International Congress of Psychology,* London, 1969. (Abstract). Published 1971.

Farren, D. C., Hirschbiel, P., & Jay, S. Toward interactional synchrony: The gaze patterns of mothers and children in three age groups. *International Journal of Behavioral Development,* 1980, *3*(2), 215–224.

Fehr, B. J. *Visual interactions in same and interracial dyads.* Unpublished master's thesis, University of Delaware, 1977.

Fehr, B. J. *The communication of evaluation through the use of interpersonal gaze in same and interracial female dyads.* Unpublished doctoral dissertation, University of Delaware, 1981.

Foddy, M. Patterns of gaze in cooperative and competitive negotiation. *Human Relations,* 1978, *31*(1), 925–938.

Fraiberg, S. Blind infants and their mothers: An examination of the sign system. In M. Lewis & L. A. Rosenblum (Eds.), *The origins of behavior* (Vol. 1): The effect of the infant on its caregiver. New York: Wiley, 1974.

Fretz, B. R., Corn, R., Tuemmler, J. M., & Bellet, W. Counselor nonverbal behaviors and client evaluations. *Journal of Counseling Psychology,* 1979, *26*(4), 304–311.

Fromme, D. K., & Schmidt, C. K. Affective role enactment and expressive behavior. *Journal of Personality and Social Psychology,* 1972, *24*(5), 413–419.

Fugita, S. S., Hogrebe, M. C., & Wexley, K. N. Perceptions of deception: Perceived expertise in detecting deception, successfulness of deception and nonverbal cues. *Personality and Social Psychology Bulletin,* 1980, *6*(4), 637–643.

Galassi, J. P., & Galassi, M. P. Behavioral performance in the validation of an assertiveness scale. *Behavior Therapy,* 1976, *7*(4), 447–452.

Gale, A., Kingsley, E., Brookes, S., & Smith, D. Cortical arousal and social intimacy in the human female under different conditions of eye contact. *Behavioral Processes,* 1978, *3,* 271–275.

Gale, A., Lucas, B., Nissim, R., & Harpham, B. Some EEG correlates of face-to-face contact. *British Journal of Social and Clinical Psychology,* 1972, *11*(4), 326–332.

Gale, A., Spratt, G., Chapman, A. J., & Smallbone, A. EEG correlates of eye contact and interpersonal distance'. *Biological Psychology,* 1975, *3*(4), 237–245.

Garratt, G. A., Baxter, J. C., & Rozelle, R. M. Training university police in black-American nonverbal behaviors. *Journal of Social Psychology,* 1981, *113,* 217–229.

Givens, D. Greeting a stranger: Some commonly used nonverbal signals of aversiveness. *Semiotica,* 1978, *22,* 351–367.

Goffmann, E. *Behavior in public places.* Glencoe, IL: Free Press, 1963.

Goldberg, G. N., Kiesler, C.A., & Collins, B. E. Visual behavior and face-to-face distance during interaction. *Sociometry,* 1969, *32,* 43–53.

Goldstein, M. A., Kilroy, M. C., & Van de Voort, D. Gaze as a function of conversation and degree of love. *Journal of Psychology,* 1976, *92*(2), 227–234.

Goodwin, C. *Conversational organization: Interactions between speaker and hearers.* New York: Academic, 1981.

Goodwin, C. Notes on story structure and the organization of participation. In J. M. Atkinson & J. E. Heritage (Eds.), *Structures of social action: Studies in conversational analysis.* Cambridge, UK: Cambridge University Press, in press.

Goodwin, M. H. *Processes of mutual monitoring implicated in the production of description sequences, Sociological Inquiry,* 1980, *50,* 303–317.

Graham, F. K. Distinguishing among orienting, defense and startle reflexes. In E. D. Kimmel, E. H. van Olst, & J. F. Orlebeke (Eds.), *The orienting reflex in humans.* Hillsdale, NJ: Lawrence Erlbaum Associates, 1979.

Greenbaum, P., & Rosenfeld, H. M. Patterns of avoidance in response to interpersonal staring and proximity: Effects of bystanders on drivers at a traffic intersection. *Journal of Personality and Social Psychology,* 1978, *36*(6), 575–587.

Greenberg, J. The role of seating position in group interaction: A review, with applications for group trainers. *Group and Organization Studies,* 1976, *1*(3), 310–327.

Griffitt, W., May, J., & Veitch, R. Sexual stimulation and interpersonal behavior: Heterosexual evaluative responses, visual behavior and physical proximity. *Journal of Personality and Social Psychology,* 1974, *30*(3), 367–77.

Haase, R. F., & Tepper, D. T. Jr. Nonverbal components of empathic communication. *Journal of Counseling Psychology,* 1972, *19*(5), 417–424.

Haley, J. *Strategies of psychotherapy.* New York: Grune & Stratton, 1963.

Hall, E. T. A system for the notation of proxemic behavior. *American Anthropologist,* 1963, *65,* 1003–1026.

Hall, K. R. L., & Devore, I. Baboon social behavior. In L. Devore (Ed.), *Primate behavior.* New York: Holt, Rinehart, & Winston, 1965.

Harper, R. G., Wiens, A. N., & Matarazzo, J. D. *Nonverbal communication: The state of the art.* New York: Wiley, 1978.

Harris, S. E. Schizophrenics' mutual gaze patterns. *Psychiatry,* 1978, *41*(1), 83–91.

Hawkes, T. *Structuralism and semiotics.* Berkeley: University of California Press, 1977.

Hedge, B. J., Everitt, B. S., & Frith, C. D. The role of gaze in dialogue. *Acta Psychologica,* 1978, *42,* 453–475.

Heider, F. *The psychology of interpersonal relations.* New York: Wiley, 1958.

Hemsley, G. C., & Doob, A. N. The effect of looking behavior on perceptions of a communicator's credibility. *Journal of Applied Social Psychology,* 1978, 8(2), 136–144.

Henley, N. *Body politics.* Englewood Cliffs, NJ: Prentice-Hall, 1977.

Hersen, M., Miller, P. M., & Eisler, R. M. Interactions between alcoholics and their wives: A descriptive analysis of verbal and nonverbal behavior. *Quarterly Journal of Studies in Alcoholism,* 1973, *34,* 516–520.

Hinchliffe, M., Lancashire, M., & Roberts, F. J. Eye-contact and depression: A preliminary report. *British Journal of Psychiatry,* 1970, *117,* 571–572.

Hinchliffe, M., Lancashire, M., & Roberts, F. J. A study of eye-contact changes in depressed and recovered psychiatric patients. *British Journal of Psychiatry,* 1971, *119,* 213–215.

Hinde, R. A. *The biological basis of human social behavior.* New York: McGraw-Hill, 1974.

Hinde, R. A. The comparative study of non-verbal communication. In J. Benthal & T. Polhemus (Eds.), *The body as a medium of expression.* New York: Dutton, 1975.

Hinde, R. A., & Rowell, T. E. Communication by posture and facial expressions in the rhesus monkey (*macaca mulatta*). *Proceedings of the Zoological Society of London,* 1962, *138,* 1–21.

Hittelman, J. H., & Dickes, R. Sex differences in neonatal eye contact time. *Merrill–Palmer Quarterly,* 1979, *25*(3), 171–184.

Ho, R., & Mitchell, S. Student's nonverbal reaction to tutors' warm/cold nonverbal behavior. *Journal of Social Psychology,* 1982, *118,* 121–130.

Hobson, G. N., Strongman, K. T., Bull, D., & Craig, G. Anxiety and gaze aversion in dyadic encounters. *British Journal of Social and Clinical Psychology,* 1973, *12,* 122–129.

Holstein, C. M., Goldstein, J. W., & Bem, D. J. The importance of expressive behavior, involvement, sex, and need-approval in inducing liking. *Journal of Experimental Social Psychology,* 1971, *7,* 534–544.

Hooff, J. A. R. A. M. van. Categories and sequences of behavior: Methods of description and analysis. In K. R. Scherer & P. Ekman (Eds.), *Handbook of method in nonverbal behavior research* (pp. 362–439). Cambridge, UK: Cambridge University Press, 1982.

Hooff, J. A. R. A. M. van. The facial displays of the catarrhine monkeys and apes. In D. Morris (Ed.), *Primate ethology.* Chicago: Aldine, 1967.

Hore, T. Social class differences in some aspects of the nonverbal communication between mother and preschool child. *Australian Journal of Psychology,* 1970, *22*(1), 21–27.

Hore, T. Visual behavior in teacher–pupil dyads. *American Educational Research Journal,* 1976, *13*(4), 267–275.

Hutt, C., & Ounstead, C. The biological significance of gaze aversion with particular reference to the syndrome of infantile autism. *Behavioral Science,* 1966, *11,* 346–356.

Hutt, C., & Vaizey, M. J. Differential aspects of group density on social behavior. *Nature,* 1966, *209,* 1371–2.

Jaffe, J., & Anderson, S. W. Communication rhythms and the evolution of language. In A. W. Siegman & S. Feldstein (Eds.), *Of speech and time.* Hillsdale, NJ: Lawrence Erlbaum Associates, 1979.

Jaffe, J., & Feldstein, S. *Rhythms of dialogue.* New York: Academic, 1970.

Jaffe, J., Stern, D., & Perry, J. C. "Conversational" coupling of gaze behavior in prelinguistic human development. *Journal of Psycholinguistic research,* 1973, *2*(4), 321–329.

Jellison, J. M., & Ickes, W. J. The power of the glance: Desire to see and be seen in cooperative and competitive situations. *Journal of Experimental Social Psychology,* 1974, *10,* 444–450.

Jones, R. A., & Cooper, J. Mediation of experimenter effects. *Journal of Personality and Social Psychology,* 1971, *20*(1), 70–74.

Johnson, K. R. Black kinesics: Some non-verbal communication patterns in the black culture. In L. A. Samovar & R. E. Porter (Eds.), *International communication: A reader* (pp. 181–189). Belmont, CA: Wadsworth, 1972.

Jurich, A. P., & Jurich, J. A. Correlations among nonverbal expressions of anxiety. *Psychological Reports,* 1974, *34*(1), 199–204.

Kelly, G. *The psychology of personal constructs* (2 vols.). New York: Norton, 1955.

Kendon, A. Some functions of gaze-direction in social interaction. *Acta Psychologica,* 1967, *26,* 22–63.

Kendon, A. The role of visible behavior in the organization of social interaction. In M. von Cranach & I. Vine (Eds.), *Social communication and movement* (pp. 29–74). New York: Academic, 1973.

Kendon, A. Looking in conversation and the regulation of turns at talk: A comment on the papers of G. Beattie and D. R. Rutter et al. *British Journal of Social and Clinical Psychology,* 1978, *17,* 23–24.

Kendon, A. The organization of behavior in face-to-face interaction: Observations on the development of a methodology. In K. R. Scherer & P. Ekman (Eds.), *Handbook of methods in nonverbal behavior research.* Cambridge, UK: Cambridge University Press, 1982.

Kendon, A., & Cook, M. The consistency of gaze patterns in social interaction. *British Journal of Psychology,* 1969, *60*(4), 481–494.

Kendon, A., & Ferber, A. A description of some human greetings. In P. M. Michael & J. H. Cook (Eds.), *Comparative ecology and behavior of primates* (pp. 591–668). London: Academic, 1973.

Keverne, E. G., Leonard, R. A., Scruton, D. M., & Young, S. K. Visual monitoring in social groups of Talapoin monkeys *(miopithecus talapoin). Animal Behavior,* 1978, *26*(31), 933–944.

Kimble, C. E., Forte, R. A., & Yoshikawa, J. C. Nonverbal concomitants of enacted emotional intensity and positivity: Visual and vocal behavior. *Journal of Personality,* 1981, *49*(3), 271–283.

Kimble, C. E., & Olszewski, D. A. Gaze and emotional expression: The effects of message positivity–negativity and emotional intensity. *Journal of Research in Personality,* 1980, *14*(1), 60–69.

Kleck, R. E. Physical stigma and nonverbal cues emitted in face-to-face interactions. *Human Relations,* 1968, *21,* 19–28.

Kleck, R. E., & Nuessle, W. Congruence between indicative and communicative functions of eye contact in interpersonal relations. *British Journal of Social and Clinical Psychology,* 1968, *7,* 241–246.

Kleinke, C. L. Compliance to requests made by gazing and touching experimenters in field settings. *Journal of Experimental Social Psychology,* 1977, *13,* 218–223.

Kleinke, C. L. Interaction between gaze and legitimacy of request on compliance in a field setting. *Journal of Nonverbal Behavior,* 1980, *5,*(1), 3–12.

Kleinke, C. L., Bustos, A. A., Meeker, F. B., & Staneski, R. A. Effects of self-attributed and other-attributed gaze on interpersonal evaluations between males and females. *Journal of Experimental and Social Psychology,* 1973, *9*(2), 154–163.

Kleinke, C. L., Desautels, M. J., & Knapp, B. E. Adult gaze and affective and visual responses of preschool children. *Journal of Genetic Psychology,* 1977, *131,* 321–322.

Kleinke, C. L., Meeker, F. B., & La Fong, C. Effects of gaze, touch, and use of name on evaluation of "engaged" couples. *Journal of Research in Personality,* 1974, *7,* 368–373.

Kleinke, C. L., & Pohlen, P. D. Affective and emotional responses as a function of other person's gaze and cooperativeness in a two-person game. *Journal of Personality and Social Psychology,* 1971, *17*(3), 308–313.

Kleinke, C. L., Staneski, R. A., & Berger, D. E. Evaluation of an interviewer as a function of interviewer gaze, reinforcement of subject gaze and interviewer attractiveness. *Journal of Personality and Social Psychology,* 1975, *31,*(1), 115–122.

Kleinke, C. L., Staneski, R. A., & Pipp, S. L. Effects of gaze, distance, and attractiveness on males' first impressions of females. *Representative Research in Social Psychology,* 1975, *6*(1), 7–12.

Knapp, M. L., Hart, R. P., Friedrich, G. W., & Schulman, G. M. The rhetoric of goodbye: Verbal and nonverbal correlates of human leave-taking. *Speech monographs,* 1973, *40,* 182–198.

Krivonos, P. D., & Knapp, M. L. Initiating communication: What do you say when you say hello? *Central States Speech Journal,* 1975, *26,* 115–125.

La France, M., & Mayo, C. Racial differences in gaze behavior during conversations: Two systematic observational studies. *Journal of Personality and Social Psychology,* 1976, *33*(5), 547–552.

La France, M., & Carmen, B. The nonverbal display of psychological androgyny. *Journal of Personality and Social Psychology,* 1980, *38*(1), 36-49.

Langer, E. J., Fiske, S., Taylor, S. E., & Chanowitz, B. Stigma, staring, and discomfort: A novel-stimulus hypothesis. *Journal of Experimental Social Psychology,* 1976, *12,* 451-463.

Leavitt, L. A., & Donovan, W. L. Perceived infant temperament, locus of control, and maternal physiological response to infant gaze. *Journal of Research in Personality,* 1979, *13,* 267-278.

Lefcourt, H. M., & Wine, J. Internal versus external control of reinforcement and the deployment of attention in experimental situations. *Canadian Journal of Behavioral Science,* 1969, *1,* 167-181.

Lefebvre, L. M. Encoding and decoding of ingratiation in modes of smiling and gaze. *British Journal of Social and Clinical Psychology,* 1975, *14*(1), 33-42.

Levine, M. H., & Sutton-Smith, B. Effects of age, sex, and task on visual behavior during dyadic interaction. *Developmental Psychology,* 1973, *9*(3), 400-405.

Lewis, S. A., & Fry, W. R. Effects of visual access and orientation on the discovery of integrative bargaining alternatives. *Organizational behavior and human performance,* 1977, *20*(1), 75-92.

Lord, C. The perception of eye contact in children and adults. *Child Development,* 1974, *45,* 1113-1117.

Lyons, J. Structuralism and linguistics. In D. Robey (Ed.), *Structuralism: An introduction.* Oxford: Clarendon, 1973.

Marler, P. Animal communication signals. *Science,* 1967, *157,* 769-774.

Martin, W. W., & Gardner, S. N. The relative effects of eye-gaze and smiling on arousal in asocial situations. *Journal of Psychology,* 1979, *102*(2), 253-259.

McBride, G., King, M. G., & James, J. W. Social proximity effects on galvanic skin responses in adult humans. *Journal of Psychology,* 1965, *61,* 153-157.

Mead, G. H. *Mind, self, and society.* Chicago: University of Chicago Press, 1934.

Milgram, S. *Obedience to authority.* New York: Harper, 1974.

Mischel, W. *Personality assessment.* New York: Wiley, 1968.

Mobbs, N. A. Eye-contact in relation to social introversion/extroversion. *British Journal of Social and Clinical Psychology,* 1968, *7,* 305-306.

Modigliani, A. Embarrassment, facework, and eye contact: Testing a theory of embarrassment. *Journal of Personality and Social Psychology,* 1971, *17*(1), 15-24.

Morris, C. *Foundations of the theory of signs.* Chicago: University of Chicago Press, 1938.

Muirhead, R. D., & Goldman, M. Mutual eye contact as affected by seating position, sex, and age. *Journal of Social Psychology,* 1979, *109*(2), 201-206.

Natale, M. A markovian model of adult gaze behavior. *Journal of Psycholinguistic Reearch,* 1976, *5*(1), 53-63.

Natale, M. Induction of mood states and their effect on gaze behaviors. *Journal of Consulting and Clinical Psychology,* 1977, *45*(5), 960.

Nevill, D. Experimental manipulation of dependency motivation and its effects on eye contact and measures of field dependency. *Journal of Personality and Social Psychology,* 1974, *29*(1), 72-79.

Newman, J., & McCauley, C. Eye contact with strangers in city, suburb, and small town. *Environment and Behavior,* 1977, *9*(4), 547-558.

Nichols, K. A., & Champness, B. G. Eye gaze and the GSR. *Journal of Experimental Social Psychology,* 1971, *7,* 623-626.

Nideffer, R. M. Test of attentional and interpersonal style. *Journal of Personality and Social Psychology,* 1976, *34,* 394-404.

Nielson, G. *Studies in self confrontation.* Copenhagen: Monksgaard, 1962.

Noller, P. Gaze in married couples. *Journal of Nonverbal Behavior,* 1980, *5*(2), 115-129.

Norton, R. W., & Pettegrew, L. S. Attentiveness as a style of communication: A structural analysis. *Communication Monographs,* 1979, *46*(1), 13-26.

O'Connor, N., & Hermelin, B. Auditory and visual memory in autistic children. *Journal of Mental Deficiency*, 1967, *11*(2), 126-131.

Osgood, C. E., Suci, G. J., & Tannenbaum, P. H. *The measurement of meaning*. Urbana: University of Illinois Press, 1957.

Patterson, M. L. Stability of nonverbal immediacy behaviors. *Journal of Experimental Social Psychology*, 1973, *9*(2), 97-109.

Patterson, M. A sequential functional model of nonverbal exchange. *Psychological Review*, 1982, *89*(3), 231-249.

Piaget, J. *Structuralism*. New York: Basic Books, 1970.

Pike, K. L. *Language in relation to a unified theory of the structure of human behavior* (2nd rev. ed.). The Hague: Mouton, 1967.

Pellegrini, R. J., Hicks, R. A., & Gordon, L. The effect of an approval-seeking induction on eye-contact in dyads. *British Journal of Social Clinical Psychology*, 1970, *9*, 373-374.

Post, B., & Hetherington, E. M. Sex differences in the use of proximity and eye contact in judgments of affiliation in preschool children. *Developmental Psychology*, 1974, *10*(6), 881-889.

Rajecki, D. W., Ickes, W., & Tanford, S. Locus of control and reactions to strangers. *Psychology and Social Psychology Bulletin*, 1981, *7*(2), 282-289.

Rosenthal, R. On the social psychology of the psychological experiment: The experimenter's hypothesis as the unintended determinant of experimental results. *American Scientist*, 1963, *51*, 268-283.

Rosenthal, R., & Jacobson, L. *Pygmalion in the classroom*. New York: Holt, Rinehart, & Winston, 1968.

Ross, M., Layton, B., Erickson, B., & Schopler, J. Affect, facial regard and reactions to crowding. *Journal of Personality and Social Psychology*, 1973, *28*(1), 69-76.

Rotter, J. B. Generalized expectancies for internal versus external control of reinforcement. *Psychological Monographs*, 1966, *80*, (Whole No. 609).

Rubin, Z. Measurement of romantic love. *Journal of Personality and Social Psychology*, 1970, *16*, 265-273.

Russo, N. F. Eye contact, interpersonal distance, and the equilibrium theory. *Journal of Personality and Social Psychology*, 1975, *31*(3), 497-502.

Rutter, D. R. Visual interaction in recently admitted and chronic long-stay schizophrenic patients. *British Journal of Social and Clinical Psychology*, 1976, *15*, 295-303.

Rutter, D. R. Visual interaction and speech patterning in remitted and acute schizophrenic patients. *British Journal of Social and Clinical Psychology*, 1977, *16*, 357-361.

Rutter, D. R. Visual interaction in schizophrenic patients: The timing of looks. *British Journal of Social and Clinical Psychology*, 1978, *17*, 281-282.

Rutter, D. R., Morely, V. E., & Graham, J. C. Visual interaction in a group of introverts and extroverts. *European Journal of Social Psychology*, 1972, *2*(4), 371-384.

Rutter, D. R., & O'Brien, P. Social interaction in withdrawn and aggressive maladjusted girls: A study of gaze. *Journal of Child Psychology and Psychiatry and Allied Disciplines*, 1980, *21*(1), 59-66.

Rutter, D. R., & Stephenson, G. M. Visual interaction in a group of schizophrenic and depressive patients. *British Journal of Social and Clinical Psychology*, 1972, *11*, 57-65. (a).

Rutter, D. R., & Stephenson, G. M. Visual interaction in a group of schizophrenic and depressive patients: A follow-up story. *British Journal of Social and Clinical Psychology*, 1972, *11*(4), 410-411. (b)

Rutter, D. R., & Stephenson, G. M. The functions of looking: Effects of friendship on gaze. *British Journal of Social and Clinical Psychology*, 1979, *18*, 203-205.

Rutter, D. R., Stehenson, G. M., Ayling, K., & White, P. A. The timing of looks in dyadic conversation. *British Journal of Social and Clinical Psychology*, 1978, *17*, 17-21.

Sacks, H. Schegloff, E., & Jefferson, G. A simplest systematics for the organization of turn-taking for conversation. *Language*, 1974, *50*, 696-735.

Sarte, J. P. *Being and nothingness.* London: Methuen, 1957.

Schaffer, H. R. Early interactive development. In H. R. Schaffer (Ed.), *Studies in mother-infant interaction.* London: Academic, 1977.

Schaller, G. *The mountain gorilla: Ecology and behavior.* Chicago: University of Chicago Press, 1963.

Schaller, G. *The year of the gorilla.* Chicago: University of Chicago Press, 1964.

Scherer, K. R., & Ekman, P. Methodological issues in studying nonverbal behavior. In K. R. Scherer & P. Ekman (Eds.), *Handbook of methods in nonverbal behavior research.* Cambridge, UK: Cambridge University Press, 1982.

Scherer, S. E., & Schiff, M. R. Perceived intimacy, physical distance and eye contact. *Perceptual and Motor Skills,* 1973, *36,* 835–841.

Schutz, W. C. *Firo: A three-dimensional theory of interpersonal behavior.* New York: Holt, Rinehart, & Winston, 1960.

Sherwitz, L., & Helmreich, R. Interactive effects of eye contact and verbal content on interpersonal attraction in dyads. *Journal of Personality and Social Psychology,* 1973, *25*(1), 6–14.

Schneider, F. W., & Hansvick, C. L. Gaze and distance as a function of changes in interpersonal gaze. *Social Behavior and Personality,* 1977, *5*(1), 49–53.

Simonds, P. E. The bonnet macaque in South India. In I. DeVore (Ed.), *Primate behavior: Field studies of monkeys and apes.* New York: Holt, Rinehart, & Winston, 1965.

Sitton, S. C., & Griffin, S. T. Detection of deception from clients' eye contact patterns. *Journal of Counseling Psychology,* 1981, *28*(3), 269–271.

Smith, B. J., Stanford, F., & Goldman, M. Norm violations, sex, and the blank stare. *Journal of Social Psychology,* 1977, *103*(1), 49–55.

Smith, J., & Sheahan, M. *Verbal and nonverbal interaction stages in human relationships.* Paper presented to the annual convention of the Eastern Communication Association, Philadelphia, May, 1979.

Snyder, M. The self-monitoring of expressive behavior. *Journal of Personality and Social Psychology,* 1974, *30,* 526–537.

Snyder, M., Grether, J., & Keller, K. Staring and compliance: A field experiment on hitchhiking. *Journal of Applied Social Psychology,* 1974, *4*(2), 165–170.

Sommer, R. *Personal space: The behavioral basis of design.* Englewood Cliffs, NJ: Prentice-Hall, 1969.

Stern, D. Mother and infant at play: The dyadic interaction involving facial, vocal and gaze behaviors. In M. Lewis & L. A. Rosenblum (Eds.), *The origins of behavior* (Vol. 1): *The effects of the infant on its caregiver.* New York: Wiley, 1974.

Stern, D. *The first relationship: Mother and Infant.* Cambridge, MA: Harvard University Press, 1977.

Stern, D., Beebe, B., Jaffe, J., & Bennett, S. The infants' stimulus world during social interaction: A study of caregiver behaviors with particular reference to repetition and timing. In H. R. Schaffer (Ed.), *Studies in mother–infant interaction.* New York: Academic, 1977.

Strongman, K. T., & Champness, B. G. Dominance hierarchies and conflict in eye contact. *Acta Psychologica,* 1968, *28,* 376–386.

Strongman, K. Communicating with the eyes. *Science Journal,* 1970, *6*(d), 47–52.

Tepper, D. T., & Haase, R. F. Verbal and nonverbal communication of facilitative conditions. *Journal of Counseling Psychology,* 1978, *25*(1), 35–40.

Thayer, S. The effect of interpersonal looking duration on dominance judgments. *Journal of Social Psychology,* 1969, *79,* 285–286.

Thayer, S. Children's detection of on-face and off-face gazes. *Developmental Psychology,* 1977, *13*(6), 673–674.

Thayer, S., & Schiff, W. Observer judgment of social interaction: Eye contact and relationship inferences. *Journal of Personality and Social Psychology,* 1974, *30*(1), 110–114.

Thayer, S., & Schiff, W. Gazing patterns and attributions of sexual involvement. *Journal of So-*

cial Psychology, 1977, 101, 235–246.

Tomkins, S. S. Affect and the psychology of knowledge. In S. S. Tomkins & C. E. Izard (Eds.), Affect, cognition, and personality. New York: Springer, 1965.

Thompson, T. L. Gaze toward and avoidance of the handicapped: A field experiment. Journal of Nonverbal Behavior. 1982, 3(3), 188–196.

Thomsen, C. E. Eye contact by non-human primates toward a human observer. Animal Behavior, 1974, 22(1), 144–149.

Tipton, R. M., & Rymer, R. A. A laboratory study of the effects of varying levels of counselor eye contact on client-focused and problem-focused counseling styles. Journal of Counseling Psychology, 1978, 25(3), 200–204.

Vallentine, M. E., The attenuating influence of gaze upon the bystander intervention effect. Journal of Social Psychology, 1980, 111(2), 197–203.

Vallentine, M. E., & Ehrlichman, H. Interpersonal gaze and helping behavior. Journal of Social Psychology, 1979, 107(21), 193–198.

Vaughn, B. E., & Waters, E. Attention structure, sociometric status, and dominance: Interrelations, behavioral correlates, and relationships to social competence. Developmental psychology, 1981, 17, 275–288.

Vine, I. Communication by facial-visual signals. In J. H. Crook, (Ed.), Social behavior in birds and mammals: Essays on the social ethology of animals and man (pp. 179–354). London: Academic, 1970.

Vine, I. Judgment of direction of gaze: An interpretation of discrepant results. British Journal of Social and Clinical Psychology, 1971, 10(4), 320–331.

Vine, I. The role of facial-visual signalling in early social development. In M. von Cranach & I. Vine (Eds.), Social communication and movement. (pp. 195–298). London: Academic, 1973.

Vlietstra, A. G., & Manske, S. H. Looks to adults, preferences for adult males and females, and interpretations of an adult's gaze by preschool children. Merrill–Palmer Quarterly, 1981, 27(1), 31–41.

Wada, J. A. Modifications of cortically induced responses in brain stem of shift of attention in monkeys. Science, 1961, 133, 40–42.

Waters, E. Matas, L., & Sroufe, L. A. Infant's reactions to an approaching stranger: Description, validation, and functional significance of wariness. Child Development, 1975, 46, 348–356.

Watson, O. M. Proxemic behavior: A cross-cultural study. The Hague: Mouton, 1970.

Watson, O. M., & Graves, T. D. Quantitative research in proxemic behavior. American Anthropologist, 1966, 68, 971–985.

Waxer, P. Nonverbal cues for depression. Journal of Abnormal Psychology, 1974, 83, 319–322.

West, C., & Zimmerman, D. H. Conversation analysis. In K. R. Scherer & P. Ekman (Eds.), Handbook of methods in nonverbal behavior research. Cambridge, UK: Cambridge University Press, 1982.

Wiemann, J. M., & Knapp, M. L. Turn-taking in conversations. Journal of Communication, 1975, 25, 75–92.

Wiener, M., Devoe, S., Rubinow, S., & Geller, J. Nonverbal behavior and nonverbal communication. Psychological Review, 1972, 79(3), 185–214.

Wiens, A. N., Harper, G., & Matarazzo, J. D. Personality correlates of nonverbal behavior. Journal of Clinical Psychology, 1980, 36(1), 205–215.

Williams, E. An analysis of gaze in schizophrenics. British Journal of Social and Clinical Psychology, 1974, 13, 1–8.

7 Pupillary Behavior in Communication

Eckhard H. Hess
The University of Chicago

Slobodan B. Petrovich
University of Maryland Baltimore County

INTRODUCTION

Even a casual review of the subject matter presented in chapters making up this volume convincingly indicates that in recent years, research in the area of nonverbal communication has made important contributions to our knowledge of human behavior. Eye behavior has also attracted much attention, and the findings reflecting on the importance of visual interaction and eye contact in interpersonal communication are extensively covered in Fehr and Exline's chapter. In this section we examine the behavior of a pupil, a component of what Magnus (1885) called "eye language."

Recorded history indicates man's preoccupation with the eye and its effects on human behavior. A few choice selections from popular literature suggest that our interest, if not our preoccupation, has not diminished: the cold look, the icy stare, shifty eyes, his eyes shot daggers, a gleam in his eye, to kill with a glance. Intimate, romantic literacy descriptions make frequent reference to large, beautiful eyes. The eye pupil has also received attention. It is interesting to note that it became popular during the middle ages for women to take belladonna in the belief that it made them look beautiful. The word "belladonna" does mean "beautiful woman" in Italian, but why was it believed that taking the drug resulted in greater beauty? Part of the answer might be that the drug served to dilate eye pupils. Atropine, a derivative of belladonna, is one of the drugs that can be used by ophthalmologists to dilate pupils for eye examinations.

There are at least two cultures (or subcultures) in which it is consciously known that pupil enlargement indicates a person's positive interest in something. Gump (1962), in writing of experiences with Chinese jade dealers, wrote that prospective buyers found it necessary to wear dark glasses to shield their eyes from astute Chinese dealers, who knew that when a buyer saw an item that he liked, his pupils would dilate. The dilation cue thus prompted the Chinese dealers to raise their prices accordingly for the item in question. Turkish rug dealers are also said to have been aware of the pupil dilation phenomenon in their dealings with European merchants. Perhaps, also, in poker playing, it may be known by some that pupil enlargement can serve to indicate to other players the nature of the hand.

Pupil change, independent of change in illumination, was noted some two hundred years ago (Loewenfeld, 1958, p. 204). However, the recent interest in pupil behavior to a large degree stems from the research carried out in our laboratories at the University of Chicago. This work has been reviewed previously (Hess, 1968, 1972). Subsequently, many other investigators have used pupil behavior as an index for assessing differential psychological responses to various stimuli, and pupillary behavior has been utilized as a measure of arousal, sensory stimulation, cognitive processes, muscular activity, attitudes, and preferences. A reasonably comprehensive coverage of this material is also available (Goldwater, 1972; Hess, 1972, 1975a; Hess & Goodwin, 1974; Janisse, 1973, 1974; Tryon, 1975; Woodmansee, 1970).

The literature reviewed and the findings presented in this chapter explicate the thesis that pupillary changes are not only relaxed to paralinguistics, but may have to be elevated, at least in some contexts, to their own level of distinction reflecting the nature of "pupil to pupil communication."

EYE PUPIL CHANGES AND INTERPERSONAL NONVERBAL COMMUNICATION

When we found in our initial and subsequent research (Hess & Polt, 1960; Hess, 1973a) that heterosexual men tended to show greater pupil dilations to pictures of women than to pictures of men or of babies, whereas heterosexual women tended to show greater pupil dilations to pictures of men or babies than to pictures of women, it appeared reasonable to explore the question of whether eye pupil size changes served as a means of nonverbal communication. Since eye pupil size changes are not under direct voluntary control, it appeared that such nonverbal communication, if it existed, probably would be largely nonconscious since most people are normally unaware of their own eye pupil size changes.

Our pilot experiment (Hess, 1965) on this question was a simple one. We selected a facial photograph of a girl who had no particularly indentifiable expression. We constructed two versions of this face: one in which the pupils of her eyes had been retouched so as to make them very small and another in which the pupils had been retouched so as to make them very large. We made slides of these two versions and projected them in our usual procedure (described in Hess, 1972, 1975a) on the screen of our pupil apparatus as part of a series of other pictures. The 20 men who saw these two pictures had twice as large increases in pupil size when viewing the picture with the large eye pupils. When the men subsequently saw photographic copies of these two pictures, some of them reported greater positive feelings toward the one with large pupils than toward the one with small pupils. Yet these men did not at all mention the fact that the eye pupil sizes were different in the two pictures and apparently thought the pictures were different in facial expression. Many of them were surprised to be told that only pupil sizes differed in the two pictures and had to be shown that this actually was the case.

Since our pilot experiment other researchers have investigated the responses of people to differences in eye pupil size in stimulus persons. Simms (1967), for example, showed two different facial photographs, one of a man and one of a woman, in two different versions each. In one version the photographs had small pupils and in the other they had large pupils. The subjects that were shown the pictures were both men and women, all married and therefore presumably heterosexual. Simms found that the subjects' pupil responses to the four photographs depended both upon the sex of the subject in relation to the photograph and upon the eye pupil size in the photograph. As might be predicted, the subjects exhibited larger pupil sizes upon viewing the photograph of the opposite sex individual that had large pupils than upon viewing the photograph of the same individual that had small pupils. Most interesting, however, were the responses of the subjects to different pupil sizes in the stimulus person of the same sex as themselves. While the male subjects' pupils did not dilate to either of the two pictures of the man, the women's pupils were the smallest in response to the picture of the woman with large pupils. Their pupil response to the picture of the woman with small pupils was the same as that to the picture of the man with the small pupils. This finding agrees with data collected by Hicks, Reaney, and Hill (1967), which inidicated that women had more positive verbal responses toward a picture of a woman when she had small pupils than for a picture of her when she had large pupils.

More recently Jones and Moyel (1971) presented photographs of different men to male subjects. Some of the photographs exhibited large pupils and some exhibited small pupils. In addition, some of the photos had light colored irises, thus making the pupil highly visible, while other photos had dark colored irises, thus making reception of the pupil size difficult. In this experiment, congruent with the finding of Hicks, Reaney, and Hill (1967), Jones and Moyel (1971) reported that photos with small pupils were verbally preferred to those with large pupils. The photos with light irises elicited somewhat more friendly responses than did the ones with dark irises, perhaps because in the latter case the pupil size would be ambiguous. This difference in response to light versus dark irises possibly may not exist in a naturalistic setting since with real persons the actual pupil size may be more readily perceived.

Work by Stass and Willis (1967) further supports the notion that pupil dilation in a stimulus person can indicate sexually toned positive interest to a perceiver. They found that pharmacologically dilating a person's pupils serves to make that person more attractive to a heterosexual opposite-sex person. They asked both male and female subjects to choose an experimental partner from two persons of the opposite sex. One of the persons offered had normal pupils while the other had dilated pupils. Both male and female subjects were more likely to pick as their partner the stimulus person with dilated pupils. Furthermore, the subjects were not found to report the use of dilated eye pupils as a criterion for having chosen their experimental partner. This data is consistent with the finding of Hess (1965), described previously in this chapter.

Earlier work by Coss (1965) demonstrated that even schematic eyes can influence pupil responses in viewers. Coss made a series of concentric circles, some with large solid inner circles and some with small solid inner circles. These circles were shown to ten men and five women in sets of one, two, or three identical stimuli in a row. When the concentric eyespots were presented in pairs, the subjects had larger pupil sizes while looking at them than they did while looking at singleton or at tripled eye spots. The finding of larger eye pupils upon the viewing of paired eye spots rather than during the viewing of tripled eye spots is of interest because the larger amount of dark area in the tripled eye spots sets is a factor that should serve to increase eye pupil size. Hence, it appears that psychological factors mediate the larger pupil size upon the viewing of paired eye spots than when singleton or tripled eye spots are seen. Among the paired eye spots, furthermore, those that most resemble eyes with dilated pupils elicited larger pupil sizes from the subjects than did those that most resembled eyes with constricted pupils.

Research in our laboratory has given even more information regarding pupil responses to schematic eye spots. We made up slides that showed a single eye spot, a pair of eye spots, or three eye spots in a row. Not only did we vary the number of eye spots shown on each slide, but also used three different "pupil" diameters, small, medium, and very large. While Coss had placed his paired eye spots quite close together, we spaced them farther apart so that they would be the same distance from each other as if they were real eyes. We did this because we reasoned that if schematic eye spots constituted a configuration that was responded to innately in the same sense that a male robin will attack a mere red feather because it resembles the breast of a territorial rival, then placing them in the proper relation to each other should enhance the pupil responses to them.

We had 20 subjects, 10 men and 10 women, and they were shown the slides of the eye spots according to our usual procedure, with appropriate control slides. Table 1 depicts the mean pupil response of the 20 subjects to single, double, and triple eye spots without regard to the "pupil size" that they had. Only the paired eye spots consistently elicited mean pupil dilations, while the singleton and tripled eye spots consistently elicited mean pupil constrictions.

Tables 2, 3, and 4 show the mean pupil responses made by the subjects to singleton, tripled, and paired eye spots as a function of different "pupil sizes." No consistent response tendencies according to "pupil size" were evident for the singletons or for the tripled eye spots. But, as Table 4 shows, both male and female subjects had larger mean pupil sizes for the medium sized "pupils" than for the small "pupils" and even larger mean pupils sizes for the largest "pupils."

These results suggest that people possess what ethologists call an innate schema for two eye spots, rather than for one or three eye spots. Jirari's (1970) findings offer some support for this thesis. On the basis of her observation of 36 neonates tested when they were under 24 hours of age, she was able to experimentally demonstrate that a schematic face (facial features, including eyes and pupils, were clearly defined and appropriately placed) was followed significantly more than a moderately scrambled face (some facial features misplaced), and the latter was followed significantly more than a scrambled, "Picasso" face. The three facial stimuli were equated for complexity, symmetry, and brightness, and thus there was probably no cue other than the form (pattern) to which the infants were responding. In another experiment, Jirari (1970) exposed 31 newborns, less than 24 hours old, to a real face and mannequin face. The real face elicited more visual following than the mannequin. Thus, babies less than a day old can differentiate complex facial stimuli, differing principally in the degree of realism.

TABLE 1
Pupil Response to Single, Double, and Triple Eyespots
Regardless of Their "Pupil Size"

	◯	◯◯	◯◯◯
Male subjects	−.039	+.008	−.056
Female subjects	−.014	+.022	−.003
All subjects	−.027	+.015	−.030

TABLE 2
Pupil Responses to Single Eyespots of Different "Pupil Size"

	◉	◉	◉
Male subjects	−.070	−.028	−.020
Female subjects	−.021	+.004	−.026
All subjects	−.046	−.012	−.023

There are psychological and psychosexual factors in an individual's pupil responses to the reception of pupil size changes in other individuals. Other research has explored various aspects of the psychosexual pupil response and demonstrated that sexual interests are indeed correlated with pupil responsiveness to the relevant sexual objects. For example, in our laboratory a study by Hess, Seltzer, and Shlien (1965) investigated the pupil responsiveness of heterosexual and homosexual men to pictures of men and women. The pupil responses of the five heterosexual men were, of course, greater to the pictures of women than to the pictures of men. Four of the five homosexual men, however, had larger pupils to the pictures of men than to the pictures of women. The fifth homosexual showed a slightly more positive response to the female pictures than to the male ones.

Atwood and Howell (1971) have further corroborated that pupil responses are correlated with sexual object interest. They studied the pupil responses of pedophiliac and nonpedophiac jail inmates to pictures of immature girls and mature women. The pedophiliacs were men that had been jailed for "non-violently" molesting young girls. They had pupil dilations to pictures of young females but slight pupil constrictions to pictures of adult females. The nonpedophiliac men, however, showed the usual adult heterosexual pupil response pattern of strong dilation to pictures of adult females and very little dilation to pictures of young females.

Unpublished research by Simms (personal communication) has indicated further aspects of the psychosexual pupil response in relation to the reception

TABLE 3
Pupil Responses to Triple Eyespots of Different "Pupil Size"

	◉◉◉	◉◉◉	◉◉◉
Male subjects	−.052	−.036	−.080
Female subjects	−.021	−.008	+.019
All subjects	−.037	−.022	−.031

TABLE 4
Pupil Response to Double Eyespots of Different "Pupil Size"

	⊙ ⊙	◉ ◉	⬤ ⬤
Male subjects	−.008	+.002	+.029
Female subjects	+.005	+.020	+.042
All subjects	−.002	+.011	+.036

of differential pupil size in stimulus persons. Simms found that male homosexuals definitely prefer a picture of a woman having constricted pupils over one of her with dilating pupils. Not only that, but men characterized as Don Juans had precisely the same pupil response patterns as the male homosexuals did. Simms suggested the possibility that male homosexuals and Don Juans both have an aversion to women who evidence sexual interest toward them. The homosexual apparently withdraws from women, whereas the Don Juan essentially appears to attack them through seduction and subsequent abandonment.

Still other research, reported by Sheflin (1969) indicates that psychosexual pupil response patterns may be very useful in understanding the nature of the psychosexual dynamics in behavior abnormalities. Sheflin found that male schizophrenics and even paranoid male schizophrenics had heterosexual pupil response patterns. Hence it suggests that notions that paranoid schizophrenics have latent or overt homosexual tendencies is open to question.

In addition, the psychosexual response pattern can be studied from a developmental viewpoint. A beginning in this area was made by Niles Bernick (1966). He showed several types of pictures to children of both sexes and of different ages. The children were students in kindergarten, first, second, fourth, eighth, tenth, and twelfth grades. They were shown pictures of men and women, mothers with a girl or a boy, fathers with a girl or a boy, boys, girls, and babies, and their pupil responses during the viewing of each of these pictures were recorded. They were also asked to tell the experimenter which pictures they liked the most and which they liked the least.

The pupil responses of the subjects to the pictures were surprisingly consistent from one age to the next and did not conform to generally assumed ideas regarding the course of psychosexual development in normal children. In the first place, the pictures of babies elicited high pupil responses from children of all ages and of both sexes. In fact, the boys had stronger pupil responses to the pictures of the babies than to other types of pictures, thus raising the question of when and why their pupil responses to babies become as small as they are in the adult men. The boys showed stronger pupil dilations to pictures of mothers than to pictures of fathers, and stronger pupil dilations to pictures of girls than to pictures of boys. Likewise, the girls showed stronger pupil dilations to pictures of fathers than to pictures of mothers, and stronger pupil dilations to pictures of fathers than to pictures of mothers, and stronger pupil dilations to pictures of boys than to pictures of girls. While the children's pupil responses to pictures of men and women were small, there was still a somewhat stronger pupil dilation to the picture of the opposite-sex adult than to the picture of the same-sex adult in the case of both boys and girls.

The verbally stated preferences of the children, however, were much more in line with the generally accepted notions regarding psychosexual development. Many of the verbally stated preferences were for same-sex pictures, particularly among the boys. The verbal preferences of boys and girls for pictures of babies were relatively high, but the verbal preference of boys and girls for pictures of mothers was extremely low. Hence while the verbal statements of the children partially conformed to the notion of the latency period in psychosexual development, their pupil responses indicated that their basic biological responses toward their own sex and toward the opposite sex remain the same from kindergarten through the twelfth grade. Thus, the hypothesis that children's verbally expressed preferences for males or females are largely determined by existent sociocultural expectations and not by actual interests must be given serious consideration. It is of considerable interest that while most boys are expected to express same-sex interests at certain ages, their pupil response patterns are actually heterosexual, so that even though homosexual preferences are essentially encouraged by the cultural milieu during the so-called latency period, most boys become overtly heterosexual in orientation rather than homosexual.

However, large pupil size in a stimulus person does not always appear to indicate sexually toned emotions in the adult sense. Several researchers have rediscovered that children have larger absolute pupil sizes than do adults and that age is inversely related to the absolute pupil size (Birren, Casperson, & Botwinick, 1950; Kumnick, 1954, 1956a, 1956b; Rubin, 1961, 1962; Silberkuhl, 1896; Wikler, Rosenberg, Hawthorne, & Cassidy, 1965). It would appear that having large pupil size would be advantageous to the child if it increases his visual appeal to caretakers. In other words, parents, parent surrogates, and other persons dealing with children would be more likely to protect, feed, and shelter children due to their visual appeal. These observations suggest to us the possibility that there has been an evolutionary, selective pressure for an innate schema that makes larger pupils in children appealing to adults. In fact, Lorenz (1943) has postulated that human adults must have built-in positive responsiveness to the characteristics of young children. Facial characteristics, including eye pupil size cues, appear to be among these appealing characteristics that promote the infant–caretaker bond. In addition the larger pupil size in young people may explain the use of belladonna.

It might simply make women look younger when their pupils are larger, in addition to providing nonverbal cues indicative of "positive affect."

An informal experiment which Hess conducted has not only indicated the positive responsiveness of adults to children but also that people actually possess nonconscious knowledge of pupil enlargement as an indicator of positive responsiveness toward whatever is being viewed. Two versions of a picture of a mother holding her baby were prepared and the mother's eye pupils were clearly visible. The one version showed her with large pupils. These pictures were presented to 16 students in a classroom who were asked the question, "Which mother loves her baby more?" Surprisingly, the students were unanimous in saying that the mother with the large pupils was the more loving, and none of them seemed to have noticed that the pupil sizes were different in the two versions until it was subsequently pointed out to them.

Experimentation currently in progress in our laboratory (Hess, 1973b) is providing further evidence of the nonconscious knowledge of eye pupil size cues. The initial study was carried out in the simplest possible way. It was an attempt to answer the question, "Do people know something about how big pupils should be under different emotional conditions?"

Two schematic outline faces that were three-quarters natural size were constructed. The eye and iris were drawn in, but not the pupil. One face, which was smiling, was called "happy," and the other face, which was frowning, was called "angry" (Figs. 1a, 1b). Several xeroxed copies of each face were made and then subjects were asked under quite informal circumstances to draw appropriately sized pupils in the two faces. For this task they were given a #2 pencil with an eraser on its end. None of the subjects professed to know anything about pupil size change phenomena.

A total of 20 subjects, 10 men and 10 women, made up the subject pool. Fifteen of the 20 subjects drew larger pupils in the "happy" face than in the "angry" face. These 15 subjects drew an average size of 2.9 mm for the pupil diameter of the "angry" face and an average size of 4.3 mm for the pupil diameter of the "happy" face.

The men and the women were not different in the way they performed, as may be seen in the upper portion of Table 5. However, there was one significant result, which was related to the ease with which the subjects' own eye pupils were visible. For example, at a distance of 5 or 6 ft the pupils of many of the subjects were easy to see. They were mainly individuals with blue, grey, light hazel, or light brown eyes. Those with dark hazel, dark brown, or almost black irises had pupils that did not show up easily. When pupils were rank ordered in terms of "ease of visibility" and correlated with the way in which the subjects had performed in the "pupil drawing" task, a correlation of .77 was obtained. This correlation was between the degree of increase of pupil size drawn for the "happy" face over those drawn for the "angry" face and the visibility of the subjects' own pupils. In fact, the four subjects who

FIG. 1   Average pupil sizes drawn in schematic faces by ten men and women. They were given the two pictures with the pupils missing and asked to draw in the appropriate sized pupils for the expression shown. Fifteen out of 20 persons drew larger pupils into the "happy" face than into the "angry" face.

drew larger pupils in the "angry" face were people whose own pupils were extremely difficult to see. This, of course, could well be an acquired cultural effect in that those individuals with very dark pupils did not have appropriate experiences in observing pupils and pupil size changes in their close relatives. This is a question that is currently being investigated. Our data indicate that the blue-eyed subjects discriminate better than the brown-eyed subjects the relationship between positive attributes of the stimulus and its large pupils as well as the gestalt involving negative stimulus attributes coupled with the small pupils. Moreover, blue-eyed subjects as compared to the brown-eyed ones are capable of manifesting a greater range of behavior as measured by their pupillary responses to picture stimuli that induce pupil dilation or constriction (Hess, 1975b).

PUPILLOMETRICS: METHODOLOGICAL CONCERNS

The review of the findings on pupillary behavior in nonverbal communication suggests that there is much to be learned about the role of the pupils in interpersonal communication. Moreover, given the limitations of the available

TABLE 5
Size of Actual Pupils Drawn by 20 Subjects
(millimeters)

Subjects	"Happy" face	"Angry" face
Ten men	4.0	2.9
Ten women	4.5	2.8
Ten subjects whose pupils were "hard to see"	3.6	3.4
Ten subjects whose pupils were "easy to see"	4.9	2.3

literature, researchers interested in pupillary behavior must be in a position to resolve some methodologically important and procedurally difficult issues if the future experimental outcomes are to be consensually valid and of promise to behavioral analysis of interpersonal communication.

We have described 17 stimulus sources that potentially can contribute to pupillary variation (Hess, 1972) and the list of variables that could confound the assessment of pupillary behavior is growing at what at times appears to be a discomforting rate (Hess, 1975a; Janisse, 1974; Tryon, 1975; see Table 6). At the same time it is encouraging to note that some of the more systematic and fruitful research efforts in pupillometrics deal with methodological concerns (Hakerem, 1967, 1974; Hess, 1972, 1975a; Janisse, 1974).

As has been illustrated, (see Table 6) there are a number of procedural concerns that require scrutiny on the part of the investigator interested in pupillary behavior. A consideration of many of these issues has generated not only methodological advances but also interdisciplinary efforts on the part of the investigators representing such areas of inquiry as ophthalmology, optometry, physiology, bioengineering, electronics, computer technology, psychology, and psychiatry (Goldwater, 1972; Hess, 1972, 1975a; Janisse, 1973, 1974). When one considers the variables (see Table 6) that contribute to pupillary behavior, it quickly becomes apparent that most of them can be experimentally controlled. Among these we would include variables such as age, sex, alcoholic intake, incentive, binocular or monocular viewing, time of testing, nature of the manual response, informational load, and the length of the testing session (Hess, 1972; Tryon, 1975). However some other variables have been the source of methodological conern and, at times, controversy. Among these we would include "inherrent pupillary variability" and various reflex responses, stimulus parameter effects, subect's level of arousal and arousal decrement, iris color, as well as the general problem of measurement especially as it relates to the constriction response (Goldwater, 1972; Hess, 1975a; Hess & Goodwin, 1974; Janisse, 1973, 1974; Loewenfeld, 1958, 1966). We hope that brief discussion of the "problem variables" will stimulate

TABLE 6
Sources of Pupillometric Variation[a]

Sources	Descriptions	Selected documentation
1. Light reflex	Pupil constricts with increased intensity of illumination and dilates with decreased intensity of illumination.	Dennison (1968); Young and Biersdorf (1954)
2. Darkness reflex	Momentary dilation due to interrupting a constant adapting light. Different from the light reflex.	Lowenstein and Loewenfeld (1964)
3. Consensual reflex	Stimulation of one eye affects both eyes equally. Failure called dynamic anisocoria.	Lowenstein and Loewenfeld (1964)
4. Near reflex	Constriction due to decreasing the point of focus.	Lowenstein and Loewenfeld (1964)
5. Lid-closure reflex	Momentary contraction followed by redilation.	DeLaunay (1949)
6. Pupillary unrest (Hippus)	Continuous changes in pupil diameter.	Duke-Elder (1971)
7. Psychosensory reflex	Restoration of diminished reflexes due to external stimulation.	Lowenstein and Loewenfeld (1952a, 1952b)
8. Age	Decreased diameter and increased variability with age.	Kumnick (1954, 1956a, b); Birren, Casperson, and Botwinick (1950)
9. Habituation	Pupil diameter decreases, speed of contraction increases, magnitude of reflex decreases.	Lowenstein and Loewenfeld (1952a); Lehr and Bergum (1966)
10. Fatigue	Diameter decreases, amplitude and frequency of hippus increases. Age amplifies these effects.	Lowenstein and Loewenfeld (1951, 1964)
11. Alertness & Relaxation	Alertness suggestions decrease and relaxation suggestions increase pupil size.	Barlett, Faw, and Leibert (1967)
12. Binocular Summation	Constriction is greater when both eyes are stimulated.	Thompson (1947)
13. Wavelength (pupilomotor Purkinje phenomena)	Larger dilation to chromatic than achromatic stimuli. As intensity of illumination is increased proportionately more constriction is elicited by shorter wavelengths.	Miller (1906); Bouma (1962)
14. Alcohol	Dilates the pupil in proportion to the percentage of alcohol in the blood.	Skoglund (1943)
15. Sexual preference	Dilation to sexually stimulating material.	Hess (1965); Simms (1967)

(continued)

TABLE 6 *(continued)*

Sources	Descriptions	Selected documentation
16. Psychiatric diagnosis	Abnormal pupillary responses in schizophrenics and neurotics.	Duke-Elder (1971); Rubin (1964)
17. Pupil size	Stimuli involving larger pupils elicit more dilation.	Hess (1965)
18. Political attitude	Dilation for preferred political figures.	Hess (1965)
19. Semantic stimuli	Small pupil diameters are associated with high recognition thresholds.	Hutt and Anderson (1967)
20. Taste	Pleasant taste elicits dilation.	Hess (1965); Hess and Polt (1964)
21. Information processing load	Increasing dilation to increasingly difficult problems.	Simpson and Hale (1969) Beatty and Kahneman (1966); Kahneman and Beatty (1966)
22. Task relevant motor response	Having to make a motor response augments pupillary responses.	Simpson (1969); Kahneman, Peavler, and Onuska (1968)
23. Incentive	Increases diameter on easy problems only.	Kahneman et al. (1968); Kahneman and Peavler (1969)
24. Verbal response requirements	Increase from baseline response.	Bernick and Oberlander (1968); Hakerem and Sutton (1966); Simpson and Paivio (1968)
25. Anxiety	Increase from baseline response.	Simpson and Molloy (1971)
26. Arousal decrement	Decrease in baseline response between onset and termination of experimental session.	Peavler and McLaughlin (1967); Peavler (1974); Shrout, Beaver, and Hess (1975)
27. Iris color	Light irises are generally larger and appear to react with larger dilation.	Gambill, Ogle, and Kearns (1967); Beck (1967) Kahn and Clynes (1969)

[a]Modified from Hess (1972) and Tryon (1975).

a more stringent scrutiny of pupillometric research and lead toward attempts at solving some of the empirical ambiguities and theoretical controversies.

Pupillary Variability

Recent research has indicated that the innervation of the iris is much more complex than had been previously imagined, consisting of a secondary neuronal network in addition to a reciprocal autonomic inervation (Hess, 1972). Moreover, Hess (1972) points out that the autonomic system is not the only source of pupillary variability. Lowenstein and Loewnfeld (1970) support this notion and indicate that the various seemingly random fluctuations in pupil size make explicit the fact that the pupil size depends on more than sympathetic and parasympathetic innervation and is profoundly influenced by states of consciousness and various neurological activities such as those involving changes in cortico-diencephalic and reticular systems. To date there are no definite remedies that would enable an investigator to filter out the "noise level" generated by these "random pupil fluctuations." Nevertheless good reliability measures have been obtained by utilizing repeated measure designs (Hakerem, 1967, 1974; Janisse, 1974). Moreover, the experimentally induced effect is of such magnitude to allow for the methodological partitioning of random fluctuations from the pupil changes that are experimentally induced.

Stimulus Parameters

Visual, acoustic, tactile, and chemical stimuli have been utilized in pupilometric research. Application of the visual stimuli has been most controversial (Loewenfeld, 1966) since control over stimulus luminance, intrastimulus brightness, and the related effects of color are not achieved easily. For example, it is difficult to equate for brightness between a control slide and a stimulus slide, particularly if one considers the intrastimulus brightness of the stimulus slide. If color slides are utilized it is difficult to tease out the confounding effects of the psychological impact stemming from "color" to that stemming from the content of the stimulus slide. Since our research has employed visual stimuli, we have extensively investigated parameters associated with utilization of the picture slide stimuli. Color, luminous flux, or overall brightness as well as intrastimulus brightness can be adequately controlled (for the extensive description and procedural guidelines see Hess, 1972, 1975a). Moreover, we have recently demonstrated that if one follows procedural safeguards for minimizing intrastimulus brightness contrast one can demonstrate that brightness contrast could not play a significant role in the pupil's response to picture slide stimuli (Hess, Beaver, & Shrout, 1975). Furthermore, it should be noted that the utility of acoustic, tactile, and chemical stimuli minimizes the methodological difficulties associated with color, luminance, and brightness contrast.

Subjects' Arousal and Arousal Decrement

The subjects' level of arousal refers to subjects' neurophysiological as well as behavioral state while processing a stimulus input. Admittedly, the arousal concept is too inclusive and does generate some ambiguities. Arousal decrement refers to the alleged loss of subjects' interest in the experimental task as well as to subjects' "habituation" as a function of time. This decrement presumably leads to the suppression of the pupil response thus generating variabilities in the measuring of the baseline levels of pupil responding.

We have demonstrated that the gradual decrease in pupil size over time is related in part to the subjects' initial apprehension of the experimental situation rather than to a loss of interest in the experimental task. Furthermore, we have shown that the arousal decrement effects can be controlled by utilizing subjects familiar with pupillometric testing or by pretesting and "adapting" the naive subjects to the basic features of pupillometric testing. In addition, baseline variation can also be controlled to a degree by the avoidance of a lengthy testing procedure or by minimizing a number of test trials. For a more extensive treatment of some of these issues the reader is referred to Hess (1972) and Janisse (1974).

Iris Color

Observations on iris color and pupillary activity (e.g., Gambill, Ogle, & Kearns, 1967; Hess, 1975a, 1975b) suggest that pupils with lighter,–less pigmented irises are larger and respond with greater dilation than do pupils with dark irises. For example Beck (1967) presented acoustic clicks of varying frequencies to a sample of blue-eyed men, blue-eyed women, brown-eyed men, and brown-eyed women. Beck found that the blue-eyed individuals gave larger pupil responses to these stimuli and that men responded with greater magnitude than women. Thus the blue-eyed men exhibited the largest response and the brown-eyed women the smallest. Since in most pupillometric experiments iris color has not been measured or adequately controlled, there is an open question as to the generalizations and utility of some of these previously published findings.

Measurement of Pupil Responses

Several techniques, ranging from photographic–manual to electronic–automated have been utilized in pupillometric research (Hakerem, 1974; Hess, 1972, 1975a). Moreover, different laboratories have employed different "yardsticks" in the assessment of pupillary changes including such measures as average pupil size, peak size, latency-to-peak size, minimum size, and variance. In summarizing on the issues of pupil measurement, it is fair to conclude that there has been *no* unanimity as to what is the most appropriate method for monitoring and assessing pupillary behavior. Further research as well as the current availability of sophisticated new instrumentation promises a resolution of these difficulties.

The Issues of Psychologically Induced Pupil Constriction

Based on data obtained in our laboratory we have advanced the thesis of bidirectionality of the pupil response. Generally, other researchers have supported our initial findings that showed that in response to stimuli indicative of positive affect there occurs pupillary dilation. At the same time our findings of constriction to negative stimuli have been the source of controversy (*e.g.*, Goldwater, 1972; Hess & Goodwin, 1974).

In addition to our findings, the support for the constriction phenomenon has come from other experimenters (Atwood & Howell, 1971; Barlow, 1969; Fredericks, 1970; Fredericks & Groves, 1971). On the other hand, as reviewed by Goldwater (1972), other investigators have failed to find a constriction response to be an index of a "negative affect." Woodmansee's carefully conducted research (Woodmansee, 1966, 1970) is often cited (e.g., Goldwater, 1972) as an example of failure to replicate a constriction response if "tight" experimental controls are utilized.

Woodmansee categorized 22 white college co-eds as "equalitarian" or "anti-Negro" according to their scores on a multifactor Racial Attitude Inventory, and then compared their pupillory responses to "racial content" picture stimuli. The interpretation that Woodmansee (1970) and others have advanced regarding his findings is different from ours. Table 7 shows data obtained by measurement of the points on Woodmansee's Fig. 2 (page 525, Woodmansee, 1970). Examination of data shows no overlap between the responses of the "equilitarian" and the "anti-Negro" treatment groups. During the viewing of the fourth picture stimulus, the "anti-Negro" subjects' pupils were "constricted" by -2.0% by comparison to the preceding control period. Since there were a total of eleven subjects in this group, some of the in-

TABLE 7

Estimated Pupil Diameter Size Changes from Control to Racial Content Test Stimuli in Eleven Equalitarian and Eleven Anti-black Female Subjects during the First Presentation of Stimuli[a]

Subjects	First stimulus (%)	Second stimulus (%)	Third stimulus (%)	Fourth stimulus (%)
Equalitarian	+3.5	+2.6	+1.7	+2.5
Antiblack	+1.9	+0.5	−0.3	−2.0

[a]Data based upon measurement of points on Fig. 2 (page 525 of Woodmansee, J. J., The pupil response as a measure of social attitudes, in: G. F. Summers, ed., *Attitude Measurement*. Chicago, Illinois: Rand McNally, 1970). The percentage changes for each stimulus were computed by taking the difference in pupil size during the viewing of the test stimulus and during the viewing of the control which preceded it, and then calculating the percentage by which the pupil changed its size from that of the control period when the test stimulus was viewed.

dividuals have probably had extensive pupil constriction for a group mean constriction of -2.0% to be obtained since pooling and averaging of data across subjects tend to minimize the manifestation of the constriction response. Woodmansee concluded that pupillary constriction does not occur in response to "negative affect" induced in "anti-Negro" subjects by their exposure to racial content test stimuli. In our opinion, the "anti-Negro" subjects' pupils dilated in response to the first test stimulus because of the arousal or "the first stimulus effects" that normally occurs in a series of stimulus presentations shown in a pupillometric apparatus. These same subjects demonstrate a slight dilation to the second picture stimulus, a slight constriction to the third stimulus and a definite constriction to the last stimulus. While arousal decrement (Woodmansee, 1970) may in part be responsible for the results that were generated, the difference in response between "equalitarian" and the "anti-Negro" subjects is strikingly bidirectional in nature.

As illustrated by the previous example, the issues of data interpretation generate a lack of consensus as well as excitement and productivity in pupil research. However, more troubling and methodologically difficult problems stem from the published record that indicates that constriction responses to psychological stimuli have involved only the use of the visual modality. This suggests that the apparent psychopupil constriction indicative of negative affects may in fact be an experimental artifact produced by utilization of particular visual stimuli. Even though there are no definitive answers on this issue, it is encouraging to note that the methodological concerns dominate current research in pupillometrics (Hess, 1972; Janisse, 1974; Woodmansee, 1970) and in our laboratory we are intensively exploring experimenal approaches toward examining the nature of the pupillory constriction phenomenon.

CONCLUDING REMARKS

As the survey of the findings presented in this chapter indicate, there is much more to be learned about the role of eye pupils in nonverbal communication. Particularly noticeable are the lacunae in the areas of cross-cultural and cross-species analysis. For example, research in our laboratory has indicated that blue-eyed individuals manifest a wider range of pupillary constriction and dilation responses than do brown-eyed individuals. In addition, blue-eyed people appear to be more sensitive to pupillary changes as indicators of a psychological state (Beck, 1967; Hess, 1975a, 1975b). It is conceivable that since the pupils of the blue-eyed individuals are more readily visable than are the pupils of brown-eyed persons, there has been an evolutionary pressure for developing and maintaining the communicative aspects of the pupil in social interactions more in blue-eyed people than in brown-eyed ones. On the other hand, brown-eyed people would probably develop other types of nonverbal signals, such as hand gestures. Thus among Europeans, eye pupil interaction in nonverbal communication should be more common among blue-eyed people of the north and not as prevalent or nonexistent among peoples of the south who, in turn, would have evolved other kinds of nonverbal signals. In addition, the interaction of pupillary behavior with other facial expressions in nonverbal communication requires further research.

Comparative literature dealing with the role of the pupil in interspecific communication is practically nonexistent. Our examples are limited to observations that pupillary changes can be used as a measure of interest and arousal in the house cat (Polt & Hess, 1963). In addition, Leyhausen (1967, p. 300) states that a sudden narrowing of the pupils announces imminent attack, especially in cats, while dilation indicates readiness for defense or escape, depending on the context. Furthermore, Leyhausen reports (personal communication) that this information is put to good use by wild cat trainers who claim that if animal pupils are large they know that they have things fairly well under control, but when the pupils narrow and become small it indeed is an indication of the animal's intention to attack.

On the productive side, it needs to be emphasized that even though the scientific interest in pupillometrics is of relatively recent origin, there is accumulating evidence for the sensitivity and potential applicability of the pupillary system as an index of various psychological states (Goldwater, 1972; Hess, 1972, 1973a, 1975a; Janisse, 1974).

However, as is the case with any new developing field, there is a need for systematic, definitive studies of basic parameters of pupillary behavior. This is particularly apparent as we glance at the literature dealing with the role of pupils in nonverbal communication. Evidence available to date ranges from anecdotal observations to scientific studies under controlled conditions. For example, Chinese jade dealers and wild cat trainers in their endeavors have apparently relied heavily on pupillary changes. A limited number of scientific, naturalistic studies (e.g., Hess, 1965) indicate the importance of pupil dilation in triggering a positive affect. Other laboratory investigations suggest that even "eye spots" can be studied as mimics of pupillary signals of some psychological states (Coss, 1970). Thus, even though available evidence is scattered across a wide range of phenomena, it does indicate that, at least in some contexts, pupillary behavior plays a role in nonverbal communication.

REFERENCES

Atwood, R. W., & Howell, R. J. Pupillometric and personality test score differences of female aggressing pedophiliacs and normals. *Psychonomic Science,* 1971, *22,* 115–116.

Barlow, J. D. Pupillary size as an index of preference in political candidates. *Perceptual and Motor Skills,* 1969, *28,* 587–590.

Bartlett,E. S., Faw, T. T., & Leibert, R. M. The effects of suggestions of alertness in hypnosis on pupillary response: Report on a single subject. *International Journal of Clinical and Experimental Hypnosis,* 1967, *15,* 189–192.

Beatty, J., & Kahneman, D. Pupillary changes in two memory tasks. *Psychnonomic science,* 1966, *5,* 371–372.

Beck, B. B. The effect of the rate and intensity of auditory click stimulation on pupil size. Paper presented at the APA annual convention, Washington, D.C., September, 1967.

Bernick, N. The development of children's preferences for social objects as evidenced by their pupil responses. Unpublished doctoral dissertation, University of Chicago, 1966.

Bernick, N., & Oberlander, M. Effect of verbalization and two different modes of experiencing on pupil size. *Perception and Psychophysics,* 1968, *3,* 327–330.

Birren, J. E., Casperson, R. C., & Botwinick, J. Age changes in pupil size. *Journal of Gerontology,* 1950, *5,* 216–221.

Bouma, N. Size of the static pupil as a function of wave-length and luminosity of the light incident on the human eye. *Nature,* 1962, *193,* 690–691.

Coss, R. G. *Mood provoking visual stimuli: Their origins and applications.* Los Angeles: Industrial Design Graduate Program, University of California, 1965.

Coss, R. G. The perceptual aspects of eye-spot patterns and their relevance to gaze behavior. In C. Hutt & S. J. Hutt (Eds.), *Behavior studies in psychiatry.* Oxford: Pergamon Press, 1970.

DeLaunay, J. A note on the photo-pupil reflex. *Journal of the Optical Society of America.* 1949, *39,* 364–367.

Dennison, B. L. A mathematical model for the motor activity of the cat iris. *Dissertation Abstracts,* 1968, *28*(8-B), 3258–3259.

Duke-Elder, S. *Systems of ophthalmology,* Vol. 12. St. Louis, Mosby, 1971.

Fredericks, R. S. Repression–sensitization and pupillary response to pleasant and unpleasant stimuli. *Dissertation Abstracts International* 1970, *31,* 2982B.

Fredericks, R. S., & Groves, M. H. Pupil changes and stimulus pleasantness. *Proceedings of the Annual Convention of the American Psychological Association,* 1971, *6,* 371–372.

Gambill, H. P., Ogle, K. N., & Kearns, T. D. Mydriatic effect of four drugs determined with pupillograph. *Archives of Ophthalmology,* 1967, *77,* 740–746.

Goldwater, B. C. Psychological significance of pupillary movements. *Psychological Bulletin,* 1972, *77,* 340–355.

Gump, R. *Jade: Stone of heaven.* New York: Doubleday, 1962.

Hakerem, G. Pupillography. In P. Venables and I. Martin (Eds.), *A manual of psychological methods.* Amsterdam: North Holland Publ., 1967.

Hakerem, G. Conceptual stimuli, pupillary dilation and evoked cortical potentials: A review of recent advances. In M. P. Janisse (Ed.), *Pupillary dynamics and behavior.* New York: Plenum Press, 1974.

Hakerem, G. & Sutton, S. Pupillary response at visual threshold. *Nature,* 1966, *212,* 485–486.

Hess, E. H. Attitude and pupil size. *Scientific American,* 1965, *212*(4), 46–54.

Hess, E. H., Pupillometric Assessment. *Research in Psychotherapy,* 1968, *3,* 573–583.

Hess, E. H. Pupillometrics: A method of studying mental, emotional, and sensory processes. In N. S. Greenfield & R. A. Sternbach (Eds.), *Handbook of psychophysiology.* New York: Holt, Rinehart & Winston, 1972.

Hess, E. H. Some new developments in pupillometrics. In: *Die normale und die gestorte Pupillenbewegung.* Symposium der Deutschen Opthalmologischen Gesellschaft, vom 10–12, März 1972, in Bad Nauheim. Munich: Bergman Verlag, 1973, pp. 246–262 (a).

Hess, E. H. What people know about the size of eye pupils. Paper presented at Eighth Pupil Colloquium, Detroit, May 26, 1973. (b)

Hess, E. H. *The tell-tale eye: How your eyes reveal hidden thoughts and emotions.* New York: Van Nostrand-Reinhold, 1975. (a)

Hess, E. H. The role of pupil size in communication. *Scientific American,* 1975, *233,* 110–119. (b)

Hess, E. H., Beaver, P. W., & Shrout, P. E. Brightness contrast effects in a pupillometric experiment. *Perception and Psychophysics,* 1975, *18,* 125–127.

Hess, E. H., & Goodwin, E. The present state of pupillometrics. In M. P. Janisse (Ed.), *Pupillary dynamics and behavior.* New York: Plenum Press, 1974.

Hess, E. H., & Polt, J. M. Pupil size as related to interest value of visual stimuli. *Science,* 1960, *132,* 349–350.

Hess, E. H., & Polt, J. M. Pupil size in relation to mental activity during simple problem solving. *Science,* 1964, *143,* 1190–1192.

Hess,E. H., Seltzer, A. L., & Shlien, J. M. Pupil responses of hetero and homosexual males to pictures of men and women: A pilot study. *Journal of Abnormal Psychology,* 1965, *70,* 165–168.

Hicks, R. A., Reaney, T., & Hill, L. Effects of pupil size and facial angle on preference for photographs of a young woman. *Perceptual and Motor Skills,* 1967, *24,* 388–390.

Hutt, L. E., & Anderson, J. P. The relationship between pupil size and recognition threshold. *Psychonomic Science,* 1967, *9,* 477–478.

Janisse, M. P. Pupil size and affect: a critical review of the literature since 1960. *Canadian Psychologist,* 1973, *14*(4), 311–329.

Janisse, M. P. (Ed.). *Pupillary dynamics and behavior.* New York: Plenum Press, 1974.

Jirari, C. Form perception, innate form preference and visually mediated head-turning in the human neonate. Chicago: The University of Chicago Press, 1970.

Jones, Q. R., & Moyel, I. S. The influence of iris color and pupil size on expressed affect. *Psychonomic Science,* 1971, *22,* 126–127.

Kahneman, D., & Beatty, J. Pupil diameter and load on memory. *Science,* 1966, *145,* 1583–1585.

Kahneman, D., & Peavler, W. S. Incentive effects and pupillary changes in association learning. *Journal of Experimental Psychology,* 1969, *79,* 312–318.

Kahneman, D., Peavler, W. S., & Onuska, L. Effects of verbalization and incentive on the pupil response to mental activity. *Canadian Journal of Psychology,* 1968, *22,* 186–196.

Kahn, M., & Clynes, M. Color dynamics of the pupil. *Annals of the New York Academy of Sciences,* 1969, *156,* 931–950.

Kumnick, L. S. Pupillary psychosensory restitution and aging. *Journal of the Optical Society of America,* 1954, *44,* 735–741.

Kumnick, L. S. Aging and pupillary response to light and sound stimuli. *Journal of Gerontology,* 1956, *11,* 38–45. (a)

Kumnick, L. S. Aging and the efficiency of the pupillary mechanism. *Journal of Gerontology,* 1956, *11,* 160–164. (b)

Lehr, D. J., & Bergum, B. O. Note on pupillary adaptation. *Perceptual & Motor Skills,* 1966, *23,* 917–918.

Leyhausen, P., The biology of expression and impression (1967). In K. Lorenz and P. Leyhausen (Eds.), *Motivation of human and animal behavior.* New York: Van Nostrand-Rheinhold, 1973.

Loewenfeld, I. E. Mechanisms of reflex dilation of the pupil. Historical review and experiment analysis. *Documenta Ophthalmologica,* 1958, *12,* 185–448.

Loewenfeld, I. E. Comment of Hess' findings. *Survey of Ophthalmology,* 1966, *11,* 293–294.

Lowenstein, O., & Loewenfeld, I. E. Types of central autonomic innervation and fatigue. *Archives of Neurology and Psychiatry,* 1951, *66,* 580–599.

Lowenstein, O., & Loewenfeld, I. E. Disintegration of central autonomic regulation during fatigue and its reintegration by psychosensory controlling mechanisms: I. Disintegration. Pupillographic studies. *Journal of Nervous and Mental Disease,* 1952, *115,* 1–21. (a)

Lowenstein, O., & Loewenfeld, I. E. Disintegration of central autonomic regulation during fatigue and its reintegration by psychosensory controlling mechanisms: II. Reintegration. Pupillographic studies. *Journal of Nervous and Mental Disease*, 1952, *115*, 121-145. (b)

Lowenstein, O., & Loewenfeld, I. E. The sleep-walking cycle and pupillary activity. *Annals of the New York Academy of Sciences*, 1964, *117*, 142-156.

Lowenstein, O., & Loewenfeld, I. The pupil. In M. H. Davson (Ed.), *The eye*, (Vol 3). New York: Academic Press, 1970.

Lorenz, K. Z. Die angeborenen Formen moglicher Erfahrung. *Zeitschrift für Tierpsychologie*, 1943, *5*, 235-409.

Magnus, H., *Die Sprache der Augen*. Wiesbaden, 1885.

Miller, R. L. The clinical validation of the pupillary response: The effect of chromatic and achromatic stimuli upon pupil responsivity. (Doctoral dissertation, Michigan State University, Ann Arbor, Michigan: University Microfilms, 1966, No. 66, 14, 152).

Peavler, W. S. Pupil size and performance. In M. P. Janisse (Ed.), *Pupillary dynamics and behavior*. New York: Plenum Press, 1974. (a).

Peavler, W. S. Individual differences in pupil size and performance. In M. P. Janisse (Ed.), *Pupillary dynamics and behavior*. New York: Plenum Press, 1974. (b)

Peavler, W. S., & McLaughlin, J. P. The question of stimulus content and pupil size. *Psychonomic Science*, 1967, *8*, 505-506.

Polt, J. M., & Hess, E. H., The pupil response as a measure of interest in the cat. *Proceedings, Eighth International Ethology Congress*, Haag, Holland, 1963.

Rubin, L. S. Patterns of pupillary dilation and constriction in psychotic adults and autistic children. *Journal of Nervous and Mental Disease*, 1961, *133*, 130-142.

Rubin, L. S. Autonomic dysfunction in psychoses: Adults and autistic children. *Archives of General Psychiatry*, 1962, *7*, 1-14.

Rubin, L. S. Autonomic dysfunction as a concomitant of neurotic behavior. *Journal of Nervous & Mental Disease*, 1964, *138*, 558-574.

Sheflin, J. A. An application of Hess' pupillometric procedure to a psychiatric population: An approach utilizing sexual stimuli. Doctoral dissertation, Purdue University, 1969. *Dissertation Abstracts International*, 1969, *29*, 1907B.

Shrout, P. E., Beaver, P. W., & Hess, E. H. Decreased "arousal decrement" as a function of subjects' experience with pupillometric experiments. Ninth pupil colloquium, Iowa City, May 1975.

Silberkuhl, W. Untersuchungen uber die physiologische Pupillenweite. *Albrecht von Graefe's Archiv für Opthalmologie*, 1896, *42*, 179-187.

Simms, T. M. Pupillary response of male and female subjects to pupillary differences in male and female picture stimuli. *Perception and Psychophysics*, 1967, *2*, 553-555.

Simpson, H. M. Effects of a task-relevant response on pupil size. *Psychophysiology*, 1969, *6*, 115-121.

Simpson, H. M., & Hale, S. M. Pupillary changes during a decision-making task. *Perceptual and Motor Skills*, 1969, *29*, 495-498.

Simpson, H. M., & Molloy, F. M. Effects of audience anxiety on pupil size. *Psychophysiology*, 1971, *8*, 491-496.

Simpson, H. M., & Paivio, A. Changes in pupil size during an imagery task without motor response involvement. *Psychonomic Science*, 1966, *5*, 405-406.

Skoglund, C. R. On the influence of alcohol in the pupillary light reflex in man. *Acta Psychologica Scandinavica*, 1943, *6*, 94-96.

Stass, W., & Willis, F. N., Jr. Eye contact, pupil dilation, and personal preference. *Psychonomic Science*, 1967, *7*, 375-376.

Thompson, L. C. Binocular summation within the nervous pathways of the pupillary light reflex. *Journal of Physiology*, 1947, *106*, 59-65.

Tryon, W. W. Pupillometry: A survey of sources of variation. *Psychophysiology,* 1975, *12,* 90–93.

Wikler, A., Rosenberg, D. E., Hawthorne, J. D., & Cassidy, T. M. Age and effect of LSD-25 on pupil size and knee jerk threshold. *Psychopharmacologia,* 1965, *7,* 44–56.

Woodmansee, J. J. Methodological problems in pupillographic experiments. Proceedings of the 74th Annual Convention of the American Psychological Association, Washington, D.C., 1966.

Woodmansee, J. J. The pupil response as a measure of social attitudes. In G. Summers (Ed.), *Attitude Measurement.* Chicago: Rand McNally, 1970, 514–533.

Young, F. A., & Biesdorf, W. R. Pupillary contraction and dilation in light and darkness. *Journal of Comparative and Physiological Psychology,* 1954, *47,* 264–268.

IV VOCAL BEHAVIOR

8 The Telltale Voice: Nonverbal Messages of Verbal Communication

Aron W. Siegman
University of Maryland Baltimore County

INTRODUCTION

The organization of this chapter reflects an historical perspective. We first address ourselves to a question that preoccupied early researchers in this area: Are there personality traits or predispositions that are associated with specific voice qualitites? We then turn to a more contemporary derivative of the same concern: What are the vocal or extralinguistic correlates of affective states, with special attention to the effects of anxiety arousal on speech. In the second half of this chapter, we discuss the effects of the social context and of cognitive planning and decision making on the encoding process — both representing recent developments in psycholinguistic research.

Before we address ourselves to these specific issues, few general observations on what we mean by the "nonverbal" aspects of spoken messages or communications are in order. The usage of the term nonverbal to designate gestural and other "purely" nonverbal correlates of human communication requires little justification. In its broadest sense, however, the term nonverbal also includes the vocal features of a message that remain after we subtract the words themselves. The more technical terms, *nonlexical, extralinguistic,* and *paralinguistic,* have been used to refer to limited aspects of the vocal, nonverbal domain. Unfortunately, there is no general agreement as to precisely which aspects of vocal nonverbal behavior are covered by these terms. Some authors use the terms interchangeably, whereas others use them to designate different but overlapping aspects of vocal, nonverbal communication. Note that all three terms imply definitions by exclusion; they refer to what is excluded rather than what is included. To a large extent, this is the case because scientific interest in this area is relatively recent, and there is no consensus as to what should be included and what should be excluded. In fact, we do not yet have a generally accepted system for classifying the nonverbal, vocal features of spoken messages, despite some efforts in that direction (e.g., Crystal & Quirk, 1964; Trager, 1958, 1961).

To imply that all the vocal "residue" of a spoken message is unrelated to the meaning of the message is, of course, incorrect, because nonverbal vocal aspects of speech, such as intonation and stress, impart both meaning and structure to spoken messages.

The following examples of how vocal emphasis can modify the meaning of a message are given by Knapp (1972):

1. *He's* giving this money to Herbie. (HE is the one giving the money; nobody else.)
2. He's *giving* this money to Herbie. (He is GIVING, not lending, the money.)
3. He's giving this money to *Herbie.*
(The recipient is HERBIE, not Lynn or Bill or Rod.)

Ambiguous sentences such as the ones preceding have been cited by Chomsky (1965) in support of the proposition that sentences with an apparently simple "surface" structure frequently conceal several underlying "deep" structures. It can be argued, however, that such ambiguities are a characteristic of the written code, but not of spoken language. The sentence, "I like Chomsky roasting" when read with equal stress on all the words, could mean: I like the fact that Chomsky is doing the roasting, or it could mean: I like the fact that Chomsky is being roasted. Vocal stress on either the word Chomsky or on the word roasting resolves this ambiguity. Similarly, intonations and stresses, pauses, and hesitations provide structure and tell us whether a statement is intended as a positive assertion or a question, or perhaps as sarcasm. It would seem fairly obvious that these nonverbal features of speech are not peripheral to but very much an integral part of spoken messages, of their meaning and structure. They certainly are nonlexical, but they are not extralinguistic. Yet traditionally the science of linguistics and the various theories and models of language have typically been based on written language and thus have failed to consider the nonverbal domain although, developmentally and historically, spoken language precedes written language; individuals and cultures speak before they write.

Not all nonverbal vocal cues are an integral part of the meaning of a message. Some may reflect the speaker's background, changes in his mood, his attitudes and feelings toward the person whom he is addressing, or even cognitive decision making. It is this category of nonverbal vocal cues, perhaps best designated as extralinguistic (or paralinguistic), that is the primary focus of interest in this chapter.

Because there does not yet exist a generally accepted system for categorizing the various vocal features that make up the extralinguistic domain, we simply list some of the more prominent variables in the extralinguistic research literature. Some are acoustic in nature, such as pitch level and pitch range, loudness and loudness range. These can be measured in terms of their physical properties or in terms of listeners' judgments. Others involve voice qualities, such as a nasal voice or a raspy voice; still others are related to the linguistic encoding process, such as speech tempo, pausing patterns, and speech disruptions. Some of these variables are discussed in greater detail in the context of specific studies.

In addition to the meaning- and syntax-related nonlexical aspects of speech and the expressive extralinguistic (or paralinguistic) aspects of speech, mention should be made of yet a third category. This category consists of vocal nonverbal cues, whose primary function is to regulate the flow of speech between two or more communicants. Of course, such regulatory cues need not be nonverbal; they can be, and frequently are, lexical in nature. They are messages about the message, and, as such, the term metalinguistic might be an appropriate designation for this category, except that one is reluctant to add to the already existing profusion and confusion of terms. This category is examined most closely by Rosenfeld and is referred to only indirectly in the present chapter.

EXTRALINGUISTIC CORRELATES OF DEMOGRAPHIC VARIABLES

Two review articles, "Speech and Personality" by Sanford (1942) and "Judgment of Personal Characteristics and Emotions from Nonverbal Properties of Speech" by Kramer (1963), summarize the early research dealing with the vocal channel. Most of these early studies address themselves to the question of whether demographic variables (such as gender, age, or occupation) can be reliably and validly inferred from the nonverbal properties of speech. In this context reliability refers to the level of listener agreement and validity to the correlation of the listeners' consensus with some independent criterion of the background or personality variable under investigation. Few of the early investigators looked at *specific* vocal correlates of demographic and personality variables. Instead, they were interested in listeners' global judgments of a speaker's background or personality characteristics, based on *all* vocal cues that remain after one removes the semantic content of the speaker's message. The limited availability of sophisticated instrumentation for the measurement and quantification of specific vocal variables was no doubt responsible, at least in part, for the methodology that characterizes the early studies. Additionally, however, the approach was justified in terms of a philosophical commitment to the superiority of "holistic" over "atomistic" studies. In order to avoid contamination of the vocal cues by the content of the message, the early investigators typically asked their speakers to read a uniform passage, frequently of a fairly innocuous nature, which, as we see later, raises serious methodological problems.

It is clear from these early studies that many demographic background variables can be reliably and validly inferred from a speaker's nonverbal vocal characteristics. In regard to personality variables, however, the results of these early studies suggest moderate to high reliability but low validity; that is, there is agreement among the judges, but there is little evidence for its objective validity. A more detailed discussion of these findings follows.

Demographic Background Variables

Gender.   Of the various background variables, gender and age are the easiest to identify on the basis of nonverbal vocal cues. However, even in relation to these variables there are as yet some unresolved issues, most of which revolve around the nature–nurture question; how much of the variability is due to anatomical and physiological differences, and how much of it is due to culture and social roles, that is, to learning.

A major difference between males and females in relation to speech involves fundamental frequency (f_o) (roughly equivalent to pitch), with females speaking with a higher pitch level than males, but there are other differences as well. There are gender differences in pronounciation, with females generally using the more standard, or the more prestigious, pronounciation (although the two are not always identical) (Bodine, 1975; Labov, 1970; Trudgill, 1975). There are gender differences in intonation patterns, with more "surprise," "hesitation," and "request for confirmation" patterns among women than men (Lakoff, 1973). There are also differences in the use of grammatical forms, although these differences are less pronounced than the differences in pronounciation, and there are differences in the choice of words and speech style. Studies conducted in the United States and elsewhere show that women use fewer profane and obscene expletives than men, although women in Brazil reported that they spoke rudely as often in front of men as in front of women, whereas men said that they refrained from using profanities and obscenities in the presence of women (Head, 1977).

Recent studies suggest that the gender differences in relation to pitch level are not wholly anatomical and physiological, although the lower fundamental frequencies of male speech are undoubtedly related to secondary sexual dimorphism at puberty, which produces a larger larynx and longer and thicker vocal cords in males than in females. Yet gender differences in frequency level are typically much greater than can be reasonably accounted for in terms of variation in vocal tract size (Mattingly, 1966). Also, judges can reliably identify the gender of preadolescents, although there is as yet no anatomical basis for the differences in formant frequency (Sachs, Lieberman, & Erickson, 1973).

It is fairly obvious that beginning at a very early age, boys and girls are socialized into different speaking styles. Much work remains to be done, however, in identifying the precise nature of these differences, and the conditions that tend to elicit them. More precise information on intracultural and intercultural variations with regard to gender-related speech differences should help shed some light on the nature–nurture issue. With respect to intracultural differences, one would want to know, for example, what relationship, if any, there is between sex-role identifications in both males and females and vocal style. Answers to this and related questions, however, must await further research. In relation to eliciting conditions, a study by Markel, Prebor, and Brandt (1972) is of interest. They report higher intensity (loudness) levels on the part of male than female interviewees, when responding to someone of their own gender. However, both male and female interviewees increase their speech intensity level when the interviewer is of the opposite gender.

Some of the other gender differences mentioned earlier also vary as a function of the listener's gender, which raises an important methodological issue. In many of the anthropological and sociolinguistic studies on gender differences in pronounciation, syntax, and word choice, the investigators were males, so that the female subjects were involved in a mixed-gender interaction, in contrast to the male subjects who were involved in a same-gender interaction. Clearly, then, listener gender needs to be controlled for before one can make valid generalizations about gender differences in speech style.

Yet another gender difference involves verbal fluency. Garai and Scheinfeld (1968), for example, report that, beginning at an early age, females display greater grammatical competence and sentence complexity, and fewer speech disabilities of all types than males. Given these findings, one could expect that women would exhibit a faster speech rate and fewer and/or shorter hesitation pauses than men. In our laboratory we have compared the verbal fluency, as measured by speech rate and related temporal indices, of college-age men and women within the context of the information-gathering type interview. In several such studies, the female students evidenced a faster speech rate, speaking with shorter and/or fewer silent pauses than the males. The results of one study, however, suggest that this gender difference in verbal fluency may very well be topic specific (limited to intimate topical areas) rather than a stable gender marker.

In this context, it should be noted that contrary to the old stereotype about female verbosity, a number of investigators have reported precisely the reverse finding, i.e., greater verbosity on the part of males and females, at least within the context of the information-gathering type interview (e.g., Heller, 1968; Siegman & Reynolds, 1984). This difference, too, however, apparently is not independent of topical focus. As with temporary fluency, this gender difference, too, apparently is limited to intimate topics, with the male interviewees being more verbose on such topics than the female interviewees (Siegman & Reynolds, 1984). One methodological implication of this finding for research on sex markers in speech is that such studies need to control not only for the nature of the interaction and listener gender but also for topical focus. Some of the speech differences between males and females referred to earlier may simply reflect the fact that in same-gender conversations males and females tend to converse about different topics (e.g., Landis, 1927; Landis & Burtt, 1924).

For a recent comprehensive review of gender differences in speech, the reader is referred to Smith (1979).

Age. It is widely agreed that f_o decreases with increasing age from infancy to adulthood in both males and females. For males there is a further slight decrease from young adulthood until about 40 to 50 years followed by an increase from 65 years on. For females, however, there apparently is no systematic further change in f_o after having reached adulthood (Helfrich, 1979).

The lowering of pitch from infancy to early adulthood is usually attributed to the ossification of the larynx structure resulting in less elasticity in the cartilages and muscles. However, the reason for the increase in pitch in older males is less obvious. One explanation is that this upward shift in older males is a result of a weakening of the gonads in secreting hormones. It is posssible, however, that the upward shift in pitch level in older males reflects not only age-related physiological changes, but also the emotional stress that is caused by factors such as forced retirement, reduced social contacts, and the decreasing self-sufficiency and status associated with old age in Western societies. That stress is associated with an increase in f_o has been shown by Scherer (1981b). The stress hypothesis may also account for the finding that in general we do not find changes in f_o in older females. Until recently most women did not work outside the home, so that for them aging was not associated with a dramatic change in life style and status as it was, and still is, for males. This stress hypothesis is supported by the results of a recent study by Heinl-Hutchinson (1975) in which she found that fundamental frequency level in older women was inversely related to number of social contacts and to life satisfaction.

Some of the other vocal characteristics that have been identified as possible cues for age judgments, particularly in the identification of older individuals, are fundamental frequency perturbations, perceived by listeners as a trembling voice, reduced loudness and articulatory control, a restricted pitch range, and a slower speech rate (Mysak, 1959).

Very little data are available on developmental changes in the extra-linguistic domain at the other end of the life-span, that is, in young children, except with regard to temporal variables. According to Goldman-Eisler (1968), pausing in speech is considered to reflect cognitive activity that is taking place at that moment in time. Frequent and/or long pauses in any stretch of speech indicate that new, creative speech is being formulated; few and/or short pauses indicate that what is being uttered is a well-practiced, habitual sequence of words. Assuming that children's repertoire of habituated word sequence increases with age, simply because they practice speaking, they should evidence fewer and/or shorter pauses as they grow older. This hypothesis is supported by recent findings (Kowal, O'Connell, & Sabin, 1975; Sabin, Clemmer, O'Connell, & Kowal, 1979), which indicate an increase in speech rate with age, due primarily to a corresponding decrease in the frequency and duration of pauses.

For a recent comprehensive review of age markers in speech, the reader is referred to Helfrich (1979).

Socioeconomic background. It is widely recognized that socioeconomic background influences a variety of speech dimensions such as vocabulary, syntax, and pronounciation. This influence is most pronounced in societies that are rigidly stratified along socioeconomic lines. There is some ambiguity, however, about what precisely is the major determinant of these differences. For a long time, it was assumed that differences in education account for most, if not all, of these social-background related speech differences. Furthermore, it was assumed that to the extent that one has had an adequate education, social-background influences on speech are negligible at best. There is mounting evidence, however, that even with education held constant, pervasive speech differences related to social background do exist. It would appear, then, that these differences have their roots in an early developmental period when language is first acquired and that they are not readily overcome by education alone. Ellis (1967), for example, had a group of college students, apparently with fairly homogeneous intelligence levels, record their impromptu versions of "The Tortoise and the Hare." Judges listened to brief selections of these recordings and then estimated the students' socioeconomic backgrounds. The judges' estimates correlated .85 with the students' socioeconomic backgrounds as measured by the Hollingshead Index. In a subsequent study, a similar group of subjects was asked to role play that they were honor students selected to conduct the University President and his guests on a tour of a new dormitory. Furthermore, the speakers were told to use their very best grammar and voice quality and to try to "fake" their voices to make them sound upper class. In this group, the judges' ratings correlated .65 with the Hollingshead Index, still an impressive correlation. A further analysis of the actual speech samples revealed that, although subjects in both socioeconomic groups used proper grammar, their choice of vocabulary, sentence length, and sentence structure varied considerably. Nevertheless, there is reason to suspect that the judges' ratings were based mostly on vocal and pronounciation cues. The basis for this hunch is another study in which the judges were asked to identify the social backgrounds of students solely on the basis of a recording in which the students counted from 1 to 10. Again, the judges' ratings correlated .65 with the Hollingshead Index. The results of the study just cited suggest that even in the United States today social background is a significant source of variance in a variety of speech dimensions, independently of the speakers' education and intelligence level.

On the basis of observations made in England, Basil Bernstein (1961) proposed two linguistic codes, one that is used primarily by members of the lower class, the other by members of the middle and upper class. The elaborated code, which is used by the middle and upper class, is characterized by the verbal elaboration of meaning and the articulation of the speaker's intent in a verbally explicit form. Furthermore, in the elaborated code, the speaker selects from a variety of lexical and syntactic alternatives and therefore the probability of predicting the pattern of what the speaker is saying is fairly low. In the restricted code, which is used by the lower class, the choice of lexical and syntactic alternatives is limited, which increases the predictability of the speaker's message. Furthermore, according to Bernstein, certain child-rearing practices found mainly among lower class families result in the child mastering only a single code — the restricted code — whereas the child-rearing practices characteristic of the middle class result in the child mastering both codes. For an elaboration of the precise nature of this relationship, the reader is referred to Bernstein's own discussions of this topic (Bernstein, 1961, 1964, 1972).

Most of the studies that have been undertaken to validate Bernstein's major hypothesis, namely, that members of the lower class and middle class typically use different codes, were conducted in England, and their relevance to the United States is open to debate. However, at least one major validating study was conducted in the United States with positive results (Hess & Shipman, 1965). Neverthless, Bernstein's contention that the lower class is locked into a single code, in contrast to the middle class, which is capable of code switching, has been challenged (Houston, 1970), and some critics have suggested that the reverse may very well be the case (e.g., Taylor & Clement,

1974). The fact is that, although widely cited, Bernstein's hypothesis has yet to be validated.

Of special interest from the point of view of the present chapter is Bernstein's hypothesis that the two codes are associated with different extralinguistic encoding patterns. The basis for this hypothesis is Goldman-Eisler's (1968) contention that cognitive planning and decision making is associated with pausing—an issue that is discussed in greater detail later in this chapter. Because the elaborated code is characterized by more complex linguistic choices than the restricted code, it should also, according to Bernstein, be associated with more pausing. In a study of the extralinguistic behavior of lower class and middle-class 16-year-olds of roughly equal intelligence, Bernstein (1962) found that the lower class group spent less time pausing and used longer phrases than the middle-class group. The former finding is, of course, consistent with Bernstein's notions, but it is less obvious how one is to view the latter finding. Since the distinguishing characteristics of the elaborated code include: (a) the elaboration of meaning and (b) complex syntactic forms, one can expect this code to be associated with relatively long utterances (due to *a*) and, if anything, relatively long rather than short phrases (due to both *a* and *b*). The finding, then, that the lower class rather than the middle class used relatively long phrases would seem to present a problem for Bernstein's position. Also, of the two socioeconomic groups matched for IQ scores, the lower class group was the more productive of the two. It must be pointed out, however, that there were only five subjects in each of these groups, hardly enough for broad generalizations about class-related speech differences. Furthermore, the fact that in this study the topic of subjects' discussions was limited to their views on capital punishment, about which subjects from different socioeconomic backgrounds may not be equally well informed, restricts the generalizability of the study's findings. It is of interest that, these methodological caveats notwithstanding, very similar findings were obtained by Howland and Siegman (1982), who analyzed the responses of 66 middle-aged American males to a structured, stress interview. As in Bernstein's study, socioeconomic status correlated positively with pause duration (.39) and negatively with length of response (−.33). Additionally, socioeconomic status correlated positively with response latency (.44) and negatively with loudness (−.46) and frequency of interruptions (−.59). Perhaps the relatively short responses of the high-status individuals reflect a conciseness of formulation rather than a dearth of information. Such an interpretation is consistent with the finding that the high-status individuals gave shorter responses and required longer response latencies than the low-status individuals. Goldman-Eisler (1968) has shown that conciseness of formulation is indeed associated with relatively long latencies. Alternatively, the longer response latencies of the high-status respondents could be due to their greater confidence in an interview situation, feeling no pressure to respond promptly.

Although the consistency between Bernstein's (1962) and Howland and Siegman's (1982) findings lends some credence to their generality, the latter findings too are subject to a number of methodological caveats. For example, the subjects in the Howland and Siegman (1982) study were interviewed by a professional psychologist, i.e., a relatively high-status person. From a socioeconomic status point of view, then, the relatively high-status interviewees interacted with a peer, but the relatively low-status interviewees interacted with someone who is of a higher status than themselves. The fact that in the Howland and Siegman (1982) study the interviewer was a female who asked challenging questions compounds the generalizability issue even further. It is by no means clear that challenging questions from a female interviewer have the same impact on high- and low-status males. Meaningful conclusions about class-related speech differences can be reached only if the topic of discussion and the social context have the same meaning to both high- and low-socioeconomic status individuals.

In an attempt to find a topic that would be of similar interest to both middle-class and working-class subjects, Brotherton (1979) compared 10-minute samples of spontaneous speech selected from interviews with five middle-class and five working-class females who were interviewed about their child-rearing practices. Again, we are dealing with limited samples, but to the extent that the differences are statistically significant, they are instructive. There were no significant class differences in the duration of silent pauses at the beginning of utterances (i.e., latencies), but significant differences were found in both the frequency and the duration of within-utterance silent pauses. As one would expect on the basis of Bernstein's theorizing, the middle-class subjects responded with more frequent and longer silent pauses than the working-class subjects. These differences occurred at both clause boundaries and within clauses. Furthermore, Brotherton was able to demonstrate that the middle-class speakers indeed produced more elaborated and less redundant responses, as well as longer lexical items than the working-class speakers. Filled pauses (ah's) were significantly more common among the middle-class than the working-class speakers both at the beginning of utterances and within clauses, suggesting a class difference in the signaling of uncertainty. Brotherton proposes that taken as a whole, the findings suggest that middle-class speakers exercise more temporal control over their linguistic resources and that they have greater processing facility in manipulating those resources than working-class speakers. However, these class differences clearly are relative. All subjects consistently displayed similar patterns and forms of speech behavior but to a greater or lesser extent, consistent with Bernstein's more recent position that code and class differences are differences of use and not of competence (Bernstein, 1973).

However, in an interview study by Siegman and Pope (1965a), with 50 female nursing students as subjects, a significant correlation (r = .28, $p < .05$) was obtained between subjects' socioeconomic background, as measured by the Hollingshead Index, and the proportion of silent pauses (2 sec and over) in subjects' responses. Contrary to the findings cited thus far (Bernstein, 1962; Brotherton, 1979; Howland & Siegman, 1982), in this study the lower and lower middle-class subject showed more pausing than the upper middle-class and upper-lcass subjects. It should be pointed out, however, that in the Siegman and Pope study, the correlation between socioeconomic background and pausing was a function of the topic under discussion. When the interviewer focused on subject's family experiences, the correlation was highly significant (r = .37, $p < .01$), but when he focused on their school experiences it was clearly not significant (r = .19, $p > .10$). Perhaps the family topic was more problematical for the lower class interviewees than for the middle-class and upper-class interviewees, or perhaps lower class individuals are less accustomed to discussing their family relations with strangers than are the others, especially in a cross-gender interactions, which was the case in this study. The significant methodological point to be made is that, in research on class-related speech differences, it is essential to control for the social context, the gender, and the status of the listener, and the meaning of the topic. In the absence of such well-controlled studies, any generalization about socioeconomic background and speech must be of a tentative nature.

EXTRALINGUISTIC CORRELATES OF PERSONALITY VARIABLES

A popular research topic from the 1920s through the 1940s was the ability of naive judges to correctly identify a speaker's personality traits from noncontent voice and speech characteristics. These studies went out of style, however, at least in part, because of the disappointing results. Typically, it was found that there was a surprisingly high level of agreement among the judges as to the speaker's position on a particular personality trait, but that it was difficult to validate this consensus on the basis of external criteria of the speaker's personality. It was widely concluded that the listeners' consensus was based on theatrical conventions for portraying certain personality types, but that it had no objective validity. Additionally, the spate of studies in the post-World War II period, which demonstrated the poor performance of the traditional personality measures — objective as well as projective — in predicting behavior, led to a reduced interest in the whole field of individual differences, and for some to a questioning of the very concept of stable personality differences or traits.

It is a fact that the early studies on the identification of personality traits from vocal characteristics were beset by many methodological problems, some of which tended to bias the results in favor of a relationship, others against it. In light of the renewed research interest in this topic, it may be useful to review the problems that plagued the early studies in this area. One major problem is the difficulty of obtaining independent, valid criteria of the speaker's position on specific personality traits.

Many of the early studies used paper-and-pencil personality tests, which were developed on an ad hoc basis, in order to measure the specific personality dimension under investigation, without any evidence that these tests met even the most basic psychometric requirements of reliability and validity.

Finally, assuming adequate reliability, it is not always clear that the judges' understanding or definition of the personality dimension that is under investigation corresponds to what is being measured by the standardized test. Such a lack of correspondence would, of course, conspire against obtaining positive results.

In order to avoid these and other problems that accompany the use of objective and projective personality tests, some investigators turned to peer evaluations. These evaluations are typically in the form of ratings obtained from the speaker's acquaintances and therefore may very well be based, at least in part, on the same cues as those used by the judges, that is, the speaker's vocal style. In other words, positive findings obtained with this method may be artifactual and spurious.

The early studies on speech and personality are beset by yet another problem, which involves the nature of the speech samples. Frequently they are not representative of natural conversation. Instead, in the typical study, a subject is asked to *read* a passage or a sentence, all too frequently of an insipid if not altogether nonsensical nature. The reason for this procedure is to eliminate content cues, but it raises a host of other problems, all of which may combine to reduce the possibility of demonstrating that personality traits or predispositions can be reliably and validly identified from a speaker's voice characteristics. First, there are systematic differences between a person's speaking voice and reading voice, and to use a sample of the latter is hardly appropriate for testing the hypothesis under scrutiny. Second, the artificial circumstances under which these speech samples are obtained may affect the speaker's voice and mask whatever vocal correlates of personality that may exist. Third, it is not unreasonable to argue that specific interpersonal conditions may be necessary for eliciting the vocal correlates of personality characteristics such as introversion–extraversion and social dominance. At the very least, speech samples should be obtained in a context of dyadic social interactions. Monologues or readings do not provide the appropriate conditions for testing the effects of personality variables such as social dominance on speech. Considering the variety of methodological problems that characterize the early studies, it was probably premature to conclude, on the basis of these studies, that naive judges cannot correctly identify a speaker's personality from his voice alone.

Following a period of quiescence, there are signs of a renewed interest in the whole question of personality and speech. The focus of interest, however, is no longer on the ability of naive judges to make accurate personality evaluations from voice qualities, although at least one investigator (Scherer, 1972, 1979) has pursued this question in a series of carefully designed studies. Instead, the focus of most of the recent studies is on identifying, by means of objective measurements, the vocal correlates of specific personality variables. The results, which are summarized later, indicate that such correlates probably do exist, at least as far as a limited number of personality variables are concerned.

Vocal correlates of extraversion–introversion.   One of the first comprehensive studies on the ability of naive subjects to make accurate personality judgments on the basis of voice quality was conducted by Allport and Cantril (1934). They used many subjects representing a wide range of backgrounds. In most of their samples, subjects were able to identify a speaker's extraversion–introversion level, as measured by Heidebreder's self-rating instrument, at better than a chance level. The authors state that they deliberately made no attempt to find out which specific aspect of the speaker's voice provided the basis for the listeners' judgments regarding his extraversion-introversion level. According to Allport and Centril (1934):

> To attempt to correlate pitch with one personal quality, speed with another and intensity with a third, would be to make the whole problem absurdly atomistic, and as is the case with all studies with such correlations between mere meaningless fragments of well structured personalities, the study would be doomed to failure. (p. 39)

They do not explain, however, why one would necessarily have to limit oneself to a single voice quality, rather than some combination thereof, which would be the proper alternative to the "atomistic" approach, if the later indeed ended in failure.

It is ironic that recent studies, which have adopted research strategies characterized by Allport and Cantril (1934) as "atomistic" and which would have been rejected by them because they are unlikely to produce positive results, have in fact produced rather encouraging results.

The results of one of the first studies to reopen the question of extraversion–introversion and speech indicate that extraverts can be distinguished from introverts by their speech style (Siegman & Pope, 1965b). In this study, Eysenck's E-scale was used to determine the speakers' extraversion-introversion levels. Previous research (Eysenck & Eysenck, 1963) suggests that this scale consists of a sociability factor and an impulsivity factor, the latter reflecting a preference for quick action versus deliberation. Considering both of these factors, it was hypothesized that extraverts would exhibit shorter latencies, speak more quickly and with fewer hesitations than introverts, especially in their initial contacts with strangers. It was felt that interviewees' verbal behavior in an initial interview situation could serve as an appropriate test for this hypothesis. The results showed that interviewees' E-scale scores correlated significantly with the following temporal indices: a latency measure, a measure of silent pauses (2 sec and over), and a measure of "filled" brief pauses (ahs and allied hesitation phenomena). All the correlations were in the predicted direction, that is, with extraversion associated with more fluent speech, i.e., shorter latencies, shorter silent pauses, and fewer hesitations.

Similar findings are reported by Ramsay (1966, 1968). Sound/silence ratios were found to be significantly higher for extraverts than for introverts. This difference occurred because the extraverts exhibited shorter silent pauses between utterances than introverts. The tasks included reading from prepared texts, reponding to interview questions, and responding to TAT cards — descriptions of the cards followed by stories about them. The difference in sound/silence ratios between extraverts and introverts increased with task complexity but seemed to be unaffected by the different levels of interpersonal involvement associated with the interview and the TAT tasks. Consequently, Ramsay suggests that it is probably the impulsivity dimension of the extraversion–introversion dimension, rather than the sociability dimension, which is the significant source of variance in relation to verbal fluency.

The results of one recent study (Siegman & Reynolds, 1985), which tried to assess the relative contribution of the sociability items of the Maudsley Extraversion scale to verbal fluency versus that of the impulsivity items, found that only the former correlated significantly with speech-rate (r (31) = .32 versus r (31) = .00). However, in another recent study (Siegman, Feldstein, & Barkley, 1984), we found a significant negative correlation between impulsivity and response latency. Perhaps impulsivity accelerates response latency, whereas sociability accelerates the temporal pacing of speech itself. However, until we have more conclusive evidence, the most reasonable position to take is that both components of extraversion, i.e., sociability and impulsivity appear to contribute to the acceleration of speech.

Yet another explanation for the positive correlation between social extraversion and verbal fluency is that social extraverts are more concerned with making a positive impression on others than are social introverts. Later in this chapter it is pointed out that in our culture fluent speech is a source of positive personality attributions and, conversely, hesitant speech, especially speech that is interrupted by long hesitation pauses, is a source of negative personality attributions. Consequently, individuals concerned with impression management are likely to attempt to speak fluently and to avoid long hesitation pauses. Although individuals' scores on Snyder's Self-Monitoring scale (Snyder, 1974), a questionnaire that was specifically developed to measure impression management, did not correlate significantly with verbal fluency indices, two of its three subscales, namely, the Extraversion scale and the Acting scale, do correlate significantly with speech rate (Siegman & Reynolds, 1983b, 1985). One implication of the impression management explanation is that the relationship between social extraversion and speech style is likely to be a function of cultural norms, with social extraverts trying to approximate the socially desirable speech style. It is of interest to note, therefore, that in a cross-cultural study by Scherer and Scherer (1981) extraversion was associated with fewer hesitation pauses for U.S. speakers but not for German speakers. In fact the German sample extraversion was associated with more frequent hesitation pauses. If the association between extraversion and relatively short silent pauses is due to the extravert's impulsivity, which according to Eysenck has a physiological basis, one would be hard put to explain such cultural differences. Such differences present no problem, however, if the association between extraversion and verbal fluency is explained in terms of impression management. It should be pointed out, however, that the association between social extraversion and fluent speech is by no means limited to U.S. speakers. The findings cited earlier by Ramsey were obtained with English (Ramsay, 1966) and Dutch (Ramsay, 1968) speakers.

In addition to the positive correlation between extraversion and verbal fluency indices, there is evidence to suggest that extraverts also speak more forcefully and more loudly than introverts (Scherer, 1979; Scherer & Scherer, 1981; Trimboli, 1973). Finally, one might expect extraverts, especially if extraversion is conceptualized in terms of sociability, to be more voluble, or talkative, than introverts. Although some investigators have found this to be the case (Campbell & Rushton, 1978; Patterson & Holmes, 1966; Rutter, Morley, & Graham, 1972), repeated attempts in our laboratory to replicate this finding have been mostly unsuccessful. In one recent study, however, we were able to obtain a significant positive correlation between extraversion and a measure of verbal productivity in females but not in males (Siegman & Reynolds, 1985). If the assumption that extraverts tend to engage in impression management is valid, then it may very well be that extraverts will moderate their talkativeness if such talkativeness could create a negative impression, which in turn is likely to depend on factors such as gender composition and the nature of the interaction. It should be noted, therefore, that, whereas the study by Campbell et al. (1978) involved conversations between females, our studies involved males interviewing females, which may have potentiated considerations of impression management and thus may have vitiated the relationship between extraversion and talkativeness.

Given that the extraversion–introversion trait is indeed associated with specific speech correlates, the next question that we should address ourselves to is: What are the speech cues that people use in making the attribution of extraversion? Are they the same as the objective correlates of extraversion–introversion, or not? If they are, such convergencies could be the basis for accurate judgments of extraversion–introversion from voice and speech characteristics. Again the evidence suggests that pauses and speech rate play a major role. In one study (Feldstein & Sloan, 1984) a group of extraverts and introverts were asked to speak as they normally do, as extraverts do, and as introverts do. Both extraverts and introverts decreased their pause durations and increased their speech rates when imitating extraverts, and increased their pause durations and decreased their speech rates when imitating introverts (although the extraverts were better at this "acting" task than the introverts). One implication of this finding is that fluent speech, free from relatively long silent pauses, is one stereotype that we attribute to the extraverted person. Another implication of this study is that people can manage or control the temporal patterning of their speech, but more about this issue later in this chapter. Other investigators too found that a relatively fast speech rate, whether on the part of males or females, is perceived as an indication of extraversion (Addington, 1968; Aronovitch, 1976). Acoustical variables also play a role in the attribution of the extraversion–introversion trait, although in relation to these variables the evidence is less consistent than it is in relation to the temporal variables. Scherer (Scherer, 1979; Scherer & Scherer, 1981) reports that fundamental frequency (f_o) (which is perceived as pitch, although the correlation between f_o and its subjective perception as pitch is far from perfect) is one acoustical cue that is used in the attribution of extraversion, provided the f_o level is not too high. A very high f_o level may be perceived as an indication of emotionality and immaturity and even of introversion (Mallory & Miller, 1958; Scherer, 1979). Aronovitch (1976) found that the variability of f_o (which is perceived as intonation), rather than the average f_o level, is the critical variable in the attribution of extraversion in male speakers. Others (Addington, 1968; Scherer, 1979) also found that the variability of f_o is associated with extraversion, although Addington (1968) reports that this was so only in the case of female speakers, but not in the case of male speakers. Intensity level (which is perceived as loudness, although here too the correlation between the physical-acoustic parameters of the stimulus and its perception by the listener as loudness is not perfect) and the variability of intensity level are yet additional cues that are used by judges in the attribution of extraversion. Aronovitch (1976) reports that intensity level is the primary cue for attributing extraversion in the case of female speakers, and variability of intensity in the case of male speakers. Scherer (1979), however, found that intensity level was also used in the attribution of extraversion to male speakers. In some of these studies (Addington, 1968; Aronovitch, 1976), there is a clear implication that different cues (or perhaps different combinations of cues) are used in the attribution of extraversion to male than to female speakers, with no consistent pattern, however, emerging from the available data.

Based on the findings reviewed so far, it would seem that there is considerable overlap between the specific speech variables that are used in the attribution of extraversion and the actual, veridical, correlates of that personality dimension. Given such overlap, it should be possible to identify a person's extraversion–introversion level on the basis of his or her speech, even if only with moderate accuracy. Why, then, were so many of the early investigators unsuccessful in their attempts to show that a person's extraversion level can be accurately judged from his voice and speech characteristics? Perhaps, as suggested earlier, these failures were due to the criteria that were used to assess the speaker's extraversion level, and/or to the failure to use meaningful, interactive speech samples, and/or to deficiencies in the judgment procedure. In a more recent study, Scherer (1972, 1979) was indeed able to show that both self and peer ratings of extraversion can be accurately inferred from voice characteristics of American speakers, although the correlations between criteria and attributions were only of a moderate level. This should not be surprising because there is only a partial overlap between the veridical correlates of extraversion and the cues that are being used in the attribution process. For example, f_o level and/or f_o variability are apparently used in the attribution of extraversion (Addington, 1968; Aronovitch, 1976), although there is no evidence that they are veridical correlates of extraversion. The relative weights that listeners assign to the different cues in the attribution of extraversion may be yet another source of error. Finally, it should be noted that, whereas listeners are fairly accurate in their judgments of loudness, they are apparently less accurate in their judgments of speech rate—they tend to estimate very fast speech as less fast than moderately fast speech (Bond & Feldstein, 1982; Feldstein & Bond, 1981). Also, a speaker's pitch and loudness levels influence the perception of that speaker's speech rate, so that speech rates of high pitched or loud speakers are perceived as faster than they really are (Bond & Feldstein, 1982; Feldstein & Bond, 1981). All these factors may reduce the accuracy of predicting a person's extraversion level on the basis of his or her vocal cues, especially on the basis of speech rate.

Vocal and speech correlates of other personality variables.   What about the stylistic speech correlates of personality traits and behavioral tendencies other than extraversion–introversion? One personality variable that reasonably can be expected to be associated with a distinctive speech style is dominance or assertiveness. The evidence for such a relationship, however, is considerably less consistent than it is for extraversion–introversion. In Scherer's cross-cultural study (Scherer, 1979) dominance was not associated with a distinctive speech style, at least not in his U.S. sample. Other evidence, however, suggests that dominance is associated with a distinctive speech style, in fact, one that very much recalls the speech style of the extravert. Thus, Mehrabian and Williams (1969) report a positive correlation between dominance, as measured by Jackson's (1967) Dominance scale, and with speech rate and speech volume. Mallory and Miller (1958) report that their subjects' scores on Bernreuter's dominance scale correlated negatively with "inadequate loudness" ($r(371) = -.32$). They also report negative correlations between their subjects' Bernreuter dominance scores and "unusually high-" pitched speech and "excessively" rapid speech. It is not quite clear that the latter finding necessarily implies a negative correlation between dominance and speech rate, but if it does, it is, of course, inconsistent with the positive correlation between dominance and speech rate reported by Mehrabian and Williams (1969). Finally, Natale, Enton, and Jaffe (1979) found that high-dominance scorers tend to engage in more interruptions and more simultaneous speech than low scorers. Thus, to the extent that the evidence suggests a distinctive speech style for dominant and assertive individuals, it overlaps with that of extraverts (loud and fluent speech in both cases). However, as pointed out earlier, the evidence for a distinctive speech style for dominance and assertiveness is not as well documented as it is for extraversion-introversion and in relation to at least one variable (speech rate) the evidence seems to be contradictory.

Recent findings suggest that there is yet another personality variable, or behavior pattern, that is associated with a distinct speech style, namely the Type-A behavior pattern. This behavior pattern has been described by Friedman and Rosenman (1974), the two individuals primarily responsible for its identification as a major independent risk factor in coronary heart disease (CHD), as "an action-emotion complex that can be observed in any person who is aggressively involved in a chronic, incessant struggle to achieve more and more in less time, and if required to do so, against the opposing efforts of other things or persons" (p. 67). They have identified competitive drive, impatience, a sense of time urgency, and hostile and aggressive behavior as the major behavioral manifestations of the Type-A behavior pattern. The results of several studies indicate that, when challenged, Type-A individuals respond with a distinctive speech style. Specifically, they respond with shorter latencies, speak more loudly, and with faster speech rates than Type-B individuals (Howland & Siegman, 1982; Scherwitz, Berton, & Leventhal, 1977; Schucker & Jacobs, 1977; Siegman & Feldstein 1984). In fact, stylistic variables, especially those involving the vocal channel, serve as the major cues for determining a person's behavior type, when such a determination is made on the basis of a person's responses to the Structured Interview (Rosenman, 1978). Again, it is of interest to note the overlap between the speech correlates of extraversion and dominance and that of the Type-A personality: namely a loud voice and a relatively fast pacing of speech. Perhaps all three personality dimensions reflect a heightened state of arousal and a tendency to respond in an active and involved manner. In fact, Scherer (1981a) reports that the activity dimension of emotional arousal is associated with loud and fast speech. Some would argue that strictly speaking the Type-A behavior pattern is not a personality trait, because the occurrence of the appropriate behavior depends on a specific situational elicitor, namely, a challenging environment. In response, it can be argued that the proper definition of any personality trait should include its environmental elicitors, and that the failure to do so may very well be responsible for the low-construct validity of many personality traits. Clearly, traits such as extraversion and dominance are no less situation specific than the Type-A syndrome, in that the behaviors that are associated with these traits are elicited by specific *social* situations.

The fact that the speech style of the extraverted and dominant individual is likely to overlap with that of the Type-A personality may help resolve two puzzling findings in the Type-A literature. The first is the apparent gradual increase of Type As in the U.S. population (Matthews, 1982). The second is that, despite efforts to standardize the administration of the Structured Interview, which is the major instrument for the assessment of the Type-A behavior pattern, and despite the efforts to make the scoring of the Structured Interview more objective and reliable, there has been no commensurate improvement in its ability to predict CHD. In fact, recently there have been a number of failures to replicate the relationship between the Type-A behavior pattern and CHD (Shekelle et al., 1984). Perhaps both of these findings are due to the fact that the Type-A assessment, when it is based on the Structured Interview, is now, more than in earlier years, heavily influenced by the interviewee's expressive vocal behavior, i.e., a loud voice and an accelerated speech style. This may confound the Type-A diagnosis with extraversion and dominance. This confounding may account for the apparent increase of Type As, and the failure of the Structured Interview to adequately predict CHD. Too many people now diagnosed as Type As may simply be outgoing and dominant individuals, who are not coronary prone.[1]

In his cross-cultural study, Scherer (1979) also investigated the vocal correlates of agreeableness and emotional stability. Of the two, only emotional stability was associated with specific voice characteristics, namely, loudness and voice contrast. Verbal productivity is yet another variable that has been associated with emotional adjustment. Cope (1969) reports that college stu-

---

[1]Another potential confound is between the subdued speech style of the Type-B behavior pattern and depression. The speech style of depressives, not unlike that of Type-B individuals, is characterized by relatively long latencies, slow speech-rates, and low volume. Clearly, if the Structured Interview is to become a more effective predictor of CHD, we need to control for such potentially confounding variables as depression and non-coronary-prone extraversion.

dents who were selected by their professors and residence hall counselors for their optimum mental health were more verbally productive, i.e., they tended to talk more, than a group of comparable controls. Campbell and Rushton (1978), who studied British, female occupational therapy students, also report a significant positive correlation between teachers' ratings of their students' emotional adjustment and the latter's verbal productivity in an interview situation. In that same study, however, there was no significant correlation between more objective indices of the subjects' emotional adjustment, such as Eysenck's and Cattell's neuroticism scales, and their verbal productivity scores — which is consistent with the results of our own studies of this relationship. In numerous interview studies conducted in our laboratory, we never found a significant correlation between subjects' objective neuroticism scores (e.g., Eysenck's Neuroticism Scale or the Taylor MAS) and their verbal productivity scores. This raises the possibility that the positive correlations between rated emotional stability and verbal productivity were artifactual, in the sense that the adjustment ratings may have been influenced by the subject's verbal productivity levels.

Let us now summarize the findings as far as the objective voice and speech correlates of personality variables are concerned. Of the traditional personality dimensions, only extraversion–introversion, whether it is defined in terms of a "paper-and-pencil" measure (e.g., the Eysenck E-scale) or in terms of peer evaluations, seems to be consistently associated with a specific speech style. As far as the other traditional personality variables are concerned, there is some evidence that dominance too may be associated with specific voice and speech-style correlates, but the evidence is less consistent than it is for extraversion. Two other dimensions that can arguably be conceptualized as personality variables, and which seem to have specific voice and speech correlates, are emotional stability and the Type-A behavior pattern, especially the latter.

The evidence in favor of specific voice and speech correlates for the preceding personality dimensions is most clearly apparent when they are defined in terms of peer evaluations. This, of course, raises the issue of confounding, because the subjects's voice and speech characteristics may have contributed to the judges' personality evaluations. On the other hand, peer evaluations may be a more reasonable and valid way to determine personality differences than the traditional self-administered paper-and-pencil questionnaires. Firstly, paper-and-pencil questionnaires are essentially self-ratings and thus are subject to the ubiquitous social desirability bias, unless specific measures are taken to correct for it. Secondly, some personality dimensions, such as extraversion and dominance, require social interactions for their activation and, therefore, may be more appropriately assessed by outside observers. There is yet another reason why peer evaluations may be more appropriate for the assessment of personality than self-evaluations. Although the discussion thus far may suggest otherwise, I do not conceive of nonverbal behavior as yet another external index of personality, on par with the traditional objective paper-and-pencil measures of personality. Instead, I view how a person moves or speaks to be the very substance of personality, and the various nonverbal indices as behavioral samples of the individual's personality. Peer evaluations may be more appropriate for the measurement of personality than self-assessments precisely because they do consider nonverbal behavior. Furthermore, to the extent that people tend not to be aware of their own nonverbal style, their self-evaluations are inadequate for the assessment of their personalities.

PERSON PERCEPTION AND SPEECH

When the early researchers discovered that listeners' personality judgments of speakers, based on the latters' voice and speech characteristics, had good interjudge reliability but presumably very little validity, they abandoned this line of research as uninteresting, and at best as the mere discovery of stereotypes of dubious validity. However, the fact that nonverbal cues, including voice, and speech characteristics elicit fairly clear-cut personality stereotypes and attitudinal attributions about a speaker has important implications for the psychology of person perception, even if these attributions lack empirical validity. The full implications of this attributional process escaped these early investigators because of their preoccupation with the validity issue. In this section, then, we discuss some of these implications and their relevance for social and clinical psychology.

The research by Brown and his associates (Brown, Strong, & Rencher, 1972, 1973, 1974) provides experimental support for the hypothesis that voice and speech characteristics are significant factors in person perception. In these studies, they used Fourier analysis and speech synthesis techniques to manipulate the rate, pitch, and intonation (variability of f_o) of simple sentences that were read by male speakers — both increasing and decreasing each of these variables from their base-line levels. These manipulated speech samples were then rated by judges on a series of competence-related and benevolence-related adjectives. The rate manipulations were found to have the largest and the most reliable effects on the judges' ratings. In one study (Brown et al., 1974), the percentage of variance accounted for in the competence ratings were 86, 4, and 3% for rate, pitch, and intonation, respectively. For the benevolence ratings, the percentage of variance accounted for were 48, 1, and 6%, respectively.

There was a monotonically increasing relationship between speech rate and evaluations of the speaker on the competence-related adjectives, with higher competence being attributed to higher speech rates, and an inverted U relationship between rate and the evaluations of the speaker on the benevolence-related adjectives, with the middle ranges of speech rate receiving the highest ratings. Only if a person's normal speech rate received less than a high benevolence rating, then increasing his speech rate would increase the judges' benevolence ratings. In a more recent study Brown and his associates (Brown, 1980) manipulated the speech rates of relatively more spontaneous speech samples. Additionally, they asked speakers to deliberately increase and decrease their speech rates. The results were essentially the same as in the earlier studies.

The results from other studies, however, suggest that there are a number of variables that may complicate these simple relationships. In the studies by Brown and his associates, the speakers were always males, but the personality attributions elicited by speech and voice characteristics such as rate and pitch may very well vary as a function of the speaker's gender. Such a gender effect, at least as far as speech rate is concerned, is suggested by the results of a study in which the authors looked at the attributions made by conversational partners about each other as a function of the time patterns of their verbal interactions (Crown, 1982; Feldstein & Crown, 1979). The participants were white and black, male and female undergraduates. Subsequent to their interactions, all partners rated each other on a variety of adjectives, which were combined into a single negative evaluation score. Speakers who spoke relatively slowly or whose speech was characterized by relatively long silences, whether within or between turns, were given negative evaluations. But this was true only for white male and black female speakers, with the relationship attenuated or even reversed in white females and black males. Siegman and Reynolds (1982) sought to determine whether lack of verbal fluency in inteviewees' speech would influence their interviewer's perception of them in a manner similar to that found in peer conversations. They report that the duration of the interviewees' silences accounted for 26% of the variance in the interviewees' ratings of their interviewers, and that the interviewees' speech rates accounted for 23% of the variance in the interviewers' positive ratings of their interviewees. By and large, interviewers made more favorable and fewer unfavorable attributions to interviewees who spoke with a relatively fast speech rate and with short silent pauses – this was so whether the interviewees were males or females.

In the Siegman and Reynolds (1982) study the interviewers' questions consisted of highly intimate as well as nonintimate queries. It is of interest to note that interviewees' slow speech rates and long silent pauses were a source of negative attributions primarily when such nonfluent speech occurred in response to the relatively neutral questions, and much less so when they occurred in response to the highly intimate questions. It is as if the interviewers discounted the interviewees' nonfluent speech when it occurred in the context of intimate communications, presumably attributing the nonfluencies to the situation rather than to stable negative characteristics of the interviewees (although this is not to suggest that the interviewers were aware of making such distinctions). Whatever the explanation may be, these findings suggest that attributions are a function not only of a speaker's demographic characteristics but also of situational variables, such as peer conversations versus interviews and the subject matter being discussed.

Role and status may also influence the attributional process. Although an interviewee's nonfluencies, at least those occurring in the context of non-intimate speech, contribute substantially to the interviewer's perception of the interviewee's personality, the reverse is not necessarily the case. In a study by Crown (1982), the *interviewers'* silent pauses and slow speech rates had no significant effect on the personality characteristics that the interviewees attributed to their interviewers. The apparent difference may reflect the different roles of interviewers and interviewees, i.e., observers and observed, respectively. Jones and Nisbett (1971) have suggested than an actor's perception of the causes of his own behavior is different from that of an observer. Whereas actors tend to attribute their behavior to situational requirements, observers tend to attribute the same behavior to stable personality dispositions. Given that interviewers assume the role of observers and interviewees that of observed—Argyle, Lalljee, and Cook (1968) report that this is true even in the case of two peers who have been arbitrarily assigned the role of interviewer and interviewee—one may expect interviewers to attribute their interviewees' nonfluencies to the interviewees' stable personality tendencies and interviewees attributing their interviewers' nonfluencies to situational variables rather than to the interviewers' personality dispositions. This distinction would explain the discrepancy between the Crown findings (1982) and those of Siegman and Reynolds (1982), although whether this is in fact the explanation must await more direct evidence.

It should be noted that even in the Siegman and Reynolds study, in which the interviewees' temporal pacing of speech contributed significantly and substantially to the interviewer's evaluations of their interviewees' personalities, the amount of variance accounted for was considerably less than in the studies by Brown and his associates. There are, of course, a number of factors that can account for this difference. For example, Brown et al. used extreme variations in speech rates whereas the Siegman and Reynolds study involved a much narrower range of variations. Also, in the Brown et al. study subjects served as their onw control whereas the Siegman and Reynolds findings are based on between-subjects comparisons. Finally, the difference may reflect the fact that in the Brown et al. studies the judges had nothing else to go on but disembodied voices varying in speech rate, whereas in the Siegman and Reynolds study the judgments were made within the context of a naturalistically occurring interaction. In such interactions many variables other than a speaker's temporal pacing of speech are likely to influence the impressions that one is going to have of that speaker, and hence the smaller amount of variance accounted for by speech rate.

There is evidence that a speaker's voice and speech characteristics elicit not only general evaluative attributions but also more specific personality attributions. Earlier in this chapter, we summarized the research evidence regarding the specific vocal and temporal indices that elicit attributions of extraversion–introversion and dominance. A study by Rose and Tryon (1979) indicates that attributions of assertiveness are also based on specific voice and speech characteristics, such as relatively short latencies and a relatively loud voice and on other nonverbal cues, such as a relatively high level of gesturing. From a clinical perspective, the importance of this latter research is that it identifies the specific behaviors that we need to focus on if we wish to intervene and modify a person's lack of assertiveness. From this perspective, the critical question is not what are the objective, veridical, correlates of assertiveness, but what are the behavioral cues that lead one to be perceived as having that behavioral tendency.

Given that a person's voice and speech characteristics are a source of personality attributions, a conclusion that is strongly supported by the early voice and personality literature, the next question that needs to be addressed is: What is the process that gives rise to such stereotypes? What is the basis for the high level of agreement among listeners that some speakers are introverts and others extraverts, some submissive and others dominant, and so on. Scherer (1979) has suggested that such personality attributions are based on culturally shared inference rules, i.e., rules about the specific voice and speech characteristics that are associated with different personality traits. Furthermore, to the extent that these inference rules are the same as the veridical voice and speech correlates of a specific personality trait, people should be able to accurately identify that personality trait in a speaker on the basis of his or her speech and voice characteristics alone.

An alternative explanation for the personality attribution process is that people simply match voices and personality traits in terms of their (connotative) meaning, so that a pleasant voice is matched with a pleasant personality trait, and an unpleasant voice with unpleasant personality traits. Of course, the evaluative dimension of voices and traits may not be the only dimension that enters into such matchings. The other two dimensions that make up connotative semantic space, namely, potency, and activity, may also enter into the matching process. For example, a pleasant, strong, active speech style is likely to be matched with personality traits that have the same connotative meaning, and so on with the different combinations of the different factors that constitute connotative semantic space. This model, then, dispenses with the assumption that people "carry around in their heads" an atlas of the voice and speech characteristics that are associated with various personality traits.

Instead, it assumes that the attribution of particular personality traits to a particular voice is a more immediate affective response that does not require complex cognitive information processing. Of course, this model needs to be empirically verified before it can be considered as a valid explanation of the process involved in the attribution of personality traits to different voice and speech styles.

Dialect and Accent as a Source of Attributions

One class of speech variables, other than the vocal and temporal character-istics of speech that has been found to be a significant source of personality attributions, involves dialects and accents. In a series of studies, Lambert and his associates (Lambert, 1967) have used a "matched-guise" technique, in order to investigate whether different personality attributions are made as a function of a speaker's language, accent, or regional dialect. These studies are typically disguised as voice and personality investigations, in which sub-jects are asked to rate the personality characteristics of what they have been led to believe are different speakers reading the same message in either differ-ent languages or different dialects. In fact, however, the various speech samples are always read by the same person who is proficient in the various languages, dialects, and so on, under investigation. The major finding is that the personality traits attributed to speakers who can be identified, on the ba-sis of their accent or dialect, as members of ethnic minority groups, or other-wise low-prestige groups, tend to be unfavorable and reflect the popular ster-eotypes associated with such groups. This is true even of individuals who on the usual ethnic prejudice questionnaires deny subscribing to such ethnic stereotypes.

Giles (1970) used the "matched-guise" technique in Britain to determine the prestige levels associated with a variety of English accents. He found that speakers could be placed on a continuum, with speakers of the standard ac-cent (Received Pronunciation, RP) accorded the highest status, regional ac-cented speakers next, and those with accents of industrial towns, the lowest status. Not all the favorable personality traits, however, were attributed to RP speakers. Although perceived as being more competent than regional speakers, the RP speakers were also perceived as having less integrity and so-cial attractiveness (sincerity, kindheartedness, etc.) than the regional speak-ers. Furthermore, Giles and his associates have also explored the behavioral implications of such attributions. In one such study, they found that argu-ments presented with the prestigious RP accent were more persuasive than ar-guments presented in a regional accent (Giles, 1973; Powesland & Giles, 1975). Requests for information in a face-to-face situation elicited longer re-sponses when made with the prestigious RP accent rather than a nonstandard urban accent (Giles, Baker, & Fielding, 1975). On the other hand, the standard English accent can be a disadvantage in areas where the local speech style serves as a marker of ethnic or national identity. Welsh bilinguals were more responsive to a request for completing a questionnaire when the request was made in Welsh rather than standard prestigeful English, whereas monolingual English-speaking Welshmen completed as many questionnaires when the request was made in accented (Welsh) English as when the request was made in standard English (Bourhis & Giles, 1976).

In a related line of research, it has been shown that subjects tend to attribute favorable personality traits to bilingual speakers who accommodate to and adopt subjects' preferred language or dialect. Moreover, subjects tend to reciprocate the accommodation, that is, they make an effort to speak the other person's preferred language or dialect. Subsequent research has shown that both responses, that is, the positive evaluation and the reciprocal accommodation, are a function of the motivations and effort attributed by subjects to the accommodating speaker. Both responses are most likely to occur if subjects believe that the speaker who accommodated himself to their preferred language or dialect had a choice in the matter, and that the accommodation required some effort on his part (Giles, Taylor, & Bourhis, 1975; Simard, Taylor, & Giles, 1976). This type of linguistic accommodation, although peripheral to the central concern of this chapter, is very much reminiscent of an accommodation process that takes place between speakers in relation to the extralinguistic aspects of communication, which is taken up later in this chapter and which may shed some light on it.

The Nonverbal Mediation of Self-Fulfilling Prophecies

A speaker's voice and speech characteristics are not only a source of personality attributions but also of attitudinal attributions, i.e., attributions about how a speaker feels about the issues being discussed and about his or her partner. Of relevance in this context are the classical studies by Rosenthal and his associates (Rosenthal, 1966, 1985) on the sources of the experimenter bias effect. This effect refers to the pervasive and powerful influence of an experimenter's hypotheses or expectations on his subjects' responses. On the assumption that this influence is mediated via nonverbal cues, Duncan and Rosenthal (1968) looked at the nonverbal and extralinguistic correlates of the instructions given to subjects by two sets of "experimenters" whose hypotheses regarding the outcome of the experiment were manipulated so that they would be divergent. Although the instructions to subjects, which included a description of their response alternatives, were standardized, each set of experimenters emphasized the response alternative that was consistent with their expectation. The correlation between differential experimenter emphasis and subject response was .72.

In a subsequent experiment, Duncan, Rosenberg, and Finkelstein (1969) experimentally manipulated the experimenters' nonverbal and extralinguistic emphasis with similar results. Their findings indicate that auditory cues alone could be sufficient mediators of the expectancy effects, although visual cues alone have been shown to be even more effective mediators of this effect (Zoble & Lehman, 1969). A study by Troffer and Tart (1964) suggests that interpersonal expectancy effects occur even when it can be assumed that the experimenters are on guard against it. In this study, the experimenters, all experienced hypnotists, were instructed to read standard passages to their subjects in two conditions, presumably varying in the subjects' suggestibility level. When the experimenters had reason to expect low-subject suggestibility scores, their voices were found to be significantly less convincing in their reading of the instructions than to the high-suggestibility subjects. This was so despite the fact that the experimenters (a) were cautioned to treat their subjects identically, (b) were told that their performance would be taperecorded, and (c) were all made aware of the problem of experimenter expectancy effects!

Perhaps the most dramatic illustration of expectancy effects and self-fulfilling prophecies involves interspecies nonverbal communication between a German mathematics teacher and his horse, Clever Hans. By tapping his foot, Hans was able to add, subtract, multiply, divide, spell, and solve a variety of problems. Hans' cleverness intrigued Pfungst and his colleague Stumpf, who undertook a systematic research program to determine the secret of Hans' cleverness. They discovered that when Hans could not see his questioner, or when the latter did not possess the answer to the problem, Hans was no longer clever. They surmised that the questioners were emitting nonverbal messages that cued Hans when to stop tapping, which was later confirmed to be the case. A forward inclination of the head of the questioner would start Hans tapping, and as the experimenter straightened up, Hans stopped tapping. Experimenting further, Pfungst discovered that only a slight upward movement of the head, or even the raising of eyebrows, could get Clever Hans to stop tapping. (For a thorough discussion of the Clever Hans phenomenon and of expectancy effects, see Rosenthal, 1981, 1985).

The effects of nonverbally mediated expectancies may be of relevance not only in the experimental laboratory but in the clinic as well. There is evidence to suggest that physician expectancy is the major factor in the placebo effect (Shapiro, 1971). To the extent that physician expectancies can be communicated by means of vocal cues, such cues may play a significant role in the placebo effect. One study conducted in Rosenthal's laboratory is suggestive of the powerful influence of extralinguistic cues in everyday social and clinical interactions. In this study (Milmoe, Rosenthal, Blane, Chafetz, & Wolf, 1967) the authors were able to postdict doctors' success in referring alcoholic patients for treatment from the level of anger and irritation in the doctors' voices when discussing their experiences with alcoholic patients. Of course, this being a postdictive-correlational study, one can only speculate about a possible causal relationship between the doctors' voice qualities and patient compliance—but it is certainly a hypothesis deserving further experimental investigation.

In the Siegman and Reynolds (1982) study, in which interviewers were found to make negative attributions about their nonfluent interviewees, at least part of the variance in the interviewees' nonfluent speech was triggered by the interviewers' own behavior (a reserved demeanor); yet they made no allowance for this fact in their attributions. As Siegman and Reynolds (1982) point out, an interviewer's nonverbally mediated warmth or reserve can trigger either a vicious or a benign cycle. An unfriendly interviewer demeanor is likely to cause interviewees to speak in a nonfluent manner, i.e., with long response latencies, frequent and/or long silent pauses, and a slow speech rate (Siegman, 1979b; Siegman & Crown, 1980), which in turn will cause them to be perceived by their interviewer in a negative light. This perception is likely to reinforce the interviewer's unfriendliness and thus perpetuate a cycle of negative interactions. It should be noted that interviewer reserve, the original behavior that triggered this vicious cycle, is encoded, at least in part, by means of voice and speech characteristics, specifically by saying relatively little and saying it in a nonfluent manner. Of course, just as an unfriendly interviewer manner is likely to trigger a vicious cycle of events, a friendly interviewer style is likely to trigger a benign cycle of events.

Nonverbal cues play a significant role not only in the inadvertent communication of attitudes but in their deliberate communication as well. In a study of Mehrabian and Williams (1969), subjects were instructed to communicate different messages with different degrees of persuasiveness. Although the desire to persuade one's audience influenced many nonverbal channels of communication, its greatest impact was on the speaker's voice and speech characteristics. Level of intonation, volume of speech, and speech rate all increased with the desire to be persuasive. Moreover, the same cues influenced the listeners' perception of the speaker's persuasiveness. Again, these findings have important clinical implications. The therapeutic enterprise has been conceptualized as an attempt at interpersonal influence and persuasion (Frank, 1961). To the extent that this is a correct assumption, the ability to behave in a persuasive manner should enhance one's therapeutic effectiveness. Unfortunately, there is little empirical data about the personal characteristics that are associated with therapeutic effectiveness. However, we do have considerable data on the nonverbal behaviors that are associated with successful interviewee behavior in employment interviews. In one such study (McGovern, 1977), personnel representatives from business and industry were asked to rate the videotaped interviews of individuals who varied in their level of nonverbal involvement. High involvement consisted of most of the nonverbal behaviors that are associated with persuasiveness: high level of eye contact, voice modulation, verbal fluency, and the absence of speech disruption. Low involvement consisted of the contrasting behaviors. One hundred percent of the evaluators who saw a low-involvement candidate rejected the candidate for a follow-up interview, but 89% of the evaluators who saw a high-involvement candidate invited the candidate for a follow-up interview. Again, these findings, and many other similar findings, have obvious and important implications for the training of effective interviewee behavior. In suggesting such impression management programs, there is the implicit assumption that nonverbal behavior is modifiable. Earlier we cited a study (Feldstein & Sloan, 1984) that indicates that people are indeed capable of controlling their speech rates. Later in this chapter we cite additional evidence for people's ability to control their speech rates and other indices of verbal fluency, although there are individual differences in people's ability to do so. The frequently made claim that nonverbal behavior, especially that of the vocal channel, cannot be readily controlled, may apply to the nonverbal correlates of emotional arousal, which is discussed shortly, and even in relation to these variables probably only to a limited degree, but it is not valid within the context of the present discussion.

By way of summary, then, it can be concluded on the basis of the studies just cited that a speaker's dialect, accent, and voice qualities (as well as the phenomenon of code switching) are all sources of personality, attitudinal, and motivational attributions made by a listener about a speaker, which in turn exert wide-ranging effects on the listener's behavior toward the speaker. Of course, vocal and other nonverbal components of the listener's response to the speaker will in turn influence the speaker's subsequent nonverbal behavior, and so on. What we have here, then, are some basic features of a quasicybernetic model of nonverbal communication. One implication of this model is that what generally goes by the term *personality* may very well be, at least in part, a product of one's nonverbal behavior, vocal and otherwise. Thus, if a person's voice and other nonverbal cues connote lack of competence, this may lead others to respond to him in a manner that tends to reinforce that quality. Of course, the cycle of events can be benign as well. To the extent that such a benign or a vicious cycle of events has in fact occurred in relation to a particular individual, judges' ratings of that person's personality based on his voice quality should show not only high reliability but also validity.

PARALINGUISTIC CORRELATES OF AFFECT

During the 1950s and 1960s studies concerned with the question of whether one can accurately identify a speaker's background and personality from his voice all but disappeared from the literature. They were replaced by an ever-increasing number of studies on the vocal correlates of transient affective states, especially anxiety. In these studies the primary interest was in the actual vocal correlates of anxiety and some other mood states, and only secondarily, if at all, in listeners' ability to accurately identify emotional states from a speaker's voice.

Several factors were responsible for this change in interest from background and personality variables to anxiety and other emotional states. First, during this period — the 1950s and 1960s — evidence began accumulating that seemed to cast serious doubt on the validity of many widely used personality measures, both of the projective and objective variety. From the evidence, it seemed that at best these personality tests account for only a very small portion of the intersubject variability on any behavior of interest to psychologists. In response to the rather dismal performance of these tests in predicting behavior, some psychologists began questioning the very concept of stable personality traits. Others simply decided to ignore the question of individual differences and instead turned their attention to experimentally manipulable variables and their effects on behavior. One such variable — a rather popular one during the 1950s — was situationally produced stress or anxiety. Anxiety is, of course, a significant construct in a number of psychological theories, but the ease with which it can be manipulated in the laboratory no doubt contributed to its popularity. Many studies were published on the effects of anxiety and stress on perception, conditioning, and serial learning, and it was inevitable that sooner or later investigators would turn their attention to its effects on speech. It is, thus, against a background of systematic theorizing about the effects of anxiety on behavior, and a considerable body of empirical findings, that investigators began to look at the effects of anxiety on speech.

There was yet another development during this period that contributed to the new interest in the nonverbal correlates of anxiety and other affective states. It is during this period that clinical psychology began coming into its own as an empirical discipline. Widely held assumptions among clinicians began to be subjected to empirical validation by research psychologists, although not always with encouraging results. Some psychologists addressed themselves to the efficacy of psychotherapy, an area that is now referred to as psychotherapy outcome research. The same period witnessed the mass production of inexpensive, high-fidelity audio and video recording devices, which made it possible to subject therapist and patient moment-by-moment interactions, their verbal and nonverbal exchanges, to careful empirical investigation. This type of investigation has come to be known as psychotherapy process research.

Because psychoanalytically based or derived psychotherapies consist essentially of verbal exchanges between patient and therapist, it is only natural that psychotherapy researchers began to conceptualize the process in terms of more general informational exchange models (e.g., Gross, 1972; Lennard

& Bernstein, 1960; Siegman & Pope, 1972). Psychoanalytically oriented psychotherapists, however, are less interested in the objective referents of their patients' communications than in the clues that they provide about the patients' unconscious motivations and about their affective states such as anxiety, anger, and depression. Because of this perspective, psychoanalytically oriented psychotherapists have become very much attuned to the nonverbal aspects of their patients' communications, including, or course, the vocal characteristics of their patients' messages. Thus, Sullivan (1954) writes:

> The beginning of my definition of the psychiatric interview states that such an interview is a situation of primarily vocal communication — not verbal communication alone. . . . But if consideration is given to the nonverbal but nontheless primarily vocal aspects of the exchange, it is actually feasible to make some sort of crude formulation of many people in from an hour and a half to, let us say, six hours of serious discourse. . . . Much attention may profitably be paid to the telltale aspects of intonation, rate of speech, difficulty in enunciation, and so on — factors which are conspicuous to the student of vocal communication. (p. 5)

Anxiety is of special interest to psychotherapists, because of its central role in psychopathology and because the occurrence of anxiety during psychotherapy is interpreted as evidence of emotional conflict. As is apparent from the preceding quotation, the assumption has been that anxiety has a disruptive effect on speech, that it is associated with difficulties in articulation, silent pauses, and other interruptions in the normal flow of speech. The following paragraphs summarize the relevant empirical studies.

The Voice of Anxiety

Anxiety and disrupted speech.   One of the first to empirically investigate the effects of anxiety on speech was George Mahl. His working hypothesis was essentially the clinically derived assumption that anxiety has a disruptive effect on the normal flow of speech. In an attempt to quantify this disruptive effect he developed the Speech Disturbance Ratio (SDR), which comprises the following categories: repetition (superfluous repetition of one or more words), sentence incompletion or reconstruction (the speaker stops leaving a sentence unfinished or starts it again), omission (the omission of a whole word or part of a word), tongue slip, stutter, intruding incoherent sounds, and "ahs," and allied hesitation phenomena ("er," "um," etc.).

In a preliminary study, Mahl (1956) divided a series of therapeutic interviews with a single patient into high-anxiety, high-conflict phases versus low-anxiety, low-conflict phases and found that the former were associated with a significantly higher SDR than the latter. It should be pointed out that for the purpose of categorizing the interviews into high and low conflict and anxiety phases he used a typescript from which all speech disturbances had been removed. Additional analyses indicated that anxiety had no effect on the occurrence of "ahs" and similar expressions, which led Mahl to remove this category from the SDR. The basic finding of a positive association between anxiety arousal and the SDR was replicated by Kasl and Mahl (1965) with a group of college students, in which anxiety arousal was manipulated by means of a stress interview. Despite an early failure to replicate Mahl's finding (Boomer & Goodrich, 1961), the results of many subsequent studies provide impressive support for the claim that anxiety arousal is associated with an increase in SDR. Furthermore, Mahl's contention that although anxiety arousal increases what he called the "Non-ah" SDR, it has no such effect on the Ah Ratio (or the Filled Pauses Ratio, as it has been referred to by others), has also been corroborated by the results of three independent investigations (Cook, 1969; Feldstein, Brenner, & Jaffe, 1963; Siegman & Pope, 1965a). All three studies experimentally manipulated their subjects' anxiety level by subjecting them to a stress and a control interview. One caveat about this procedure is that it confounds anxiety arousal with interviewer topical focus, for the interviewer's questions in the stress interview typically concern different topical areas than his questions in the control interview. Because there is evidence, as is shown later in this chapter, that the SDR increases as a function of the cognitive difficulty of the task, it is not unreasonable to argue that interviewer topical focus could be a significant source of variance in interviewee's SDR, independent of anxiety arousal.

There is, however, at least one study that suggests that there may be a relationship between anxiety arousal and the SDR, independent of topical focus. In this study (Pope, Siegman, & Blass, 1970), an experimental group and a control group of student volunteers were interviewed twice. The second interview was a repeat performance of the first and was justified to the subjects on the basis that the tape recording of the first interview was accidentally erased. It was expected that for the control subjects the second interview, being a repeat of the first and therefore involving practice, would show a significant decrease in the SDR, which it did. Subjects in the experimental group, however, whose anxiety level was aroused prior to the second interview by being informed that their test responses revealed serious psychological problems, showed no decrease in their SDR during the second interview. In other words, the effects of practice and anxiety were cancelled by each other. These findings suggest that the association between anxiety arousal and the SDR is indeed independent of the particular topic under discussion.

Anxiety and the temporal pacing of speech.   In his study of the effects of anxiety on speech within the context of psychotherapeutic interviews, Mahl (1956) looked not only at its effects on speech disruption but also on silent pauses. He assumed that the high-anxiety, high-conflict phases would be associated with longer silent pauses than the low-anxiety, low-conflict phases, which he found to be the case. Mahl himself did not pursue this issue further in his subsequent studies, but others who did obtained contradictory findings. In some studies anxiety was associated with longer pauses and generally with a slowing down of speech, and in others with the very opposite pattern. We describe these studies in some detail because, hopefully, they will help us in developing a model that will allow us to predict when anxiety is likely to have a generally accelerating effect on speech and when it is likely to have a generally decelerating effect on speech.

One of the early experimental investigations of the effects of anxiety arousal on the temporal structure of speech within the context of the initial interview is by Siegman and Pope (1965a, 1972). Differential anxiety levels were aroused in the interviews by means of a topical manipulation. Specifically, interviewees were selected so that questions focusing on their family relations would be more anxiety provoking than questions focusing on their school experiences. A post-interview questionnaire revealed that this objective was achieved, although the topical manipulation produced only mild anxiety arousal. Before presenting the results of this study, however, we need to digress and discuss the indices that were used in that study for measuring the temporal structure of speech. From the very beginning of our research, we have viewed silent pauses in speech not as empty, meaningless, holes, but as an integral part of human speech, which in alternation with vocalizations create the temporal structure and rhythm of human speech. To index the temporal patterning of speech, we typically have looked at response latency, within-response silent pausing — its duration and frequency — and speech rate. *Response latency,* or *reaction-time* (RT) is defined as the silent interval between the last word of the interviewer's question and the first word of the interviewee's response. Early in our research, when the relevant time measurements were made by hand with a stopwatch, the *silence quotient* (SQ) was used as an index of the duration of within-response silent pauses. This quotient was obtained by summating all silent pauses 2 sec and longer and dividing that by the total response duration. Ever since we have started to measure the relevant time intervals automatically, by means of the Automatic Vocal Transaction Analyzer (for a detailed description, see Chapter 9), we have used the average of all silent pauses 300 msec and more (APD) as an index of within-response silent pausing. The correlation (r) between these two indices (SQ and APD) is mostly between .7 and .8, and occasionally even higher than that. Pause frequency is, of course, self-explanatory. This measure, however, needs to be adjusted for response duration, which we have done either by expressing the former as a ratio, with the latter as the denominator, or by using the latter as a covariate for the former. Unfortunately, these two measures do not correlate very well and can yield different results. Speech rate, which is obtained by dividing the total number of words in a response by the response duration, correlates about .5-.6 — with indices of within-response pause duration. More recently we have been using the proportionality constant ratio (PCR), which is the ratio of the proportionality constant of a speaker's vocalizations to the proportionality constant of his pauses, as an estimate of speech rate. The PCR has been found to be highly correlated with words per minute (Feldstein, 1976) and can, therefore, serve as an automated index of speech rate. Typically, the PCR correlates fairly highly with indices of silent pausing. This is to be expected given that speech rate is, at least in part, a function of the duration of within-response silent pauses, plus, presumably, the time it takes to articulate speech. Otherwise, the intercorrelations of the preceding temporal indices are modest at best, suggesting that they index different aspects of the temporal structure of speech. It should be noted, however, that the magnitude of these intercorrelations tends to vary as a function of topical focus, (Siegman & Reynolds, 1984) and the nature of the interviewer–interviewee relationship (Siegman, 1980). One other temporal measure that we have used in our early studies is *articulation rate* (AR), which is obtained by dividing the total number of words in a response by the total response time minus the silent pauses. We have since dropped this index because it confounds "pure" articulation time with *short* silent pauses (under 2 sec or under 300 msec). It should be pointed out, however, that in our early studies we have consistently obtained nonsignificant zero order correlations between the articulation-rate and speech-rate indices, which is surprising considering that both measure within-response silent pauses, the former, at least in part, relatively short ones and the latter relatively long ones. These findings would suggest independence between the relatively short and long silent pauses in speech, which has been confirmed in a study by Levin and Silverman (1965).

Let us now return to the Siegman and Pope (1965b, 1972) study on the effects of anxiety on the temporal patterning of speech. The results show that the anxiety-arousing topic, in contrast to the neutral one, was associated with a shorter RT $(.05 < p < .10)$, a slower SQ $(p < .02)$, a higher speech rate $(.05 < p < .10)$, and a higher articulation rate (not significant), altogether with accelerated rather than with decelerated speech. Using a similar experimental paradigm, Feldstein et al. (1963) also found that the anxiety-arousing interview topics were associated with a higher speech rate (or verbal rate, as they refer to it) than the neutral interview topics. Cook (1969) obtained similar results, but only with low trait-anxiety subjects (i.e., subjects obtaining low scores on inventories measuring chronic anxiety level), whereas the opposite trend was obtained with high trait-anxiety subjects. Perhaps beyond a certain optimum level, anxiety no longer accelerates speech but has the opposite effect — a possibility that is discussed in greater detail shortly. If this is so, it may explain why the anxiety manipulation in the Cook study did not produce a facilitating, or accelerating, effect in the high trait-anxiety subjects because for them the manipulation may have produced more than the optimum level of anxiety arousal.

One serious problem with the aforementied studies is that the anxiety arousal was achieved via topical manipulation. This confounding between anxiety arousal and topical focus presents a serious methodological problem because one cannot be certain that the results of these studies reflect variations in anxiety arousal rather than variations in topical focus. There are, however, other findings that indicate that experimentally produced anxiety arousal is in fact associated with an acceleration of verbal tempo, independent of topical focus. Perhaps the most convincing evidence comes from a series of word association studies by Kanfer (1958a, b), in which subjects were administered intermittent electric shocks, which were preceded by an auditory warning signal. Subjects showed an increase in post-tone speech rate, i.e., in anticipation of the shock, and a decrease in post-shock speech rate, indicating that anxiety arousal has an accelerating effect on speech. These findings are not especially surprising if we think of anxiety arousal in terms of a heightened drive level. Conceptualizing anxiety in terms of drive, Spence and his associates hypothesized that anxiety arousal would facilitate simple conditioning and simple serial learning and would interfere with complex serial learning (Taylor, 1951;Taylor & Spence, 1952). This hypothesis is based on the Hullian postulate that response strength is a multiplicative function of habit strength and drive. Thus, anxiety arousal should facilitate learning in situations in which the dominant response is the correct one, that is in simple learning tasks, and impede the learning process in situations involving multiple conflicting response tendencies, that is complex learning tasks. The results of a number of investigations have confirmed this hypothesis (e.g., Montague, 1953; Siegman, 1957). By the same token, anxiety arousal should accelerate speech tempo, provided the speaker is not faced with conflicting response tendencies.

The findings in the Siegman and Pope (1966b, 1972) interview study that mild anxiety arousal was associated not only with a faster speech tempo but also with an increase in interviewee productivity (longer responses) and vocabulary diversity are also consistent with a drive–activation–arousal conceptualization of anxiety and stress. It should be noted that the results of subsequent studies indicate that the facilitative effect of anxiety on productivity (Pope, Siegman, & Blass, 1970) and vocabulary diversity (Sunshine & Horowitz, 1968) is independent of topical manipulation. A positive correlation between anxiety arousal and productivity is, of course, to be expected on the basis of the Hull–Spence–Taylor position, which clearly states that anxiety arousal will make previously below-threshold responses suprathreshold. The positive correlation between anxiety arousal and vocabulary diversity suggests that the facilitative effect of anxiety arousal may involve not only autonomic but also cortical arousal. This is, of course, a highly speculative hypothesis, and it should be noted that other investigators have reported negative correlations between anxiety and vocabulary diversity.

Although it is clear that anxiety arousal can have a facilitating and accelerating effect on speech, it is equally true that it can have the opposite effect as well. We have already discussed Mahl's (1956) study, in which he found that anxiety arousal was associated with an increase in silent pauses in speech. We now discuss a number of other studies that found anxiety arousal to be associated with a slowing-down effect on speech and attempt to develop a model that allows us to predict when anxiety is likely to have an accelerating effect and when it is likely to have a decelerating effect.

The inverted U hypothesis.   In discussing the energizing-facilitating effects of arousal on behavior, a number of authors have argued that this effect is likely to reach an asymptote with increasing levels of arousal, and that eventually it reverses itself (Duffy, 1962; Fiske & Maddi, 1961; Hebb, 1955). If this is indeed the case, then even if mild and moderate levels of anxiety arousal tend to accelerate speech, very high levels of anxiety arousal should be associated with slower speech, more pauses, and so forth. This hypothesis, although reasonable from a commonsense and perhaps even from a theoretical viewpoint, is difficult to test empirically. It is difficult to calibrate levels of anxiety arousal and to identify in advance precisely which anxiety levels will produce a facilitating effect and which will produce the reverse effect. The failure to obtain the hypothesized asymptote or reversal in any particular study can always be attributed, post hoc, to insufficient arousal.

Perhaps the most clear-cut evidence in favor of the inverted U hypothesis comes from a study by Fenz and Epstein (1962), in which the authors obtained stories in response to TAT-like stimulus cards from a group of novice parachutists on their day of jumping and from a control group. In addition to the control group of nonparachutists, the parachutists served as their own controls by responding to the cards on a nonjumping day. Subjects always responded to three kinds of cards: neutral (no relevance to parachute jumping), low relevance, and high relevance. The data clearly suggest that anxiety arousal has an activating effect on response latency. Conditions that can be assumed to have aroused mild-to-moderate anxiety were associated with a decrease in RT. On the other hand, the one condition that probably aroused very high anxiety levels, namely the high-relevance cards on the day of jumping, was associated with a steep increase in RT (Fig. 8.1). Pauses in the parachutists' stories on the day of jumping also showed an activation effect, with lower SQs in the low-relevance than the neutral cards, and higher SQs in the high-relevance than the low-relevance cards. There were no significant differences in the control group. Subjects' verbal-rate data also follow a similar pattern, but these differences are not significant. By and large, the results of

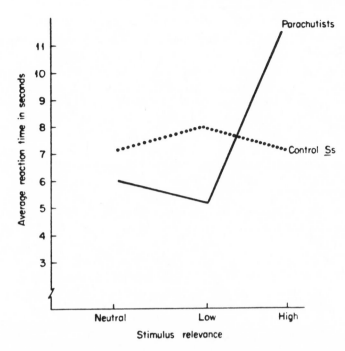

FIG. 8.1 Reaction time as a function of experimental group and stimulus relevance (from Fenz & Epstein, 1962. Copyright 1962 by Duke University Press).

the Fenz and Epstein study support the inverted U hypothesis, as far as anxiety and temporal indices of speech are concerned.

There is one study, however, the results of which appear to be inconsistent with the inverted U hypothesis. In this study (Pope, Blass, Siegman, & Raher, 1970), six psychiatric, hospitalized patients spoke into a tape recorder each morning for the entire period of their hospitalization, describing for about 10 min their experiences during the preceding day. The patients were also rated each day by a team of trained nurses on a number of manifest anxiety scales. The speech samples recorded during each patient's 8 most anxious and 8 least anxious days were compared. It should be noted that all patients had psychosomatic diagnoses and that occasionally they all manifested extreme anxiety, as well as stretches of calm and relaxed behavior. The results are based on a within-subjects' comparison (high-anxiety versus low-anxiety days) and are not confounded by subjects' psychiatric diagnoses. Speech samples recorded during subjects' high-anxious days, in contrast to speech samples recorded during subjects' low-anxious days, were associated with a significantly faster speech rate and lower SQs. These findings, then, suggest that even high-anxiety arousal—it is not unreasonable to assume that during the high-anxiety days these patients were very anxious indeed—is associated with a higher speech rate, because of a reduction in long pauses. But, as is argued in the following paragraph, even this finding can be reconciled with the inverted U hypothesis, provided it is limited to speaking tasks involving choices between conflicting response tendencies, that is, to complex speaking tasks.

Anxiety, speech tempo, and the nature of the task. Strangely enough, most of the studies investigating the effects of anxiety arousal on speech have ignored the role of task complexity. As was pointed out earlier, however, whether anxiety arousal is likely to have a disruptive or a facilitative effect on behavior, at least within the Hullian framework, is primarily a function of the nature of the task. The same level of anxiety arousal that facilitates simple learning tasks (tasks in which the predominant response tendency is the correct one) will interfere with complex learning tasks (tasks that elicit competing response tendencies) (Siegman, 1957; Taylor & Spence, 1952). By the same token the effects of anxiety arousal and stress on tempo should also be a function of the nature of the speaking task. The same arousal level that accelerates highly habituated speech sequences or "automatic" speech, such as is involved in discussing a familiar topic, is likely to slow down speech that requires planning and decision making, such as is involved in making up stories in response to TAT cards. This would account for the fact that even fairly high-anxiety levels accelerated patients' speech when they were asked to talk about their experiences during the preceding day but had the opposite effect on the subjects in the Fenz and Epstein study who were asked to make up creative stories about ambiguous TAT-like cards.

Audience Anxiety and Speech

Public speaking is an anxiety-arousing situation for many people, and its effects on speech have been investigated in a series of studies by Levin and Paivio and their associates. Considering the effects of situational anxiety on speech summarized earlier in this chapter, one would expect public speaking, to the extent that it is in fact anxiety arousing, to be associated with speech disturbances as measured by Mahl's SDR. Second, public speaking should be associated with an accelerated speech tempo if the speaking task is a complex one. Third, public speaking should be associated with a relatively high productivity. The actual findings are reviewed separately for each of the three speech variables.

In a study by Levin and Silverman (1965) on the effects of audience anxiety on speech in children, subjects were asked to complete story stems (a story completion task) either in front of an audience of four adults, or to a microphone while no one was listening. The public-speaking condition was found to be associated with significantly more brief pausing (less than 1 sec) and more filled pauses (which approached significance) but had no effect on relatively long pauses.

Reynolds and Paivio (1968) looked at the effects of audience anxiety on speech in a group of college students, whose task was to define a series of abstract and concrete nouns. In the audience condition subjects sat facing 10–15 peers; in the control condition they talked to the experimenter. The experimental manipulation had no independent significant effect on either of the two temporal indices: response latency and silence pause ratio. There was, however, a significant interaction between subjects' scores on an inventory designed to measure audience sensitivity (ASI) and the experimental manipulation on the silence ratio. High-ASI scorers showed an increase in silent pauses from the control to the public-speaking condition, low-ASI scorers a decrease. Moreover, in the control condition the high-ASI scorers obtained lower silent pause ratios than the low-ASI scorers (see Fig. 8.2). A similar interaction between subjects' ASI scores and public versus private speaking is reported by Paivio (1965) in relation to speech rate. On the assumption that

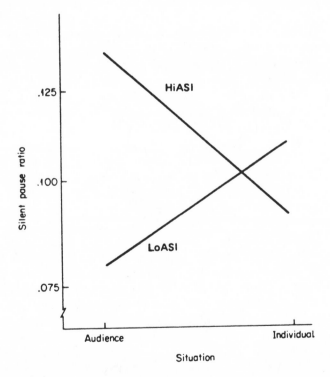

FIG. 8.2   Silent pause ratio as a function of audience sensitivity level and audience situation (from Reynolds & Paivio, 1968).

the public-speaking situation produced mild anxiety arousal in the low-ASI scorers and fairly high anxiety levels in the high-ASI scorers, the results of these two studies are consistent with the inverted U hypothesis, namely, that mild anxiety arousal accelerates speech and that strong arousal has the reverse effect.

By and large, then the evidence indicates that low levels of audience anxiety accelerates speech but that high levels of audience anxiety have a decelerating effect, which is consistent with a drive activation approach to anxiety. In other studies, however, high levels of audience anxiety apparently had a slowing down effect on speech, even when the speech task was not a complex one. In both the Paivio (1965) study and the Reynolds and Paivio (1968) study, subjects were assigned both simple and complex speaking tasks; yet there was no evidence that audience anxiety facilitated speech in relation to the simple speaking tasks, in the sense of reducing silent pauses and accelerating speech rate. Perhaps people who know that they become *very* anxious when they have to speak in public deliberately adopt a slow and careful speech style so as to reduce potential speech disruptions to a minimum. It is interesting that, of the several investigators who looked specifically at the impact of audience anxiety on Mahl's SDR or on its separate major component categories, none obtained the expected disruptive effect (Geer, 1966; Levin & Silverman, 1965; Paivio, 1965; Reynolds & Paivio, 1968). Considering the consistency with which situational anxiety has been found to be associated with an increase in the SDR, this is a rather puzzling finding. All the findings, however, fall into place if we assume that people who suffer extreme "stage fright" try to cover up their disability by adopting a deliberate, slow, and careful speech style. It might also explain why public speaking apparently is associated with reduced productivity (Levin, Baldwin, Gellwey, & Paivio, 1960), rather than with an increase in productivity, as was the case in the Siegman and Pope (1972) interview study. To the extent that a speaker wishes to cover up his anxiety, he is, of course, well advised to curtail the length of his speech.

Some methodological observations. It must be remembered that because most of the audience anxiety studies involve complex speaking tasks, such as making up stories, interpreting cartoons, providing definitions, and so on, one cannot readily generalize from these findings to the more general issue of the effects of anxiety on everyday speech, which typically involves "automatic," simple speech. Other methodological problems concern the proper condition for evaluating the effects of audience anxiety. In some of the studies (e.g., Levin & Silverman, 1965; Reynolds & Paivio, 1968) the control condition required that subjects speak into a tape recorder, with no other person present. This presents at least two problems. First, speaking into a tape recorder, certainly if it is for the first time, can be a stressful experience

(Sauer & Marcuse, 1957). Second, as is shown later in this chapter, the mere presence of another person or persons produces pressures on a speaker that he does not have to contend with if he is left alone. It can be argued, therefore, tha the proper control condition for audience anxiety is one in which the speaker addresses one other person. A parametric study, in which audience size is systematically varied from a single listener to a large group would, of course, be ideal. Finally, there is the problem that in some studies there is a confounding between audience size and status. Thus in one study (Levin & Silverman, 1965), in which the speakers were children, the audience consisted of higher status adults, and in another study (Reynolds & Paivio, 1968), in which the audience condition consisted of peers, the control condition involved the presence of a high-status experimenter. Considering the evidence, to be presented later, that listener status influences a speaker's paralinguistic behavior, such confounding between audience size and status presents a serious problem.

Vocal Correlates of Lying

One area of nonverbal behavior research that has flourished since the first edition of this book involves the nonverbal correlates of deception. On the assumption that, as far as most individuals are concerned, lying is a stressful and anxiety-arousing experience, this research should be of relevance to how anxiety-arousal affects the vocal and temporal aspects of speech. The assumption that lying is anxiety arousing for most people has in fact informed many of the hypotheses regarding the nonverbal correlates of deceptive communications. The findings have been summarized in a comprehensive review by Zuckerman, DePaulo, and Rosenthal (1981), and they have been brought up to date in a subsequent review article by Zuckerman and Driver (1985). The conclusions regarding the effects of deception on noncontent, or paralinguistic, speech variables are based on the results obtained in 11–17 independent studies, the precise number of studies depending on the variable being investigated, except for pitch, for which there were only four independent studies. Compared to truthful communications, deceptive ones are relatively short, high pitched, contain many speech disruptions, as indexed by Mahl's SDR (1956), and many hesitations (ah's, etc.), with the latter being more strongly and more significantly associated with lying than any other nonverbal measure except pupil dilation. As far as the temporal aspect of speech is concerned, however, no clear-cut pattern seems to emerge from the various studies. It is possible, however, that for a variety of reasons these deception studies cannot provide us with critical information about the effects of anxiety arousal on nonverbal behavior. First, in almost all these studies the subjects are instructed by the experimenter to give truthful responses to some questions and to lie in response to others. To the extent that subjects were instructed by their experimenter to lie, they should have little reason to be anxious about lying, or so it would seem on first glance. In justifying the relevance of these laboratory studies to lying in the real world, which can be a source of considerable anxiety arousal, it has been argued that, if lying has been conditioned to anxiety in the past, deception in the lab is likely to be at least minimally anxiety arousing even when sanctioned by the experimenter. Also, in order to increase subjects' anxiety level, some experimenters tell their subjects that the ability to deceive is associated with intelligence and professional success. Even so, the relevance of such laboratory paradigms to naturalistic lying that involves considerable anxiety arousal is debatable. A second problem is that in some of these deception studies the deceptive communications were obtained from subjects talking into a tape recorder or to a video camera rather than addressing another person. Again, the relevance of such studies to naturalistic lying, which typically is face-to-face — a condition that may be essential for producing the anxiety arousal and the other negative affects usually associated with lying — is open to debate. A third problem is that in many of the deception studies the participants are required to spontaneously make up a fictitious response. The making up of such fictitious responses is cognitively more demanding than simply telling the truth, which may explain why in some deception studies lying was associated with slower speech than the truthful responses. In fact, when Zuckerman and Driver (1985) grouped the deception studies into those in which subjects had no opportunity to plan and to rehearse their deceptive communications and those in which the subjects were given an opportunity for such preplanning, they found that whereas in the former set of studies there was a significant negative correlation between lying and speech-rate in the latter there was a significant positive correlation between the two. A recent study (Reynolds, Siegman, & Demorest, 1983) tried to assess the temporal pacing of speech in deceptive communications using a design that is not subject to any of the preceding strictures. The lying was unfeigned, it caused subjects to be fairly anxious (it was not sanctioned by the experimenter), it was face-to-face and not particularly cognitively demanding. Nevertheless, lying was found to be associated with relatively long response latencies relatively frequent and long pauses, and a relatively slow speech rate. The authors suggest that the subjects of this study found themselves in a conflict whether to respond truthfully or to lie, and that this approach-avoidance conflict reversed the otherwise positive association between anxiety arousal and speech. Furthermore, what was said earlier within the context of audience anxiety, namely, that individuals who suffer from such anxieties frequently try to cover up their anxiety symptoms and in so doing they may overshoot the mark, may be of relevance in deceitful communications as well. People are likely to want to cover up the nonverbal manifestations of their deceitfulness and in so doing overshoot the mark. Of course, from a lie-detection point of view, it does not matter whether the individual speaks more quickly or more slowly than usual — as long as the deviation is an indication that the person is lying.

Yet one other finding obtained within the context of deceptive communications is of relevance to the broader issue of the nonverbal vocal correlates of anxiety arousal, specifically, to the role of cognition in expressive nonverbal behavior. It has been claimed that whereas verbal behavior is a product of cognitive activity, nonverbal behavior, especially expressive nonverbal behavior, represents a direct expression of affective experience, relatively free from cognitive control. Recent evidence, however, suggests that such nonverbal behavior is far from being a pure expression of affect, uncontaminated by cognitive processes. For example, as part of the aforementioned deception study, Siegman and Reynolds (1983b) investigated the relationship between personality variables and lying skills, with the latter operationally defined as the ability to control one's temporal pacing of speech so that it would be nearly the same when lying as when telling the truth. There were three separate indices for measuring the participants' lying skills, based respectively on their reaction times, silent pauses, and speech rates when lying as compared to their truthful responses. The lower the discrepancy, the better one's lying skill. Of particular interest was the relationship between Snyder's Self-Monitoring Scale (SMS) (Snyder, 1974) and lying skills, because this scale was designed to measure, at least in part, the ability to control, or to regulate, one's expressive, self-presentation behavior. Whereas subjects' overall SMS scores correlated significantly with only one out of the three indices measuring lying skills, their scores on two SMS subscales — Extraversion and Acting skills — correlated significantly with all three indices designed to measure lying skills. Specifically, the extraverts and subjects with good acting skills were more successful liars than the introverts and the individuals with poor acting skills. These findings, which have been replicated in a subsequent study (Siegman & Reynolds, 1984), indicate that people can and do regulate their expressive nonverbal behavior, and that this ability involves specific social skills. It is suggested that what Paul Ekman (1978) has proposed about the expression of emotion in face, namely, that such expressions reflect both biologically preprogrammed responses as well as cultural display rules, is probably true of expressive nonverbal behavior in general, except that we need to add the individual's personal input as well, with cognitive appraisal factors having a significant role in the latter two contributions.

Trait Anxiety and Speech

Personality dimensions other than self-monitoring may also influence how people deal with anxiety arousal and its nonverbal correlates. A number of investigators have looked at the relationship between dispositional anxiety or trait anxiety, as measured by the Taylor Manifest Anxiety Scale, or MAS, and similar measures, and some of the speech parameters discussed in this chapter. By and large the relationships between predispositional anxiety and speech found in these studies seems to differ from that of experimental, or situational, anxiety, and speech. For example, although situational anxiety and stress have consistently been found to be associated with speech disruptions, as measured by Mahl's SDR (Cook, 1969; Kasl & Mahl, 1965; Siegman & Pope, 1972), there is no evidence for a similar positive correlation between trait anxiety and SDR. As far as the relationship between trait anxiety and the temporal pacing of speech is concerned, the evidence is somewhat puzzling. A review article by Murray (1971) cites six studies that correlated measures of trait anxiety and response latency. All six correlations were negative, three significantly so. Given this negative correlation between trait anxiety and response latency—which is consistent with a drive conceptualization of anxiety–one could expect a similar negative correlation between trait anxiety and within-response silent pauses, because the evidence suggests a moderate positive correlation between RT and within-response silent pauses (e.g., Siegman, 1979b). In fact, however, trait anxiety correlated positively with a measure of within-response silent pauses in an early study by Siegman and Pope (1965b), a finding that has frequently been reconfirmed in our laboratory, and by Helfrich and Dahme (1974) in Germany, although they suggest that this correlation obtains only in high anxiety-arousing situations. Equally paradoxical are the findings of Preston and Gardner (1967) who obtained negative correlations between various indices of trait anxiety and the *frequency* of pauses 1.5 sec and over, but also a positive correlation between the same indices and the *average duration* of all pause 1.5 sec and over.

However, these findings may not be as paradoxical as they appear to be on first glance if we assume that high trait-anxiety scorers pause relatively infrequently but when they do pause, it is for a relatively long period of time. As pointed out earlier, if we think of anxiety in terms of arousal and drive level, it should not be surprising that high trait-anxiety scorers respond more quickly and with fewer silent pauses than low trait-anxiety scorers. Under these circumstances, high trait-anxiety individuals should also exhibit more nonfluencies than low trait-anxiety individuals, given their lack of planning time, but, as pointed out earlier, this apparently is not the case. Perhaps one strategy that high trait-anxiety individuals have learned to use in order to avoid excessive nonfluencies is to do their planning during a few but relatively long silent pauses. In other words, the relatively long pauses of high trait-anxiety speakers may serve to compensate for their relatively short latencies and generally accelerated speech tempo under conditions of high-anxiety arousal. It is of interest to note that parallel results were obtained in a recent study with Sarason's Test Anxiety Questionnaire. High scorers on this test responded with significantly shorter latencies but spoke with longer silent pauses in an interview than the low scorers. The significance of this study is that both findings, i.e., the short latencies and the long silent pause were obtained within the same study. Yet another explanation for these paradoxical findings has been offered by Scherer (1979). He suggests that high trait-anxiety scorers are excessively sensitive to other people's evaluations, and that their accelerated speech tempo represents an attempt to avoid negative evaluations from their listeners. Of course, by the same token they should avoid engaging in long silent pauses. According to Scherer, they fail to do this for one of two reasons. One is that because of their sensitivity to listener evaluations, unexpected listener signals such as a frown of doubt or disapproval should intervene with their ongoing thought processes, requiring long silent pauses to reorient and restructure their cognitive planning. An alternative explanation is in terms of cognitive overload and the compensatory mechanism mentioned earlier. To test these alternate explanations one would need fairly complex interaction-oriented designs. So much seems fairly clear, however, that in addition to the factors mentioned earlier in this chapter as moderators between anxiety arousal and speech one also needs to consider the individual's learned strategies to cope with anxiety arousal and stress.

Anxiety and Speech: Some General Observations

In the early literature on anxiety and speech, especially in the clinical literature, it was assumed that the effects of anxiety on speech are exclusively of a disruptive and disorganizing nature. If the authors of this literature had major reservations about this generalization, they certainly were not very explicit about them. The experimental data indicate that the picture is much more complex than is suggested by the aforementioned literature. Suffice it to cite the finding that within the context of the initial interview mild anxiety arousal was found to be associated with relatively productive interviewee responses and with an accelerated speech tempo free of long silent pauses, to indicate that the consequences of anxiety arousal are not exclusively disruptive in nature. In fact, conceptualizing anxiety in terms of drive and arousal, it was suggested that anxiety arousal per se is associated with an accelerated speech pattern. There are, however, a number of factors that can moderate or even reverse this relationship. For example, one implication of conceptualizing anxiety in terms of drive, in the Hullian sense, is that the effects of anxiety on speech are a function of task difficulty, a variable that has all but been ignored in the literature on anxiety and speech. Clearly, we need more studies to clarify the effects of task difficulty, of anxiety level, and of the interaction between these two variables on speech.

Another factor affecting the relationship is the level of anxiety arousal, with very high levels reversing the relationship from a positive to a negative one. Also, anxiety arousal, even in mild or moderate degrees, is likely to decelerate rather than accelerate speech if the anxiety produces an approach-avoidance conflict. Also, for a variety of reasons, people may want to cover up the fact that they are anxious. Under such circumstances, anxiety arousal may produce paradoxical behavior, i.e., a deliberate and slow pacing of speech, relatively few speech disruptions, and reduced productivity. The very intensity of subjects' anxiety arousal may motivate the subject to hide it, which may be yet another reason why the usual positive relationship between anxiety arousal and speech tempo tends to break down under extreme arousal.

Finally, any model for the effects of anxiety arousal on speech should allow for individual differences, that is, for different learned response tendencies to anxiety. There is evidence, for example, that the speech behavior of chronically anxious individuals parallels the speech behavior produced by situational anxiety arousal in some respects but not in others. Thus, chronically anxious individuals tend to speak with an accelerated speech tempo, which parallels the findings obtained with situational anxiety. There are, however, two notable exceptions to this parallelism. First, the speech of chronically anxious individuals apparently tends to be punctuated by relatively long silent pauses, and, second, it has no more speech disruptions than the speech of nonanxious individuals. It was suggested that perhaps chronically anxious individuals have learned to compensate for their accelerated speech tempo with relatively few but long silent pauses so as to avoid too many speech disruptions.

In the literature on nonverbal communication one frequently comes across the statements to the effect that expressive nonverbal behavior is at best only minimally controllable. Presumably this is so because people have no awareness of their expressive, nonverbal behavior patterns. This assumption regarding the lack of awareness is debatable. There is evidence that trained actors do very well in mimicking or simulating the extralinguistic features of anxiety arousal and of other emotional states (Feldstein, 1964). There is also evidence that people accurately identify the emotions that the actors portrayed, and that on this task laymen do as well as trained psychiatrists (Feldstein, Jaffe, & Cassotta, 1964). Clearly, then, people must be aware of the extralinguistic correlates of anxiety arousal and other emotional states, at least when they occur in others.

Yet another reason for the alleged "leakiness" of expressive nonverbal behavior is that such behavior is a direct expression of effective arousal, without intervening cognitive processes. We have argued earlier that this is not the case, but even if it were, the work of Neal Miller and many others on biofeedback indicates that even autonomic nervous system correlates are not beyond self-control. The findings obtained by Siegman and Reynolds (1983b) suggest that some people do monitor and successfully control their expressive nonverbal behavior in anxiety-arousing situations.

Vocal Correlates of Depression and Anger

Investigators have also looked at the vocal correlates of emotional states, other than anxiety. These studies have recently been reviewed by Scherer (1981a) and by Williams and Stevens (1981). Table 8.1, provided by Scherer (1981a), summarizes the findings. An examination of this table suggests a fairly high degree of covariation between the various vocal measures, with one pattern consisting of high fundamental frequency (F_o), a wide range and variability of F_o, high intensity and a fast tempo, and another pattern consisting of a low fundamental frequency, a narrow range and small variability of F_o, low intensity and slow tempo. These two patterns could very well represent different levels of arousal, with the first pattern indicating a high level of arousal (because this pattern of vocal behavior is also associated with the activation dimension of emotional experiences) and the second pattern indicating low arousal. As pointed out by Scherer (1981a), it is not clear, therefore, from these findings whether the emotions that have been studied in these investigations merely vary in terms of their location on the arousal dimension or whether they are in fact associated with discrete vocal patterns, which distinguish among the various emotional experiences. A fundamental

TABLE 8.1
Summary of Results on Vocal Indicators of Emotional States

Emotion	Pitch Level	Pitch Range	Pitch Variability	Loudness	Tempo
Happiness/joy	High	?	Large	Loud	Fast
Confidence	High	?	?	Loud	Fast
Anger	High	Wide	Large	Loud	Fast
Fear	High	Wide	Large	Loud	Fast
Indifference	Low	Narrow	Small	?	Fast
Contempt	Low	Wide	?	Loud	Slow
Boredom	Low	Narrow	?	Soft	Slow
Grief/Sadness	Low	Narrow	Small	Soft	Slow
Evaluation	?	?	?	Loud	?
Activation	High	Wide	?	Loud	Fast
Potency	?	?	?	Loud	?

Source: Revised from Scherer, 1981a, p. 206. Reprinted with permission of Grune & Stratton, Inc.

methodological problem with some of these studies is that the data were obtained from individuals who were instructed to read standard passages in a manner that would convey a specific emotional state. We cannot be certain, therefore, that the findings represent veridical correlates of these emotional states, or mere theatrical stereotypes. With the exception of anxiety, there are only few experimental studies of the vocal correlates of emotional and affective states. The reasons for the dearth of such experimental data are complex. As far as the negative emotions, such as anger and sadness are concerned, it is, in part, due to ethical constraints in subjecting people to experiences that produce such emotions. There is also a methodological consideration, which makes the results of experimental studies of emotions difficult to interpret. Even when experimenters are quite careful in standardizing the conditions that presumably produce a specific emotion such as anger, for example, one cannot be certain that the same conditions did not also produce other emotions such as anxiety, depression, or perhaps even surprise, or a combination of these emotions. The same reservation, only more so, applies to naturalistic or seminaturalistic studies of emotion, which rely on spontaneous reactions to films or to specific experiences, such as childbirth (Brown, 1980).

There is reason to believe, however, that at least some of the findings that have been obtained in studies using feigned expressions of sadness–grief represent more than mere theatrical stereotypes. For example, in the study by Pope, Blass, Siegman, and Raher (1970) with psychiatric patients, which was described earlier, a group of trained nurses made daily ratings of their patient's depression level. Audio recordings obtained from each patient during his 8 most depressed and his 8 least depressed days over a period of 3 months were then analyzed in terms of their temporal and other extralinguistic characteristics. On the basis of the widely held clinical judgment that slow and retarded speech is a prominent symptom of depressed patients, and on the basis of findings obtained with feigned sadness–grief, it was expected that the patients' speech samples obtained during the high-depression days would be associated with a slower speech rate than those obtained during the low-depression days. This expectation was fully confirmed. Additional analyses suggest that this difference is due primarily to an increase in the frequency and the duration of long silent pauses during periods of depression rather than to an increase in the frequency of very short pauses. The Filled Pauses, or Ah Ratio, did not discriminate between the speech samples of the high- and low-depression days. It was expected that it might discriminate, because it is usually associated with cautious and hesitant speech. This suggests that the relatively slow speech rate during depression is not an indication of cautious speech, but perhaps of a low-energy and activation level. Finally, as in Feldstein's (1964) study with feigned sadness and depression, depression had no significant effect on the patient's Speech Disruption Ratios.

That depression is associated with a slower speech rate and a higher silence ratio was also noted in a study by Aronson and Weintraub (1972), who compared depressed and other patient groups, as well as normal controls, on several extralinguistic as well as content-oriented variables. In terms of the extralinguistic measures, the depressed group could be readily distinguished from the others on the basis of reduced productivity, a slower speech rate, and higher silence ratios. Finally, in a group of patients with various psychiatric diagnoses, Kanfer (1960) obtained a significant negative correlation between their scores on the Depression scale of the MMPI and speech rates.

The empirical data, then, consistently indicate that the experience of depression, in depressed patients and in others who do not carry such a diagnostic label, is associated with more and/or longer pauses, resulting in a slower speech rate. As to the cause of these findings, we can only speculate. It is argued later in this chapter that the mere presence of another person in dyadic conversation has the effect of reducing the frequency and duration of silent pauses in speech. The social withdrawal of depressed patients, therefore, could have the effect of increasing the frequency and duration of silent pauses in dyadic conversation. It is recalled, however, that the speech samples obtained by Pope et al. (1970) involved essentially monologue-type speech and yet, here too, depression was associated with a slow speech tempo. Physiological factors, such as underarousal, could, of course, account for these findings.

Current clinical thinking distinguishes between various types of depression, e.g., between unipolar versus bipolar and endogenous versus exogenous depression, each apparently associated with somewhat different clinical syndromes. The studies cited previously did not make such distinctions, although they all apparently focus on relatively mildly depressed patients. In studying the nonverbal correlates of depression future investigators will be well advised to keep the aforementioned distinctions in mind. One recent study (Jaffe & Anderson, in press) found that the speech rates of severely depressed patients predicted their response to the tryciclids. Surprisingly, patients with the slowest speech rates showed a better recovery than patients with relatively faster speech rates.

Although sadness/grief may not be the same as clinical depression, it is of interest to note that there is considerable overlap between the temporal pacing of speech in clinical depression and in feigned sadness–grief.

Considering the importance of anger and hostility in traditional theories of psychopathology and the current research interest in angry, aggressive behavior on the part of social psychologists, the dearth of studies on the nonverbal correlates of anger is surprising. The need for such information is made even more urgent by recent findings that have implicated anger and hostility in a variety of major health problems, especially hypertension and coronary heart disease (Diamond, 1982; Williams, 1983; Williams, Barefoot, & Shekelle, 1984).

The available evidence suggest that anger is associated with a high-pitched and loud voice and with a fast speech tempo (Scherer, 1981a). Most of the available studies, however, have used simulated anger. The results of such studies are suggestive at best, because they may merely reflect people's theatrical stereotypes of how other people talk when angry rather than the veridical correlates of anger. However, the results of two studies conducted in our laboratory confirm Scherer's conclusions, at least as far as the temporal pacing of speech and loudness are concerned. In one study, Crown, Feldstein, and Siegman (1979) found that subjects who were thwarted in a teaching task, and who presumably were more angry than their colleagues in the control group, spoke with significantly shorter pauses than the controls. In another recent study, male interviewees who were rated as being high in anger and hostility spoke more loudly, more quickly, and interrupted their interviewer more often than male interviewees who were judged as having a low potential for anger and hostility (Siegman, 1985). However, these expressive correlates of anger and hostility were attenuated in females. Given our cultural norms, which expect women to control their anger, it is not surprising that the expressive vocal correlates of anger are less pronounced in females than in males.

In addition to anger and hostility scores, the participants in the aforementioned study were also assigned covert anger, or anger-in scores, according to criteria developed by Dembroski and MacDougall (1983). The correlations between the participants' anger-in scores and their vocal behavior indicate that the associations between anger and speech that have been noted thus far are limited to overt anger, and do not hold for covert anger, or anger-in. By and large, the speech style associated with anger-in was in the opposite direction from that associated with anger-out. In fact, there were significant negative correlations between anger-in and frequency of interruptions for both males and females. There are two ways that one can interpret these findings. One is basically that anger manifests itself in a loud, accelerated, and interruptive speech style. However, such behavioral manifestations can be inhibited, and this is what we see in covert anger. Alternatively, it can be argued that loud and accelerated speech is no more a direct manifestation of anger arousal than is a more subdued speech style; each simply represents a different coping mechanism with anger. According to this point of view, expressive behavior — vocal or otherwise — is not to be seen as an immediate manifestation of affective experiences, unencumbered by cognitive processes, but rather as the manifestation of an individual's coping style. In fact, there is evidence to suggest that this is so not only on the behavioral level but on the physiological level as well. Thus, Diamond (1982) cites evidence that overt anger (anger-out) and covert anger (anger-in) are associated with different cardiovascular responses, with the cardiovascular correlates of covert anger resembling those of anxiety and fear more than those of overt anger. These data suggest that even the physiological correlates of anger may reflect one's coping strategies, which influence one's affective experiences on the most fundamental level.

THE SOCIAL AND INTERPERSONAL CONTEXT

Although the early literature on the extralinguistic aspects of speech focused primarily on the role of personality differences and the effects of emotional arousal, it is becoming increasingly clear that there are other factors that are of equal if not of greater significance in terms of their contribution to the total variance of the extralinguistic domain. The remainder of this chapter is devoted to two such factors: the social-interpersonal context and cognitive processes.

There are some fairly obvious reasons for assuming that the social context is a significant contributor to the variance in the extralinguistic domain. Speech, whether directed to one individual or to a larger audience, is clearly an interpersonal activity. It can be argued that even monologues have an implicit audience. It would seem, therefore, only reasonable to assume that the demographic characteristics of one's audience and the relationship between speaker and audience will determine not only what is being said but also how it is encoded. It is surprising, therefore, that the literature concerned with the effects of the speaker's and listener's demographic backgrounds and of their relationship to each other on extralinguistic variables is fairly sparse.

Extralinguistic Behavior in Mixed Company

At the beginning of this chapter, evidence was cited suggesting that gender is a significant source of variance in the extralinguistic domain. For example, there is evidence that men speak more loudly than women. It was also pointed out, however, that this relationship tends to vary as a function of situational variables. One such variable, in dyadic interactions, is the gender of the other speaker. There is evidence to suggest that both men and women speak differently when addressing a member of their own sex than when speaking to a member of the opposite sex. Thus, both men and women apparently speak more loudly when addressing someone of the opposite sex as opposed to someone from their own sex (Markel, Prebor, & Brandt, 1972). In relation to some extralinguistic behaviors, however, the mixed-gender situation may have different effects on males than on females. For example, in one interview study (Siegman, 1975) conducted in our laboratory, female interviewees were found to speak with shorter silent pauses than male interviewees when responding to relatively intimate questions. However, this difference obtained only in same-gender dyads, with precisely the opposite difference obtaining in opposite-gender dyads, i.e., the males speaking with shorter pauses than the females. In this study, then, the mixed-gender situation produced more than a simple exaggeration of base-line gender differences. In fact, different motivating factors may have been at work for males and females — precisely which factors, however, remain an issue for further investigation. One important implication of these findings is that in studies that involve dyadic verbal interactions, and in which the focus of interest is subjects' extralinguistic behavior, it is not enough to control for subjects' gender but is also imporant to control for their partners' gender. Otherwise what may appear as subject-gender differences may in fact reflect differences in same-gender versus opposite-gender interactions. Moreover, the effects of gender composition (same vs. opposite-gender) may be different for males than for females. Unfortunately, this is rarely taken into consideration, which may account for the many unreplicated and contradictory findings in this field.

Also relevant in this context are the results of a study (Siegman, 1975) that was designed to assess the social reinforcement value of eye contact between interviewer and interviewee, when cues other than eye contact, such as verbal signals, are used to regulate the initiation and termination of both the interviewer's and interviewee's comments. Interviewees, both males and females, rated their interviewer as warmer and they were more attracted to their interviewer when there was eye contact between them than when it was eliminated, independent of the interviewer's gender. In relation to interviewees' productivity levels, however, there was a significant interaction between the gender composition of the interviewer–interviewee dyad and eye contact. Elimination of eye contact inhibited productivity in same-gender dyads and facilitated productivity in mixed-gender dyads. Although this finding deals with productivity, whose status as an extralinguistic variable may be somewhat marginal, it has significant methodological implications. It suggests that gender composition is, in the terminology of Kogan and Wallach (1964), a significant moderator variable. Relationships obtained in same-gender dyads may not be obtained, or may even be reversed, in mixed-gender dyads. In studies with a single experimenter, male or female and male and female subjects, potentially significant results may simply cancel each other out, unless separate analyses are made for the male and the female subjects.

Voices of Love and Power

Factorial analyses of dyadic interactions involving such diverse relationships as parent–child, husband–wife, employer–employee, and interviewer-interviewee consistently have identified two basic dimensions: power or dominance and love or warmth (Foa, 1961; Pope & Siegman, 1972). It is not unreasonable to assume that the opposite poles of these dimensions are likely to be associated with varying nonverbal behaviors. In fact, this has been shown to be the case in relation to eye contact (see Exline & Fehr, 1978). Very little experimental research, however, has been done on the effects of different affective or status relationships on extralinguistic behavior, except within the context of initial interviews. In the following paragraphs, we summarize the findings of a number of such studies conducted in our laboratory.

Warmth and the flow of communication in the initial interview. Textbooks on the initial interview, written from a clinical perspective, typically exhort the novice interviewer to be warm, friendly, and understanding rather than neutral and reserved, and certainly not outright cold, challenging, and rejecting. This advice is based on the general assumption that interviewees will be more attracted to a warm than to a cold interviewer, and on the further assumption that such attraction is likely to enhance interviewee productivity and self-disclosure. The latter assumption is frequently couched in social-reinforcement theory terms. Interviewees, it is said, should want to prolong exchanges that are pleasant and rewarding, and to terminate those that are unpleasant and painful, either of which can be achieved by the proper manipulation of productivity level. As to self-disclosure, it is argued that the risk of rejection is the most obvious reason why people tend to withhold information that is of an intimate nature and potentially self-damaging. Of course, this risk is less of a consideration if an interviewer is warm and accepting rather than reserved and neutral. It is somewhat less clear what effects warmth and attraction are likely to have on the extralinguistic domain. One possibility is that people are likely to feel more relaxed with a warm than a cold interviewer and therefore will tend to adopt a less formal style, or a less "elaborated code," to use Bernstein's (1961) terminology. If so, interviewees may be more fluent, that is, exhibit fewer and shorter silent pauses, when addressing a warm rather than a cold interviewer. What does the evidence suggest in relation to these expectations?

The expectation that interviewees would feel more attracted to a warm than to a cold interviewer was confirmed in numerous studies conducted in our laboratory and elsewhere (Heller, 1968; Johnson & Dabbs, 1976) and is consistent with a conceptualization of interpersonal attraction in terms of social reinforcement theory (Byrne, 1971). The expected positive relationship between interpersonal attraction and the temporal pacing of speech was confirmed in four studies conducted in our laboratory that addressed themselves to this question. In our first study of the initial interview, which was described in greater detail earlier in this chapter (p. 383), an attempt was made to assess interviewees' attraction to their interviewers. To that end, each interviewee was administered an adaptation of the Libo Picture Impressions

Test (Libo, 1956) pre and postinterview, with the change in scores constituting interviewee's attraction scores. The correlation between subjects' attraction scores and a pausing index, combining latency and within-utterance pauses, was significant ($r = -.38$, $N = 50$, $p < .01$). The correlation between interviewees' attraction scores and a hesitation index, combining "ahs" and relatively brief pauses, fell short of significance ($r = -.25$, $.05 < .10$), but the correlation between their attraction scores and the Ah ratio alone was significant ($r = -.28$, $p < .05$). There was no significant correlation, however, between subjects' attraction scores and their SDRs (Pope & Siegman, 1966).

The results of our first experimental study of the effects of interviewer warmth obtained essentially similar results. Interviewer warmth had a clearly significant effect on an index that combined response latency and between-utterance pauses, a borderline effect on the latency index, and no significant effect on the silent pauses ratio (Siegman, 1979a, p. 94). In a subsequent experiment, however, interviewer warmth, in contrast to interviewer reserve, was associated with a significantly lower silent pause ratio as well as with a faster speech rate. On the other hand, the inverse relationship between warmth and response latency obtained only during the first half of the interviews and dissipated as the interviews progressed (Siegman, 1979a, pp. 99–100). In our most recent experiment, interviewer warmth was associated with relatively few silent pauses and with relatively short latencies (Siegman & Crown, 1980). This last experiment differed from those that preceded it in that the interviewer's questions were only partially preprogrammed. Also, unlike in the previous studies, the interviewees were not given specific instructions about the interviewer's style, i.e., whether the interviewer would be warm or reserved. Perhaps these differences account for the fact that in this last study the differences were less dramatic than in some of the preceding ones. Nevertheless, it is fair to conclude that interviewer warmth is associated with a faster pacing of speech, expressing itself in shorter latencies, and/or shorter silences, and/or fewer silences, depending on the nature of the interpersonal interaction.

The expectation that interviewer warmth would facilitate interviewee productivity level fared less well. In four out of five studies that were conducted in our laboratory and that addressed themselves to this issue, and in two studies conducted elsewhere (Heller, 1968; Johnson & Dabbs, 1976), no evidence was found to support the hypothesis that interviewer warmth per se facilitates interviewee productivity or that interviewer coldness per se has an inhibiting effect. Although reinforcement theory is occasionally invoked in order to explain the presumptive beneficial effect of interviewer warmth on interviewee productivity, it can be argued that this represents an unjustified application of the theory. Reinforcement, properly understood, is the rewarding of an operant response. Therefore, for an increase in interviewee productivity to occur, it is necessary that social reinforcers be dispensed on a contingent basis, that is, only after the occurrence of productive interviewee responses. The indiscriminate (noncontingent) dispensation of social reinforcers on the part of an interviewer may very well create a general ambience of friendliness and warmth, and our studies indicate that they do, but there is no basis in reinforcement theory for the assumption that such ambience is likely to enhance interviewee productivity.

Of course, in real life, people, including interviewers, are rarely consistently warm or reserved, rather, they tend to fluctuate between the two affective states. Therefore, in our most recent study of interviewer warmth, we investigated not only the effects of consistent interviewer warmth and reserve but also that of warmth followed by reserve and vice versa. The results suggest that interviewer *reserve* following a previous period of warmth significantly enhances interviewee productivity, especially when the questions focus on intimate topics. Similar results were obtained in earlier studies on the effects of interviewer "mm-hmms." Although the indiscriminate, or noncontingent, use of these verbal reinforcers had no facilitating effect on interviewees' productivity, the withholding of these responses after an earlier period of responding periodically with "mm-hmm" tended to increase interviewees' productivity (Siegman, 1972, 1976). Presumably, the withholding of social reinforcers, following a previous period during which such responses were freely dispensed, is interpreted by interviewees as a sign of interviewer displeasure. This in turn may motivate interviewees to give more information or to explain and justify their previous remarks in order to restore the interviewer's friendly approval, all of which, of course, will tend to increase the interviewees' productivity. In fact, there is replicated evidence that explicitly challenging interviewer remarks tend to have a facilitating rather than an inhibiting effect on interviewee productivity (Heller, 1968; Siegman, 1972). To summarize, whereas indiscriminate interviewer friendliness apparently does not facilitate interviewee productivity, there is evidence to suggest that interviewee productivity can be maximized by a proper alternation between friendliness and reserve, although the identification of the most effective pattern of social reinforcement requires further research.

It should be noted, however, that the generalization that indiscriminate interviewer warmth does not have a facilitating effect on interviewee productivity may not apply to all populations. For example, there is evidence to suggest that people who admit to having many personal problems tend to respond favorably even to indiscriminate interviewer warmth (Heller, 1968), and the same may be true of hospitalized mental patients as well (Heller, 1972, p. 21). Clearly, we need further research on the effect of psychopathology and of demographic and personality variables on the relationship between interviewer warmth and interviewee productivity.

If noncontingent interviewer warmth and friendliness does not facilitate interviewee productivity, why do the textbooks on interviewing recommend such behavior, and why do interviewers follow it? Perhaps it is related to the fact that clinicians work mostly with disturbed populations. Or perhaps it is related to the finding that interviewer friendliness and warmth is reciprocated in kind; even interviewers want to be liked rather than disliked. In fact, in our laboratory, we found it difficult to train interviewers to behave in a reserved manner, even on a partial schedule. Also, it should be pointed out that whereas interviewer warmth per se does not enhance interviewee productivity nor interviewer reserve per se inhibit it, interviewees who expect their interviewer to be warm and friendly and instead find him to be reserved do in fact respond with reduced productivity (Siegman, 1979a). To the extent, then, that interviewees expect their interviewers to be warm and friendly, and the evidence suggests that they do, a reserved interviewer demeanor can have a chilling effect on interviewee's productivity.

To summarize, then, it would appear that interviewer warmth is reciprocated in kind, that its effect on interviewee productivity is fairly complex, and that its most unambiguous effect, as far as interviewee vocal behavior is concerned, involves the temporal pacing of speech. This latter finding has implications for other areas in social psychology as well. For example, social psychologists today are very much concerned with the determinants of interpersonal attraction, but most of the data in this research area are derived from simple rating scales in which subjects indicate how much they liked their partner in an experimental task and whether they would like to work with him again. These measures, however, are vulnerable to acquiescence and related response biases. Clearly, what is needed in this research area is a behavioral index of interpersonal attraction. A study (Siegman, 1979a) that was designed to test Aronson's (1969) gain–loss model of interpersonal attraction supplemented conventional rating scales with the Silence Quotient (SQ) as an index of interpersonal attraction. The results obtained with the SQ cast doubt on the validity of the loss part of the gain–loss hypothesis. More importantly, the use of extralinguistic indices of attraction made it possible to monitor changes over time, something that cannot be done very well with the usual rating scales.

Power and the flow of communication in the initial interview.   A major dimension of interviewees' perceptions of their interviewer involves status or competence. It is not unreasonable to expect, therefore, that an interviewer's status or perceived competence could influence an interviewee's extralinguistic behavior, although precisely in what way is not clear. It may be that people are likely to adopt a more formal style when addressing a high-status person than when conversing with a peer. If so, one can also expect people to speak more carefully, with more hesitations and perhaps with more silent pauses, when addressing a high-status as opposed to a low-status person. Specifically in terms of the interview, perhaps one can expect interviewees to speak more freely about intimate matters to a high-status than to a low-status interviewer.

The results of a study (Pope & Siegman, 1972) that addressed itself to the preceding questions provide partial support for both hypotheses. In this study, 32 female nursing students were interviewed twice, once by someone introduced as a senior professor and experienced interviewer and once by someone introduced as a beginning novice. Two interviewers alternated between the high-status and the low-status role. In order to protect the credibility of the status manipulation, the two interviewers — who differed in age — conducted the interviews from behind a screen. The subjects never did see their interviewers. The manipulation also provided a plausible cover story, namely, that the purpose of the study was to investigate the effects of the screen on the interviewee. The interview itself was divided into two segments, one focusing on interviewee's family relations, the other on interviewee's school experiences. Of the two syntactic variables presumably related to speech formality, that is, the subordinate clause ratio and the passive-verb ratio, only the latter was significantly affected by interviewer status. As expected, the interviewees showed a higher passive-verb ratio when responding to the high-status than to the low-status interviewer. Interviewees also responded with significantly shorter response latencies (RTs) but with higher SQ's to the high-status than to the low-status interviewer, suggesting that in addressing a high-status person, one is under pressure to respond promptly, but that the response itself is associated with more pausing, perhaps because of its more formal style. A further analysis indicated that these effects did not occur across the board in the two interview segments. Rather, they were limited to the segment focusing on the interviewee's school experiences, perhaps because it was to this segment that the interviewer's status as a professor was most salient. There was one other significant finding in this study: The high-status interviewer elicited significantly fewer speech disruptions in the family relations topic than the low-status interviewer, suggesting that perhaps interviewees found it less anxiety arousing to discuss this topic with the high-status than with the low-status interviewer. On the other hand, high-interviewer status did not facilitate interviewees' productivity in response to questions dealing with family relations, although it did have such a facilitating effect on interviewees' productivity in response to questions dealing with their academic experiences. In a more naturalistic study of the effects of interviewer status, Pope and his associates (Pope, Nudler, Norden, & McGee, 1976; Pope, Nudler, VonKorff, & McGee, 1974) did not find that interviewer status facilitated either interviewees' productivity or their self-disclosure.

On the whole, then, the impact of interviewer status on interviewees' speech was fairly minimal, less than was expected. Perhaps in an interview situation, any interviewer, whether a professor or a student, is in a dominant position vis-a-vis the interviewee. In other words, perhaps the crucial factor is not one's social status but one's role in a specific dyadic interaction. Clearly, more information is needed to clarify how status and power relationships between communicants affect the encoding process and the flow of communication.

The Role of the Other Person in Dyadic Interactions

The discussion thus far, especially the findings on the effects of interviewer warmth and interviewer status, may lead some readers to conclude that the other partner in a dyadic conversation has only a marginal impact on the speaker's extralinguistic behavior. Dramatic evidence to the contrary is provided by a phenomenon variously called synchrony or congruence. It is a common observation that we tend to adjust the loudness level of our speech to that of our conversational partner. Recent evidence indicates that such congruence of synchrony between partners occurs in relation to many other speech variables as well. In one of the early studies of synchrony, Matarazzo and Wiens (1972) found that interviewees tend to match the duration of their responses to that of the interviewer. Long interviewer remarks are followed by relatively lengthy interviewee responses, and short interviewer queries are followed by brief interviewee replies. Controlling for potentially confounding influences, such as interviewer ambiguity–specificity level and topical focus, Siegman, Pope, and Blass (1969) still obtained the synchrony phenomenon, although the effect was weaker than in the Matarazzo studies and obtained only within the first of two interview sequences. The expectation that the magnitude of the synchrony effect would be a function of the interviewer's status — that is, experienced professor versus student novice — did not materialize. This, however, could be due to the possibility that was mentioned earlier, that the interviewer is always in a dominant position vis-a-vis the interviewee, independent of the former's social status. More recently, Howland and Siegman (1982) also found that interviewers and interviewees accommodate to each other as far as productivity, response latency, and average duration of vocalization are concerned.

In a study of informal conversations, Feldstein (1968) did not find the kind of moment-to-moment matchings found by Matarazzo and his associates within the context of structured interviews. He did find, however, that the average duration of a speaker's utterances covaried with those of his partners, when matched with different partners in a series of conversations.

Synchrony or congruence has also been found in relation to response latency (Howland & Siegman, 1982; Matarazzo & Wiens, 1972), interruptions (Matarazzo & Wiens, 1972), duration of silent pauses (Feldstein, 1972), rate of speech — defined as number of syllables divided by phonation time —

(Webb, 1972), loudness (Welkowitz, Feldstein, Finkelstein, & Aylesworth, 1972; Natale, 1975), and precision of articulation (Tolhurst, 1955). Finally, the language and dialect accommodation phenomenon discussed at the beginning of this chapter can also be understood in terms of a synchrony effect, analogous to that found with extralinguistic variables.

A detailed discussion of the synchrony or congruence phenomenon can be found in Feldstein and Welkowitz's chapter in this book. Whatever its explanation may be, the synchrony phenomenon certainly illustrates the profound interactional nature of dyadic speech

Speaking without seeing. There is yet another way in which the "other" partner in a dyadic conversation influences the speaker's extra-linguistic behavior. If conversation is to proceed in an orderly fashion, without the participants talking to each other at the same time, there must be an orderly exchange of speaker and listener roles. The speaker must provide the listener with appropriate cues indicating when he is ready to relinquish the floor, and he must also monitor the listener for indications that he wants to assume the floor. The cues that serve this regulatory function are complex and are discussed in some detail in Chapter 12. For our purposes, suffice it to say that although these cues are mostly visual in nature they also involve some of the extralinguistic vocal variables discussed thus far. For example, according to Maclay and Osgood (1959) ahs or filled pauses serve, at least in part, as signals to the listener that the speaker is not yet ready to give up the floor. According to Maclay and Osgood, then, filled pauses are the speaker's responses to his own silences.

concern over "losing" the floor probably also determines the duration of one's silent pauses. When one has reason to fear "losing" the floor, silent pauses are likely to be reduced to a minimum, accompanied by an increase in filled pauses. A comparison of pausing behavior in interviews as opposed to TAT responses indicates that the latter are associated with fewer filled pauses but more silent pauses (Siegman & Pope, 1966a). The relatively high pausing ratio in the TAT responses can, of course, be attributed to task difficulty which, however, does not account for the relatively low incidence of filled pauses. A parsimonious explanation for both findings is that in the TAT situation there is less pressure on the subject to respond promptly and to go on talking lest he lose the floor than in the interview situation and, hence, the fewer "ahs" and increased pausing. Similarly, in monologues, where there is no concern about being interrupted, there is a dramatic increase in the duration of between-utterance silent pauses (e.g., Siegman & Reynolds, 1983c).

What extralinguistic effects are likely to occur if the participants in a dyadic conversation cannot see each other? If it is indeed correct that in normal conversation a speaker relies primarily on visual cues, such as eye contact, to indicate whether or not he is ready to relinquish the floor, and only secondarily — during times when he needs to pause — on filled pauses, on "ahs," then it seems reasonable to assume that situations in which visual cues are unavailable to a speaker, for example, in telephone or telephone-like conversations, there will be an increase in filled pauses. The evidence indicates that dyadic conversation without face-to-face contact is, in fact, associated with an increase in the Filled Pauses Ratio (Kasl & Mahl, 1965; Siegman & Pope, 1972). That it is indeed the possibility of being interrupted that is responsible for the increase in filled pauses when visual cues are unavailable is supported by the finding that when the speaker knows that he will not or cannot be interrupted, the same circumstance (i.e., absence of speaker–listener visual contact) produces a significant decrease in filled pauses. This finding has been reported by Feldstein et al. (1963) and has been replicated in our laboratory, in a study to be described in some detail later in this section.

A study by Siegman and Reynolds (1983a) asked the question: What is the effect of eliminating visual feedback in circumstances where the synchronization of role taking is not an issue, for example, when role synchronization is accomplished by means of prearranged verbal cues. The results indicate, that even so, the elimination of visual feedback inhibits productivity and increases the duration of within-utterance silent pauses of female interviewees. The same manipulation, however, had no deleterious effects on the productivity levels and the extralinguistic variables of male interviewees. A similar gender effect was noted by Ellsworth and Ross (in Ellsworth & Ludwig, 1972), who found that a reduction of visual feedback reduced self-disclosure in females but not in males. At least as far as females, then, are concerned, visual feedback serves functions other than the synchronization of role switching. At least one such function is to provide feedback how the participants feel about each other and what they are saying. This kind of feedback from one's conversational partner, interviewer, or experimenter may play a role in yet another phenomenon, which was noted in the TAT study, cited earlier (Siegman & Pope, 1966a). As subjects progressed in their task of making up stories, there were changes on a number of extralinguistic variables, simply as a function of time. Response latencies became somewhat longer but speech increased in fluencey: fewer filled and unfilled pauses. Similar results were obtained by Lalljee and Cook (1973) without the context of the initial interview. Moreover, they found that this apparent adaptation effect takes place within the first 3 min of the interview, after which there is a leveling off in interviewee's fluency level. One possible explanation for this phenomenon is that in any encounter between strangers the participants tend to experience a certain uncertainty, which is reduced by feedback from their partners, and which is reflected in their extralinguistic behavior. It is of interest that, in addition to an intrasession adaptation effect, there apparently is also an intersession adaptation process (Siegman, 1974b). As subjects return for a second interview or testing session, they show less hesitation — as indexed by the aforementioned extralinguistic variables – than they do at the very ouset of their first session, but more than they show after having leveled off.

The studies discussed thus far involve mutual or symmetrical invisibility, i.e., there is equal reduction in visual feedback for both partners. What, however, if the reduction in visual feedback is asymmetrical, so that one cannot see one's partner but one is seen by him? Argyle, Lalljee, and Cook (1968) provide data that indicate that this can be extremely disconcerting, whether one is a male or a female. They suggest that this is so because it places one of the partners in an inferior or submissive relation to the other partner. Clearly, such an asymmetrical relationship interferes with the communication process, although its precise effects on the extralinguistic variables discussed here remains to be investigated.

Although as a rule the elimination of visual feedback has a disruptive effect on communication, under certain circumstances, it can have a beneficial effect as well. This was suggested by a study conducted in our laboratory in which one half the subjects were interviewed in the usual manner, that is, interviewer and interviewee confronting each other, the other half with the participants sitting in adjoining rooms. Prior to the interview, subjects in both conditions were requested to use the word "finished" to indicate when they had completed their response to the interviewer's queries. It was made clear to them that the interviewer would not interrupt them, nor proceed with the next question, until they had used the agreed upon cue to indicate that they had completed their response. Because all the interviewer's communications were in the form of questions, it was always clear to the interviewees when he was finished with his messages. For all interviewees, one half the interviewer questions were of a personal character, the others impersonal. Furthermore, there were three types of response conditions: speaking, dictation, and writing. Both the separation of interviewer and interviewee and the mode of response (speaking versus dictating versus writing) moderated the impact of topical focus on interviewees' productivity level. In the face-to-face interview condition, subjects were less productive when replying to highly personal than to impersonal interview questions. This is consistent with other findings and is to be expected considering that people tend to be defensive about highly personal matters. This effect, however, was attenuated, and eventually reversed, as the interview situation and response mode became more impersonal. Interviewees' reluctance to talk about intimate matters dissipated when the usual interpersonal pressures that exist in face-to-face communications were removed, either by separating the participants or by giving the interviewee the opportunity to respond in writing. Also, in this study, in which interviewees did not have to contend with the possibility of being interrupted, the primary effect of eliminating visual contact between the communicants was to reduce the interviewees' filled pauses to half ($F = 10.65$, $df = 1/16$, $p < .01$). The facilitating effect of interviewer absence on interviewee productivity in relation to intimate material was confirmed in a recent study (Siegman & Reynolds, 1983c). In this study, the subjects responded to questions, some highly intimate, others impersonal, under two different conditions: with the interviewer in the room reading the questions to the interviewees from a set of cards or with the interviewees themselves reading the questions from the cards without benefit of interviewers (who were not in the room). In the interviewer-present condition, cues other than eye contact were used to regulated speaker–listener transitions. As in the previous study, interviewer absence facilitated interviewee productivity but only in response to the intimate questions. It should be pointed out, however, that this facilitating effect of interviewer absence apparently is limited to circumstances in which the interviewer is completely out of the room. A mere reduction of visual feedback, with the interviewer remaining in the room and interacting with the interviewee, will, as discussed earlier, restrict interviewee productivity, at least in the case of female interviewees.

By way of summary then, it can be said that conversation is a social activity par excellence. Perhaps the findings that illustrate this observation most dramatically are those that go by the name of synchrony or congruence, but there is other evidence as well. For conversation to proceed in an orderly fashion, the participants must let each other know whether they wish to hold on, relinquish, or take over the floor. This they usually do by means of visual and extralinguistic cues. It is not surprising, therefore, that as a rule, communication proceeds more smoothly with than without visual contact between participants. There are, however, circumstances when the absence of face-to-face contact facilitates communication—for example, when the topic of discussion is potentially embarrassing to the participants. Finally, it was hypothesized that the demographic characteristics of one's conversational partner affect one's extralinguistic behavior. Clearly, people speak differently when they talk to someone of like gender than to someone of the opposite gender. There is also evidence that interpersonal attraction affects a number of extralinguistic variables. It was suggested that code formality may be the intervening variable, with people adopting a less formal style when addressing someone they like and are attracted to than when talking to someone about whom they are indifferent.

COGNITION AND HESITATION

Preceding sections focused on the role of personality factors, affective states, and the social context in extralinguistic behavior. There is increasing evidence, however, that there is yet another major source of variance in the extralinguistic domain, especially in relation to the fluency and hesitation indices that have been the focus of this chapter. The results of recent research leave little doubt that cognitive processes play a significant role in extra-linguistic behavior, and an increasing number of researchers are now attempting to clarify the precise nature of this relationship.

This "new look" in psycholinguistic research no doubt reflects the general *Zeitgeist,* with its emphasis on cognition. Nevertheless, considerable credit for the shift in emphasis from affective to cognitive factors must go to the work of Goldman-Eisler (1968), even though it has been questioned on a variety of methodological grounds (see Boomer, 1970).

In an early study Goldman-Eisler used a guessing technique in order to determine the predictability of words following hesitations (pauses) in a speaker's communication. She found that "where guessers found themselves at a loss for predicting the next word as spoken originally . . . the original speaker also seemed to have been at a loss for the next word, for it was at these points that he tended to hesitate" (Goldman-Eisler, 1968, p. 42). On the basis of these findings Goldman-Eisler concludes that hesitation pauses reflect the speaker's lexical decision-making process, that is, his word choices.

Boomer (1970), who has questioned Goldman-Eisler's work on a variety of methodological grounds, believes that such pauses involve primarily structural syntactic decisions. In part, his position is based on the finding that hesitation pauses tend to cluster immediately following the first word in a phonemic clause. Perhaps the hesitation pauses at the very beginning of a clause do involve syntactic planning, in contrast to subsequent hesitation pauses that involve lexical decisions. Goldman-Eisler (1968), however, states that syntax is a matter of habit or skill rather than of cognitive planning:

> The examination of sentence structure in the light of the concomitant hesitation pauses showing an absence of any relationship between the two indicates that the hierarchical structuring of sentences and embedding of clauses is more a matter of linguistic skill than of planning. Syntactical operations had all the appearance of proficient behaviour as distinct from the volitional aspect of lexical and semantic operations. (p. 80)

Perhaps comparing the frequency of pauses in sentences with and without subordinate clauses — which is what Goldman-Eisler did — is too crude a test of the hypothesis that syntactic complexity involves cognitive planning. Moreover, as is shown later in this chapter, the silent pause clearly is only one of many manifestations of cognitive activity.

In another frequently cited study, Goldman-Eisler (1961a, b, 1968) compared the ratio of silent and filled pauses in speech associated with tasks of varying levels of difficulty. Specifically, she asked subjects first to describe and then to interpret a series of *New Yorker* cartoons. Each subject was given the following instructions: "You will be shown a series of cartoon stories with no verbal captions. You are asked to have a good look at them. As soon as you have got the point, say 'Got it' and proceed to describe the content of the story as depicted in the pictures before you; conclude by formulating the general point, meaning, or moral of the story in as concise a form as you can." A comparison of the descriptions and the interpretations showed that the latter were associated with a significantly higher silent-pause ratio (but not filled-pause ratio) than the former. This was true not only of the group as a whole, but every single subject in the study evidenced a higher silent-pause ratio in the interpretations than in the descriptions. Although the RTs or initial delays for the descriptions (the period from when the subject said "Got it" to the first word of the description) were roughly the same as the initial delays for the interpretations, Goldman-Eisler argues that it took subjects proportionately more time to plan and to organize the interpretations than the descriptions, because the former contained fewer words than the latter (fewer than a third). This argument is based on the assumption that everything else being equal there should be a positive correlation between RT and subsequent productivity—an assumption that is clearly contradicted by data obtained in our laboratory.

Be that as it may, it is Goldman-Eisler's position that because interpretation is a more complex task than description it also requires longer planning than description and that this planning takes place during the initial delays. Furthermore, this planning during the initial delays involves primarily content and semantic decisions in contrast to within-utterance pauses, which involve primarily lexical choices. That the interpretations were associated with more hesitant speech than the descriptions is clear, but precisely what is responsible for the hesitations is less clear. The pauses could, of course, reflect lexical decision making, as Goldman–Eisler believes they do, because the words generated in the interpretations were in fact less predictable than those of the description. However, the interpretations were also syntactically more complex than the descriptions, which may account for the difference in the silent-pause ratio associated with the two tasks. Goldman-Eisler considered this possibility but dismissed it because interview responses are associated with a lower silent-pause ratio than the cartoon interpretations, despite the fact that the two are of equal syntactic complexity. To this one can reply that:

1. The interview responses probably contain a higher ratio of over-practiced word sequences or automatic speech than the cartoon interpretations.

2. In the interview situation, syntactic complexity may be associated with other types of hesitation phenomena, such as filled pauses and speech disruptions.

Yet another possible explanation for the higher pause ratio of the interpretations than the descriptions may be the fact that subjects were instructed to formulate the interpretations in as *concise* a form as possible. As a matter of fact, Goldman-Eisler reports that in the interpretations (but not in the descriptions) there was a positive correlation between conciseness or brevity of expression and silent-pause ratio. Apparently the attempt to eliminate redundancy and to formulate concise responses is associated with an increase in salient pauses.

The confouding, in Goldman-Eisler's study, between the experimental manipulation (description versus interpretation) and the requirement to be concise, plus negative results obtained by Rochester, Thurston, and Ruff (1977) prompted Siegman (1979a) to attempt to replicate Goldman-Eisler's findings. In this study 12 male and 12 female subjects were asked to *describe* four *New Yorker* cartoons and two TAT cards, and to *formulate* the meaning of four other cartoons as well as to *make up a story* about two other TAT cards. The order of experimental task — description versus interpretation and story-making — and the two sets of stimuli were counterbalanced between subjects. Furthermore, for one half of the subjects, the instructions for *both* tasks included the requirement that they formulate their responses in a concise manner. The dependent variables were: response latency, average duration of pauses, pause frequency, and within-response pausing time, with the latter two adjusted for response duration.

The nature of the task, that is, description versus interpretation, was a significant source of variance in relation to all the dependent variables except pause frequency, with longer pauses associated with the interpretations than the descriptions. This effect, however, was significantly stronger for the cartoons than the TATs. On the whole, then, the results of this study replicate Goldman-Eisler's findings that cognitive planning and decision making is associated with hesitation pauses.

A question that remains to be answered is: Why did the experimental manipulation have a significantly weaker effect when the stimuli involved TAT cards rather than cartoons? Perhaps formulating the meaning of cartoons, which presumably have only a single correct meaning, is a more complex task than making up stories for TAT cards, where the subject is under relatively few constraints once he has decided on a theme. This speculation is supported by the finding that the average pause duration was significantly higher for the cartoon interpretations than for the TAT stories.

It may very well be the case that in order for an increase in task difficulty to produce hesitation pauses, the subject must be operating at or near his information-processing capacity. If the more difficult of the two tasks is relatively undemanding, the experimental manipulation may have no significant effect on subjects' pausing behavior. This situation probably occurred in the study by Rochester et al. (1977), and hence their failure to replicate Goldman-Eisler's findings.

It should be noted that although the description versus story-making manipulation had only a weak effect on subjects' within-response pauses in the

TAT, it did have a clear-cut impact on subjects' SDRs. Subjects showed significantly higher SDRs in the story-making task than in the description task.

That cognitive complexity can affect a rather wide range of hesitation phenomena, not just silent pauses, is indicated by the results of yet another study. Reynolds and Paivio (1968) asked subjects to define a series of abstract and concrete nouns. The abstract definitions, in contrast to the concrete ones, were associated with longer latencies, silent pauses exceeding 1.5 sec, filled pauses. It is fairly clear, then, that cognitive complexity or difficulty is associated with a relatively high level of pre and within-utterance pausing, as well as other hesitation indices. The specific hesitation indices affected may, of course, be a function of the kind of decision to be made, but they may also be a function of the social context. Cognitive planning and decision making is more likely to be manifested by silent pausing in some situations, such as cartoon interpretations and story-making, than in others, such as dyadic conversations.

As pointed out earlier, Goldman-Eisler is of the opinion that all semantic planning takes place during the silent pause before a person starts speaking. Brotherton (1979), however, has shown that such planning also occurs during within-utterance pauses. In an analysis of interviewer–interviewee exchanges, she found that many of the interviewees' responses to the interviewer's questions occurred without any measurable initial delays. In fact there were even a few interviewee responses without either initial delays or within utterance pauses. Although these silence-free responses contained newly generated information, they were all relatively short. Longer responses were inevitably associated with within-utterance pauses, most of them occurring at clause boundaries. These silent pauses between clauses may very well serve the function of semantic planning.

Cognition and hesitation in the initial interview.   Siegman and Pope (1965a, 1972) looked at the effect of cognitive planning and decision making on hesitation indices within the context of the initial interview. Specifically they investigated the effects of ambiguous versus specific interviewer questions on a broad sampling of hesitation phenomena. An ambiguous interviewer remark was defined as one that requires that the interviewee decide between many response alternatives (that is, one requiring planning and decision making). "Tell me about your family" is one example of a moderately ambiguous interviewer question. By way of contrast, a specific interviewer remark is one to which there is only one or a restricted number of response alternatives. Thus, "What kind of work do you do?" is an example of a highly specific interviewer question. In the first of a series of studies (Siegman & Pope, 1965a) ambiguous interviewer probes were found to be associated with more frequent filled and unfilled brief pausing than specific interviewer probes. Interviewer ambiguity, however, was not related to relatively long silent pauses, as indexed by the RT and SQ measures, nor was it related to the SDR.

In subsequent studies, however, ambiguous interviewer remarks, in contrast to specific ones, also elicited longer latencies and silences in interviewees' responses (Pope, Blass, Bradford, & Siegman, 1971; Siegman & Pope, 1972). The discrepancy between the first and the later studies may very well be the result of a procedural difference between them. In the first study the decision as to when an interviewee had completed his or her response to the interviewer's query was left to the subjective decision of the interviewer. In subsequent studies, however, interviewers were either instructed to wait a fixed period of time after each interviewee response before proceeding to the next question, or they were told not to begin their response until signaled by the interviewee that he had finished his. It is not unreasonable to assume, therefore, that in the first study subjects were under greater pressure than in subsequent studies to respond promptly and to refrain from long silent pauses, lest they lose the floor. This may explain why in the first study interviewer ambiguity did not affect interviewees' response latencies nor their silent-pause ratios. It should be pointed out that in none of the studies, however, did we find a significant relationship between interviewer ambiguity and interviewee speech disruptions.

In another study, Siegman and Pope (1966a) investigated the effects of stimulus ambiguity in the TAT on hesitation phenomena in subjects' story completions. Stimulus ambiguity was defined in terms of the variability of themes evoked by the different cards. In this study, stimulus ambiguity was associated not only with an increase in the various hesitation indices listed earlier but also with an increase in the SDR. Perhaps speaker uncertainty is more likely to be associated with speech disruptions in tasks requiring new word combinations, as is the case in the TAT, than in the interview that, as pointed out earlier, involves a considerable amount of "automatic speech," that is, habituated or overpracticed word sequences.

In a recent study, Rochester and Gill (1973) found that sentences containing noun-phrase complements (NPC) were associated with more speech disruptions than sentences containing relative clauses (Rel. Cl.). The magnitude of this effect, however, was a function of the speech context, in this case, dialogues versus monologues, with the difference more pronounced in the latter than in the former. Furthermore, speech context interacted with the location of disruptions. For dialogues, disruption location was of little consequence. In monologues, however, disruption location was a critical variable. When disruptions were measured at clause boundaries, there was a 30-percentage-point spread between the proportions of disrupted NPC sentences and disrupted Rel Cl. sentences. But when disruptions were measured at other locations, the proportion of disrupted sentences were about the same regardless of type of sentence. The authors attribute the difference in speech disruption frequency in the two types of sentences to the fact that complement-type constructions are syntactically more complex than relative clause constructions. The fact that this difference was most pronounced in monologues suggest to Rochester and Gill that the role of syntax may recede as one moves from monologues to dialogues.

An alternate possibility is that syntactic complexity is associated with different hesitation phenomena in monologues than in dialogues. The previously cited studies by Siegman and Pope argue strongly in favor of the proposition that cognitive planning and decision making can produce a variety of hesitation phenomena, depending on the nature of the task and on the interpersonal context. For example, when a speaker feels constrained not to remain silent for too long, cognitive decision making manifests itself by an increase in brief filled or unfilled pauses rather than long silent pauses. Similarly, syntactic complexity may be associated with speech disruptions in monologues, but with some other hesitation phenomenon in dialogues, in which disruption-free speech is at a greater premium. In other words, with regard to hesitation phenomena, we are proposing a form of "symptom equivalence."

One obvious methodological implication of the previously cited Siegman and Pope study is that in investigating the effects of cognitive planning and decision making on speech one needs to sample a wide range of hesitation phenomena, not just pausing, as did Goldman-Eisler (1968) or speech disruptions, as did Rochester and Gill (1973).

In their studies on stimulus ambiguity and verbal fluency, Siegman and Pope (1965a, 1966a) also addressed themselves to the potential role of anxiety as a mediating variable. It has been suggested that cognitively complex tasks are more anxiety arousing, and that such affective arousal may account for the hesitant speech. In order to test whether the effects of interviewer ambiguity on interviewee verbal fluency are in fact mediated by anxiety arousal, one half of the interviewer's questions were designed to be anxiety arousing, the other neutral. Moreover, subjects were divided, on the basis of their Taylor Manifest Anxiety Scale scores into an anxious and nonanxious group. Should the effects of interviewee ambiguity be mediated by anxiety-arousal, then these effects should be more pronounced in the anxiety-arousing than in the neutral questions, and for the anxious than for the nonanxious subjects. This was clearly not the case. In the TAT too, the effects of stimulus ambiguity on verbal fluency were independent on the anxiety-arousing characteristics of the cards. The latter were determined by a content analysis of subjects' stories, and held constant by means of an analysis of covariance. It seems fairly clear, then, that the hesitation phenomena associated with uncertainty and cognitive planning are not mediated by anxiety arousal.

On the other hand, some silent pauses in speech that are frequently attributed to affective arousal may in fact reflect cognitive activity going on at the time of the pausing. For example, Siegman and Reynolds (1984) have shown that interviewees' responses to intimate interviewer questions are associated with longer response latencies, more frequent and longer within-response silent pauses, and a slower speech rate than their responses to relatively nonintimate questions. Although these differences can be explained in terms of affective arousal, a more parsimonious explanation is in terms of an increase in information processing, due to the self-censoring activities that are elicited by intimate questions (Siegman & Reynolds, 1984).

Intelligence Test Scores and Hesitation Phenomena

Considering the rather clear-cut evidence that cognitive planning and decision making are associated with hesitant speech, it is only reasonable to speculate about the role of intelligence in the various hesitation indices. Do individuals who obtain high vocabulary test scores speak more fluently, with fewer silent pauses, than low scorers? If Goldman-Eisler is correct in her assertion that within-utterance silent pauses reflect lexical decision making, one could argue that the answer to the previous question should be in the affirmative. On the other hand, both high and low scorers may be equally involved in lexical decision making, but on different levels of difficulty. In that case there may be no significant correlation between vocabulary skill and the silent-pause ratio. Similar questions can, of course, be asked in relation to the SDR, the Filled-Pauses Ratio, and other hesitation indices. Furthermore, to the extent that a speaker's decisions involve not only lexical choices but also structure and syntax, intelligence measures other than vocabulary scores — perhaps measures of abstraction ability — may be significant sources of variance in the various hesitation indices.

Data obtained as part of the interview study described earlier (Siegman & Pope, 1965a) provide partial answers to the preceding questions. In this study all interviewees took the Shipley Hartford Retreat Scale, which consists of a vocabulary subtest and a subtest designed to measure the ability to find higher order commonalities among diverse visual patterns. The interview itself, it is recalled, consisted of both ambiguous and specific interviewer remarks. To the extent that there is a relationship between vocabulary skill and the absence of hesitation phenomena, it was expected to be strongest in response to interviewer questions that involved planning and decision making. The results indicate that the expected negative relationship between vocabulary test scores and hesitation — response latency and silent pauses — was obtained, but only in the interview segment consisting of specific interviewer probes (Table 8.2). Significant negative correlations between vocabulary proficiency and within-utterance silent pauses have also been reported by Preston and Gardner (1967). In contrast to the findings of our interview study that vocabulary proficiency rather than abstraction ability is the significant source of variance in hesitation pauses, Bernstein (1962) reports data suggesting the very opposite to be the case. On the basis of his findings

TABLE 8.2
Correlations (rs) between Shipley-Hartford Scales and Pausing

Shipley-Hartford Scales	Reaction-Time		Silence-Quotient	
	Specific Qs	Ambiguous Qs	Specific Qs	Ambiguous Qs
Vocabulary	−.355**	−.109	−.318*	−.252
Abstraction	−.072	−.228	−.146	−.136

$*p < .05$
$**p < .01$

Bernstein concludes that hesitation pauses are related to code complexity rather than simple vocabulary choice. However, considering the contradiction in the data base, his conclusion may have been a bit premature.

Finally, it would seem that neither vocabulary nor abstraction skills are related to the frequency of speech disruptions or the frequency of filled pauses in speech — a conclusion that is supported by the findings of other investigators (Feldstein et al., 1963; Preston & Gardner, 1967).

Silent Pauses — a Window to Cognitive Activity in the Brain

If excessively long silent pauses in speech — excessive in terms of group and/or personal norms — are viewed as an indication that the speaker is experiencing encoding difficulties, then such pauses may serve important diagnostic functions. Earlier we cited evidence of an increase in speech rate with aging. It has been suggested that subtle changes in pausing behavior may very well precede the more obvious manifestations of mental deterioration in the aged (Siegman, 1978, 1979a). An analysis of pausing behavior and of other hesitation phenomena may also be in assessing the effects of drugs on cognitive functioning. For example, in one study (Siegman & Pope, 1967) it was found that even relatively small dosages of alcohol were associated with an increase of subjects' silent-pause ratios and other hesitation phenomena, even before there was any indication of subjects' intoxication in their blood alcohol levels. It has also been suggested that an analysis of silent pauses and other hesitation phenomena in youngsters with learning disabilities in the verbal area may help define the nature of their problems in that area (Siegman, 1979a).

SOME CONCLUSIONS AND SUGGESTIONS FOR FURTHER RESEARCH

In relation to many of the issues discussed in this chapter, there is either insufficient evidence or evidence that is too contradictory for any definite conclusions to be drawn. In relation to some issues, however, the data allow for at least some tentative conclusions.

Personality as a source of variance in extralinguistic behavior. Despite the near contempt with which some contemporary experimental psychologists view this issue, a number of investigators have reopened the question and are bringing to bear on it considerable methodological and conceptual sophistication. Of course, the mere failure to find significant correlations between personality test scores and extralinguistic variables should not necessarily be viewed as evidence against the hypothesis that personality is a significant source of variance in extralinguistic behavior. A plausible alternative is that the personality tests do not really measure what they are supposed to measure. They certainly have no greater face validity than the psycholinguistic behaviors that they are supposed to validate. But, even so, there are a number of significant correlations between personality test scores and extralinguistic variables. Thus far, the most promising personality variable seems to be extraversion–introversion, and the most promising extralinguistic variables involve the temporal pacing of speech — with extraverts showing a more accelerated pacing than introverts. An interesting question in relation to this finding concerns the mediating process or processes. Extraverts are reputed to be more socially at ease than introverts. This tendency could very well have the effect of reducing long silent pauses and accelerating speech tempo in social interactions. On the other hand, extraverts are also reputed to be more impulsive and less reflective in their responses. This too could reduce silent pauses and other hesitation phenomena. It remains, then, for further experimental research to clarify which of these factors, independently or in combination, mediate the relationship between extraversion-introversion and the temporal pacing of speech. One more point on this issue: Speech tempo is a very broad category, which could be affected by a variety of temporal speech variables (for example, an increase or decrease in long pauses, or in short pauses, or in word articulation). We need to know more about which of these are related to the extraversion–introversion dimension. Yet another possibility is that extraverts are more concerned with making a favorable impression on others and therefore avoid long silent pauses.

There is considerable evidence that listeners tend to agree among themselves about a speaker's personality traits — other than extraversion-introversion — although researchers have yet to demonstrate the validity of these judgments. Nevertheless, this by no means is a trivial finding because such listener attributions can have serious consequences for the speaker. To account for the high level of interjudge reliability, it is suggested that voice types and personality traits are matched on the basis of their similarity in semantic space. Furthermore, it is suggested that personality, attitudinal, and motivational attributions that a listener makes about a speaker influence the listener's verbal and nonverbal behavior to the speaker. Consistent personality attributions can, therefore, initiate a process of self-fulfilling prophecies.

Anxiety and speech. Early investigators of the effects of anxiety on speech approached the issue from a clinical pserspective. Accustomed to think of anxiety as a source of symptoms and pathology, they assumed that its effects on speech are likely to be of a disruptive nature. They expected anxiety arousal to be associated with speech disruptions, with hesitant speech, and with frequent and long silent pauses. The evidence is farily consistent with the expectation regarding speech disruptions but not with the other expectations, where the evidence, at least on first glance, seems contradictory. In order to account for these contradictions we proposed a model that, hopefully, can predict when anxiety is likely to have an accelerating effect on speech and when it is likely to have a slowing down effect. Mild anxiety arousal is likely to have an accelerating affect on speech, provided the speech task does not involve complex decision making, i.e., it is not a difficult task. Extreme anxiety may slow down speech even if it does not involve complex choices. The positive relationship between anxiety arousal and the temporal pacing of speech can be attenuated or even reversed if the speaker finds himself in conflict about whether to speak or not to speak (as can be the case in deceptive communications) or if he is motivated to cover up his anxiety (as can be the case in lying or in anxiety associated with public speaking).

Although it is fairly clear that at least mild anxiety arousal accelerates speech involving overlearned word sequences, provided the speaker is not in an approach–avoidance conflict situation or trying to cover up his anxiety, the precise temporal parameters that are affected may very well vary as a function of the social context.

Finally, although we have argued for some sort of functional equivalence among the various hesitation phenomena, their location may make a difference. Therefore, future studies on anxiety and speech should not only distinguish among the various hesitation indices but also determine whether they are located, for example, within clauses or at their boundaries.

The findings in the Siegman and Pope interview study (1966b, 1972) showed that mild anxiety arousal is associated with an increase in interview productivity (longer responses) and with vocabulary diversity are consistent with a drive-activation-arousal conceptualization of anxiety and stress. It should be noted that subsequent studies indicate that the facilitative effect of anxiety on productivity (Pope, Siegman, & Blass, 1970) and vocabulary diversity (Sunshine & Horowitz, 1968) is independent of topical manipulation. A positive correlation between anxiety arousal and productivity is, of course, to be expected on the basis of the Hull–Spence–Taylor position, which clearly states that anxiety arousal will make previously below-threshold responses suprathreshold. The positive correlation between anxiety arousal and vocabulary diversity suggests that the facilitative effect of anxiety arousal involves

not only autonomic but also cortical arousal. This is, of course, a highly speculative hypothesis, and it should be noted that other investigators have reported negative correlations between anxiety and vocabulary diversity.

Social context.   The presence of other people influences our vocal behavior in subtle yet powerful ways. One need only to look at the data on the
mutual accommodation phenomena (congruence in the temporal pacing of
speech and in relation to other vocal parameters) to be convinced of this generalization. There is evidence to suggest that the mere presence of another
person from whom one can expect visual and other feedback facilitates the
flow of communication in dyadic conversations. If, however, the topic of
conversation is potentially embarrassing, the mere presence of such a person
can inhibit the flow of communication because of the speaker's expectation
of negative feedback.

Gender composition may very well be one of the most profound influences
on extralinguistic behavior in dyadic conversation. Both males and females
speak differently when addressing members of their own sex than when addressing persons of the opposite sex. Equally important, from a methodological point of view, is the finding that gender composition is a significant moderator variable. Relationships between social-psychological variables and
extralinguistic behavior that are obtained in same-gender groups can be attenuated and even reversed in opposite-gender groups, and vice versa.

Finally, there is evidence that both interpersonal attracton and status influence vocal behavior in dyadic interactions, although we have more empirical
evidence about the former than the latter. Interpersonal attraction, which
can be readily controlled in the laboratory by manipulating the level of
friendliness, is associated with more fluent and less hesitant speech, in the
sense of shorter latencies and fewer and/or shorter silent pauses. Presumably
this is so because people engage in less self-monitoring and censoring when
interacting with someone they like than when talking to someone they do not
like.

Cognition and hesitation.   The evidence concerning the effects of cognitive planning and decision making on speech is much more clear-cut than is
the evidence in relation to anxiety and speech. Cognitive planning clearly is
associated with a variety of hesitation phenomena, such as silent pauses,
speech disruptions, and filled pauses. The precise indices that are affected depend on the nature of the decision-making process, for example, choosing
among several alternative responses to an ambiguous question, or choosing
among syntactic alternatives, and on situational constraints. A speaker is under greater pressure, for instance, to avoid long silent pauses in dialogues
than in monologues or when asked to make up stories in response to TAT
cards. Therefore, in dialogues, hesitation is much less likely to take the form
of long unfilled pauses than in the latter situations. This, of course, is the

principle of the functional equivalence of hesitation indices referred to earlier. The methodological implication should be obvious. In trying to determine whether a speaker is engaged in cognitive planning and decision making on the basis of the presence or absence of speech hesitation, it is important to choose the appropriate hesitation index. If there is clear-cut empirical basis for such a choice, the investigator has no alternative but to sample a broad range of hesitations indices. Many classical studies in this area are subject to the criticism that they did not sample a sufficiently wide range of hesitation indices.

One of the still unsettled issues is the basic question of how sentences are generated. There is no question that lexical decision making is associated with hesitation in speech, but whether these hesitations indicate proximal decision, that is, decisions about the word immediately following the hesitation, or more distal decisions, is as yet unclear. Also to be settled is the question whether structural-syntactic decisions are a matter of learned habits, as is claimed by Goldman-Eisler or of cognitive decision making, as is claimed by her critics. If the latter is the case, we need to know what type of structural-syntactic decisions are made at which point of the encoding process.

Despite all these unanswered basic questions, we have come a long way from the days when hesitation phenomena were conceptualized *exclusively* in terms of anxiety and emotional arousal. The clinical observation that emotional conflicts are associated with hesitant speech is probably an accurate one, but precisely because such conflicts also involve difficult cognitive choices and decision making. To the extent that there is an association between emotional conflict and hesitation, the relationship is frequently mediated by cognitive factors, rather than by anxiety arousal. In fact, as was pointed out earlier, anxiety arousal per se is likely to accelerate rather than slow down speech, unless difficult cognitive decision making is involved.

It may be worth noting several recurrent themes in this chapter. One is the moderating effect of topical focus on many of the relationships that we have examined in this chapter. Another is the importance of cognition in extralinguistic behavior. Finally, there is the prominence of temporal variables. Whether we looked at personality and speech, the effects of anxiety arousal on speech, or the effects of the social context and of cognition on speech, the significant dependent variables invariably involved the temporal dimension. Perhaps this reflects nothing more than the relative ease with which the temporal dimension can be quantified, or nothing more than the role of fadism in social science research. On the other hand, it may illustrate the profound importance of temporal patterning in human speech.

Although we have come a long way in the measurement and understanding of silent pauses and other hesitation phenomena, much remains to be done. For example, we have only fragmentary evidence regarding the independence of short versus long silent pauses, and we need to know more about that. We also need to know more about the interaction of pauses (and other hesitation phenomena) and their location. There is some evidence that the implications of silent pauses at clause junctures are different from those within clauses, but there have been only few systematic investigations of this issue. Finally, two individuals may have comparable total pausing times and average pause durations and yet speak with different temporal rhythms. We need to identify the basic varieties of such rhythms, their veridical behavioral correlates, and the attributions that they elicit.

In the course of this chapter we have tried to identify the vocal-nonverbal correlates of personality, of different affective states, and of behaviors such as deception and the Type-A behavior pattern. But does not the very discovery of the nonverbal correlates of these traits and states undermine their usefulness as detectors of these traits and states? The more people know about their nonverbal behavior when, for example, they are anxious, the easier it may be for them to counteract it. The same, of course, applies to deception and to the Type-A behavior pattern. But the problem goes beyond the narrow issue of the detection of anxiety, deception, and the Type-A behavior pattern. It has been said, and rightly so, that the nonverbal channels of communication, which in contrast to the verbal channel are inherently ambiguous and communicate meaning implicitly rather than explicitly, analogically rather than digitally, serve several critically important functions. First of all, they allow us to express our feelings, be they like or dislike, respect or contempt, without taking full responsibility for them. It is undeniably easier to retract what has been expressed nonverbally than what has been expressed verbally, precisely because of the relative ambiguity of the nonverbal channels. This ability to disown nonverbally expressed affect can spare us much grief in daily interpersonal interactions. Secondly, the evocative and analogical nature of nonverbal cues allows us to communicate a dimension of our experience, which those of us who are not poets find difficult to put into words. With the appropriate modulation of voice and with the proper expressive movements, prose can become poetry. But as our research findings allow us to eliminate the ambiguity of nonverbal cues and to explicate their meaning, i.e., to transform the nonverbal channel into yet another digital code, they may lose these adaptive functions. But, then, mankind is likely to discover new codes to serve these same vital functions, scientists will try to explicate the meanings of these newly emerging codes, and the cycle will begin all over again.

REFERENCES

Addington, D. W. The relationship of selected vocal characteristics to personality perception. *Speech Monographs,* 1968, *35,* 492–503.

Allport,G., & Cantril, H. Judging personality from the voice. *Journal of Social Psychology,* 1934, *5,* 37–55.

Aronovitch, C. D. The voice of personality: Stereotyped judgments and their relation to voice quality and sex of speaker. *Journal of Social Psychology,* 1976, *99,* 207-220.

Aronson, E. Some antecedents of interpersonal attraction. In W. J. Arnold & D. Levine (Eds.), *Nebraska Symposium on Motivation* (Vol. 17). Lincoln: University of Nebraska Press, 1969.

Aronson, E., & Weintraub, W. Personal adaptation as reflected in verbal behavior. In A. W. Siegman & B. Pope (Eds.), *Studies in dyadic communication.* New York: Pergamon, 1972.

Argyle, M., Lalljee, M., & Cook, M. The effects of visibility on interaction in a dyad. *Human Relations,* 1968, *21,* 3-17.

Bernstein, B. Social class and linguistic development: A theory of social learning. In A. H. Halsey, J. Floud, & A. Anderson (Eds.), *Economy, education and society.* Glencoe, IL: Free Press, 1961.

Bernstein, B. Linguistic codes, hesitation phenomena and intelligence. *Language and Speech,* 1962, *5,* 31-46.

Bernstein, B. Elaborated and restricted codes: Their social origins and some consequences. *American Anthropologist,* 1964, *66,* Part II, 55-64.

Bernstein, B. Social class, language and socialization. In S. Moscovici (Ed.), *The psychology of language.* Chicago: Markham, 1972.

Bernstein, B. Postscript to the Paladin edition of *Class, codes and control* (Vol. 1). St. Albans, Hertfordshire: Paladin, 1973.

Bodine, A. Sex differences in language. In B. Thorne & N. Henley (Eds.), *Language and sex: Difference and dominance.* Rowley, MA: Newbury House, 1975.

Bond, R. N., & Feldstein, S. Acoustical correlates of the perception of speech rate: An experimental investigation. *Journal of Psycholinguistic Research,* 1982, *11,* 539-557.

Boomer, D. S. Review of Goldman-Eisler, Psycholinguistics: Experiments in spontaneous speech. *Lingua,* 1970, *25,* 152-164.

Boomer, D. S., & Dittmann, A. T. Hesitation pauses and juncture pauses in speech. *Language and Speech,* 1962, *5,* 215-220.

Boomer, D. S., & Goodrich, D. W. Speech disturbance and judged anxiety. *Journal of Consulting Psychology,* 1961, *25,* 160-164.

Bourhis, R. Y., & Giles, H. The language of cooperation in Wales: a field study. *Language Sciences,* 1976, *42,* 13-16.

Brotherton, P. Speaking and not speaking: Processes for translating ideas into speech. In A. W. Siegman & S. Feldstein (Eds.), *Of speech and time.* Hillsdale, NJ: Lawrence Erlbaum Associates, 1979.

Brown, B. L. The detection of emotion in vocal qualities. In H. Giles, W. P. Robinson, & P. M. Smith (Eds.), *Language: Social psychological perspectives.* Oxford: Pergamon, 1980.

Brown, B. L., Strong, W. J., & Rencher, A. C. Acoustic determinants of perceptions of personality from speech. *International Journal of the Sociology of Language,* 1972, *6,* 11-32.

Brown, B. L., Strong, W. J., & Rencher, A. C. Perceptions of personality from speech: Effects of manipulations of acoustical parameters. *Journal of the Acoustical Society of America,* 1973, *54,* 29-35.

Brown, B. L. Strong, W. J., & Rencher, A. C. Fifty-four voices from two: The effects of simultaneous manipulations of rate, mean fundamental frequency and variance of fundamental frequency on ratings of personality from speech. *Journal of the Acoustical Society of America,* 1974, *55,* 313-318.

Byrne, D. *The attraction paradigm.* New York: Academic, 1971.

Campbell, A., & Rushton, J. R. Bodily communication and personality. *British Journal of Social and Clinical Psychology,* 1978, *17,* 31-36.

Cassotta, L., Feldstein, S., & Jaffe, J. *The stability and modifiability of individual vocal characteristics in stress and nonstress interviews.* Unpublished manuscript, The William Alanson White Institute, 1967.

Chomsky, N. *Aspects of the theory of syntax.* Cambridge, MA: MIT Press, 1965.

Cook, M. Anxiety, speech disturbances and speech rate. *British Journal of Social and Clinical Psychology*, 1969, *8*, 13-21.

Cope, C. S. Linguistic structure and personality development. *Journal of Counseling Psychology*, 1969, *16*, 1-19.

Crown, C. L. Impression formation and the chronography of dyadic interactions. In M. Davis (Ed.), *Interaction rhythms: Periodicity in communicative behavior*. New York: Human Sciences, 1982.

Crown, C. L., Feldstein, S., & Siegman, A. W. *Speech sounds and silences in nonsimulated expressions of anger*. Paper presented at the Eastern Psychological Association, Philadelphia, 1979.

Crystal, D., & Quirk, R. *Systems of prosaic and paralinguistic features in English*. The Hague: Mouton, 1964.

Dembroski, T. M., & McDougall, J. M. Behavioral and psychophysiological perspectives on coronary prone behavior. In T. M. Dembroski, T. H. Schmidt, & G. Blumchen (Eds.), *Behavioral bases of coronary heart disease*. New York: Karger, 1983.

Diamond, E. L. The role of anger and hostility in essential hypertension and coronary heart disease. *Psychological Bulletin*, 1982, *92*, 410-433.

Duffy, E. *Activation and behavior*. New York: Wiley, 1962.

Duncan, S., Jr., & Rosenthal, R. Vocal emphasis in experimenters' instruction reading as unintended determinant of subjects' responses. *Language and Speech*, 1968, *11*, 20-26.

Duncan, S., Jr., Rosenberg, N. J., & Finkelstein, J. The paralanguage of experimenter bias. *Sociometry*, 1969, *32*, 207-219.

Ekman, P. Facial expression. In A. W. Siegman & S. Feldstein (Eds.), *Nonverbal behavior and communication*. Hillsdale, NJ: Lawrence Erlbaum Associates, 1978.

Ellis, D. S. Speech and social status in America. *Social Forces*, 1967, *45*, 431-437.

Ellsworth, P. C., & Ludwig, L. M. Visual behavior in social interacton. *The Journal of Communication*, 1972, *22*, 375-403.

Exline, R. V., & Fehr, B. J. Applications of semiosis to the study of visual interaction. In A. W. Siegman & S. Feldstein (Eds.), *Nonverbal behavior and communication*. Hillsdale, NJ: Lawrence Erlbaum Associates, 1978.

Eysenck, H. J., & Eysenck, S. B., G. On the dual nature of extroversion. *British Journal of Social and Clinical Psychology*, 1963, *2*, 46-55.

Feldstein, S. Vocal patterning of emotional expression. In J. H. Masserman (Ed.), *Science and psychoanalysis* (Vol. 7). New York: Grune & Stratton, 1964.

Feldstein, S. Interspeaker influence in conversational interaction. *Psychological Reports*, 1968, *22*, 826-828.

Feldstein, S. Temporal patterns in dialogue: Basic research and reconsiderations. In A. W. Siegman & B. Pope (Eds.), *Studies in dyadic communication*. New York: Pergamon, 1972.

Feldstein, S. Rate estimates of sound-silence sequences in speech. *Journal of the Acoustical Society of America*, 1976, *60*, (Supplement No. 1) S46. (Abstract)

Feldstein, S., & Bond, R. N. Perception of speech rate as a function of vocal frequency and intensity. *Language and speech*, 1981, *24*, 385-392.

Feldstein, S., Brenner, M. S., & Jaffe, J. The effect of subject sex, verbal interaction, and topical focus on speech disruption. *Language and Speech*, 1963, *6*, 229-239.

Feldstein, S., & Crown, C. L. *Interpersonal perception in dyads as a function of race, gender, and conversational time patterns*. Paper read at the Eastern Psychological Association, Philadelphia, April, 1979.

Feldstein, S., Crown, C. L., & Siegman, A. W. *Silence, self-esteem and nonsimulated verbal expressions of anger*. Unpublished manuscript, University of Maryland Baltimore County, 1980.

Feldstein, S., & Jaffe, J. The relationship of speech disruption to the experience of anger. *Journal of Consulting Psychology*, 1962, *26*, 505-509.

Feldstein, S., Jaffe, J., & Cassotta, L. *A profile analysis of affective expression in speech*. Unpublished manuscript, The William Alanson White Institute, 1964.

Feldstein, S., & Sloan, B. Actual and stereotyped speech patterns of extraverts and introverts. *Journal of Personality*, 1984, *52*, 188-204.

Fenz, W. D. J., & Epstein, S. Measurement of approach-avoidance conflict along a stimulus dimension by a thematic apperception test. *Journal of Personality*, 1962, *30*, 613-632.

Fiske, D. W., & Maddi, S. R. (Eds.). *Functions of varied experience*. Homewood, IL: Dorsey, 1961.

Foa, U. Convergences in the analysis of the structure of interpersonal behavior. *Psychological Review*, 1961, *5*, 341-353.

Frank, J. D. *Persuasion and healing*. Baltimore: Johns Hopkins Press, 1961.

Friedman, M., & Rosenman, R. *Type-A behavior and your heart*. New York: Knopf, 1974.

Garai, J. E., & Scheinfeld, A. Sex differences in mental and behavioral traits. *Genetic Psychology Monographs*, 1968, *77*, 169-299.

Geer, J. H. Effects of fear arousal upon task performance and verbal behavior. *Journal of Abnormal Psychology*, 1966, *71*, 119-123.

Giles, H. Evaluative reactions to accents. *Educational Review*, 1970, *22*, 211-227.

Giles, H. Communicative effectiveness as a function of accented speech. *Speech Monographs*, 1973, *40*, 330-331.

Giles, H., Baker, S., & Fielding, G. Communication length as a behavioral index of accent prejudice. *International Journal of the Sociology of Language*, 1975, *6*, 73-78.

Giles, H., Taylor, D. M., & Bourhis, R. Towards a theory of interpersonal accommodation through language: Some Canadian data. *Language in Society*, 1975, *2*, 177-192.

Goldman-Eisler, F. Hesitation and information in speech. In C. Cherry (Ed.), *Information theory*. London: Butterworths, 1961. (a)

Goldman-Eisler, F. A comparative study of two hesitation phenomena. *Language and Speech*, 1961, *4*, 18-26. (b)

Goldman-Eisler, F. *Psycholinguistics: Experiments in spontaneous speech*. New York: Academic, 1968.

Gross, H. S. Toward including listening in a model of the interview. In A. W. Siegman & B. Pope (Eds.), *Studies in dyadic communication*. New York: Pergamon, 1972.

Hargreaves, W. A., & Starkweather, J. A. Collection of temporal data with the duration tabulator. *Journal of Experimental Analysis of Behavior*, 1959, *2*, 170.

Head, B. *Sex as a factor in the use of obscenity*. Paper presented at the Linguistic Society of America Summer Meeting, Honolulu, 1977.

Hebb, D. O. Drives and the CNS (conceptual nervous system). *Psychological Review*, 1955, *62*, 243-254.

Heinl-Hutchinson, M. *Untersuchung zur Sprechweise und deren Beziehung zur Lebenszufriedenheit bei älteren Menschen*. Master's thesis, University of Giessen, 1975.

Helfrich, H. Age markers in speech. In K. R. Scherer & H. Giles (Eds.), *Social markers in speech*. Cambridge: Cambridge University Press, 1979.

Helfrich, H., & Dahme, G. Sind Verzogerungsphanomene bein spontanen Sprechen Indikatoren personlichkeitsspezifischer Angstverarbeitung. *Zeitschrift fur Socialpsychologie*, 1974, *5*, 55-65.

Heller, K. Ambiguity in the interview interaction. In J. M. Shlien (Ed.), *Research in psychotherapy*. Washington, DC: American Psychological Association, 1968.

Heller, K. Interview structure and interview style in initial interviews. In A. W. Siegman & B. Pope (Eds.), *Studies in dyadic communication*. New York: Pergamon, 1972.

Hess, R. D., & Shipman, V. C. Early experience and the socialization of cognitive modes in children. *Child Development*, 1965, *36*, 869-888.

Houston, S. A re-examination of some assumptions about the language of the disadvantaged child. *Child Development*, 1970, *41*, 947-962.

Howland, E. W., & Siegman, A. W. Toward the automated measurement of the Type-A behaior pattern. *Behavioral Medicine,* 1982, *5,* 37–54.

Jackson, D. N. *Manual for the personality research form.* London, Canada: University of Western Ontario Press, 1967.

Jaffe, J., & Anderson, S. Speech rate studies in major depressive disorders: Prediction of early response to medication. In S. Feldstein, C. L. Crown, & J. Welkowitz (Eds.), *Speech sounds and silences: A social-psychophysical approach to clinical concerns.* Hillsdale, NJ: Lawrence Erlbaum Associates, in press.

Johnson, C. F., & Dabbs, J. M., Jr. Self-disclosure in dyads as a function of distance and the subject–experimenter relationship. *Sociometry,* 1976, *39,* 257–263.

Jones, E. E., & Nisbett, R. E. *The actor and the observer: Divergent perceptions of the causes of behavior.* General Learning Press, 1971.

Kanfer, F. H. Effect of a warning signal preceding a noxious stimulus on verbal rate and heart rate. *Journal of Experimental Psychology,* 1958, *55,* 78–80. (a)

Kanfer, F. H. Supplementary report: Stability of a verbal rate change in experimental anxiety. *Journal of Experimental Psychology,* 1958, *56,* 182. (b)

Kanfer, F. H. Verbal rate, content, and adjustment ratings in experimentally structured interviews. *Journal of Abnormal and Social Psychology,* 1959, *58,* 305–311.

Kanfer, F. H. Verbal rate, eyeblink, and content in structured psychiatric interviews. *Journal of Abnormal and Social Psychology,* 1960, *61,* 341–347.

Kasl, S. V., & Mahl, G. F. The relationship of disturbances and hesitations in spontaneous speech to anxiety. *Journal of Personality and Social Psychology,* 1965, *1,* 425–433.

Knapp, M. L. *Nonverbal communication in human interaction.* New York: Holt, Rinehart, & Winston, 1972.

Kogan, N., & Wallach, M. A. *Risk-taking: A study in cognition and personality.* New York: Holt, Rinehart, & Winston, 1964.

Kowal, S., O'Connell, D. C., & Sabin, E. J. Development of temporal patterning and vocal hesitations in spontaneous narratives. *Journal of Psycholinguistic Research,* 1975, *4,* 195–207.

Kramer, E. Judgment of personal characteristics and emotions from nonverbal properties of speech. *Psychological Bulletin,* 1963, *60,* 408–420.

Labov, W. The study of language in its social context. *Studium Generale,* 1970, *23,* 66–84.

Labov, W. *Sociolinguistic patterns.* Philadelphia: University of Pennsylvania Press, 1972.

Lakoff, R. Language and woman's place. *Language in Society,* 1973, *2,* 45–79.

Lalljee, M., & Cook, M. Uncertainty in first encounters. *Journal of Personality and Social Psychology,* 1973, *26,* 137–141.

Lambert, W. E. A social psychology of bilingualism. *Journal of Social Issues,* 1967, *23,* 99–100.

Landis, C. National differences in conversation. *Journal of Abnormal and Social Psychology,* 1927, *21,* 354–375.

Landis, M. H., & Burtt, H. E. A study of conversation. *Journal of Comparative Psychology,* 1924, *4,* 81–89.

Lee, R. R. Dialect perception: A critical review and re-evaluation. *Quarterly Journal of Speech,* 1971, *57,* 410–417.

Lennard, H. L., & Bernstein, A., *The anatomy of psychotherapy.* New York: Columbia University Press, 1960.

Levin, H., Baldwin, A. L., Gallwey, M., & Paivio, A. Audience stress, personality, and speech. *Journal of Abnormal and Social Psychology,* 1960, *61,* 469–473.

Levin, H., & Silverman, I. Hesitation phenomena in children's speech. *Language and Speech,* 1965, *8,* 67–85.

Libo, L. M. *Manual for the Picture Impression Test.* University of Maryland School of Medicine, Baltimore, 1956.

Maclay, H., & Osgood, C. E. Hesitation phenomena in spontaneous English speech. *Word,* 1959, *15,* 19–44.

Mahl, G. F. Disturbances and silences in the patient's speech in psychotherapy. *Journal of Abnormal and Social Psychology,* 1956, *53,* 1–15.

Mallory, E., & Miller, V. A. A possible basis for the association of voice characteristics and personality traits. *Speech Monographs,* 1958, *25,* 255–260.

Markel, N. N., Prebor, L. D., & Brandt, J. F. Biosocial factors in dyadic communication: Sex and speaking intensity. *Journal of Personality and Social Psychology,* 1972, *23,* 11–13.

Matarazzo, J. D., & Wiens, A. N. *The interview: Research on its anatomy and structure.* Chicago: Aldine-Atherton, 1972.

Matthews, K. A. What is the Type A (coronary-prone) behavior pattern from a psychological perspective? *Psychological Bulletin,* 1982, *91,* 293–323.

Mattingly, I. G. Speaker variation and vocal tract size. *Journal of the Acoustical Society of America,* 1966, *39,* 1219.

McGlone, R. E., & Hollien, H. Vocal pitch characteristics of aged women. *Journal of Speech and Hearing Research,* 1963, *6,* 164–170.

McGovern, T. V. The making of a job interviewee: The effect of nonverbal behavior on an interviewer's evaluations during a selection interview. Doctoral dissertation, Southern Illinois University, 1976. *Dissertation Abstracts International,* 1977, *37,* 4740B–4741B. (University Microfilms No. 77-6239)

Mehrabian, A., & Williams, M. Nonverbal concomitants of perceived and intended persuasiveness. *Journal of Personality and Social Psychology,* 1969, *13,* 37–58.

Milmoe, S., Rosenthal, R., Blane, H. T., Chafetz, M. E., & Wolf, I. The doctor's voice: Postdictor of successful referral of alcoholic patients. *Journal of Abnormal Psychology,* 1967, *72,* 78–84.

Montague, E. K. The role of anxiety in serial learning. *Journal of Experimental Psychology,* 1953, *45,* 91–96.

Murray, D. C. Talk, silence and anxiety. *Psychological Bulletin,* 1971, *75,* 244–260.

Mysak, E. D. Pitch and duration characteristics of older males. *Journal of Speech and Hearing Research,* 1959, *2,* 46–54.

Natale, M. Convergence of mean vocal intensity in dyadic communication as a function of social desirability. *Journal of Personality and Social Psychology,* 1975, *32,* 790–804.

Natale, M., Enton, E., & Jaffe, J. Vocal interruptions in dyadic communication as a function of speech and social anxiety. *Journal of Personality and Social Psychology,* 1979, *37,* 865–878.

Osgood, C. E., Suci, G. J., & Tannenbaum, P. H. *The measurement of meaning.* Urbana: The University of Illinois Press, 1957.

Paivio, A. Personality and audience influence. In B. A. Maher (Ed.), *Progress in experimental personality research* (Vol. 2). New York: Academic, 1965.

Patterson, M., & Holmes, D. S. Social interaction correlates of the MMPI extraversion-introversion scale. *American Psychologist,* 1966, *21,* 724–725. (Abstract)

Pope, B., Blass, T., Bradford, N. H., & Siegman, A. W. Interviewer specificity in semi-naturalistic interviews. *Journal of Consulting and Clinical Psychology,* 1971, *36,* 152.

Pope, B., Blass, T., Siegman, A. W., & Raher, J. Anxiety and depression in speech. *Journal of Consulting and Clinical Psychology,* 1970, *35,* 128–133.

Pope, B., Nudler, S., Norden, J. S., & McGee, J. P. Changes in nonprofessional (novice) interviewers over a 3-year training period. *Journal of Consulting and Clinical Psychology,* 1976, *44,* 819–825.

Pope, B., Nudler, S., VonKorff, M. R., & McGee, J. P. The experienced professional interviewer versus the complete novice. *Journal of Consulting and Clinical Psychology,* 1974, *42.,* 680–690.

Pope, B., & Siegman, A. W. Interviewer-interviewee relationship and verbal behavior of interviewee. *Psychotherapy,* 1966, *3,* 149–152.

Pope, B., & Siegman, A. W. Relationship and verbal behavior in the initial interview. In A. W. Siegman & B. Pope (Eds.), *Studies in dyadic communication.* New York: Pergamon, 1972.

Pope, B., Siegman, A. W., & Blass, T. Anxiety and speech in the initial interview. *Journal of Consulting and Clinical Psychology*, 1970, *35*, 233–238.

Powesland, P. F., & Giles, H. Persuasiveness and message accent incompatibility. *Human Relations*, 1975, *28*, 85–93.

Preston, J. M., & Gardner, R. C. Dimensions of oral and written language fluency. *Journal of Verbal Learning and Verbal Behavior*, 1967, *6*, 936–945.

Ramsay, R. W. Personality and speech. *Journal of Personality and Social Psychology*, 1966, *4*, 116–118.

Ramsay, R. W. Speech patterns and personality. *Language and Speech*, 1968, *11*, 54–63.

Reynolds, A., & Paivio, A. Cognitive and emotional determinants of speech. *Canadian Journal of Psychology*, 1968, *22*, 164–175.

Reynolds, M. A., Siegman, A. W., & Demorest, M. E. *The voice of deception: The temporal pacing of speech in unfeigned lying.* Unpublished manuscript, University of Maryland Baltimore County, 1983.

Robinson, W. P. *Language and social behavior.* London: Penguin, 1972.

Rochester, S. R., & Gill, J. Production of complex sentences in monologues and dialogues. *Journal of Verbal Learning and Verbal Behavior*, 1973, *12*, 203–210.

Rochester, S. R., Thurston, S., & Rupp, J. Hesitation as clues to failures in coherence: A study of the thought-disordered speaker. In S. Rosenberg (Ed.), *Sentence production: Developments in theory and research.* Hillsdale, NJ: Lawrence Erlbaum Associates, 1977.

Rose, Y. J., & Tryon, W. W. Judgments of assertive behavior as a function of speech loudness, latency, content, gestures, inflection, and sex. *Behavior Modification*, 1979, *3*, 112–123.

Rosenman, R. H. The interview method of assessment of the coronary-prone behavior pattern. In T. M. Dembroski, S. M. Weiss, J. L. Shields, S. G. Haynes, M. Feinleir (Eds.), *Coronary-prone behavior.* New York: Spinger-Verlag, 1978.

Rosenthal, R. *Experimenter effects in behavioral research.* New York: Appleton-Century-Crofts, 1966.

Rosenthal, R. Nonverbal cues in the mediation of interpersonal expectancy effects. In A. W. Siegman & S. Feldstein (Eds.), *Multichannel integrations of nonverbal behavior.* Hillsdale, NJ: Lawrence Erlbaum Associates, 1985.

Rosenthal, R. Pavlov's mice, Pfungst's horse, and Pygmalion's PONS: Some models for the study of interpersonal expectancy effects. In T. A. Sebeok & R. Rosenthal (Eds.), *The clever Hans phenomenon. Annals of the New York Academy of Sciences,* No. 364, 1981.

Rutter, D. R., Morley, J. E., & Graham, J. C. Visual interaction in a group of introverts and extraverts. *European Journal of Social Psychology*, 1972, *2*, 371–384.

Sabin, E. J., Clemmer, E. J., O'Connell, D. C., & Kowal, S. A pausological approach to speech development. In A. W. Siegman & S. Feldstein (Eds.), *Of time and speech: Temporal speech patterns in interpersonal contexts.* Hillsdale, NJ: Lawrence Erlbaum Associates, 1979.

Sachs, J., Lieberman, P., & Erickson, D. Anatomical and cultural determinants of male and female speech. In R. Shuy & R. W. Fasold (Eds.), *Language attitudes: Current trends and prospects.* Washington, DC: Georgetown School of Language, 1973.

Sanford, F. H. Speech and personality. *Psychological Bulletin*, 1942, *30*, 811–845.

Sauer, R. E., & Marcuse, F. L. Overt and covert recording. *Journal of Projective Techniques*, 1957, *21*, 391–395.

Shapiro, A. K., Placebo effects in medicine, psychotherapy and psychoanalysis. In A. E. Bergin & S. L. Garfield (Eds.), *Textbook of psychotherapy and behavior change: Empirical analysis.* New York: Wiley, 1971.

Shekelle, R. B., et al. The MRFIT behavior pattern study: II. Type A behavior pattern and incidence of coronary heart disease. *CVD Epidemiology Newsletter*, January 1984, p. 34.

Scherer, K. R. Judging personality from voice: A cross-cultural approach to an old issue in interpersonal perception. *Journal of Personality*, 1972, *40*, 191–210.

Scherer, K. R. Personality markers in speech. In K. R. Scherer & H. Giles (Eds.), *Social markers in speech.* Cambridge: Cambridge University Press, 1979.

Scherer, K. R. Speech and emotional states. In J. K. Darby (Ed.), *Speech evaluation in psychiatry.* New York: Grune & Stratton, 1981, (a)

Scherer, K. R. Vocal indicators of stress. In J. K. Darby (Ed.), *Speech evaluation in psychiatry.* New York: Grune & Stratton, 1981. (b)

Scherer, K. R., London, H., & Wolf, T. J. The voice of confidence: Paralinguistic cues and audience evaluation. *Journal of Research in Personality,* 1973, *7,* 31–44.

Scherer, K. R., & Scherer, U. Speech behavior and personality. In J. K. Darby (Ed.), *Speech evaluation in psychiatry.* New York: Grune & Stratton, 1981.

Scherwitz, L., Berton, B. S., & Leventhal, H. Type-A assessment and interaction in the behavior pattern interview. *Psychosomatic Medicine,* 1977, *39,* 229–240.

Schucker, B., & Jacobs, D. R. Assessment of behavioral risk for coronary disease by voice characteristics. *Psychosomatic Medicine,* 1977, *39,* 219–228.

Siegman, A. W. *Some relationships of anxiety and introversion–extraversion to serial learning.* Unpublished doctoral dissertation, Columbia University, 1957.

Siegman, A. W. A cross-cultural investigation of the relationship between introversion–extraversion, social attitudes and anti-social behavior. *British Journal of Clinical and Social Psychology,* 1962, *2,* 196–208.

Siegman, A. W. Do interviewer mm-hmm's reinforce interviewee verbal productivity? *Proceedings of the 80th Annual Convention of the American Psychological Association,* 1972, *7,* 323–324. (Summary)

Siegman, A. W. *Interview-conversations as testing ground for psychological theories.* Symposium paper presented at the annual meetings of the American Psychological Association, New Orleans, Louisiana, August, 1974. (a)

Siegman, A. W. The gain–loss principle and interpersonal attraction in the interview. *Proceedings of the Division of Personality and Social Psychology,* 1974, 85–88. (b)

Siegman, A. W. *Some effects of eliminating eye-contact in the interview.* Paper read at annual meeting of the Eastern Psychlogical Association, New York, April, 1975.

Siegman, A. W. Do noncontingent interviewer mm-hmm's facilitate interviewee productivity? *Journal of Consulting and Clinical Psychology,* 1976, *44,* 171–182.

Siegman, A. W. The meaning of silent pauses in the initial interview. *Journal of Mental and Nervous Disease,* 1978, *166,* 642–654.

Siegman, A. W. Cognition and hesitation in speech. In A. W. Siegman & S. Feldstein (Eds.), *Of time and speech: Temporal speech patterns in interpersonal contexts.* Hillsdale, NJ: Lawrence Erlbaum Associates, 1979. (a)

Siegman, A. W. The voice of attraction: Vocal correlates of interpersonal attraction in the interview. In A. W. Siegman & S. Feldstein (Eds.), *Of time and speech: Temporal speech patterns in interpersonal contexts.* Hillsdale, NJ: Lawrence Erlbaum Associates, 1979. (b)

Siegman, A. W. Interpersonal attraction and verbal behavior in the initial interview. In R. St. Clair & H. Giles (Eds.), *The social and psychological contexts of language.* Hillsdale, NJ: Lawrence Erlbaum Associates, 1980.

Siegman, A. W. Expressive correlates of affective states and traits. In A. W. Siegman & S. Feldstein (Eds.), *Multichannel integrations of nonverbal behavior.* Hillsdale, NJ: Lawrence Erlbaum Associates, 1985.

Siegman, A. W., & Crown, C. Interpersonal attraction and the temporal patterning of speech in the initial interview: Replication and clarification. In W. P. Robinson, H. Giles, & P. M. Smith (Eds.), *Language: Social-psychological perspectives.* London: Pergamon, 1980.

Siegman, A. W., & Feldstein, S. *The vocal stylistics of the Type-A behavior pattern, as measured by Jenkins Activity Scale.* Unpublished manuscript, University of Maryland, 1984.

Siegman, A. W., & Pope, B. The effects of ambiguity and anxiety on interviewee verbal behavior. In A. W. Siegman & B. Pope (Eds.), *Studies in dyadic communication.* New York: Pergamon, 1972.

Siegman, A. W., & Pope, B. Personality variables associated with productivity and verbal fluency in the initial interview. *Proceedings of the 73rd annual convention of the American Psychological Association,* 1965, 273–274. (b)

Siegman, A. W., & Pope, B. Ambiguity and verbal fluency in the TAT. *Journal of Consulting Psychology,* 1966, *30,* 239–245. (a)

Siegman, A. W., & Pope, B. The effect of interviewer ambiguity–specificity and topical focus on interviewee vocabulary diversity. *Language and Speech,* 1966, *9,* 242–249. (b)

Siegman, A. W., & Pope, B. *The effects opf alcohol on verbal productivity and fluency.* Paper presented at the annual meetings of the Eastern Psychological Association, Boston, April, 1967.

Siegman, A. W., Pope, B., & Blass, T. Effects of interviewer status and duration of interviewer messages on interviewee productivity. *Proceedings of the 77th annual convention of the American Psychological Association,* 1969, 541–542.

Siegman, A. W., & Reynolds, M. *Gender differences in pausing behavior: Stable markers or situation specific?* Symposium paper presented at the 87th Annual Meetings of the American Psychological Association, New York, September, 1979.

Siegman, A. W., & Reynolds, M. A. Interviewer–interviewee nonverbal communications: An interactional approach. In M. Davis (Ed.), *Interaction rhythms: Periodicity in communicative behavior.* New York: Human Sciences Press, 1982.

Siegman, A. W., & Reynolds, M. A. Effects of mutual invisibility and topical intimacy on verbal fluency in dyadic communication. *Journal of Psycholinguistic Research,* 1983, *12,* 443–455. (a)

Siegman, A. W., & Reynolds, M. A. Self-monitoring and speech in feigned and unfeigned lying. *Journal of Personality and Social Psychology,* 1983, *45,* 1325–1333. (b)

Siegman, A. W., & Reynolds, M. A. Speaking without seeing or the effect of interviewer absence on interviewee disclosure time. *Journal of Psycholinguistic Research,* 1983, *12,* 595–602. (c)

Siegman, A. W., & Reynolds, M. A. The facilitating effects of interviewer rapport and the paralinguistics of intimate communications. *Journal of Clinical and Social Psychology,* 1984, *2,* 89–96.

Siegman, A. W., & Reynolds, M. A. *Personality and speech in truthful and deceptive communications.* Unpublished manuscript, University of Maryland Baltimore County, 1985.

Simard, L. M., Taylor, D. M., & Giles, H. Attribution processes and interpersonal accommodation in a bilingual setting. *Language and Speech,* 1976, *19,* 374–387.

Smith, P. M. Sex markers in speech. In K. R. Scherer & H. Giles (Eds.), *Social markers in speech.* Cambridge: Cambridge University Press, 1979.

Snyder, M. Self-monitoring of expressive behavior. *Journal of Personality and Social Psychology,* 1974, *30,* 526–537.

Sullivan, H. S. *The psychiatric interview.* New York: Norton, 1954.

Sunshine, N. J., & Horowitz, M. K. Differences in egocentricity between spoken and written expression under stress and nonstress conditions. *Language and Speech,* 1968, *11,* 160–166.

Taylor, D. M., & Clement, R. Normative reactions to styles of Quebec French. *Anthropological Linguistics,* 1974, *16,* 202–217.

Taylor, J. A. The relationship of anxiety to the conditioned eyelid response. *Journal of Experimental Psychology,* 1951, *41,* 81–92.

Taylor, J. A., & Spence, K. W. The relationship of anxiety level to performance in serial learning. *Journal of Experimental Psychology,* 1952, *44,* 61–64.

Tolhurst, G. C. *Some effects of changing time patterns and articulation upon intelligibility and word perception.* Contract N6 onw-22525, Project No. NR 145-993. NMRI Project NM 001 104 500 40. U.S. Naval School of Aviation Medicine, Naval Air Station, Pensacola, Florida, and Ohio State University Research Foundation, Columbus, Ohio, January, 1955.

Trager, G. Paralanguage: A first approximation. *Studies in Linguistics,* 1958, *13,* 1–12.

Trager, G. The typology of paralanguage. *Anthropological Linguistics,* 1961, *3,* 17–21.

Trimboli, F. Changes in voice characteristics as a function of trait and state personality variables. *Dissertation Abstracts International,* 1973, *33,* 3965.

Troffer, S. A., & Tart, C. T. Experimenter bias in hypnotist performance. *Science,* 1964, *145,* 1330-1331.

Trudgill, P. Sex, covert prestige and linguistic change in the urban British English of Norwich. In B. Thorne & N. Henley (Eds.), *Language and sex: Difference and dominance.* Rowley, MA: Newberry House, 1975.

Webb, J. T. Interview synchrony: An investigation of two speech rate measures in an automated standardized interview. In A. W. Siegman & B. Pope (Eds.), *Studies in dyadic communication.* New York: Pergamon Press, 1972.

Welkowitz, J., Feldstein, S., Finkelstein, M., & Aylesworth, L. Changes in vocal intensity as a function of interspeaker influence. *Perceptual and Motor Skills,* 1972, *35,* 715-718.

Williams, C. E., & Stevens, K. N. Vocal correlates of emotional stress. In J. K. Darby (Ed.), *Speech evaluation in psychiatry.* New York: Grune & Stratton, 1981.

Williams, R. B., Jr. Behavioral correlates of angiographic findings. In T. M. Dembroski, T. H. Schmidt, & G. Blumchen (Eds.), *Biobehavioral bases of coronary heart disease.* New York: Karger, 1983.

Williams, R. B., Barefoot, J. C., & Shekelle, R. B. The health consequences of hostility. In M. A. Chesney, S. E. Goldstein, & R. H. Rosenman (Eds.), *Anger, hostility and behavioral medicine.* New York: Hemisphere/McGraw-Hill, 1984.

Zoble, E. J., & Lehman, R. S. Interaction of subject and experimenter expectancy effects in a tone length discrimination task. *Behavioral Science,* 1969, *14,* 357-363.

Zuckerman, M., DePaulo, B. M., & Rosenthal, R. Verbal and nonverbal communication of deception. In L. Berkowitz (Ed.), *Advances in experimental social psychology* (Vol. 14). New York: Academic, 1981.

Zuckerman, M., & Driver, R. E. Telling lies: Verbal and nonverbal correlats of deception. In A. W. Siegman & S. Feldstein (Eds.), *Multichannel interpretations of nonverbal behavior.* Hillsdale, NJ: Lawrence Erlbaum Associates, 1985.

9 A Chronography of Conversation: In Defense of an Objective Approach

Stanley Feldstein
University of Maryland Baltimore County

Joan Welkowitz
New York University

Conversational interaction is increasingly being viewed as a singularly intriguing and rich interpersonal process. Consider the astonishing variety of behaviors that can occur within the confines of even a single conversation. Mouths open narrowly or widely; voices emerge to utter sounds, grow loud and soft, and high and low; lips curl and stretch; teeth grind; nostrils twitch; eyes blink; pupils dilate; eyebrows lift, foreheads crease, heads nod; shoulders shrug; arms wave; hands turn; fingers flex; legs cross; feet shuffle, bodies shift, and—through it all perhaps—eyes may watch; ears may listen; noses may sniff. The list is not exhaustive. But amidst such a bustle of activity, it is relatively easy to overlook one of the basic dimensions of conversational interaction, that is, the temporal organization of its sounds and silences. It is this temporal organization, indexed by the chronography of conversation, with which the present chapter is concerned.

The importance of time as a psychologically meaningful dimension of human behavior cannot seriously be questioned. Time as a succession, time as duration, time as rhythm, are aspects of all the ventures of human existence (e.g., Fraser, 1966). Formal studies of the perception of time form a body of psychological literature that is probably smaller than it ought to be. But studies of the time it takes to do or say something, or to begin doing or saying something represent a quite sizable portion of the literature of psychology. Nonetheless, although the formal investigation of the time patterns of verbal interaction began several decades ago, it has only recently begun to develop in ways that are of more general psychological interest. It is probably fair to say that this development was stimulated in large part by the coupling of a markedly increased concern about the details of interpersonal behavior with, as Rosenfeld (Chapter 12) suggests, a technological sophistication that made the adequate recording and analysis of such behavior possible. That this concern has focussed, in part, upon conversation implies two basic and related notions. The first is that conversation might usefully be considered a microcosm of social interaction; the second, that characteristic patterns of individual behavior are most clearly displayed in social interactions.

The working expectations that underlie much of the research in conversation chronography have to do with the possibilities that the pacing of a conversational exchange not only modifies (along with other coverbal behavior) the lexical message embedded in it, but in part communicates and is determined by aspects of the participants' personalities and by dimensions of their relations with each other. These possibilities are enchanced by the fact that such pacing is not ordinarily under deliberate control. On the other hand, the adequacy with which the possibilities can be explored very much depends upon the adequacy with which the pacing is described. This chapter is concerned primarily with some of the major issues involved in such a description. To that end, it reviews the temporal classifications that initiated the area of conversation chronography and an alternative classification preferred by the authors. It then compares, in some detail, the implications of recent definitions of turn-taking behavior (which is viewed as the behavior that centrally characterizes conversation) and briefly describes some investigations of talking in and out of turn. Finally, the chapter presents a series of studies that have to do with the tendency of conversational participants to match each other's speech patterns during the course of one or more conversations. Inasmuch as the primary purpose of the chapter is to argue for a particular approach to the investigation of conversational time patterns, it makes no attempt to review exhaustively the increasing number of relevant studies that have begun to appear in the literature.

INITIAL APPROACHES

To what does the "chronography" of a conversation refer, that is, exactly what aspects of a conversation are timed? The earliest answer was provided by Norwine and Murphy (1938): "In the simplest case of conversational interchange each party speaks for a short time, pauses, and the other party replies. The time intervals are then simply the lengths of time each party speaks and the lengths of the pauses between speeches" [p. 282]. They called the speeches *talkspurts* and defined a single *talkspurt* as the ". . . speech of one party, including his pauses, which is preceded and followed, with or without intervening pauses, by speech from the other party perceptible to the one producing the talkspurt" [p. 282]. They also noted that there are instances in which, instead of alternating, the speakers engage in simultaneous talk-spurts, which they named *double talking*. Their recognition of the fact that there are pauses within talkspurts was formalized by labeling such pauses *resumption times*. However, the pauses that separated the talkspurts of different speakers were called *response times*.

Norwine and Murphy worked for the Bell Telephone System and the data they used to formulate a description of conversational time patterns were recorded telephone interactions. The apparent clarity of their categories was marred by the ambiguity they introduced into their discussion of *response time,* which, they asserted, ". . . ordinarily occurs at the end of a talkspurt but may be a pause followed by a resumption of speech by the first talker" [p. 282]. The qualification implies that either an arbitrary duration must be set beyond which a resumption time becomes a response time, or the classification of silences must be a matter of judgment. Either way, the objectivity of the talkspurt and silence categories are compromised.

A quite different method of timing conversational interactions was offered by the anthropologist, Eliot Chapple, who was concerned with cross-cultural comparisons. Chapple (1939, 1940) asserted that the timing of the "acts" of one individual in interaction with another could provide psychology with an objective and reliable method of assessing personality. To examine the assertion, he constructed the Interaction Chronograph (Chapple, 1949), which is simply an instrument used by an observer to record the occurrences and durations of the "actions" and "inactions" of each participant in an interaction, as well as "interruptions (when both act)" and "failures to respond (when both are silent)." Although the method utilized verbal behavior as its primary data, it included all gestural behavior that was judged by the observer to be part of the interaction. Average scores of 12 presumably different measures could be derived from the record of the Interaction Chronograph, although it might be noted that of the 66 coefficients obtained by intercorrelating the measures, only 17 were nonsignificant and 14 were ±.70 or above; no one of the measures was statistically independent of all the others (Matarazzo, Saslow, & Hare, 1958, p. 421). Nevertheless, they were thought to be conceptually different from each other.

It must be stressed that Chapple was concerned with interpersonal action rather than interpersonal verbal behavior. The Chronograph was intended for the study of "action" units rather than speech units, and observers were instructed to score an action as finished only when "all facial (and other) muscle activity" had ceased (Chapple, 1939). Theoretically, an action could include the occurrence of speech but does not necessarily imply it. In point of fact, however, Chapple and his colleagues used as their interactional contexts interviews and, occasionally, somewhat less constrained types of conversations (e.g., Chapple & Harding, 1940). Moreover, the action units served as the basis for scoring "utterance" and "silence" durations. It seems quite appropriate, therefore, to regard Chapple's research as embodying a model of conversational time patterns. The research that, in fact, took this position with respect to Chapple's work was begun in 1954 by Matarazzo and his colleagues (Matarazzo & Wiens, 1972). They used the Chronograph to describe the temporal patterning of interviews as a method of examining the "emotional, attitudinal, or motivational state" of the interviewees.

Originally, Matarazzo and his associates utilized the measures devised by Chapple, but they then discovered that most of the variance associated with the 12 measures could be accounted for by just two variables, namely *speech* and *silence* (Matarazzo et al., 1958). To facilitate obtaining the values of these variables directly, they designed a system (Johnston, Jensen, Weitman, Hess, Matarazzo, & Saslow, 1961) that recorded and automatically scored sequences of verbal interactions. As does the Chronograph, the system, called the Interaction Recorder, requires a human observer. However, the observer is not required to view the interacting individuals but simply to hear them. In 1966, Wiens, Molde, Holman, and Matarazzo reported that the exclusion of all bodily gestures from the decisions involved in the utilizing of verbal behavior yielded utterance durations that differed very little from those that included gestural behavior. Thus, they characterize the verbal interactions in an interview in terms of four measures: *utterances, interruptions, reaction time latencies,* and *initiative time latencies.* According to Matarazzo and Wiens (1972), ". . . *an utterance (or speech unit) is recorded as the total duration of time it takes a speaker to emit all the words he is contributing in that particular unit of exchange (as this would be judged by common social standards)"* [p. 6, original italics]. *Interruptions* are defined as instances of simultaneous speech. A *reaction time latency* is the interval of silence between the end of one person's utterance and the beginning of the other person's utterance. Finally, an *initiative time latency* is the silence that occurs between two consecutive utterances of the same speaker. They are silences that ". . . precede the introduction of new ideas or thoughts by the same individual *without an intervening comment by the other interview participant . . ."* [p. 8, original italics].

These four parameters are less ambiguous than the earlier measures used by Matarazzo and his colleagues by virtue of the fact that their delineation is not dependent upon gestural information. According to its definition, however, an utterance is still determined by an observer's judgment about the semantic content of what a speaker says. The observer probably also uses the pitch and intensity contours of the speaker's voice to make his determination. At the same time, Matarazzo and Wiens indicate that, in practise, an utterance that can be judged incomplete by virtue of its content is recorded as completed if it is interrupted by the comment of another speaker.

Note that the labels, *reaction time latency* and *response time,* while they may not necessarily imply a strict stimulus-response model of interactional behavior, do assign responsibility for the silence indicated to the person whose speech follows the silence. The assumptions that underlie the assignment may or may not characterize interviews; in the absence of systematic evidence, they cannot be said to characterize conversations in general.

Judgmental variables are problematical. They can, of course, be shown to be reliable in the sense that the same judge, given the same data and sufficient training, will tend to make the same judgment from one time to the next. Moreover, different judges can usually be trained to make the same, or similar judgments about the same data. Nevertheless, judgments are rarely as satisfying as objective measurements if only because it is never clear how the various sorts of information used to make judgments were weighted, or whether all of the available information is even used.

AN EMPIRICAL CLASSIFICATION

In 1963, Jaffe and Feldstein began to explore the possibility of using interaction chronography to study psychopathological communication. They made two decisions, however, which determined the course of their research and differentiated it from previous chronographic research. The first decision was to describe a set of temporal categories that carried no inferential baggage, was concerned only with verbal behavior, and could be obtained automatically from live or audiotaped dialogues (or multilogues). The second was based upon the realization that to learn anything about the relation of dialogic time patterns to psychopathology, they would need to know much more than was known about the patterns of nonpathological interactions. Thus, they decided to examine the temporal structure of conversations by individuals not considered psychologically disturbed.

The decision to study the temporal patterns of verbal interactions empirically was also made — at about the same time — by a number of other investigators. Brady (1965, 1968, 1969) developed a completely automated system for detecting what he calls the "on-off patterns" of speech. His concern, as had been that of Norwine and Murphy, was with the patterns of telephone conversations rather than with face-to-face interactions. Nevertheless, the care and sophistication of his approach to the area and particularly to aspects of instrumentation design that affect the interpretation of the on-off patterns have been instructive. Similarly, Hayes and Meltzer and their associates approached the empirical analysis of conversational time patterns as a way of studying the details of social behavior (e.g., Hayes, 1969; Meltzer, Hayes, & Shellenberger, 1966). They have been sufficiently impressed with the usefulness of the approach and the importance of physicalistic cues (e.g., amplitude, duration) in social interaction to propose that the study of such cues warrants the formation of a subdivision of social psychology called "social psychophysics" (Meltzer, Morris, & Hayes, 1971).

The AVTA System

An empirical analysis of conversational time patterns can be accomplished most easily by an electronic system capable of automatically detecting and recording the presence and absence of speech. The investigators mentioned above have developed their own instruments for the purpose. Only one system, the Automatic Vocal Transaction Analyzer, or AVTA (Cassotta, Feldstein, & Jaffe, 1964; Jaffe & Feldstein, 1970), will be described here, firstly because it broadly illustrates the type of system needed, and secondly because the description will clarify the nature of the data used by Jaffe and Feldstein to categorize conversational time patterns.

AVTA does not require the use of a human observer.[1] It includes a component[2] that "perceives" the verbal behavior of each participant in an audiotaped or ongoing conversation simply as a sequence of sounds and silences. The component is essentially an analogue-to-digital converter with voice relays and a cancellation network that electronically cancels the spill of each speaker's voice into the other speaker's microphone. It functions by "inquiring" about the state of the relays associated with each speaker at a predetermined rate that can range from 100 to 1000 msec. The initial studies (Jaffe & Feldstein, 1970) used an inquiry rate of 300 msec., that is, the state of the relays were monitored 200 times per minute. Subsequent studies have used inquiry rates of either 100 or 300 msec. Comparisons have indicated that the two inquiry rates yield results that, in terms of average values per time interval, are not markedly different (Jaffe & Feldstein, 1970). The information obtained from the relays is transmitted to a computer component of the system which provides a computer-readable record of the digitalized sound-silence sequences and descriptive statistics summarizing the parameter values derived from them.

One other technical point should be made clear. Although no one is required to monitor the verbal interactions processed by AVTA, a person with unimpaired hearing is needed to determine the level of vocal intensity that AVTA is to accept as a speech sound, thereby enabling AVTA to decide

---

[1]Welkowitz and Martz (unpublished data) recently completed a software version of AVTA for use with the PDP/12 computer (Digital Equipment Corporation). The hardware version uses a PDP/8.

[2]Another component analyzes the amplitude, or intensity level, of the voices in a conversation.

which behavior is to be assigned to what temporal category. The purpose of this procedure is to generate a description of the time patterns of verbal interactions as perceived by a human listener and, presumably, by the speakers themselves.

Parameters of Conversational Time Patterns

Jaffe and Feldstein (1970) segmented the conversational speech stream into five empirically defined categories or parameters: *speaker switches, vocalizations, pauses, switching pauses,* and *simultaneous speech.* The intervals of time between successive speaker switches were rather awkwardly called "floor times." It is more convenient — and consistent with other parameter definitions — to consider "speaker switches" and "floor times" two aspects of a single parameter that may be called *speaking turns,* or more simply, *turns.* Speaker switches index the frequency of turns, and floor times their durations. A *turn* begins the instant one participant in a conversation starts talking alone and ends immediately prior to the instant another participant starts talking alone. It is, in other words, the time during which a participant has the floor. The parameter, *turns,* is the crux of the temporal classification inasmuch as it indexes the feature that defines a conversation, that is, the fact that its participants alternate, or take turns speaking. It is also the superordinate member of the classification in that the other parameters represent events that occur during each participant's turn. Thus, a *vocalization* is a continuous (i.e., uninterrupted) segment of speech (sound) uttered by the person who has the floor. A *pause* is an interval of joint silence bounded by the vocalizations of the person who has the floor and is, therefore (as are the vocalizations), credited to him. A *switching pause* is an interval of joint silence bounded by the vocalizations of different participants, that is, it follows a vocalization by the participant who has the floor and is terminated by the vocalization of another participant who thereby obtains the floor. Thus, the switching pause is a silence that marks a switch of speakers or, alternatively, the end of one turn and beginning of another. Since it occurs during the turn of the person who relinquished the floor, it is credited to him.

Simultaneous speech is speech uttered by a participant who does *not* have the floor during a vocalization by the participant who does have the floor. On the basis of its outcome, simultaneous speech may be divided into two types: interruptive and noninterruptive (Feldstein, BenDebba, & Alberti, 1974). *Noninterruptive simultaneous speech* begins and ends while the participant who has the floor is talking. *Interruptive simultaneous speech* is part of a speech segment that begins while the person who has the floor is talking and ends after he has stopped. Only that portion of the segment uttered while the other person is still talking is considered interruptive simultaneous speech. The remaining portion, inasmuch as it is a unilateral utterance, marks the beginning of a turn for the participant who initiated the simultaneous speech and is considered, therefore, his vocalization. Thus interruptive simultaneous speech culminates in a change of which participant has the floor while noninterruptive simultaneous speech does not.[3] Figure 9.1 graphically illustrates the five temporal parameters.

Parameter Characteristics

Inasmuch as the parameters were quite different from those involved in previous classifications of interactional time patterns, studies were conducted to investigate the extent to which they are independent of each other and reliable. The studies are described in detail elsewhere (e.g., Jaffe & Feldstein, 1970) and their results need only be reviewed briefly here. It should be noted, however, that these results are concerned primarily with the average durations of pauses, switching pauses, and vocalizations. Only later were more extensive analyses of the characteristics of speaking turns and simultaneous speech conducted, and the results of those analyses are reported in greater detail.

Most of the results presented here are from one study, both for the sake of brevity and because the study was the one best suited to examine the interrelationships and reliabilities of the parameters. However, the results are representative of those obtained in previous and subsequent investigations. The study (Marcus, Welkowitz, Feldstein, & Jaffe, 1970) examined the verbal ex-

---

[3]The distinction between interruptive and noninterruptive simultaneous speech is identical to that made by Meltzer *et al.* (1971) between successful and unsuccessful interruptions. The difference in terminology, which may seem to make for an unnecessary proliferation of names for the same events, appears to reflect a basic difference in approach. The names *interruptive simultaneous speech* and *noninterruptive simultaneous speech* are purely descriptive; the occurrence of simultaneous speech either terminates in an interruption (the participant who has the floor stops talking) or does not. Such names communicate no preconceptions that are likely to bias inquiries about the events they describe and/or needlessly complicate the ways in which the results of the inquiries can be interpreted. On the other hand, the names *successful interruptions* and *unsuccessful interruptions* are meaningful only when viewed as abbreviations of successful- and unsuccesful-interruption attempts. But the name *interruption attempts* implies knowledge about the intentions of those participants who happen to speak simultaneously. Indeed, Meltzer and his colleagues frame the paper in words and phrases (for example, win, lose, defender, contest for the floor, wrest the floor away) that assume that the intentions of the speakers play a motivational role in the occurrence of simultaneous talking. They even speculate about whether such brief utterances as "yes" and "uh-huh" should be classified as "interruptions" (when they occur as simultaneous speech) inasmuch as they ". . . are obviously not attempts to take over the floor . . ." (Metzler *et al.,* 1971, p. 395). Since they provide no evidence for such a position, it can only be considered to reflect their preconceptions about a possibly important but still unexplored dimension of the issues they investigated. The point here is not to denigrate an otherwise excellent paper, but to suggest that the meaning of parameters might better be established by research than by fiat.

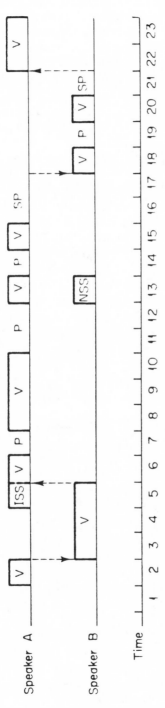

FIG. 9.1 A diagrammatic representation of a conversational sequence. The numbered line at the bottom represents time in 300-msec units. V stands for *vocalization*, P for *pause*, and SP for *switching pause* (the silence that frequently occurs immediately prior to a change in the speaking *turn*). The arrows that point down denote the end of speaker *A*'s turns; the arrows that point up denote the end of speaker *B*'s turns. ISS and NSS stand for *interruptive and noninterruptive simultaneous speech*, respectively. (Adapted from Figure II-2 of Jaffe and Feldstein, 1970).

443

changes of 24 female college students who had been divided into six equal groups. The design required that each subject meet individually with each of the three other subjects in her group for half an hour a day for eight consecutive weekdays. She was told that the purpose of the study was to provide information about how people get to know each other through conversation, and she was asked to use the half-hour periods with each partner to talk about whatever might further that goal. Thus, the subjects engaged in 36 dialogues on each of eight occasions. (Inasmuch as the groups each consisted of four subjects, they were called quartets while the study was being conducted, and the informal name, *quartet study,* will be used here as a convenient reference label.)

Pauses, switching pauses, and vocalizations. The first question that had to be answered was whether the parameters — although they clearly represent different events — could be considered distinct aspects of the time structure of conversation. The results of the quartet study and previous studies (Cassotta, Feldstein, & Jaffe, 1967; Feldstein, Jaffe, & Cassotta, 1967) indicated that only pauses and switching pauses are significantly related to each other and then only within the context of relatively unstructured conversations; the comparisons of pauses and switching pauses yielded product-moment *rs* of .60 and .66 for the conversations and .23 for interviews. That the magnitude of their relationship distinguished two different types of dialogue seemed to justify maintaining their separate identities. Subsequent studies (to be discussed later) have confirmed the usefulness of that decision.

Several types of reliability were examined. One that need only be mentioned is the reliability of the AVTA system. Research (Cassotta *et al.,* 1964) demonstrated not only the capability of the system to replicate accurately the analysis of a given conversation, but also the superiority of its performance to that of a human observer. The remaining types of reliability involve the consistency of the parameter values within single conversations and their stability from conversation to conversation.

The following types of reliability were evaluated: (a) the consistency of the parameter values from the first to the second 15 min. of a conversation; (b) the stability of the parameter values from one conversation to another involving the same participants; and (c) the stability of the parameter values from one conversaton to another in which only one of the participants is the same. For the first type of reliability, the evaluation yielded average estimates of .71 for pauses, .72 for switching pauses, and .76 for vocalizations. For the second type, it yielded average estimates of .65 for pauses, .66 for switching pauses, and .68 for vocalizations. Assessment of the third type yielded average estimates of .33 for pauses, .33 for switching pauses, and .72 for vocalizations. The estimates suggest that the ways in which individuals time their verbal participation in conversational exchanges remain quite consistent during the course of a conversation and, with the same partners, stable from one conversation to the next. However, when the different conversations involve different partners, only the average durations of their vocalizations remain stable. A possible explanation for the unreliability of the average silence durations in such a context will be offered later.

Speaking turns and simultaneous speech. Information about the descriptive characteristics of speaking turns and simultaneous speech (as defined earlier) has, for the most part, not yet appeared in print. It may be useful, therefore, to present such information before going further. Table 9.1 lists the means and standard deviations that were derived from the conversations obtained in the quartet study. Note again that the conversations were relatively unconstrainted and might be expected to differ in frequencies and durations of turns and simultaneous speech from other types of dialogues. Indeed, in the interviews examined by Cassotta *et al.* (1967), too little simultaneous speech occurred to warrant its analysis.

Initially, it seemed a potentially fruitful strategy to explore both the frequencies and durations of turns and simultaneous speech, if only to obtain the sort of descriptive statistics presented in Table 9.1. There is, of course, a necessary and inverse relation between the average duration of an individual's turn and the number of turns he has taken within a given unit of time. In the quartet study, the correlation of turn frequencies and turn durations yielded an average coefficient of $-.54$. On the other hand, there is no necessary relation between the number of times people engage in simultaneous speech and the durations of their engagements; It may well be that the two aspects of simultaneous speech reflect different processes and/or person characteristics. The extent of the relation between the frequencies and durations of simultaneous speech (in the quartet study) is indexed by correlation coefficients of .22 for noninterruptive simultaneous speech (NSS) and .11 for interruptive simultaneous speech (ISS). It may be more likely, though, that the magnitude of these coefficients is primarily a function of the inconsistency of the NSS and ISS durations. The consistency with which the women who took part in the quartet study utilized NSS and ISS durations during the course of a conversation was examined by comparing the first and second 15 min. of their conversations on each occasion. As can be seen in Table 9.2, the consistency estimates for the durations of NSS and ISS are markedly lower than are those for the frequencies of NSS and ISS; indeed, the estimates for the ISS durations hover about zero. It is not clear why the durations are unreliable. The durations used in the study ranged (given the constraint of the AVTA inquiry period) from one 300-msec. unit to three 300-msec. units. Most of the women engaged in one- and two-unit segments; whether they used one or the other was apparently fortuitous. Similarly, assessments of the stability of

TABLE 9.1

Means (M) and Standard Deviations (SD) of the Frequencies and Average Durations of Interruptive and Noninterruptive Simultaneous Speech (ISS and NSS, respectively) and Speaking Turns within and across the Eight Occasions of the Quartet Study

Parameters			1	2	3	4	5	6	7	8	Average
						Occasions					
Frequency	ISS	M	24.6	27.3	28.2	27.6	29.3	30.6	29.4	29.0	28.3
		SD	13.8	15.0	15.0	13.3	15.2	14.7	14.5	15.0	14.7
	NSS	M	43.1	45.0	44.6	48.8	48.4	45.8	42.5	41.6	45.0
		SD	29.7	29.5	22.8	36.6	25.0	19.2	21.2	19.5	26.0
Duration	ISS	M	.416	.422	.422	.461	.425	.436	.425	.419	.428
		SD	.062	.059	.048	.236	.059	.077	.069	.065	.084
	NSS	M	.397	.403	.398	.425	.410	.403	.412	.407	.407
		SD	.047	.049	.048	.166	.050	.043	.053	.061	.065
Turn frequency		M	188.9	193.4	187.8	185.5	192.9	191.2	191.6	198.9	191.3
		SD	41.5	32.8	35.6	38.5	45.0	40.6	42.1	46.2	40.3
Turn duration		M	4.983	4.749	4.958	5.008	4.877	4.938	4.893	4.708	4.889
		SD	2.045	1.707	1.797	1.776	1.819	2.160	1.952	1.931	1.898

Note: The durations are given in seconds. The quartet study (Marcus *et al.*, 1970) is described in the text.

TABLE 9.2
Reliability Estimates for the Comparison of the First and Second Fifteen Minutes Within each Occasion of the Quartet Study for the Frequencies and Average Durations of Interruptive and Noninterruptive Simultaneous Speech (ISS and NSS, respectively) and Speaking Turns

Parameters		*1*	*2*	*3*	*4*	*5*	*6*	*7*	*8*	*Average*
						Occasions				
Frequency	ISS	.70	.59	.78	.65	.63	.64	.66	.70	.67
	NSS	.82	.66	.79	.64	.69	.53	.64	.51	.67
Duration	ISS	.17	.02	.06	.29	.32	− .06	− .02	.35	.15
	NSS	.17	.38	.25	.53	.22	.26	.31	.36	.31
Turn Frequency		.69	.56	.54	.54	.75	.57	.64	.69	.63
Turn Duration		.74	.63	.58	.51	.59	.60	.77	.56	.63

Note: The reliability estimates are zero order product-moment correlation coefficients. The *df* for each comparison is 22. A coefficient of .40 is needed for significance at the .05 level (two-tailed).

NSS and ISS durations over time yielded low, nonsignificant coefficients[4] of .20 for the NSS segments and .06 for the ISS segments. Thus, the amount of time spent in each occurrence of simultaneous speech varied inconsistently not only within single conversations but also from conversation to conversation (in which the same participants were involved).

A comparison of the mean durations of the NSS and ISS segments (averaged over the eight occasions) indicated that there is neither a significant relationship nor an appreciable difference between them. This lack of a difference seems to suggest that the duration of simultaneous speech does not determine its outcome, that is, whether it becomes interruptive or noninterruptive. This suggestion, as well as the fact that the average durations of the NSS and ISS segments obtained in the quartet study are brief and indistinguishable, are at variance with the findings of Meltzer *et al.* (1971). They obtained simultaneous speech segments that lasted as long as 6 sec. Moreover, their report seems to imply that the durations of the ISS and NSS segments they obtained (the "successful" and "unsuccessful" interruptions, to use their own words) were different. This difference in the results of the two studies may be a function of gender and/or task; Meltzer, Morris, and Hayes used

---

[4]Remember that each dyad conversed once each day for eight days. Thus, the study permitted an examination of stability over varying time intervals, the shortest being that between two consecutive conversations and the longest between the first and the last conversation. The eight occasions allow for 28 "between-occasions" comparisons, and they were made by means of product-moment correlations. The resulting coefficients were transformed to *z*'s before being averaged.

male as well as female participants, and asked them to engage in problem-solving discussions. It seems likely, however, that the nature of the conversation is the more important determinant. Apparently, social conversatons that are essentially not task oriented do not elicit sustained instances of simultaneous speech. In any case, that the studies obtained different results argues for a systematic look at the duration of simultaneous speech as a function of different conversational contexts and structures.

The frequency with which simultaneous speech occurred in the quartet study was both consistent within conversations (Table 9.1) and stable across conversations; the stability estimate for NSS is .48 and for ISS is .61. It is particularly interesting to note the considerable variation in the frequencies with which individuals engaged in the two types of simultaneous speech. NSS was initiated by one of the participants only three times during the course of a conversation and by another, 201 times. The frequencies with which the participants initiated ISS ranged from 1 to 87 per conversation. In others words, there was one person who initiated NSS on an average of about every 9 sec. and another person who actually interrupted her partner an average rate of approximately once every 21 sec.! A comparison of the NSS and ISS frequencies, averaged over the eight occasions, yielded a correlation coefficient of .62 (Feldstein, BenDebba, & Alberti, 1974), indicating that those persons who tended to initiate NSS often also tended to initiate ISS often and vice versa. The magnitude of the relationship raises some questions about the viability of differentially categorizing segments of simultaneous speech simply on the basis of their consequences. But that, after all, is the basis upon which pauses and switching pauses are distinguished; they are silences which have different outcomes. It has yet to be demonstrated clearly, however, that the distinction between NSS and ISS is more than topographical, although some efforts relevant to the issue will be explored later.

Intercorrelations between the two types of simultaneous speech and pauses, switching pauses, and vocalizations yielded the coefficients presented in Table 9.3. It is worth noting that, although all of the coefficients are low, the majority are negative, and especially that those participants who tended to initiate ISS more frequently tended also to have shorter pauses and switching pauses.

Not only is it interesting to note the wide range of frequencies with which individuals initiate simultaneous speech, but also the markedly different frequencies with which turns are initiated (or relinquished) in relatively unrestrained conversations. (It is necessarily the case that the number of turns taken by one participant in a dialogue cannot differ from that taken by the other participant by more than 1. On the other hand, the average amount of time a participant keeps the floor once he has acquired it can be very different from that of the other participant.) The one 30-min. conversation of the quartet study that had the fewest number of turns had 96; the one with the

TABLE 9.3
Comparisons of the Frequencies and
Average Durations of Interruptive and
Noninterruptive Simultaneous Speech
(ISS and NSS, respectively) with the
Average Durations of Pauses (P),
Switching Pauses (SP) and
Vocalizations (V)[a]

		P	SP	V
Frequency	ISS	− .39	− .37	.01
	NSS	− .18	− .26	.34
Duration	ISS	− .18	− .26	.34
	NSS	− .23	− .29	.19

[a]Note: The values in the table are zero-order product-moment correlation coefficient averaged (using z transformations) over the eight occasions of the quartet study. The df for each comparison is 22. A coefficient of .40 is required for significance at the .05 level (two tailed).

most had 312. The average duration of turns within a single conversation ranged from approximately 1.5 sec. to 15 sec. As can be seen in Table 9.1, however, the average (over eight occasions) number of turns initiated during the course of a conversation was approximately 191, and the average duration of each turn was about 5 sec. It is, moreover, clear from Table 9.2 that the frequencies with which the women of the study took the floor and the lengths of time they held it were quite consistent within conversations. Indeed, they also remained stable from one conversation to another; the stability estimates are .61 for turn frequencies and .64 for turn durations.

Pauses, switching pauses, and vocalizations are the events of which most speaking turns are comprised, although it should be clear that a turn may consist of a single vocalization, a vocalization and a switching pause, or only vocalizations and pauses. Nevertheless, one might suppose that the average durations of the three events account for much of the variability associated with the average durations of turns. Comparisons between turn durations and the durations of vocalizations, pauses, and switching pauses, using the data from the quartet study, yielded zero-order correlation coefficients of .44, .34, and .12, respectively. However, the multiple correlation (R) of the three parameters with turns is .66 ($F_{3.20} = 17.32; p < .001$) indicating that, in the quartet study, the three parameters accounted for 43% of the variability of turns. Of the 43%, vocalizations contributed 19%, pauses 22%, and switching pauses only 2%. (The relation between pauses and switching pauses yielded an R of .66). Notice, then that the *duration* of turns does not appear to be entirely accounted for by durations of its components; indeed, a good bit of its variability remains unexplained. The findng tends to support the notion, implicit in the empirical classification of time patterns, that the parameter, speaking turns, carries information that is not fully shared by the other parameters.

Not surprisingly, the contribution of the durations of pauses, switching pauses, and vocalizations to the *frequency* of turns was much smaller. The coefficients indexing the relations between turn frequency and the durations of the three parameters are $-.08$ for vocalizations, $-.31$ for pauses, and $-.40$ for switching pauses. Together, they account for 19% of the variability of turn frequencies ($F_{3,20} = 5.43; p < .05$) but of that, switching pause durations are responsible for 16%. The more active the interaction in a dialogue (the larger is its number of turns), the more likely it is that the participants will have shorter switching pauses.

Simultaneous speech is not a component of the turn. However, the strong relation between the frequencies of turns and of interruptive simultaneous speech ($r = .75$) is not unexpected. By definition, the more interruptive simultaneous speech individuals engage in, the more frequently they obtain the floor. The addition of noninterruptive simultaneous speech frequencies to this relationship is inconsequential in its effect. On the other hand, the frequencies of both ISS and, particularly, NSS are highly related to the *duration* of turns. NSS frequencies account for 38% of the variability of turn durations in the data from the quartet study, and ISS frequencies account for an additional and significant 6%. There does not appear to be a necessary relation between the frequency with which people initiate NSS and the average duration of their turns, but the analysis indicates that the more the participants of the study did initiate NSS the shorter were the average durations of their turns. Similarly, the more ISS they initiated, the shorter were their turns on the average.

Turn durations were also significantly related to the *durations* of both NSS and ISS, but given the unreliability of simultaneous speech durations, it is not clear that the relationship is meaningful.

TURN-TAKING BEHAVIOR: DISAGREEMENTS AND DIRECTIONS

A growing number of investigations have become interested of late in the fact that people alternate—take turns—speaking when they engage in conversation. (Even the participants in a conversation recognize the importance of such alternation and will occasionally comment on its absence with the observation, "This seems to be a one-sided conversation.") Schegloff (1968) asserted that the phenomenon be considered a basic rule of conversation and, more than a decade ago, Miller (1963) suggested that the taking of turns in conversation may warrant the status of a language universal.

Definitional Differences

Offhand, one would think it easy to know who in a conversation has the turn and who does not. It is, therefore, surprising to find so little agreement about not only what a turn is, but when it occurs and who has it. "Difficult as it might be to realize, a major hurdle to research on human speech (whether involving content or noncontent approaches) has been the lack of agreement among investigators on how to define the basic unit or units to be studied" (Matarazzo & Wiens, 1972, pp. 3–4). As was said earlier, the turn in the pivotal unit in conversation. The fact that different investigators define the unit in different ways *but refer to it by the same name* can only make for an increasing amount of confusion and noncomparable research findings. The position taken here is (as might be expected) that the turn is best defined empirically and the fact that turn-taking behavior is receiving increased research attention justifies a comparison of some recent definitions of the turn with that presented earlier.

Semantic information and gestural behavior as unitizing criteria. As Rosenfeld (Chapter 12) notes, the definitions of a turn vary from those that rely heavily upon the judgments of the investigators to that determined solely by the objective measurement of speech onset and termination. However, the issue is not sufficiently clarified by labeling one approach subjective and the other objective. One position within the former approach views the turn as a unit the boundaries of which are determined primarily by gestural information. What the gestures are, however, and the precise delineation of their characteristics as well as of the points at which they need to occur in the speech stream in order to serve as turn signals, are decisions currently based upon investigators' judgments. Another, not entirely independent position, views conversation as a vehicle for the exchange of "information" and a turn as the mechanism for ordering the flow of information in a way that will insure maximum comprehensibility. It must be said that the latter view of a conversational exchange appears intuitively reasonable, and not necessarily subjective. The approach, however, further assumes that if, indeed, turns serve such an end, their delineation must be determined primarily by the semantic content of the exchange and, to some degree, the "amount" of information implied by the content. However, the differentiation of content and amount of information can, at this point, only be subjective. Thus, for example, Yngve (1970) suggests three structural categories to which utterances can be assigned: "back-channel" messages, "having the turn" and "having the floor". A participant has the floor when his utterances represent a substantive amount of information, a "topic" appears to be Yngve's term. Having the turn involves the communication of less informative messages, perhaps "subtopics." Yngve (1970) states that ". . . dialogue appears to be organized by topics which they [the participants] take turns pushing forward by means of subtopics . . ." [p. 575]. Back-channel messages are remarks made by the person who does not have the floor and, perhaps, not even the turn. Yngve does not make the latter distinction clear. Nor does he clearly indicate whether back-channel messages are less informative than those communicated by turns. He does say that back-channel activity is "quite varied" and includes gestural and vocal behavior, and that the vocal comments range from vocal segregates to short remarks and questions. However, his report represents an initial and somewhat informal inquiry into the structure of conversation.

Duncan (1972), who is concerned with the signals that regulate the "turn system" (Duncan, 1973, 1974; Duncan & Niederehe, 1974), asserts that a back-channel remark constitutes neither a turn nor a claim for a turn. He notes that back-channel communication includes gestural activity, vocal segregates and other short utterances, and suggests that it may also include many other conversational control signals. He proposes that the back channel be expanded to include, among other things, requests for clarification, brief restatements by one participant of immediately preceding statements by the other participant, and completions by one participant of sentences begun by the other participant. Implied in his discussion of back-channel communication, however, is that it is less informative than communication by turns. Duncan's position allows him to divide simultaneous speech into two categories: *simultaneous talk* and *simultaneous turns*. Simultaneous talk occurs when the person who does not have the turn utters a back-channel remark while the person who has the turn is talking. If, however, the remark uttered by the person who does not have the turn can be considered a turn or a claim for a turn, the resulting simultaneous speech is classified as simultaneous turns. Whether or not the remark is consigned to the back channel, or designated a turn or claim for a turn, seems to depend upon the appearance or nonappearance of "turn-yielding" and/or "attempt-suppressing" signals sent by the participant who has the turn. Here, the amount of information conveyed by the remark may be secondary; the point is not explicated.

It is Rosenfeld (Chapter 12) who most explicitly combines the notion that conversation is structured in terms of informational units with the suggestion that the flow of such units is regulated by nonverbal signals. He is, however, very much aware of the definitional problems involved in such a position. In his discussion of these problems he makes the point that utternace duration as a criterion of amount of information (the longer the utterance the greater the amount of information) has the advantages of being precisely and reliably measurable. But the basic question is not whether duration of utterance and amount of information are related; it is whether, for the purpose of describing the semantic content of natural conversation, the term "information" can be defined in a way that renders it both meaningful and measurable. If the answer is negative, as it is at the present time, then unitizing the time patterns of a conversation in terms of something that cannot be adequately defined does not seem likely to be very useful.

None of this is meant to deny the probable value of viewing conversation as an information exchange process. To be sure, the study of conversation from such a perspective would be tellingly facilitated were a technique devised for objectively assessing the informational characteristics of a conversational exchange. But the important point is that, given such a perspective, it is not surprising that the units that are used to describe the exchange are primarily informationl and only secondarily temporal. A turn cannot simply be taken; it has to be earned. Or to put it another way, one takes a turn not by talking but by saying something! (It is only half jesting to comment that long experience in listening to casual conversations suggests that if informativeness were the criterion that identified a turn then most conversations involve people who do a great deal of talking without ever having a turn!)

Speaker switching as a sole criterion.   Consider, instead, the possibility that the (speech) sounds and silences of a conversational exchange have a coherent structure of their own that can be described without recourse to information from other dimensions of the exchange, such as the words or body movements. The only information needed for the description that is extrinsic to the sounds and silences is the knowledge of their source, that is, knowing by whom they were generated. Thus, no preconceptions are incorporated into the description about the "meaning" of its components or parameters. Initially, at least, a sound is just a sound, a silence just a silence. Only source and structure are used to differentiate categories of sound and/or silence, or configurations of sounds and silences.

The approach makes no assumptions about the function of conversational interaction, nor is it designed to facilitate the study of a particular function. It seems quite likely that conversation serves a variety of ends, and may even satisfy more than one at the same time. Its most apparent function, for example (although not necessarily its most frequent), is to communicate cognitive and affective information. It is probably also used, and perhaps frequently, as simply a form of interpersonal contact in which the participants attend primarily to the sound of each other's voice and minimally to the words that are uttered — a sort of auditory stroking. There is even some indication (Cobb, 1973) that persons who know each other and are together in an appropriate situation tend to engage in conversation at predictably regular intervals of time. That conversational interaction should exhibit such periodicity was recently suggested by Chapple (1970), who views it as controlled by endogenous factors. The position argues that the mere occurrence of conversational behavior satisfies a biologically programmed need.

The approach translates a conversation into a string or sequence of sounds and silences, each of which is identified by its source. The knowledge of their sources allows for the formulation of a rule that provides the string with a coherent structure. This "alternation rule" is that a participant takes a turn by vocalizing alone and loses it when another participant begins to vocalize alone. The rule thus unambiguously assigns the turn and transforms the string into a chain of concatenated events. One way to describe the structure of these "events" is in terms of the classification presented earlier.[5] But how seriously are these events, these segments of speech sounds and silences and their combinations, to be taken? They are indexed by their durations and/or frequencies. Are their durations (and therefore their frequencies) primarily a function of their having been processed by a "threshold device" such as AVTA (Hayes, Meltzer, & Wolf, 1970)? Are the durations, in other words, arbitrary and their fluctuations random with respect to the durations of the preprocessed events? It seems unlikely. As pointed out earlier, the threshold intensity of the AVTA system is determined by a person of unimpaired hearing in order to enable AVTA to "hear" what presumably would be heard by all persons with unimpaired hearing. The event durations generated by AVTA are intended to be their "perceived" durations rather than their "true" durations. Moreover, the average duration of each of these events (other than that of simultaneous speech) has been shown to reliably characterize individuals in the sense that different individuals tend to use consistently different average durations in their conversational interactions. Finally, it has been shown thus far (Jaffe & Feldstein, 1970) that the average durations of vocalizations, pauses, and switching pauses, and even the frequency of vocalizations (BenDebba, 1974), can be systematically modified. At the very least, these findings argue that the components of the classification offered here—an objectively temporal description of the verbal interaction of a conversation—are very much worth further investigation.

In this approach, then, a turn is taken by the participant who begins to talk while the other participant is silent. It does not matter what he talks about, or whether the talk is informative or uninformative. Nor does it matter whether he speaks only very briefly or at length. A vocal segregate can serve as a turn even though it takes only a fraction of a second to utter. It would be easy to exclude it; AVTA (or any similar automated data processor) could be instructed to not classify as turns utterances that meet the other criteria but are shorter than a specified duration. But there is no adequate reason to do so at present, certainly none that has any convincing evidence to support it. On the contrary, if the having of discernible consequences were considered a reasonable justification, there is evidence to support the inclusion of such a turn.

---

[5]Models have been presented elsewhere which attempt to account for the structure mathematically (Jaffe, 1970: Jaffe & Feldstein, 1970) and recursively (Feldstein, 1972).

Not only have segregates such as "mm-hmm" been shown to serve as effective reinforcers in the control of certain syntactical classes of words (e.g., Greenspoon, 1955; Salzinger, Portnoy, Zlotogura, & Keisner, 1963), but BenDebba (1974) has demonstrated that "mm-hmm" can be used, in a way that renders it a turn, to increase a participant's rate of vocalizations in a verbal exchange. In short, the categorization of very brief utterances as turns is troublesome only if the turn is considered an informational unit rather than a temporal unit.

One other issue deserves mention. It seems to be assumed by many of those concerned with identifying the nonverbal signals that function as conversational control mechanisms that the alternation that occurs in a conversation is one that involves the roles of "speaker" and "listener" or "auditor." The roles are not meant just to indicate who is speaking and who is silent. An "auditor" may speak and remain an auditor if what he says is judged to be a back-channel communication (Duncan, 1972) or a "listener response" (Dittman & Llewellyn, 1968). And although he may not be talking at any particular moment, a participant can remain the "speaker" for as long as he has the turn. The "speaker," then, is the participant who conveys information and the "listener" is the one who receives it (Rosenfeld, Chapter 12). The attribution of such roles implies, of course, the position that conversation is an information exchange system. But, if the participant who is judged to be conveying information is thereby considered to be having a turn (or the floor), it is not clear that anything more is gained by also considering him to be the "speaker." In other words, the essential characteristics of the role of "speaker" are talking (much of the time) and conveying information. However, the essential characteristics of the state of "having the turn" are also talking and conveying information. Thus, the state of "having the turn" and the role of "speaker" are equivalent. But is the role of "listener" the same as the state of *not* "having the turn?" The participant who, at a particular time in the conversation, does not talk much and does not convey much information even when he does talk cannot, presumably, be considered to have the floor. Thus, he is the participant who does not have the floor. To say, however, that he is not talking much and not conveying information does not appear to be the same as saying that he is listening and receiving information, both of which are the essential characteristics of the "listener" role. Attributing the role of "listener" to the participant who does not have the turn implies that instead of simply not being engaged in one set of activities he is engaged in another set of activities, that he is, if you will, taking a turn at listening and receiving infromation. The distinction, then, between not having the turn an being a "listener" appears to be substantive, but it is also problematical. While it may not be clear, in many if not most ordinary conversations, that when a "speaker" is talking he is conveying information, it is obvious at least that he is talking. It is frequently not at all clear, however, that a "listener" is either listening or receiving information! In any case, the position holds that the participants in a conversation alternate in the taking of the roles. Thus, the roles are considered to be temporal units as well as informational untis. Unfortunately, given the lack of reliable criteria for evaluating amount of information, it becomes more than occasionally difficult to determine which participant is filling which role at which moment.

The alternation rule simply determines who has the floor in a conversation. It does not allot roles to the participants such that the one who has the floor is the "speaker" and the other is the "listener." The total amount of time a participant spends in not having the floor is, of course, equivalent to the sum of the durations of the other participant's turns and is, therefore, not separately indexed. The use of the descriptive category of simultaneous speech rather than "listener response" to take into account the speech of the participant who does not have the floor entails considerably fewer assumptions.

It may well be that the attribution of a listener role, or alternatively, the categorization of time spent not having the floor, is a necessary (or useful) step in accounting for the temporal structure of verbal interaction. Jaffe (1970), for example, proposed a Markov-based model of dialogic time patterns that posits two silence "states" and one sound "state." The silence states are pausing and "listening." He demonstrated that, given the three parameters that index these states for each participant, one can quite nicely approximate the actual transition probabilities generated by the sound-silence sequences of the two participants. The assumption of a listening state (in addition to the pausing and sound states for each participant) not only reduces the eight parameters of an alternative model to six parameters, but also markedly reduces the sizes of the discrepancies between actual transition probabilities and those predicted by the alternative model. However, it seems clear that, apart from the substantive issues involved in combining certain of the original parameters to make possible the reduction, the posited listening *state* is not meant to approximate the listening *role* discussed above. It accounts only for the time spent in silence while not having a turn. Moreover, the model dictates that the likelihood that one of the participants will remain silent during the time he does not have a turn is almost wholly dependent upon the behavior of the other participant.[6]

---

[6]In Chapter 1, Jaffe talks about "speaker" and "listener" in ways that seem to imply that the two are role behaviors. He even talks about the "listener's response" and "listeners' interjections." He does, however, regard the interjection as a speaker switch, that is, a change in who has the speaking turn. On the other hand, the following remarks make his position vaguely reminiscent of Yngve's (1970) distinction between "having the turn" and "having the floor": "To pursue the metaphor of parliamentary procedure, the listener has been briefly recognized by the chairman, *but the longer term sending-receiving configuration is preserved"* (italics ours).

In short, the disagreements about what constitutes a turn reflect different approaches to the study of conversational time patterns. The positions that comprise one approach assume, implicitly or explicitly, that the primary function of conversation is to exchange information, and that the characteristics of, and interrelations among, the various dimensions of a conversation are determined by that function. The other approach assumes that the dimensions of a conversational exchange can be defined and examined independently of each other and without regard to the function of the conversation. It does not imply that the dimensions are unrelated to each other or that their characteristics are not influenced by the function, but that such relationships and influence must be demonstrated rather than assumed. It does imply that a particular dimension may be subject to influences other than that wielded by the function of a conversation and may carry information different from and even contradictory to that carried by other dimensions.

Research Directions

To date, few studies of turn-taking behavior have been concerned with much more than the relations between turns (defined in various ways) and types of nonverbal behaviors and initiation strategies (Schegloff, 1968). Fewer still have investigated turns and simultaneous speech as they are defined in this chapter. These few are worth reviewing if only to demonstrate that the parameters, although empirically defined, bear consistent and meaningful relationships to other behaviors of interest.

A preliminary study by Alberti (1974) explored the notion that the amount of interaction in a dialogue may be related to the time, or time frame, to which the semantic content of the dialogue refers. He therefore compared the frequency of turns per minute, which he used as an index of amount of interaction, with the frequencies of past, present, and conditional verbs, which he used as estimates of referred time. The conversations used in the study were four task-oriented dialogues (involving college students) that were randomly selected from a much larger number of recorded dialogues. Analyses of the data indicated that the use of the present tense was positively related to the frequency of turns per minute. The frequencies with which past and conditional tenses were used were not found to be related to the frequency of turns. Thus, while a rapid exchange in a dialogue may mean that the discussion is referring to what, for the participants, can be considered the present time, a slow interaction may not necessarily imply a discussion of the past or future.

A most imaginative experiment by Martindale (1971) examined the effects of territorial dominance on turn-taking behavior in a simulated legal bargaining situation. Martindale used as his subjects 60 male college students who lived in dormitories on their campus. The students were randomly divided into equal numbers of "defense attorneys" and "prosecuting attorneys." Each defense attorney was asked to meet for half an hour with a prosecuting attorney to argue — out of court — the prepared case of a defendent known to be guilty. The attorneys were instructed to negotiate a prison term for the defendent, with the prosecuting attorneys arguing for the maximum allowed by law and the defense attorneys arguing for the minimum. The critical experimental manipulation was that half of the 30 dialogues were conducted in the dormitory rooms (home territory) of the defense attorneys and half in the rooms of the prosecuting attorneys! It was hypothesized that when attorneys are negotiating on their own territory they (a) hold the floor longer and (b) are more successful than the attorneys with whom they are negotiating. It should also be mentioned that the students were given, prior to their negotiating sessions, the Dominance Scale of the California Personality Inventory.

The results supported both hypotheses. The average turn durations of those students who negotiated the case on their own territory (in their own rooms) were significantly longer than were the turn durations of the students with whom they negotiated, regardless of which role they were playing. They were also the students whose negotiations were more successful. The average prison term agreed upon by the two attorneys on the territory of the defense attorneys was 22 months; the average term agreed upon on the territory of the prosecuting attorneys was 60 months!

The correlation between territory and the average turn durations statistically controlled for the scores the students received on the Dominance Scale of the CPI. Interestingly, however, the personality characteristic presumably indexed by the scores did not markedly affect how long on the average, the students kept the floor each time they took it, although it was related to the total amount of time the students held the floor during their negotiations.

Talking out of turn.   Talking at the same time as a speaker who has the floor is talking (i.e., simultaneous speech) is, in effect, talking out of turn. It seems perfectly appropriate that such behavior be discussed within the context of talking about turns.

If, as Schegloff (1968) suggested, the taking of turns is considered a basic conversational rule, then talking out of turn, is a violation of the rule. It is a violation that often disrupts the flow of an interaction. Yet, the frequencies with which individuals engage in such behavior, that is, initiate simultaneous speech, have been shown earlier to be characteristic of their conversational styles, which suggest, at the least, that they merit further exploration.

Meltzer *et al.* (1971), in the study mentioned earlier, concern themselves with the question of what determines the outcome of a segment of simultaneous speech. Why do some segments terminate in a change of which speaker has the floor while others do not? The investigators explored the possibility that vocal amplitude (intensity) plays a role in determining outcome. To obtain their data, they randomly selected one participant in each of 60 problem-solving dialogues as the target and identified all instances in which the target person initiated simultaneous speech. They then computed the proportion of these instances that were successful interruptions," that in the classification preferred here would be considered instances of interruptive simultaneous speech (ISS). These proportions of ISS for the target persons were used as the dependent variable in a stepwise multiple regression analysis in which 10 vocal amplitude variables were used as the predictors. The analysis revealed that only two of the 10 predictors were significantly related to the proportions of ISS and together accounted for 62% of their variance, although they were unrelated to each other. One predictor variable was the average difference between the vocal amplitudes of each target person and his conversational partner while they were engaged in simultaneous speech; the larger the difference and louder the partner's voice, the less likely it was that the simultaneous speech of the target person would interrupt his partner. The other variable was the mean difference between the amplitude of the partner's voice immediately prior to the occurrence of simultaneous speech and its amplitude during the simultaneous speech. The relation indicated that the greater increase in amplitude from before to after the onset of simultaneous speech, the less likely was it that the latter would culminate in an interruption.

The investigators suggest that most instances of simultaneous speech are of too short a duration for their outcomes to be determined by the semantic content of what is being said, hence, the importance of physicalistic cues. They did, however, find instances of simultaneous speech that lasted for as long as 6 sec. They therefore examined the comparative utility of the two amplitude variables in predicting the outcome of simultaneous speech segments of various durations. As had been expected, they found that both variables became less effective in predicting outcome as the durations of the segments increased. The decline in effectiveness, however, was much less marked for the variable indexing the average amplitude differential between the voices of the two speakers during simultaneous speech than for that indexing the change in vocal amplitude following the onset of simultaneous speech made by the speaker who had the floor.

Although the results are excitingly provocative, Meltzer, Morris, and Hayes point out that the study leaves unsettled the question of whether semantic content plays any role in determining the outcome of brief segments of simultaneous speech. That is, amplitude may function as a mediating factor that allows speakers to respond quickly to content, or it may be so highly related to content (e.g., the greater the semantic information, the higher the amplitude) that its role is determining outcome is artifactual. The position of the investigators is that amplitude operates independently of content. The results seem to justify the position although the correlation method of the study might be viewed as limiting their conclusiveness. An experimental verification of part of these results was provided by another excellent study conducted by Morris (1971).

Working within the conceptual framework of the earlier study (Meltzer *et al.,* 1971), Morris views the participant in a conversation who initiates simultaneous speech as the "interrupter" and the participant who had the floor prior to its initiation as the "defender." His experiment tested three hypotheses. The first is that amplitude is causally related to the outcome of simultaneous speech such that increases in vocal amplitude by the defender during occurrences of simultaneous speech ". . . significantly increase his ability to successfully defend the floor" (Morris, 1971, p. 320). Put more empirically, the causal relationship is such that the more likely it is that a participant who has the floor raises his voice during the occurrence of simultaneous speech, the more likely he is to have the floor at the end of its occurrence. The second hypothesis is that, whereas amplitude increments by the defender during simultaneous speech are effective in helping him keep the floor, amplitude increments by the interrupter during simultaneous speech do not affect the likelihood of his obtaining the floor. The implication here is that the determination of who *will* have the floor is influenced primarily by the behavior of the participant who *does* have the floor. Finally, the study posits that those participants who intiate simultaneous speech that tends to terminate noninterruptively (without their having obtained the floor) tend, over time, to increase the amplitude of their voices upon the initiation of simultaneous speech by their partners and are, thereby, more likely over time to retain the floor following occurrences of simultaneous speech.

The study utilized two experimental and one control condition with 11 dyads in each condition. The discussions of the control dyads were allowed to proceed without experimental intervention. In one experimental condition, the vocal amplitude of one of the participants in each dyad was electronically increased, prior to its reception (via earphones) by the other perticipant, during 50% of the instances in which the *other* participant initiated simultaneous speech. In the other experimental condition, the vocal amplitude of one of the participants in each dyad was increased during 50% of the instances in which *he* initiated simultaneous speech. To use the investigator's terms, the former experimental condition was one in which the defender's amplitude was boosted whereas the latter was one in which the interrupter's amplitude was boosted.

The results appear to support the first two hypotheses fully and the third one partially. That is, the increase in amplitude during simultaneous speech over time described by the first half of the third hypothesis is only significant (at the .05 point) when evaluated by a one-tailed test (the use of which is no more justified in evaluating this result than it would have been in evaluating the other results). The results confirm the basic findings of the Meltzer, Morris, and Hayes study (although not the interaction of amplitude and duration), and make clear that vocal amplitude, or intensity, operates as a critical interpersonal cue in determining the outcome of a majority of instances of simultaneous speech. Although Morris concedes that semantic content may play some role in such determinations, he justifiably points out that the role cannot be considered decisive.

It is also of interest that amplitude is effective as a determinant primarily when it is used by the participant who has the floor. One of the suggestions Morris offers to account for its asymmetrical effectiveness is that the amplitude increase by the participant who has the floor forces the participant who initiated the simultaneous speech to recognize that he is violating a conversational rule, that is, that he is being rude, and thereby it decreases the likelihood of his persisting. Morris also assumes that the amplitude increase expresses the intention of the participant who has the floor to continue talking, and that it is so interpreted by the violator. It is not clear that the assumption is either warranted or necessary. The amplitude increment may well be an automatic response to a competing acoustical input and serve to maintain the previous signal-to-noise ratio. It is conceivable that the increment is viewed as a reminder of the violation rather than as a statement of intent.

In any case, the results of both of the two studies described above are important, and the studies themselves suggest research paradigms that may be useful in exploring other aspects of temporal behavior and its correlates. As both studies indicate, however, the outcome of simultaneous speech is not wholly determined by change in vocal amplitude. Semantic content is not completely ruled out as a determinant. But more important, perhaps, are personality characteristics.

It may be inferred from the reliability data presented earlier that there are consistent differences among individuals in the extent to which they initiate ISS and NSS in conversations. The inference raises two questions: Do personality characteristics play a role in the initiation of simultaneous speech, and do they influence its outcome? Although there have been few speculations about what "kinds" of people tend to talk while someone else is talking, it has been suggested that the outcome of such simultaneous speech may be a function of dominance and submissiveness (Gallois & Markel, 1975). Meltzer *et al.* (1971) do, in fact, wonder whether ". . . the *outcome* of an interruption (who "wins" the floor) may be a more valid indicator of dominance than the occurrence of an interruption" [p. 393].

Using the data from the quartet study described earlier, Feldstein, Alberti, BenDebba, and Welkowitz (1974) compared the frequencies with which the participants initiated simultaneous speech with those of their personality characteristics indexed by the Cattell Sixteen Personality Factor Questionnaire or the 16PFQ (Cattell, Eber, & Tatsuoka, 1970). The 16PFQ was completed by the subjects (along with Witkin's (1950) form of Embedded Figures Test, of which more will be said later) prior to their participation in the experimental conversations. The study asks three questions. Do personality characteristics influence the frequencies with which individuals initiate simultaneous speech? Are the frequencies with which individuals initiate simultaneous speech influenced by the personality characteristics of their conversational partners? Are the two possible outcomes of simultaneous speech (ISS and NSS) differentially related to personality characteristics?

The relations between the simultaneous speech frequencies and the 16 personality factors were compared by means of 16 hierarchical multiple regression analyses. Each regression equation used the initiation frequencies as its dependent variable and had seven independent variables, the order of which was specified in advance by the investigators (Cohen & Cohen, 1975). The first variable to enter the equation identified which of the frequencies of the dependent variable were ISS and NSS. The second variable consisted of the factor scores of the participants, and the third, those of their conversational partners. The remaining four variables are product variables which, as a function of their order in the equation, examined possible interaction effects among the participants, their partners, and the outcome of simultaneous speech.

The analyses indicated that it was the participant who received low scores on factors L, O, and Q_4, and high scores on Factor I, who more frequently initiated simultaneous speech. According to the *handbook* of the 16PFQ (Cattell *et al.*, 1970), persons who obtain low scores on the first three factors can be characterized as easygoing, relaxed, conciliatory, complacent, secure, and relatively insensitive to the approbation or disapprobation of others. The interpretations of Factor I are discussed shortly.

The analyses also indicated that the participants who initiated more simultaneous speech had partners who received high scores on Factors A, C, and F and low scores on Factor Q_2, who, in other words, could be described as good-natured, cooperative, attentive to people, emotionally mature, realistic, talkative, cheerful, and socially group-dependent. They were partners who also received high scores on Factor H. However, the analyses revealed that the participants' initiation of simultaneous speech was also influenced by interactions among certain aspects of their personalities with those of their partners. The interactions involve Factors H, I, and M. The *Handbook* describes persons who score high on Factor H as adventurous, "thick skinned," genial, and socially bold, whereas persons who score low are described as shy, timid, restrained, and sensitive to threat. The results show that although in general, the participants initiated more simultaneous speech while talking to partners who scored high on Factor H than to partners who scored low, the initiation frequencies of participants who received low scores—the shy, timid, restrained participants—were considerably more affected by how their partners scored on Factor H than were those of participants who received high scores.

Those participants who scored low on Factor I—participants described as "tough minded," unsentimental, self-reliant, and practical—initiated, on the average, *less* simultaneous speech than did participants with high scores on Factor I—those described as sensitive, dependent, insecure, attention seeking, and imaginative. However, the initiation frequencies of participants who scored high on the factor were apparently unaffected by the factor scores of their partners, whereas those of participants who scored low on the factor show a significant positive relation to the factor scores of their partners.

Finally, the analysis of Factor M indicates that those participants who scored high on the factor—characterized by the *Handbook* as imaginative, unconventional, absent-minded, absorbed, and fanciful—initiated more simultaneous speech when talking to partners who scored high than to partners who scored low. On the other hand, those participants with low scores on the factor—subjects characterized as "down-to-earth," conventional, prosaic, earnest, and concerned with immediate interests and issues—initiated more simultaneous speech with partners who had low scores.

Of considerable interest is the fact that the results provide no evidence that those personality characteristics of the participants and their partners that are measured by the 16PFQ had any influence on the outcome of their simultaneous speech!

One further regression equation was computed which included all those factors shown by the previous analyses to be related to the initiation of simultaneous speech. The solution yielded a significant multiple correlation of .55, indicating that the personality factors in the equation accounted for approximately 30% of the variability in the frequencies with which simultaneous speech was initiated. The personality characteristics of the participants contributed 8% of the variance, those of their partners accounted for 16% of the variance, and the interactions among these two sets of characteristics accounted for 6%. Each of these contributions is significant.

Obviously, the study needs to be cross-validated and extended to men. The results do suggest, however, that the extent to which a woman initiates simultaneous speech in a conversation—the extent to which she talks out of turn—is not only influenced by aspects of her own personality, but also by those of her conversational partner. Women who are relaxed, complacent, secure, and not overly dependent upon the approval of others tend to initiate more simultaneous speech than women who are generally apprehensive, self-reproaching, tense, and frustrated. But apart from their own characteristics, women tend to initiate more simultaneous speech when they converse with others who are aloof, critical, emotionally labile, introspective, silent, and self-sufficient.

What is surprising is that none of the 16 personality factors were related to the *outcome* of simultaneous speech. It seems so much more likely that the outcome, rather than simply the initiation of simultaneous speech, would be influenced by personality characteristics. It may be the case, however, that the presumed relation between personality and outcome is dependent upon contextual, or situational, variables. One such variable might be the stated purpose of a discussion. The dialogues of the study were casual and unconstrained. It is possible, however, that only task-oriented and/or argumentative dialogues permit personality dimensions to influence the outcome of simultaneous speech. The implication here is that there is an interaction of outcome, personality, and conversational demands such that personality is differentially related to ISS and NSS only in certain types of conversations.

Gallois and Markel (1975) conducted a study of the relation between turn-taking behavior and "social personality." Inferring from the other research that the personality of a bilingual individual varies according to which of his languages he is using, they requested each of 13 bilingual men to converse (on separate occasions) with two friends, one who primarily spoke English and the other Spanish. Although the investigators defined turns as they are defined in this chapter, their analyses involved not the durations of turns but the amount of speech in the turns. They did, however, use the frequency of turns and the frequency of turns following simultaneous speech in examining another aspect of the study. Frequency of turns following simultaneous speech sounds very like an estimate of ISS.

For their analyses, the authors segmented each conversation into the first 5 min., the last 5 min. and 5 min. from the exact center of the conversation. In comparing these three "sections" of the dialogues, they found turns occurred more frequently during the opening section than during the closing section. In addition, a higher frequency of turns following simultaneous speech occurred in the middle section than in either the first or last sections. They conclude that people are more interactive at the beginnings of conversations and more interruptive during the middle of conversations. They speculate that obtaining the floor by means of simultaneous speech may reflect ". . . heightened involvement in the conversation" [p. 1139].

Crown and her colleagues (Crown, Feldstein, & Bond, 1982) recently reported an observational study concerned with the roles of interruptive and noninterruptive behavior in the forming of interpersonal impressions. Sixty-seven male and 103 female university students participated in the study. Of the women, 53 were white and 50 were black; of the men, 43 were white and

24 were black. The students were assembled into pairs that represented all possible combinations of race and gender, although the numbers of pairs were not the same for all the combinations. The members of each pair were asked to engage in a 20-minute conversation that would enable them to become better acquainted. After their conversation was finished, they were asked to describe themselves and each other in terms of a set of 20 seven-point, bipolar adjective scales. An independent group of judges rated which pole of each scale was negative and which was positive. The positive pole was given a score of "1" and the negative pole a score of "7."

Multiple regression equations compared the two types of simultaneous speech to each of the 20 scales and included race and gender as predictor variables. The results of the analyses indicated that, in general, the interpersonal impressions elicited by the interruptive and noninterruptive behaviors of the conversational partners were dependent on their race and gender. Positive impressions were formed of white men who tended to engage in noninterruptive simultaneous speech and for white women who engaged in interruptive simultaneous speech. The black participants, both men and women, were viewed in more positive ways when they tended to refrain from using either type of simultaneous speech.

To account for the results, the authors suggested that the use of interruptive speech by white women may have been seen as assertive rather than impolite and that the use of noninterruptive speech by men may have been viewed as indicative of support and interest. They did not interpret the findings associated with the black participants. It could be that blacks are expected to abide much more closely than are whites to the rules of polite conversation. It should be noted, however, that the impressions elicited by the study about the black participants were (as were those about the white participants) from conversational partners who were black as well as white. Thus, it seems unlikely that simple interpretations can account for any of the results.

More than two talking. The studies reviewed thus far have been concerned with turn-taking in dialogues. A very interesting issue that has been raised recently is whether the speaking turn, as defined earlier in this chaper, adequately describes the ways in which speakers share the floor in conversations involving more than two persons. Dabbs and his colleagues have begun to examine the temporal characteristics of group interactions (Dabbs & Ruback, 1984; Dabbs & Swiedler, 1983) and discuss their approach and some of their findings in Chapter 10 of this book. An earlier attempt was made by Lustig (1980), who demonstrated that the transition matrix that Jaffe and Feldstein (1970) used to describe dialogues could be extended to describe three-person interactions. In doing so, he maintained the same definition of the speaking turn proposed by Jaffe and Feldstein. *"Possession of the floor* [original italics] is obtained by the person who utters the first unilateral

sound. Once possession is obtained, it is maintained until another person utters a unilateral sound, at which time the former loses and the latter gains
possession of the floor" (Lustig, 1980, p. 4). He did, however, provide a category of "unclassifiable events." His example of such an event is one in which
speakers A, B, and C speak simultaneously although A is the turn-holder. A
then stops speaking and B and C continue. Lustig indicated that the event is
not classifiable apparently because once A dropped out of the interaction,
possession of the floor could not be determined. Another category used by
Lustig that differs from that of Jaffe and Feldstein is that of *simultaneous
speech.* When two or three of the speakers talk simultaneously, the simultaneous speech is credited to the speaker who has the floor rather than to the
speakers who do not have the floor. The latter speakers are credited with
"talk-overs." Lustig said that simultaneous speech refers to the "target" of
what he called a "multiple speech act," whereas talk-overs refer to the initiation of the act.

Dabbs and his colleagues (Chapter 10) provide a different resolution of the
problems involved in classifying the temporal patterning of multipersona interactions, or *multilogues.* Their perceptions of the difficulties presented by
the classification of turn-taking and simultaneous speech in such interactions
prompted them to formulate two sets of parameters, one for dyadic and one
for group interactions. Thus, in addition to a speaker turn, there is a "group
turn," which occurs when two or more people in a group are talking at the
same time and none of them can be considered to have the floor because none
of them started speaking first. There are also pause, switching pause, and vocalization parameters that characterize group rather than dyadic
interactions.

It seems clear that the time patterns of a multilogue are, at least empirically, considerably more complex than those of a dialogue, and it is quite possible that the parameter set that describes a dialogue needs to be expanded to
accommodate the patterns of a multilogue. It seems less clear that the basis of
the parameters used to describe such patterns should be primarily empirical.
Lustig's classification may be considered a potentially stochastic model and
all but one of its parameters appear to form a coherent set. The exception is
the parameter, *talk-over,* which seems to be an effort to cope with the occurrence of interruptive behavior. The talk-over involves an extrainteractional
piece of information that is neither defined nor discussed, i.e., the "designated subject." It is this "designated subject" that distinguishes a talk-over
from simultaneous speech. But how is a designated subject determined and
who makes the determination? On the other hand, are there vocal behaviors
in a multilogue that legitimately can be considered interruptive or, in terms of
the dyadic model, simultaneous but noninterruptive?

No distinction is made between interruptive and noninterruptive simultaneous speech when several individuals are talking at the same time in the

"grouptalk" model of Dabbs et al. (Chapter 10), and the simultaneous speech simply indexes who are talking during a group vocalization (although the distinction is maintained for the dyadic parameters of the model). The group parameters of the model are based largely upon the empirically observed sound–silence patterns of group interactions and there appears to be no logically necessary connection between the group and dyadic parameters. Nevertheless, the model fulfills an important need for the extension to groups of a level of analysis that continues to contribute to an understanding of dyadic exchanges.

CONVERSATIONAL CONGRUENCE: CORRELATES ANDD CONCERNS

It was noted earlier that comparisons of successive conversations involving the same individuals have indicated that the stability of their average silence durations depend upon whether their partners were the same in the different conversations; the participation of different partners resulted in markedly lower stability. The loss of stability appears, at least in part, to be a function of the propensity of conversational participants to vary the time patterns of their verbal contributions such that their patterns became increasingly similar during the course of a conversation. This mutual influence apparently exerted by speakers upon one another seems to reflect the more general tendency, on the part of interacting individuals, to develop orientations and interpersonal behavior that become more similar the more frequently the individuals interact (e.g., Homans, 1950; Newcomb, 1953). The expression of this tendency in terms of a variety of the dimensions of verbal interaction has been observed by a number of investigators (e.g., Feldstein, 1968; Jaffe, 1964; Jaffe & Feldstein, 1970; Kendon, 1967; Lennard & Bernstein, 1960; Marcus *et al.,* 1970; Matarazzo, 1965; Welkowitz & Feldstein, 1969). The phenomenon has been variously labeled *synchrony* (e.g., Webb, 1972), *symmetry* (Meltzer *et al.,* 1971), *pattern matching* (Cassotta *et al.,* 1967), and *congruence* (Feldstein, 1972). In his discussion of synchrony, Webb (1972) reviews some mechanisms that may account for its occurrence and asserts that synchrony exists ". . . when intensity, frequency, or durational characteristics of one's behavior rhythmically agree with similar characteristics of ambient stimuli, whether personal or impersonal in origin" [p. 125]. Although the definition is general, Webb confines his discussion to what he calls "verbal synchrony" and is concerned with speech rates within interview contexts. A closely related phenomenon — the development of similar accents during the course of a conversation — has been described by Giles, Taylor, and Bourhis (1973) as *interpersonal accommodation.* This description has been broadened recently (Crown & Feldstein, 1981) to imply the phenomenon to which all the other terms refer.

Congruency (or pattern matching) can be defined much like synchrony but is more restricted in its reference. It is used to describe the occurrence, within the span of one or more conversations, of similar intensity, frequency, or durational values for the participants on one or more of the parameters that characterize temporal patterning. Almost all of the studies conducted thus far by the authors and their associates have indicated that the parameters are, in one way or another, susceptible to the type of interspeaker influence reflected by congruence.

The first study (Feldstein *et al.*, 1967) to examine the occurrence of congruence in conversations rather than interviews involved task-oriented conversations. Thirty-two men and 32 women participated in the study, and each engaged in one conversation with each of the two different members of his or her own sex and one with a member of the opposite sex. The dyad participants were asked to resolve differences in their answers to an attitude questionnaire. (The study is more fully described by Jaffe & Feldstein, 1970, as Experiment 2.) Comparisons of the average durations of pauses and switching pauses of the dyad participants yielded congruence coefficients[7] of .56 and .55, respectively. However, a comparison of the average durations of their vocalizations yielded a coefficient of − .04. Whereas the conversational participants were apparently able to influence the durations of each other's silences, they were unable to influence the durations of each other's vocalizations. These findings were confirmed by subsequent studies. In the quartet study described earlier, for example, the congruence coefficients obtained by comparing the mean durations of the pauses and switching pauses of the conversational participants, averaged over the eight occasions of the study are .43 and .62, respectively; that for their mean durations of vocalizations is .08. A preliminary study conducted by Welkowitz and Feldstein (1969) also indicated that durations of vocalizations used by each participant in the dialogues were not markedly affected by those of the other. Interestingly, however, a trend analysis of the absolute differences between the average durations of the members of participant pairs did show that their average durations were more similar by the end of their third conversation than by the end of their first. That is, the duration of their vocalizations had converged by the end of the third conversation. Perhaps durations of vocalizations sim-

---

[7]Degree of congruence has been frequently indexed by an intraclass correlation coefficient (Haggard, 1958) that, when so used, has been called for convenience, a congruence coefficient. For the purpose of explication, consider one participant of a dialogue the speaker and the other participant the partner. Then, for a particular parameter and group of dialogues involving different participant pairs, the appropriate values of the speakers (e.g., their average pause durations) are correlated with those of their partners. The intraclass correlation assesses the similarity of not only the shapes of the distributions under scrutiny but also their means. The significance of an intraclass correlation coefficient is indexed by its associated F ratio. A more recent measurement technique is discussed toward the end of the chapter.

ply take longer to influence than do those of pauses and switching pauses. The finding needs to be replicated.

Although the durations of vocalizations do not appear to be readily susceptible to interspeaker influence, the intensiy levels of vocalizations do. Vocal intensity, measured in terms of the average amplitude of speech for a given time unit, roughly corresponds to what is subjectively perceived as the "loudness" of speech. There is both anecdotal and systematic evidence to suggest that intensity congruence occurs in unconstrained conversations. Try, for example, to begin a conversation by speaking very softly or whispering. As likely as not, the person you speak to will respond in an equally soft voice. And it will probably take a few minutes before he realizes what the two of you are doing (given that the circumstances do not appear to call for it) and request an explanation. There is a body of observational and experimental studies that indicates that speakers adjust the intensity of their voices according to the amount of noise present in the situations in which they find themselves talking (e.g., Charlip & Burk, 1969; Garnder, 1966; Hanley & Steer, 1949; Kryter, 1946; Webster & Klump, 1962) and to the intensity levels of their own voices and those of people talking to them (e.g., Baird & Tice, 1969; Black, 1949a, b; Jacobson, 1968; Lane & Tranel, 1971). None of the latter studies had to do with conversational interactions. Of particular relevance to the issue of mutual interspeaker influence of vocal intensity is the finding reported by Meltzer *et al.* (1971) in a footnote (p. 396) of what they call *symmetry,* that the correlation of one person's amplitude in a conversation with that of the other person yielded a coefficient of .57. This incidental discovery that conversational participants tend to match the intensity levels of their voices was confirmed in a subsequent, independent exploration of the issue (Welkowitz, Feldstein, Finkelstein & Aylesworth, 1972). Whereas the former study involved problem-solving discussions, the latter study asked the participants to talk about anything they wished. The latter study was also concerned with the effects of interpersonal perception upon intensity congruence. Specifically, one group of participants was informed that its members had been paired on the basis of having similar personality characteristics while the other group was told that its members had been randomly paired. Intensity congruence occurred in the conversations of those who presumably perceived each other as similar. However, it occurred only in a second conversation in which the participant pairs engaged. It is worth noting that the study also demonstrated that the average intensity levels used by speakers remain quite consistent during the course of conversation.

A more thoroughgoing investigation of the congruence of vocal intensity in conversations was conducted by Natale (1976b) Two experiments were involved. The first one used a modified standardized interview to test the expectation that the vocal intensities of interviewees would match the experimentally controlled changes in the vocal intensity of the interviewer. The second experiment examined the notions that (a) the degree to which the vocal intensity levels of participants in unconstrained conversations become congruent is directly related to their "social desirability" (measured by the Marlowe-Crowne Scale), and (b) the vocal intensity levels of the participants converge over the course of three conversations. The results support the three expectations. Of importance is the fact that the dialogue participants were in separate booths and could not see each other. While such a procedure may make the generalizability of the results to "ordinary face-to-face conversations" somewhat precarious, it serves the purpose of controlling for the possible influence of nonverbal cues. Together with the findings of Meltzer *et al.* (1971) and Welkowitz and her associates (1972), the Natale study establishes the viability of vocal intensity as a behavior systematically susceptible to interpersonal (or interspeaker) influence.

Some Correlates and Questions

Early research on durational congruence (Cassotta *et al.,* 1967) and the recent research on intensity congruence (Natale, 1975b; Welkowitz *et al.,* 1972) strongly suggest that there are notable differences in the extent to which conversational pairs achieve congruence. It may then be that the degree to which their pauses and switching pauses become mutually modified is dependent upon certain of their personality characteristics, on their perceptions of themselves and each other, or on some aspects of their relationship to each other. A number of studies have concerned themselves with these possibilities.

Interpersonal perception. There is a considerable history of research concerned with the role of interpersonal perception in attitude change (e.g., Berscheid, 1966; Brock, 1965; Dabbs, 1964), in facilitating communication (e.g., Runkel, 1956), in interpersonal attraction (e.g., Byrne, 1961; Byrne, Griffitt, & Stefaniak, 1967; Griffitt, 1966), and in self-perception (e.g., Stotland, Zander, & Natsoulas, 1961; Burnstein, Stotland, & Zander, 1961). Dabbs (1969) has also briefly reported two experiments that examined the effects of gestural similarity on interpersonal perception. The experiments, in which confederate interviewees mimicked the gestures of interviewing subjects, yielded results that indicated that those subjects who were mimicked tended to view the confederates as more persuasive, better informed, and more similar to themselves than did subjects who were not mimicked. Even apart from the experimental evidence, it is difficult to imagine how many of the ways in which people behave toward each other could *not* be influenced by the ways in which they perceive each other. Welkowitz and Feldstein (1969), in an exploratory study, examined the possibility that the degree to which interacting speakers achieve temporal congruence depends upon whether they perceive each other's "personality" as similar or dissimilar.

The subjects of the study were asked to complete a battery of personality test and were then randomly assembled into 40 same-sex dyads, or pairs, with one of the following explanations: The members in each of 15 of the dyads were told that they had been paired with each other because their performances on the personality tests indicated that they were very much alike. Those in 15 other dyads were informed that they were paired because the tests indicated that they were different from each other. The subjects in the remaining 10 dyads were told that they had been randomly paired. The subjects were also informed that the purpose of the experiment was to attempt an assessment of "how people who are similar (dissimilar, or randomly paired) get to know each other." The dyads met for an hour a week for three consecutive weeks. Prior to each conversation, each member of a dyad was placed in a separate room which allowed him only verbal communication with the other member of his dyad. The recorded conversations were processed by AVTA and the average durations of pauses, switching pauses, and vocalizations were subjected to separate statistical analyses.

The analyses confirmed the consistency and stability of the parameters. In addition, they also confirmed the finding of previous studies that the vocalization durations of conversationalists do not become similar within the course of single conversations although, as was noted earlier, they did become more similar by the end of the third conversation. The coefficients that indexed the congruence of the vocalizations, averaged over the three occasions on which the subjects conversed, were .24 for the "similar" group, .22 for the "different" group, and .25 for the "random" group. The averaged congruence coefficients for pauses and switching pauses were .58 and .53, respectively, for the "similar" group, .45 and .48 for the "different" group, and .29 and .33 for the "random" group. Although only the .58 is significant, it seems very likely on the basis of prior and subsequent research, that the magnitude of the coefficients are at least in part a function of the small number of dyads in each group (with its resulting low statistical power). It may well be, however, that the low coefficients of the group of randomly paired dyads are not as much a result of the number of dyads as of an actual lack of congruence. Analyses of variance and the absolute differences between the average durations of pauses, switching pauses, and vocalizations of the dyad members indicate the average difference of the "random" group is almost four times as large as those of the other groups for pauses, almost three times as large for switching pauses, and about twice as large for vocalizations. The average intradyad differences of the "similar" and "different" groups are not significantly different for any of the parameters.

That the randomly paired dyads did not achieve congruence becomes intriguing when one considers that in most subsequent correlational studies the dialogue participants were almost always randomly paired but did achieve congruence. Somehow, the explicit knowledge of having been randomly paired seems to have made the difference. The results begin to suggest that not only are the silence durations of a conversationalist capable of being modified by those of his partner in the conversation, but that the extent of the modification is capable of reflecting their interpersonal perceptions.

One other finding of the study may be worth mentioning as a possible source of future research. The analyses of pauses and switching pauses yielded significant interactions among the groups and occasions. Whereas the average intradyad differences associated with the two parameters decreased from the first to the second conversation (occasion) for both the "different" and "random" groups, those for the "similar" group increased. Could it have been that the dyad members in the similar group discovered by the end of their first conversation that they were not as similar as they were led to expect, and that the discovery was responsible for the increased differences of their second conversation? What, to put it more generally, is the effect on congruence of a marked change in an individual's perception of his conversational partner? A postexperimental inquiry might have shed some light on the question, but none was conducted.

The relation between congruence and interpersonal perception was directly investigated in a study concerned with the time patterns of Chinese and Canadian conversations (Feldstein, Hennessy, & Bond, 1981). The participants were 11 pairs of Canadian and 11 pairs of Oriental men. The Canadian dyads engaged in two 8-minute English dialogues and the Oriental dyads in one 8-minute English and 8-minute Chinese dialogue.

Congruence coefficients computed for the Chinese and English conversations separately yielded estimates for pauses and switching pauses, respectively, of .42 and .78 for the Canadian conversations, .40 and .48 for the English conversations of the Orientals, and .78 and .79 for the Chinese conversations of the Orientals. It had been decided, in view of the results of the Welkowitz and Feldstein (1969) study described earlier, that a criterion level of .10 would be used to evaluate statistical significance. The p values of the coefficients .40 and .42 were .08 and .09, respectively. The p values of the remaining estimates were below .05.

After their conversations were completed, the participants were asked to describe their conversational partners in terms of a set of 24 bipolar, six-point adjective scales selected from a larger set developed by Goldberg (1976). In order to explore the relation between temporal congruence and interpersonal perception, it was necessary to derive scores that indexed the similarity (or dissimilarity) of the pauses and switching pauses of conversational partners and the similarity of their interpersonal perceptions. The absolute difference between the average pause durations and between the average switching-pause durations of each pair of partners was used to represent the degree to which their pause and switching-pause durations were similar. Obviously, the smaller the difference, the more similar were the durations. Also, the absolute difference between the ratings given to each other by a pair of conversational partners on a particular adjective scale was used to represent the extent to which the ratings were similar; again, the smaller the difference, the more similar were the ratings. The absolute differences between the ratings were summed over the 24 scales and the resulting total differences for the 11 Canadian and 11 Oriental pairs were correlated with their absolute pause and switching-pause differences. These comparisons yielded significant product-moment coefficients of .68 and .69, respectively, for the Canadian conversations and .59 and .69 for the English conversations of the Oriental partners. Comparisons of the scale difference with the pause and switching-pause differences from the Chinese conversations yielded rs of only .16 and .14, respectively.

It is consistent with the previous research that it was the conversational silences that became similar during the course of the conversations and that switching pauses, which can be considered *inter*personal silences, were matched better than were pauses, which are *intra*personal silences. It is also important for what was the primary purpose of the study that the Chinese interactions also exhibited temporal congruence. More important in terms of exploring the relations between congruence and interpersonal perception is the suggestive finding that those participants who achieved similar durations of silences tended also to perceive each other in similar ways! It is not clear, however, why this similarity of perception appeared to be reflected only by the similarity of silence durations in the English conversations. Perhaps the similarity of the silence durations of the Oriental speakers who talked together in Chinese was primarily a function of the structure of the language. It may be that the silences in Chinese are not especially susceptible to interpersonal factors that are not part of the language structure. An experimental test of the possibility is obviously needed.

Psychological differentiation.   It seems hardly likely that the occurrence of congruence is fully explained by conversationalists' perceptions of each other. If congruence can be viewed as reflecting susceptibility or sensitivity to interpersonal influence, then it may be related to personality charcteristics that presumably measure such sensitivity. The first study to pursue this possibility was the quartet study described earlier and referred to so often. The major purpose of the quartet study was not, in fact, to confirm the occurrence of congruence, but to investigate the relation of congruence to the personality characteristic that has been called *psychological differentiation* (Witkin, Dyk, Faterson, Goodenough, & Karp, 1962). Although the construct, *psychological differentiation,* is presumably quite similar to that labeled *field dependence* it is not clear that they are identical. Both, however, basically refer to the differential responsiveness of individuals to internal and external cues. More psychologically differentiated individuals have been found to be more responsive to internal and less responsive to external cues than are less differentiated individuals. (Psychological differentiation is inversely related to field dependence.) However, the justification for examining the relation between psychological differentiation and congruence is that a host of studies (e.g., Bieri, Bradburn, & Galinsky, 1958; Crutchfield, Woodworth, & Albrecht, 1958; Fitzgibbons, Goldberger, & Eagle, 1965; Konstadt & Forman, 1965; Wallach, Kogan, & Burt, 1967) have shown that less psychologically differentiated persons are the more responsive to, interested in, and aware of others in interpersonal contacts, and are more likely to be influenced by others. The general hypothesis of the quartet study was that there is an inverse relationship between the degrees of psychological differentiation of participants in dialogues and the extent to which their dialogues exhibit temporal congruence.

Degree of psychological differentiation was estimated by the individual form of the Embedded Figures Test (Witkin, 1950), or EFT.[8] The score used to index the degree of congruence that occurred in a dialogue was the absolute difference between the average parameter duration of one conversational participant and that of her conversational partner. Thus, the higher the score (that is, the greater the difference), the less the congruence. Such *congruence scores* were obtained for the parameters of pauses and switching pauses. Since the durations of the participants' vocalizations tended not to become congruent during the course of a conversation, the relation of their differences to psychological differentiation was not investigated. The general hypothesis was tested in terms of the congruence of pauses and switching pauses by means of separate hierarchical multiple regression analyses in which the order of the entering independent variables was specified in advance (Cohen & Cohen, 1975). The independent variables (in the order in which they entered the regression equation) were the EFT scores of the subjects, the EFT scores of their conversational partners, and the products of the two sets of scores. By dint of their position in the equation, the product scores indexed the interaction of the subjects' and partners' scores.

In effect, the results of the analyses supported the hypothesis, although not quite in the way anticipated. One analysis indicated that the degrees of psychological differentiation of the subjects and of their partners separately and significantly affected the congruence of their pauses such that the greater the differentiation of the subject or her partner, the less similar did their pause

---

[8]Inasmuch as Witkin and his associates (Witkin *et al.*, 1962) found that the correlation of the EFT with the Block Design subtest of the WAIS yielded an *r* of .80, the EFT scores of the subjects in the quartet study were statistically adjusted for the subjects' performance of the BD subtest. That is, the subjects' BD scores were covaried out of their EFT scores.

durations become. Presumably, then, dyads in which both participants are highly differentiated achieve less pause congruence in their conversations than do dyads in which only one of the participants is highly differentiated, and considerably less pause congruence than do dyads in which neither of the participants is highly differentiated. The other analysis, however, indicated that only the interaction of the subjects' and partners' EFT scores was effectively related to the congruence of their switching pauses. In other words, the level of psychological differentiation of one or the other conversational participant was not, in itself, sufficient to influence the extent to which their interaction achieved congruence. Instead, the congruence they achieved depended upon the joint effect of both their levels of differentiation. Specifically, the relation was such that although the degree of congruence achieved by the more differentiated subjects and their partners was not markedly affected by their partners' level of differentiation, the less differentiated subjects achieved a greater degree of congruence with partners who were less differentiated.

In view of the findings of others that persons who are more sensitive to interpersonal cues tend to be less psychologically differentiated, the relation of the construct to congruence makes sense. It also makes sense that the congruence of switching pauses is related only to configurations of *both* participants' levels of differentiation since switching pauses are primarily *inter*personal silences whereas pauses are primarily *intra*personal silences. The results, then, do suggest that temporal congruence is more likely to occur during the conversations of persons who are interpersonally responsive, or sensitive, than during the conversations of persons who are not. But is it simply the greater awareness of interpersonal cues that makes for congruence? Might it be that other interpersonal dynamics either enhance the effectiveness of such awareness in bringing about congruence or independently contribute to its occurrence? At the present time, there are no proper answers to these questions, although a tentative indication, again from the quartet study, suggests that they may be worth investigating.

Social contact. At the end of their participation in the quartet study, the subjects were asked to rate each of their three conversational partners on a seven-point scale which had to do with whether or not they liked the contact they had with their partners. The seven statements of the scale proceeded from "I disliked the contact with her very much." to "I enjoyed the contact with her very much." The scales provided four scores for each subject. Three of the scores indicated the degree to which she enjoyed her contact with each of her partners and were called *contact enjoyment* scores. The fourth, a *general contact enjoyment* score, was the sum of the three contact enjoyment scores.

The analyses of the scores revealed that the extent to which the average switching pause durations of the conversational participants became similar depended, in part, upon the interaction of their contact enjoyment scores. It should be noted that almost all the participants tended to enjoy their contacts with their partners. However, those participants who expressed greater enjoyment achieved congruence with partners who expressed greated enjoyment than with partners who expressed less enjoyment. The degrees of congruence achieved by the dialogues of those who tended to enjoy their contacts less were not materially affected by the extent of enjoyment claimed by their partners. Interestingly, the levels of psychological differentiation of the subjects were not related to the extent to which they claimed to enjoy their contact with each of their partners, although they were positively related to the general levels of enjoyment they expressed. Apparently, psychological differentiation and contact enjoyment as measured in the quartet study independently contribute to the occurrence of switching pause congruence. Can the same be said of psychological differentiation and interpersonal perception? Another pilot study was conducted (Welkowitz & Feldstein, 1970) to examine the relation of *perceived* differences and similarities of personality to the congruence of pauses and switching pauses after *actual* differences and similarities of psychological differentiation are taken into account. The design of the study replicated that of the Welkowitz and Feldstein (1969) study described earlier. However, the battery of personality tests included the individual form of the EFT. In addition, the "similar," "different," and "random" groups each had 20 dyads. Finally, each dyad met for only two 60-min. conversations spaced one week apart. Multiple regression analyses were performed in which the levels of psychological differentiation of the subjects and their conversational partners (and the product scores for the interaction) were entered into equations prior to entering the variables that assessed the contributions to pause and switching pause congruence of the three groups.

Coefficients of congruence were computed and found to be significant for the pauses and switching pauses of the "similar" and "different" groups only. No significant relations, however, were found between the levels of psychological differentiation of the participants and either pause or switching pause congruence. There were much larger differences (congruence scores) between the average pause and switching pause duration of conversational participants in the "random" group than in the other two groups and those of the "different" group were larger than those of the "similar" group. The vocalization congruence scores of the "random" group were larger than those of the similar group only. As with the earlier study, the results should be viewed as no more than suggestive. Although, for example, there were both male and female dyads, the analyses did not take gender into account. Could it be that differences between the levels of psychological differentiation of males and females were responsible for the failure to find a relationship between psychological differentiation and the congruence scores?

Social desirability. A correlational study published by Natale (1975a) attempted to explore the relation between social desirability and the congruence of pauses and switching pauses. Marlowe and Crowne (1960) originally thought that their Social Desirability Scale measured a need for social approval, which they considered indicative of a readiness to engage in socially conforming behavior and responsiveness to social influence. Natale, suggesting that congruence can be viewed as an instance of conforming behavior, reasoned that persons who score high on the Social Desirability Scale contribute more to the occurrence of congruence than those who score low.

The subjects were college students who were assembled into eight male and five female dyads each of which was asked to engage in two half-hour dialogues scheduled a week apart. To test the expectation of the study, the social desirability scores of the participants were subjected to multiple regression analyses in which the congruence scores of pauses and switching pauses were entered as the dependent variables. The results of the analyses seem[9] to support the expectation only with respect to the congruence of switching pauses and only for the second occasion on which the participants conversed. As noted earlier, switching pauses are interpersonal silences that might be expected to be more sensitive to interpersonal processes than pauses. The results make sense whether the Marlow-Crowne estimate of social desirability is viewed as indexing a need for social approval or a need for avoiding feelings of rejection (Crowne & Marlowe, 1964) if the latter need makes for socially compliant behavior. The results are seemingly at variance, however, with an interpretation of the estimate as reflecting a defensiveness that, as it increases, is expressed in the avoidance of interpersonal contact (Jacobson & Ford, 1966; Jacobson, Berger, & Millham, 1970). It may well be, of course, that individuals whose defensiveness leads them to ordinarily avoid interpersonal situations are compliant when they find themselves within the context of such situations. However complex the psychodynamic correlates of high

---

[9]Natale reports what may be considered a significant main effect that indexes the relation between the subjects' social desirability and the congruence scores for switching pauses. However, the relationship is apparently modified by an interaction of the social desirability of the subjects with that of their conversational partners, although it is not clear from the degrees of freedom associated with the *F* ratio he reports for the interaction effect, that Natale entered the partners' social desirability scores as a variable in the regression equation. Assuming, however, that he did (and in the proper order), he misinterprets the meaning of the interaction effect. It seems likely, from the information given, that the interaction indicates that, compared to subjects with low social desirability scores, those with high scores achieved much more congruence with partners who had high social desirability scores than with partners who had low scores.

scores on the Marlow-Crowne Scale may be, such scores do appear to be positively associated with the congruence of switching pause durations and vocal intensity (Natale, 1975b).

Interpersonal warmth.   The greater sensitivity of switching pauses to interpersonal processes emerged in still another study conducted by Welkowitz and Kuc (1973). One of the aims of the study was to examine the relation of temporal congruence to the extent to which conversational participants rate each other as "warm," "genuine," and "empathic" *and* the extent to which independent observers so rate them. Extrapolating from the position that such qualities enhance effectiveness and communication within therapeutic dyads (e.g., Rogers, 1958, 1961; Truax & Carkhuff, 1967), the authors suggest that the same qualities should make for mutual satisfaction in ordinary impersonal exchanges, and they note that temporal congruence was found to be related to mutual satisfaction (Marcus *et al.,* 1970).

College students were assembled into 16 male and 16 female dyads and the members of each dyad were asked to talk to each other about whatever interested them. The dyads met once for a 45-min. conversation. Following their conversations the participants were requested to complete a number of scales which included the rating of their conversational partners on items (Truax & Carkhuff, 1967) related to empathy, warmth and genuineness as defined by Rogers (1961). The same items were used by three independent observers who rated each participant after listening to the recorded conversations.

Appropriate multiple regression equations were used to evaluate the relations between the ratings and temporal congruence. In addition, the ratings made by the dyad members about each other were compared with those made by the independent observers and found to be unrelated. The only significant result of the regression analyses that is of interest here indicates that the participants who received higher ratings of warmth *from the independent observers* contributed more to the congruence of switching pauses than did those who received lower ratings.

One of the questions raised by the results is why congruence was not related to the participants' rating of each other. Earlier exploratons (Welkowitz & Feldstein, 1969, 1970) suggest that congruence is, in part at least, a function of interpersonal perception, although the perception was global and experimentally induced. In this study, the participants had to formulate their own perceptions of each other and do so in terms of specific characteristics. However, their perceptions were solicited *after* the conversations had taken place and it may very well be that it was the inquiry that made the participants aware of their impressions of each other. Is it possible that interpersonal perceptions affect the time patterns of a conversation only if the participants are aware of them?

Interpersonal relations. It might be thought that two individuals who share, or believe that they share, a relationship would certainly accommodate to each other in their interactions to a greater extent than would interacting individuals who do not know each other. This expectation was embodied in a study conducted by Crown (1984), the intent of which was to examine interpersonal accommodation within the conversational interactions of pairs who liked each other, pairs who disliked each other, and pairs who were not acquainted with each other. Although the accommodative behavior that Crown investigated was the temporal pacing of both gazes and speech, it is the latter that is of primary concern here. It should be noted, however, that one of the major goals of the study was to integrate two important channels of nonverbal communication: vision and voice.

The participants in the study were 76 women who were all residents of women's dormitories at the Univeresity of Delaware. They were selected from a much larger group, each member of whom completed a sociogram about all the other women who resided on her floor. The sociogram was concerned with the extensiveness and quality of her interrelationship with each of those other women and the pairings described earlier were made on the basis of the sociogram ratings. Of the 38 pairs, 12 were of participants who liked each other, 13 were of those who disliked each other, and 13 were of participants who were unaquainted with each other. The members of each pair were simply asked to talk with each other for 30 minutes.

For the vocal behavior of the pairs, the study analyzed only pauses, switching pauses, and vocalizations in terms of their average duration and proportion of occurrence for each minute of an interacton. Thus, for each 30-minute interaction, the analysis yielded 30 pairs of durations and 30 pairs of proportions per parameter. The 30 pairs of durations and proportions were then subjected to separate time-series regression analyses (which are discussed in some detail later). These analyses yielded estimates of interpersonal accommodation for each participant in the study. The durations of the temporal parameters yielded significant estimates for 21 of the 76 participants. In addition, there was a nonartifactual, marked similarity between the estimates of dyad members, indicating that the accommodation tended to be mutual for the majority of dyads. The same similarity characterized those estimates derived from the proportions of the temporal parameters. Moreover, those estimates were significant for 68 of the 76 participants!

Two multivariate analyses of variance were used to compare the estimates of the "like," "dislike," and "unacquainted" groups: One was used for the estimates derived from the durations and the other for the estimates derived from the proportions. The former yielded a multivariate F ratio that was nonsignificant. The latter yielded a significant multivariate F but, of the step-down unvariate F ratios, only that for pause accommodation was significant. Surprisingly, those dyad members who were not acquainted with each other and those who disliked each other achieved greater accommodation in their interactions with each other than did those dyad members who liked each other. This same pattern of results characterized the gaze behaviors of the dyad members and their combined gaze and vocal behaviors.

An even more interesting finding was the interaction obtained between the degree of pause accommodation of the three groups and the scores of a factor derived from the dyad members' postinteractional impressions of each other. Their impressions were obtained in terms of a set of 20 ten-point adjective scales, and the adjectives that defined the factor involved in the interaction effect were self-assured, sensitive, courteous, intelligent, liberal, spontaneous, appealing, friendly, responsive, and attractive. The interaction effect was such that the relation between degree of pause accommodation of the factor scores was positive for the unacquainted group and negative for the "like" group. In other words, those dyad members in the unacquainted group who viewed their conversational partners more positively (i.e., rated them higher on the factor) tended to accommodate *more* than those members who viewed their partners less positively. On the other hand, among those dyads in which the members liked each other, those participants who rated their partners more positively accommodated *less* than the participants whose impressions of their partners were less positive.

Crown points out that the results are at variance with her initial expectation and she interprets the findings in terms of the sequential functional model proposed by Patterson (1982). The model is described to some extent later in this chapter and to a much greater extent in Chapter 11 of this book. Suffice it here to say that Crown suggests that the results are more readily understandable if the temporal patterning of the voice and gaze behaviors in the dyadic interactions of her study are considered to have served a regulatory function intended to perpetuate the conversations and maintain the comfort of the participants. From such a perspective, it does not seem especially odd that conversationalists who like each other do not need to accommodate to each other very much to continue to interact comfortably. Nor would it be surprising to find that the more positive were their evaluations of each other, the less they felt the need to accommodate. On the other hand, according to Crown (1984):

> People who do not like each other or do not know each other are not, under ordinary circumstances, likely to engage in interactions. However, when they are constrained to do so, as they were in the prsent study, it seems reasonable to assume that they will engage in whatever behaviors keep the interaction going and comfortable. It might be expected, therefore, that both types of interactions would exhibit greater accommodation than that achieved by interactants who like each other. (p. 80)

It might also be expected that, in such types of interactions, those participants who evaluate their partners more positively employ more accommodative behaviors, particularly if they were previously acquainted.

The Crown study was the first major effort to assess the influence of the affective tone of a dyadic relationship upon congruence, or interpersonal accommodation, in which the latter is measured by a time-series regression analysis per dyad. That the results of the study appear to be "explained" rather nicely by Patterson's theory is interesting in its implications for the phenomenon of temporal accommodation and for the theory. It should be clear, however, that the "explanation" is post hoc, and that the study was not intended as a test of the Patterson theory. An important implication of the results for future investigations of interpersonal accommodation derives from the study's use of proportions of time rather than average durations. The use of proportions was suggested by the literature concerning visual attention (see Chapter 11) and they appear, in the Crown study, to reflect the occurrence of accommodation more sensitively than do average durations of the temporal behaviors.

Socialization level. At the very least, the occurrence of congruence implies that the participants in the dialogues have heard each other It might be argued, however, that its occurrence is a consequence not simply of the participants having heard each other, but also of their ability to attend to each other, to take each other's contribution into account. What Piaget (1955) in his discussion of children's language, calls *socialized* speech, can be viewed as an aspect of this ability. *Socialized* speech, in contrast to *egocentric* speech, indicates that the child is capable of taking his listener into account to the extent of recognizing his point of view and engaging in an exchange of ideas. Note that the difference between the two types of speech is in terms of their semantic content. Welkowitz, Cariffe, and Feldstein (1976) suggest that the distinction can also be related to temporal congruence. They assert that the distinction made by Piaget reflects a difference in degree of socialization, and they posit that the emergence of congruence in children's conversation parallels the progression from an egocentric to a sociocentric orientation. Thus, they hypothesize that for children the occurrence of congruence is positively related to age.

Two groups of children participated in the experiment. Each consisted of 10 same-gender dyads. The younger group involved children whose ages ranged from 5.4 to 6.1 years, the older children whose ages ranged from 6.4 to 7.2 years. Each pair of children met on two occasions, spaced one week apart, and on each occasion, engaged in a 20-min. dialogue.

The average durations of the children's pauses were found to be both consistent during the course of each conversation and stable from one conversation to the other. Interestingly, the consistency of the younger group increased significantly from the first to the second conversation. The average durations of switching pauses were consistent only for the older group on the first occasion but for both groups on the second occasion. On the other hand, it was only the switching pause durations that yielded significant congruence coefficients for both groups on both occasions. The younger group did not achieve pause congruence on either occasion.

That the pause durations of the younger group were not susceptible to interpersonal influence provides partial support for the hypothesis that the emergence of congruence in children's conversations is a function of age. The findings also suggest that switching pause durations reflect interpersonal influence earier than do pause durations. It is apparent, however, that to test more adequately the general notion that the occurrence of congruence is related to level of socialization rquires a look at the verbal interactions of children younger than those who took part in this study, and, more importantly perhaps, a direct comparison of the occurrence of congruence in children's dialogues with the semantic content of the dialogues classified in terms of the Piagetian categories. Even more telling would be a comparison of the occurrence of congruence with estimates of the children's levels of socialization, although it is not at all clear how the latter might be formulated.

Garvey and BenDebba (1974) assembled middle-class children between the ages of about 3.5 and 5.7 years into 12 triads and had each child talk to each other member of this triad. Three of the resulting dyads were male, nine were female, and 24 were mixed. The children in the dyads were previously acquainted with each other.

The authors examined the relation of the ages of the children to the numbers of utterances they produced within a 5-min. period and to their average numbers of words per utterance. Of interest is the finding that the sex of the dyad was not related to either variable. Of greater interest are the findings that (1) a comparison of the numbers of utterances produced by the members of the dyads yielded a significant intraclass (congruence) coefficient, and (2) the absolute differences between the numbers of utterances produced by the dyad members are significantly and negatively related to their ages. The latter finding suggests that older children more closely match the frequencies of their utterances to those of their conversational partners than do younger children.

One problematical aspect of the study is that its definition of an "utterance" makes it an ambiguous unit. An utterance is considered to be any segment of the speech of one person that is bounded on each end by *either* the speech of another person or a silence of one or more seconds. Thus, an utterance is a speech sound, or a sequence of speech sounds separated by one or more silences each of less than one second duration, embedded in one of four possible boundary configurations. The use of another person's speech as a boundary condition is difficult to argue with. But using a duration of 1 sec. as the criterion that distinguishes between boundary and nonboundary silences seems to imply that silences of 1 sec. or more have correlates and/or functions that differ from those of briefer silences. The more general implication is that there are "long" and "short" silences that reflect different states and/or processes. The possibility has been explored by Siegman and his associates (Siegman, Chapter 8). They, however, have used silences of 2 or more seconds as their "long" silences. On the other hand, it may be recalled from the brief review presented earlier, that Matarazzo and his colleagues also use silence as an utterance boundary. They call such silences *initiative time latencies,* and report (Matarazzo & Wiens, 1972, p. 42) that their durations tend to range between 1 and 2 sec. Presumably, however, it is not the duration of the latencies that defines them but semantic (and perhaps paralinguistic) characteristics of the surrounding utterances. In any case, given the seemingly arbitrary duration of the silences that Garvey and BenDebba use to help define an utterance unit, it is difficult not to consider the unit an at least partially arbitrary segment.

The study cannot be directly compared with that reported by Welkowitz *et al.* (1976). The results of the two studies, however, make more credible the notion that the extent to which children match the temporal patterns of each other's speech in their interactions is related to their levels of socialization.

Some Issues of Concern

At least two further issues about congruence merit discussion. One has to do with its measurement and the other with its mechanism. A number of investigators are currently exploring the relative utility of several data-analytic procedures for assessing the achievement of congruence. The mechanism or mechanisms that make for the matching of time patterns are still unknown, although a number of theories that have been proposed very recently are worth considering.

Measurement issues and efforts.   In most of the studies reviewed previously, the occurrence of congruence was indexed by an intraclass correlation coefficient. The coefficient is computed for a group of dyads and says little about the extent to which each dyad has achieved congruence. A somewhat more direct tack has been taken by Natale (1975b) in his investigation of vocal intensity. The first experiment he reports examined the effect of systematic changes in the vocal intensity level of an interviewer upon the average intensity level of not only a group of interviewees but each of the interviewees in the group. He found a significant and positive relation between the vocal intensity level of the interviewer and that of 17 of the 21 interviewees. Similar investigations involving free dialogues and the analyses of other aspects of the temporal parameters would be valuable.

The notion that dyads "achieve" congruence implies, in part, that the parameter values of their members not only become increasingly similar during the course of a conversation, but that they become more similar to each other than to the values of other dyads. These kinds of similarity are indexed by the intraclass correlation coefficient. Part of the implication, then, is that the parameters values of the participant in conversations are, at the start of the conversations, different from and relatively unrelated to those of their partners. But what are the parameter values of participants who have not yet begun to converse? They can be the parameter values obtained by the participants in previous conversations with other persons. Marcus *et al.* (1970) used such parameter values to examine the notion that the parameter values of persons who have not yet begun their first conversations tend not to exhibit the similarities indexed by a significant congruence coefficient. The average durations of the pauses, switching pauses, and vocalizations obtained by the 24 women who participated in the quartet study were assembled into 36 random pairs for each of the eight occasions. That is, the average parameter durations obtained by each participant were randomly paired with those of three other participants such that none of the pairs were drawn from persons who had actually conversed together. Moreover, the random pairs were different in the different occasions.

The reason for replicating the design of the original study (with regard to the number of pairs per occasion) was to make possible at least an inspectional comparison of the congruence coefficients yielded by the randomly paired durations with those by the appropriately paired durations. Intraclass analyses of the random pairs yielded coefficients (averaged over the eight occasions) of $-.14$ for pauses, $-.03$ for switching pauses, and $-.04$ for vocalizations. None of the coefficients on any of the occasions was significant; those for pauses and switching pauses ranged from $-.25$ to $.15$. Recall that the average congruence coefficients for pauses, switching pauses, and vocalizations obtained in the original study were $.43$, $.62$, and $.08$, respectively. Thus, the results seem to provide some indirect evidence in support of the notion.

Perhaps more direct evidence could be obtained by dividing dialogues into several segments, calculating for each dyad a congruence score per segment, and computing a trend analysis of the congruence scores from the first to last segment. Such a procedure has been used to study the *convergence* of parameter values over successive conversations by the same dyads (Welkowitz & Feldstein, 1969). One should expect a general decrease in congruence scores (that is, an increase in congruence) from the first to last segment. The shape of the trend may even help to answer the question — raised by the notion of achieving congruence — of whether there is a particular point in time at which congruence occurs in conversations. One difficulty is raised by the possibility that both participants begin with durations that are relatively similar. Another difficulty with the procedure is deciding what ought to be the duration of the segments. Should each one be 5 min., 10, 15? Jaffe and Breskin (1970) assert that 5-min. speech samples seem to characterize the temporal parameters reliably, but should reliability be the sole basis for such a decision? Should the duration of the segments vary according to the type of dialogues that are to be examined? It is not clear, for example, that the duration of the speech sample needed for reliable estimates of the parametesr is independent of the type of dialogue being examined. One probably useful consideration is that the segments be long enough to allow for a trend analysis of the segment means of individual dyads.

It is conceivable, of course, that dialogues can be divided into segments that consist, for instance, of only a single turn. The analysis of this kind of moment-to-moment tracking involves a correlation of the turn durations of one participant in a dyad with those of the other. Such was the strategy used in the studies of Ray and Webb (1966) and Feldstein (1968). Neither study found evidence of moment-to-moment influence. Recently, however, Cappella and Planalp (1981) used a similar but more sophisticated procedure to measure such influence. The procedure is known as time-series regression (TSR) analysis that, in the type of research of concern here, is essentially a method of comparing the sequence of one person's moment-to-moment behavior with that of another person after controlling for the effect of each person's prior behavior on his present behavior.

Employing time-series regression procedures, Cappella and Planalp analyzed twelve 20-minute conversations in terms of a continuous turn-by-turn version and a categorical probability version. In the first version, the turn was the unit of measurement such that the vocalizations, pauses, and switching pauses per turn of each speaker were compared with those of his (or her) conversational partner. In the second version, each conversation was divided into ten 2-minute segments and, for each segment of each speaker, the probabilities of talking, listening, both talking, and both silent were computed. These parameters and others derived from them were then used as variables in separate regression equations that compared conversational partners with each other in terms of the parameters. The results of these analyses indicated that the partners tended to match the durations of their switching pauses, their probabilities of continuing to speak simultaneously, and their probabilities of ending mutual silences.

Neither the study nor the procedure is without problems. Relatively speaking, for instance, turns are so short an event that their use in a time-series regression analysis was (and is) likely to introduce a large proportion of random variance. The use of 2-minute probabilities on the other hand, yielded too few observations (10 pairs for each 20-minute dialogue) for an adequate analysis of the 12 dialogues. The observations of the 12 dialogues were, therefore, concatenated to yield 120 pairs of observations (two observations per pair of speakers) for the analysis of each variable. The results of such concatenated sequences can quite appropriately be generalized to the individual dialogues that comprise the sequences, although with somewhat less confidence than could separate analyses of the individual dialogues. Moreover, differences among the dialogues in the direction of influence are lost. Nevertheless, given a sufficiently long conversation or, possibly, probabilities based upon shorter time units, time-series regression procedures are particularly suited to the analysis of interspeaker influence in single dialogues.

Crown and Feldstein (1981) reported a constructive replication of the Cappella and Planalp study that used 14 dialogues, each of which was 60 minutes long. The time unit for their analyses was 1 minute and their variables, computed per minute, were the averages and proportionality constants of pauses, switching pauses, and vocalizations. The participants were males and females who had been assembled into same-gender pairs. Each dialogue was analyzed separately in terms of each of the three variables (pauses, switching pauses, and vocalizations). The analyses used a time lag of one step to remove autocorrelational effects; the issue of such effects are discussed shortly. Although it was not reported, it might be noted that a reanalysis of the first 30 minutes of each dialogue yielded the same results as those obtained from the full 60-minute analyses.

Of the 28 participants in the study, 19 obtained significant regression coefficients (used as indices of interspeaker influence or interpersonal accommodation), indicating that the durations or probabilities of their pauses, switching pauses, or vocalizations converged with, or diverged from, those of their partners. The accommodation implied by the coefficients was in the direction of convergence for the silences of the dialogues and of divergence for the vocalizations.

Essentially, the results of the Crown and Feldstein study replicated those of the Cappella and Planalp investigation and helped to confirm the usefulness of time-series regression analysis as a technique for examining interpersonal accommodation. The subsequent study by Crown (1984), described earlier, offers further evidence in support of the technique but suggests that the proportion of time that an individual engages in a particular vocal behavior may provide a measure of that behavior that more adequately reflects accommodation than the average duration of that behavior.

There are good reasons why time-series regression analysis promises to be a very useful procedure for measuring congruence, or interspeaker influence. It is potentially capable of providing not only an analysis of individual dialogues, but also an estimate of the degree to which each participant in the dialogue was influenced by his or her partner. Moreover, the algebraic sign of a participant's estimate indicates whether his or her behavior has *converged* with that of the other participant (i.e., whether the behavior of the two participants has become similar), or whether it has *diverged* from that of the other participant (i.e., whether their behaviors have become less similar or more dissimilar). Both types of behavior represent accommodative strategies. An estimate that is not statistically significant presumably reflects a lack of evidence that accommodation, or interspeaker influence, has occurred.

However, the application of time-series regression analysis to the measurement of interspeaker influence involves a number of problems, some of which are discussed briefly by Cappella and Planalp (1981). The primary ones concern the choice of which class of regression models to use and of which particular model within that class. Another has to do with the need to remove, from the relation of the behaviors of the two persons, the influence of each one's past behavior upon his or her present behavior. Such self-influence are called *autocorrelational effects.* The problem is to determine the optimal number of prior steps in time — or, put another way, the optimal time lag — needed to remove sizeable autocorrelational effects. (The question of what are "sizeable" effects is also problematical.) The optimal number of steps is probably best determined empirically at present, although it might also be determined theoretically under various assumptions (Gottman, 1981; Ostrom, 1978). Still another issue is concerned with discovering the best estimate of interspeaker influence that can be derived from the time-series regression equation. Cappella and Planalp used the regression coefficient as their index of "self" and "other" influence but did not specify whether the coefficient they used was raw or standardized. Crown and Feldstein (1981) used raw regression coefficients as their indices. Crown (1984) then found that the standardized partial regression coefficient provides a more adequate estimate of interpersonal accommodation than does the raw coefficient. It is possible that another term yielded by the solution of the equation can provide an even more useful estimate; the issue warrants further inquiry.

Mechanisms of temporal matching.   Until recently, very few extensive efforts had been made to account for the matching of time patterns in conversational interactions. Webb (1972) noted the inadequacies of the reinforcement paradigm offered by Matarazzo (1965) and the more recent suggestions by Matarazzo and Wiens (1967) that temporal synchrony may be viewed as an outcome of "modeling" (Bandura, 1965) on the parts of one or both participants. His preference is for an activation-level approach (Fiske & Maddi, 1961) which assumes that organisms have characteristic levels of activity that respond in kind to the varying impacts of both interpersonal and impersonal stimuli. Since it is difficult to believe that the physiological activity level of an organism does not play some role in all or most of its interactions with its environment, the appeal of the model is understandable. However, it views the occurrence of interpersonal congruence as the outcome of a more or less automatic response of each individual to the impact of the particular aspect of the other individual's behavior that is being matched. Such a position seems too simplistic to be useful.

Natale (1975b) claimed that synchronous behavior can be explained by a "communication model" he adopted from Lane and Tranel (1971). The latter authors theorized that the autoregulation of vocal intensity in the direction of matching the vocal intensity level of another voice represents a speaker's attempt to achieve or maintain intelligibility. Natale speculated that the model accounts equally well for the congruence of the temporal aspects of verbal interaction, although his argument in support of the assertion is not entirely convincing. Nonetheless, the model is promising and deserves serious investigation. Its implications are perhaps more complex than is immediately apparent.

One implication of the model is that a speaker anticipates (although without necessarily being aware of it) that a failure on his part to match the temporal and/or intensity patterns of the speech of his conversational partner will render his message less intelligible. What is the basis for such an expectation? Is it actually likely that the intelligibility of a verbal exchange is noticeably enhanced by the presence or diminished by the absence of congruence? That one participant in a dialogue speaks loudly, for example, and the other speaks softly does not, at first glance, seem likely to affect the intelligibility of either speaker's message unless both talk at the same time. If the pauses of one speaker are very long and those of the other quite short, will they fail to understand each other adequately? Or fully?

In point of fact, no reliable data are available that could help answer such questions. It seems possible that noncongruous interactions are less communicative than they might be, or that their messages are in some way distorted. It is conceivable, for example, that noncongruent patterns elicit attitudes and/or affective responses that interfere with message reception. Or it may be that congruence (or the lack of it) serves as a form of metacommunication, especially perhaps in those cases in which the verbal message is not the *raison d'etre* of the exchange. And the metacommunication may be as much concerned with the sustaining of a conversation as with the maintaining of its intelligibility. All of these possibilities are empirically testable.

Beginning in the early 1970s, Giles and his colleagues (e.g., Bourhis, Giles, & Lambert, 1975; Giles, 1973, 1977, 1977b, 1980; Giles & Powesland, 1975; Giles & Smith, 1979; Giles, Taylor, & Bourhis, 1973) developed a theory of "speech accommodation." It was originally concerned with speech accent but was soon broadened to encompass a host of linguistic and acoustic features that it characterizes as "speech style." The theory attempts to account for speech *convergence* and *divergence*. Convergence refers to what has here been called congruence, pattern matching, synchrony, etc. Divergence refers to the finding that in certain circumstances individuals deliberately strive to maintain their own speech styles as distinct from the styles of those with whom they ar interacting. The original propositions of the theory hold that convergence reflects the need or desire of individuals and groups for social identification and/or integration, whereas divergence is a strategy used by individuals and groups to affirm their distinctiveness from others. The propositions are derived from the notion that interpersonal attraction is positively related to interpersonal similarity (e.g., Bishop, 1979; Byrne, 1969; Lott & Lott, 1965; Newcomb, 1961; Tedeschi, 1974) and from the notion that, in certain situations, individuals regard each other in terms of their group affiliations rather than in terms of their individual characteristics (e.g., Tajfel, 1974, 1979; Tajfel & Turner, 1978; Turner, 1975). However, in a chapter that has appeared recently, Thakerar, Giles, and Cheshire (1982) present a reformulation of the theory and its propositions. The reformulation is based upon three conclusions drawn from the body of research reviewed by the chapter. One is that *linguistic* and *psychological* convergence and divergence are independent of each other. Linguistic convergence and divergence can be divided into *objective* and *subjective* convergence and divergence. Objective convergence and divergence refer to speakers' actual speech behavior, whereas subjective convergence and divergence refer to whether speakers think they are (or were) converging or diverging linguistically. Psychological convergence and divergence apparently refer to whether speakers think, or believe, that they are "integrating with" or "differentiating from" those with whom they interact.

The second conclusion is that speakers are not necessarily aware of their linguistic convergence or divergence. Thirdly, subjective linguistic convergence, when it implies psychological convergence, serves different functions for different speakers. Following these conclusions, the authors present six reformulated propositions that take into account: (a) the expectations of the interacting speakers about each other's characteristic speech patterns; (b) the anticipated costs and rewards of linguistic convergence and divergence in terms of social approval, communicational efficiency, and group identification; (c) the role of personality and environmental factors as well as of the breadth of speakers' repertoires in determining the extent of subjective linguistic convergence and divergence; and (d) the factors that make for positive and negative evaluations of objective linguistic convergence and divergence. The propositions do not radically alter the original assumptions of the theory. Instead, they represent changes suggested by empirical research findings and recognition of a cognitive component in the processes of speech accommodation that is presumably implied by the research findings.

The theory is an important effort to understand behaviors that most investigators in the area have observed to occur in each of the verbal and vocal channels of speech. The orientation of the theory is distinctly social psychological in its primary concern with social motives and attributions. The theory has not yet been extended to encompass the vocal–verbal interactions of children (Garvey & BenDebba, 1974; Welkowitz, Cariffe, & Feldstein, 1976) or of infants and mothers (e.g., Beebe, Stern, & Jaffe, 1979; Stern, 1974, 1977; Stern, Jaffe, Beebe, & Bennett, 1975), but it seems likely that it could be so extended with, perhaps, some revision of its motivational explanation. The usefulness of the theory is a function of not only its ability to account for the type of temporal matching with which this chapter is primarily concerned, but also its ability to generate hypotheses that can be and have been empirically tested.

A second major theory was proposed recently by Cappella and Greene (1982). The theory offers a "discrepancy-arousal-affect explanation" of the occurrence of interspeaker influence in expressive behavior. *Expressive behavior* is meant to include all the objective aspects of speech and the voice that have been discussed here as well as smiling, laughter, gaze and proxemic behavior, body position, touch, orientation, and facial displays. The authors also include verbal intimacy. Such behaviors, singly or in combination, are viewed as an indication of involvement or responsiveness. *Expectation* is presumed to be a "cognitive representation" held by each speaker of the degree of involvement of the speaker with whom he or she interacts. Within the context of a dyad, in other words, expectation refers to the anticipation, on the part of each speaker, about the amount of expressive activity in which the other speaker will engage. It is assumed that these expectations are formed by experience with a particular speaker, personal preferences, and the social norms of particular situations. *Discrepancy* refers to the difference between the expected and actual amounts of expressive activity. *Arousal* is defined as a physiological response of the autonomic nervous system that may be measured in terms of a variety of psychophysiological indices. Finally, *affect* refers to the experiencing, by each speaker, of pleasant (positive) or aversive (negative) feelings during an interaction.

The theory most directly represents a modification and generalization of the discrepancy-arousal model proposed by Stern (1974) to account for the interactive facial displays and gaze patterns of infants and mothers. The model assumes that increasing arousal is associated with a moderate to excessive increase in the discrepancy between a mother's actual behavior and her infant's expectations about her behavior. It also assumes that moderate arousal is pleasurable and excessive arousal is unpleasant. This relation, then, between discrepancy — believed to be cognitively determined — and affect is mediated by psychological excitation.

However, the Cappella and Greene theory also has its roots in the "arousal-labeling" model presented by Patterson in 1976. The model asserts that changes in affiliative, or intimacy, behaviors on the part of one person in an interaction induce changes in arousal on the part of the other person in the interaction. These changes in arousal are then labeled by the person experiencing them as positive or negative, depending on the context of the interaction, the type of relationship between the participants, and the cognitive cues afforded by the situation (Schachter & Singer, 1962). Positively labeled arousal makes for the reciprocation of affiliation, or intimacy, whereas negatively labeled arousal results in those compensatory behaviors needed to restore the equilibrium level of affiliation that is assumed to have existed previously (Argyle & Cook, 1976; Argyle & Dean, 1965).

In describing their theory, Cappella and Greene (1982) asserted, essentially, that Patterson's model overemphasizes the role of labeling in convergent and divergent behavior and underemphasizes the importance of arousal. They also suggested that the model needs to be extended, not only to include what they called "behaviors indicative of generalized involvement" rather than "affiliative" behaviors alone, but also to encompass infant–adult as well as adult–adult interactions. Ellsworth (1977) also raised questions about the theory and, finally, some of Patterson's recent work (Patterson, Jordan, Hogan, & Frerker, 1981) failed to support predictions based upon the model. Patterson (1982) has just published a reformulation of the model that attempts to cope with these criticisms and questions. It does not, however, attribute greater importance to the role of arousal. Instead, it provides a fivefold classification of the functions that are served by what Patterson calls *nonverbal involvement behaviors* and a three-fold categorization of factors that are antecedent to all interactions. These involvement behaviors and antecedent factors are incorporated into a "sequential functional model of nonverbal exchange" that is intended to account for the convergence and divergence of a wide variety of nonverbal behaviors in interpersonal interactions. The reader is referred to Chapter 11 (Patterson & Edinger) for a detailed description of the model. It is interesting to note, given the position of the present chapter, that the first issue Patterson (1982) clarifies in developing his model is definitional and concerns the distinction between behaviors and their functions. "This might seem like a trivial concern," he states, "but the assumptions resulting from the use of particular terms or labels can substantially affect our approach to researching various issues" (p. 232). He proposes *nonverbal involvement behaviors* as a more "neutral" label than *intimacy* or *affiliative* behaviors and describes the functions of such behaviors separately.

It is probably fair to say that the theories of Giles and his associates, of Cappella and Greene, and of Patterson are the three major efforts to explain and predict the occurrence of changes in the nonverbal behavior of interacting speakers toward increased similarity or dissimilarity as their interaction proceeds. There are, of course, problems associated with demonstrating the viability of each of the theories. Thakerar and Giles (1981), for example, define *subjective* convergence and divergence in terms of speakers' beliefs, in terms, concretely, of self-reports. It is difficult to imagine that (unless they are primed to make such self-observations) speakers have any but the vaguest notion about whether their speech actually moved towards or away from the speech of persons with whom they interact, unless the features about which they are asked are quite obvious or are easy to manipulate deliberately. As was mentioned earlier, Cappella and Greene (1982) talk about the relation of the discrepancy between actual and expected expressive behavior to arousal. However, the impact of the discrepancy is mediated by an "acceptance region," which apparently is a region that defines, or is defined by, the allowable magnitudes of discrepancies from expectation. Thus, an expressive behavior that is "outside of" the acceptance region (i.e., too far above or below it) is highly arousing and affectively negative, whereas a behavior "within" the region is only mildly arousing and affectively positive. Moreover, those behaviors outside the region elicit *compensation* (divergence), whereas those within elicit *reciprocation* (convergence). But can the acceptance region be mapped in a way, or ways, other than by observing which intensities of which behaviors are or are not highly arousing, i.e., can the region be mapped independently of the expressive behavior and arousal? Instead of referring to an "acceptance region," Patterson (1982) refers to a "range of appropriate involvement" that each participant in an interaction uses to gauge each other's nonverbal behaviors. This range represents an expectation level. The magnitude of the discrepancy between one participant's expectation of appropriate involvement and the other's actual level of involvement presumably determines the stability of the interaction and degree of stability influences the extent of cognitive-arousal mediation processes that may initiate cognitive-affective reassessment of the interaction. Specifying the "range of appropriate involvement" is likely to be as problematical as mapping Cappella and Greene's "acceptance region" in spite of the electrophysiological and "thought-listing" techniques to which Patterson refers in his discussion of possible measurement procedures. It is, however, not the intent of the present chapter to offer a detailed critique of the three theories. Suffice it to say that they are important attempts to uncover the mechanisms underlying the occurrence of nonverbal congruence, synchrony, convergence, reciprocation, or accommodation, during the course of an interpersonal interaction.

CONCLUDING COMMENTS

The chapter has tried to make two major and, to some extent, related points. The first is that it is possible to consider the temporal patterning of a conversation a dimension in its own right, one that is not dependent on the other dimensions of the conversation for the definitions of its parameters. The second point is that the parameters of a chronography of conversation should be defined such that they empirically describe the behaviors they are supposed to tag, and incorporate no presumptions about the intentions of the participants that are based primarily upon the expectancies and intiutions of the investigator. In short, the parameters ought to be defined as objectively as possible. The reason for making these points is that the investigation of conversation chronography can still be considered a relatively new area of study, and its development ought not to be hampered — as is the case with so many other areas of psychology — by measurement procedures and a terminology that include by definition unnecessary and unwarranted preconceptions. As was said earlier in the chapter, the importance and utility of a temporal classification of dialogue should be established by research rather than by fiat.

On the other hand, one reason for studying the various channels of communication is to provide a more complete picture of their separate and combined contributions to the total communicative act. It is an ambitious goal and there are no well-defined ways to accomplish it. The work of Crown, Duncan, Kendon, Rosenfeld, Yngve, and others who explore the simultaneous interplay of several channels represents a seemingly more direct, perhaps richer, approach to the goal than that advocated in this chapter. It is an approach that demands very careful and exceedingly detailed analyses of the data and is not, therefore, undertaken lightly. It may well be the more fruitful approach.

The chapter has also presented some of the directions researchers have taken in their efforts to examine the relevance of conversation chronography to issues and events of more traditional psychological interest. In doing so, the chapter raised questions that were intended to serve as markers of possible paths for further inquiries.

The statement of the authors' position presented in this chapter may appear to be unnecessarily strong. After all, it is, in essence, a reiteration of the familiar argument that objectivity and precision are among the characteristics usually considered fundamental to a scientific investigation. It is not clear, however, that the familiarity of the argument makes its emphasis less useful.

ACKNOWLEDGMENT

The authors gratefully acknowledge the computing assistance of Mary June Fowler, the extended discussions with Mohamed BenDebba, and the generous amount of computer time provided by the Statistics Center of UMBC. They are particularly indebted to Dr. Sherry Rochester for her constructively critical reading of a prepublication draft of the chapter.

REFERENCES

Alberti, L. *Some lexical correlates of speaker switching frequency in conversation.* Paper read at the Eighteenth International Congress of Applied Psychology, Montreal, July, 1974.
Argyle, M, & Cook, M. *Gaze and mutual gaze.* London: Cambridge University Press, 1976.

Argyle, M., & Dean, J. Eye contact, distance, and affiliation. *Sociometry,* 1965, *28,* 289–304.

Baird, J. D., & Tice, M. Imitative modeling of vocal intensity. *Psychonomic Science,* 1969, *19,* 219–220.

Bandura, A. Behavior modification through modeling procedures. In L. Krasner & L. P. Ullman (Eds.), *Research in behavior modification.* New York: Holt, Rinehart & Winston, 1965.

Beebe, B., Stern, D., & Jaffe, J. The kinesic rhythm of mother–infant interactions. In A. W. Siegman & S. Feldstein (Eds.), *Of speech and time.* Hillsdale, NJ: Lawrence Erlbaum Associates, 1979.

BenDebba, M. *Vocalization rate as a function of contingent "mm-hmms."* Paper presented at the annual meeting of the Eastern Pschological Association, Philadelphia, April, 1974.

Berscheid, E. Opinion change and communicator-communicatee similarity and dissimilarity. *Journal of Personality and Social Psychology,* 1966, *4,* 670–680.

Bieri, J., Bradburn, W. M., & Galinsky, M. D. Sex differences in perceptual behavior. *Journal of Personality,* 1958, *26,* 1–12.

Bishop, G. D. Perceived similarity in intersocial attitudes and behaviors: The effects of belief and dialect style. *Journal of Applied Social Psychology,* 1979, *9,* 446–465.

Black, J. S. The intensity of oral responses to stimulus words. *Journal of Speech and Hearing Disorders,* 1949, *14,* 16–22. (a)

Black, J. S. Loudness of speaking: The effect of heard stimuli on spoken responses. *Journal of Experimental Psychology,* 1949, *39,* 311–315. (b)

Bourhis, R. Y., Giles, H., & Lambert, W. E. Social consequences of accommodating one's style of speech: A cross-national investigation. *International Journal of the Sociology of Language,* 1975, *6,* 53–71.

Brady, P. T. A technique for investigating on-off patterns of speech. *Bell System Technical Journal,* 1965, *44,* 1–22.

Brady, P. T. A statistical analysis of on-off speech patterns in 16 conversatons. *Bell System Technical Journal,* 1968, *47,* 73–91.

Brady, P. T. *A model for generating on-off speech patterns in two-way conversation.* Paper presented at the annual meeting of the Acoustical Society of America, Philadelphia, April, 1969.

Brock, T. C. Communicator-recipient similarity and decision change. *Journal of Personality and Social Psychology,* 1965, *1,* 650–653.

Burnstein, E., Stotland, E., & Zander, A. Similarity to a model and self-evaluation. *Journal of Abnormal and Social Psychology,* 1961, *62,* 257–264.

Byrne, D. Interpersonal attraction and attitude similarity. *Journal of Abnormal and Social Psychology, 1961, 62,* 713–715.

Byrne, D. Attitudes and attraction. *Advances in Experimental Social Psychology,* 1969, *4,* 35–89.

Byrne, D., Griffitt, W., & Stefaniak, D. Attraction and similarity of personality characteristics. *Journal of Personality and Social Psychology,* 1967, *5,* 82–90.

Cappella, J. N., & Greene, J. O. A discrepancy-arousal explanation of mutual influence in expressive behavior for adult and infant–adult interaction. *Communication Monographs,* 1982, *49,* 89–114.

Cappella, J. N., & Planalp,S. Talk and silence sequences in informal conversations, III: Interspeaker influence. *Human Communication Research,* 1981, *7,* 117–132.

Cassotta, L., Feldstein, S., & Jaffe, H. AVTA: A device for automatic vocal transaction analysis. *Journal of Experimental Analysis of Behavior,* 1964, *7,* 99–104.

Cassotta, L., Feldstein, S., & Jaffe, J. *The stability and modiviability of individual vocal characteristics in stress and nonstress interviews.* Research Bulletin No. 2. New York: William Alanson White Institute, 1967.

Cattell, R. B., Eber, H. W., & Tatsuoka, M. M. *Handbook for the Sixteenth Personality Factor Questionnaire.* Champaigne, Illinois: Institute for Personality and Ability Testing, 1970.

Chapple, E. D. Quantitative analysis of the interaction of individuals. *Proceedings of the National Academy of Sciences,* 1939, *25,* 58–67.

Chapple, E. D. "Personality" differences as described by invariant properties of individuals in interaction. *Proceedings of the National Academy of Sciences,* 1940, *26,* 10–16.

Chapple, E. D. The Interaction Chronograph: Its evolution and present application. *Personnel,* 1949, *25,* 295–307.

Chapple, E. D. *Culture and biological man: Explorations in behavioral anthropology.* New York: Holt, Rinehart and Winston, 1970.

Chapple, E. D., & Harding, C. F., III. Simultaneous measures of human relations and emotional activity. *Proceedings of the National Academy of Sciences,* 1940, *26,* 319–326.

Charlip, W. S., & Burk, K. W. Effects of noise on selected speech parameters. *Journal of Communication Disorders,* 1969, *16,* 267–270.

Cobb, L. *Time series analysis of the periodicities of casual conversations.* Unpublished doctoral dissertation, Cornell University, 1973.

Cohen, J., & Cohen, P. *Applied multiple regression/correlation analysis for the behavioral sciences.* Hillsdale, New Jersey: Lawrence Erlbaum Associates, 1975.

Crown, C. L. *Interpersonal accommodation of vision and voice as a function of interpersonal attraction.* Unpublished doctoral dissertation, University of Delaware, 1984.

Crown, C. L., & Feldstein, S. *Conversational congruence: Measurement and meaning.* Paper read at the Eastern Psychological Association, New York, April, 1981.

Crown, C. L., Feldstein, S., & Bond, R. N. *Effects of simultaneous speech on interpersonal perception.* Paper read at the Eastern Psychological Association, Baltimore, April, 1982.

Crowne, D. P., & Marlow, D. *The approval motive.* New York: Wiley, 1964.

Crutchfield, R. S., Woodworth, D. G., & Albrecht, R. E. *Perceptual performance and the effective person.* Lackland Air Force Base, Texas: Personnel Laboratory, WADC-TN-58-60, ASTIA Doc. No. AD 151 039, 1958.

Dabbs, J. M., Jr. Self-esteem communicator characteristics, and attitude change. *Journal of Abnormal and Social Psychology,* 1964, *69,* 173–181.

Dabbs, J. M., Jr. Similarity of gestures and interpersonal influence, *Proceedings of the 77th Annual Convention of the American Psychological Association,* 1969, *4,* 337–338.

Dabbs, J. M., Jr. & Ruback, R. B. *Vocal patterns in male and female five-person groups.* Paper read at the American Psychological Association, Toronto, August, 1984.

Dabbs, J. M., Jr. & Swiedler, T. C. Group AVTA: A microcomputer system for group voice chronography. *Behavior Research Methods and Instrumentation,* 1983, *15,* 79–84.

Dittmann, A. T., & Llewellyn, L. G. Relationship between vocalizations and head nods as listener responses. *Journal of Personality and Social Psychology,* 1968, *9,* 79–84.

Duncan, S., Jr. Some signals and rules for taking speaking turns in conversations. *Journal of Personality and Social Psychology,* 1972, *23,* 283–292.

Duncan, S., Jr. Toward a grammar for dyadic conversations. *Semiotica,* 1973, *9,* 29–46.

Duncan, S., Jr. On the structure of speaker-auditor interaction during speaking turns. *Language in Society,* 1974, *3,* 161–180.

Duncan, S., Jr., & Niederehe, G. On signaling that it's your turn to speak. *Journal of Experimental Social Psychology,* 1974, *10,* 234–247.

Ellsworth, P. C. *Some questions about the role of arousal in the interpretation of direct gaze.* Paper presented at the annual meeting of the American Psychological Association, San Francisco, August 1977.

Feldstein, S., Interspeaker influence in conversational interaction. *Psychological Reports,* 1968, *22,* 826–828.

Feldstein, S. Temporal patterns of dialogue. Basic research and reconsiderations. In A. W.

Siegman & B. Pope (Eds.), *Studies in dyadic communication*. New York: Pergamon, 1972. Pp. 91–113.

Feldstein, S., Alberti, L., BenDebba, M., & Welkowitz, J. *Personality and simultaneous speech*. Paper presented at the annual meeting of the American Psychological Association, New Orleans, August, 1974.

Feldstein, S., BenDebba, M., & Alberti, L. *Distributional characteristics of simultaneous speech in conversation*. Paper presented at the Acoustical Society of America, New York, April, 1974.

Feldstein, S., Hennessy, B., & Bond, R. N. *Conversation chronography and interpersonal perception in Chinese and English dyads*. Paper read at the American Psychological Association, Los Angeles, August, 1981.

Feldstein, S., Jaffe, J., & Cassotta, L. The effect of mutual visual access upon conversational time patterns. *American Psychologyist*, 1967, *23*, 595. (Abstract)

Fiske, D. W., & Maddi, S. R. A conceptual framework. In D. W. Fiske & S. R. Maddi (Eds.), *Functions of varied experience*. Homewood, Illinois: Dorsey, 1961. Pp. 11–56.

Fitzgibbons, D. L., Goldberger, L., & Eagle, M. Field dependence and memory for incidental material *Perceptual and Motor Skills*, 1965, *21*, 743–749.

Fraser, J. T. (Ed.). *The voices of time. A cooperative survey of man's views of time as expressed by the sciences and by the humanities*. New York: Braziller, 1966.

Gallois, C., & Markel, N. N. Turn taking: Social personality and conversational style. *Journal of Personality and Social Psychology*, 1975, *31*, 1134–1140.

Gardner, M. B. Effect of noise, system gain, and assigned task on talking level in loud-speaker communication. *Journal of the Acoustical Society of America*, 1966, *40*, 955–965.

Garvey, C., & BenDebba, M. Effects of age, sex and partner on children's dyadic speech. *Child Development*, 1974, *45*, 1159–1161.

Giles, H. Accent mobility: A model and some data. *Anthropological Linguistics*, 1973, *15*, 87–105.

Giles, H. Social psychology and applied linguistics: Towards an integrative approach. *ITL: Review of Applied Linguistics*, 1977, *35*, 27–42. (1)

Giles, H. (Ed.) *Language, ethnicity and intergroup relations*. European Monographs in Social Psychology (No. 13). London: Academic, 1977. (b)

Giles, H. Accommodation theory: Some new directions. IN S. de Silve (Ed.), *Aspects of linguistic behavior*. York, England: University of York, 1980.

Giles, H., & Powesland, P. F. *Speech style and social evaluation*. European Monographs in Social Psychology (No. 7). London: Academic, 1975.

Giles, H., & Smith, P. M. Accommodation theory: Optimal levels of convergence. In H. Giles & R. St. Clair (Eds.), *Language and social psychology* (pp. 45–65). Oxford: Blackwell, 1979.

Giles, H., Taylor, D. M., & Bourhis, R. Y. Towards a theory of interpersonal accommodation through language: Some Canadian data. *Language in Society*, 1973, *2*, 177–192.

Goldberg, L. R. Language and personality: Toward a taxonomy of trait descriptive terms. *Istanbul Studies in Experimental Psychology*, 1976, *12*, 1–23.

Gottman, J. M. *Time-series analysis: A comprehensive introduction for social scientists*. New York: Cambridge, 1981.

Greenspoon, J. The reinforcing effect of two spoken sounds on the frequency of two responses. *American Journal of Psychology*, 1955, *68*, 409–416.

Griffitt, W. Interpersonal attraction as a function of self-concept and personality similarity-dissimilarity. *Journal of personality and Social Psychology*, 1966, *4*, 581–584.

Haggard, E. A. *Interclass correlation and the analysis of variance*. New York: Dryden, 1958.

Hanley, T. D., & Steer, M. Effect of level of distracting noise upon speaking rate, duration, and intensity. *Journal of Speech and Hearing Disorders*, 1949, *14*, 363–368.

Hayes, D. P. The Cornell datalogger. *Administrative Science Quarterly*, 1969, *14*, 222–223.

Hayes, D., Meltzer, L., & Wolf, G. Substantive conclusions are dependent upon techniques of measurement. *Behavioral Science,* 1970, *15,* 265–269.

Homans, G. C. *The human group.* New York: Harcourt Brace, 1950.

Jacobson, L. I., Berger, S. E., & Millham, J. Individual differences in cheating during a temptation period when confronting failure. *Journal of Personality and Social Psychology,* 1970, *15,* 48–56.

Jacobson, L. I., & Ford, L. H., Jr. Need for approval, defensive denial, and sensitivity to cultural stereotypes. *Journal of Personality,* 1966, *34,* 596–609.

Jacobson, R. *Child, language, aphasia, and phonological universals.* The Hague: Mouton, 1968.

Jaffe, J. Computer analysis of verbal behavior in psychiatric interviews. In D. Rioche & E. A. Weinstein (Eds.), *Disorders in communication: Proceedings of the Association for Research in Nervous and Mental Diseases,* Vol. 42. Baltimore, Md.: Williams & Wilkens, 1964. Pp. 389–399.

Jaffe, J. Linked probablistic finite automata: A model for the temporal interaction of speakers. *Mathematical Biosciences,* 1970, *7,* 191–204.

Jaffe, J., & Breskin, S. Temporal patterns of speech and sample size. *Journal of Speech and Hearing Research,* 1970, *13,* 667–668.

Jaffe, J., & Feldstein, S. *Rhythms of dialogue.* New York: Academic, 1970.

Johnston, G., Jansen, J., Weitman, M., Hess, H. F., Matarazzo, J. D., & Saslow, G. A punched tape data preparation system for use in psychiatric interviews. *Digest of the International Conference on Medical Electronics,* 1961, p. 17.

Kendon, A. Some functions of gaze direction in social interaction. *Acta Psychologica,* 1967, *26,* 22–63.

Konstadt, N., & Forman, E. Field dependence and external directedness. *Journal of Personality and Social Psychology,* 1965, *1,* 490–493.

Kryter, K. D. Effects of ear protective devices on the intelligibility of speech in noise. *Journal of the Acoustical Society of America,* 1946, *18,* 412–417.

Lane, H. L., & Tranel, B. The Lombard reflex and the role of hearing in speech. *Journal of Speech and Hearing Research,* 1971, *14,* 677–709.

Lennard, H. L. & Bernstein, A. *The anatomy of psychotherapy.* New York: Columbia University Press, 1960.

Lott, A. J., & Lott, B. E. Group cohesiveness as interpersonal attraction: A review of relationships with antecedent and consequent variables. *Psychological Bulletin,* 1965, *64,* 259–310.

Lustig, M. W. Computer analysis of talk-silence patterns in triads. *Communication Quarterly,* 1980, *28,* 3–12.

Marcus, E. S., Welkowitz, J., Feldstein, S., & Jaffe, J. *Psychological differentiation and the congruence of temporal speech patterns.* Paper presented at the meeting of the Eastern Psychological Association, Atlantic City, April, 1970.

Marlowe, D., & Crowne, D. P. A new scale of social desirability independent of psychopathology. *Journal of Consulting Psychology,* 1960, *24,* 349–354.

Martindale, D. A. *Effects of environmental context in negotiating situations: Territorial dominance behavior in dyadic interactions.* Unpublished doctoral dissertation, City University of New York, 1971.

Matarazzo, J. D. The interview. In B. B. Wolman (Ed.), *Handbook of clinical psychology.* New York: McGraw-Hill, 1965. Pp. 403–450.

Matarazzo, J. D., Saslow, G., & Hare, A. Factor analysis of interview interaction behavior. *Journal of Consulting Psychology,* 1958, *22,* 419–429.

Matarazzo, J. D., & Wiens, A. N. Interviewer influence on durations of interviewee silence. *Journal of Experimental Research in Personality,* 1967, *2,* 56–69.

Matarazzo, J. D., & Wiens, A. N. *The interview: Research on its anatomy and structure.*

Chicago: Aldine-Atherton, 1972.

Meltzer, L., Hayes, D. P., & Shellenberger, D. *Consistency of vocal behavior in discussions.* Paper presented at the meeting of the American Psychological Association, Chicago, September, 1966.

Meltzer, L., Morris, W., & Hayes, D. Interruption outcomes and vocal amplitude: Explorations in social psychophysics. *Journal of Personality and Social Psychology,* 1971, *18,* 392–402.

Miller, G. A., Speaking in general. Review of J. H. Greenberg (Ed.), *Universals of language. Contemporary Psychology,* 1963, *8,* 417–418.

Morris, W. N. Manipulated amplitude and interruption outcomes. *Journal of Personality and Social Psychology,* 1971, *20,* 319–331.

Natale, M. Social desirability as related to convergence of temporal speech patterns. *Perceptual and Motor Skills,* 1975, *40,* 827–830. (a)

Natale, M. Convergence of mean vocal intensity in dyadic communication as a function of social desirability. *Journal of Personality and Social Psychology,* 1975, *32,* 790–804. (b)

Newcomb, T. M. An approach to the study of communicative acts. *Psychological Review,* 1953, *15,* 393–404.

Newcomb, T. M. *The acquaintance process.* New York: Holt, Rinehart, & Winston, 1961.

Norwine, A. C., & Murphy, O. J. Characteristic time intervals in telephonic conversation. *Bell System Technical Journal,* 1938, *17,* 281–291.

Ostrom, C. W., Jr. *Time-series analysis: Regression techniques.* Beverly Hills, CA: Sage, 1978.

Patterson, M. L. A sequential functional model of nonverbal exchange. *Psychological Review,* 1982, *89,* 231–249.

Patterson, M. L., Jordan, A., Hogan, M. B., & Frerker, D. Effects of nonverbal intimacy on arousal and behavioral adjustment. *Journal of Nonverbal Behavior,* 1981, *5,* 184–198.

Piaget, J. *The language and thought of the child.* New York: World, 1955.

Ray, M. L., & Webb, E. J. Speech duration effects in the Kennedy news conferences. *Science,* 1966, *153,* 899–901.

Rogers, C. A process conception of psychotherapy. *American Psychologist,* 1958, *13,* 142–149.

Rogers, C. *On becoming a person.* Boston: Houghton Mifflin, 1961.

Runkel, P. Cognitive similarity in facilitating communication. *Sociometry,* 1956, *19,* 178–191.

Salzinger, K., Portnoy, S., Zlotogura, P., & Keisner, R. The effect of reinforcement on continuous speech and on plural nouns in grammatical context. *Journal of Verbal Learning and Verbal Behavior,* 1963, *1,* 477–485.

Schachter, S., & Singer, J. E. Cognitive, social, and physiological determinants of emotional state. *Psychological Review,* 1962, *69,* 379–399.

Schegloff, E. A. Sequencing in conversational openings. *American Anthropologist,* 1968, *70,* 1075–1095.

Stern, D. N. Mother and infant at play: The dyadic interaction involving facial, vocal, and gaze behavior. In M. Lewis & L. A. Rosenblum (Eds.), *The effect of the infant on its caregiver.* New York: Wiley, 1974.

Stern, D. N. *A first relationship: Mother and infant.* Cambridge, MA: Harvard University Press, 1977.

Stern, D. N., Jaffe, J., Beebe, B., & Bennett, S. L. Vocalizing in unison and in alternation: Two modes of communication within the mother–infant dyad. *Annals of the New York Academy of Sciences,* 1975, *263,* 89–100.

Stotland, E., Zander, A., & Natsoulas, T. Generalization of interpersonal similarity. *Journal of Abnormal and Social Psychology,* 1961, *62,* 250–256.

Tajfel, H. Social identity and intergroup behavior. *Social Science Information,* 1974, *13,* 65–93.

Tajfel, H. (Ed.). *Differentiation between social groups: Studies in the social psychology of intergroup behavior.* European Monographs in Social Psychology (No. 14). London: Academic, 1979.

Tajfel, H., & Turner, J. C. An integrative theory of intragroup conflict. In W. G. Austin & S. Worschel (Eds.), *The social psychology of intergroup relations.* Monterey, California: Brooks/Cole, 1978.

Tedeschi, J. L. Attributions, liking and power. In T. L. Huston (Ed.), *Foundations of interpersonal attraction.* New York: Academic Press, 1974.

Thakerar, J. N., & Giles, H. They are — so they spoke: Noncontent speech stereo-types. *Language and Communication,* 1981, *1,* 255–262.

Thakerar, J. N., Giles, H., & Cheshire, J. Psychological and linguistic parameters of speech accomodation theory. In C. Fraser & K. R. Scherer (Eds.), *Advances in the social psychology of language.* Cambridge: Cambridge University Press, 1982.

Truax, C. B., & Carkhuff, R. R. *Toward effective counseling in psychotherapy.* Chicago: Aldine, 1967.

Turner, J. C. Social comparison and social identity: Some prospects for intergroup behavior. *European Journal of Social Psychology,* 1975, *5,* 5–34.

Wallach, M. A., Kogan, N., & Burt, R. B. Group risk taking and field dependence-independence of group members. *Sociometry,* 1967, *30,* 323–338.

Webb, J. T. Interview synchrony: An investigation of two speech rate measures. In A. W. Siegman & B. Pope (Eds.), *Studies in dyadic communication.* New York: Pergamon, 1972. Pp. 115–133.

Webster, J. C., & Klump, R. G. Effects of ambient noise and near-by talkers on a face-to-face communication task. *Journal of the Acoustical Society of America,* 1962, *34,* 936–941.

Welkowitz, J., Cariffe, G., & Feldstein, S. Conversational congruence as a criterion of socialization in children. *Child Development,* 1976, *47,* 269–272.

Welkowitz, J., & Feldstein, S. Dyadic interaction and induced differences in perceived similarity. *Proceedings of the 77th Annual Convention of the American Psychological Association,* 1969, *4,* 343–344.

Welkowitz, J., & Feldstein, S. Relation of experimentally manipulated interpersonal perception and psychological differentiation to the temporal patterning of conversation. *Proceedings of the 78th Annual Convention of the American Psychological Association,* 1970, *5,* 387–388.

Welkowitz, J., Feldstein, S., Finkelstein, M., & Aylesworth, L. Changes in vocal intensity as a function of interspeaker influence. *Perceptual and Motor Skills,* 1972, *35,* 715–718.

Welkowitz, J., & Kuc, M. Interrelationships among warmth, genuineness, empathy, and temporal speech patterns in interpersonal interaction. *Journal of Consulting and Clinical Psychology,* 1973, *41,* 472–473.

Welkowitz, J., & Martz, M. J. WELMAR: Computer programs to analyze dialogic time patterns. Unpublished manuscript, New York University, 1975.

Wiens, A. N., Molde, D., Holman, D., & Matarazzo, J. D. Can interview interaction measures be taken from tape recordings? *Journal of Psychology,* 1966, *63,* 249–260.

Witkin, H. A. Individual differences in ease of perception of embedded figures. *Journal of Personality,* 1950, *19,* 1–15.

Witkin, H. A., Dyk, R. B., Faterson, H. F., Goodenough, D. R., & Karp, S. S. *Psychological differentiation.* New York: Wiley, 1962.

Yngve, V. H. On getting a word in edgewise. In M. A. Campbell *et al.* (Eds.), *Papers from the Sixth Regional Meeting, Chicago Linguistic Society.* Chicago: University of Chicago Department of Linguistics, 1970. Pp. 567–578.

10 "Grouptalk": Sound and Silence in Group Conversation

James M. Dabbs, Jr.
R. Barry Ruback
Mark S. Evans
Georgia State University

Group conversations are a mixture of simple and complex patterns of sounds and silence. In some cases the conversation is a series of monologues; group members take turns talking and these turns are separated by silence. In more complex cases, the speakers interrupt one another, and sometimes several or even all group members speak at once. In this chapter we discuss an automatic technique we have been using to gain some understanding of the nature and effect of conversations in groups. We have focused on group conversations because we believe they are useful indicators of group interaction.

Over the past 50 years, there have been repeated calls in social psychology for studies of the process of group interaction, the verbal and nonverbal means by which members communicate with and influence one another (Dashiell, 1935; Kelley & Thibaut, 1954; McGrath & Kravitz, 1982). A major problem has been the lack of agreement on how "process" should be defined. In the absence of a satisfactory definition of process, research on groups has tended toward a black-box approach. It has been assumed that certain inputs (e.g., group size or leadership) produce certain outcomes (e.g., performance on a task or cohesiveness) by means of some process that mediates between inputs and outcomes (Hackman & Morris, 1975). Although the precise nature of this group process is unclear (Hackman, 1983), the importance of interaction appears central. Indeed, Hackman and Morris (1975) accept interaction as equivalent to process and have specified how certain inputs are linked through group interaction to certain outputs, though they do not offer an independent definition of interaction. We propose here to define interaction in terms of objective, content-free measures of vocal behavior. Our approach stands in marked contrast to a tradition of studying the meaning of

501

what people say during interaction (e.g., Bales & Cohen, 1979). Our approach has not been widely used and therefore requires some justification, which is presented here.

BACKGROUND

Traditional Measures of Group Process

Group research has been criticized because it focuses more upon the outcome than the process of group interaction (McGrath & Kravitz, 1982). This emphasis has undoubtedly come about because process is so difficult to study. In analyzing group discussion, one must deal with an enormous and complex amount of data.

The best known research on group interaction is probably that of Bales (1950, 1970; Bales & Cohen, 1979), which reduces the total flow of conversation to a relatively few underlying categories. Bales' (1950) original observational coding system, the Interaction Process Analysis, classified behaviors by each group member into one of 12 categories, 6 reflecting socioemotional activity and 6 reflecting task activity. Subsequently, Bales (1970) identified three dimensions on which group interaction could be scored: dominant/submissive, friendly/unfriendly, and instrumentally controlled/emotionally expressive.

Although the Bales scoring system has been used for over 30 years, there are problems with using it for other than the self-analytic and observer groups for which it was designed. One problem is that the system does not permit the coding of actions that occur very quickly. Bales and Cohen (1979) state that "messages" can be coded at the rate of "about one per minute, and by good scorers considerably faster" (p. 164). If one assumes that some significant group phenomena might be over in less than a minute, or even in less than 30 seconds or 15 seconds or 5 seconds, it becomes readily apparent that the Bales system is inadequate.

A second problem is that the Bales system cannot code the simultaneous behaviors of two or more individuals. In our research on 60 five-person groups we found simultaneous speech occurring from 5 to 15% of the time. Even if simultaneous behaviors could be coded, perceptual limitations would make it difficult for an observer to determine whether three or four or five individuals were participating at one time. The problem of coding multiple participation would still exist if five or six observers were used (as recommended by Bales and Cohen), because messages are coded by minute rather than by second and one could not determine whether or not messages coded for the same minute were simultaneous.

Content-Free Measures of Group Discussion

A simpler means of data collection and analysis comes from the work of Jaffe and Feldstein (1970) and that of Chapple (1949). This approach deals with the temporal organization of sound and silence. Rather than listening to words or emotional tones, Jaffe and Feldstein focused upon the timing of vocalizations and pauses. The question immediately arises as to whether content-free measures can reveal important or interesting findings. Content-free measures ignore what is traditionally thought of as "meaning." However, research summarized by Cappella (1981), Feldstein and Welkowitz (this volume), Lustig (1980), and Siegman and Feldstein (1979) has shown such measures can be useful. Content-free measures have been related to stress, personality differences, the relationship between partners, and the winning and losing of arguments. Our proposal would extend this approach from dyads to groups, somewhat as Lustig (1980) has done with triads. Measures based upon the amount and timing of sound and silence might indicate whether group conversation moves quickly or slowly, speakers are talkative or laconic, listeners are responsive or dull, and the overall interaction is smooth or clumsy.

The Jaffe and Feldstein model. The raw data used by Jaffe and Feldstein consisted of on–off patterns of sound and silence from each speaker. Jaffe and Feldstein used the Automatic Vocal Transaction Analyzer (AVTA) both to gather and summarize raw data. AVTA (Cassotta, Feldstein, & Jaffe, 1964) automatically detects and records the presence and absence of speech. The system includes analog-to-digital converters and a cancellation network to eliminate the spillover of one person's voice into another person's microphone. It determines the on–off state of each voice at each moment and transforms these data into psychologically meaningful scores.

We hear conversation, however, not as simple sound and silence but as a pattern of alternation among speakers. The basic parameter in the Jaffe and Feldstein scheme is the individual *turn,* which is made up of a speaker's *vocalizations* and *pauses.* Silence that ends a turn is a *switching pause,* and it is always followed by the beginning of the other speaker's turn. When one person has the turn and is speaking and the other joins in, this speech on the part of the second person is called simultaneous speech; *interruptive simultaneous speech* leads to a change of turn, and *noninterruptive simultaneous speech* does not.

The "Grouptalk" model. The situation is more complicated when more than two people are conversing. In a dyad one partner's turn begins when that partner speaks alone and ends the instant the other partner speaks alone. But in groups larger than dyads a turn-taker may fall silent while several others are speaking at once, in which case there is no obvious way to decide who has the turn. No new turn-taker has emerged (no one else is speaking alone), but it hardly seems appropriate to continue crediting the turn to the original speaker, who is now silent while others are speaking. Another problem with using the concept of alternating individual turns in groups arises when there is silence for a moment following a speaker, and then two or more speakers begin at once. The Grouptalk model proposes the notion of *group turn* to cover these contingencies.

A group turn begins when an individual turn-taker has fallen silent and two or more other persons are speaking. The other persons may have interrupted the original turn-taker, or they may simultaneously have begun to speak following a silence. The group turn ends the instant an individual again speaks alone. Analogously to individual turns, group turns may contain *group vocalizations* and *group pauses* and end with *group-switching pauses*. During a group turn the set of people who are speaking together may vary, but no one will be speaking alone. In our research we have found that group turns occupy about 4% of the total discussion time.

The Grouptalk model includes six Jaffe and Feldstein codes and the four group turn codes (noted previously). Our definition of an individual turn differs from Jaffe and Feldstein's in that under our definition an individual turn ends when an individual turn-taker has fallen silent and two or more others are speaking together, rather than continuing through this multiple speaking to the moment a new turn-taker appears.

Some critics (e.g., Strodtbeck, 1972) have argued that written transcripts contain as much information as the Jaffe and Feldstein type of on–off data, but some kinds of information would be quite difficult to analyze from transcriptions of group conversations. For example, simultaneous speech of two or more individuals at once would be difficult to capture in a transcript, as would the pauses between vocalizations. Moreover, producing and analyzing transcripts is costly in time and money. Precise measures of the amount and timing of talk cannot be obtained wthout automatic equipment.

An overview of the Grouptalk model is shown in Fig. 10.1. The left side of Fig. 10.1 is essentially the Jaffe and Feldstein model, in which conversation stays within the turns of individual subjects. Conversation moves among vocalizations, pauses, switching pauses, and, when other partners join the current turn-taker, the two kinds of simultaneous speech. The right side of Fig. 10.1 shows group turns, when the floor cannot be attributed to a single person. A group turn may be regarded as something negative, with members battling for the floor, or as something positive, with members enthusiastically joining in together. For now, we wish to avoid evaluative interpretations and treat group turns and individual turns as if they were coequal. Later findings may tell us more about the psychological significance of group turns.

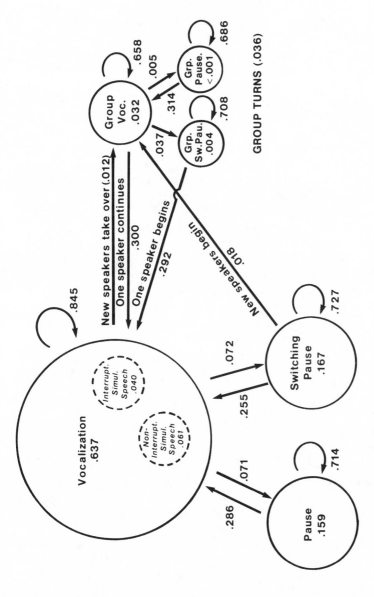

INDIVIDUAL TURNS (.964)

GROUP TURNS (.036)

FIG. 10.1 Diagram of conversational states in the Grouptalk model. Solid circles constitute a mutually exclusive and exhaustive set of states. Dashed circles are additional events that may occur during the vocalizing state. Numbers inside circles are simple probabilities of the occurrence of each state or event. Numbers beside arrows are transitional probabilities of each state occurring at the next point in time. The data come from 20 five-person group conversations, lasting an average of 15 minutes each, in which the conversational state was coded every quarter second.

505

Conversation moves back and forth between individual and group turns and, within these turns, among the vocalization, pause, and switching pause states. The numbers included in Fig. 10.1 are probabilities, based upon observations every quarter second for 300 minutes of group conversation in a study described in the next section. The numbers within the circles are simple probabilities of the occurrence of each code, and the numbers beside the arrows are transitional probabilities of each state following each state at the next point in time. Where states cannot follow each other (for example, a pause cannot follow a switching pause), no arrow is shown.

Group Structure and Grouptalk Model

A major impetus for developing the Grouptalk model lies in the need for measures of group processes (McGrath & Kravitz, 1982). It is relatively easy to measure individuals, but measuring a group, as something different from the sum of its members, is more difficult. The Grouptalk model can describe both individuals and groups. Scores describing individuals come mostly from the left side of Figure 10.1. They include turns, vocalizations, pauses, switching pauses, and the two kinds of simultaneous speech. For each subject we can summarize the percentage of time, number of episodes, and mean duration of each of these states. Scores describing the group as a whole can be produced by summarizing the states of all individuals from the left side of Fig. 10.1, or by summarizing the group turn states from the right side of Fig. 10.1. Groups vary in the amount of time occupied by group turns, and we can examine the percentage of time, number of episodes, and mean duration of group turns, group vocalizations, group pauses, and group switching pauses. Group scores can also be produced by the way in which conversational states are ordered in time. Following is a more detailed discussion of dependent variables that might be derived from our grouptalk codes.

A Markov model of turn taking. Jaffe and Feldstein (1970) show that the alternation of sound and silence in monologues and dialogues approximates a first-order Markov process. This is a process in which the future state, given the present state, is independent of past history in other words, it is a process in which knowledge of a single state can allow one to make a statistical prediction about future states. Whereas people remember a great deal about the content of what they have been saying, their on–off vocalizations at a given moment appear to emerge unaffected by their earlier patterns of on–off vocalizations.

Our grouptalk model contains, for a five-person group, six mutually exclusive and exhaustive turn states, these being the turn states of the individuals in the group plus the groupturn state. If one wishes to examine turns only among individuals, the data can be recast into a set of five states, with each group turn recorded as part of the preceding individual turn state. Our data management system preserves the vocal date on its original time base, and such recoding is relatively easy. Adequacy of a first-order Markov model can be tested (for either the five- or the six-state turn set) by examining the transitional matrix showing the probability of each turn following each other turn at each moment in time. Observed probability values in the transitional matrix at a time lag $t + 1$ are tested against predicted values (which are given by the original matrix squared; Jaffe & Feldstein, 1970, p. 66). Because group conversations seem to us basically similar to dyadic conversations, we expect a first-order Markov model to fit our data.

Time to stationarity. If turn transitions approximate a Markov process, then time to stationarity should be a useful dependent variable. Time to stationarity is the number of time intervals it takes for the process to reach the point at which predictions of who speaks next converge upon their simple expected probability values. Jaffe, Cassotta, and Feldstein (1964) found monologues that were more "spontaneous" reached stationarity faster, and we would expect shorter time to stationarity in group conversations where there is more emphasis upon superficial social exchange and less upon intellectual problem solving.

H and T. The information theory statistics H and T (Attneave, 1959) can be computed from the transitional matrix of turn taking. H is a measure of uncertainty, which is approximately equivalent to variance and the opposite of predictability, order, structure, or stereotypy. With regard to group conversation, H indicates how similar the amount of vocalization is among group members. H is computed from the marginals of the transitional matrix. T is a measure of sequential ordering and is computed from the marginals minus the cells. H and T have been used by Davis (1963) to assess order in a sociometric matrix and by Gottman and Bakeman (1979) to analyze predictability in a stream of behavior. In our data, H indexes uncertainty in who on the average speaks at a given moment, and T indexes uncertainty in who follows whom at the next moment. H and T can be computed for each group.

The uncertainty H in knowing who will be talking at any given moment can be computed from the simple probabilities of each member's talking, using the formula $H = - \Sigma p_i \log (2) p_i$. H will vary from 0 (when one member does all the talking) to $\log (2)N$ (when all N members talk equally). The uncertainty T in knowing who will follow whom can be computed from the transitional probabilites in the turn-taking matrix, where rows represent the person speaking at time t and columns represent the person speaking at time $t + 1$. Using the formula for H aforementioned, T is equal to H for row totals, plus H for column totals, minus H for cells. T is much like the chi-square statistic, and it shows the degree of contingency in the sequential ordering of turns. T will be high when there is predictability, or order, in who speaks next. Order might be caused by one speaker always following another or by two speakers following each other. T will be low if transitions are not predictable, that is, where there is little or no statistical contingency between the rows and columns of the matrix. It is possible for order to change over time, as when a homogeneous group evolves into a set of independent dyads and triads. Order can also exist in larger sets of transitions as, say, in a family where father always speaks to mother and mother to child, but father and child do not speak to each other directly. An exploration of such patterns in families is provided by Parker (1984).

A–B–A sequences. The statistic T, analogously to chi-square, provides information on the overall sequential dependency to the pattern of turn taking across a whole group conversation. Davis (1963) suggests that T be used for initial screening of data, and that subsets of the overall pattern be examined to provide a detailed picture of what is going on. Parker (1984) argues that much of group conversation is made up of brief periods of turn taking between pairs of members within the overall group. Parker has used such pairings to characterize the conversations of disturbed families.

Such pairings within our data can be tabulated, using Roger Bakeman's ESEQ ("Event Sequences") program. ESEQ will, among other things, take as input the string of turns from subjects A, B, C, D, and E, count all two-person chains of the form A–B–A, A–C–A, A–D–A, . . . , E–C–E, E–D–E, and compute z-scores to indicate whether each kind of chain occurs more or less frequently than expected by chance. The resulting scores can tell us the total amount of such dyadic sequential patterning that occurs in a group. Like the statistic T, these chains might be used to define the overall sequential patterning in a group. The ESEQ scores can also be summarized to show the role of each individual within the group. Summaries characterizing individuals could be correlated with peer ratings to show how members feel about persons who tend to be at the beginning and end (e.g., "A" in "A–B–A") or the center (e.g., "B" in "A–B–A") of sequential chains.

Fourier analysis of rhythm. Fourier analysis decomposes a complex wave form into its cyclical components. The vocal record of group conversations can be represented by a time series of numbers, the numbers indicating how many people (from 0 to 5) were vocalizing at each point in time. Plotted graphically, this curve would rise when several subjects speak at once and fall when there is silence. With such a data record as input, the computer program BMDP-1T will perform a Fourier analysis and determine the relative power of each component wavelength of the overall curve. This technique has been used by Dabbs (1983) and by Warner, Waggener, and Kronauer

(1983) to examine cycles of sound and silence in dyadic conversations. Fourier analysis would determine the most characteristic cyclical wavelength of the alternation of sound and silence in each group, which would then be related to members' evaluation of the group. We suspect that groups with shorter cycles seem to their members to be moving at a faster "pace" and therefore members find them more exciting and like them better.

The intraclass correlation coefficient. Intraclass r provides an index of similarity among members within a group. Feldstein and Welkowitz (Chapter 9) used intraclass r to define "congruence" in the vocal behavior of two members of a dyad, and they report that pauses and switching pauses were the vocal parameters that showed highest congruence. In extending the intraclass r measure from dyads to five-person groups, Dabbs and Ruback (1984) found high intraclass r's in switching pauses and simultaneous speech. The intraclass r is plausibly a measure of group cohesiveness, because it indexes the degree to which group members are behaving similarly to one another, and there is extensive literature relating similarity to liking. We think that cohesiveness, and the intraclass r, will increase with arousal.

Computer graphics. The statistics described previously, and the traditions from which they arise, are not part of the normal research vocabulary for many social psychologists. Further, they provide summary scores that are rich with meaning but often hard to visualize. There would be a two-fold advantage in developing more readily comprehensible ways of displaying data from group conversation. First, group members could see their own behavior in a feedback session and learn more about the group process and their role in it. And second, an investigator could change the time base in playing back the recorded data, to discover patterns that only become apparent at certain speeds (Dabbs, 1982). Once such patterns become visible to an investigator, more traditional statistical techniques can be used to define them and examine their significance.

We now have a program that displays a strip chart on the microcomputer screen showing the pattern of each group member's vocalization and silence, and much more impressive graphic displays would be relatively easy to produce. For example, a sociogram could be constructed in real time or during playback in faster than real time. A set of five spots could represent the five members of a group. Each spot could shimmer and grow in size as that member speaks, and a flying cursor could trace turn transitions among members. The cursor could grow wider with each transition, so that the final picture would have larger spots and wider lines to show which group members have spoken more and been involved more often in transitions with the other members. A graphics printer could make a copy of this picture available to group participants. The cost of this kind of display would be slight, and it could well have practical usefulness.

Data Collection

Equipment. Developing a conceptual model is only one necessary step in studying the patterns of sound and silence in group conversation. There is also the practical problem of how to collect and manage large amounts of data. Data collection is more complicated with a group than with a dyad. The system must recognize a person speaking alone and also recognize several persons speaking at once. The task is difficult, because each subject's voice will also be heard on the microphones of other subjects, and the crosstalk cancellation network used in Jaffe and Feldstein's AVTA cannot readily be applied to more than two microphones. The system we use was developed by Dabbs and Swiedler (1983), following the general approach of a system developed by Brown (1979).

Subjects in a group wear small lavaliere microphones. An electronic device continuously compares each microphone signal to a standard "trigger" level, which corresponds to the level of a very soft voice. Signals above the trigger level are amplified to 5 volts and monitored through the parallel input port of an Apple II computer. These signals reveal which microphones are active at a given moment, but more information is needed to identify which *subjects* are active, (i.e., to determine whether a sound on a given microphone comes from the person wearing the microphone or from someone else).

The relative intensity of microphone signals provides this information. Each speaker's voice will be louder and thus will be above the trigger level more of the time, on his or her microphone than on any of the other microphones. The computer checks each microphone line about eight times per millisecond. Every 10 milliseconds, the computer summarizes its findings and designates the microphone that has been above the trigger level most often as belonging to the true speaker. The computer cancels isolated spikes of noise and fills in brief (300 millisecond) pauses within and between the speaker's words.

This same procedure allows the computer to recognize several subjects speaking at once. When people speak together, their voices are not perfectly syncrhonized. In the continuous mix of syllables, accents, and brief pauses, even the softest-spoken speaker will have moments of being loudest. In picking the most active microphone every 10 milliseconds, the computer under these conditions will find rapid alternation in which of several microphones is most active; the computer then "looks over" its current array and designates all these microphones as belonging to active speakers. The same procedure that filled brief gaps in the speech of a single person will now fill gaps caused by the computer's alternation among the microphones of the several simultaneous speakers. Every quarter second the computer saves one 8-bit byte, each bit representing the on–off state of one person's voice in a group of up to eight members.

Data Management

Enough data are produced by the on–off patterning of a group of voices to overwhelm an unwary investigator. Without careful planning of how to handle the data, many analyses become difficult or impossible to perform (Bakeman & Dabbs, 1976). The data acquisition system described by Brown (1979) has not led to much research, perhaps because of problems in storing and analyzing data. We have employed a data management approach that generally follows the approach outlined by Bakeman and Dabbs (1976).

The voice data, sampled every quarter second, produces 2400 samples for every 10 minutes of conversation. Each sample is stored as an 8-bit number that describes the on–off states of the voices of up to eight subjects. The data are stored on disk by the Apple II computer and later transferred to a mainframe computer, where a Pascal program called GRPTFD transforms the data into the codes that define the Grouptalk model. GRPTFD operates by tracing changes in the raw on–off voice signals through the possible states and transitions of the Grouptalk model, emitting codes to describe each subject and the group as a whole at each quarter-second moment.

The resulting Grouptalk codes are stored in a computer file using Bakeman's (1975) Time Frame Data (TFD) format. Each line in TFD shows how long the conversational state of a group remained unchanged and what codes characterized the group during this time. Any change in the conversation (any change in the on–off state of any microphone) produces a new line in TFD. TFD provides an efficient format for storing data and providing input into several programs for summarizing data written by Roger Bakeman: STRIP, DFREQ, JOINT, and ESEQ. STRIP generates a strip chart showing the moment-by-moment state of any specified set of behavioral codes. It provides an overview of the data and helps the investigator detect glaring errors. A strip chart of a three-person group could show transitions among A's Turn, B's Turn, C's Turn, and Group Turn. DFREQ summarizes durations and frequencies of each behavioral code. In the three-person group, DFREQ could compute time vocalizing, number of vocalizations, and mean length of vocalizations of Subject A, Subject B., Subject C, and Group. JOINT computes simple probabilities of events, conditional probabilities of co-occurring events, and transitional probabilities of events following each other at specified lags in time. (The simple and conditional probabilities shown in Fig. 10.1 were computed using JOINT.) ESEQ analyzes specified sequences of events. For example, ESEQ could count occurrences of the sequence "A's

Turn–C's Turn–B's Turn" and compute the expected probability of this number of occurrences.

Any collateral data collected during group interaction (e.g., the moments that ideas appeared in brainstorming sessions) can be merged with the vocal codes in the Time Frame Data file. Summary vocal statistics characterizing each individual and each group can then be computed and placed in a separate computer file, along with questionnare data, peer ratings, and judges' evaluations of each individual and group. This latter file provides the input for SPSS and BMDP correlational and analysis of variance programs. Peer ratings can be corrected using Kenny's SOREMO program (Kenny, Lord, & Garg, 1983) to control for the bias caused by missing self-ratings in a round-robin design. The analysis of hierarchical, nested round-robin designs implemented by Kenny's LEVEL (Kenny & Stigler, 1983) program can be used to contrast individual-level with group-level effects.

Example: Group Problem Solving

Twenty problem-solving groups were studied to test the adequacy of the data acquisition and management system and the usefulness of the Group-talk model. The primary focus of the study concerned leadership and group cohesion.

Method. Mixed-sex groups of five undergraduate subjects each spent 10–30 minutes working on the Desert-Survival Problem (Lafferty & Pond, 1974). In this task subjects play the role of being stranded in the desert after a plane crash. A brief written description sets the stage, and subjects were given a list of 15 items (e.g., knife, compass, water) that have survived the crash. Subjects first ranked the 15 items, as individuals, in terms of their importance for survival, then discussed the problem to reach group consensus on the importance of each item. Finally, subjects completed questionnaires giving their reactions to each other and to the group as a whole.

Vocal, visual, and self-report measures were obtained. The subjects wore lavaliere microphones leading to the microcomputer system in an adjacent room. A videotape recording was made with the subjects' knowledge using a single microphone and a television camera mounted near the ceiling on one side of the room. Self-report measures were obtained with postexperimental questionnaires, on which the subjects gave their reactions to each other and to the group as a whole.

Questionnaire items included six 7-point adjective scales for rating the group and six peer-rating scales for rating each member of the group. The peer-rating scales included two items each on leadership, task performance and likeability. Individual peer-rating responses were processed by Kenny, Lord, and Garg's (1984) SOREMO program, which corrects for a bias that is produced by missing self-ratings in round-robin designs such as the present one. Pearson correlation coefficients among the six corrected peer ratings across the 100 subjects were very high, ranging from .74 to .95, and the ratings were therefore combined into an overall single mean peer rating given each group member. Group-rating scales included two items each on group likeability, quality of group performance, and group spirit. Intercorrelations among these items were lower than for the peer-rating scales, ranging from .22 to .69, and responses of the five-group members were combined into mean ratings of group likeability, performance, and spirit. Voice data were collected with the Group AVTA system, and Grouptalk codes for each quarter second were determined and stored in Time Frame Data (TFD) format. The program DFREQ examined the TFD file and computed the percentage of each session occupied by each Grouptalk code. DFREQ summaries for each individual and each group were used as input into SPSS statistical programs for further analysis.

Results. We first examined how subjects' vocal behavior was related to ratings received from their peers. Pooled within-group correlations were computed to eliminate the effect of mean differences among groups. The correlations revealed a pervasive relationship: Talking is associated with positive ratings. We therefore went one step further and computed partial correlations to control for overall amount of talking in the relationships between Grouptalk scores and peer ratings. The correlations and partial correlations are shown in Table 10.1, along with the mean percentage of session time occupied by each grouptalk code for each subject.

TABLE 10.1
Individual Vocal Behavior and Pooled Within-Group Correlations with Rating by Peers

Grouptalk Code	Mean % of Session	Pearson r with Peer Ratings	Partial r Controlling for Talk
Total talk	16.3	.80[b]	—
Turn	19.2	.79[b]	.05
Vocalization	12.1	.79[b]	−.07
Pause	3.2	.67[b]	−.06
Switching pause	3.9	.69[b]	.27[b]
Latency before turn	3.8	.57[b]	.21[a]
Noninterrupt. simul. speech	1.7	.16	.05
Interrupt. simul. speech	1.0	.53[b]	.14
Group simul. speech	1.4	.33[b]	.01

[a]p .05
[b]p .01

Note: There were 20 groups of 5 subjects each. Degrees of freedom are 79 for the Pearson r's and 78 for the partial r's.

It is apparent from Table 10.1 that talking in groups is desirable, but this has long been known (Stein & Heller, 1979). Unfortunately, our peer ratings were so highly intercorrelated that we could not examine whether talking was differentially related to leadership and to likeability. The Grouptalk codes are all generally associated with overall amount of talk, and controlling for overall talk tends to remove the significant relationships between Grouptalk codes and peer ratings. An exception lies in the pauses around a speaker's turn. Speakers who spend more time in switching pauses after their turns are rated more highly. One might say that these speakers "give pause" to the group when they speak; others are a little slower to respond, producing a longer switching pause. Higher ratings are also related to the latency before a speaker's turn; higher rated speakers are themselves a little slower to speak than are other members of the group. The picture suggested here is one of a slight aloofness, or separation from others in the ongoing vocal stream, on the part of the more highly rated group members.

We next examined how the vocal behavior of the group was related to evaluations given to the group by its members. It seemed likely to us that the members' evaluations of a group would be related to the amount of talking in the group and to how often several individuals talked at once.

The percentage of time each group spent in each of the Grouptalk codes was correlated with members' mean ratings of the group's likeability, performance, and spirit. These correlations are shown in Table 10.2, along with the mean percentage of the session time that someone (anyone) was emitting one of the Grouptalk codes. Because total talking was not as strongly related to group ratings as it had been to peer ratings (see line 1 of Table 10.2) and because of the lower power of statistical tests based upon 20 groups than upon 100 subjects, total talking was not partialed out of any of the relationships shown in the table.

The pattern of findings was different for groups than for individuals. Overall talking was significantly related to group spirit but not to group likeability or performance. Group spirit was negatively related to pausing and positively related both to individual vocalizations and to simultaneous speech and group vocalization. Group performance was related only slightly to the Grouptalk parameters.

Finally, we examined how the unpredictability of talking, which we suspect reflects an egalitarian quality of a conversation, was related to members' evaluations of their groups. We expected members to like groups more in which members' participation was about equal. The information statistic H was computed for each group based upon the distribution of turns among the five members. For each member, the probability p represented the number of time frames occupied by that member's speaking turns, divided by the total number of time frames in the conversation. For this analysis, time frames oc-

TABLE 10.2
Group Vocal Activity and Between-Group Correlations with Member Ratings of Group
Likability, Performance, and Spirit

Grouptalk Code	Mean % of Session	Likeability	Pearson r with: Performance	Spirit
Talk	81.5	.35	−.18	.66[b]
Individual turn	96.0	−.28	.18	−.35
Vocalization	60.6	.29	−.05	.52[b]
Pause	15.9	−.48[a]	−.09	−.62[b]
Switching pause	19.5	−.12	.17	−.32
Noninterrupt. simul. speech	5.6	.41[a]	−.06	.70[b]
Interrupt. simul. speech	3.7	.37	−.18	.59[b]
Group turn	4.0	.28	−.17	.35
Group vocalization	3.1	.27	−.27	.58[b]
Group pause	.1	.03	−.41[a]	.11
Group switching pause	.9	.12	.11	−.24

[a]p .05
[b]p .01
Note: Degrees of freedom are 18.

cupying a group turn were recoded as part of the immediately preceding individual turn.

Correlations were computed between H and members' mean ratings of the group's likeability, performance, and spirit. The correlation with group spirit was positive and significant, $r = .49$ 18 df, $p < .05$. The correlations with likeability and performance also were positive (rs = .35 and .27, respectively) but not statistically significant. It appears that H does provide a group index that is related to the psychological reactions of group members. Variations in T based on this same set of data were not related to members' evaluations of their group.

In summary, the microcomputer efficiently processed a large amount of data, and the Grouptalk model organized these data in a meaningful and comprehensive manner. The familiar finding that leadership and talking are related (e.g., Stein & Heller, 1979) was made with more precision than in previous studies, and we found that beyond the simple amount of talking there were significant differences among the Grouptalk codes. A more equal ("uncertain") distribution of talking was desirable. Analysis at the group level showed that members enjoyed groups in which there was a lot of talking and little pausing, although analysis at the individual level showed pauses before and after turns were more important than vocalizations in producing high ratings.

Other Applications

These findings indicate that the Grouptalk model and data acquisition system can provide useful information about individual differences and group processes. We have been pursuing applications to other kinds of groups.

Brainstorming and creativity. "Brainstorming" has been studied for well over 20 years, but patterns of vocalization during brainstorming have not been examined. The most widely reported finding in the area is that real groups produce fewer ideas than "nominal" groups made up of the same number of individuals working alone, although findings regarding the *quality* of ideas produced are less clear (Lamm & Trommsdorff, 1973). It is sometimes hypothesized that groups produce less because not everyone can talk at once or because others inhibit new ideas, although Stroebe (1982) has proposed an explanation based upon social loafing, which arises when each subject in a group knows he or she does not have to produce. An objective chronography of the vocal patterns in brainstorming groups could bear upon the question of competition for available speaking time among group members. It might also tell us what speech patterns are associated with the production of ideas.

In our research (Ruback, Dabbs, & Hopper, 1984), 20 groups of five persons each were asked to find ways to increase the number of tourists visiting the United States each year. The four principles of brainstorming were explained to subjects: no criticism, freewheeling welcome, quantity wanted, and combination and improvement sought. Grouptalk, video, and audio recordings of each session were made. A pair of judges identified the speaker and the precise time of occurrence of each new idea, and this information was entered along with the stream of vocal parameters into the Time Frame Data file.

Analyses focused upon leadership and upon vocal behavior around the appearance of new ideas. Leaders talked more than others and, even controlling for amount of talk, leaders spent more time in turns and in the pauses before and after their turns. Ideas tended to appear in the stream of conversation following periods of increased pausing between speakers rather than periods of increased talk. Subjects liked groups more that talked more, and they specifically preferred groups that spent more time vocalizing and less time in switching pauses. Productivity was affected quite differently by talking, with more ideas produced when there was less talking.

Observations of these groups suggest that characteristics of emergent leaders vary considerably. Often there is no leader, but the leaders who do appear are oriented toward task or social concerns. Sometimes the same person embodies both concerns, encouraging and cajoling others along toward solving the problem. But we have seen frustration on the part of a task leader who kept trying to bring the group back toward solving the problem whereas a social leader ignored task demands and helped the group have fun. Analysis of cases like these may begin to reveal differences in the characteristic vocal patterns of the two kinds of leaders.

Juvenile delinquency and family patterns. Grouptalk measures obtained on juvenile delinquents and their families may provide information about how delinquents communicate with their families and how their families react differently to them and to other siblings. Prior research suggests that communication patterns differ depending on whether or not the family contains a juvenile delinquent. For example, delinquents appear more inclined either to interrupt the conversations of others or to remain silent throughout a conversation than do nondelinquents (Haley, 1980). In a study of the content of family conversations, Alexander (1973) found that normal families had high rates of supportive communications (characterized by information seeking, information giving, empathy, and equality), whereas delinquent families had high rates of defensive communications (characterized by punishment and threats). Moreover, there tended to be a difference in the reciprocity of communication: Normal families showed parent–child reciprocity in supportive communications but not in defensive communications, whereas delinquent families showed reciprocity in defensive communications but not in supportive communications. Parker (1984) reports that families with a delinquent member are more highly ordered in their communication patterns than are normal families, with the mother a center of communication and little direct communication between father and child. The reciprocity of communication between family members or lack of it might be reflected in some of the content-free Grouptalk parameters. Differences in the communication links between the delinquent and each of the two parents might become visible over the course of a long session. Changes in the Grouptalk variables over several sessions might show changes as the delinquency situation improves or deteriorates.

Other research. Using other populations we can study vocal patterns in group psychotherapy and family therapy. In pretests we have noticed that discussion in some groups seems to be limited to same-sex group members. It might be worthwhile to arrange groups with a single male or single female member to study the effects of minority membership. A jury decision-making paradigm (Davis, Holt, Spitzer, & Stasser, 1981) would allow us to use the Grouptalk measures to reveal what types of individuals will lead the jury deliberations or have the most or least influence on the jury's final judgment. In examining same-sex five-person groups (Dabbs & Ruback, 1984) we have found that females talked more than males; specifically, they spent more time vocalizing and less time in switching pauses than males did. This finding, at variance with results of most studies, may have been due to the fact that same-sex rather than mixed-sex groups were used and that these groups were discussing social rather than intellectual topics.

The use of content-free vocal parameters to examine the functioning of a group also has practical as well as theoretical appeal. This approach could benefit any organization that depends on small group meetings to produce ideas and solve problems that range from easy to hard, routine to novel, or casual to life threatening. If vocal parameters are "read" correctly, they may indicate how a group is functioning and whether its behavior is appropriate for the problem at hand. Objective measures of vocal parameters could provide feedback to a group while it is functioning. They could keep a leader aware of each member's degree of participation, which might be especially important when new ideas are needed and some members are silent because their ideas conflict with what is being discussed. Vocal scores might provide an index of group spirit or be manipulated to vary group spirit, which could have different effects depending on whether the task at hand is performed better at high or low levels of group spirit. These practical applications should bear upon the functioning of groups that have meetings and discussions to deal with problems of varying complexity and novelty.

There are many questions and populations to study. Our current aim is a dual one of validating the Grouptalk model as a description of group conversation and using the model to gather data on substantive issues.

REFERENCES

Alexander, J. F. Defensive and supportive communications in normal and deviant families. *Journal of Consulting and Clinical Psychology,* 1973, *40,* 223-231.

Attneave, F. *Applications of information theory to psychology.* New York: Henry Holt, 1959.

Bakeman, R. *Data analyzing procedures* (Tech. Rep. 1). Atlanta, Georgia State University, Infancy Laboratory, 1975.

Bakeman, R., & Dabbs, J. M., Jr. Social interaction observed: Some approaches to the analysis of behavior streams. *Personality and Social Psychology Bulletin,* 1976, *2,* 335-345.

Bales, R. F. *Interaction process analysis: A method for the study of small groups.* Cambridge, MA: Addison-Wesley, 1950.

Bales, R. F. *Personality and interpersonal behavior.* New York: Holt, Rinehart, & Winston, 1970.

Bales, R. F., & Cohen, S. P. *SYMLOG: A system for the multiple level observation of groups.* New York: Free Press, 1979.

Brown, E. F. Apparatus for collecting voice chronography data. *Behavior Research Methods and Instrumentation,* 1979, *11,* 553-557.

Capella, J. N. Mutual influence in expressive behavior: Adult-adult and infant-infant dyadic interaction. *Psychological Bulletin,* 1981, *89,* 101-132.

Cossotta, L., Feldstein, S., & Jaffe, J. AVTA: Device for automatic vocal transaction analysis. *Journal of Experimental Analysis of Behavior,* 1964, *7,* 99-104.

Chapple, E. D. The interaction chronograph: Its evolution and present application. *Personnel,* 1949, *25,* 295-307.

Dabbs, J. M., Jr. Making things visible. In J. Van Maanen, J. M. Dabbs, Jr., & R. R. Faulkner, *Varieties of qualitative research.* Beverly Hills, CA: Sage, 1982.

Dabbs, J. M., Jr. Fourier analysis and the rhythm of conversation. Atlanta, GA: Georgia State University, 1983 (ERIC Document Reproduction Service No. ED 222 959).

Dabbs, J. M., Jr., & Ruback, R. B. Vocal patterns in male and female groups. *Personality and Social Psychology Bulletin,* 1984, *10,* 518–525.

Dabbs, J. M., Jr., & Swiedler, T. C. Group AVTA: A microcomputer system for group voice chronography. *Behavior Research Methods and Instrumentation,* 1983, *15,* 79–84.

Dashiell, J. F. Experimental studies of the influence of social situations on the behavior of individual human adults. In C. Murchison (Ed.), *Handbook of social psychology.* Worcester: Clark University Press, 1935.

Davis, J. H. The preliminary analysis of emergent social structure in groups. *Psychometrika,* 1963, *28,* 189–199.

Davis, J. H., Holt, R. W., Spitzer, C. E., & Stasser, G. The effects of consensus requirements and multiple decisions on mock juror verdict preferences. *Journal of Experimental Social Psychology,* 1981, *17,* 1–15.

Gottman, J. M., & Bakeman, R. The sequential analysis of observational data. In M. E. Lamb, S. J. Suomi, & G. R. Stephenson (Eds.), *Social interaction analysis: Methodological issues.* Madison, WI: University of Wisconsin Press, 1979.

Hackman, J. R. *Theory and method in group effectiveness research.* Paper presented at the annual meeting of the American Psychological Association, Anaheim, CA, August, 1983.

Hackman, J. R., & Morris, C. G. Group tasks, group interaction process, and group performance effectiveness: A review and proposed integration. In L. Berkowitz (Ed.), *Advances in experimental social psychology* (Vol. 8). New York: Academic, 1975.

Haley, J. *Leaving home: The therapy of disturbed young people.* New York: McGraw–Hill, 1980.

Jaffe, J., Cassotta,L., & Feldstein, S. A Markovian model of time patterns in speech. *Science,* 1964, *144,* 884–886.

Jaffe, J., & Feldstein, S. *Rhythms of dialogue.* New York: Academic, 1970.

Kelley, H. H., & Thibaut, J. W. Experimental studies of group problem solving and process. In G. Lindzey (Ed.), *Handbook of social psychology* (Vol. 2). Cambridge, MA: Addison–Wesley, 1954.

Kenny, D. A., Lord, R. G., & Garg, S. A. Social relations analysis of peer ratings. Unpublished manuscript, University of Connecticut, 1983.

Kenny, D. A. Lord, R. G., & Garg, S. A. *A social relations model of peer rating.* Unpublished manuscript, University of Connecticut, 1984.

Kenny, D. A., & Stigler, J. W. LEVEL: A FORTRAN IV program for correlational analysis of group-individual structures. *Behavior Research Methods and Instrumentation,* 1983, *15,* 606.

Lafferty, J. C., & Pond, A. *The desert survival situation.* Plymouth, MI: Human Synergistics, 1974.

Lamm, H., & Trommsdorff, G. Group versus individual performance on tasks requiring ideational proficiency (brainstorming): A review. *European Journal of Social Psychology,* 1973, *3,* 361–388.

Lustig, M. W. Computer analysis of talk–silence patterns in triads. *Communication Quarterly,* 1980, Fall, 3–12.

McGrath, J. E., & Kravitz, D. A. Group research. In M. R. Rosenzweig, & L. W. Porter (Eds.), *Annual review of psychology* (Vol. 33). Palo Alto, CA: Annual Reviews, 1982.

Parker, K. C. H. *Speaking sequence based models of group interaction: Relational dominance and involvement in groups and families.* Unpublished doctoral dissertation, University of Waterloo, 1984.

Ruback, R. B., Dabbs, J. M., Jr., & Hopper, C. H. The process of brainstorming: An analysis using individual and group vocal parameters. *Journal of Personality and Social Psychology,* 1984, *47,* 558–567.

Siegman, A. W., & Feldstein, S. (Eds.). *Of speech and time: Temporal speech patterns in interpersonal contexts.* Hillsdale, NJ: Lawrence Erlbaum Associates, 1979.

Stein, R. T., & Heller, T. An empirical analysis of the correlations between leadership status and participation rates reported in the literature. *Journal of Personality and Social Psychology, 37,* 1993–2002, 1979.

Strodtbeck, F. L. Techniques for stimulating family interaction in the laboratory and methodological problems of conducting experiments with families. In J. L. Framo (Ed.), *Family interaction: A dialogue between family researchers and family therapists.* New York: Springer, 1972.

Stroebe, W. *Motivational determinants of group productivity.* Paper presented at the Second International Conference on Social Processes in Small Groups, Nags Head, NC, June 1982.

Warner, R. M., Waggener, T. B., & Kronauer, R. E. Synchronized cycles in ventilation and vocal activity during spontaneous conversational speech. *Journal of Applied Physiology: Respiratory, Environmental, and Exercise Physiology,* 1983, *54,* 1324–1334.

V FUNCTIONAL PERSPECTIVES

11 A Functional Analysis of Space in Social Interaction

Miles L. Patterson
Joyce A. Edinger
University of Missouri-St. Louis

In the earlier edition of this book, this discussion of space and social interaction focused on two general issues: (a) correlates of spatial behavior and (b) the consequence of manipulating spatial arrangements. That provided a practical and convenient way of dividing the research on spatial behavior, but it lacked an integrative theoretical theme. In the present chapter we hope to correct that shortcoming by developing our discussion around a broad functional perspective. It is interesting to note that the final discussion in the previous chapter anticipated the functional approach that we take in this chapter. Specifically, in the section on future prospects were the following comments by Patterson (1978):

> Another general concern which deserves more attention in the future is to examine the use of space in terms of its functions. We know, for example, that, among other purposes, interpersonal space can be manipulated to communicate intimacy, to upset or threaten someone, or to achieve relative isolation or privacy. In order to understand better the influence of space in social situations, we should know what, if any, purpose is intended by the participants in differing arrangements. (p. 285)

Recently we have developed different aspects of a functional approach to nonverbal behavior (Edinger & Patterson, 1983; Patterson, 1982a, b); that functional perspective provides an organizing theme in the present chapter for our analysis of research on spatial behavior. Before reviewing that body of research, it is necessary to discuss briefly the essentials of the functional model (Patterson, 1982b).

AN OVERVIEW OF THE FUNCTIONAL MODEL

The functional model of nonverbal exchange is based on a general assumption that similar forms and levels of nonverbal involvement can serve very different functions in social interaction. For example, a smile may be used to (a) indicate liking, (b) deceive another, or (c) facilitate an interactive exchange. Conversely, component behaviors contributing to nonverbal involvement may be interchangeable in serving the same function or purpose. Thus, liking may be indicated by a smile, an extended gaze, moving close to another, or a gentle touch. Of course, these components may well be integrated into a coordinated pattern that is more intense than any one of the components.

The functional model identifies five general functions of nonverbal involvement. Specifically, those functions include (a) the informational function, (b) interaction regulation, (c) expressing intimacy, (d) social control, and (e) the service-task function. Technically, all nonverbal behavior might be described as potentially informative. However, it seems useful to partition those informational behaviors that specifically aid in the regulation of interaction. Consequently, the regulation function might be viewed as a special case of the informational function. For example, a head nod, a pause, or a specific gesture might serve to coordinate the give and take in conversational exchange. Although each of those behaviors is informative in some way, it is probably more important to stress their regulatory impact in the interaction.

It is assumed that the informational and interaction regulation functions are molecular in focus; that is, they may be used to describe isolated behavioral patterns that occur in interaction. In contrast, the intimacy, social control, and service-task functions are molar in focus. Those functions may be used to describe the motives or purposes underlying an interaction or, at least, a substantial part of interaction. We describe the molar functions after making one additional distinction about the informational function. Identifying a given behavioral sequence as informational (i.e., not regulating interaction) is not, in itself, a particularly important distinction. However, a contrast proposed between informative behavior that is *communicative* and that which is *indicative* is quite important. MacKay's (1972) emphasis on communication as purposive behavior underlies this distinction. MacKay suggests that communicative behavior is initiated for some purpose or goal, whereas indicative behavior is not. A communicative pattern would include some evaluation of whether or not the specific behavior achieved its purpose. Presumably then, a communicative pattern would involve some greater awareness of one's behavior and its implications. In contrast, an indicative pattern is relatively spontaneous, not goal directed, and less likely to be prominent in cognitive awareness.

The communication-indication contrast is particularly important in differentiating between the molar functions of intimacy and social control. Intimacy might be described as a bipolar dimension that reflects union with, openness toward, or commitment to another person. Typically, increased intimacy is the result of increased liking or love for another individual. Depending on the situational constraints, cultural norms, or individual difference factors, increased intimacy is usually manifested by increased nonverbal involvement with another, e.g., close approach, smiling, touch. The functional model assumes that the behavioral manifestations of some level of intimacy is usually indicative; that is, such a pattern does not necessitate cognitive awareness or deliberation. Thus, there is consistency between the perceived intimacy and nonverbal involvement. Of course, such a generalization has to be tempered by the constraining influences of situation. In contrast, the social control function identifies the use of increased or decreased nonverbal involvement in the service of some interpersonal goal. Such behavior may be characterized as purposive. That purposive pattern is presumed to be represented within awareness more clearly than is the intimacy pattern. Furthermore, in contrast to the intimacy function, the social control function may involve inconsistency between underlying affect toward the other person and the nonverbal involvement initiated toward that person.

Examples of the operation of each of these functions may clarify the distinction between them. A specific exchange between good friends may typically be dominated by a high level of liking that spontaneously leads to increased involvement in the form of a close approach, postural openness, increased gaze, and occasional smiling. In this intimacy exchange, the increased involvement occurs relatively automatically with little or no cognitive awareness of one's behavior. If the same individuals were not friends, but rather a personnel manager and a prospective employee engaged in a job interview, the resulting exchange would probably reflect a social control function. A sensitive applicant in this situation is likely to manage his or her behavior very carefully in order to create a desirable impression. Consequently, the applicant might choose to sit moderately close to the personnel manager, be directly oriented, lean forward slightly, initiate a high level of gaze, and smile and nod frequently in response to the manager's comments. Such a moderately high level of overall involvement may occur even though the applicant strongly dislikes the personnel manager. The behavioral routine described here becomes a means to the end of influencing the personnel manager's decision. In this case there is a clear inconsistency between the underlying affect and the overt behavior of the applicant. Obviously, the fact that one has either a personal (intimate) relationship with another or a relationship that is completely utilitarian does not mean that the former is limited only to intimacy exchanges and the latter only to social control exchanges.

Most married couples can attest to the occasional manipulative (social control) exchanges that occur in intimate relationships.

The final molar function, the service-task function, describes those exchanges that are based primarily on the constraints of the service or task characteristics that underlie the interaction. In this case the bases for nonverbal involvement are essentially impersonal and reflect little about the personal relationship between the interactants. Heslin (1974) has described such service exchanges with respect to the use of touch. For example, physician-patient, barber/hairdresser–customer, or tailor–customer exchanges often involve the initiation of relatively "intimate" forms of touch. However, that touch is merely a means to the end of treating or serving the needs of the patient–customer and is not relevant for assessing the underlying intimacy between individuals. Thus, the situational norms or expectancies for service-task exchanges determine the appropriate level of involvement, independent of affective reactions toward the other person. As those norms are more clearly shared by each interactant, the opportunity for misattribution from the behaviors becomes lessened.

The molar functions of intimacy, social control, and the service-task function are central in this model's explanation of nonverbal exchange. However, the initiation and development of these functions are mediated by various factors antecedent to the interaction. Figure 11.1 provides an illustration of the sequential steps proposed in the functional model. The antecedent factors include personal variables such as culture, gender, and personality. In addition, past experience and relational-situational characteristics may be categorized as antecedent factors. The effect of the antecedent factors is manifested in terms of behavioral predispositions, arousal change, and cognitive expectancies. Those preinteraction mediators determine the functional perspectives of interactants and their initial levels of nonverbal involvement at the interaction stage. When the result is an unstable exchange, arousal change and cognitive assessment should lead to an adjustment in the perceived function of the exchange and/or an adjustment in the level of nonverbal involvement. The model predicts that unstable exchanges should move toward stability over time through the mediating influence of cognitions and arousal. However, if an unstable exchange cannot be moved toward stability (comfort, predictability), then it will probably be terminated sooner than a stable exchange would be.

The basic structure of the functional model should provide a useful means for organizing this discussion of spatial behavior; that is, the model's focus on the functions of nonverbal behavior and the manner in which those functions are affected by antecedent variables provides a basis for reviewing and analyzing spatial behavior. Although our review is limited to spatial behavior, it is important to realize that a broad understanding of social behavior requires sensitivity to a variety of other behaviors that moderate the influence

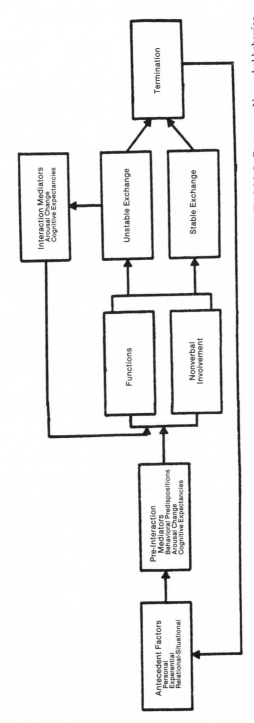

FIG. 11.1 A diagram of the sequential functional model of nonverbal exchange. (Reproduced from R. Heslin & M. L. Patterson, Nonverbal behavior and social psychology. New York: Plenum, 1982, with permission of publisher.)

527

of space. This concern is reflected throughout this chapter in our discussion of the research on space.

OVERVIEW OF RESEARCH ON SPACE

A great deal of the research on the social use of space has developed around the concepts of territoriality and personal space. Territoriality may be defined as the demarcation and defense of a fixed geographical area. The use of the concept of territory seems to be generally consistent across animal research (Hediger, 1961) and human research (Altman & Haythorn, 1967). Sommer and Becker (1969) have extended the definition, however, to include temporary territories such as chairs or tables in public settings. They note that the increasing use of public spaces often requires the marking of places with coats or other materials to insure the holding of a chair or table. Even with this extended definition of the term, territoriality is not nearly as pervasive a concern for social interaction as is personal space. The term *personal space* has been used to describe the limiting distance that separates individuals when interacting with one another. Personal space has been likened to a bubble or sphere that serves to protect the individual from intrusion by others. Hall (1966, p. 119) has used a similar term, personal distance, to refer to a range from 1.5 to 4 ft that serves to separate individuals comfortably. Although one might disagree with the specific limits of such a range, the recognition of variability in this protective distance is important. Occasionally, one will encounter discussions of personal space that imply that a single fixed interaction distance may be identified for each individual. It should become clear as we progress through this chapter that a number of factors exercise considerable influence on the interaction distances chosen in various settings. Consequently, a single estimate of personal space for an individual is not really possible. In fact, the notion of a personal space seems to add little to our understanding of space in social interaction (Patterson, 1975). Consequently, we use terms such as *interaction distance* or *interpersonal distance* in our discussion. Practically, those terms reflect what is actually measured or observed in research and at the same time avoid reifying distance into a personal space that surrounds each individual.

Measurement Issues

The investigation of interaction distance has been attempted in a variety of ways. Before covering the substantive issues, it may be useful to describe some of the general techniques employed to study spatial behavior. Most frequently used is the direct or estimated measurement of individuals in live interactions, whether in a field or laboratory setting. A modification of this interaction procedure is the observation of approaches by an individual to a target person. With this technique, a subject is usually asked simply to approach another person from one or more directions until he or she begins to feel uncomfortable (e.g., Frankel & Barrett, 1971). Further removed from the live interaction is a type of role-playing procedure in which a person is instructed to imagine another individual in a specific location and approach him or her according to some instructional set (e.g., Mehrabian, 1968a). Another group of methods for studying interaction distance might be called representational or symbolic procedures because they are designed to approximate the live interaction. The questionnaire method as used by Sommer (1965) requires respondents to indicate their preferred seating arrangements in specific situations. A diagram of a table or set of tables allows the subject to visualize his or her alternative seating choices, given some limits set by the instructions. Frequent use has been made of miniaturized human figures or silhouettes that may be arranged on some background to simulate a real interaction. Usually the figures are two-dimensional cloth or cardboard cutouts (Kuethe, 1962), but three-dimensional scaled figures (Desor, 1972) have also been used. A final type of symbolic procedure is a paper-and-pencil variant of the limiting approach technique (Duke & Nowicki, 1972). In this procedure a central point on a diagram is used to represent the individual. Eight radii emanate from the central point representing the angles of approach by an imaginary person. A simple mark along each radius defines the limit of a comfortable interpersonal distance (CID).

Because there are a variety of substantially different techniques employed in the research on space, the question of the validity of these procedures becomes an important one. There are a number of studies that have examined the validity issues, but the results are not consistent. Little (1965) has reported a very high correlation between the placement of doll figures and live actresses in the simulation of various relationships. Other research has also reported substantial correlations between paper-and-pencil symbolic techniques and actual behavioral approaches (Duke & Kiebach, 1974; Duke & Nowicki, 1972; Haase & Markey, 1973; Pedersen, 1973a). Specific support for the validity of Duke and Nowicki's CID measure has also been found in the results of other studies (Veitch, Getsinger, & Arkkelin, 1976; White & Lira, 1978). Other researchers have found, however, that various representational measures are not consistently related to behavioral measures (Alovisetti, 1977; Aronow, Reznikoff, Tryon, & Rauchway, 1977; Dosey & Meisels, 1969; Love & Aiello, 1980; Slane, Petruska, & Cheyfitz, 1981). In an examination of different techniques for studying reactions to spatial invasion, Becker and Mayo (1970) reported significant differences between several different measures. Further evidence for differences between measurement techniques was indicated in an investigation of nine different procedures, that yielded an average intercorrelation between pairs of measures of only $r = .21$ (Knowles & Johnsen, 1974). More recently Knowles (1980) has suggested that low correlations among different measures should not be the sole criterion for judging the convergent validity of the representational measures. Instead, he proposes that convergence of results from different, but uncorrelated, measures is sufficient evidence for the generalizability or external validity of different measures; that is, even if a representational measure is not correlated with a behavioral measure, the presence of similar effects argues for the representational measure's external validity.

Although the evidence is conflicting, there are a couple of points that may help in coming to an evaluation of different procedures. First, most of these studies require the testing of the same subjects over different measures. Once subjects become aware of the purpose of the investigation—and that is difficult to conceal—it is quite possible that they may attempt to respond consistently, even though the instructions may not direct that. If that happens, then the correlations between different measures will be artificially high and thereby overestimate the real similarity between measures. Even though Knowles (1980) has reported convergence of effects across representational and live measures of interaction distance (in spite of low correlations among the different measures), the overall pattern of results across studies is not one that instills confidence in the utility of the representational measures. Consequently, in this review we emphasize the results from studies using actual distances in live interactions. A final qualification has to be noted here too. Some of the live measures can be very reactive. For example, distance measures that request subjects to stop approaching the experimenter or confederate sensitize the subjects to judgments that may normally be outside their awareness. These measures, like the representational measures, almost certainly have less external validity than do spontaneous, unobtrusive measures.

Our emphasis on the functional perspective in this review begins with an analysis of the role of the antecedent factors in spatial behavior. Prominent among the antecedent influences are (a) the personal factors of culture, gender, and personality; (b) the experiential factor, and (c) the relational-situational factor.

PERSONAL FACTORS

Culture

Cross-cultural comparisons. The work of E. T. Hall has been very critical in bringing to light the importance of cultural influences on spatial behavior. Hall (1963, 1966) has suggested that the use of space, like the use of language, is culturally specific. He believes that people from dissimilar cultures not only use and structure space differently but actually experience it differently. In fact, Hall (1968) suggests that these differences between cultures have their basis in the selective programming of sensory capacities of the individuals in each culture. We might use a general contact–noncontact dimension to describe the interpersonal use of space in various cultures. At the extreme of those preferring very close contact are Arabs, who typically interact at distances close enough to permit feeling the other's breath (Hall, 1966, pp. 159–160). Hall claimed that this tendency may be the result of the Arab's appreciation of olfactory and tactile cues in interaction. Latin American and Mediterranean people could also be described as being high-contact groups. Hall suggests that the other extreme of interactive involvement includes the English and some North European people whose aloofness and reserve may be linked to their preference for distant interactions. In contrast to the role of olfactory and tactile feedback regulating interpersonal distance in the contact groups, the interaction distance in the noncontact groups may be regulated by visual feedback. According to Hall, such visual feedback may include feedback from the muscles around the eyes, ease of focusing on the other person, or size of the retinal image (Hall, 1968). Although Hall's observations of cultural differences are very interesting, a note of caution should be sounded about their generalizability. From Hall's descriptions, most of the samples he observed seem to be middle- or upper-class males. Social class and sex differences within culture may moderate the general patterns Hall describes.

Hall's personal reports of substantial cultural differences in the use of space have been investigated empirically in several studies. Although some of the evidence supports the hypothesis of cultural variability in the use of space, the results are not consistent. The close and intense interactions among Arabs that Hall reported have been systematically observed in the laboratory setting where pairs of male college students were brought together for discussions. The Arab pairs not only sat closer together but had more directly confronting body orientations, greater eye contact, and spoke in louder voices than did American pairs (Watson & Graves, 1966). It is also interesting to note that the Arab pairs showed occasional, though apparently accidental, touching that was never present among the American pairs. In a very similar study, using Latin American students as representative of a contact culture, no differences were found relative to the North American students (Forston & Larson, 1968). Although no differences were observed in the structured sessions in that study, the authors reported that before and after the discussion the Latin Americans appeared to stand closer together than the North American pairs did. In an observational study of subjects from Costa Rica, Panama, and Columbia, Shuter (1976) found that the Costa Ricans preferred higher levels of involvement than did the Columbians. Apparently, Latin Americans are not as homogeneous in their interaction patterns as outsiders might assume. Some evidence for preferred higher levels of contact among people of the southern Mediterranean countries can be found in a study by Shuter (1977). In that study, Italians were found to interact more closely during conversations than did Germans or Americans.

In some cases the cross-cultural differences in spacing do not seem to be indicative of consistent differences in nonverbal involvement. For example, in two studies by Noesjirwan (1977, 1978), Indonesian pairs sat closer together in public settings than did Australian pairs. Furthermore, the Indonesians in both studies also touched and smiled more than did the Australians. However, in the second study (Noesjirwan, 1978) Australian males sat in more directly facing orientations and initiated higher levels of gaze than did the Indonesians. Noesjirwan proposed that the high involvement of the Indonesians in the form of close approaches, touch, and smiling may have reflected a high level of affiliation, whereas the direct body orientation and high gaze of the Australians may have reflected dominance. In a study by Sussman and Rosenfeld (1982), Venezuelan foreign students sat relatively close and Japanese foreign students sat relatively distant when they were speaking their own languages. However, the difference between the two cultural groups faded when both groups spoke English. Furthermore, American subjects speaking English sat at a distance comparable to the Venezuelan and Japanese subjects who spoke English. Thus, the Venezuelan and Japanese subjects closely approximated the American conversational distance when they spoke English, but not when they spoke their native languages. Presumably, the spoken language and the behavioral norms associated with it affect the spacing choices individuals initiate.

The results of the Sussman and Rosenfeld study are particularly interesting because, in this case, they suggest that Hall's hypothesis of differential sensory programming across cultures is not an adequate explanation of the differential use of space; that is, if the Venezuelan and Japanese spacing patterns were a function of their experiencing different sensory inputs, then simply changing the language spoken should not affect those sensory experiences. In contrast to Hall's proposal, the differences in the Sussman and Rosenfeld study suggest that the spacing preferences may be very much situationally determined.

Subcultural comparisons.   The apparent differences in interaction distances as a function of national origin have implications for potential subcultural differences in a country like the United States with its diverse population. Hall's (1966, pp. 172–173) suggestion that Puerto Ricans and blacks have much greater involvement than do New Englanders and Americans of Northern European stock would lead us to expect that the blacks and Puerto Ricans interact more closely than whites. There is mixed support for that prediction. In two similar studies, black children in the first and second grade have been found to interact more closely than white children of the same age (Aiello & Jones, 1971; Jones & Aiello, 1973). However, Jones and Aiello (1973) found that those differences were reduced and apparently beginning to reverse themselves by the time the children were at the fifth-grade level. In both of these studies, it is important to note that socioeconomic level differences were confounded with race. In fact, Scherer (1974) examined the role of socioeconomic level and race in spacing in children and found that social class, but not race, affected interaction distances. Specifically, lower-class students stood closer to one another than did middle-class students. However, in another study that controlled for socioeconomic level, Mexican–American second graders related to one another at closer distances than did the white students (Ford & Graves, 1977). Consistent with the Jones and Aiello (1973) results, the ethnic differences disappeared in Ford and Graves' eighth-grade students. Ethnic differences have been found for older school children in at least one study. McGurk (1976) found, in a sample of fifth- through eighth-grade students, that Puerto Rican children reacted most favorably toward a counseling encounter when the counselor was seated 2.5 ft from them, whereas the Anglo children reacted most favorably when the counselor was seated 4 ft from them.

Further support for the hypothesis of closer interaction among blacks than whites was found in a study measuring the approaches of college students toward a confederate of their own race and sex (Bauer, 1973). Unfortunately, no information was available on the socioeconomic levels of the subjects in this study. Bauer was rather cautious in interpreting the very close approaches by black subjects (9.8 in vs. 15.6 in for whites) as really representing the minimal comfortable approach distance. He suggested that instructions asking subjects to "approach as close as you feel comfortable" may have been interpreted by blacks as a challenge and consequently led to closer approaches. When socioeconomic level was equated in another study of spatial preferences in adults, no differences were found among Black, Puerto Rican, Italian, and Chinese groups (Jones, 1971).

With the exception of Bauer's results that may reflect more than racial differences in approach distances, the pattern of findings from the other studies might suggest that differential spatial preferences across subcultures are learned early in life but gradually become more similar by exposure to a common cultural norm. However, Baxter (1970) has found differences in proxemic behavior that contrast with the results of both Aiello and Jones' studies on children. Baxter's observations of pairs of individuals at a zoo indicated shorter interaction distances for white adults than for black adults. An interesting speculation was offered by Jones and Aiello (1973) in trying to resolve these inconsistencies. This speculation revolved around the nature of the interaction in each of these settings. Jones and Aiello observed that blacks, when not actually communicating, were more likely to move away from one another than whites were. Because their own distance measures

ken only during periods when children were talking, whereas a sub-
number of Baxter's observations must have been taken during intervals when pairs were not talking, the different studies may have capitalized
on situational differences between blacks and whites; that is, Jones and
Aiello may have sampled a situation predisposing blacks to interact relatively
closely, whereas Baxter may have sampled a contrasting situation in which
blacks were relatively distant. The issue of potential subcultural differences
will probably not be adequately clarified until a systematic consideration of
developmental, situational, and socioeconomic determinants resolves the
present inconsistencies.

Gender Differences

The gender of the interactants in a social situation seems to be an important
factor in determining spatial patterning, but its effects are complex. In same-
sex dyads, females have been found to interact more closely than do males
(Adler & Iverson, 1974; Aiello & Jones, 1971; Dosey & Meisels, 1969; Evans
& Cherulnik, 1980; Pellegrini & Empey, 1970). Similar patterns have been
found for groups larger than dyads (Mehrabian & Diamond, 1971; Patterson
& Schaeffer, 1975). Presumably, the expression of intimacy in same-sex
groups has traditionally been more acceptable for females than for males,
and these interaction distance differences may reflect that. The picture becomes a little more complicated in the case of opposite-sex pairings. For example, in the Dosey and Meisels (1969) study, females who approached
standing males remained more distant than those who approached females.
In contrast, male subjects approached males and females at comparable distances. Similarly, others have found that females typically allow closer approaches to themselves than do males (Crowe, 1977; Hartnett, Bailey, &
Gibson, 1970; Mehrabian & Friar, 1969; Tennis & Dabbs, 1975; Willis,
1966). Here again, traditional sex-role differences seem indicated; that is, females appear to be more reserved than males, both in actively approaching
someone of the opposite sex and in passively limiting the closer approach of
such a person. This generalization is probably more representative of interactions between strangers or casual acquaintances of the opposite sex than it is
for those romantically involved (or married).

The differences suggested between males and females in their preferred interaction distances with others of the same sex are consistent with the results
of two experiments on crowding. In those two studies, females reacted more
positively to others of the same sex under crowded than uncrowded conditions, whereas males reacted in just the opposite way (Freedman, Levy,
Buchanan, & Price, 1972; Ross, Layton, Erickson, & Schopler, 1973). Other
researchers, however, have failed to replicate this effect (Marshall & Heslin,
1975; Stokols, Rall, Pinner, & Schopler, 1973). The Marshall and Heslin ex-

periment is particularly interesting because the experimenters found results directly opposing those of the Freedman et al. (1972) and Ross et al. (1973) studies. Specifically, Marshall and Heslin found that for a relatively long (1.5 hr) and highly involving task, males reacted more positively to the crowded condition, whereas females reacted more positively to the uncrowded condition. The authors suggested that for males in the crowded condition the combination of the longer duration and the necessity for cooperation in the task reduced the initial aggressiveness and defensiveness. In their place a feeling of camaraderie was instilled for accomplishing a common goal. For females in the crowded condition, the extension of a task-oriented interaction over a considerable period of time may have led to some frustration because a warm, sociable interaction was thereby prevented. Certainly results such as these suggest that much more needs to be known about the way that situational determinants affect sex differences.

A further complication in the differences between males and females in homogeneous sex groups is that the sex of the subject is confounded with the sex of the partner. Dabbs (1977) has proposed that the sex of the partner may be a more important determinant of reactions to crowding than is sex of the subject. Some support for that notion can be found in a study from our laboratory. In that study, males' ratings were unaffected by either the sex of the partners or the arrangement of the chairs (circular or L-shape) in a high-density condition. However, female subjects rated the circular arrangement more positively when they were with other females, but more negatively when they were in mixed-sex groups (Patterson, Roth, & Schenk, 1979). In this instance, the sex of the partner was more important than the sex of the subject. Consistent with that finding are the results of two other studies on small group interaction. In both studies, subjects in three-person same-sex groups, regardless of their sex, preferred closer seating to a female than to a male group moderator (Giesen & Hendrick, 1977; Giesen & McClaren, 1976).

For the most part, the illustrations of gender differences in spatial behavior discussed up to this point have come from studies in which the subjects were not acquainted with one another. There is reason to believe that these patterns may be modified when the interactants are acquainted, especially for opposite-sex pairs. For example, Cook (1970) found, in both field observations and surveys, that opposite-sex pairs sat closer together in restaurants than same-sex pairs. Given the setting of this particular study, it is likely that pairs dining together would at least be friends. A similar result has been noted in the observation of pairs of individuals visiting a zoo. Cross-sex pairs stood closer than same-sex pairs in the adolescent and adult age groupings (Baxter, 1970). Again, in this setting, it is probable that most pairs walking together would be more than casual acquaintances. Further evidence for the effect of relationship on sex differences in spacing can be found in a study by Heshka and Nelson, 1972). Significantly closer approaches in outdoor settings were observed in pairs of friends or relatives than in pairs of strangers. Interaction distances in male–male dyads were similar for stranger and friend groups, but both male–female and female–female dyads interacted at closer distances in friend pairs than stranger pairs. Thus, in studies that sample pairs who are likely to be well acquainted, female and mixed-sex pairs typically interact more closely than do male pairs.

The role of the gender of the interactants is complex, but some general statement can probably be made on the basis of the research up to this point. In same-sex groups, females typically interact more closely than do males. Closer approaches by females may be a product of greater emphasis on affiliative and dependent relationships in the socialization process of females. In addition, the stigma of homosexuality that might be inferred from very close interactions between males probably serves to limit close approaches between males. Support for this latter factor can be seen in the similar approach distances for friend and stranger pairs among males. Females, in contrast, approach female friends much more closely than female strangers. Interaction distance in cross-sex pairs, like that in female pairs, seems to be clearly affected by degree of acquaintance. Relatively distant patterns are common for interactions between unacquainted males and females, whereas much closer patterns are typical between close friends or lovers. There are undoubtedly other limiting factors for which there is not much information yet available. For example, Baxter's (1970) study suggests that gender differences in spacing may be minimal until the adolescent years, but Aiello and Jones (1971) have found differences in 6- to 8-year-olds. It is also possible, as Marshall and Heslin (1975) have found, that differences in the purpose and duration of an interaction may affect the general patterns suggested as a function of gender. A particularly useful way of pursuing gender differences may be in terms of sex-role orientations. That consideration is beyond the scope of this chapter, but the interested reader might examine Ickes' (1981) model of sex-role influences on interaction.

Personality

Stability of spatial preferences. It is common in much of the material written about human spatial behavior to make assumptions about individual differences in spacing. It is often suggested that such differences are a product of personality differences between individuals. It does seem clear that over time in similar situations preferred interaction distances are quite stable. The correlations between approaches in two interview sessions, in one case separated by 20 min and in another by 1 week, were essentially identical, $r = .96$ and $r = .97$, respectively (Patterson, 1973a). In another study using an interview format, approaches to the same interviewer separated by 1 or 2 weeks produced correlations of approximately $r = .90$ (Daniell & Lewis,

1972). When different interviewers were employed, the correlations over similar intervals averaged approximately $r = .80$. The stability in spatial behaviors across time seems to be present as early as 4 or 5 years of age (Eberts & Lepper, 1975). Although these results suggest that spatial preferences are stable over time, that may be less characteristic of individuals who score highly on neuroticism (Long, Calhoun, & Selby, 1977). Nevertheless there seems to be sufficient stability over time to pursue the issue of identifying specific characteristics that could be responsible for individual spatial preferences.

Normal-abnormal differences.   At a fairly general level, there is some evidence suggesting that psychiatric patients may differ from normal subjects in the use of space in social interactions. Specifically, in two studies schizophrenics compared to normals have shown greater avoidance of others, as indicated by increased interpersonal distance (Horowitz, Duff, & Stratton, 1964; Sommer, 1959). However, Aronow (1974) found no differences among process schizophrenics, reactive schizophrenics, and normal hospital employees on one live and three representational measures of spacing. Aronow suggested that the considerable degree of structure inherent in these various measures may facilitate the appropriate behavior from the schizophrenic subjects. A second experiment in Sommer's (1959) article may represent a less structured task. In that experiment, schizophrenics who were instructed to approach a seated decoy tended to sit adjacent to rather than opposite from the decoy as most normals did. In this case, a relatively close but nonconfronting arrangement selected by schizophrenics may serve to minimize interaction just as avoidance does; that is, adjacent seating does not facilitate interaction as much as opposite seating does. Sommer suggested that these distortions in use of space also result in causing others to withdraw. Such inappropriate spatial interaction is generally consistent with the pattern of deficient social skills typically noted in schizophrenics.

Extreme interpersonal distances have been noted in another very select group of individuals—violent prisoners. A comparison between groups of violent and nonviolent inmates indicated that in order to feel comfortable the violent prisoners required approximately four times as much area around themselves as the nonviolent prisoners did (Kinzel, 1970). This difference was particularly striking when the experimenter approached from behind the prisoner. Kinzel interpreted the larger separation for violent prisoners in approaches from behind as being an indication of a high level of homosexual anxiety. It would generally be expected, however, that violent-prone individuals would require a greater margin of safety from others, especially from behind, even if their fears did not specifically relate to homosexual assaults. A number of other studies have similarly reported preferences for greater interpersonal distances among violent than nonviolent prisoners including (a) black South African prisoners (Roger & Schalekamp, 1976), (b) New

Zealand prisoners (Gilmour & Walkey, 1981), and (c) female prisoners (Rubinstein, 1975). In another experiment, an electrodermal measure of arousal provided comparable results to those found with a verbal "stop" measure; that is, the violent prisoners not only required more distance around them, but they also showed higher levels of arousal for similar approaches than did the nonviolent prisoners (Curran, Blatchley, & Hanlon, 1978). Finally, results from two studies indicate that violent adolescents require more space than do their less violent peers (Booraem, Flowers, Bodner, & Satterfield, 1977; Newman & Pollack, 1973). In all these studies, however, little support was found for Kinzel's findings of the differences being greatest in approaches from behind the subjects.

Normal personality differences.   Given the rather extreme differences between psychiatric and normal groups or violent and nonviolent individuals, it is probably not very surprising that differences exist in their spatial behavior. The attempts to relate differential spacing behavior, however, to personality characteristics among normal individuals have not been consistently successful. One group of personality variables, including extraversion, affiliation, and social anxiety, has indicated some predictive utility for spatial behavior. A questionnaire procedure involving the choice of seating arrangements from diagrams indicated that extraverts, in contrast to introverts, tended not only to sit closer to others, but also to choose positions allowing greater eye contact (Cook, 1970). The preference for closer seating with increased levels of extraversion has also been found in actual interview sessions (Patterson & Holmes, 1966). Similarly, closer comfortable approach distances have been related to higher levels of extraversion (Pedersen, 1973b). In another investigation of the relationship of extraversion to interpersonal distance, no differences were found between introverts and extraverts in their degree of approach to an interviewer (Williams, 1971). However, when the initiation of the approach was reversed, Williams found that extraverts permitted closer approaches to themselves than did introverts.

A second personality factor that may be a determinant of differential spacing behavior is social anxiety. Patterson (1973a, 1977) found marginally significant correlations between social anxiety and the subject's approach in an interview session, indicating that those scoring higher on social anxiety tended to remain more distant from the interviewer than did lower scorers. Consistent with this relationship was the tendency for the more distant subjects to rate themselves as less at ease than the closer subjects (Patterson, 1973a). In a second experiment in the same study, no personality measures were taken, but the more distant subjects again rated themselves as less at ease than the closer ones. It is possible that the relationship between social anxiety and avoidance is bidirectional; that is, social anxiety might induce avoidance, but, given the avoidance, anxiety may also be produced, especially if such avoidance behavior is seen as inappropriate.

Another personality variable that should be relevant for social behavior is affiliation. Two different studies have provided data indicating that those higher on affiliation prefer greater proximity to others than do those low on affiliation. Clore (1969) examined the relationships between need affiliation of subjects and their approaches to the chair of a "stranger" whom they were about to meet. In fact, the stranger never appeared, but approaches to the chair, marked with a coat, were closer for high affiliators than for low affiliators. In one of the few studies focusing on the spatial behaviors of groups, Mehrabian and Diamond (1971) observed seating arrangements in four-person groups gathered together supposedly to evaluate some musical selections. Those scoring high on affiliation sat significantly closer to others than did those low on affiliation. Mehrabian has suggested elsewhere, however, that closeness of approach is not really part of a general affiliation factor for interpersonal behavior but may be more consistent with an intimacy or liking factor (Mehrabian & Ksionzky, 1972).

The evidence relating the role of any one of these personality variables to spatial behavior is certainly not so compelling as to generate unqualified confidence. The number of studies is relatively small and the relationships found are not particularly strong. It is important to note, however, that there is evidence indicating very substantial correlations among test measures of extraversion, affiliation, and social anxiety (Patterson & Strauss, 1972). In fact, a majority of items from each of these three dimensions loaded on a common social approach–avoidance factor. Thus, the separate results, showing that extraversion, affiliation, and lack of social anxiety predict close approaches, may be overlapping and representative of a more general social approach–avoidance dimension.

There are several other dimensions that have been examined for their potential relationship to spatial behavior, but the evidence is not as substantial as with the social approach–avoidance variables. Some of these results indicate closer approaches may be related to high self-esteem (Frankel & Barrett, 1971; Kissell, 1974), low authoritarianism (Frankel & Barrett, 1971), high exhibitionism and impulsivity (Sewell & Heisler, 1973), high self-concept (Stratton, Tekippl, & Flick, 1973), low test anxiety in an evaluative setting (Karabenick & Meisels, 1972), high dominance (Fromme & Beam, 1974), and, in mixed-sex pairs, higher levels of heterosexuality (Hartnett et al., 1970) and lower levels of shyness (Carducci & Webber, 1979). One of the more theoretically interesting findings involves results relating approach distance to the internal–external control dimension. On a symbolic approach task, both the internal- and external-control individuals approached friends and relatives at similar distances, but internals approached strangers much more closely than did externals (Duke & Nowicki, 1972; Heckel & Hiers, 1977). Duke and Nowicki explained these differences in terms of expectancies of the two groups in various situations. In dealing with friends and relatives, both groups acted similarly because clear expectancies were formed on the basis of adequate past experience. However, with strangers, externals, who lack confidence in their own abilities to affect situations, remained relatively distant whereas internals, expecting to control the situation, came much closer. One set of results has failed to support these predictions (Edwards, 1977) and, consequently, the generality of Duke and Nowicki's proposed dynamics might be questioned.

The studies reviewed that do indicate potential personality determinants of spatial behavior are by no means representative of all the investigations focusing on individual differences. In direct contrast to other results, Patterson (1973a) and Meisels and Canter (1970) found no relationship between interaction distance and extraversion. Several other variables might intuitively be expected to influence spatial behavior in social settings. Some of the variables that have been examined and found not predictive of interpersonal distance are sensitivity to rejection (Mehrabian & Diamond, 1971), social desirability (Patterson, 1973a; Patterson & Holmes, 1966), and body image boundary and anxiety as measured by the Rorschach (Dosey & Meisels, 1969).

The personal factors in the form of culture, gender, and personality do influence the spacing patterns of individuals in social interaction. Other factors such as age, socioeconomic status, religion, or occupation may also contribute to differences in the use of space. Furthermore, it seems likely that a general understanding of the role of the personal factors requires a sensitivity to the interaction effects produced by the various factors. In addition, the impact of the personal factors may also be qualified by their interaction with the other antecedents — experiential and relational-situational factors.

EXPERIENTIAL FACTOR

The experiential factor focuses on the residual influence of recent and/or similar experiences on subsequent interactions. Although there is little empirical research on the role of past experience on later interactive behavior, an obvious case can be made for the importance of experience. One general mechanism that may mediate the effect of recent experience is some learning-reinforcement process. This process might be activated directly or vicariously through observing the consequences of the behavior of others. In general, spatial patterns that are reinforced, either directly or vicariously, will tend to be repeated.

The mediation of experiential effects might also take the form of some stimulation-regulation process. For example, close approaches may produce overstimulation (Milgram, 1970) that later leads to some sort of compensatory adjustment. This process is a kind of homeostatic mechanism, similar to that proposed in Argyle and Dean's (1965) equilibrium theory. However, in this case the compensatory adjustments may be seen as extending over time in an attempt to correct some over or understimulation. One experiment might be cited here. Specifically, interpersonal distance was found to increase following an insult, compared to a no-insult control (O'Neal, Brunault, Carifio, Troutwine, & Epstein, 1980). This effect was greater when the experimenter who made the insult was approached than when an assistant was approached. However, the effect was present even for the assistant.

An alternate stimulation-regulation process is Helson's (1964) adaptation level (AL) approach. In fact, AL theory would seem to predict adjustments that are oppposite those of a stimulation-based homeostatic model. Specifically, repeated deviations from the AL of previous approaches should result in a new AL for distance that is closer to the more recent approaches. Thus additional experiences of close (or distant) interaction distances should be perceived as less extreme and produce smaller adjustments.

It is not surprising that little systematic research on experience exists because such research typically requires the measurement and/or manipulation of distance over time and across situations. Nevertheless, experience is an important antecedent that should be considered in evaluating spatial preferences.

RELATIONAL-SITUATIONAL FACTOR

The relational-situational factor refers to the interaction effect of relationship by situational influences on patterns of nonverbal involvement. These separate elements are grouped into this common category because the effect of the relationship between individuals is often modified by the situational circumstances surrounding an interaction. Little research has been conducted, however, on the interactive influence of relationship by situation for the same reason that there is little research on the experiential factor—it requires repeated measurement or manipulation over different circumstances.

There is a considerable literature on the influences of relationship on spatial behavior. Much of that has developed out of Byrne's (1969, 1971) similarity-attraction paradigm. Typically, in that paradigm, similarity in attitudes was manipulated by the experimenter and its effects noted on various ratings. However, the generalizability of the relationship between similarity and attraction has been extended by behavioral measures of attraction, including interpersonal distance. In general, as the degree of attraction between two individuals increases, the approach distance between them decreases. This result has been supported both in a laboratory setting where an individual was forced to sit close to either a similar or dissimilar stranger (Byrne, Baskett, & Hodges, 1971) and in an analysis of behavior following computer-dating matches (Byrne, Ervin, & Lamberth, 1970). In an interview situation, Clore (1969) found only a slight tendency for increased attraction to result in closer approaches, but he did find that with increased attraction approaches were more directly confronting. Other studies have shown that increasing the degree of liking toward an imagined other, in a role-playing situation, produced linear decreases in distance to the imagined other (Mehrabian, 1968a; Mehrabian & Friar, 1969). Consistent with the preceding evidence are the findings that those intending to indicate disapproval from another (Mehrabian & Ksionzky, 1972) remain more distant from that person than those indicating or receiving approval.

In addition to the degree of liking or attraction, the specific type of relationship between individuals also influences their spatial interaction. However, the type of relationship and degree of attraction are obviously not independent of one another. For example, very high levels of attraction in opposite-sex pairs may lead to a marital relationship. Conversely, the development of a specific relationship, such as that between a parent and newborn infant, usually leads to high attraction and love. It is not surprising that those in more intimate relationships typically sit closer (Cook, 1970) or stand closer (Heshka & Nelson, 1972; Willis, 1966) to one another when initiating conversations than do those in less intimate relationships. Again, as discussed in the section on gender differences, increased friendship or intimacy in male-female and female–female pairs typically leads to closer interaction distances. The absence of closer approaches between males, who are even good friends, may be due to a greater concern about homosexuality among males than females. Further support for the indication of deeper relationships through closer interactions has also been found by Little (1965) who used line drawings, silhouettes, and live pairs of individuals. Across these differing methods, friends interacted at closer distances than acquaintances, who, in turn, interacted more closely than did strangers.

There are a few other relationship dimensions that may influence spatial patterning. For example, approaches to others were found to be closer if the others are (a) age peers rather than those younger or older (Latta, 1978; Willis, 1966), (b) of similar rather than different race (Campbell, Kruskal, & Wallace, 1966; Hendricks & Bootzin, 1976; Willis, 1966), and (c) of similar rather than different status (Lott & Sommer, 1967). In another study that examined status differences, no effects were found in approach distances. However, in that study equal-status employees stood in more directly facing orientations than did unequal-status employees (Jorgenson, 1975). Even these diverse findings may be interpreted in terms of the general hypothesis of increased liking or attraction leading to closer spatial arrangements. It seems quite clear, as Byrne and his associates have found, that similarity in beliefs or attitudes leads to attraction that, in turn, is manifested behaviorally by closer interactions. However, in many situations, especially with those individuals about whom we know very little, inferences about similarity must be made on minimal information. It has been found that, with little or no information about beliefs of others, evaluations may be determined by other salient characteristics of the individuals such as race (Stein, Hardyck, & Smith, 1965). Given little knowledge of others' beliefs, similarities in race, age, or status may serve to indicate something about the broader, more critical similarities in beliefs; that is, similarities in race, age, or status may lead to inferences of similarities in beliefs. The resulting conclusions of similarity or dissimilarity may determine attraction and indirectly affect interpersonal distance. Obviously, other factors besides perceived similarity influence attraction toward others. Physical attractiveness (Berscheid & Walster, 1978), power, or ability to reward others can add to one's attractiveness. If such qualities do increase a person's attractiveness, that should lead others to prefer a higher level of involvement with that individual.

Although research has not focused on relationship influences as a function of situation, it is not difficult to imagine the interactive effect of these two factors. The norms associated with different situations often provide different constraints on the manifestation of nonverbal involvement. The superior–subordinate relationship at a place of business may require a very formal and distant interactive pattern. However, the same individuals will probably interact more closely when they leave the work setting for an after-hours cocktail. An important setting-based element that may also interact with the type of relationship is that of territory. Individuals who are on their own territories are typically more comfortable and more controlling in an interaction than are visitors. Thus, a territory-holder may take the initiative in setting the limits of appropriate involvement in an interaction.

One approach that may be useful in analyzing situational variables is the behavior setting perspective of ecological psychology (Barker, 1968; Wicker, 1979). The behavior-setting approach emphasizes the homogeneity in behavior across people as a function of selection mechanisms and physical and social constraints in a setting; that is, because individuals typically migrate to settings that are compatible with their interests, and the settings, in turn, often selectively admit individuals, there is considerable pressure for homogeneity in behavior. That homogeneity is increased by the physical constraints and social norms affecting everyone in the setting. The result of these converging setting pressures is that the effect of relationships on social behavior is moderated by the setting itself.

MEDIATION OF ANTECEDENT INFLUENCES

In this review of the antecedent factors that affect spatial behavior, we have identified three general categories of variables — personal, experiential, and relational-situational variables. The functional model assumes that the influence of these antecedent factors is mediated more directly by behavioral predispositions, arousal change, and cognitive assessment. In general it is assumed that the personal factors such as culture, gender, and personality contribute to relatively stable behavioral predispositions for particular levels of nonverbal involvement. These predispositions can be seen as habitual patterns of relating to other people that require little or no cognitive input. For example, the extraverted person who approaches others closely and engages in a highly involved interaction typically operates at an "automatic," nonreflective level. As long as others do not react too extremely or the interaction is not an unusual one (e.g., a conversation with a very important person), the actor's dominant pattern of high involvement evolves with little cognitive awareness.

The experiential and relational-situational factors are assumed to exert their influence primarily through the mediators of arousal change and cognitive assessment; that is, the residue of past experience and the anticipation of specific interpersonal and situational circumstances can contribute to arousal change and to cognitive expectancies about the impending interaction. The link between the arousal and cognitive activity is probably a bidirectional one. Arousal change can signal the need for some cognitive evaluation (Schachter & Singer, 1962), or the nature of the cognitive expectancy can, in turn, precipitate a change in arousal. The coordinated cognitive-affective activity might lead to specific expectancies or strategies for involvement that substantially determine an actor's behavior in an interaction. For example, the expectancy of meeting a good friend predictably leads to closer approaches and greater involvement than does the expectancy of meeting a disliked acquaintance. However, sometimes the affective reaction toward another person is not a good predictor of behavior toward that individual. One might *behave* in a close and friendly manner with the disliked superior for the simple reason of protecting one's job. In a general fashion, the cognitive expectancies about an interaction determine the anticipated functions underlying an interaction. Those functions and their influence on spatial behavior are the next concern of this discussion.

FUNCTIONS OF SPATIAL BEHAVIOR

Informational Function

In the earlier discussion of the functional model we suggested that the identification of the informational function is practically less important than the contrast between the communicative and indicative categories of that function; that is, with the exception of those occurrences in which nonverbal behavior serves a specific regulatory function, all behavior might be described as informational. Although the informational category may not be a very discriminating classification, some examples relating to spatial behavior may be useful.

The more obvious instances in which spatial behavior is clearly informative are in the formation of impressions. For example, closer approaches by an individual toward another person typically leads third-party observers to judge the approaching person more favorably (Kelly, 1972; Mehrabian, 1968b). A close approach and a light touch (on the back) by a confederate has also been found to produce more favorable reactions from subjects (Jourard & Friedman, 1970). Individuals who approach more closely are usually judged more favorably (Patterson & Sechrest, 1970). Obviously if the approaching person comes too close and invades another's space, then reactions can become very negative. We discuss the effects of spatial invasion in the review of the social control function.

A person's spatial behavior and other nonverbal behavior can be potentially informative in a number of ways. The few examples cited here relate specifically to impression formation, and that is a basic and important consideration in relating to others. The distinction proposed earlier regarding informational behaviors that may be either communicative or indicative is critical to the process of forming impressions. When an individual behaves in a spontaneous or indicative fashion, reactive attributions typically result that identify aspects of the environment as potential causes for behavior. In contrast, if an individual behaves in an intentional or communicative fashion, purposive attributions typically result that focus on potential reasons underlying the behavior (Schneider, Hastorf, & Ellsworth, 1979, pp. 123–128). The contrast between indicative and communicative patterns is discussed further in the review of intimacy and social control functions.

Regulating Interaction

Spatial arrangements obviously play a major role in the regulation of interaction. Hall's (1966, 1968) discussions of distance zones and Argyle and Kendon's (1967) analysis of standing and dynamic features of interaction both emphasize the important role of space in social behavior. More recently Kendon (1976, 1977) has stressed the importance of arrangement or orientation in the development of interactions. Kendon has proposed that common to almost all focused interactions is a basic facing or F-formation. The F-formation is present when the forward orientations (transactional segments) of each interactant overlap, and each person has easy visual access to the other group members. Consistent with Kendon's speculations, the results of two studies show that individuals who are most central, physically or visually, in small groups initiate and receive more comments (Michelini, Passalacqua, & Cusimano, 1976; Silverstein & Stang, 1976). The apparent functions of an F-formation include the following: (a) defines the normalcy of an interaction; (b) identifies the number of interactants; (c) creates a favorable communication network; (d) promotes the equality of the participants; and (e) creates a boundary between the group and the surrounding environment (Ciolek & Kendon, 1980). In other words, the F-formation promotes adaptive adjustments that facilitate coordinated and undisturbed interactions.

A considerable amount of research has focused on the specific effects of distance and arrangement on social interaction. One general assumption related to space and social interaction is that there exists an optimal distance and arrangement for specific types of interactions. This is reflected in Hall's (1966, 1968) classification of the intimate, personal, social-consultive, and public zones of interaction. As one moves from the intimate to public zones, interactions become more formal, less personal, and less intense. Argyle and Dean's (1965) equilibrium model of nonverbal intimacy might be seen as proposing a specific adaptive mechanism designed to compensate for inappropriate distances or arrangements; that is, given a particular function for a specific interaction, inappropriately close or far distances should lead to compensatory behavioral adjustments. Two reviews (Cappella, 1981; Patterson, 1973b) report fairly broad support for the predictions of equilibrium theory, although there may be other reasons for questioning the adequacy of that theory (Cappella & Greene, 1982; Patterson, 1976, 1982b).

There are a number of empirical studies that offer support for the existence of some optimal distance in specific interactions. For example, two studies show that a moderate distance (5 ft) between interactants may decrease anxiety (Rogers, Rearden, & Hillner, 1981) and increase verbal productivity (Stone & Morden, 1976) relative to close (2 ft) and far (9ft) distances. Supportive of those results are the findings of a study that attempted to determine the range of comfortable interaction distances. In that study subjects were instructed to approach first at a most comfortable seated distance and then move closer (farther) and farther away (closer) until they began to feel uncomfortable. The average of the most comfortable distance was 4.7 ft, whereas the average close and far approaches were 3.1 and 9.1 ft, respectively (Patterson, 1977). Similarly, Thompson, Aiello, and Epstein (1979) found that in seated interactions of two to four people of the same sex, intermediate distances in the 4–8 ft range were preferred over closer or farther distances. In addition, moderate distances in therapy or counseling exchanges may be preferred by clients and therapists (Knight & Bair, 1976; Lassen, 1973). Of course, what is moderate or optimal for one type of interaction in one setting may be extreme for another type of interaction in a different setting. For example, the studies cited thus far do not involve intimate exchanges between good friends or family members. In two studies of *standing* distances between either opposite-sex friends or strangers, the friend pairs expressed more comfort at closer distances (1-2 ft) but less comfort at farther distances (5-10 ft) than did the stranger pairs (Ashton, Shaw, & Worsham, 1980; Baker & Shaw, 1980).

A final issue with respect to regulating interaction is the role of distance in maintaining the boundaries and integrity of a group space. In studies that have examined the permeability of group space, it seems clear that the closer the interacting individuals, the less likely it is that they will be split or invaded by a passerby (Bouska & Beatty, 1978; Cheyne & Efran, 1972). Furthermore, with an increase in group size (Knowles, 1973) and apparent status (Bouska & Beatty, 1978), the likelihood of intrusion decreases. In addition, when it is obvious that a group is actively conversing, it is less likely that it will be invaded (Cheyne & Efran, 1972).

Expressing Intimacy

Much of the research on nonverbal behavior in social interaction has been interpreted in terms of expressing intimacy. Argyle and Dean (1965) and Patterson (1976) have used the term *intimacy* to refer both to the underlying affiliative needs that motivate nonverbal behavior and to the behaviors themselves (distance, gaze, smiling, verbal intimacy). Recently, Patterson (1982b) has proposed that the distinction between the underlying motives for behavior and the behaviors themselves be clarified. Specifically, he suggested that intimacy identify one of several general motives that underlie nonverbal exchange, whereas the term *nonverbal involvement* might be used to denote the set of behaviors that manifest those different motives. A more specific description of intimacy would identify it as the consequence of a basic affective or evaluative reaction toward another person. Practically, that positive affective reaction would involve liking, love, concern for, or commitment to the other person. Such a positive reaction would typically lead to the initiation of higher levels of nonverbal involvement. In terms of our earlier distinction between communication and indication, a high level of involvement would *indicate* high positive intimacy. Of course, intimacy is a bipolar dimension that reflects a range from intense liking or love at one end to intense disliking or hate at the other. Just as high involvement would indicate positive intimacy, avoidance characterized by low involvement would indicate negative intimacy.

The research that may be most informative regarding intimacy and the use of space is the work on the encoding of first impressions of others. In one study, liking was manipulated in opposite-sex interactions by bogus feedback regarding attitude similarity. Both male and female subjects sat closer to a liked than to a disliked opposite-sex confederate (Allgeier & Byrne, 1973). In another study feedback about attitude similarity was used factually in a study of "computer-dating" matches (Byrne, Ervin, & Lamberth, 1970). For both males and females, increased attraction to the partner was predictive of closer interpersonal distances during a period in which subjects received final instructions from the experimenter. In addition, proximity was related to the rated physical attractiveness of females, but not of males. This suggests that interpersonal distance may have been more under the control of the male than the female in each pair (Byrne et al., 1970). Other research cited in the discussion of the relational-situational factor clearly indicates that increased liking or attraction to others typically leads to closer interaction distances (Cook, 1970; Heshka & Nelson, 1972; Mehrabian, 1968a; Mehrabian & Friar, 1969; Willis, 1966).

Explicitly negative experiences or expectancies may precipitate decreased involvement, just as positive experiences and expectancies can precipitate increased involvement. For example, subjects who were told to expect a hostile group discussion chose more distant seating arrangements than those who were told to expect a friendly group discussion (Barrios & Giesen, 1977). Similarly, interpersonal distance can increase following an insult (O'Neal, Brunault, Carifio, Troutwine, & Epstein, 1980) or disapproval (Mehrabian & Ksionzky, 1972), and when subjects expect an abrupt and rude exchange (Feroleto & Gounard, 1975).

It is presumed that the intimacy function is more likely to be dominant in exchanges that are less structured and less evaluative in nature. Casual, informal interactions between acquaintances, conversations around the water cooler at work, or exchanges between family members at home are examples of circumstances that may facilitate the intimacy function. Under such conditions, it is assumed that the liking, love, or concern for the other person is manifested in a relatively spontaneous, nonreflective fashion. An important caution should be noted. The fact that an interaction occurs between individuals who hold strong and unambiguous affective reactions toward one another is not assurance that the intimacy function is necessarily primary. Very managed and manipulative behavioral strategies may be used on loved ones as well as on strangers. This should be more apparent in our discussion of the social control function.

Social Control

In some circumstances the influence of interpersonal affect may be minimal relative to the effect of specific goals or purposes of an interaction. On those occasions, the pattern of nonverbal involvement may be dominated by social control motives. Social control describes a range of motives that have a common focus of trying to influence the reactions of another person. The goal of trying to influence another person is manifested through the managed expression of nonverbal involvement. In contrast to the intimacy function in which cognitive awareness presumably plays a minimal role, the social control function often involves an awareness of the purpose of one's behavior. We have recently discussed the role of nonverbal involvement in social control (Edinger & Patterson, 1983) and do not attempt such a comprehensive review in this chapter. However, our sample of the research on spatial behavior and social control should provide a representative picture of that work.

Spatial invasion. The initiation of close approaches to unsuspecting subjects represents a technique that has been commonly used in studying the dynamics of spatial behavior. We have chosen to describe this research as an example of social control because the extremely close approaches of spatial invasions would normally seem to be the result of relatively deliberate attempts to influence others. In many cases, such close approaches may reflect attempted aggression, intimidation, or, perhaps, a form of ingratiation. The primary focus of the research on spatial invasions is on behavioral responses to the intruder and what those responses apparently indicate about cognitive-affective reactions toward the intruder. A characteristic response to very close approches from a stranger is an increased frequency and/or decreased latency of flight reactions (Felipe & Sommer, 1966; Koneni, Libuser, Morton, & Ebbesen, 1975; Smith & Knowles, 1978, 1979). This typical pattern may be influenced by the sex composition and ages of the individuals involved. For example, subjects may react more strongly to a spatial invasion from a male than from a female (Bleda & Bleda, 1978). Furthermore, male subjects may react more strongly to the invasions of other males. In one study, younger male adults (compared to older male adults) responded more aggressively by staring back a the intruder, inflating their posture, or even counterapproaching him (Veno, 1976). In another study, male intruders who approached subjects from behind on an escalator produced quicker flight from and more glances back toward the intruder among male than female subjects (Harris, Luginbuhl, & Fishbein, 1978). Furthermore, invasions may be more aversive when the intruder is not an age peer (Mishara, Brawley, Cheevers, Kitover, Knowles, Rautiala, & Suvajian, 1974). Willis and his colleagues (Dean, Willis, & LaRocco, 1976; Fry & Willis, 1971) have found that spatial intrusions by younger children (5 years of age) are apparently less aversive than those by older children (10 years of age). In those studies intrusions of 5-year-olds typically resulted in reciprocated involvement in the form of smiling, touch, or conversation, whereas the intrusion of 10-year-olds typically resulted in avoidance by adults.

In some circumstances of spatial invasion, the closeness of the intruder may not be intense enough to produce flight reactions. Alternately, the situation may prevent people from easily leaving the setting. In either case, alternate forms of compensatory adjustment to an intruder are possible. In a study of spatial invasions in a library, compensatory adjustments increased as subjects were approached more closely by a confederate (Patterson, Mullens, & Romano, 1971). The adjustments took the form of increased "blocking" of the intruder (i.e., turning away or using an arm and hand to screen the intruder). Fisher and Byrne (1975) have found that males and females differ in their reactions to intruders in the library setting. Specifically, males rated the situation most negatively when the invader sat directly opposite them, whereas females rated the situation most negatively when the invader was immediately adjacent. Furthermore, Fisher and Byrne observed that males typically placed their books and materials more forward and opposite themselves, whereas females typically placed their books and materials in an adjacent position. The latter results suggest that subjects anticipate the possibility of an intrusion and set up barriers in locations where they feel most vulnerable.

In general, the results of the research on spatial invasions suggest that close approaches by strangers are usually very uncomfortable. A situational factor that may moderate attributions following such approaches is the density of individuals in the setting. Practically, high density may make close approaches inevitable, with the consequence that intruders are held less responsible for such approaches. Active flight from an intruder or the more subtle compensatory responses may be interpreted as attempts to maintain some comfortable level of involvement (Argyle & Dean, 1965). In some circumstances, the intruder's close approach may be countered with a stare, a still closer approach or an aggressive posture. From the intruder's perspective the close approach to another would typically involve a deliberate, managed pattern designed to assert some advantage over that person. In the following sections we examine more subtle variations in distance that focus on specific types of social control motives.

Persuasion.   The persuasiveness of a communicator seems to be related to the distance he or she maintains from another person, but the results of research on this problem are not consistent. Mehrabian and Williams (1969) found that perceived persuasiveness of a communicator increased directly as a function of proximity to the target person. In contrast, Albert and Dabbs (1970) found that attitude change decreased as a function of proximity. The procedural differences between these two studies are substantial and may account for the conflicting results. Mehrabian and Williams used a perceived persuasiveness evaluation of a speaker videotaped at 4 vs. 12 ft from the camera. Albert and Dabbs examined actual attitude change following live interactions at 1–2, 4–5, and 14–15 ft. In another study, Goldman (1980) examined the effects of gaze and distance on the effectiveness of verbal reinforcement of an attitude. The results indicated that attitude change was greater at a moderate (4–5ft) distance than at a close (2–3 ft) distance. Compliance with a mundane request, however, seems to increase as the requester approaches a subject more closely (Ernest & Cooper, 1974).

The role of nonverbal involvement in attitude change and compliance is an interesting issue. It is generally assumed that increased power or pressure from a person in a position of authority will typically increase the behavioral compliance of an audience. If a close approach is intimidating, it is reasonable to assume that behavioral compliance should increase with increased proximity (touch or gaze). The underlying attitude change, however, will probably be adversely affected by increased pressure or stress and reactance against the communication will develop (Brehm, 1972).

Impression management. The use of distance in impression management implies that an individual deliberately manages his or her proximity to another for the purpose of creating a particular impression. In general, an individual's closer approach to another person usually produces more favorable reactions. Kelly (1972) found support for this relationship in patients' judgments of photographs of therapy interactions that were taken at varying distances.

In a study employing a simulated interview format, closer approaches by a confederate increased ratings on the dimensions of friendliness, extraversion, dominance, and aggression (Patterson & Sechrest, 1970). This pattern held over a range of 8, 6, and 4 ft but then reversed when the confederate approached at the 2 ft distance. Very close approaches, especially those approximating the invasion conditions described earlier, might clearly produce less positive ratings, e.g., on friendliness ratings. If that were the case, however, in the Patterson and Sechrest study, one might still expect rated extraversion, dominance, and aggressiveness to increase also. One alternate interpretation is that the confederates (in spite of instructions and training) compensated for their close approach at 2 ft and consequently were less behaviorally involved with the subjects. Here again, examining distance alone without monitoring other involvement behaviors may give an incomplete picture of an interaction.

Moderately close approaches may be most effective in creating positive impressions in others. That generalization has to be qualified by the nature of the setting and the relationship between the interactants. For example, in interactions between superiors and subordinates, superiors have greater license in determining the preferred distances. In fact, in one study in which subordinates initiated interactions with superiors, distance increased with increased discrepancy in rank (Dean, Willis, & Hewitt, 1975). In this case a moderately close approach by a low-ranked subordinate to a high-ranked superior would probably be seen as inappropriate by the superior.

In conclusion, it should be emphasized that the purposeful management of distance and other involvement behaviors can be very effective in determining the affective and behavioral reactions of others. Very close approaches, characteristic of those used in spatial invasion studies, can reflect motives such as aggression, dominance, or intimidation. Individuals who are approached very closely by strangers often show either flight reactions or distinct compensatory adjustments to the intruder, in addition to negative affective reactions. Moderately close approaches may typically generate more positive reactions than those that are too close or too far.

Service-Task Function

In some settings interaction distance is determined more by the nature of the service or task underlying a particular social exchange; that is, interpersonal motives reflecting either an intimacy or social control focus are less important than the service or task demands. Most people have occasional interpersonal contacts that are based on very explicit service goals. Heslin (1974) used the term *functional-professional* to describe a category of service relationships in classifying the use of touch. In these service exchanges Heslin notes that the relationship is basically one between the actor as an agent or manipulator and the client as an object.

Some obvious examples of service-based exchanges are those between physician and patient, dentist and patient, tailor and customer, and even teacher and student. In these exchanges a close approach and touch are often basic elements in providing the desired service. For those who are knowledgeable about the norms for these service exchanges, the high involvement required is usually seen as a necessary service component that is irrelevant to any interpersonal evaluation. In the case of the service component, the focus is on the use of nonverbal involvement in explicit or focused interactions. In the case of the task component, the management of nonverbal involvement typically serves to maximize the privacy of those who share a common presence with others but do not directly interact with those around them. In some cases the task function is facilitated by the design of the setting, whereas in other cases individual behavioral adjustments alone determine appropriate involvement levels.

Waiting areas or lounges in airports or train stations are examples of settings in which people share a common presence but do not typically intend to interact with one another. Sommer (1974, pp. 73–75) notes that the common design in many airport waiting areas involves straight-line seating in rows facing in the same direction. The chairs are usually hard plastic and are bolted to the floor. Although such arrangements may deter comfortable interaction among members of a group, they do contribute to the privacy that isolated individuals may prefer.

Studying is an example of a task or activity that often requires a moderate degree of privacy. Results from several studies of the use of college libraries show that students are most concerned with finding a quiet location away from others and distractions and not with proximity to reference materials

(Schaeffer & Patterson, 1977; Sommer, 1966, 1968, 1970). In this instance, seating choices often involve relatively remote locations and/or those that face away from various distractions. Sommer and Becker (1969) have examined differences between subjects who were instructed to retreat from others versus actively defend against others in choosing a seating location. Retreat subjects typically chose a seat in the rear of the room, on the aisle, and facing away from the doorway. Active defense subjects typically chose a nonaisle seat that faced the door. Although Sommer and Becker were not interested in the specific motives that might stimulate either a retreat or active defense strategy, it seems likely that the retreat strategy would be more characteristic of an individual who was serious about studying.

In many cognitive and motor tasks, performance may be affected by the arrangements under which individuals work. For example, there are results indicating that closer arrangements may produce greater decrements on more difficult learning tasks (Katsikitis & Brebner, 1981). In the elementary school classroom, study behavior and task involvement seem to be better when students are arranged in rows rather than facing one another around tables (Axelrod, Hall, & Tams, 1979; Wheldall, Morris, Vaughan, & Ng, 1981). The results found in the research on arrangement and performance might be interpreted in terms of arousal-mediated effects such as those described by Zajonc (1965) in social facilitation theory. Specifically, if increased involvement in the form of closer and/or more directly facing arrangements does increase arousal (Patterson, 1976), then contrasting effects might be found in the learning and performance of simple versus difficult tasks; that is, on more difficult tasks increased arousal will tend to produce a decrement whereas on easier tasks increased arousal will tend to improve performance.

The service-task function describes the instrumental use of nonverbal behavior in professional service encounters and in various task or setting-determined activities. Typically, the interpersonal affect and motivation that are basic to the intimacy and social control functions have little relevance for the level of involvement required for various service or task exchanges. Although individuals may have some influence on the level of involvement they initiate in service and task exchanges, in many circumstances the norms of the service or task activity determine what is appropriate. When the levels of nonverbal involvement are clearly a product of the service or task norms, we would expect interpersonal attributions for behavior to be minimized.

AN OVERVIEW OF THE FUNCTIONAL APPROACH

The functional model has provided an integrative perspective for reviewing the research on spatial behavior. We have suggested that interpersonal distance and other involvement behaviors may be examined in terms of five basic functional categories: (a) providing information, (b) regulating interaction, (c) expressing intimacy, (d) social control, and (e) the service-task function. The last three categories are especially important in describing the molar functions characteristic of social behavior. The distinctions among these molar functions are facilitated by a contrast proposed between informative behavior that is communicative and that which is indicative. It is presumed that spatial patterns that serve the intimacy function are characterized by the relatively spontaneous and indicative use of distance that results from interpersonal affect. In contrast, it is presumed that the managed and communicative use of distance for social control motives results from a relatively purposeful goal or objective. In the latter case, interpersonal affect may be independent of what is behaviorally expressed.

A number of antecedent factors that an individual brings to a social setting may influence his or her characteristic use of space and the manner in which specific functions are activated. The personal factors of culture, gender, and personality have been extensively researched. Each of these factors contributes to consistent differences in the use of space in social interaction. For the most part it is assumed that the personal factors produce their influence in relatively stable behavioral predispositions. These habitual patterns of spatial involvement are relatively automatic tendencies that are typically not well represented in cognitive awareness. In contrast, the experiential and relational-situational antecedents are assumed to exert their influence through cognitive and affective mediation; that is, past experience of a particular type or expectancies focusing on the relationship or situation can generate cognitive strategies relating to the expressive or managed use of spatial behavior. In addition, the expectancies about an impending interaction are often directly relevant to the initiation of specific functions. For example, an anticipated meeting with a loved one will probably result in a spontaneously close approach (intimacy), whereas an anticipated job interview will probably result in a managed moderate approach (social control).

The functional orientation described in this chapter was anticipated in the conclusion of the chapter on space in the first edition of this book. In a similar fashion, in concluding this discussion, it might be useful to chart some tentative directions for future research from this revised perspective. First, it would seem desirable to emphasize questions that deal with the experiential and relational-situational determinants of spatial behavior. The vast majority of research on spatial behavior may be characterized as focusing on one or more of the personal factors—culture, gender, personality, age. Relatively little work has focused either on past experience or on the relational-situational factors even though their role in cognitive and affective reactions seems to be a critical one. Second, greater attention should be paid to the measurement of mediating cognitive and affective reactions in social interaction. Various techniques exist for the assessment of cognitions (Cacioppo &

Petty, 1981), and the technology for measuring physiological reactions has become more sophisticated. Because many hypotheses about interpersonal distance or other nonverbal behaviors implicitly or explicitly identify cognitive or affective mediators, the measurement of those reactions is especially important. Finally, a recommendation from the first edition of this chapter bears repetition and elaboration. Specifically, we feel that a comprehensive understanding of the role of nonverbal behavior in social interaction requires a multivariate description and analysis. It is convenient in the context of this book to isolate specific chapters on single channels such as gaze, distance, or facial expression, but that approach makes it difficult to appreciate the coordinated, multichannel reactions that occur in live interactions. An orientation that is grounded in multivariate constructs such as intimacy (Argyle & Dean, 1965; Patterson, 1976), immediacy (Mehrabian, 1969), proxemics (Hall, 1966), or nonverbal involvement (Patterson, 1982b) can better approximate the complexity of multichannel patterns of behavior. If this suggestion caught on, we might look for a third edition of this book in which each chapter would provide a coordinated, multichannel analysis of various social psychological processes such as attraction, interpersonal influence, impression management, aggression, etc. That should constitute a demanding criterion for the success of our charting future directions in research.

REFERENCES

Adler, L. L., & Iverson, M. A. Interpersonal distance as a function of task difficulty, praise, status orientation, and sex of partner. *Perceptual and Motor Skills,* 1974, *39,* 683–692.

Aiello, J. R., & Jones, S. E. Field study of the proxemic behavior of young school children in three subcultural groups. *Journal of Personality and Social Psychology,* 1971, *19,* 351–356.

Albert, S., & Dabbs, J. M., Jr. Physical distance and persuasion. *Journal of Personality and Social Psychology,* 1970, *15,* 265–270.

Allgeier, A. R., & Byrne, D. Attraction toward the opposite sex as a determinant of physical proximity. *Journal of Social Psychology,* 1973, *90,* 213–219.

Alovisetti, M. C. An investigation of a simulated spatial technique as a measure of interpersonal distancing behavior (Doctoral dissertation, University of Rhode Island, 1977). *Dissertation Abstracts International,* 1977, *38,* 1945B. (University Microfilms No. 77-22, 541)

Altman, I., & Haythorn, W. The ecology of isolated groups. *Behavioral Science,* 1967, *12,* 169–182.

Argyle, M., & Dean, J. Eye-contact, distance, and affiliation. *Sociometry,* 1965, *28,* 289–304.

Argyle, M., & Kendon, A. The experimental analysis of social performance. In L. Berkowitz (Ed.), *Advances in experimental social psychology* (Vol. 3). New York: Academic, 1967.

Aronow, E. The interpersonal distance of process and reactive schizophrenic males (Doctoral dissertation, Fordham University, 1973). *Dissertation Abstracts International,* 1974, *34,* 4032B–4033B. (University Microfilms No. 74-2774)

Aronow, E., Reznikoff, M., Tryon, W., & Rauchway, A. On construct validity of the concept of interpersonal distance. *Perceptual and Motor Skills,* 1977, *45,* 550.

Ashton, N. L., Shaw, M. E., & Worsham, A. N. Affective reactions to interpersonal distances by friends and strangers. *Bulletin of the Psychonomic Society,* 1980, *15,* 306–308.

Axelrod, S., Hall, R. V., & Tams, A. Comparison of two common classroom seating arrangements. *Academic Therapy,* 1979, *15,* 29–36.

Baker, E., & Shaw, M. E. Reactions to interpersonal distance and topic intimacy: A comparison of strangers and friends. *Journal of Nonverbal Behavior,* 1980, *5,* 80–91.

Barker, R. G. *Ecological psychology: Concepts and methods for studying the environment of human behavior.* Stanford, CA: Stanford University Press, 1968.

Barrios, B., & Giesen, M. Getting what you expect: Effects of expectation on intragroup attraction and interpersonal distance. *Personality and Social Psychology Bulletin,* 1977, *3,* 87–90.

Bauer, E. A. Personal space: A study of blacks and whites. *Sociometry,* 1973, *36,* 402–408.

Baxter, J. C. Interpersonal spacing in natural settings. *Sociometry,* 1970, *33,* 444–456.

Becker, F. D., & Mayo, C. *Measurement effects in studying reactions to spatial invasions.* Paper presented at the meeting of the Eastern Psychological Association, New York, April, 1970.

Berscheid, E., & Walster, E. *Interpersonal attraction* (2nd ed.). Reading, MA: Addison–Wesley, 1978.

Bleda, P. R., & Bleda, S. E. Effects of sex and smoking on reactions to spatial invasion at a shopping mall. *Journal of Social Psychology,* 1978, *104,* 311–312.

Booraem, C. D., Flowers, J. V., Bodner, G. E., & Satterfield, D. A. Personal space variations as a function of criminal behavior. *Psychological Reports,* 1977, *41,* 1115–1121.

Bouska, M. L., & Beatty, P. A. Clothing as a symbol of status: Its effect on control of interaction territory. *Bulletin of the Psychonomic Society,* 1978, *11,* 235–238.

Brehm, J. *Responses to loss of freedom: A theory of psychological reactance.* Morristown, NJ: General Learning, 1972.

Byrne, D. Attitudes and attraction. In L. Berkowitz (Ed.), *Advances in experimental social psychology* (Vol. 4). New York: Academic, 1969.

Byrne, D. *The attraction paradigm.* New York: Academic, 1971.

Byrne, D., Baskett, G. D., & Hodges, L. Behavioral indicators of interpersonal attraction. *Journal of Applied Social Psychology,* 1971, *1,* 137–149.

Byrne, D., Ervin, C. R., & Lamberth, J. Continuity between the experimental study of attraction and real-life computer dating. *Journal of Personality and Social Psychology,* 1970, *16,* 157–165.

Cacioppo, J. T., & Petty, R. E. Social psychological procedures for cognitive response assessment: The thought listing technique. In T. V. Merluzzi, C. R. Glass, & M. Genest (Eds.), *Cognitive assessment.* New York: Guilford Press, 1981.

Campbell, D. T., Kruskal, W. H., & Wallace, W. P. Seating aggregation as an index of attitude. *Sociometry,* 1966, *29,* 1–15.

Cappella, J. N. Mutual influence in expressive behavior: Adult–adult and infant–adult dyadic interaction. *Psychological Bulletin,* 1981, *89,* 101–132.

Cappella, J. N., & Greene, J. O. A discrepancy-arousal explanation of mutual influence in expressive behavior for adult and infant–adult interaction. *Communication Monographs,* 1982, *49,* 89–114.

Carducci, B. J., & Webber, A. W. Shyness as a determinant of interpersonal distance. *Psychological Reports,* 1979, *44,* 1075–1078.

Cheyne, J. A., & Efran, M. G. The effect of spatial and interpersonal variables on the invasion of group controlled territories. *Sociometry,* 1972, *35,* 477–489.

Ciolek, T. M., & Kendon, A. Environment and the spatial arrangement of conversational encounters. *Sociological Inquiry,* 1980, *50,* 237–271.

Clore, G. *Attraction and interpersonal behavior.* Paper presented at the annual meeting of the Southwestern Psychological Association, Austin, 1969.

Cook, M. Experiments on orientation and proxemics. *Human Relations,* 1970, *23,* 61–76.

Crowe, W. L. The relationship between self-disclosure, locus of control, personal space, social risk-taking, desire-for-novelty, novelty-experiencing, and biographical variables: A multivariate approach (Doctoral dissertation, York University, 1975). *Dissertation Abstracts International,* 1977, *37,* 4642B.

Curran, S. F., Blatchley, R. J., & Hanlon, T. E. The relationship between body buffer zone and violence as assessed by subjective and objective techniques. *Criminal Justice and Behavior,* 1978, *5,* 53–62.

Dabbs, J. M., Jr. Does reaction to crowding depend upon the sex of subject or sex of subject's partners? *Journal of Personality and Social Psychology,* 1977, *35,* 343–344.

Daniell, R. J., & Lewis, P. Stability of eye contact and physical distance across a series of structured interviews. *Journal of Consulting and Clinical Psychology,* 1972, *39,* 172.

Dean, L. M., Willis, F. N., & Hewitt, J. Initial interaction distance among individuals equal and unequal in military rank. *Journal of Personality and Social Psychology,* 1975, *32,* 294–299.

Dean, L. M., Willis, F. N., & LaRocco, J. M. Invasion of personal space as a function of age, sex, and race. *Psychological Reports,* 1976, *38,* 959–965.

Desor, J. A. Toward a psychological theory of crowding. *Journal of Personality and Social Psychology,* 1972, *21,* 79–83.

Dosey, M. A., & Meisels, M. Personal space and self-protection. *Journal of Personality and Social Psychology,* 1969, *11,* 93–97.

Duke, M. P., & Kiebach, C. A brief note on the validity of the Comfortable Interpersonal Distance Scale. *Journal of Social Psychology,* 1974, *94,* 297–298.

Duke, M. P., & Nowicki, S. A new measure and social-learning model for interpersonal distance. *Journal of Experimental Research in Personality,* 1972, *6,* 119–132.

Eberts, E. H., & Lepper, M. R. Individual consistency in the proxemic behavior of preschool children. *Journal of Personality and Social Psychology,* 1975, *32,* 841–849.

Edinger, J. A., & Patterson, M. L. Nonverbal involvement and social control. *Psychological Bulletin,* 1983, *93,* 30–56.

Edwards, D. J. A. Perception of crowding and personal space as a function of locus of control, arousal seeking, sex of experimenter, and sex of subject. *Journal of Psychology,* 1977, *95,* 223–229.

Ernest, R. C., & Cooper, R. E. "Hey mister, do you have any change?": Two real world studies of proxemic effects on compliance with a mundane request. *Personality and Social Psychology Bulletin,* 1974, *1,* 158–159.

Evans, R. M., & Cherulnik, P. D. Sex composition and intimacy in dyads: A field study. *Journal of Social Psychology,* 1980, *110,* 139–140.

Felipe, N. J., & Sommer, R. Invasion of personal space. *Social Problems,* 1966, *14,* 206–214.

Feroleto, J. A., & Gounard, B. R. The effects of subjects' age and expectations regarding an interviewer on personal space. *Experimental Aging Research,* 1975, *1,* 57–61.

Fisher, J. D., & Byrne, D. Too close for comfort: Sex differences in response to invasions of personal space. *Journal of Personality and Social Psychology,* 1975, *32,* 15–21.

Ford, J. G., & Graves, J. R. Differences between Mexican–American and White children in interpersonal distance and social touching. *Perceptual and Motor Skills,* 1977, *45,* 779–785.

Forston, R. F., & Larson, C. U. The dynamics of space: An experimental study in proxemic behavior among Latin Americans and North Americans. *Journal of Communication,* 1968, *18,* 109–116.

Frankel, A. S., & Barrett, J. Variations in personal space as a function of authoritarianism, self-esteem and racial characteristics of a stimulus situation. *Journal of Consulting and Clinical Psychology,* 1971, *37,* 95–98.

Freedman, J. T., Levy, A., Buchanan, R., & Price, J. Crowding and human aggressiveness. *Journal of Experimental Social Psychology,* 1972, *8,* 549–557.

Fromme, D. K., & Beam, D. C. Dominance and sex differences in nonverbal responses to differential eye contact. *Journal of Research in Personality,* 1974, *8,* 76–87.

Fry, A. M., & Willis, F. N. Invasion of personal space as a function of the age of the invader. *Psychological Record,* 1971, *21,* 385–389.

Giesen, M., & Hendrick, C. Physical distance and sex in moderated groups: Neglected factors in small group interaction. *Memory and Cognition,* 1977, *5,* 79–83.

Giesen, M., & McClaren, H. A. Discussion, distance and sex: Changes in impressions and attraction during small group interaction. *Sociometry,* 1976, *39,* 60–70.

Gilmour, D. R., & Walkey, F. H. Identifying violent offenders using a video measure of interpersonal distance. *Journal of Consulting and Clinical Psychology,* 1981, *49,* 287–291.

Goldman, M. Effect of eye contact and distance on the verbal reinforcement of attitude. *Journal of Social Psychology,* 1980, *111,* 73–78.

Haase, R. F., & Markey, M. J. A methodological note on the study of personal space. *Journal of Consulting and Clinical Psychology,* 1973, *40,* 122–125.

Hall, E. T. A system for the notation of proxemic behavior. *American Anthropologist,* 1963, *65,* 1003–1026.

Hall, E. T. *The hidden dimension.* New York: Doubleday, 1966.

Hall, E. T. Proxemics. *Current Anthropology,* 1968, *9,* 83–108.

Harris, B., Luginbuhl, J. E. R., & Fishbein, J. E. Density and personal space in a field setting. *Social Psychology,* 1978, *41,* 350–353.

Hartnett, J. J., Bailey, K. G., & Gibson, F. W., Jr. Personal space as influenced by sex and type of movement. *Journal of Psychology,* 1970, *76,* 139–144.

Heckel, R. V., & Hiers, J. M. Social distance and locus of control. *Journal of Clinical Psychology,* 1977, *33,* 469–471.

Hediger, H. P. The evolution of territorial behavior. In S. L. Washburn (Ed.), *Social life of early man.* Chicago: Aldine, 1961.

Helson, H. *Adaptation-level theory.* New York: Harper & Row, 1964.

Hendricks, M., & Bootzin, R. Race and sex as stimuli for negative affect and physical avoidance. *Journal of Social Psychology,* 1976, *98,* 111–120.

Heshka, S., & Nelson, Y. Interpersonal speaking distance as a function of age, sex, and relationship. *Sociometry,* 1972, *35,* 491–498.

Heslin, R. *Steps toward a taxonomy of touching.* Paper presented at the annual meeting of the Midwestern Psychological Association, Chicago, May, 1974.

Horowitz, M. J., Duff, D. F., & Stratton, L. O. Body-buffer zone. *Archives of General Psychiatry,* 1964, *11,* 651–656.

Ickes, W. Sex role influences in dyadic interaction: A theoretical model. In C. Mayo & N. M. Henley (Eds.), *Gender and nonverbal behavior.* New York: Springer–Verlag, 1981.

Jones, S. E. A comparative proxemics analysis of dyadic interaction in selected subcultures of New York City. *Journal of Social Psychology,* 1971, *84,* 35–44.

Jones, S. E., & Aiello, J. R. Proxemic behavior of black and white first-, third-, and fifth-grade children. *Journal of Personality and Social Psychology,* 1973, *25,* 21–27.

Jorgenson, D. O. Field study of the relationship between status discrepancy and proxemic behavior. *Journal of Social Psychology,* 1975, *97,* 173–179.

Jourard, S. M., & Friedman, R. Experimenter–subject "distance" and self-disclosure. *Journal of Personality and Social Psychology,* 1970, *15,* 278–282.

Karabenick, S. A., & Meisels, M. Effects of performance evaluation on interpersonal distance. *Journal of Personality,* 1972, *40,* 275–286.

Katsikitis, M., & Brebner, J. Individual differences in the effects of personal space invasion: A test of the Brebner–Cooper model of extraversion. *Personality and Individual Differences,* 1981, *2,* 5–10.

Kelly, F. D. Communicational significance of therapist proxemic cues. *Journal of Consulting and Clinical Psychology,* 1972, *39,* 345.

Kendon, A. The F-formation system: The spatial organization of social encounters. *Man–*

Environment Systems, 1976, *6,* 291–296.

Kendon, A. Spatial organization in social encounters: The F-formation system. In A. Kendon (Ed.), *Studies in the behavior of social interaction.* Lisse, Holland: Peter deRidder Press, 1977.

Kinzel, A. Body-buffer zone in violent prisoners. *American Journal of Psychiatry,* 1970, *127,* 59–64.

Kissell, P. D. The relationship of self-esteem, programmed music, and time of day to preferred conversational distance among female college students (Doctoral dissertation, New York University, 1974). *Dissertation Abstracts International,* 1974, *35,* 2280B. (University Microfilms No. 74-25,001)

Knight, P. H., & Bair, C. K. Degree of client comfort as a function of dyadic interaction distance. *Journal of Counseling Psychology,* 1976, *23,* 13–16.

Knowles, E. S. Boundaries around group interaction: The effect of size and status. *Journal of Personality and Social Psychology,* 1973, *26,* 327–331.

Knowles, E. S. Convergent validity of personal space measures: Consistent results with low intercorrelations. *Journal of Nonverbal Behavior,* 1980, *4,* 240–248.

Knowles, E. S., & Johnsen, P. K. *Intrapersonal consistency in interpersonal distance.* Paper presented at the Eastern Psychological Association meeting, Philadelphia, 1974.

Konečni, V. J., Libuser, L., Morton, H., & Ebbesen, E. B. Effects of a violation of personal space on escape and helping responses. *Journal of Experimental Social Psychology,* 1975, *11,* 288–299.

Kuethe, J. L. Social schemas. *Journal of Abnormal and Social Psychology,* 1962, *64,* 31–38.

Lassen, C. L. Effect of proximity on anxiety and communication in the initial psychiatric interview. *Journal of Abnormal Psychology,* 1973, *81,* 226–232.

Latta, R. M. Relation of status incongruence to personal space. *Personality and Social Psychology Bulletin,* 1978, *4,* 143–146.

Little, K. B. Personal space. *Journal of Experimental Social Psychology,* 1965, *1,* 237–247.

Long, G. T., Calhoun, L. G., & Selby, J. W. Personality characteristics related to cross-situational consistency of interpersonal distance. *Journal of Personality Assessment,* 1977, *41,* 274–278.

Lott, D. F., & Sommer, R. Seating arrangement and status. *Journal of Personality and Social Psychology,* 1967, *7,* 90–95.

Love, K. D., & Aiello, J. R. Using projective techniques to measure interaction distance: A methodological note. *Personality and Social Psychology Bulletin,* 1980, *6,* 102–104.

MacKay, D. M. Formal analysis of communicative processes. In R. A. Hinde (Ed.), *Non-verbal communication.* Cambridge, England: Cambridge University Press, 1972.

Marshall, J. E., & Heslin, R. Boys and girls together: Sexual composition and effect of density and group size on cohesiveness. *Journal of Personality and Social Psychology,* 1975, *31,* 952–961.

McGurk, W. T. Anglo and Puerto Rican client attitudes generated by varied interaction distances and counselor ethnicity in the dyadic counseling interaction (Doctoral dissertation, University of Massachusetts, 1976). *Dissertation Abstracts International,* 1976, *37,* 136A. (University Microfilms No. 76-14,707)

Mehrabian, A. Relationship of attitude to seated posture, orientation, and distance. *Journal of Personality and Social Psychology,* 1968, *10,* 26–30. (a)

Mehrabian, A. Inference of attitudes from the posture, orientation and distance of a communicator. *Journal of Consulting and Clinical Psychology,* 1968, *32,* 296–308. (b)

Mehrabian, A. Some referents and measures of nonverbal behavior. *Behavior Research Methods and Instrumentation,* 1969, *1,* 203–207.

Mehrabian, A., & Diamond, S. G. Seating arragnement and conversation. *Sociometry,* 1971, *34,* 281–289.

Mehrabian, A., & Friar, J. T. Encoding of attitude by a seated communicator via posture and position cues. *Journal of Consulting and Clinical Psychology,* 1969, *33,* 330-336.

Mehrabian, A., & Ksionzky, S. Some determinants of social interaction. *Sociometry,* 1972, *35,* 588-609.

Mehrabian, A., & Williams, M. Nonverbal concomitants of perceived and intended persuasiveness. *Journal of Personality and Social Psychology,* 1969, *13,* 37-58.

Meisels, M., & Canter, F. M. Personal space and personality characteristics: A non-confirmation. *Psychological Reports,* 1970, *27,* 287-290.

Michelini, R. L., Passalacqua, R., & Cusimano, J. Effects of seating arrangement on group participation. *Journal of Social Psychology,* 1976, *99,* 179-186.

Milgram, S. The experience of living in cities. *Science,* 1970, *167,* 1461-1468.

Mishara, B. L., Brawley, P., Cheevers, M., Kitover, R. M., Knowles, A. M., Rautiala, P., & Suvajian, A. Encroachments upon the body buffer zones of the young and old woman: A naturalistic study. *International Journal of Aging and Human Development,* 1974, *5,* 3-5.

Newman, R. C., & Pollack, D. Proxemics in deviant adolescents. *Journal of Consulting and Clinical Psychology,* 1973, *40,* 6-8.

Noesjirwan, J. Contrasting cultural patterns of interpersonal closeness in doctors' waiting rooms in Sydney and Jakarta. *Journal of Cross-Cultural Psychology,* 1977, *8,* 357-368.

Noesjirwan, J. A laboratory study of proxemic patterns of Indonesians and Australians. *British Journal of Social and Clinical Psychology,* 1978, *17,* 333-334.

O'Neal, E. C., Brunault, M. A., Carifio, M. S. Troutwine, R., & Epstein, J. Effect of insult upon personal space preferences. *Journal of Nonverbal Behavior,* 1980, *5,* 56-62.

Patterson, M. L., Stability of nonverbal immediacy behaviors. *Journal of Experimental Social Psychology,* 1973, *9,* 97-109. (a)

Patterson, M. L. Compensation in nonverbal immediacy behaviors: A review. *Sociometry,* 1973, *36,* 237-252. (b)

Patterson, M. L. Eye contact and distance: A re-examination of measurement problems. *Personality and Social Psychology Bulletin,* 1975, *1,* 600-603.

Patterson, M. L. An arousal model of interpersonal intimacy. *Psychological Review,* 1976, *83,* 235-245.

Patterson, M. L. Interpersonal distance, affect, and equilibrium theory. *Journal of Social Psychology,* 1977, *101,* 205-214.

Patterson, M. L. The role of space in social interaction. In A. W. Siegman & S. Feldstein (Eds.), *Nonverbal behavior and communication.* Hillsdale, NJ: Lawrence Erlbaum Associates, 1978.

Patterson, M. L. Personality and nonverbal involvement: A functional analysis. In W. Ickes & E. S. Knowles (Eds.), *Personality, roles, and social behavior.* New York: Springer-Verlag, 1982. (a)

Patterson, M. L. A sequential functional model of nonverbal exchange. *Psychological Review,* 1982, *89,* 231-249. (b)

Patterson, M. L., & Holmes, D. S. *Social interaction correlates of the MPI extraversion-introversion scale.* Paper presented at the annual meeting of the American Psychological Association, New York, 1966.

Patterson, M. L., Mullens, S., & Romano, J. Compensatory reactions to spatial intrusion. *Sociometry,* 1971, *34,* 114-126.

Patterson, M. L., Roth, C. P., & Schenk, C. Seating arrangement, activity and sex differences in small group crowding. *Personality and Social Psychology Bulletin,* 1979, 100-103.

Patterson, M. L., & Schaeffer, R. E. *Effects of size and sex composition on interaction distance, participation, and satisfaction in small groups.* Paper presented at the annual meeting of the Rocky Mountain Psychological Association, Salt Lake City, May, 1975.

Patterson, M. L., & Sechrest, L. B. Interpersonal distance and impression formation. *Journal of Personality,* 1970, *38,* 161-166.

Patterson, M. L., & Strauss, M. E. An examination of the discriminant validity of the social-avoidance and distress scale. *Journal of Consulting and Clinical Psychology,* 1972, *39,* 169.

Pedersen, D. M. Relations among sensation seeking and simulated and behavioral personal space. *Journal of Psychology,* 1973, *83,* 79–88. (a)

Pedersen, D. M. Correlates of behavioral personal space. *Psychological Reports,* 1973, *32,* 828–830. (b)

Pellegrini, R. J., & Empey, J. Interpersonal spatial orientation in dyads. *Journal of Psychology,* 1970, *76,* 67–70.

Roger, D. B., & Schalekamp, E. E. Body-buffer zone and violence: A cross-cultural study. *Journal of Social Psychology,* 1976, *98,* 153–158.

Rogers, P., Rearden, J. J., & Hillner, W. Effects of distance from interviewer and intimacy of topic on verbal productivity and anxiety. *Psychological Reports,* 1981, *49,* 303–307.

Rosenfeld, H. M. Effect of an approval-seeking induction on interpersonal proximity. *Psychological Reports,* 1965, *17,* 120–122.

Ross, M., Layton, B., Erickson, B., & Schopler, J. Affect, facial regard, and reactions to crowding. *Journal of Personality and Social Psychology,* 1973, *28,* 69–76.

Rubinstein, E. S. Body buffer zones in female prisoners (Doctoral dissertation, Long Island University, The Brooklyn Center, 1975). *Dissertation Abstracts International, 1975, 36,* 1456B–1457B. (University Microfilms No. 75-20, 503).

Schachter, S., & Singer, J. E. Cognitive, social, and physiological determinants of emotional state. *Psychological Review,* 1962, *69,* 379–399.

Schaeffer, G., & Patterson, M. L. Studying preferences, behavior, and design influences in a university library. In P. Suedfeld, J. A. Russell, L. M. Ward, F. Szigeti, & G. Davis (Eds.), *The behavioral basis of design* (Book 2). Stroudsberg, PA: Dowden, Hutchinson, & Ross, 1977.

Scherer, S. E. Proxemic behavior of primary school children as a function of their socioeconomic class and subculture. *Journal of Personality and Social Psychology,* 1974, *29,* 800–805.

Schneider, D. J., Hastorf, A. H., & Ellsworth, P. C. *Person perception* (2nd ed.). Reading, MA: Addison–Wesley, 1979.

Sewell, A. F., & Heisler, J. T. Personality correlates of proximity preferences. *Journal of Psychology,* 1973, *85,* 151–155.

Shuter, R. Proxemics and tactility in Latin America. *Journal of Communication,* 1976, *26,* 46–52.

Shuter, R. A field study of nonverbal communication in Germany, Italy, and the United States. *Communication Monographs,* 1977, *44,* 298–305.

Silverstein, C. H., & Stang, D. J. Seating position and interaction in triads: A field study. *Sociometry,* 1976, *39,* 166–170.

Slane, S., Petruska, R., & Cheyfitz, S. Personal space measurement: A validational comparison. *Psychological Record,* 1981, *31,* 145–151.

Smith, R. J., & Knowles, E. S. Attributional consequences of personal space invasions. *Personality and Social Psychology Bulletin,* 1978, *4,* 429–433.

Smith, R. J., & Knowles, E. S. Affective and cognitive mediators of reactions to spatial invasions. *Journal of Experimental Social Psychology,* 1979, *15,* 437–452.

Sommer, R. Studies in personal space. *Sociometry,* 1959, *22,* 247–260.

Sommer, R. Further studies in small group ecology. *Sociometry,* 1965, *28,* 337–348.

Sommer, R. The ecology of privacy. *Library Quarterly,* 1966, *36,* 234–248.

Sommer, R. Reading areas in college libraries. *Library Quarterly,* 1968, *38,* 249–260.

Sommer, R. The ecology of study areas. *Environment and Behavior,* 1970, *2,* 271–280.

Sommer, R. *Tight spaces: Hard architecture and how to humanize it.* Englewood Cliffs, NJ: Prentice-Hall, 1974.

Sommer, R., & Becker, F. Territorial defense and the good neighbor. *Journal of Personality and Social Psychology,* 1969, *11,* 85–92.

Stein, D. D., Hardyck, J. A., & Smith, M. B. Race and belief: An open and shut case. *Journal of Personality and Social Psychology,* 1965, *1,* 281–289.

Stokols, D., Rall, M., Pinner, B., & Schopler, J. Physical, social and personal determinants of the perception of crowding. *Environment and Behavior,* 1973, *5,* 87–115.

Stone, G. L., & Morden, C. J. Effect of distance on verbal productivity. *Journal of Counseling Psychology,* 1976, *23,* 486–488.

Stratton, L. O., Tekippl, D. J., & Flick, G. L. Personal space and self-concept. *Sociometry,* 1973, *36,* 424–429.

Sussman, N. M., & Rosenfeld, H. M. Influence of culture, language, and sex on conversational distance. *Journal of Personality and Social Psychology,* 1982, *42,* 66–74.

Tennis, G. H., & Dabbs, J. M., Jr. Sex, setting and personal space: First grade through college. *Sociometry,* 1975, *38,* 385–394.

Thompson, D. E., Aiello, J. R., & Epstein, Y. M. Interpersonal distance preferences. *Journal of Nonverbal Behavior,* 1979, *4,* 113–118.

Veitch, R., Getsinger, A., & Arkkelin, D. A note on the reliability and validity of the Comfortable Interpersonal Distance Scale. *Journal of Psychology,* 1976, *94,* 163–165.

Veno, A. E. Response to approach: A preliminary process-oriented study of human spacing. *Social Science Information,* 1976, *15,* 93–115.

Watson, M. O., & Graves, T. D. Quantitative research in proxemic behavior. *American Anthropologist,* 1966, *68,* 971–985.

Wheldall, K., Morris, M., Vaughan, P., & Ng, Y. Y. Rows versus tables: An example of the use of behavioural ecology in two classes of eleven-year-old children. *Educational Psychology,* 1981, *1,* 171–184.

White, M. J., & Lira, F. T. A comparison of two measures of interpersonal distance. *Journal of Social Psychology,* 1978, *104,* 151–152.

Wicker, A. W. *An introduction to ecological psychology.* Monterey, CA: Brooks/Cole, 1979.

Williams, J. L. Personal space and its relation to extraversion–introversion. *Canadian Journal of Behavioural Sciences,* 1971, *3,* 156–160.

Willis, F. N. Initial speaking distance as a function of the speakers' relationship. *Psychonomic Science,* 1966, *5,* 221–222.

Zajonc, R. B. Social facilitation. *Science,* 1965, *16,* 269–274.

12 Conversational Control Functions of Nonverbal Behavior

Howard M. Rosenfeld
The University of Kansas

INTRODUCTION

The scientific study of human social interaction recently has undergone dramatic changes. Interpersonal behavior, like other natural phenomena, is being analyzed in ever-increasing detail. Just as the invention of the microscope permitted the identification of intricate physical processes, the recent development of sophisticated apparatus for the recording and analysis of social behavior has enabled the exploration of previously undetected interpersonal processes. While the behaviors involved in social interaction must be perceived at some level by the persons who are affected by them, they often are too complex in structure and too rapid in occurrence to be adequately recorded through direct observation. However, through detailed analysis of audio-visual records and with the aid of high-speed computers, the structures and functions of many fleeting interpersonal events now can be analyzed objectively and efficiently. Although such explorations still are in an early stage, some consensual discoveries are beginning to emerge. Thus, this is an opportune time to pull together some of the results of research, evaluate its progress and suggest promising directions for future study.

Participants in social interaction must manage a wide variety of interpersonal tasks (Goffman, 1967). In larger social assemblies, persons who wish to converse with each other give signals of orientation by which to initiate a focused relationship (Kendon, 1970). Once oriented, the participants typically must go through certain phases such as the semiritualistic exchange of greetings, which may determine the possibilities of further phases (Kendon & Ferber, 1973, Schegloff, 1968), the conduct of the major items of business that constitute the main body of the interaction (Bales, 1955), and an exchange of farewells, which permits them to terminate the encounter to their mutual satisfaction (Knapp, Hart, Friedrich, & Shulman, 1973; Schegloff & Sacks, 1973). Particularly throughout the more central phases of interaction, the participants are faced with the persistent problem of how to facilitate the virtually continuous flow of information.

The successful conversant must be skillful in the management of all of these requirements. Thus, a comprehensive theory of social interaction ultimately must integrate the diverse findings that are being generated, rather piecemeal, by research on the various subproblems. There also is a need for more thorough understanding of circumscribed aspects of the total conversational process. In this chapter we focus our attention on the fundamental problem of how conversants use nonverbal behavior to regulate the flow of information throughout the main body of their interaction. We will refer to this particular usage of nonverbal behavior as its "conversational control function". First, we outline a perspective that is intended to incorporate current conceptions of the process. in subsequent sections we review and evaluate research that bears upon the perspective.

A PERSPECTIVE ON
CONVERSATIONAL CONTROL PROCESSES

We are particularly concerned with face-to-face interactions of pairs of persons in which a major purpose of the participants is to exchange information that is encoded primarily through spoken language, and in which both participants are relatively free to select their means of accomplishing this task. Perhaps the most common variety of such interactions is the problem-oriented discussion. More constricted forms are structured interveiws and psychotherapy sessions. Activities excluded by this emphasis are highly ritualistic or ceremonial exchanges in which reactions are preprogrammed, and occasions in which a person is concerned only with showing off in the presence of an audience and not with their reaction to his particular behaviors. Emotional aspects of communication (Dittman, 1972b), while they may be informative, are dealt with only tangentially in our analysis.

No precise method has been devised for categorizing and quantifying the information exchanged throughout natural conversations. Yet it is commonly assumed that conversational behavior does consist of units of information that are at least informally or indirectly definable. We colloquially refer to such units as "ideas," "facts," and "opinions," and we assume that the flow of "new" information in an interaction sequence is at least grossly detectable. Even though we may not yet be able to confidently quantify the rates at which information is exchanged in conversations, recent research indicates that we now are able to identify reliably behavioral units into which information is organized by participants.

Our basic proposition is that conversations can productively be viewed as orderly structures of informational units. The orderly structure itself is the result of a collaborative exchange of signals by the participants that function to regulate the flow of informational units. While the presentation of complex information in human interactions is most efficiently carried out via the verbal–linguistic channel (speech), we will argue that the orderly flow of verbal information is influenced in large part by simpler signals carried in the nonverbal channels. Of particular importance in this control process are the vocal and kinesic channels, which refer to nonlinguistic properties of vocal behavior and to observable bodily activities, respectively.

Our emphasis on nonverbal behavior is not meant to imply that a substantial amount of control is not also carried out by verbal–linguistic behavior. Spoken language is clearly better suited for the provision of complex, differentiated commentaries upon specific items of information and thus for the control of the content of subsequent informational units. Psycholinguists, sociolinguists, and social psychologists, among others, are making progress toward the analysis of the ways in which conversants process information. However, they have not reached consensus on ways of determining the content and quantity of information transmitted in natural conversations. In addition, their work has proceeded substantially in isolation from research on nonverbal aspects of communication. Ultimately, this artificial separation of the communication process will have to be integrated.

The tendency for conversations to be structured into orderly sequences of units can be attributed primarily to the widely recognized necessity for conversants to alternate in speaking turns if they are to understand each other. It is difficult, if not impossible, for a pair of persons to exchange complex information if they are both talking at the same time. Somehow they must manage to coordinate complementary roles, analogous to the need for pedestrians or drivers approaching each other from opposite directions on a narrow road to avoid a collision (cf. Goffman, cited in Duncan, 1972). Specifically, they must assume reciprocal roles for periods of time, during which one participant is primarily the conveyor of verbal information and the other primarily the receiver.

To understand how the above role-complementarity is accomplished throughout conversation, it is necessary to detect the exchange of two kinds of control signals. We must recognize the signals that indicate when it is appropriate and those that indicate when it is inappropriate for the participants to switch speaker–listener roles. These two kinds of controlling signals do not occur at random in the conversational process, for they are intimately connected to the process of information exchange. They occur primarily at the ends of coherent units of verbal information. At the junctures terminating these units, the speaker typically seeks some indication of his success in conveying information. The reaction sought from the listener may be simply a brief signal of attention, or perhaps a further indication of whether or not the listener has understood the message or agrees with it. Or a more elaborate reaction may be called for, in which case the listener and speaker may have to signal an impending switch in speaker–listener roles.

Certain nonverbal cues at natural junctures in speech are important components of the responses that indicate whether speaker–listener roles should continue versus whether they should switch, and whether or not the listener is satisfied with the prior utterance of the speaker. The nonverbal cues can occur singly or in combinations, and with or without verbal accompaniment. Some different-appearing cues are functionally equivalent or substitutable, while some similar-appearing cues serve separate functions.

Although our focus will be upon nonverbal processes that control the orderly flow of information in conversations, we know that not all conversations proceed smoothly. One reason is that participants do not always agree about when speaker–listener roles should shift. Thus, they may give conflicting signals or they may even choose to ignore clear signals. Another possible reason is that the participants fail to interpret each other's signals in the same way. The latter may be the result of mental retardation or deficient socialization experiences. It may also occur when the participants are normal members of different cultural groups, each of which has its own signaling system.

If participants are from different linguistic communities, it is obvious that they will have difficulties understanding messages transmitted by the verbal–linguistic channel. But what is the likelihood of comparable difficulties in the exchange of nonverbal controlling signals? We review a body of evidence that indicates there should be considerable commonality in the performance of nonverbal controlling signals across linguistic communities. This commonality should result from the involvement of certain physiological mechanisms in speech processing. Even though there is increasing evidence that virtually any physical response may be modifiable through experience with the environment (Miller, 1969), the occurrence of common innate dispositions in humans may function to limit variability in the actual distribution of controlling cues across social groups.

SEGMENTATION AND CLASSIFICATION
OF CONVERSATIONAL BEHAVIOR

The analysis of conversational control functions of nonverbal behavior requires that conversations be segmented into certain classes of units. First the flow of verbal–linguistic behavior must be divided into successive periods in which one subject is considered to be in the speaker role and the other subject simultaneously in the listener role. Within each of these complementary role periods, the utterances of the speaker must be subdivided into informational units. The informational units, in turn, must be classified into those whose endings indicate that the participants should shift speaker–listener roles, and those that indicate that the present role-relationship should continue. Listener signals at the ends of the speaker's informational units also must be classified into those that indicate a desire to maintain versus switch roles, as well as those that indicate satisfaction or disattisfaction with the preceeding speech unit.

Units of Complementary Verbal Participation

We have noted that there is consensus that participants in a conversation must segment their time into complementary speaker–listener roles. This may appear at first glance to be a simple distinction to make. However, there is much disagreement about what constitutes a speaking turn. Definition and procedures for determining turns have ranged from dependence upon simple physical criteria to complex judgemental criteria. Part of the problem appears to be that as one approaches a more intuitively meaningful definition, the efficiency and reliability of its implementation decreases. The ideal definition would be both reliable and comprehensive. Inasmuch as consensual decisions about how to define speaker-listener periods are critical to progress in the understanding of conversational control functions, we will now review different approaches in some detail.

In the most objective approach (Feldstein, 1972; Jaffe & Feldstein, 1970), speaking turns are defined on the basis of the automated measurement of who is vocalizing, beyond a specified threshold of intensity, at each moment in time. It should be noted that the vocalizations of the participants are recorded in situations in which vocal responses can reasonably be assumed to be primarily linguistic, in contrast to humming, grunting, and the like. Also the threshold of intensity for each speaker's voice is set at a level at which the voice is intelligible to a normal listener. Speaker–listener roles are determined with the aid of a computer that assesses whether or not each participant is vocalizing in each successive, brief time interval (for example, .3 sec).

In this automated method of analysis, a person may be considered to maintain the speaker role until the other person becomes the sole vocalizer. Thus, occasional occurrences of simultaneous speaking, and more common occurrences of simultaneous silence, would be considered part of the turn of the preceding sole speaker. We will have relatively little to say in this chapter about the interesting process by which "contests" for gaining or rejecting the speaker role occur and are resolved. Rather, we will emphasize the processes by which smooth turn-taking is accomplished However, it should be noted that automated measures of relative intensity of vocalization of participants during periods in which simultaneous speech occurs have been utilized to determine how the outcome is resolved (Morris, 1971). It also should be noted that periods of rapid alternation of vocalization between speakers might be considered to constitute contests for the floor. In such a case, a switch in speaker–listener roles might not be considered to occur until the computer detects that a certain minimal duration of speech occurs by the prior listener only.

Verbal Responses of Listeners

A more significant problem in the determination of speaker–listener periods concerns the classification of brief verbal responses by the listener following an informational unit by the speaker. By the automated criterion we have just discussed, the brief verbalization would be considered a shift in the speaker–listener role. However, other investigators hold that certain minimally informative verbal and vocal responses should be considered as continuations of the listener role. From this latter perspective, the brief utterances by listeners are interpreted as methods by which they help maintain the speaker in this role. A familiar example is the "mm-hmm," which commonly is considered functionaly equivalent to the silent head nod as a signal not to change speaker–listener roles.

The differentiation of verbal responses into those that constitute speaker responses and those that constitute listener responses presents some serious problems for reliability of measurement. Still, it has considerable intuitive appeal. Yngve (1970) has proposed that a participant in a conversation "holds the floor" as long as he maintains primary responsibility for presenting a body of information. During this period the listener may occasionally engage in "back-channel" verbalizations that function to aid the floor-holder in the communication of his position. However, we have argued that satisfactory measures of the content of information in conversation have not been devised. Thus, how can we determine the conditions under which a verbal response should be defined, paradoxically, as a listener response?

Researchers have varied in criteria for identifying verbal listener responses. The most common basis is the judgment by the coder that the content of the verbal response indicates that the responder wishes to remain in a listener role. Many simple verbalizations are assumed to indicate that the responder is simply attending to the speaker or acknowledging the occurrence of the speaker's prior utterance (Rosenfeld, 1966a; Snyder, 1945). The most notorious examples are the "mm-hmm," or "uh-huh." These "vocal identifiers" (Pittenger & Smith, 1957) have been viewed linguistically as members of a larger class of common nonlexical "vocal segregates" (Bateson: see Trager, 1958, p. 6). Attentional functions also have been attributed to brief lexical terms such as "yeah" and "I see."

Some researchers have proposed that certain more evaluative or informative messages also should be categorized as listener responses. For example, Kendon (1967) gave the examples of "mm yes" and "that's true" as point granting or assenting signals by listeners, and contrasted them with the simple attentional usage of "mm-hmm." However, his tentative classification scheme also took into account the degree to which the prior speaker appeared to be trying to elicit assent by the listener. Thus, it is not clear whether or not the form of the verbal listener response is in itself a sufficient basis for making the distinction, or if further verbal context is necessary. In addition, the intonational qualities of such responses may or may not confirm their substantive implications.

Another argument for the inclusion of brief verbal responses within the listener role is that their brevity itself excludes them from consideration as substantive informational units. Research on the temporal properties of speech indicates that informative utterances of greater complexity require more time for preparation and production (Goldman-Eisler, 1968). On the basis of such evidence, Kendon (1967) included among listener responses speech that lasted less than an arbitrary minimum of 5 sec. While the wisdom of selecting this particular length may be argued, length of utterance, in contrast to judged meaning of utterance, does have the current advantage of being assessable with high reliability.

One additional set of criteria that should be considered in determining whether a verbal response should be categorized as speaker or listener behavior is the kinesic accompaniments of the utterance. In general, speakers avert gaze more than do listeners in dyadic interaction (Exline, 1963; Nielsen, 1962). In particular it has been found that more complex utterances, which supposedly require both more concentration for their formulation and absence of interruption for their performance, tend to be initiated with orientation of the speaker's eyes away from the listener (Day, 1964; Duke, 1968; Kendon, 1967). Conversely most brief vocal–verbal responses, including attention signals, laughs, short questions, and exclamations, were observed by Kendon to be accompanied by gaze directed toward the other person. (Exceptions were verbal assenting signals, which typically were accompanied by a brief dropping of the eyelids, thereby interrupting gaze and negative exclamations.) Furthermore, the initiation of more complex units of speech tends to be accompanied by gesticulatory activity (Dittmann & Llewellyn, 1969). In contrast, gestural activity rarely occurs as an accompaniment of brief listener verbalizations (Gunnell & Rosenfeld, 1971). Rosenfeld and Hancks (in preparation), as part of an ongoing study to be described more fully later, compared the nonverbal accompaniments of brief listener verbalizations with the nonverbal concomitants of the first two words of the speaker's next utterance. The relative frequencies of speech-related nonverbal signals of listeners and speakers obtained from 250 such comparisons representing 20 independent conversational dyads were as follows: movements of the head away from the other person, 22/104; initiations of gesticulations of the hand or arm, 2/14. In contrast, the comparable frequencies for head nodding were 188/6. Thus, longer utterances initiated with gaze avoidance and gesticulation are especially indicative of the speaker role.

The use of length of utterance and kinesic concomitants as criteria for defining listener verbalizations may not be applicable if complex utterances are included within the definition of listener responses. Rosenfeld and Hancks found that only 6% of listener responses that were composed of simple segmentals or simple lexical items were accompanied by shifts in gaze away from the speaker, whereas 25% of the listener responses consisting of multiple lexical items (for example, "that's very very true") were associated with gazes away. Duncan and Niederehe (1974) have reported some difficulty in distinguishing between speaker and listener responses when applying the broad conception of listener behavior suggested by Yngve, which includes asking questions, making comments, and filling in information initiated by the speaker.

In the present writer's view, progress in understanding conversational control processes requires greater attention to the reliability of definitions of verbal listener responses. It is necessary to give as complete a specification of defining criteria as possible. These might profitably include audio or visual tape-recorded examples that serve as models of subtle paralinguistic and kinesic qualifications of content. Of course, the ultimate criterion for validating a verbal act as a listener response should be evidence of its role in the process of conversational control. This will be considered in a later section, along with nonverbal aspects of listener behavior.

INFORMATIONAL UNITS WITHIN SPEAKER ROLES

Now that we have a general idea about how conversations can be segmented into complementary speaker–listener periods, we can turn our attention to the task of subdividing those periods into informational units of speech. Recall the conception of the conversational process as organized to facilitate the flow of such units. It was proposed that nonverbal control processes will be activated primarily around the junctures that separate the units. At such junctures the participants should transmit nonverbal information that indicates whether they should switch or maintain speaker–listener roles, as well as what general form of informational content is needed in subsequent utterances. We now face the problem of deciding what criteria should be used for segmenting speaker periods into informational units. Once again, we review some of the major options that have been proposed.

Semantic and Quantitative Analysis of Information

Ideally, we would like to describe conversational units in terms of the substantive information they convey. In particular it would be advantageous to determine how much of a total body of information to be transmitted from one participant to another actually is conveyed in each unit. From the formal perspective of information theory, this decision depends upon both the message sent (encoded) by the speaker and its reception (decoding) by the listener. The communication engineer has a precise definition of the transmission of information. The basic unit H, refers to the receiver's uncertainty about a message prior to its successful transmission by the sender (Shannon & Weaver, 1949). Unfortunately, we do not know how to apply the measure of information to the flow of natural conversational behavior. To do so would require prior knowledge of what the participants initially do and do not know about a topic, how they encode their informational repertoires into measurable units of speech, and the degree to which their knowledge is affected by each other's utterances (Haas & Wepman, 1972; MacKay, 1972).

It is possible to track *roughly* the flow of information in conversations by artificially controlling the ideational input available to participants, assessing its subsequent verbal performance, and testing for its acquisition following the interaction (Rosenfeld & Sullwold, 1969). However, the validity of inferences about the amount of information that is transmitted during the conversation is limited by the possibility of covert, higher level integration by the participants of the discrete units of informational input.

More precise records of informational flow can be obtained through restricting conversations by means of structured "referential communication" tasks (Glucksberg, Krauss, & Higgins, 1975; Rosenberg, 1972). Such paradigms allow one to keep better track of informational production of speakers and its effects upon listeners by placing rather severe constraints upon not only the contents available for discussion, but also upon the occasions for performing them. Within the restricted range of response opportunities available to participants, this research has indicated that lack of comprehension by listeners affects the subsequent informational output by speakers. For example, experimentally induced noncomprehension by listeners has resulted in substantive descriptions by speakers that were more slowly spoken, lengthier, and more redundant (Longhurst & Siegel, 1973). While such research procedures seldom have been employed for detecting the effects of nonverbal signals upon the flow of information in conversations, they might productively be adapted for that purpose.

Using transcriptions of speech in unconstrained conversations, various efforts have been made to define information on the basis of the linguistic content. For example, the "type-token" ratio — the number of different kinds of words divided by the total number of words spoken over a specified sample of speech — has been widely applied as a general index of amount of information or nonredundancy. Distinctions between the contents of words, individually as well as in phrases and sentences, within a corpus of speech have been used for differentiating classes and amounts of information by means of automated computer analysis (Stone, Dunphy, Smith, & Ogilvie, 1966; Psathas, 1969). More subjective definitions hav been used in the designation of subtle variations in informational content, such as changes in ideas (Horowitz & Newman, 1964) or topic (Ervin-Tripp, 1969), the occurrence or subordinate "side sequence" phrases of conversation (Jefferson, 1972), as well as more elaborate listings of varieties of substantive units (Pace & Boren, 1973). Different scoring systems have been designed for application to different structures or purposes of conversation, such as interviews (Hawes, 1972), psychotherapy (Snyder, 1945), and conferences (Bales, 1955).

Particularly promising have been recent efforts to incorporate the larger conversational context and the task requirements of participants in the interpretation of messages (Carswell & Rommetveit, 1971; Glucksberg, Trabasso, & Wald, 1973), and to compare sequences of syntactic utterances on the basis of their fundamental ideational correspondences (Schank, 1972). Some common forms of sequential relations between the contents of utterances of alternating speakers in conversation have been identified, such as question–answer sequences, elliptical references to prior utterances, and extensions of the other person's utterance (Speier, 1972). However, at this time it seems safe to conclude that less progress has been made in semantic bases for constructing conversational units than in grammatical approaches.

Syntax and Pausing

A problem with all of the above semantically based measures of information when applied to natural conversations is that they provide no valid basis for segmenting a speaker's behavior into functional communicative units. There is increasing evidence that minimally meaningful units of conversational information are structured in units larger than single words (Goldman-Eisler, 1972), but determination of the appropriate size of unit remains a problem. Definitions of minimal units of utterance commonly have been based upon the criteria of grammatical completion and subsequent pausing (Davis, 1937, p. 44). However, a minimal functional requisite for validating a definition of a unit of spoken information in conversation should be that noticeable changes in listener behavior typically occur near the boundaries of the units. Both grammatical phrase endings and pauses contribute to the predictability of speaker switching (see Jaffe & Feldstein, 1970, pp. 49–50). Yet, these measures are insufficient for defining a conversational speech unit. Kendon (1967) reported that only 49% of verbal "accompaniment" signals by listeners occurred at "phrase boundary pauses," leaving 51% unaccounted for. Similar results were presented in a case study by Yngve (1970). While the occurrence of grammatical junctures, especially when followed by pauses, is a better predictor of listener reactions that are nonjunctural locations or hesitation pauses within phrases, none of these appears to be an adequate basis for unitization of conversation.

The Phonemic Clause

A promising minimal unit is the "phonemic clause," a rhythmic segment of speech consisting of short strings of words, identified by a single primary stress which is followed by a slowing or stretching of speech (Boomer, 1978; Dittmann & Llewellyn, 1967; Trager, 1962; Trager & Smith, 1951). The stressed word typically is the highest "information" word, in contrast to "function" words which serve to hold the information words together. Listener responses rarely occur at locations other than the junctures that separate phonemic clauses. The association between junctures and such listener responses as "mm-hmm's" and head nods has been statistically significant in virtually every individual conversation in which it has been tested.

Phonemic clauses that terminate with a rising or falling pitch change — called "final" junctures (Dittmann, 1972a) — regularly precede verbal and nonverbal listener responses (Dittmann & Llewellyn, 1967, 1968). Compared to sustained-pitch junctures, final junctures increased the predictability of brief verbal listener responses by 21% in the 1967 verbal interaction study. Postjunctural pauses accounted for 18% of the listener responses, but when juncture type was held constant, the juncture pauses were found to contribute only an additional 10% to the predictability of the verbal listener responses. Final junctures terminated half of the phonemic clauses scored in the 1968 face-to-face interaction study. With an average of five words per clause such junctures should have occurred an average of once every 10 words in their data.

Most smooth speaker switches also occur in the junctures that follow phonemic clauses (Duncan, 1972, 1973). Duncan included some sustained as well as final junctures in his predictive units, but only when the sustained junctures were accompanied by such additional cues as head turning toward the listener, termination of movement or relaxation of the hand, unfilled pause, drawl, and drops in pitch or loudness. Of 2,481 phonemic clauses he scored, 885 (36%) met his criteria for predictive units. With an average length of 2.8 clauses, we would estimate his selected speech units to average about 14 words in length. Although the junctures that separate phonemic clauses are not sufficient for the prediction of major listener responses in free conversations, they do appear to be virtually necessary. Thus, the phonemic clause meets a major requisite for a minimal information unit, even though its definition does not identify the amount or content of information contained in the unit. It is apparent that phonemic clauses are related to semantic and syntactic properties of conversational speech, but the precise nature of the relationship is not yet clear.

Kinesic Concomitants

We mentioned earlier that common nonverbal orientational and gesticulatory behaviors can aid in discriminating between speaker and listener verbal responses. Similarly, gaze avoidance and gesticulation constitute criteria for identifying the initiation of separate units *within* a speaking turn.

On the basis of preliminary observations of normal speakers of American English, Birdwhistell (1970, pp. 110–143) has proposed that kinesic activities serve to demarcate, distinguish between, and interrelate grammatical and semantic units of speech ranging from sublexical components to strings of sentences. Units comparable to phonemic clauses, which we have found to meet the functional requisites of minimal communicative units, were observed by Birdwhistell to be regularly accompanied by kinesic stress and juncture markers involving the head, eyes, hands, and feet of the speaker.

Observations of sound films of conversations between psychotherapists and their clients led Scheflen (1964) to emphasize higher order units. The "point," which may be roughly defined as a coordinated set of phonemic clauses that correspond to colloquial notions of "making a point," was characterized by persistent head and eye activities. Different individuals were found to utilize small and sometimes idiosyncratic kinesic repertoires, but with variations within the repertoires demarcating adjacent points. Examples of activities associated with points were the tilting, turning, cocking, and extension of the head. Some correspondence also was noted between the nonverbal characteristics of a point and the substantive content of its verbal component. The next higher level, the "position," comprising a sequence of points, was marked by a gross shift in posture, and typically lasted from .5 to 6 min. Finally, the "presentation" consisted in all positions of a speaker in a continuous discourse and was marked by a complete change in location.

Kendon (1972; 1973) performed a comprehensive microanalytic analysis of speech rhythms and body movement on a sound film of a 1.5-min segment of informal conversation in a group setting. He identified a five-level hierarchy of intonationally defined speech units (see Crystal, 1969) which appeared to correspond to levels of substantive complexity. The units, in ascending order of size, are the "prosodic phrase" (compare the phonemic clause), the "locution" (similar to the written sentence), the "locution group," the "locution cluster" (similar to the written paragraph), and finally the entire "discourse" or total verbal participation of the speaker. Speech units both within and between levels were differentiated by kinesic activities.

Larger movements, involving more body parts, were associated with more comprehensive verbal structures. Smaller and more rapidly changing movements accompanied the simpler, faster changing levels. In the example described by Kendon, movements of the face (eyes, brows, mouth) occurred at higher rates than did head movement; the wrists and fingers moved more frequently than did the forearms; and the forearms more than the upper arms. Distinctive movements characterizing each phrase appeared to be predominantly organized — that is, to "peak" — around the major stressed syllable, which we previously noted is typically located in the highest information word of a phonemic clause. Each speech unit was preceded by a form of nonverbal "speech preparatory" activity (cf. Dittmann & Llewellyn, 1969), and the latency of speech following the preparatory movements increased with the comprehensiveness of the unit. Within a level of speech complexity, similar body parts were employed across units, but with distinctive patterns per unit.

If these limited but promising observations prove to be characteristic of conversations in general, they should lead to a much more elaborated and exact system for the segmentation of informational units of speech than currently is available. From the present perspective, it is particularly important to determine the ways in which the different kinds of speaker units affect the responses of listeners.

NONVERBAL LISTENER RESPONSES

We have defined the role of listener as the total period of time during which the other person is the dominant speaker. If there are no periods of role-indeterminacy or floor-negotiation, then the listener period is bound by the listener's own speaker roles. At the verbal level, the listening period is characterized primarily by substantive verbalizations of the speaker and silence by the listener, with possible segments of silence by the speaker and brief verbalization by the listener. We already have discussed vocal and verbal aspects of listener responses. Throughout the listening period the listener can engage in a wide range of kinesic responses that are capable of serving conversational control functions. Junctures between phonemic clauses of speakers are particularly critical occasions for the performance of major listener reactions.

Just as the speaker provides responses that can be conceptually separated into information-encoding and listener-controlling functions, so too might the listener provide both decoding cues and speaker-controlling cues. On the basis of the oberservation that movements of listeners are synchronized somewhat independently with the vocal and the visible behavior of speakers, Kendon (1970) has speculated that listeners may provide distinctive nonverbal cues that they are decoding the speaker's utterances at various hierarchical levels of organization. Dittmann (1972c) similarly has suggested that listener responses may reflect not only a social reaction to the speaker, but also energy expended in the decoding process—analogous to the kinesic activity of speakers that is associated with the encoding of utterances (Dittmann & Llewellyn, 1968; Moscovici, 1967).

There is no standard lexicon of nonverbal listener responses, and the literature on listener behavior varies widely in the range of responses that have been included in the concept. However, there is an emerging consensus about what components are most centrally involved in the control process. One of the most widely utilized kinesic response by listeners is the head nod. We will discuss the functions of its variations as well as the implications of its occurrence alone versus with verbal concomitants. As is the case with speakers, listeners also can exert control by means of visual orientation and gesticulation, although they do so at a lower rate. We will pay less attention to a variety of less common kinesic listener reactions, such as postural changes, small head movements, frowns, eyebrow flashes, and small smiles. Finally, we will consider the conversational control functions of the failure of listeners to provide distinctive responses at clear junctures in the speaker's behavior.

NONVERBAL CONTROL PROCESSES

The behaviors by which conversants influence each other's orderly participation and their progression toward substantive goals falls within a more general class of interpersonal control signals referred to as "regulators" or "integration signals" (Scheflen, 1963, 1968). According to Ekman and Friesen (1969), "Regulators are acts which maintain and regulate the back-and-forth nature of speaking and listening. . . . They tell the speaker to continue, repeat, elaborate, hurry up, become more interesting, less salacious, give the other a chance to talk, etc. They can tell the listener to pay special attention to wait just a minute more to talk, etc. [p. 82]." From common experience it is not difficult to conjure up familiar nonverbal responses by which these respective outcomes are solicited. For example, the listener could communicate the above sequence of reactions by silent visual attention or small periodic nods, a cocking of the head while cupping an ear, a puzzled expression, speech-accompanying head nods that recycle beyond the rate of stresses of the speaker, yawning, opening the mouth and raising a hand, and so on. And we can imagine the speaker communicating his respective desires by tapping the listener with a finger, raising a hand in an emblem of "wait," and so forth. In fact, as Scheflen as well as Ekman and Friesen have pointed out, virtually any category of nonverbal behavior can serve as a regulator in some circumstances.

Thus, to provide a comprehensive list of nonverbal regulators virtually would require a complete dictionary of nonverbal communication. Even if such a horrendous task were possible, the accompanying inference that "all nonverbal behavior is regulatory behavior" is too general to be of value. The solution chosen by Ekman and Friesen (1969) was to limit regulators to those nonverbal behaviors that did not fit into their four other major categories of nonverbal usage—emblems, affect displays, illustrators, and adaptors. From their perspective, which implicitly emphasizes the interpretive—communicative functions of nonverbal behavior more than its social-behavioral consequences, this was a sensible decision. However, it left the category of nonverbal regulator impoverished with little more than the listener head nod as an entry, except under special circumstances (See Ekman & Friesen, 1972, p. 359, regarding overlap between regulators and speech-illustrative movements).

From the present perspective there is another solution. While recognizing that all elementary nonverbal acts may have multiple social meanings or usages, their specific functions as regulators may be identified through the addition of contextual cues. By contextual cues we refer to the larger array of behavior of conversants within which a specific nonverbal act is performed. For example, a smile initiated by a listener in the middle of a phonemic clause may differ in function from one emitted after a final-sounding juncture. Another way of utilizing the concept of context in the identification of regulators is to include configurations of multiple nonverbal activities that occur in close temporal association. Thus, we are suggesting that the nonverbal behaviors that serve different social functions be viewed not as mutually exclusive, but rather as imbedded in mutually exclusive contexts or behavioral configurations.

It should be noted that the degree to which the *forms* of common classes of nonverbal responses might subtly vary with the *contexts* in which they are performed is not yet well-understood. Birdwhistell (1970) has described extremely wide variations in the forms of head nods (pp. 158–166) and smiles (pp. 29–39). Gunnell and Rosenfeld (1971) found that smiles typically differ contextually from head nods and brief verbal listener responses in that only the last two occurred predominantly in listening periods. Yet Dittmann (personal communication) has observed that listeners occasionally give brief smiles at junctures, which differ in form from speech-associated smiles by their smallness and quickness of termination. Also Rosenfeld and McRoberts (in preparation) found that positivity ratings of head nods were predictable from such features as initial direction and duration, as well as presence of concomitant smiles.

THE DATA BASE

Conversational control functions of nonverbal behavior have been referred to, at least in passing, in numerous studies. However, only a few studies have been oriented primarily toward their analysis. For the present chapter, we will emphasize available studies that have been dedicated to a temporal analysis of interpersonal control processes within face-to-face conversations. The studies we review generally fall into two classes: extensive behavioral measurement of small numbers of subjects, and limited behavioral measurement of larger numbers of subjects. Possibly because of limitations in the time available to investigators, some tradeoff has occurred between comprehensiveness of behavioral assessment and breadth of sampling of subjects.

The studies, taken as a whole, are a rather fragmentary assortment, yet the consensual findings that have emerged from them attest to the robustness of certain processes of conversational control. On the other hand, the very limited sampling of subject populations and situations clearly indicates a need for much more research in the area. The research has been based almost exclusively upon polite conversations among American or English adults of the middle or upper-middle class. Thus, the scholar seeking definitive documentation of conversational control processes may well be disappointed. However, the discovery-oriented researcher may be encouraged by the range of territory remaining to be explored.

One of the most detailed analyses was performed upon sections of a 16 mm sound motion picture of a multiperson conversation in an English pub. Portions of the film were analyzed by Kendon (1970, 1972), frame by frame, for all changes of movements of the head, hands, arms, and trunk, and for the correspondence of these movements with the phonetically transcribed speech of the participants. Another comprehensively analyzed set of data, coded by more molar and eclectic categories, consisted of two videotaped 19-min conversations among adults, with one person in common in the two dyads (Duncan, 1972, 1973, 1974; Duncan & Niederehe, 1974). These painstaking studies required years of analysis to reach their present state of completion. In addition to deriving important heuristic hypotheses about the variables involved in conversational control, their authors were able to aid future researchers by indicating which miniature behaviors are unlikely to be implicated.

More selective nonverbal measurements have been applied to larger samples consisting of college students. The relationship of interpersonal visual orientation to molar categories of verbal behavior was studied in 5-min samples of coordinated audiotape and film (two frames per second) records of seven dyads in which the participants were getting acquainted (Kendon, 1967). Unfortunately, in none of the publications identified so far in this section on the data base was any assessment of intercoder reliability coefficients reported for the various behavioral categories. However, it is evident that meticulous attention was required for the detailed, temporal scoring of these studies and that multiple coders were involved, who at least resolved disagreements through discussion.

The relationship of phonemic junctures to verbal listener responses and head nods was investigated in 20 dyads by Dittmann and Llewellyn (1968). Automated procedures were employed to aid in the objective detection of head nods and their coordination with reliably assessed units of speech. All of the studies mentioned so far in this section consisted of descriptive analyses of relatively unrestricted conversations. A relatively comprehensive molar analysis also has been performed on nonverbal behavior reliably assessed from videotapes of six college students in a more restricted condition (Gunnell & Rosenfeld, 1971; Rosenfeld, 1972). Each student spent about 45 min interviewing the same actress–confederate who was trained to perform fluent and disfluent utterances on a random schedule and to terminate her utterances with clear junctures at which she gazed at the listener and paused. Rates of each category of nonverbal behavior by interviewers were compared at junctures versus between junctures of the interviewee.

While we had arbitrarily decided to emphasize the role of body motion and, to a lesser extent, brief verbal listener responses in conversational control, it should be mentioned that thorough analyses have been performed on another important dimension of nonlinguistic behavior. The structure of the purely temporal properties of vocal behavior in conversations has been extensively analyzed in repeated samples (Feldstein, 1972; Jaffe & Feldstein, 1970; also see relevant chapters in this book). Automated measurement assured high reliability.

Finally, it should be noted that relatively comprehensive analyses of nonverbal control processes have been initiated on larger samples of subjects and situations. For example, Duncan (personal communication) is replicating his study on six additional dyads. Twenty-six videotapes of half-hour conversations also are being analyzed in the present author's laboratory. All conversants were carefully selected for their mutual involvement in the topic of their discussion. High-resolution videotape records were obtained, with split-screen full-face images of each participant, permitting the scoring of such details as gaze direction, in addition to head movement. Pam Gunnell is comparing nonverbal behavior in samples of speaker switching and "mm-hmm" listener responses from twenty of the conversations. Rosenfeld and Margaret Hancks are studying the same tapes to compare the nonverbal concomitants and consensually judged functions of several levels of complexity of verbal listener response, including vocal segregates (for example, "mm" or "mm-hmm"), simple lexical items (for example, "yeah" or "I see"), and multiple lexical items (for example, "yeah, okay").

The other six half-hour videotapes, collected by Rosenfeld and Diane Beecher, have one person in common to the six dyads. In two conversations he was predominantly in a learner role, in two a teacher, and in two others a codiscussant. The study was designed to include some control over individual differences in interpreting different control functions of nonverbal behavior.

Because these studies were accessible to the writer, completed analyses from some of them will be mentioned in this chapter. Any omissions of other relevant research is unintentional.

CONTROL FUNCTIONS OF NONVERBAL BEHAVIORS

Speakers and listeners probably monitor each other's behavior regularly, if not continuously, throughout most conversations. Thus, any clear behavior change by one participant at any point in the interaction could produce a noticeable effect on the behavior of the other. In the typical polite conversation, however, the relationship between speaker and listener behavior *prior* to junctures probably reflects little more than their coordinated effort to mutually track the subphrase elements of the speaker's utterance and to signal each other that they are doing so. Such "synchrony" has been noted between nonverbal movements of listeners and the phonic, syllabic, and lexical units of speakers (Condon & Ogston, 1966).

However, on the basis of very limited numbers of thoroughly analyzed interactions, Kendon (1970) has described ways in which synchronization prior to the juncture may lead to more molar variations in the conversational process. For example, synchronization of the listener's movements with the elements of the speaker's utterance near the end of a phonemic clause may serve to signal the speaker that the listener has comprehended the speaker's meaning prior to the completion of the speaker's utterance. Such prejunctural signaling by the listener may indicate that the speaker should either provide new information or else let the listener take on a more dominant role in the conversation.

The role of prejunctural head nodding in this process has been suggested and illustrated by Birdwhistell (1970), Dittmann and Llewellyn (1968), and Rosenfeld (1972). If such prejunctural signaling should prove to be common, then the assumption of discrete alternation in turns, which typifies theories of conversation, may convey an oversimplified perspective. In fact, the nature of most of the conversations that have been analyzed indicates a bias toward an overemphasis on polite, cooperative social encounters.

In current analyses at our laboratory, Gunnell has found significantly more smooth speaker switches among dyads who were given complementary conversational goals than among those given less compatible tasks. Also, Duncan and Niederehe (1974) report that nonverbal efforts by listeners to gain control of the floor sometimes are initiated prior to the completion of the speaker's utterance, and that such listener behaviors affect the likelihood of disruptive versus smooth transitions between speaking turns. In larger data samples reported by Jaffe and Feldstein (1970), more simultaneous speech occurred in conversations based on attitudinal discrepancies than in interviews. Also, within the attitude discrepancy study simultaneous speech varied with changes in partner and topic. Finally, it is noteworthy that both simultaneous speech and pauses were shorter in duration among conversants in their study between whom a visual barrier had been inserted than between those who conversed face to face. One might speculate that the screen eliminated nonverbal cues that otherwise would have perpetuated conflicting floor claims and would have allowed a speaker to hold the floor for longer pause durations.

Speaker Elicitation of Listener Behavior

First let us consider how the speaker signals that he does *not* wish to switch speaking roles at the juncture. Inasmuch as speakers tend to look away from listeners when formulating or initiating complex speech units, we would expect gaze avoidance to inhibit listener responses. Kendon (1967) investigated this process in two conversations. He reported that when the speaker ended his utterance without looking at the listener, 71% of the time the listener either gave no subsequent speech or else "delayed" his speech. When the speaker ended with an extended look at the listener, the listener followed with no speech or delayed speech only 29% of the time.

Duncan (1972, 1973) found one speaker behavior that was particularly effective in preventing the listener from taking over the floor, even after the listener signaled a wish to do so. This cue was a hand gesticulation by the speaker that was maintained or not returned to resting state through the juncture. Of 361 junctures that contained the gesticulation plus at least one additional cue that otherwise tended to predict turn switching, only two of the junctures resulted in speaker switching. Of 416 junctures containing a turn-switching cue but which lacked gesticulation, 86 resulted in changes in speaking turn. It will be recalled that gesticulation, like gaze avoidance, also is characteristic of the invitation of complex utterances. The possibility of its intentional use as a switch-suppressing signal may derive from its natural usage in speech formulation (Dittmann & Llewellyn, 1969) and illustration (Ekman & Friesen, 1972).

How does a speaker indicate that he wants, or is available for, a listener reaction? We previously noted that a "final" pitch ending of the speaker's phonemic clause itself is a predictor of listener responses. Dittmann and Llewellyn (1968) compared falling, rising, and sustained endings for their prediction of listener head nods and brief vocalizations. One or both of these listener responses occurred after 37% of falling, 26% of rising, and only 6% of sustained junctures. Similarly Duncan (1972, 1973) listed rising or falling pitch, but not sustained pitch, as one of six speaker behaviors at the juncture that predicted the occurrence of speaker switches.

Dittmann and Llewellyn (1968) also compared the probability of occurrence of head nods or verbal listener responses at junctures versus at nonjuncture locations of speech. The ratio between the two was 15:1 (50:1 for head nods alone), indicating that performing the body of the phonemic clause in itself is a major inhibitor of listener responses. Inasmuch as pausing is more common after final than sustained junctures, one might expect that pausing itself accounts for listener responses. However, while pausing after the final juncture increases the probability of listener responses, pausing within the juncture (hesitation) has little if any effect. In telephone-type conversations studied by Dittmann and Llewellyn (1967), the ratio of the probabilities of verbal listener responses after juncture pauses versus after hesitation pauses was 20:1.

Dittmann and Llewellyn (1968) showed that final junctures, in contrast to sustained junctures, almost always preceded head nods or brief vocalizations by listeners. However, the occurrence of final junctures was not sufficient for predicting *when* the listener responses would occur. The listener responses occurred after only 37% of falling junctures and 26% of rising junctures.

Comparable results were found by Duncan, who used an overlapping but more complex definition of junctures at which cues permitting listener reactions were provided by speakers. His study indicated that a maximum of only 29% of the speaker signals were followed by listener responses (Duncan, 1974), and that only an additional 11% were followed by floor switches (Duncan, 1972). Thus, a liberal estimate of the degree to which all possible opportunities for reaction provided by speakers are responded to by listeners is about 40%.

Duncan identified several speaker cues, in addition to the junctures that terminate phonemic clauses, which preceded listener responses and speaker switching. His major finding was that the greater the *number* of speaker cues at the juncture, the greater was the probability of the listener taking over the speaker role. Six cues were involved. We already have noted that one cue was the final ending of the juncture (rising or falling pitch). Duncan's other five speaker cues at junctures that preceded switching included only one kinesic variable—the termination of any hand gesticulation or the relaxation of a tensed hand position used in the prior speech unit. This cue, of course, would include the termination of the hand gesticulation that serves as a turn-suppressing signal. Another of the cues was grammatical completion; but inasmuch as the same cue also predicted the occurrence of listener responses, it was not uniquely either a turn-predicting cue or a listener response cue. Rather, it enabled either response. The remaining three cues were drawl on the final or stressed syllable of the phonemic clause, the occurrence of a verbal "sociocentric sequence" (for example, "and so on" or "you know"; see the reassurance-seeking "sympathetic circularity" sequence described by Bernstein, 1962), or a combination of a sociocentric sequence and a drop in pitch or loudness below the levels characteristic of the clause.

None of the six cues was found to be more predictive than the others. The correlation between number of speaker cues at the juncture and the probability of floor switching was .96. However, the size of this rank-order correlation should be interpreted with caution because the occurrence of more than four cues was too infrequent to be reliable. A more accurate picture of the effect of number of cues is reflected in the substantial increases in prediction occurring between one and two cues and between two and three cues. Both zero cues and one cue were followed by switching only 10% of the time. With two cues, the prediction increased to 17%; and with three or four cues it was about 33%.

Duncan's results and interpretations imply that the final juncture occurring *alone* (one turn-offering cue) is no more predictive than a sustained juncture alone (zero turn cues). Yet, in the telephonelike conversations studied by Dittmann and Llewellyn (1967) final junctures predicted listener responses substantially better than did sustained junctures. Reconcilliation of the two studies would seem to require that in Dittmann and Llewellyn's study final junctures had to be associated with additional cues in the vocal or linguistic channels. While the latter authors did find that postjunctural pausing was confounded with finality of juncture and that it added modestly to the prediction of listener responses, pauses were not included in Duncan's set of speaker cues. Other vocal–verbal possibilities from Duncan's list include grammatical completion, drawl, sociocentric sequence, and decreasing loudness.

Also, as one would expect, the *fewer* the speaker's eliciting cues the more likely it was that an attempt by the listener to speak would result in simultaneous talk — a breakdown in the turn-taking mechanism. But in this case the critical numbers of cues were not quite the same as for the prediction of smooth switches. Listener attempts at speaking resulted in simultaneous talk 100% of the time after zero cues, 17% after one cue, 8% after two or three cues, and not at all after four or more cues.

Duncan (1974) also claimed that two nonverbal cues by speakers at junctures additively predicted listener responses (to be discriminated from floor-switching responses or no response at all). The cues were grammatical completion of clauses and turning of the speaker's head toward the listener. However, neither of these cues is capable of differentially predicting whether a listener response or a turn-switch is more likely to result. Grammatical completion also was one of the six cues that predicted switches. The head-turning cue was not included as a predictor of switches by Duncan because it did not differentiate between smooth versus contested varieties of speaker switching, and apparently not because it failed to differentiate speaker continuation versus switching at the juncture.

On the basis of Duncan's data let us assume that visual orientation and grammatical completion by speakers at junctures indicate that the listener should make *some* kind of response, but does not specify whether it should be a listener response or a switch from the listener to the speaker role. The decision, then, must be left up to the listener. The option the listener selects should depend upon its relative potential for facilitating the flow of information in the conversation. If the speaker is generating new information at an adequate rate the listener should be expected to signal the speaker to continue via a simple listener response. If the listener wishes to give a more complicated commentary on the information he has been receiving than could be provided by a listener response, he would be expected to attempt to take over the speaking role. In other words, we are proposing that the decision of the listener whether or not to give a listener response depends upon his success in processing information, which in turn is affected by variables outside of the scope that we have been considering.

Still, the *form* of the listener response, if it occurs, may be affected by nonverbal cues of the speaker. Earlier we suggested that nonverbal listener responses can provide various simple messages to the speaker, including degree of attentiveness, understanding, and agreement. In the next section we will review evidence concerning the nonverbal composition of these different messages and how their occurrence may be selectively influenced by nonverbal signals from the speaker. We have reviewed evidence that several kinds of speaker cues apparently are functionally equivalent, or substitutable, in their capacity to evoke some form of listener behavior. Is it also true that different forms of listener responses are functionally equivalent? The most readily available evidence by which to answer this question involves head nods and brief verbal responses.

First there is clear evidence from two studies that the two kinds of listener response occur together at junctures more often than would be expected from chance combinations of their individual occurrences. Dittmann and Llewellyn (1968) found that their co-occurrence constituted 22% of listener responses, compared to 60% for vocalizations alone and 18% for head nods alone. The significant proportion of co-occurrences was upheld within the responses of each of 14 subjects for whom it was testable. Gunnell and Rosenfeld (1971) found the same result in four of five subjects on whom it was testable. The significant co-ocurrences indicate that the combination of nods and verbal responses have a communicative function that is not served by the individual components.

Next, it should be noted that while nods and brief verbal responses typically occurred at or near junctions in both studies, the two forms of response differed in time of occurrence relative to the juncture. In both studies, when the two responses occurred at the same juncture, the nod typically preceded the verbal portion of the listener response. Dittmann (personal communication) found that 23% of listener nods versus only 6% of "mm-hmms" preceded phonation stops of the speaker. He also found that the average latencies of the two responses after junctures were 10 versus 30 msec, respectively. Similar results were obtained by Rosenfeld (1972) in an analysis of head nodding from the Grunnell and Rosenfeld (1971) videotapes. A sample of 126 listener nods from the six dyads was studied in detail. Seven of the 31 nods that occurred in conjunction with verbal listener responses and an additional 31 nods that occurred alone were initiated prior to the completion of the speaker's terminal clause. Verbal listener responses, on the other hand, rarely occurred prior to the juncture. The difference may be attributable to the likelihood that a verbal listener response, in contrast to a nod, would disrupt the utterance of the speaker.

Finally, there was evidence in Rosenfeld's analysis that particular speaker behaviors evoked the nods prior to the junctures. Most of the listener nods that preceded the speaker's juncture were themselves preceded by the initiation of one of the following speaker behaviors: a filled hesitation pause ("ah" type) accompanied by a hand gesticulation, a filled pause accompanied by a head movement (usually a nod or shake), or a phrase whose content was redundant with the preceding phrase. Several other listener nods started during sociocentric sequences (especially "y'know") by the speaker. Dittmann and Llewellyn (1968) also found that nods were elicited by "y'know." They also observed that the joint occurrence of nods and brief verbalizations tended to be preceded by speaker behaviors requiring a relatively vigorous type of listener response. For example, the joint listener responses occurred after the speaker asked a question but before the listener gave a reply, or after the speaker answered a brief question previously asked by the listener. Dittmann and Llewellyn estimated that simple attentional functions were performed by only 30% of the joint responses, compared to 51% of the single responses. Thus, it would appear that the joint listener response tends to indicate understanding or agreement, whereas the individual occurrence of the head nod or "mm-hmm" is more likely to indicate simple attention.

Rosenfeld and Hancks sought to determine the degree to which nonverbal behaviors of speakers accounted for the "complexity" of subsequent verbal listener responses ("mm-hmm" or other segmentals, simple lexical responses and more elaborate forms). Although only accounting for about 18% of the variance in the complexity of 250 verbal listener responses from 20 dyads (using a hierarchical analysis of variance statistic), they found the following speaker behaviors to contribute: pointing of the head or initiating low-amplitude head nods prior to the juncture, and raising the head after the juncture. Again, it would appear that the noticeability of a listener response is at least partly attributable to elicitations of the speaker. This interpretation is enhanced by the further finding that more complex verbal listener responses, compared to simpler ones, tended to be louder and were more likely to be accompanied by eyebrow flashes and repetitive nods.

A variety of examples of possible nonverbal signals were given earlier in this chapter to illustrate the diversity of controlling messages that may be given by the speaker and listener. Rosenfeld and Hancks attempted to determine which nonverbal behaviors of listeners were indicative of attention, understanding, and agreement, and how these behaviors were affected by speakers. Five independent observers of the audio–video records were asked to take the role of the speaker and to rate the 250 listener responses on each of the three dimensions using a four-point scale. Certain nonverbal activities of both listener and speaker were found to be associated with each of the averaged judgments.

Behaviors of the listener that were associated with judgments of "agreement" were complex verbal listener responses and multiple head nods. The agreeing-type listener response was found to predictably follow the speaker's pointing of his head in the direction of the listener. In contrast, judgments that the listener was indicating understanding were associated with repeated small head nods by the listener prior to the speech juncture, and did not involve any apparent speaker signals. Thus, signals of understanding, in contrast to agreement, appear to be more subdued in form and more likely to be initiated by the listener than elicited by the speaker. Finally, judgments of listener attention were associated with forward leaning of the listener prior to the speaker's juncture, audibility of verbal listener response after the juncture, and initiation of gesticulation by the speaker after the juncture but prior to resuming speech. While the implications of the judgment study should be taken only as suggestive, they support the contention that distinctive configurations of nonverbal listener responses communicate different types of feedback to speakers, some of which are elicited by the speakers and some of which are initiated by the listeners.

Effects of Listener Responses on Speaker Behavior.

It is the listener's responsibility to aid the speaker in conveying verbal information as well as to collaborate in the process of speaker switching. We will deal with the latter problem first. To the degree that the speaker provides the turn-switching cues we have discussed, the listener merely has to decide whether or not to take advantage of the opportunity. If he does, he thereby contributes to putting the former speaker into a listener role. However, the listener may wish to take over the speaking role in the absence of such "permission" by the speaker. In such cases, the listener can engage in turn-claiming cues, which, if acknowledged by the speaker, will lead to a smooth switch.

Duncan and Niederehe (1974) detected four such turn-claiming cues by listeners in the two conversations they studied. Two were nonlinguistic vocal cues: overloudness and a sharp, audible inhalation. The other two were kinesic: a shift of the head away from the speaker and the start of a gesticulation. The two kinesic cues were more effective than the two vocal cues. Their usage should be familiar to the reader by now; the head-away cue and the gesticulation were previously found to be associated with the preparation and initiation of speech. In one of the two dyads at least one of the four turn-claiming cues was found to precede 95% of the smooth turn switches, but only 19% of the listener response junctures. In the other dyad, the comparable percentages were 72 and 9%. The cues were even more strongly involved in the resolution of simultaneous talking. There were 18 occasions of simultaneous speech in the study in which the number of turn-claiming cues minus the number of turn-yielding cues favored one participant over the other. Each participant was favored in a substantial number of the occasions. In all 18 cases, the favored participant took over the speaking role at the end of the simultaneous talking.

Duncan (1974) also found that when listener responses occurred prior to the completion of speaking units, the speaker was more likely to emit floor-retaining cues. On 63% of such occasions the speaker turned his head away or gesticulated, in contrast to only 24% of the occasions in which the listener response had followed the completion of the speech unit. Presumably, the early listener response indicates that the listener has already comprehended the speaker's information prior to the completion of the utterance within which it was encoded. This could be threatening to the speaker in two ways — by inferring that the speaker has been unnecessarily slow or overly redundant in presenting information and by increasing the probability that the listener intends to take over the speaker role before the speaker is ready to give it up. This could explain why the early listener response leads the speaker to insert a floor-retaining signal that otherwise would have been omitted.

It is likely that rather minor variations in the timing of brief listener signals, as well as in their content, can function as "feedback," indicating a need for the speaker to modify his flow of information. Nonverbal feedback signals, especially in the context of the verbal content of speech, can provide the speaker with more or less specific information about what modifications are needed.

Consider the possible variants of the head nod. Its general form has been technically defined (McGrew, 1972): "The head is moved forward and backward on the condyles resting on the atlas vertebra, resulting in the face moving down and up [p. 57]." Variations in performance of the act occur along such dimensions of velocity, amplitude, and frequency of cycles (Birdwhistell, 1970, pp. 160–165). Birdwhistell has proposed that different forms of the head nod are involved in different control functions. He differentiated functional classes of head nods by normal listeners in terms of the number and timing of repetitions and their relationship to speaker behavior. What we have referred to as a simple attentional signal was attributed to brief single head nods by listeners that occur repeatedly during the speaker's utterance. Longer lasting single nods were claimed to result in disruption of the flow of speech and justification of prior substantive points. Double head nods were said to either modify the vocalization rate of the speaker upward or downward, or else to evoke an elaboration of the substance of the speaker's prior utterance. Triple head nods at nonprimary-stress points in a phonemic clause were claimed to produce hesitations and, if the cycles were very brief, to result in termination of speech or an inquiry into the listener's problem. These interesting observations should be verified in formal research on larger samples.

The possible feedback implications of less common listener movements at nonswitching junctures also should be further explored. For example, in an ethological approach to the analysis of interviews, Grant (1968) identified a cluster of correlated nonverbal responses that were associated with point-making by speakers and attention by listeners. This "contact" cluster included the head bob and flashing and raising of the eyebrows. Wiener, Devoe, Rubinow, and Geller (1972) claimed that the raised eyebrow or frown of a listener typically leads the speaker to reiterate or correct his message (p. 208). They also asserted that the listener's smile, when accompanied by eye contact, signals comprehension but with an unwillingness to speak. Even the horizontal head shake, recognized as a common multicultural emblem of negation by Darwin (1872/1965), has been attributed the function of reassurance in certain social contexts (McGrew, 1972).

The effects of another kind of listener state at nonswitching junctures also deserves greater attention — the absence of a noticeable listener response at the juncture. Occasions in which the listener fails either to "comment" or take over the floor are likely to be bothersome to the speaker. According to Wiener et al. (1972) the speaker will either give a louder repetition of his message, make an attention-eliciting sound, or quit talking altogether. However, we have noted that most junctures are not followed by verbal listener responses or head nods (Dittmann & Llewellyn, 1968; Duncan, 1972). Perhaps the absence of additional reaction by the listener is aversive to the speaker to the degree that it is preceded by speaker signals which normally evoke more active listener responses.

Our general proposition is that *a listener response which is insufficient relative to the level of evocation by the speaker will be interpreted by the speaker as a negative response.* Experimental research on learning by children has shown that they interpret the absence of response by the experimenter as meaning the opposite of the typical kind of response provided by that experimenter (Crandall, Good, & Crandall, 1964). If the experimenter's mode of operation had been to reward the child after a correct response, then the subsequent occurrence of no response was reacted to as if it were a punishment. The opposite reaction occurred if the experimenter had previously only punished the child for poor responses.

Negative interpretations of videotapes of neutral face–head behaviors of teachers occurred in a developmental study of judge reactions only among judge groups beyond the first grade of elementary school (Rosenfeld, Shea, & Greenbaum, 1975). This finding has been replicated in nonnormal populations as well. There is evidence that persons are more likely to give positive reactions to desirable behavior than negative reactions to undesirable behavior in polite social situations (Rosenfeld, 1966a) and elsewhere (Boucher & Osgood, 1969). Thus, as children become increasingly exposed to social evaluations, they are more likely to interpret nonreactions as the opposite of the positive reactions to which they have become accustomed.

Rosenfeld (1972, pp. 433–434) has described a microanalysis of a videotaped episode in which a listener failed to reciprocate the smile initiated by a speaker at three consecutive junctures, responding instead with a head turn and side glance toward the speaker. Following each successive juncture the speaker modified the substance of his comment (which apparently was unintentionally insulting to the listener) into an increasingly less offensive form and also produced a weaker and briefer smile. Finally, the listener gave a strong smile. The speaker then smiled broadly and quickly suggested that they discuss a different topic. A more extreme example of the disruptive effects of insufficient responsiveness is the actual awkward exodus of speakers from a conversational setting in which the listener was an operant conditioner preprogrammed to shift into a strict extinction period (Ulrich, 1962).

We end our discussion of short-term nonverbal controlling processes in face-to-face interaction by noting that many general rules governing conversational participation in such situations can be generated from the linguistic channel alone (Sacks, Schegloff, & Jefferson, 1974). However, given the considerable independent and interactive effects of the nonverbal channel it is quite clear that both channels of communication must be integrated into a comprehensive theory of conversational structure and process.

LONGER-TERM EFFECTS OF LISTENER RESPONSES

Thus far, our conception of control processes has emphasized the immediate or short-term consequences of a specific signal. We have viewed conversations as if control processes operate independently at each juncture. But there are also likely to be longer term effects as a result of the pattern of signals given over extended time periods. The important problem of how speakers and listeners cumulatively influence the structure of their interaction has been approached from a variety of perspectives. Thus far, however, the comprehensive temporal analyses needed for clear understanding of this process have not been performed.

There is abundant evidence that participants in conversations tend to become more similar in their nonverbal behaviors over time. Most of this evidence has consisted of correlations between behaviors that have been summarized over large blocks of time. Thus, it is difficult to determine what specific social influence mechanisms might have contributed to the obtained relationships. At the vocal level of significant similarity between members of dyads has been found in pause length (Jaffe & Feldstein, 1970) as well as loudness, articulatory precision, and duration of utterance (see review in Webb, 1972). At the kinesic level, interpersonal gazing has been found to be significantly correlated in amount (Argyle & Ingham, 1972; Kendon, 1967) and in mutuality beyond that expected on the basis of amount of gazing by each participant (Stephenson, Rutter, & Dore, 1972).

The time required for nonverbal correspondences to develop varies between response categories. Rosenfeld (1966b) found that smile rates were significantly related within the first 5 min of casual get-acquainted sessions among pairs of college students; however, head nod rates were not significantly correlated between the participants until the third 5-min session, which was held two weeks later. In the case of smiling, the degree of correlation was consistently so high that one might expect smiling to have strong effects on the control of conversation only when nonreciprocated.

In an example described earlier we noted how the repeatedly nonreciprocated smile was followed by reformulations of a substantive statement into increasingly more agreeable forms. There is more extensive evidence that repeated failure to reciprocate nonverbal elicitations is upsetting and disruptive to the recipient. In a study by Rosenfeld (1967) adult experimenter-interviewers of young teenagers repeatedly withheld smiles, head nods, and brief verbal listener responses at the junctures following the subjects' responses. This resulted not only in a significant reduction of subject smiles and nods, but also in an increase of self-stimulatory responses and non-"ah" types of verbal disfluencies. Other research has shown that rates of verbal and kinesic attentional responses are among the strongest determinants of positive impression formation (Rosenfeld, 1966a). Perhaps also relevant in this vein is the finding by Argyle, Lalljee, and Cook (1968) that speech is disrupted when a subject is put into a condition in which he can be seen by the other conversant but cannot see the latter. These studies are consistent with our proposition that nonresponses are viewed as negative responses, especially when they occur in reaction to cues that normally evoke positive responses.

The cumulative effects of negative nonverbal responses and neutral responses of listeners on the reduction of nonverbal responses of speakers are interpretable within an operant conditioning paradigm as instances of punishment and extinction. Similarly, the modification of the content of speaker utterances in response to differential evaluative reactions by listeners could be attributable to selective reinforcement. Insufficient research has been done by which to determine the degree to which differential reinforcement processes can account for the cumulative effects of nonverbal control processes on conversational content or on the nature of the control process itself. However, existing data are compatible with the hypothesis that the behaviors involved in interpersonal control tend to becme more simplified and efficient throughout interaction (MacKay, 1972; Ruesch, 1973; Scheflen, 1963; Vine, 1970).

There is substantial experimental evidence that nonverbal reinforcement processes can affect verbal behavior in face to face interaction. Rates of occurrence of arbitrarily designated classes of verbal response have been increased by providing such listener consequences as head nods, smiles, and leaning forward (Krasner, 1958, p. 152). Early efforts to apply operant conditioning principles, that were initially developed in animal laboratories, to human conversations led to some oversimplified conclusions. Later research, in which certain structural features of conversation were taken into account, has corrected some of the earlier misconceptions. Matarazzo and his colleagues (1964a, b) found that more or less continuous head nodding or "mm-hmming" by interviewers resulted in substantial increases in utterance duration. However, in similar studies in which the interviewee was permitted to state when he had complemented his utterance and in which kinesic cues were not transmitted, no such effects of noncontingent "mm-hmms" were found (Siegman, 1973). In fact, there was a tendency for nonresponsiveness to lead to an increase in utterance length, possibly because it signaled that the speaker's response was incomplete.

From an operant conditioning perspective, it is critical to establish both that one has an effective reinforcer and that it is made contingent upon the occurrence of a particular class of response. In future research on the conditioning of conversational content more attention should be paid to evidence that the content and intonation of verbal responses have different reinforcing capacities in different demographic groups (Brooks, Brandt, & Wiener, 1969; Stevenson, 1965). Also, the occurrence of junctures and other natural configurations of speech should be considered in defining a unit of response. In semicontrolled two-person interactions, subtle verbal conditioning of the lexical content of brief utterances has been established (Rosenfeld & Baer, 1969, 1970). However, it subsequently was found that such conditioning is less likely to work if an attempt is made to modify the normal usage of established communicative habits (see Rosenfeld, 1972). Subtle modifications in the contents of utterances can be conditioned within the range of normal usage, but it is difficult to subtly influence a normal conversant into uttering meaningless messages.

THE ORIGINS OF CONVERSATIONAL CONTROL
SIGNALS

Inasmuch as the nonverbal behaviors we have found to be involved in conversational control processes were assessed in studies of primarily middle class American and English subjects, we have not established the degree to which they are characteristic of other social and linguistic groups. If the behavioral codes by which control functions are carried are as arbitrary as linguistic codes, then we would expect little similarity across linguistic communities. If, on the other hand, the control code is inherently related to universal requisites for human verbal communication, then there may be common usages across linguistic communities. This is not to deny the increasing evidence that most if not all human behavior is subject to modification through experience. Yet a natural linkage between a particular behavior form and the requisites of effective conversation should give that form a higher likelihood of usage than arbitrarily encoded forms. Similarity in conversational control signals across linguistic communities could be of great advantage in promoting understanding between members of the different groups.

Probably the most regularly employed nonverbal control signal is visual orientation — toward or away from the person with whom one is conversing. The high proportion of conversational time in which listeners look at speakers is attributable to more than signaling attention and observing kinesic activity of the speaker. It also is explainable in terms of an acoustic orienting reflex characteristic of humans and other species. When not directly facing a speaker (or other generator of vocal signals), a sound shadow at the far ear can block or alter many high-tone inputs. Binaural balance is achieved by means of a reflexive "noncompensatory nystagmus which moves the eyes toward the locus of the perceived sound source" (Diebold, 1968, p. 555). In this way the visual–kinesic and vocal–auditory systems become linked early in the developmental process. Significant "coupling" between the gaze of infant and mother appears early in the infant's first year (Jaffe, Stern, & Peery, 1973; Stern, 1974), as does the connection of gaze with the turn-taking pattern of vocalization (Bateson, 1971).

Periodic gaze avoidance also may reflect more than the conventional signaling of floor-maintaining or floor-taking interests, or of covert verbal encoding processes. In several species the head is oriented away from a threatening animal. This "cut-off" posture (Chance, 1962; see Hutt & Ounsted, 1966) has been interpreted as a means of preventing excessive stimulation which could inhibit the threatened animal from taking adaptive action. In primates, "cut-off" behavior may take a variety of forms all of which decrease visual input. These forms include facing at an oblique angle, head turning, lowering of eyes, partially closing the eye lids, or covering the eyes with the hand.

Ellsworth and Ludwig (1972) and Coss (1973) have reviewed evidence that adults increase in autonomic arousal when stared at, which may relate to the widespread cultural "taboos" on staring and to the flight reactions that often follow staring episodes. In the conversational process we have noted that there is considerable mutual gazing, controlled mainly by changes in gaze orientation of the speaker. Perhaps the ability of speaker gazes (particularly when accompanied by feedback eliciting cues) to evoke listener responses or speaker switching is partially explainable as the product of escape or avoidance conditioning. By engaging in listener responses or speaker-switching cues, the listener thereby sets the occasion for at least one of the participants to avert gaze and thereby to terminate the uncomfortable pressure of the speaker's coercive visual signals.

An additional impetus to the development of the visual–attentional behaviors that charcterize conversation is the apparently innate attention-evoking function of eyelike stimuli in many animals and in humans (Ahrens, 1954; Hindmarch, 1973). Once the attention of the developing child is thereby drawn to the face area, the varied stimulus properties associated with the face (movements, and later, structural configurations) become increasingly attractive (Walters & Parke, 1965). Vine (1970) has further argued that the evolution of the head and face area as a dense source of a variety of nonverbal signals, such as cross-culturally common displays of emotion, may be associated with the fact that the human visual apparatus can only focus upon a limited area of the visual field.

Perhaps the next most strongly implicated kinesic activity in the conversational control processes we have discussed is the gesticulation — particularly whether or not hand motion is in process versus returned to a resting state. There are wide individual differences in the form and quantity of gesticulation in the conversational process, indicating that it may not have a strong inherent relationship to conversational control.

The role of cultural factors in the acquisition of gesticulatory habits was clearly demonstrated by Efron (1941/1972). Large differences in gestural style were observed by Efron and his associates in New York City between unassimilated members of two European cultures — Southern Italian and Eastern European Jewish. Many of these cultural differences were related to the conversational control process. For example, the traditional Jews characteristically conversed at very close distances. This proximity was associated with a high degree of gesturing, often via head movements because of the restricted opportunities for arm motion. Manual contact betwen conversants was common both as an attention-eliciting device by speakers and as a means of gaining the speaking turn by listeners. One humorous observation was reported of a speaker actually gesticulating in a berating manner with the arm of the listener. Simultaneous gesturing was common and was associated with simultaneous talking. The traditional Italian displayed more fluid and controlled gesticulatory habits, and tended to use termination of gestural movement as a floor-seeking signal. Comparisons of assimilated Jews and Italians in New York City, from the same European ancestory as the unassimilated groups, revealed virtually no differences in gestural style.

In addition to arm movements, Dittmann and Llewellyn (1969) found that head and foot movements of speakers were most common at the initiation of phonemic clauses in conversation. The occurrence of *some* kind of noticeable kinesic activity at the beginning of complex speech units is likely to be common cross-culturally. This would be expected on the basis of the hypothesis that the process of speech encoding involves tension or energy expenditure which tends to be manifest in kinesic activity (Dittmann, 1972c; Kendon, 1970), as well as by the turn-regulating capacity of such responses. Hand and arm movements provide a convenient, although not necessary, means of engaging in such activity.

Certain components of facial affect displays that are optionally employed in conversational regulation — for example, eyebrow flashes, small smiles, or frowns — have been considered to have derived from related functions in prehuman primates and other mammals (see McGrew, 1972; Vine, 1970). If so, they are likely to be correctly interpretable across many linguistic communities, even though there are substantial cultural differences in display rules (Ekman, 1972). It also has been argued that the head nod and head shake occur too frequently across cultures as signals of affirmation and negation to be considered arbitrary signals (Darwin, 1872/1965). Spitz (1957) has offered developmental evidence to support the theory, previously proposed by Darwin, that the affirmative function of the head nod derives from the reciprocating horizontal motion of the head of the infant in the reflexive sucking process, while the head shake derives independently from the infant's rejection of attempts to feed him.

LaBarre (1954), on the other hand, has argued that variations in the ways that affirmation and negation are expressed cross-culturally are inimical with a universalistic interpretation. For example, he noted that in the Punjab and Sind, affirmation is expressed by "throwing the head back in an oblique arc to the left shoulder, one time, somewhat 'curtly' and 'disrespectfully' to our taste"; and in Ceylon it is expressed by "curving the chin in a downward leftward arc . . . , often accompanied by an indescribably beautiful parakineme of back-of-right-hand cupped in upward-facing-palm of the left hand, plus-or-minus the additional kineme of a crossed-ankle curtsey [p. 198]." Other societies are even reputed to use the horizontal head shake as a sign of affirmation.

While no extensive efforts are here being made to provide sufficient evidence to resolve the controversy over how much nature and nurture contribute, we will retain the conservative proposition that *the nonverbal signals involved in conversational control are less arbitrarily coded than are the linguistic contents with which they are associated.* In this context we will add that there is considerable evidence indicating that in the communication of positivity and negativity, the visual–kinesic channel typically dominates the verbal–auditory channel (Bugental, Kaswan, & Love, 1970a: Burns & Beier, 1973; Levitt, 1964; Zaidel & Mehrabian, 1969). Finally, if it may be assumed that the major messages involved in conversational control consist of binary opposites (speak–listen, approve–disapprove, etc.), then even arbitrary forms may be easily learned by observers through brief exposure to their contextual usages as suggested by Leach (1972).

Little is known about the contribution of developmental processes in the acquisition of conversational control skills. We have noted that elementary school children begin to recognize the communicative functions of neutral and subtle negative facial reactions (Rosenfeld *et al.,* 1975). This, and additional evidence that the dominance of nonverbal over verbal cues of positivity and negativity increases with age among linguistically competent persons (Bugental, Kaswan, Love, & Fox, 1970b), may be attributable to the effect of gradual social learning of the referential meanings and normative social reactions to subtle nonverbal signals in conversation. An initial descriptive study of young children in conversations indicated that their listener responses are more latent and less common than are those of adults (Dittmann, 1972a). Experimental research also indicates that younger children are less likely to reformulate their utterances in response to nonverbal or minimal verbal expressions of noncomprehension (Peterson, Danner, & Flavell, 1972). The degree to which the deficiencies in nonverbal control of conversation in children can be attributed to less well-developed information processing skills (cf. Glucksberg, Krauss, & Higgins, 1975) and to less well-established social habits has not been determined.

SUMMARY AND CONCLUSIONS

The era of serious research on conversational control functions of nonverbal behavior is well under way. A small number of limited studies has produced encouraging results. Some of the results have been replicated sufficiently to be considered confirmed. These include the role of phonemic clause endings as major occasions for the occurrence of nonverbal controlling activities and the use of head and eye orientation and of gesticulation in the maintenance and change of speaker roles. It also is evident that nonverbal control signals by listeners may or may not occur in conjunction with verbal listener responses and that combinations of listener activities have stronger or different effects than do isolated activities. In addition, evidence was offered in favor of the proposition that nonverbal listener reactions that are insufficient relative to the nonverbal evocations of speakers are similar in function to active negative reactions. Research also was reviewed in support of the proposition that there are some physiological reasons for the widespread, if not inevitable, occurrence of certain nonverbal controlling cues in the conversational process.

Other discoveries concerning the roles of a variety of small movements of the head and face need further confirmation. More research also is needed on the determination of functional equivalences and differences in the usage of various forms of nonverbal response. Progress in this rapidly developing field of inquiry should be particularly enhanced by efforts to overcome certain methodological limitations of much of the current body of evidence. These requisites include the wider sampling of subject populations and situations, greater attention to the production of comprehensive coding systems that are reliably communicable; and the precise temporal analysis of multivariate data for short-term and cumulative effects. Finally, progress toward the understanding of the role of nonverbal activities in the exchange of information requires greater integration with new developments in the area of verbal information processing.

REFERENCES

Ahrens, R. Beitrag zur entwicklung des physiognomie-und mimikerkennens. *Zeitschrift fur Experimentelle und Angewandte Psychologie,* 1954, *2,* 412–454.

Argyle, M., & Ingham, R. Gaze, mutual gaze, and proximity. *Semiotica,* 1972, *6,* 32–49.

Argyle, M., Lalljee, M., & Cook, M. The effects of visibility on interaction in a dyad. *Human Relations,* 1968, *21,* 3–17.

Bales, R. F. How people interact in conferences. *Scientific American,* 1955, *192,* 31–35.

Bateson, M. C. Epigenesis of conversational interaction. Paper presented to the Society for Research in Child Development, Minneapolis, April 4, 1971.

Bernstein, B. Social class, linguistic codes, and grammatical elements. *Language and Speech,* 1962, *5,* 221–240.

Birdwhistell, R. L. *Kinesics and context: Essays on body motion communication.* Philadelphia: University of Pennsylvania Press, 1970.

Boomer, D. S. The phonemic clause: Speech unit in human communication, In A. W. Siegman & S. Feldstein (Eds.), *Nonverbal behavior and communication.* Hillsdale, N.J.: Lawrence Erlbaum Associates, 1978.

Boucher, J., & Osgood, C. W. The Pollyana hypothesis. *Journal of Verbal Learning and Verbal Behavior,* 1969, *8,* 1–8.

Brooks, R., Brandt, L., & Wiener, M. Different responses to two communication channels: Socioeconomic class differences in response to verbal reinforcers communicated with and without tonal inflection. *Child Development,* 1969, *40,* 453–470.

Bugental, D. E., Kaswan, J. W., & Love, L. R. Perception of contradictory meanings conveyed by verbal and nonverbal channels. *Journal of Personality and Social Psychology,* 1970, *16,* 647–655. (a)

Bugental, D. E., Kaswan, J. W., Love, L. R., & Fox, M. N. Child versus adult perception of evaluative messages in verbal, vocal and visual channels. *Developmental Psychology,* 1970, *2,* 367–375. (b)

Burns, K. L., & Beier, E. G. Significance of vocal and visual channels in the decoding of emotional meaning. *Journal of Communication,* 1973, *23,* 118–130.

Carswell, E. A., & Rommetveit, R. (Eds.), *Social contexts of messages.* New York: Academic Press, 1971.

Chance, M. R. A. An interpretation of some agonistic postures: The role of "cutoff" acts and postures. *Symposia of the Zoological Society of London,* 1962, *8,* 71–89.

Condon, W. S., & Ogston, W. D. Sound film analysis of normal and pathological behavior patterns. *Journal of Nervous and Mental Disease,* 1966, *143,* 338–347.

Coss, R. G. The cutt-off hypothesis: Its relevance to the design of public places. *Man-Environment Systems,* 1973, *3,* 417–440.

Crandall, V. C., Good, S., & Crandall, V. J. Reinforcing effects of adult reactions and nonreactions on children's achievement expectatons; A replication study. *Child Development,* 1964, *35,* 485–497.

Crystal, D. *Prosodic systems of intonation in English.* London: Cambridge University Press, 1969.

Darwin, C. *The expression of the emotions in man and animals.* Chicago: The University of Chicago Press, 1965. (Originally published London: Murray, 1872).

Davis, E. A. *The development of linguistic skill in twins, singletons with siblings, and only children from five to ten years.* Minneapolis: University of Minnesota Press, 1937.

Day, M. E. An eye movement phenomenon relating to attention, thought and anxiety. *Perceptual and Motor Skills,* 1964, *19,* 443–446.

Diebold, R. A., Jr. Anthropological perspectives: Anthropology and the comparative psychology of communicative behavior. In T. A. Sebeok (Ed.), *Animal communication: Techniques of study and results of research.* Bloomington: Indiana University Press, 1968.

Dittmann, A. T. Developmental factors in conversational behavior. *The Journal of Communication,* 1972, *22,* 404–423. (a)

Dittmann, A. T. *Interpersonal messages of emotion.* New York: Springer, 1972. (b)

Dittmann, A. T. The body movement–speech rhythm relationship as a cue to speech encoding. In A. W. Siegman & B. Pope (Eds.), *Studies in dyadic communication.* New York: Pergamon Press, 1972. (c)

Dittmann, A. T., & Llewellyn, L. G. The phonemic clause as a unit of speech decoding. *Journal of Personality and Social Psychology,* 1967, *6,* 341–349.

Dittmann, A. T., & Llewellyn, L. G. Relationship between vocalizations and head nods as listener responses. *Journal of Personality and Social Psychology,* 1968, *9,* 79–84.

Dittmann, A. T., & Llewellyn, L. G. Body movement and speech rhythm in social conversation. *Journal of Personality and Social Psychology,* 1969, *11,* 98–106.

Duke, J. D. Lateral eye movement behavior. *Journal of General Psychology,* 1968, *78,* 189–195.

Duncan, S., Jr. Some signals and rules for taking speaking turns in conversations. *Journal of Personality and Social Psychology,* 1972, *23,* 283–292.

Duncan, S., Jr. Toward a grammar for dyadic conversations. *Semiotica,* 1973, *9,* 129–46.

Duncan, S., Jr., On the structure of speaker-auditor interaction during speaking turns. *Language in Society,* 1974, *2,* 161–180.

Duncan, S., Jr., & Niederehe, G. On signaling that it's your turn to speak. *Journal of Experimental Social Psychologyk,* 1974, *10,* 234–247.

Efron, D. *Gesture, race, and culture.* The Hague: Mouton, 1972 (Originally published as *Gesture and environment.* New York: King's Crown Press, 1941).

Ekman, P. Universals and cultural differences in facial expressions of emotion. In J. K. Cole (Ed.), *Nebraska Symposium on Motivation*, (Vol. 19). Lincoln: University of Nebraska Press, 1972.

Ekman, P., & Friesen, W. V. The repertoire of nonverbal behavior: Categories, origins, usage, and coding. *Semiotica*, 1969, *1*, 49–98.

Ekman, P., & Friesen, W. V. Hand movements. *The Journal of Communication*, 1972, *22*, 353–374.

Ellsworth, P. C., & Ludwig, L. M. Visual behavior in social interaction. *The Journal of Communication*, 1972, *22*, 375–403.

Ervin-Tripp, S., Sociolinguistics. In L. Berkowitz (Ed.), *Advances in experimental social psychology* (Vol. 4). New York: Academic Press, 1969.

Exline, R. V. Explorations in the process of person perception: Visual interaction in relation to competition, sex, and need for affiliation. *Journal of Personality*, 1963, *31*, 1–20.

Feldstein, S. Temporal patterns of dialogue: Basic research and reconsiderations. In A. W. Siegman & B. Pope (Eds.), *Studies in dyadic communication*. New York: Pergamon Press, 1972.

Glucksberg, S., Trabasso, T., & Wald, J. Linguistic structures and mental operations. *Cognitive Psychology*, 1973, *5*, 338–370.

Glucksberg, S., Krauss, R., & Higgins, E. T. The development of referential communication skills. In F. D. Horowitz, M. E. Hetherington, S. Scarr-Salapatek, & G. M. Siegel (Eds.), *Review of Child Development Research*, Vol. 4. Chicago: University of Chicago Press, 1975.

Goffman, E. *Interacton ritual: Essays on face-to-face behavior*. Garden City, New York: Doubleday, 1967.

Goldman-Eisler, F. *Psycholinguistics: Experiments in spontaneous speech*. New York: Academic Press, 1968.

Goldman-Eisler, F. Segmentation of input in simultaneous translation. *Journal of Psycholinguistic Research*, 1972, *1*, 127–140.

Grant, E. C. An ethological description of non-verbal behavior during interviews. *British Journal of Medical Psychology*, 1968, *41*, 177–184.

Gunnell, P., & Rosenfeld, H. M. Distribution of nonverbal responses in a conversational regulation task. Paper presented to Western Psychological Association, San Francisco, California, April, 1971.

Haas, W. A. & Wepman, J. M. Information theory measures of grammatical goodness of fit. *Journal of Psycholinguistic Research*, 1972, *1*, 175–181.

Hawes, L. C. Development and application of an interview coding system. *Central States Speech Journal*, 1972, *23*, 92–99.

Hindmarch, I. Eyes, eye-spots and pupil dilation in nonverbal communication. In M. von Cranach & I. Vine (Eds.), *Social communication and movement: Studies of interaction and expression in man and chimpanzee*. New York: Academic Press, 1973.

Horowitz, M. W., & Newman, J. B. Spoken and written expression: An experimental analysis. *Journal of Abnormal and Social Psychology*, 1964, *68*, 640–647.

Hutt, C., & Ounsted, C. The biological significance of gaze aversion with particular reference to the syndrome of infantile autism. *Behavioral Science*, 1966, *11*, 346–356.

Jaffe, J., & Feldstein, S. *Rhythms of dialogue*. New York: Academic Press, 1970.

Jaffe, J., Stern, D. N., & Peery, J. C. "Conversational" coupling of gaze behavior in prelinguistic human development. *Journal of Psycholinguistic Research*, 1973, *2*, 321–329.

Jefferson, G. Side sequences. In D. N. Sudnow (Ed.), *Studies in social interaction*. New York: Free Press, 1972.

Kendon, A. Some functions of gaze-direction in social interaction. *Acta Psychologica*, 1967, *26*, 22–63.

Kendon, A. Movement coordination in social interaction: Some examples described. *Acta Psychologica*, 1970, *32*, 100–125.

Kendon, A. Some relationships between body motion and speech: an analysis of an example. In A. W. Siegman & B. Pope (Eds.), *Studies in dyadic communication*. New York: Pergamon Press, 1972.

Kendon, A. The role of visible behavior in the organization of social interaction. In M. von Cranach & I. Vine (Eds.), *Social communication and movement: Studies of interaction and expression in man and chimpanzee*. London: Academic Press, 1973.

Kendon, A., & Ferber, A. A description of some human greetings. In R. P. Michael & J. H. Crook (Eds.), *Comparative ecology and behaviour of primates*. London: Academic Press, 1973.

Knapp, M. L., Hart, R. P., Friedrich, G. W., & Shulman, G. M. The rhetoric of goodbye: verbal and nonverbal correlates of human leave-taking. *Speech Monographs*, 1973, *40*, 182–198.

Krasner, L. Studies of the conditioning of verbal behavior. *Psychological Review*, 1958, *55*, 148–170.

LaBarre, W. Paralinguistics, kinesics, and cultural anthropology. In T. A. Sebeok, A. S. Hayes, & M. C. Bateson (Eds.), *Approaches to semiotics*. The Hague: Mouton, 1964.

Leach, E. The influence of cultural context on nonverbal communication in man. In R. A. Hinde (Ed.), *Non-verbal communication*. Cambridge: Cambridge University Press, 1972.

Levitt, E. A. The relationship between abilities to express emotional meanings vocally and facially. In J. R. Davitz (Ed.), *The communication of emotional meaning*. New York: McGraw-Hill, 1964.

Longhurst, T. M., & Siegel, G. M. Effects of communication failure on speaker and listener behavior. *Journal of Speech and Hearing Research*, 1973, *16*, 128–140.

MacKay, D. M. Formal analysis of communicative processes. In R. A. Hinde (Ed.), *Nonverbal communication*. Cambridge, England: Cambridge University Press, 1972.

Matarazzo, J. D., Saslow, G., Wiens, A. N., Wietman, M., & Allen, B. V. Interviewer head nodding and interviewee speech durations. *Psychotherapy: Theory, Research and Practice*, 1964, *1*, 54–63. (a)

Matarazzo, J. D., Wiens, A. N., Saslow, G., Allen, B. V., & Weitman, M. Interviewer mm-hmm and interviewee speech durations. *Psychotherapy: Theory, Research and Practice*, 1964, *1*, 109–114. (b)

McGrew, W. C. *An ethological study of children's behavior*. New York: Academic Press, 1972.

Miller, N. E. Learning of visceral and glandular responses. *Science*, 1969, *163*, 434–445.

Morris, W. N. Manipulated amplitude and interruption outcomes. *Journal of Personality and Social Psychology*, 1971 *20*, 319–331.

Moscovici, S. Communication processes and the properties of language. In L. Berkowitz (Ed.), *Advances in experimental social psychology*, Vol. 3. New York: Academic Press, 1967.

Nielsen, G. *Studies in Self Confrontation*. Copenhagen: Munksgaard, 1962.

Pace, R. W., & Boren, R. R. *The human transaction: Facets, functions, and forms of interpersonal communication*. Glenview, Illinois: Scott, Foresman, 1973.

Peterson, C. L., Danner, F. W., & Flavell, J. H. Developmental changes in children's response to three indications of communicative failure. *Child Development*, 1972, *43*, 1463–1468.

Pittenger, R. E., & Smith, H. L., Jr. A basis for some contributions of linguistics to psychiatry. *Psychiatry*, 1957, *20*, 61–78.

Psathas, G. Analyzing dyadic interaction. In G. Gerbner, O. R. Holsti, K. Krippendorff, W. J. Paisley, & P. J. Stone (Eds.), *The analysis of communication content: Developments in scientific theories and computer techniques*. New York: Wiley, 1969.

Rosenberg, S. The development of referential skills in children. In R. L. Schiefelbusch (Ed.), *Language of the mentally retarded*. Baltimore: University Park Press, 1972.

Rosenfeld, H. M. Approval-seeking and approval-inducing functions of verbal and nonverbal responses in the dyad. *Journal of Personality and Social Psychology*, 1966, *4*, 597–605. (a)

Rosenfeld, H. M. Instrumental affiliative functions of facial and gestural expressions. *Journal of Personality and Social Psychology*, 1966, *4*, 65–72. (b)

Rosenfeld, H. M. Nonverbal reciprocation of approval: An experimental analysis. *Journal of Experimental Social Psychology,* 1967, *3,* 102–111.

Rosenfeld, H. M. The experimental analysis of interpersonal influence processes. *The Journal of Communication,* 1972, *22,* 424–442.

Rosenfeld, H. M. & Baer, D. M. Unnoticed verbal conditioning of an aware experimenter by a more aware subject: The double-agent effect. *Psychological Review,* 1969, *76,* 425–432.

Rosenfeld, H. M., & Baer, D. M. Unbiased and unnoticed verbal conditioning: The double-agent robot procedure. *Journal of the Experimental Analysis of Behavior,* 1970, *14,* 99–107.

Rosenfeld, H. M., & Hancks, M. The association of nonverbal behaviors of speakers and listeners with judgments of listener attention, understanding, and agreement (in preparation).

Rosenfeld, H. M., McRoberts, R. Effect of topographical features and nonverbal context of ratings of teacher head nods. (in preparation)

Rosenfeld, H. M., Shea, M., & Greenbaum, P. Developmental trends in the recognition of normative facial emblems of "right" and "wrong" by normal children from grades 1 to 5. Paper presented to Society for Research in Child Development, Denver, April 1975.

Rosenfeld, H. M., & Sullwold, V. Optimal informational discrepancies for persistent communication. *Behavioral Science,* 1969, *14,* 303–315.

Ruesch, H. *Therapeutic communication.* New York: Norton, 1973.

Sacks, H. Schegloff, E. A., & Jefferson, G. A simplest systematics for the organization of turn-taking for conversation. *Language,* 1974, *50,* 696–735.

Schank, R. C. Conceptual dependency: A theory of natural language understanding. *Cognitive Psychology,* 1972, *3,* 552–631.

Scheflen, A. E. Communication and regulation in psychotherapy. *Psychiatry,* 1963, *26,* 126–136.

Scheflen, A. E. The significance of posture in communication systems. *Psychiatry,* 1964, *27,* 316–331.

Scheflen, A. E. Human communication: Behavioral programs and their integration in interaction. *Behavioral Science,* 1968, *13,* 44–55.

Schegloff, E. A. Sequencing in conversational openings. *American Anthropologist,* 1968, *70,* 1075–1095.

Schegloff, E. A., & Sacks, H. Opening up closings. *Semiotica,* 1973, *8,* 289–327.

Shannon, C. E., & Weaver, W. *The mathematical theory of communication.* Urbana: University of Illinois Press, 1949.

Siegman, A. W. Effect of noncontingent interviewer mm-hmms on interviewee productivity. *Proceedings, 81st Annual Convention, American Psychological Association,* 1973, *8,* 559–560.

Snyder, W. U. An investigation of the nature of non-directive psychotherapy. *Journal of General Psychology,* 1945, *33,* 193–223.

Speier, M. Some conversational problems for interactional analysis. In D. N. Sudnow (Ed.), *Studies in social interaction.* New York: Free Press, 1972.

Spitz, R. A. *No and yes: On the genesis of human communication.* New York: International Universities Press, 1957.

Stephenson, G. M., Rutter, D. R., & Dore, S. R. Visual interaction and distance. *British Journal of Psychology,* 1972, *64,* 251–257.

Stern, D. N. Mother and infant at play: The dyadic interaction involving facial, vocal and gaze behaviors. In M. Lewis & L. Rosenblum (Eds.), *The effect of the infant on its caregiver.* New York: Wiley, 1974.

Stevenson, H. W. Social reinforcement of children's behavior. In L. P. Lipsitt & C. C. Spiker (Eds.), *Advances in child development and behavior,* Vol. 2, New York: Academic Press, 1965.

Stone, P. J., Dunphy, D. S., Smith, M. S., & Ogilvie, D. M. *The general inquirer: A computer approach to content analysis.* Cambridge, Massachusetts: M.I.T. Press, 1966.

Trager, G. L. Paralanguage: A first approximateion. *Studies in Linguistics*, 1958, *13*, 1-12.

Trager, G. L. Some thoughts on 'juncture'. *Studies in Linguistics*, 1962, *16*, 11-22.

Trager, G. L., & Smith, H. L., Jr. *An outline of English structure*. (Studies in Linguistics: Occasional Papers, 3). Norman, Oklahoma: Battenberg Press, 1951. (Republished: New York: American Council of Learned Societies, 1965).

Ulrich, R. Conversational control. *Psychological Record*, 1962, *12*, 327-330.

Vine, I. Communication by facial-visual signals. In J. H. Crook (Ed.), *Social behaviour in birds and mammals: Essays on the social ethology of animals and man*. London: Academic Press, 1970.

Walters, R. H., & Parke, R. D. The role of the distance receptors in the development of social responsiveness. In L. P. Lipsitt & C. C. Spiker (Eds.), *Advances in child development and behavior*, Vol. 2. New York: Academic Press, 1965.

Webb, J. T. Interview synchrony: An investigation of two speech rate measures. In A. W. Siegman & B. Pope (Eds.), *Studies in dyadic communication*. New York: Pergamon Press, 1972.

Wiener, M., Devoe, S., Rubinow, S., & Geller, J. Nonverbal behavior and nonverbal communication. *Psychological Review*, 1972, *79*, 185-214.

Yngve, V. H. On getting a word in edgewise. In M. A. Campbell *et al.* (Eds.), *Papers from the sixth regional meeting, Chicago Linguistic Society*. Chicago: University of Chicago Department of Linguistics, 1970.

Zaidel, S. F., & Mehrabian, A. The ability to communicate and infer positive and negative attitudes facially and vocally. *Journal of Experimental Research in Personality*, 1969, *3*, 233-241.

Author Index

Block, J., 275, *316*
Blumer, D. P., 29, *33*
Blumstein, S., 30, *32*
Blurton Jones, N. G., 102, 103, *138,* 144, 162, 167, 173, *206*
Bodine, A., 354, *426*
Bodner, G. E., 538, *556*
Bolinger, D., 65, *94*
Bolles, R. C., *206*
Bond, R. N., 367, *426,* 464, 472, *495, 496*
Bonit, R. N., *427*
Boomer, D. S., 29, *32,* 58, 382, 413, *426,* 573, *596*
Booraem, C. D., 538, *556*
Bootzin, R., 542, *558*
Boren, R. R., 572, *599*
Borke, H., 165, *206*
Borod, J. C., 148, 184, *206*
Botwinick, J., 334, 338, *345*
Boucher, J. D., *6,* 157, 158, 160, 192, *206,* 589, *596*
Bouma, N., 338, *345*
Bourhis, R. Y., 376, *426, 428,* 467, 488, *494, 496*
Bouska, M. L., 547, *556*
Bowden, R. E. M., 152, *206*
Bower, T. G. R., 162, *206*
Bowers, D., 187, *209*
Bowlby, J., 162, 166, *206*
Boyd, E. F., 170, *213*
Bradburn, W. M., 474, *494*
Bradford, N. H., 417, *430*
Bradshaw, J. L., 144, 187, *206*
Brady, P. T., 439, *494*
Brain, W. R., 30, *32*
Brandt, J. F., 355, 401, *430*
Brandt, L., 591, *596*
Brannigan, C. R., 102, 103*n, 138,* 144, 174, *206*
Bratzlavsky, M., 151, 152, 195, *206, 207*
Brawley, P., 549, *560*
Brazelton, T., 163, 166, *207*
Brebner, J., 553, *558*
Breed, G., 269, 271, *316*
Brehm, J., 551, *556*
Brenner, M. S., 382, 384, 410, 420, *427*
Breskin, S., 485, *497*
Briem, V., 186, *207*
Brigham, J. C., 186, *207*
Brock, T. C., 470, *494*
Brodal, A., 146, *207*
Broman, M., 187, *207*

Brookens, N. L., 151, *210*
Brookes, S., 161, 283–84, *319–20*
Brooks, J., 167, 168, 198, *216*
Brooks, R., 591, *596*
Brotherton, P., 360, 361, 416, *426*
Brown, B. L., 371, 372, 398, *426*
Brown, E. F., 510, 511, *518*
Brown, R., 39, *63,* 304, 313, *316*
Brown, S. L., 149, 150, 179, *207, 220*
Brunault, M. A., 541, 548, *560*
Bruner, J. S., 75, *94,* 143, 144, 151, *207*
Brunner, C. C., 277, *317*
Brunori, P., 185, *207*
Bruyer, R., 148, 187, *207*
Buchanan, D. R., 274, 293, *316*
Buchanan, R., 534, 535, *557*
Buchtel, H., 189, *207*
Buck, R. A., 74, *94,* 165, 172, 185, 186, 196, 198–200, *207*
Bugental, D. B., 166, *220, 221*
Bugental, D. E., 52,*n,* 189, 190, *207–8,* 595, *597*
Bull, D., 277, *321*
Bulwer, J., 65, *94*
Burk, K. W., 469, *495*
Burke, D., 152, *221*
Burke, P. H., 147, *208*
Burns, J. A., 287, 314, *316*
Burns, K. L., 189, *208,* 595, *597*
Burnstein, E., 470, *494*
Burt, R. B., 474, *499*
Burtt, H. E., 356, *429*
Bustos, A. A., 302, 303, *322*
Buzby, D. E., 186, *208*
Byck, R., 203, *208*
Byrne, D., 403, *426,* 470, 489, *494,* 541, 542, 547, 548, 550, *555, 556, 557*

C

Cacioppo, J. T., 148, 179, 182, *208,* 554–55, *556*
Cann, A., 187, *216*
Calhoun, L. G., 537, *559*
Callan, H. M., 255, 280–81, 295, 314, *316*
Campari, F., 189, *207*
Campbell, A., 365, 370, *426*
Campbell, B. E., *316*
Campbell, D. T., 135, *139,* 542, *556*
Campbell, R., 148, 187, *208*
Campos, J. J., 161, 163, 168–70, 197, *208, 214, 215, 221*

Subject Index